Politics:
Canada

**FOURTH
EDITION**

McGraw-Hill Ryerson Series in Canadian Politics
Paul W. Fox, *General Editor*

Forthcoming

Politics: Canada

FOURTH EDITION

Paul W. Fox
Principal
Erindale College
University of Toronto

McGRAW-HILL RYERSON LIMITED

Toronto Montreal New York London Sydney Johannesburg
Mexico Panama Düsseldorf Rio de Janeiro New Delhi
Auckland São Paulo

POLITICS: CANADA
Fourth Edition

1 2 3 4 5 6 7 8 9 10 BP 6 5 4 3 2 1 0 9 8 7

Hardcover ISBN: 0-07-082500-9

Softcover ISBN: 0-07-082454-1

Printed and bound in Canada

Canadian Cataloguing in Publication Data

Main entry under title:

Politics: Canada
(McGraw-Hill Ryerson series in Canadian Politics)

Includes bibliographies.
ISBN 0-07-082500-9 bd. ISBN 0-07-082454-1 pa.

1. Canada — Politics and government — 1963
— Addresses, essays, lectures.* I. Fox, Paul W., 1921-

JL11.P65 1977   320.9'71'064   C77-001279-5

PREFACE TO THE FOURTH EDITION

This book began fifteen years ago as a collection of readings to supplement and update existing textbooks in Canadian government. Now in its fourth edition *Politics: Canada* seems to have grown into a textbook itself.

Once again and since the third edition in 1970, the chapters have increased in number, in length, and in scope. Together they cover most aspects of our federal system of government. Individually, each chapter tries to offer a comprehensive review of the particular subject, bringing the topic up-to-date at the time of writing.

In each edition more and more of the material has become original, appearing for the first time in this book. Thus new items have been added to this edition while at the same time most of the articles which were published originally in previous editions have been revised and updated for the present edition.

Among the material now presented for the first time are the following: Professor David Bell, "Regionalism in the Canadian Community"; Professor John McMenemy, "Influence and Party Activity in the Senate: A Matter of Conflict of Interest?"; Professor Peter Russell, "The Supreme Court Since 1960"; Kenneth G. Tilley, "Ministerial Executive Staffs"; and Loren M. Simerl, "A Survey of Canadian Provincial Election Results, 1905-1976." To each of these authors I would like to offer my special thanks for allowing me to publish their articles in this book. Mr. Simerl deserves a particular word of gratitude, I believe, from me and from all students of Canadian government since he has produced a meticulously detailed and definitive compilation of provincial election results. It is a unique set of data which is not available elsewhere.

I should like to express my thanks also to those authors who contributed original work to previous editions and who have taken the trouble to update their articles for this edition. Their names and their articles are as follows: Professor Juris Dreifelds, "Nationalism and Socialism in French Canada"; Professor Hugh Whalen, "The Perils of Polling"; Dr. David Surplis, "Concentration and Control in Canadian Media"; Dr. Mark MacGuigan, M.P., "Backbenchers, the New Committee System, and the Caucus"; Professor Peter Russell, "The Supreme Court's Interpretation of the Constitution from 1949 to 1960"; and Professor Brian Land, "A Description and Guide to the Use of Canadian Government Publications."

Finally, I wish to thank all those other authors and their publishers who have given me permission to include their work in this edition. I appreciate that they have allowed me to edit their articles and on occasion to alter the titles of their works so that some selections could be cast in the form of a controversial dialogue. I have found that this arrangement makes the book particularly useful for academic discussion groups.

For pedagogic reasons I have added to this edition much more illustrative material: diagrams, charts, tables, and data. I hope that teachers and students will find, as I have, that this material is very useful for instructional purposes.

My introductory remarks to each chapter are intended to serve the same end. I have tried to provide a brief summary of the substance of each topic, noting in particular recent developments in the field and how the items in the chapter fit together. Within chapters I have frequently added some items which I have prepared to supply contemporary information that I thought would be interesting and helpful to students. Most of it involves descriptive or factual material which was difficult to locate elsewhere, for example, a compendium of the salaries and allowances of MPs and MLAs.

The bibliography which concludes each chapter gives references to major books and articles in the respective subject. Although the bibliographies have been brought up to date and are reasonably comprehensive, they make no claim to being exhaustive.

A word should be added about abbreviations. Some of the sources which recur frequently have been reduced to initials in order to save space. Thus *C.J.E.P.S.* stands for the *Canadian Journal of Economics and Political Science*, *C.J.P.S.* for the *Canadian Journal of Political Science*, *C.P.A.* for *Canadian Public Administration*, and *Q.Q.* for *Queen's Quarterly*. When a selection from an article or book has been included within a chapter of *Politics: Canada* and identified by a footnote, the reference is not repeated in the relevant bibliography, although the item may appear as a cross-reference in another bibliography.

I have omitted from the fourth edition some material that appeared in previous editions of *Politics: Canada*. But in each instance I have noted in the introduction to the particular chapter the omission and the previous location of the material so that readers may find it if they wish to consult it.

Some of the items have been omitted because the subjects have now been dealt with more fully in other publications, particularly in companion books in the McGraw-Hill Ryerson Series in Canadian Government and Politics. This Series has grown rapidly in recent years. A complete list of the works in the Series appears elsewhere in this book. The Series is open-ended and new works will continue to be published in it.

Since the field of Canadian government and politics keeps on growing and changing, there may be further editions of *Politics: Canada* in the future.

Erindale College,
University of Toronto

Paul Fox,
April 15, 1977.

CONTENTS

Politics: Canada

FOURTH EDITION

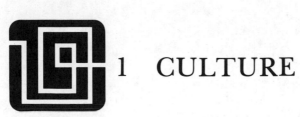 1 CULTURE

1

POLITICAL SCIENCE

Professor Dahl's article is a useful introduction to the study of political science. It touches on most of the basic questions that arise in connection with political science and outlines the major aspects of the discipline. The bibliography includes references to some recent works in the analysis of political systems and some general works dealing with behavioural aspects of political science, though specific Canadian political behavioural studies are noted in the bibiliography to Chapter 10.

WHAT IS POLITICAL SCIENCE?*

Robert A. Dahl

What is political science?

To begin, political science is, of course, the study of politics. One might better say, it is the *systematic* study of politics, that is, an attempt by systematic analysis to discover in the confusing tangle of specific detail whatever principles may exist of wider and more general significance.

At the very outset, then, we must distinguish political science as the systematic *study* of politics from the *practice* of politics.

The same person may of course both study and practise politics. The student of politics may serve as an adviser to the political practitioner. Plato, the great Greek philosopher and political theorist, is said to have

* From *American Politics and Government*, the Forum Lectures broadcast and published by the Voice of America, Washington, D.C., 1965, pp. 1-19. By permission.

gone to Syracuse, in Sicily, in 367 B.C. to advise the ruler of that city—who, I am sorry to say, was a tyrant. . . .

Sometimes, though less often, a political scientist may be not only an adviser but also an active practitioner of the political arts. That astounding man of the Italian Renaissance, Niccolo Machiavelli, served as a secretary of the Republic of Florence for fourteen years. . . . [He also wrote] such masterpieces of political science as *The Prince* and *The Discourses* and even a great comic and rather scabrous play, *La Mandragola*. Machiavelli's descriptions and prescriptions are so lacking in ordinary standards of morality that his name has come to be associated with notions of ruthless egoism in politics. To many people, I imagine, he represents the essence of political evil. Yet the man himself loathed despotism and believed devoutly in the virtues of republican institutions. . . .

Machiavelli began his career as a politician and became a political scientist when his political career ended; with Woodrow Wilson the sequence was just the reverse. Wilson was a historian and political scientist long before he began the political career that propelled him into the White House. . . . It has sometimes been said that Wilson himself unfortunately ignored his own advice when he became President. But the practising politician often does ignore the political scientist—even, as in Wilson's case, when the political scientist happens to be himself.

I mention these examples less to show that political scientists are typically involved in politics than the contrary. I want to emphasize that actually engaging in politics is not at all the same thing as studying politics in order to develop principles of general relevance. Political science means the study, not the practice, of politics.

An Ancient Study

As you may have noticed from these examples, the study of politics is an ancient field of learning. It is also a study that has received unusual emphasis in those Western cultures that derive from the worlds of Greek and Roman civilization. For the Greeks and Romans were immensely concerned with political things.

The modern study of politics, in fact, can be traced to that magnificent and unbelievably creative people, the Greeks of the fifth and the fourth centuries before Christ and, most of all, to the Athenians. It was in Athens that Socrates, Plato, and Aristotle raised to the highest level of intellectual endeavour the kinds of questions about politics that concern thoughtful men down to the present day. I have in mind such questions as:

> How do we acquire knowledge about politics and about political life? How do we distinguish politics from other aspects of human life? In what ways are political systems similar to one another? In what ways do political systems differ from one another? What is the role of authority and power in political systems? How do men behave in politics? What are the special characteristics, if any, of *homo politicus*, political man? What kinds of conditions make for stability, for change, or for revolution in a political system? What is required if social peace is to be maintained and violence to be avoided? What sort of political system is

the best? How should we and how do we decide questions about what is "the best" in politics?

Every age has produced one or two men who provide great answers to these great questions . . . [such as] the three Greeks: Socrates, Plato, and Aristotle. Let us consider several others. Cicero, who was both witness to and participant in the death agony of the Roman Republic; St. Augustine, born in North Africa in the fourth century; St. Thomas Aquinas, born near Naples in the thirteenth century; Machiavelli, born in Florence in the fifteenth century; Thomas Hobbes, the Englishman, born in the next century; John Locke, also an Englishman, born in the seventeenth century; at the end of the seventeenth century, a Frenchman, Montesquieu, who greatly influenced the men who drafted the United States Constitution; in the eighteenth century, another Frenchman, Rousseau; in the nineteenth century the Germans, Hegel, Marx, and Engels, the Englishmen Jeremy Bentham and John Stuart Mill, the Frenchman Alexis de Tocqueville. . . .

What Is Politics?

What is politics? This innocent question is rather like asking a biologist, "What is life?" Biology, it is said, is the science of life or living matter in all its manifestations. Very well. But what is living matter? It turns out that this question is extremely difficult to answer and that biologists do not exactly agree on the answer. Yet they are quite confident that some kinds of matter—one-celled animals, for example—are clearly at the centre of biology, while others—a piece of granite, for example—are clearly outside the field. So, too, in political science. We pretty well agree on the kinds of things that are definitely political. Thus the governments of the United States, the Soviet Union, and any other nation, province, state, city, town, or colony are unquestionably political and therefore in the domain of political science. The government of an ant colony is not; at any rate I have not noticed any of my colleagues writing about party politics or imperialism in ant colonies. Yet if we can say with confidence what lies at the centre of politics, we are, like the biologist confronted with the question of life, not so sure of the exact boundaries.

Let me therefore describe what is at the centre. To begin, wherever we find politics, most authorities agree, we necessarily encounter human beings living together in some kind of an association. . . . Wherever we find politics we encounter some special relationship among the human beings living together, a relationship variously called "rule," "authority," or "power". To refer once again to Aristotle, the very first page of the *Politics* contains references to different kinds of authority, what distinguishes the authority of the statesman from the authority of the head of the household or of the master over his slave, and the like. Wherever we find politics we discover conflict and ways in which human beings cope with conflict. Indeed, when human beings live together in associations and create rules, authorities, or governments to deal with these conflicts, the very attempts to rule also help to generate conflicts. Which comes first, power or conflict, need not detain us; we find both conflict and power wherever human beings live together. Politics arises, then, whenever there are people living together in associations, whenever they are involved in conflicts, and wherever they are subject to some kind of power, rulership, or authority.

These phenomena exist everywhere, therefore politics is everywhere. But not all associations have equal power. You can very easily test this —though I strongly urge you not to try—by having your family, which is one association, attempt to take over your neighbour's property, which, I am sure, happens to be protected by a more powerful association, the national state in which you reside. The state is the association that has the greatest power within some particular territory. Thus the *government* of the state is obviously at the very centre of politics, and therefore of political science. And the various organized institutions that make up the government of a state—the executive, the legislature, the judiciary, regional organizations, provinces, and local governments—all involve politics.

There are associations, organizations, and institutions that help to determine what the organs of government actually do; what rules the government adopts and enforces. In the modern world the most important are obviously political parties, such as the Republican and Democratic parties in the United States, Conservatives, Labourites, and Liberals in Britain, the Communist party in the Soviet Union, and so on. In many countries the political parties are so influential that one can consider them as a kind of informal government that rules the rulers. Thus political parties are pretty clearly at or near the centre of politics and therefore of political science.

In addition to the parties, other organizations help to determine what the state does, even though they may not run candidates in elections and are not directly and openly represented in parliament. These associations are sometimes called interest groups; any association that tries to secure from the state policies favourable to its members or followers is an interest group. In the United States interest groups include such organizations as the American Medical Association, which represents physicians and has been involved in the struggle over a national program of medical care; labour unions, including the great national organization, the AFL-CIO, which frequently descends on Congress in an attempt to secure legislation favourable to trade unions in particular and the working people in general; farm organizations, which seek to gain favourable treatment for farms. One could go on endlessly simply listing examples of interest-group organizations in the United States. Not long ago the United States House of Representatives debated and passed a bill increasing the legal authority of the federal government to protect the rights of Negroes. A recently published list of the groups who were actively working in Washington to persuade congressmen to support the bill shows: six civil rights organizations, fifteen labour unions, nineteen religious organizations, and ten other groups.

Neither can we ignore ordinary citizens. Election, voting, and other forms of participation by citizens in civic life are also elements of politics.

Have we now reached the boundaries of politics? Hardly. In fact some political scientists would extend the meaning of politics to include *any* activity involving human beings associated together in relationships of power and authority where conflicts occur. In this sense, politics truly does exist everywhere: within trade unions, within the interest-group organizations of doctors or farmers, in business organizations, even in private clubs, indeed anywhere that human beings assemble together. Viewed in this way, the domain of politics and therefore of political science does not stop simply with the institutions of the state, or even with such familiar political institutions as political parties and organized interest groups, but extends to an enormous range of human activity. The question of how far the boundaries of political science extend is a lively one among political scientists at the present time, but we need not linger over it any more. For it is perfectly obvious that no matter how they draw their boundaries, political scentists have more than enough to do.

Is Politics a Science?

. . . In what sense is the study of politics a science? In what sense *can* it be? Even if it can be, should it be a science? These questions, as you might imagine, are also the subjects of a great deal of discussion; it is not too much to say that the discussion has gone on for a very long time, if not, in fact, from the time of the Greeks.

The term "science" has, of course, many meanings. And the word does not mean quite the same thing in one language as it does in another. In some countries, scholars do not consider that political science is a single subject, like biology, but many subjects. Some scholars speak not of political science but of the political *sciences*. In France, until recently, one heard of *les sciences politiques* and in Italy *le scienze politiche*—that is, the political sciences. What do we mean, then, by the *science* of politics? To some people the word "science" simply means any systematic approach to human knowledge; so that one could speak of the science of physics, the science of mathematics, or perhaps even a science of theology. To others, and this is a good deal more common in English-speaking countries nowadays, the word "science" tends to be restricted to the natural sciences, studies that involve the observation of nature and the development of laws and theories explaining the phenomena of nature such as chemistry, physics, and the biological sciences. In recent years, particularly in the United States, we have come to speak of the social and behavioural sciences, that is, those that seek by observation to develop explanations of human behaviour.

To confuse the matter even more, science is thought of sometimes as an achievement in being, sometimes as a method, and sometimes as a goal.

Physics is a science in the first sense. When one speaks of physics as a "real" science, he probably does not mean that physicists are simply hoping to develop theories that someday will explain the nature of physical reality; he means that they already have such theories, and they are of impressive power to explain the physical world.

But science also refers to the *methods* by which scholars investigate their subject. One might say that a century ago medicine was not very "scientific" because its methods were extremely crude; it was difficult to distinguish the charlatan from the honest inquirer after medical knowledge. Today, on the contrary, medical research in the most advanced laboratories uses highly sophisticated methods of inquiry very much like those used in physics, chemistry, and biology. Yet almost everyone would agree that in its laws, theories, and explanations medicine is not so far advanced as, say, physics.

One might also think of science as a goal, as something to be arrived at by rigorous methods of inquiry, even if present knowledge is somewhat sparse.

In which of these three senses is the study of politics a science? Despite the fact that the best minds of every age have tended to turn their attention to the study of politics, as I pointed out above, certainly the study of politics is not an already achieved science like physics. We simply do not have a body of theories about political systems that enables us to predict the outcome of complex events with anything like the reliability that a physicist, a chemist, or even a biologist generally can predict the outcome of complex events in his field. If you believe that there is such a theory in politics, I am bound to say that you are, in my opinion, deluding yourself. It is true that from time to time a writer, sometimes even a great writer, has claimed that he possesses a full-fledged predictive science of politics. So far, however, no comprehensive theory of politics that undertakes to predict the outcome of complex events has stood the test of experience. The most notable modern example of failure is, I think, Marx. If you examine his predictions carefully and test them against actual developments, he proves to be wrong in so many cases that only those who regard Marxism as a kind of religion to take on faith, and against all evidence, can remain persuaded that it is a truly predictive scientific theory. Nonetheless, political scientists do have an enormous amount of knowledge about politics, much of it extremely reliable knowledge.

•   •   •

We can say, then, that political science is the study of politics by methods and procedures designed to give us the greatest reliability in a highly complex world. As a body of knowledge, modern political science is definitely not a highly perfected science like physics or chemistry. Our knowledge of politics is continually and rapidly growing; however, this knowledge is of varying degrees of reliability, for some of it is highly speculative and about as reliable as anything one is ever likely to learn about human beings.

Matters Studied

What objects or phenomena do we actually study in political science? I have already mentioned most of these when I discussed the boundaries of politics, but let me now enumerate the main phenomena, the "objects" of political science. First, we study individual citizens, voters, leaders.

Strange as it may seem, study of the ways in which individuals actually behave in politics is one of the newest developments in the field. It is true, of course, that the behaviour of individuals in politics has never been ignored. Machiavelli's *The Prince* describes how many Renaissance political leaders did act and prescribes how they had to act if they were to succeed in the ruthless and tempestuous political jungle that was Renaissance Italy. Even though few writers had as much to say about the seamy side of political life as did Machiavelli, insights about man's political behaviour are scattered in works over the centuries.

Our understanding of man has made a quantum jump since Sigmund Freud and the advent of modern psychology, psychoanalysis, and psychiatry made us all acutely aware of man's capacity for irrational, nonrational, impulsive, neurotic, and psychotic action—in politics, unfortunately, as much as elsewhere. Partly as a result of this change, in the last several decades political scientists have begun to observe individuals and politics with a concern for detail and accuracy that, if not entirely new, is at least highly uncommon. What is new, perhaps, is a search for reliable generalizations. We are no longer content to observe a few individuals engaged in politics and to describe their behaviours, to investigate a few great, unusual leaders or a few simple yet possibly rare citizens. Rather, we want to know how widely our generalizations apply.

. . . [For instance] the independent voter is often thought to be, at least by comparison, a model citizen, rational, thoughtful, responsible, open-minded, in contrast to the partisan who, it is often thought, is less reflective, less thoughtful, and perhaps even less interested in a campaign because he made up his mind long ago and nothing will budge him. The view is, surely, plausible. Beginning with the presidential election of 1940, however, studies by American social scientists began to destroy this happy picture of the independent voter. In one study after another it was discovered that, far from being a thoughtful, attentive, responsible citizen, a person who lacks any spirit of partisanship more than likely has no great interest in politics, is quite ignorant about politics, does not pay much attention to political campaigns, and makes up his mind at the last possible moment, frequently on the basis of rather trivial or accidental influences. . . .

This finding has forced us to do some rethinking of our notions about the roles of the partisan and independent in American politics and perhaps in democratic systems in general. We cannot yet be sure how widespread this phenomenon is. Some studies indicate that it holds in certain European countries, in nations as different, for example, as Britain and Italy. But it may not hold in others. A recent analysis suggests that perhaps our model citizen, the thoughtful, reflective, interested man who does not make up his mind until he has tried to hear both sides of the argument, does actually exist in the United States and may play no negligible role in elections, even though his numbers are pretty tiny.

A second phenomenon studied by political scientists is the private or semipublic associations to which many individuals belong. The most visible of these, as I suggested earlier, are political parties. There are a vast number of studies of political parties throughout the world: how they are organized, how nominations are made, what the parties do in campaigns and elections, the characteristics of party leaders, members, and followers, and differences and similarities in the party systems of various countries.

Perhaps the most significant development during the last several decades has been the discovery of the tremendous importance of interest groups, particularly in the United States. Because class lines are rather weak, vague, and uncertain in this country, despite considerable differences in social standing, prestige, and income, and because our political parties, unlike many European parties, are neither tightly organized nor highly centralized, it was natural, I suppose, that American political scientists were the first to turn their attention to interest groups. It is fair to say, in fact, that they pioneered investigation in this area. In the last decade, however, concern with the role of interest groups in politics has spread to European political scientists, who have also begun to demonstrate that social classes and political parties are by no means the only significant political forces in European politics and that a variety of interest groups are active in the political parties and influence cabinet ministers, the civil servants, and other governmental officials. It would be impossible to understand the operation of any democratic system if one ignored the decisive role often played by representatives of the party of interests that exists in a modern industrialized and urbanized society.

A third focus for study is, of course, the political institutions themselves—the parliaments, the cabinets, the courts, the civil service, and the like. These are such obvious and familiar subjects for political science, therefore, that I will not comment on them further.

A fourth focus is a political system as a whole. A lively question of enduring interest to American political scientists is how to distinguish democracies from other systems and, perhaps more important, what conditions are required for the stability of democratic institutions. As political scientists learn more about the actual operation of democratic political systems, it becomes obvious that ... the ideals formulated by classical spokesmen for democracy, such as Locke, Rousseau, and Jefferson, are not only a long way from achievement (a fact that in itself would hardly be a new discovery) but may even have to be reformulated for fear that, as unattainable and utopian goals, they serve merely to discredit democracy as an ideal.

The existence of many new nations only recently liberated from colonial rule and still struggling with problems of independence, internal peace, and self-government presents as great an intellectual challenge to political scientists as they have ever faced: to discover the conditions under which these countries can develop stable constitutional governments based on the consent and support of the bulk of the population and capable of an orderly solution to staggering problems of economic growth and social development. It is fair to state that the study of politics in its 2,000-year development in the West has been rather parochial.

Now that we are confronted by the need for moderately reliable knowledge about the political systems developing in Africa, Asia, and even in Latin America, we find that facts and theories drawn from the experience of European and English-speaking countries are inadequate. As a consequence, during the last decade or so tremendous efforts have been made in the United States to develop scholars with an understanding of the problems and politics of the non-Western world. . . .

I must discuss one other focus of political science that is so painfully important to all of us that it might even be placed at the very centre of the stage. I have in mind, of course, the relation among political systems, that is, international relations. Here, too, the challenge strains our capacities to the very limit if not, indeed, beyond. In their attempt to grapple with the portentous and enormously complicated problems of international politics, political scientists in recent years have resorted to an amazing variety of techniques of inquiry and analysis, not excluding even the use of electronic computers to simulate negotiation and conflict among several countries in international politics. Although some of these efforts might seem absurd and unrealistic, my view is that we are so desperately in need of solutions that we can ill afford to mock any serious intellectual effort to discover them; and help may come from quite unexpected quarters.

Methods of Study

These, then, are some of the phenomena studied by modern political scientists. You might want to know *how* we study these things? To answer this question properly would require many chapters. Politics, as everyone knows, is not something one can directly observe in either a laboratory or a library. Indeed, direct observation of politics is often extremely difficult or downright impossible. Consequently, we often have to study politics by indirect observation, through historical materials, records, papers, statistical data, and the like. This process, I have no doubt, conveys the customary image of nearsighted scholars consulting the works of one another without ever emerging from the library into the heat and turmoil of political life. Yet one of the oldest though often neglected traditions of political science is the tradition of direct observation.

It is worth recalling that the great Greek students of politics, Socrates, Aristotle, and Plato, were able to and did observe politics in the compact laboratory of the city-state. They did not make the sharp division that modern scholars often make between the world of books and study and the world of affairs. Eighteen centuries later, Machiavelli was able to observe the political life of Renaissance Italy from his post in the Republic of Florence. I rather think there are many scholars today who believe that their fragile dignity would be damaged should they leave their libraries to mingle with the ordinary folk in the noisy byways of politics. Nonetheless, a most interesting development over the last several decades has been the growing insistence that wherever possible the scholar should observe as directly as he can the objects of his study. As a result, never before in history have there been so many scholars seeking to interview politicians, civil servants, and ordinary citizens.

. . . This development is, in my view, an enormously healthy one, for just as the biologist is no less a biologist, but a good deal more, because he observes in his laboratory the organisms with which he works, and just as the physician gains knowledge from studying patients and not merely from reading what others have written about disease, so too the study of political science has gained from the growing conviction that one cannot know politics merely by traversing the path between the classroom and the library. Yet to observe politics directly is much more difficult for us than it was for Aristotle or for Machiavelli; for the world we study is larger and more complicated, the population is greater, and the slice of the world we see—we now know—is not likely to be truly representative of the world.

The political scientist's laboratory, then, is the world—the world of politics. And he must work in that laboratory with the same caution and the same rigorous concern for the accuracy and reliability of his observation that is true of the natural scientist in his laboratory; with a good deal less chance, nonetheless, of succeeding. Because direct observation is no simple matter of casual and accidental interview, the political scientist finds that for every hour he spends observing politics he may have to spend a dozen analyzing his observations. Raw observations are all but useless, so the scholar still must work at his desk, in the silence of his study, reading and reflecting, trying to pierce the veil that seems always to keep truth half-hidden. Now that we have brought our political scientist back to his desk, far from the hurly-burly of politics, let us leave him there. But if he is to study politics he cannot stay there long. You may run into him at the next political meeting you attend.

BIBLIOGRAPHY

Alker, H. R., Jr., *Mathematics and Politics*, Toronto, Collier-Macmillan, 1965.

Almond, G., "A Development Approach to Political Systems," *World Politics*, Vol. XVII, No. 2, January, 1965.

Backstrom, C. H., and Hursh, G. D., *Survey Research*, Chicago, Northwestern University Press, 1963.

Benson, O., *Political Science Laboratory*, Columbus, Charles E. Merrill, 1969.

Bergeron, G., Painchaud, P., Sabourin, L., Tournon, J., *L'état actuel de la théorie politique*, Ottawa, 1964, Vol. I, Cahiers de la Société Canadienne de Science Politique.

Bluhm, W. T., *Theories of the Political System: Classics of Political Thought and Modern Political Analysis*, Englewood Cliffs, N.J., Prentice-Hall, 1965.

Cairns, A. C., "Alternative Styles in the Study of Canadian Politics", *C.J.P.S.*, Vol. VII, No. 1, March, 1974.

Charlesworth, J. C. (ed.), *A Design for Political Science: Scope, Objectives, and Methods*, [A Symposium], Monograph 6 in a Series sponsored by The American Academy of Political and Social Science, Philadelphia, 1966.

Connery, R. H. (ed.), *Teaching Political Science: A Challenge to Higher Education*, Don Mills, Burns & MacEachern Ltd., 1965.

Dahl, R. A., *Modern Political Analysis*, Englewood Cliffs, N.J., Prentice-Hall, 1963.

Dion, L., *Le statut théorique de la science politique*, Montréal, le centre de documentation et de recherches politiques, Collège Jean-de-Brébeuf, 1964.

Duverger, M., *The Idea of Politics, The Uses of Power in Society*, Toronto, Methuen, 1966.

Easton, D., *A Framework for Political Analysis*, Englewood Cliffs, N.J., Prentice-Hall, 1965.

Easton, D., *A Systems Analysis of Political Life*, New York, Wiley and Sons, 1965.

Easton, D., *The Political System, An Inquiry Into the State of Political Science*, New York, Knopf, 1953.

Golembiewski, R. T., Welsh, N. A., Crotty, W. J., *A Methodological Primer for Political Scientists*, Chicago, Rand McNally, 1969.

Gould, J., and Kolb, W. L., (eds.), *A Dictionary of the Social Sciences*, New York, The Free Press, 1964.

Isaak, A. C., *Scope and Methods of Political Science*, Homewood, Illinois, Dorsey, 1975.

Kalvelage, C., Segal, M., and Anderson, P. J., *Research Guide for Undergraduates in Political Science*, Morristown, N.J., General Learning Press, 1972.

Khan, R. A., MacKown, S. A., and McNiven, J. D., *An Introduction to Political Science*, Georgetown, Ontario, Irwin-Dorsey, 1972.

Merritt, R. L., and Puszka, G. J., *The Student Political Scientist's Handbook*, Cambridge, Mass., Schenkman, 1969.

Polsby, N., Dentler, R., Smith, P., *Politics and Social Life: An Introduction to Political Behaviour*, Boston, Houghton Mifflin, 1963.

Ranney, A., *The Governing of Men: An Introduction to Political Science*, New York, Holt, Rinehart, and Winston, 1966, rev. ed.

Sorauf, F. J., *Political Science, An Informal Overview*, Columbus, Charles E. Merrill, 1965.

Strum, P., and Shmidman, M. D., *On Studying Political Science*, California, Goodyear, 1969.

Wallis, W. A., and Roberts, H. V., *The Nature of Statistics*, New York, The Free Press, 1965.

Wiseman, H. V., *Political Systems, Some Sociological Approaches*, London, Routledge, Kegan, Paul, 1966.

2

THE CONSTITUTION, REVIEW, AND FORMAL AMENDMENT

This chapter provides a review of the nature of the Canadian constitution and reproduces the highlights in recent attempts to revise the constitution and achieve both "patriation" and a new method of amendment. It also lists the five recent amendments of the B.N.A. Act which the Canadian Parliament has enacted under the power given to it in 1949.

The first item is taken from the *Final Report* of the Special Joint Committee of the Senate and the House of Commons on the Constitution, which was published in 1972. This selection gives an admirable brief review of the Canadian constitution, distinguishing between the basic document, the Britsh North America Act, and the other components. It also presents the relevant recommendations of the Joint Committee which strongly urged the creation of a new Canadian constitution.

In 1968 in the wake of Ontario Premier Robarts' Confederation for Tomorrow Conference, the federal government and the provinces embarked on a protracted series of conferences devoted to reviewing the Canadian constitution. The aims were several: to modernize the B.N.A. Act by deleting anachronistic clauses and adding sections dealing with current concerns such as civil and language rights and regional economic disparities, and to "patriate" the B.N.A. Act by transferring the domicile of the Act, and especially the process of formal amendment, from Britain to Canada while at the same time establishing a new formula for amendment. The seven constitutional conferences which were held between 1968 and 1971 are summarized in a page taken from the first edition of Professor Donald Smiley's book, *Canada in Question: Federalism in the Seventies*.

At their final meeting in Victoria, B.C., in June 1971 the federal government and the ten provinces very nearly reached agreement on a new constitution. The document which emerged from that conference was entitled the Canadian Constitutional Charter, although it is more popularly known as the Victoria Charter. It failed to be implemented when the government of Quebec subsequently rejected it, but its clauses have continued to provide the basis for discussions between Ottawa and the provinces since then. This chapter reproduces the Statement of Conclusions of the Victoria Conference and the verbatim draft of the Charter.

Disappointment engendered by the failure of the Victoria Charter led to a cessation of negotiations between 1971 and 1975. However, in April of the latter year Prime Minister Trudeau reopened the subject with the provincial premiers. In March 1976 he wrote a long letter to them, urging patriation of the B.N.A. Act and enclosing a draft of a modification of the Victoria Charter. His letter, somewhat abridged, and the changes the draft made in the Constitutional Charter are included in this chapter. During the summer and fall of 1976 the provincial premiers discussed the prime minister's proposals for both patriation and amendment but as this edition goes to press, no agreement has yet been reached.

Since the federal and provincial governments have been trying for nearly fifty years to devise a method of formal amendment of the B.N.A. Act by Canadians within Canada, it is worthwhile to review the problem briefly. Most sections of the B.N.A. Act remain amendable by the United Kingdom Parliament, acting usually upon a Joint Address from the Canadian Parliament. An amendment to the B.N.A. Act (No. 2, 1949) permitted the Canadian Parliament to amend certain aspects of the Act which are under federal jurisdiction, but this power has been used sparingly. The five instances of Canadian Parliamentary amendment to date are summarized by the editor in an item in this chapter.

The various attempts to achieve a method of formal amendment have been described in texts such as Dawson and Ward, *The Government of Canada*, and Smiley, *Canada in Quebec: Federalism in the Seventies*. Previous editions of *Politics: Canada* have reproduced some of the more recent documentation. See, for instance, the first edition, pp. 81-90, for the steps prior to 1960; *ibid.*, 91-94, for the "Fulton Formula" in 1960, and *ibid.*, pp. 94-98, for an abridgement of Saskatchewan's objections to it.

In 1964 the then federal minister of justice, the Honourable Guy Favreau, presented a revised proposal known as the "Fulton-Favreau Formula". It too failed to achieve adoption, largely because of the objections of the government of Quebec. For the F-F Formula, see the third edition of this book, pp. 463-469, where it is reprinted verbatim in company with two other items: an explanation from Ottawa's comprehensive White Paper, *The Amendment of the Constitution of Canada, 1965*, and a passage from an N.D.P. spokesman's criticism of the proposal. Quebec's objections to the F-F Formula were contained within an exchange of correspondence between Quebec's Premier Jean Lesage and Prime Minister L. B. Pearson which has been reprinted in the second edition of *Politics: Canada*, pp. 146-150.

From 1967 to 1971 the search for an agreed method of formal amendment was included within the general review of the constitution conducted in the series of federal-provincial conferences noted above. Part IX of the Canadian Constitutional Charter of 1971 proposed a method of formal amendment of the new constitution. Part X and the Schedule indicated what sections of the B.N.A. Act would be repealed and how the B.N.A. Act and its amendments would be renamed. However, as mentioned, the Victoria Charter failed to be implemented. In 1975 and 1976 the subject was revived in the manner described above.

The final item in this chapter contains a selection from the Report of the Second Bilingual Districts Advisory Board which outlines the nature of the Official Languages Act passed by Parliament in 1969. For verbatim relevant passages from the text of the Act, see *Politics: Canada*, third edition, pp. 65-68.

The bibliography for this chapter is lengthy. For convenience it is divided into five sections: the constitution, federal problems, current constitutional documentation, bilingualism and biculturalism, and amending the constitution. Two books in the McGraw-Hill Ryerson Series should be consulted for excellent brief accounts of the matters dealt with in this chapter. They are Donald V. Smiley, *Canada in Question: Federalism in the Seventies*, second edition, 1976, and R.I. Cheffins and R. N. Tucker, *The Constitutional Process in Canada*, second edition, 1976.

CANADA'S CONSTITUTION—CHANGE REQUIRED*

Joint Committee on the Constitution

The Constitution and the B.N.A. Act

The Canadian Constitution may be said to be at present principally contained in the British North America Act of 1867. But we must note the limitations of this statement. The original Act has itself been subject to direct amendment many times, and it has also been indirectly amended by the United Kingdom Parliament, by the Parliament of Canada, and by the Provincial Legislatures according to their respective powers. In addition, the effect of its various sections has been greatly altered by decisions of the Judicial Committee of the Privy Council and, since 1949, of the Supreme Court of Canada. It has also been affected by a myriad of administrative arrangements which have been worked out between the Federal and the Provincial Governments, including the establishment of Federal-Provincial Conferences. Moreover, it has been touched by the ebb and flow of political and economic power between the central and the regional governments under the influence of wars, developments in transportation and communication, changes in business organization, and changing tax yields. Finally, the theory and practice of responsible government, which is the heart of our whole system of government, was ignored entirely by the B.N.A. Act and left to the realm of constitutional conventions.

Clearly, then, the B.N.A. Act has never been taken to be the whole of

---

* From the *Final Report* of the Special Joint Committee of the Senate and the House of Commons on the Constitution of Canada, Ottawa, Information Canada, 1972. Reproduced by permission of the Minister of Supply and Services Canada. (The order of the pages quoted has been changed to pp. 6-7, 1-2, 8-12.)

the Canadian Constitution. Moreover, it has not remained static even as law, and its total significance has been considerably altered by socio-economic events. Nevertheless, as formally amended and realistically interpreted, it is substantially the whole of our written constitution and, more important, is the fundamental framework in relation to which every part of the total constitution must be seen. Rights and privileges of all kinds, even responsible government itself, exist only insofar as they are not altered by the Act. We must therefore judge the adequacy of our present Constitution by reference to the adequacy of the B.N.A. Act.

To take the position that the present Canadian Constitution is to be judged on the basis of the British North America Act is not to confuse the totality of the Constitution with the Act. The Act is the keystone of the constitutional arch, and its weaknesses are transmitted to the whole structure. Thus the inadequacies of the B.N.A. Act are those of the Constitution itself.

The measure of the inadequacy of the British North America Act is that it does not serve Canadians fully as either a mirror of ourselves or as an inspirational ideal. As enacted in 1867, it did not attempt explicitly to set forth any values or goals of that time except to adopt "a Constitution similar in Principle to that of the United Kingdom." Whatever values it recognizes are implicit in that statement, or have to be inferred from the governmental structure and division of powers it establishes.

Even the distribution of powers between the Imperial and Canadian governments and between the Federal and Provincial governments does not reflect the Canadian reality of today: an independent, democratic, officially bilingual, multicultural, federal state. The imperial power of London over Ottawa in the Act was matched by that of Ottawa over the provincial capitals. As one witness remarked, "In the early years after Confederation, the provinces were treated like colonies of Ottawa with limited powers of self-government."

The B.N.A. Act can still be directly amended by an act of the United Kingdom Parliament. The royal power to disallow any Federal law within two years of its passage (s. 56) and the Federal power similarly to disallow any Provincial law (s. 90) are anachronistic today. They would make a mockery of Canadian independence, and of the distribution of governmental powers within Canada. In the case of the royal power the British Government undertook at the London Conference of 1929 not to use it again, but it has not been removed from the Act. The Federal power of disallowance has not been used since 1943, but also remains in the Act.

The role of the Supreme Court of Canada, the final interpreter of all our laws since 1949, is nowhere mentioned in the Act. Moreover, although Canada officially ceased to be part of the British Empire with the Statute of Westminster in 1931, the only treaty power which is provided for in the Act is that of implementing Empire treaties (s. 132). Then, too, the very limited provisions of section 133, guaranteeing the right to the use of the English and French languages in the Parliament of Canada and in the Legislature of Quebec and in Federal and Quebec courts, are no longer sufficient in a state dedicated to two official languages. Finally, the division of powers no longer appears to be sufficiently functional.

Need for Change

Although the constitution of a colony is not an adequate constitution for a nation, the British North America Act could not be said to have been a failure. It was an adequate enough constitution for the Canada of 1867—perhaps, the only possible constitution for that day—and, it has served us well as a basic framework of government—though increasingly less well as the years have gone by. In taking the position that Canada needs a new Constitution *now*, we are far from criticizing what our statesmen have wrought in the past.

●   ●   ●

Recommendations

1. Canada should have a new and distinctively Canadian Constitution, one which would be a new whole even though it would utilize many of the same parts. (See Chapter 3 as well as Chapter 1).
2. A new Canadian Constitution should be based on functional considerations, which would lead to greater decentralization of governmental powers in areas touching culture and social policy and to greater centralization in powers which have important economic effects at the national level. Functional considerations also require greater decentralization in many areas of governmental administration.

●   ●   ●

One of the most pressing needs is the protection of the individual person, through a comprehensive Bill of Rights and through linguistic guarantees to individuals. Equally pressing is the need for the recognition and protection of minority ethnic groups, including the native peoples. Their contribution to our country should be formally recognized and their natural vitality encouraged.

The most acute cultural-linguistic crisis is that of the French minority in Canada. . . .

We acknowledge a cultural imperative for Quebec: it must have sufficient control over its collective life to ensure the preservation and development of French-Canadian culture. Put another way, the Constitution must guarantee the preservation of the collective personality of French Quebec. In the expansion of provincial powers which we propose, Quebec would gain new powers to achieve these ends.

●   ●   ●

We have spoken of the need for an increase in both centralization and decentralization, depending on functional considerations. In our view greater decentralization in areas of culture and social policy would benefit all the Provinces. We propose such decentralization for reasons of functionalism and flexibility, and to meet the regional differences which became obvious to us in the course of our hearings. Consequently we propose an expansion of Provincial powers in areas like income support, criminal law, marriage and divorce, educational television, taxing powers, and international arrangements, and we support limitations on Federal powers with respect to appointments to the Senate and the Supreme Court, and with respect to Federal spending in fields of Provincial jurisdiction.

On the other hand, greater centralization is necessary in the regulation of the economy. Hence there should be a transfer of some existing Provincial powers to the Federal Parliament. We have in mind, particularly, an increase in Federal jurisdiction over air and water pollution, international and interprovincial trade and commerce, incomes, securities regulation, financial institutions, unfair competition, and foreign ownership.

At the same time, we favour considerable administrative decentralization in the operations of the Federal Government. This change of administrative direction requires no change in the Constitution. It does require a change of heart. It involves the recognition that geographically Canada is a very, very large country. From its extremities the centre of the nation looks and feels very far away. The injection of the judgments and feelings of Canadians from these areas into a more regionalized government service, would be tangible proof that the central government wishes to reach out to all Canadians. . . .

These power transfers and administrative rearrangements would necessitate not only a new spirit of cooperation among the eleven governments of Canada, but also new cooperative structure. We do not think it wise to theorize too much in the area of governmental structures. But we shall have some suggestions to make. One objective is to avoid increasing governmental structures solely for the purpose of creating intellectually tidy superstructures. We would also recognize that the Government of Canada should in the future exercise leadership principally by persuasion rather than by directive.

•   •   •

Recommendations

3. The Canadian Constitution should be patriated by a procedure which would provide for a simultaneous proclamation of a new Constitution by Canada and the renunciation by Britain of all jurisdiction over the Canadian Constitution.

•   •   •

4. The formula for amending the Constitution should be that contained in the Victoria Charter of June 1971. . . .

•   •   •

5. The Canadian Constitution should have a preamble which would proclaim the basic objectives of Canadian federal democracy.

In the course of this Report we make a number of references to matters which ought to be included in the preamble to a new Canadian Constitution. We thus propose the inclusion in the preamble of the following basic objectives of our society: a federal system of government within a democratic society; the enhancing of basic human rights; developing Canada as a bilingual and multicultural country; recognition of Canada's native people; the promotion of economic, social and cultural equality; the reduction of regional disparities; the advancement of Canada as a free and open society based on the consent of its people; the striving for world peace and security.

As we have mentioned earlier, a Constitution ought to reflect its community. The preamble in any Constitution can play an important role as a source of inspiration to a country. It can state in the broadest possible terms the objectives and aspirations of the society it governs. . . .

The details of our recommendations in connection with the Preamble are set out below, particularly in recommendations 6, 10, 27, 29, 30, 31 and 32.

[For a complete list of the Joint Committee's Recommendations, which totalled 105, see its *Final Report*, pp. 95-101.]

CONSTITUTIONAL CONFERENCES, 1967-1971*

Donald V. Smiley

[*November 27-30, 1967*—Confederation for Tomorrow Conference convened by the government of Ontario.]

February 5-7, 1968—First Meeting of the Constitutional Conference. A Continuing Committee of Officials established and also a Constitutional Secretariat authorized. The following questions to be examined in the future process of review: official languages, fundamental rights, distribution of powers, reform of institutions linked with federalism including the Senate and Supreme Court of Canada, regional disparities, amending procedure and provisional arrangements and mechanisms of federal-provincial relations.

February 10-12, 1969—Second Meeting of the Constitutional Conference. Four ministerial committees established for the study of official languages, fundamental rights, the judiciary and the Senate. The Continuing Committee authorized to give immediate attention to the distribution

* From *Canada in Question: Federalism in the Seventies*, Toronto, McGraw-Hill Ryerson, first edition, 1972, p. 52. By permission. (For a much more detailed list and chart, see Canadian Intergovernmental Conference Secretariat, *The Constitutional Review 1968-1971: Secretary's Report*, Ottawa, Information Canada, 1974, pp. 497 *et. seq.*)

of powers, particularly the taxing and spending powers and constitutional aspects of regional disparities.

June 11-12, 1969—First Working Session. Discussions of taxing and spending powers and regional disparities. Reports from Continuing Committee of Officials.

December 8-10, 1969—Third Meeting of the Constitutional Conference. Discussion of the distribution of powers in relation to income security and social services, the spending power and regional disparities.

September 14-15, 1970—Second Working Session. Priority to be given to study of amending procedures and mechanisms for inter-governmental relations. Discussion of constitutional aspects of regional disparities.

February 8-9, 1971—Third Working Session. Preliminary agreement on "elements which might be incorporated into the Constitution at time of early patriation." Agreement on proposed amending formula as a "feasible approach."

June 14-16, 1971—Fourth Constitutional Conference. Discussion of what subsequently emerged as the "Victoria Charter."

CONSTITUTIONAL CONFERENCE VICTORIA, B.C., JUNE 14-16, 1971*

Statement of Conclusions

1. The 7th meeting of the Constitutional Conference was held in Victoria on June 14-16, 1971, on the occasion of the 100th anniversary of the entry of British Columbia into Confederation.
2. The Conference discussions dealt with constitutional provisions as set forth in a Charter which is based on the consensus arrived at in the Working Session of the Constitutional Conference in February 1971. . . . If the Charter, which is to be treated as a whole, is accepted, and this acceptance is communicated to the Secretary of the Constitutional Conference by Monday, June 28th, 1971, governments will recommend the Charter to their Legislative Assemblies and, in the case of the federal government, to both Houses of Parliament.
3. The acceptance of the Charter by both Houses of Parliament and by the Legislative Assemblies would enable the necessary action to be taken to patriate the Canadian Constitution, so that the power to amend and to enact constitutional provisions will rest exclusively with the Canadian people.
4. The proposed Charter also contains the terms of a formula for amending the Constitution entirely within Canada, and a number of other

* From, *Constitutional Conference Proceedings, Victoria, B.C., 1971, June 14, 1971*, Ottawa, Information Canada, 1971. Reproduced by permission of the Minister of Supply and Services Canada.

provisions to be incorporated into the Constitution at the time of patriation. These provisions are concerned with certain basic political and language rights, regional disparities, the Supreme Court of Canada, federal-provincial consultation, and the repeal of reservation and disallowance. In addition, a number of steps would be taken to bring the language of the Constitution up to date, including the renaming of certain enactments, and the deletion of spent and irrelevant provisions.

5. The Constitutional Conference also discussed the subject of social policy. It agreed to include in the proposed Charter an amendment to Section 94A of the B.N.A. Act by adding to its provisions family, youth, and occupational training allowances. In addition, a new sub-section is to be added requiring consultation by the Government of Canada with Provinces on any proposed legislation in relation to a matter covered by the revised section.

6. An early meeting of First Ministers will be held to discuss all aspects of federal-provincial fiscal arrangements, including tax reform, shared-cost programs, equalization and tax sharing. . . .

CANADIAN CONSTITUTIONAL CHARTER (THE VICTORIA CHARTER) 1971*

Part I: Political Rights

Art. 1. It is hereby recognized and declared that in Canada every person has the following fundamental freedoms: freedom of thought, conscience and religion, freedom of opinion and expression, and freedom of peaceful assembly and of association; and all laws shall be construed and applied so as not to abrogate or abridge any such freedom.

Art. 2. No law of the Parliament of Canada or the Legislatures of the Provinces shall abrogate or abridge any of the fundamental freedoms herein recognized and declared.

Art. 3. Nothing in this Part shall be construed as preventing such limitations on the exercise of the fundamental freedoms as are reasonably justifiable in a democratic society in the interests of public safety, order, health or morals, of national security, or of the rights and freedoms of others, whether imposed by the Parliament of Canada or the Legislature of a Province, within the limits of their respective legislative powers, or by the construction or application of any law.

Art. 4. The principles of universal suffrage and free democratic elections to the House of Commons and to the Legislative Assembly of each Province are hereby proclaimed to be fundamental principles of the Constitution.

Art. 5. No citizen shall, by reason of race, ethnic or national origin, colour, religion or sex, be denied the right to vote in an election of

* From, *Constitutional Conference Proceedings, Victoria, B.C., 1971, June 14, 1971*, Ottawa, Information Canada, 1971. Reproduced by permission of the Minister of Supply and Services Canada.

members to the House of Commons or the Legislative Assembly of a Province, or be disqualifed from membership therein.

Art. 6. Every House of Commons shall continue for five years from the day of the return of the writs for choosing the House and no longer, subject to being sooner dissolved by the Governor General, except that in time of real or apprehended war, invasion or insurrection, a House of Commons may be continued by the Parliament of Canada if the continuation is not opposed by the votes of more than one-third of the members of the House.

Art. 7. Every Provincial Legislative Assembly shall continue for five years from the day of the return of the writs for the choosing of the Legislative Assembly, and no longer, subject to being sooner dissolved by the Lieutenant-Governor, except that when the Government of Canada declares that a state of real or apprehended war, invasion or insurrection exists, a Provincial Legislative Assembly may be continued if the continuation is not opposed by the votes of more than one-third of the members of the Legislative Assembly.

Art. 8. There shall be a session of the Parliament of Canada and of the Legislature of each Province at least once in every year, so that twelve months shall not intervene between the last sitting of the Parliament or Legislature in one session and its first sitting in the next session.

Art. 9. Nothing in this Part shall be deemed to confer any legislative power on the Parliament of Canada or the Legislature of any Province.

Part II: Language Rights

Art. 10. English and French are the official languages of Canada having the status and protection set forth in this Part.

Art. 11. A person has the right to use English and French in the debates of the Parliament of Canada and of the Legislatures of Ontario, Quebec, Nova Scotia, New Brunswick, Manitoba, Prince Edward Island and Newfoundland.

Art. 12. The statutes and the records and journals of the Parliament of Canada shall be printed and published in English and French; and both versions of such statutes shall be authoritative.

Art. 13. The statutes of each Province shall be printed and published in English and French, and where the Government of a Province prints and publishes its statutes in one only of the official languages, the Government of Canada shall print and publish them in the other official language; the English and French versions of the statutes of the Provinces of Quebec, New Brunswick and Newfoundland shall be authoritative.

Art. 14. A person has the right to use English and French in giving evidence before, or in any pleading or process in the Supreme Court of Canada, any courts established by the Parliament of Canada or any court of the Provinces of Quebec, New Brunswick and Newfoundland, and to require that all documents and judgments issuing from such courts be in English or French, and when necessary a person is entitled to the services of an interpreter before the courts of the other Provinces.

Art. 15. An individual has the right to use of the official language of his choice in communications between him and the head or central office of every department and agency of the Government of Canada and of the Governments of the Provinces of Ontario, Quebec, New Brunswick, Prince Edward Island and Newfoundland.

Art. 16. A Provincial Legislative Assembly may, by resolution, declare that any part of Articles 13, 14, and 15 that do not expressly apply to that Province shall apply to the Legislative Assembly, and to any of the provincial courts and offices of the provincial departments and agencies according to the terms of the resolution, and thereafter such parts shall apply to the Legislative Assembly, courts and offices specified according to the terms of the resolution; and any right conferred under this Article may be abrogated or diminished only in accordance with the procedure prescribed in Article 50.

Art. 17. A person has the right to the use of the official language of his choice in communications between him and every principal office of the departments and agencies of the Government of Canada that are located in an area where a substantial proportion of the population has the official language of his choice as its mother tongue, but the Parliament of Canada may define the limits of such areas and what constitutes a substantial proportion of the population for the purposes of this Article.

Art. 18. In addition to the rights provided by this Part, the Parliament of Canada and the Legislatures of the Provinces may, within their respective legislative jurisdictions, provide for more extensive use of English and French.

Art. 19. Nothing in this Part shall be construed as derogating from or diminishing any legal or customary right or privilege acquired or enjoyed either before or after the coming into force of this Part with respect to any language that is not English or French.

Part III: Provinces and Territories

Art. 20. Until modified under the authority of the Constitution of Canada, Canada consists of ten Provinces, named Ontario, Quebec, Nova Scotia, New Brunswick, Manitoba, British Columbia, Prince Edward Island, Saskatchewan, Alberta and Newfoundland, two Territories, named the Northwest Territories and the Yukon Territory, and such other territory as may at any time form part of Canada.

Art. 21. There shall be a Legislature for each Province consisting of a Lieutenant-Governor and a Legislative Assembly.

Part IV: Supreme Court of Canada

Art. 22. There shall be a general court of appeal for Canada to be known as the Supreme Court of Canada.

Art. 23. The Supreme Court of Canada shall consist of a chief justice to be called the Chief Justice of Canada, and eight other judges, who shall, subject to this Part, be appointed by the Governor General in Council by letters patent under the Great Seal of Canada.

Art. 24. Any person may be appointed a judge of the Supreme Court of Canada who, after having been admitted to the Bar of any Province, has, for a total period of at least ten years, been a judge of any court in Canada or a barrister or advocate at the Bar of any Province.

Art. 25. At least three of the judges of the Supreme Court of Canada shall be appointed from among persons who, after having been admitted to the Bar of the Province of Quebec, have, for a total period of at least ten years, been judges of any court of that Province or of a court established by the Parliament of Canada or barristers or advocates at that Bar.

Art. 26. Where a vacancy arises in the Supreme Court of Canada and the Attorney General of Canada is considering a person for appointment to fill the vacancy, he shall inform the Attorney General of the appropriate Province.

Art. 27. When an appointment is one falling within Article 25 or the Attorney General of Canada has determined that the appointment shall be made from among persons who have been admitted to the Bar of a specific Province, he shall make all reasonable efforts to reach agreement with the Attorney General of the appropriate Province, before a person is appointed to the Court.

Art. 28. No person shall be appointed to the Supreme Court of Canada unless the Attorney General of Canada and the Attorney General of the appropriate Province agree to the appointment, or such person has been recommended for appointment to the Court by a nominating council described in Article 30, or has been selected by the Attorney General of Canada under Article 30.

Art. 29. Where after the lapse of ninety days from the day a vacancy arises in the Supreme Court of Canada, the Attorney General of Canada and the Attorney General of a Province have not reached agreement on a person to be appointed to fill the vacancy, the Attorney General of Canada may inform the Attorney General of the appropriate Province in writing that he proposes to convene a nominating council to recommend an appointment.

Art. 30. Within thirty days of the day when the Attorney General of Canada has written the Attorney General of the Province that he proposes to convene a nominating council, the Attorney General of the Province may inform the Attorney General of Canada in writing that he selects either of the following types of nominating councils:

(1) a nominating council consisting of the following members: the Attorney General of Canada or his nominee and the Attorneys General of the Provinces or their nominees;

(2) a nominating council consisting of the following members: the Attorney General of Canada or his nominee, the Attorney General of the appropriate Province or his nominee and a chairman to be selected by the two Attorneys General, and if within six months from the expiration of the thirty days they cannot agree on a Chairman, then the Chief Justice of the appropriate Province, or if he is unable to act, the next senior Judge of his court, shall name a Chairman;

and if the Attorney General of the Province fails to make a selection within the thirty days above referred to, the Attorney General of Canada may select the person to be appointed.

Art. 31. When a nominating council has been created, the Attorney General of Canada shall submit the names of not less than three qualified persons to it about whom he has sought the agreement of the Attorney General of the appropriate Province to the appointment, and the nominating council shall recommend therefrom a person for appointment to the Supreme Court of Canada; a majority of the members of a council constitutes a quorum, and a recommendation of a majority of the members at a meeting constitutes a recommendation of the council.

Art. 32. For the purpose of Articles 26 to 31 "appropriate Province" means, in the case of a person being considered for appointment to the Supreme Court of Canada in compliance with Article 25, the Province of Quebec, and in the case of any other person being so considered, the Province to the bar of which such person was admitted, and if a person was admitted to the bar of more than one Province, the Province with the bar of which the person has, in the opinion of the Attorney General of Canada, the closest connection.

Art. 33. Articles 26 to 32 do not apply to the appointment of the Chief Justice of Canada when such appointment is made from among the judges of the Supreme Court of Canada.

Art. 34. The judges of the Supreme Court of Canada hold office during good behaviour until attaining the age of seventy years, but are removable by the Governor General on address of the Senate and House of Commons.

Art. 35. The Supreme Court of Canada has jurisdiction to hear and determine appeals on any constitutional question from any judgment of any court in Canada and from any decision on any constitutional question by any such court in determining any question referred to it, but except as regards appeals from the highest court of final resort in a Province, the Supreme Court of Canada may prescribe such exceptions and conditions to the exercise of such jurisdiction as may be authorized by the Parliament of Canada.

Art. 36. Subject to this Part, the Supreme Court of Canada shall have such further appellate jurisdiction as the Parliament of Canada may prescribe.

Art. 37. The Parliament of Canada may make laws conferring original jurisdiction on the Supreme Court of Canada in respect of such matters in relation of the laws of Canada as may be prescribed by the Parliament of Canada, and authorizing the reference of questions of law or fact to the court and requiring the court to hear and determine the questions.

Art. 38. Subject to this Part, the judgment of the Supreme Court of Canada in all cases is final and conclusive.

Art. 39. Where a case before the Supreme Court of Canada involves questions of law relating to the civil law of the Province of Quebec, and involves no other question of law, it shall be heard by a panel of five judges, or with the consent of the parties, four judges, at least three of whom have the qualifications described in Article 25, and if for any reason three judges of the court who have such qualifications are not available, the court may name such *ad hoc* judges as may be necessary to hear the case from among the judges who have such qualifications serving on a superior court of record established by the law of Canada or of a superior court of appeal of the Province of Quebec.

Art. 40. Nothing in this Part shall be construed as restricting the power existing at the commencement of this Charter of a Provincial Legislature to provide for or limit appeals pursuant to its power to legislate in relation to the administration of justice in the Province.

Art. 41. The salaries, allowances and pensions of the judges of the Supreme Court of Canada shall be fixed and provided by the Parliament of Canada.

Art. 42. Subject to this Part, the Parliament of Canada may make laws to provide for the organization and maintenance of the Supreme Court of Canada, including the establishment of a quorum for particular purposes.

Part V: Courts of Canada

Art. 43. The Parliament of Canada may, notwithstanding anything in the Constitution of Canada, from time to time provide for the constitution, maintenance, and organization of courts for the better administration of the laws of Canada, but no court established pursuant to this Article shall derogate from the jurisdiction of the Supreme Court of Canada as a general court of appeal for Canada.

Part VI: Revised Section 94A

Art. 44. The Parliament of Canada may make laws in relation to old age pensions and supplementary benefits including survivors' and disability benefits irrespective of age, and in relation to family, youth, and occupational training allowances, but no such law shall affect the operation of any law present or future of a Provincial Legislature in relation to any such matter.

Art. 45. The Government of Canada shall not introduce a bill in the House of Commons in relation to a matter described in Article 44 unless it has, at least ninety days before such introduction, advised the government of each Province of the substance of the proposed legislation and requested its views thereon.

Part VII: Regional Disparities

Art. 46. The Parliament and Government of Canada and the Legislatures and Governments of the Provinces are committed to:

1) the promotion of equality of opportunity and well being for all individuals in Canada;
2) the assurance, as nearly as possible, that essential public services of reasonable quality are available to all individuals in Canada; and
3) the promotion of economic development to reduce disparities in the social and economic opportunities for all individuals in Canada wherever they may live.

Art. 47. The provisions of this Part shall not have the effect of altering the distribution of powers and shall not compel the Parliament of Canada or Legislatures of the Provinces to exercise their legislative powers.

Part VIII: Federal-Provincial Consultation

Art. 48. A Conference composed of the Prime Minister of Canada and the First Ministers of the Provinces shall be called by the Prime Minister of Canada at least once a year unless, in any year, a majority of those composing the Conference decide that it shall not be held.

Part IX: Amendments to the Constitution

Art. 49. Amendments to the Constitution of Canada may from time to time be made by proclamation issued by the Governor General under the Great Seal of Canada when so authorized by resolutions of the Senate and House of Commons and of the Legislative Assemblies of at least a majority of the Provinces that includes

1) every Province that at any time before the issue of such proclamation had, according to any previous general census, a population of at least twenty-five per cent of the population of Canada;
2) at least two of the Atlantic Provinces;
3) at least two of the Western Provinces that have, according to the then latest general census, combined populations of at least fifty per cent of the population of all the Western Provinces.

Art. 50. Amendments to the Constitution of Canada in relation to any provision that applies to one or more, but not all, of the Provinces may from time to time be made by proclamation issued by the Governor General under the Great Seal of Canada when so authorized by resolutions of the Senate and House of Commons and of the Legislative Assembly of each Province to which an amendment applies.

Art. 51. An amendment may be made by proclamation under Article 49 or 50 without a resolution of the Senate authorizing the issue of the proclamation if within ninety days of the passage of a resolution by the House of Commons authorizing its issue the Senate has not passed such a resolution and at any time after the expiration of the ninety days the House of Commons again passes the resolution, but any period when Parliament is prorogued or dissolved shall not be counted in computing the ninety days.

Art. 52. The following rules apply to the procedures for amendment described in Articles 49 and 50:

1) either of these procedures may be initiated by the Senate or the House of Commons or the Legislative Assembly of a Province;
2) a resolution made for the purposes of this Part may be revoked at any time before the issue of a proclamation authorized by it.

Art. 53. The Parliament of Canada may exclusively make laws from time to time amending the Constitution of Canada, in relation to the executive Government of Canada and the Senate and House of Commons.

Art. 54. In each Province the Legislature may exclusively make laws in relation to the amendment from time to time of the Constitution of the Province.

Art. 55. Notwithstanding Articles 53 and 54, the following matters may be amended only in accordance with the procedure in Article 49:

1) the office of the Queen, of the Governor General and of the Lieutenant-Governor;
2) the requirements of the Constitution of Canada respecting yearly sessions of the Parliament of Canada and the Legislatures;
3) the maximum period fixed by the Constitution of Canada for the duration of the House of Commons and the Legislative Assemblies;
4) the powers of the Senate;
5) the number of members by which a Province is entitled to be represented in the Senate, and the residence qualifications of Senators;
6) the right of a Province to a number of members in the House of Commons not less than the number of Senators representing the Province;
7) the principles of proportionate representation of the Provinces in the House of Commons prescribed by the Constitution of Canada; and
8) except as provided in Article 16, the requirements of this Charter respecting the use of the English or French language.

Art. 56. The procedure prescribed in Article 49 may not be used to make an amendment when there is another provision for making such amendment in the Constitution of Canada, but that procedure may nonetheless be used to amend any provision for amending the Constitution, including this Article, or in making a general consolidation and revision of the Constitution.

Art. 57. In this Part, "Atlantic Provinces" means the Provinces of Nova Scotia, New Brunswick, Prince Edward Island and Newfoundland, and "Western Provinces" means the Provinces of Manitoba, British Columbia, Saskatchewan and Alberta.

Part X: Modernization of the Constitution

Art. 58. The provisions of this Charter have the force of law in Canada notwithstanding any law in force on the day of its coming into force.

Art. 59. The enactments set out in the first column of the Schedule, hereby repealed to the extent indicated in the second column thereof, shall continue as law in Canada under the names set forth in the third column thereof and as such shall, together with this Charter, collectively be known as the Constitution of Canada, and amendments thereto shall henceforth be made only according to the authority contained therein.

Art. 60. Every enactment that refers to an enactment set out in the Schedule by the name in the first column thereof is hereby amended by substituting for that name the name in the third column thereof.

Art. 61. The court existing on the day of the coming into force of this

Charter under the name of the Supreme Court of Canada shall continue as the Supreme Court of Canada, and the judges thereof shall continue in office as though appointed under Part IV except that they shall hold office during good behaviour until attaining the age of seventy-five years, and until otherwise provided pursuant to the provisions of that Part, all laws pertaining to the court in force on that day shall continue, subject to the provisions of this Charter.

This schedule is NOT final, subject to confirmation

SCHEDULE

Enactments	Extent of Repeal	New Name
British North America Act, 1867, 30-31 Vict., c. 3 (U.K.).	Long title; preamble; the heading immediately preceding section 1; sections 1, 5, the words between brackets in section 12; sections 19, 20, 37, 40, 41, 47, 50, the words "and to Her Majesty's Instructions" and the words "or that he reserves the Bill for the Signification of the Queen's Pleasure" in section 55; sections 56, 57, 63; the words between brackets in section 65; sections 69, 70, 71, 72, 73, 74, 75, 76, 77, 78, 79, 80, 83, 84, 85, 86; the words "the Disallowance of Acts, and the Signification of Pleasure on Bills reserved" and the words "of the Governor General for the Queen and for a Secretary of State, of One Year for Two Years, and of the Province for Canada" in section 90; head (1) of section 91; head (1) of section 92; 94A; sections 101, 103, 104, 105, 106, 107, 119, 120, 122, 123; the words between brackets in section 129; sections 130; 134, 141, 142; the heading immediately preceding section 146; sections 146, 147; the First Schedule; the Second Schedule.	Constitution Act, 1867.
An Act to amend and continue the Act 32 and 33 Victoria chapter 3; and to establish and provide for the Government of the Province of Manitoba, 1870, 33 Vict., c. 3 (Can.).	Long title; Enacting clause; sections 3, 9, 10, 11, 12, 13, 14, 15, 16, 18, 19, 20, 25.	Manitoba Act, 1870.

Order of Her Majesty in Council admitting British Columbia into the Union, dated the 16th day of May 1871.	The whole except terms 4, 9, 10, 13, 14 in the Schedule.	British Columbia Terms of Union
British North America Act, 1871, 34-35 Vict., c. 28 (U.K.), and all acts enacted under section 3 thereof.	Long title; preamble, enacting clause; sections 1, 6.	Constitution Act, 1871.
Order of Her Majesty in Council admitting Prince Edward Island into the Union, dated the 26th day of June, 1873.	The whole, except the conditions in the schedule relating to the provision of steam service and telegraphic communication between the Island and the mainland, the condition respecting the constitution of the executive authority and the Legislature of the province, and the condition applying the British North America Act, 1867 to the province.	Prince Edward Island Terms of Union
Parliament of Canada Act, 1875, 38-39 Vict., c. 38 (U.K.).	Long title; preamble, enacting clause.	Parliament of Canada Act, 1875.
Order of Her Majesty in Council admitting all British possessions and Territories in North America and islands adjacent thereto into the Union, dated the 31st day of July, 1880.	The whole, except the last paragraph.	Adjacent Territories Order.
British North America Act, 1886, 49-50 Vict., c. 35 (U.K.).	Long title; section 3.	Constitution Act, 1886
Canada (Ontario Boundary) Act, 1889, 52-53 Vict., c. 28 (U.K.).	Long title; preamble; enacting clause.	Canada (Ontario Boundary) Act, 1889.
Canadian Speaker (Appointment of Deputy) Act, 1895, Session 2, 59 Vict., c. 3 (U.K.).	Long title; preamble, enacting clause, Section 2.	Canadian Speaker (Appointment of Deputy) Act, 1895.
Alberta Act, 1905, 4-5 Edw. VII, c. 3 (Can.).	Long title; enacting clause, sections 4, 5, 6, 7, 12, 13, 15, 16(2), 18, 19, 20, Schedule.	Alberta Act.
Saskatchewan Act, 1905, 4-5 Edw. VII, c. 42 (Can.).	Long title; enacting clause; sections 4, 5, 6, 7, 12, 13, 14, 15, 16(2), 18, 19, 20, Schedule.	Saskatchewan Act.

British North America Act, 1907, 7 Edw. VII, c. 11 (U.K.).	Long title; preamble, enacting clause, section 2, Schedule.	Constitution Act, 1907.
British North America Act, 1915, 5-6 Geo. V. c. 45 (U.K.).	Long title; enacting clause, section 3.	Constitution Act, 1915.
British North America Act, 1930, 20-21 Geo. V, c. 26 (U.K.).	Long title; fourth paragraph of preamble, enacting clause, section 3.	Constitution Act, 1930.
Statute of Westminster, 1931, 22 Geo. V, c. 4 (U.K.). in so far as it applies to Canada.	Long title; the words "and Newfoundland" in section 1 and 10(3); section 4 in so far as it applies to Canada; section 7(1).	Statute of Westminster, 1931.
British North America Act, 1940, 3-4 Geo. VI, c. 36 (U.K.).	Long title; preamble, enacting clause, section 2.	Constitution Act, 1940.
British North America Act, 1943, 7 Geo. VI, c. 30 (U.K.).	The whole.	
British North America Act, 1946, 10 Geo. VI, c. 63 (U.K.).	Long title; preamble, enacting clause, section 2.	Constitution Act, 1946.
British North America Act, 1949, 12 and 13 Geo. VI, c. 22 (U.K.).	Long title; third paragraph in preamble; enacting clause; sections 2, 3; terms 6(2), (3), 15(2), 16, 22(2), (4), 24, 27, 28, 29 in the Schedule.	Constitution Act, 1949.
British North America (No. 2) Act, 1949 (U.K.). 13 Geo. VI, c. 81 (U.K.)	The whole.	
British North America Act, R.S.C. 1952, c. 304 (Can.).	Section 2.	Constitution Act, 1952.
British North America Act, 1960, 9 Eliz. II, c. 2 (U.K.).	Long title; preamble; enacting clause; sections 2, 3.	Constitution Act, 1960.
British North America Act, 1964, 12 and 13, Eliz. II, c. 73 (U.K.).	Long title; enacting clause; section 2.	Constitution Act, 1964.
British North America Act, 1965, 14 Eliz. II, c. 4, Part I, (Can.).	Section 2.	Constitution Act, 1965.

LETTERS TO THE PREMIERS CONCERNING "PATRIATION" OF THE BNA ACT*

Pierre-Elliott Trudeau

(Same letter sent to Premiers Schreyer, Hatfield, Moores, Regan, Davis, Campbell, Blakeney. An appropriately modified form was sent to Premiers Bennett and Bourassa.)

CONFIDENTIAL

Ottawa, K1A 0A2
March 31, 1976

The Honourable Peter Lougheed,
Premier of Alberta,
Legislative Building,
Edmonton, Alberta.

My dear Premier:
   I had been hoping to be in touch with you well before this to advise you about progress in the exercise we started last April, with our discussion at 7 Rideau Gate, for "patriation" of the B.N.A. Act. . . .
   You will recall that we started with agreement in principle on the desirability of "patriating" the B.N.A. Act and, at the same time, establishing as law the amending procedure that had been agreed to in Victoria in 1971. We also agreed that we would not, in the present "patriation" exercise, consider substantive changes to the B.N.A. Act itself since any entry on that course would, as the discussions from 1968 to 1971 had shown, make early action impossible. Mr. Bourassa indicated, however, that it would be difficult for his government to agree to this, unless the action also included "constitutional guarantees" for the French language and culture. We agreed that our general acceptance of the plan, in principle, would be subject to more precise exploration and definition, and this was the purpose of the discussions Mr. Robertson [secretary to the cabinet] had with you on my behalf. . . .
   It quickly became apparent in Mr. Robertson's discussions that the action for "patriation" and establishment of the amending procedure would be more meaningful for, and more acceptable to, a number of provinces if certain other alterations in our constitutional situation could be established at the same time. Most of these alterations, with the exception of Mr. Bourassa's "constitutional guarantees", were among the things that had been included in the Victoria Charter. They included the provision for consultation with the provinces about appointments to the Supreme Court of Canada and the special handling of cases arising from the civil law of Quebec. They included also the provision concerning the reduction of regional disparities. Certain of the western provinces wanted

---

* Letter and "Draft Proclamation" tabled in the House of Commons, April 9, 1976, and published in *House of Commons Debates*, April 9, pp. 12696-12699 and pp. 12701-12705. Reproduced by permission of the Minister of Supply and Services Canada.

to have the amending procedure itself modified so that the requirement with regard to consent from the four western provinces would be the same as that for the four eastern provinces. This would mean deletion of the population provision respecting the western provinces that was inserted at Victoria.

The main problem was the definition of the "constitutional guarantees" to which Mr. Bourassa had referred at the outset. Mr. Robertson found that the Premiers he spoke to after the initial discussions with Mr. Bourassa in May had no objection in principle to "constitutional guarantees", although all made it clear that they would want to consider them in detail once they had been worked out with Quebec and reduced to writing.

I will not go into all the difficulties that are presented by the concept of "constitutional guarantees"; they are many and complex. Discussions with Mr. Bourassa's representatives finally led to a formulation that was included in a document sent to him in November, 1975. I am enclosing a copy of the full document herewith. I would draw your attention especially to Parts IV and VI. The formulation of the principal "constitutional guarantee" is Part IV (Article 38). It is buttressed by Part VI (Article 40) and also by the provisions concerning language in Part III.

As I have mentioned, the "constitutional guarantee" was a concept raised by Mr. Bourassa and stated by him to be essential. Articles 38 and 40 attempt to cover the points made by his representatives. Mr. Bourassa knows that my colleagues and I share some conern about the Articles, and he understands that it will fall to him to explain them to his fellow Premiers, in the light of the facts relating to the position of the French language and culture in Canada.

I should emphasize that the document, while it is styled a "Draft Proclamation", was put in this form simply to show with maximum clarity what the result would be if all the proposals, as they had emerged in the course of Mr. Robertson's consultations, were found acceptable by all governments. It should not be regarded as a specific proposal or draft to which anyone is committed at this stage, since there has not been agreement to the totality of it by anyone. It is rather in the nature of a report on the various ideas, including Mr. Bourassa's "constitutional guarantee", as they developed in the course of the informal discussions from April to November, 1975.

As I stated earlier, most of the "Draft Proclamation" consists of provisions of the Victoria Charter which various Premiers have asked to have included in any action we take. In some cases there are adjustments of the Victoria provisions in order to take into account altered circumstances since 1971 and to benefit by some hind-sight. The new parts of this "report" are the Parts IV and VI to which I have already referred. For ease of reference the main elements are:

(a) A Preamble. This is entirely new and is simply an idea of the way a total presentation might look.

(b) Part I is the amending formula contained in the Victoria Charter made applicable to those parts of the Constitution not now amendable in

Canada. Thus Articles 49, 50, 51, 52, 56 and 57 of Part IX of the Victoria Charter are included, while Articles 53, 54 and 55, which were designed to replace Articles 91(1) and 92(1) of the British North America Act, are not. The amending formula has not been modified to take account of the views expressed by certain Western Premiers concerning the population qualification for agreement by the Western provinces. I suggest that this might be a matter that, in the first instance, the four Western Premiers might attempt to solve among themselves.

(c) Part II, which is Part IV of the Victoria Charter concerning the Supreme Court, with a final Article (included in another Part of the Victoria Charter) to protect the status of Judges already appointed.

(d) Part III, which is a modified version of Part II of the Victoria Charter concerning language rights. It would entrench the constitutional status of the English and French languages federally. It would not affect the provinces, but it would permit a province, under Article 35, to entrench its own provision if it so wished.

(e) Part IV, which is the "guarantee" designed to protect the French language and culture against adverse action by the Parliament and Government of Canada.

(f) Part V, which is essentially Part VII of the Victoria Charter on Regional Disparities. The presentation has been slightly altered but there is no change in substance whatever.

(g) Part VI, which is a new Article designed to indicate the spirit in which Governments may enter into agreements. In two of the three areas specifically mentioned, major agreements with Quebec have been concluded over the past two years (family allowances and consultation on immigration).

Mr. Bourassa advised me in our conversation on March 5th that the things he considers to be necessary might well go beyond what we, in the federal government, have understood to be involved in the present exercise. In part they might relate to the distribution of powers. I advised him that the Government of Canada, for its part, feels that it can go no further as part of this exercise than the constitutional guarantees that are embodied in the document and that indeed even they might find difficulty of acceptance in their present form. To go further would involve entry upon the distribution of powers, with the consequences to which I have referred. We must, then, consider three alternatives that are open to us in these circumstances.

Let us begin with the simplest alternative. The Government of Canada remains firmly of the view that we should, as a minimum, achieve "patriation" of the B.N.A. Act. It is not prepared to contemplate the continuation of the anomalous situation in which the British Parliament retains the power to legislate with respect to essential parts of the constitution of Canada. Such "patriation" could be achieved by means of an Address of the two Houses of the Canadian Parliament to the Queen, requesting appropriate legislation by the British Parliament to end its capacity to legislate in any way with respect to Canada. Whereas unanimity of the federal government and the provinces would be desirable even for so limited a measure, we are satisfied that such action by the Parliament of

Canada does not require the consent of the provinces and would be entirely proper since it would not affect in any way the distribution of powers. In other words, the termination of the British capacity to legislate for Canada would not in any way alter the position as between Parliament and the provincial legislatures whether in respect of jurisdictions flowing from Sections 91 and 92 or otherwise.

However, simple "patriation" would not equip us with an amending procedure for those parts of our constitution that do not come under either Section 91(1) or Section 92(1) of the B.N.A. Act. To meet this deficiency, one could provide in the Address to the Queen that amendment of those parts of the constitution not now amendable in Canada could be made on unanimous consent of Parliament and the legislatures until a permanent formula is found and established. In theory this approach would introduce a rigidity which does not now exist, since at present it is the federal Parliament alone which goes to Westminster, and the degree of consultation of or consent by the provinces is a matter only of convention about which there can be differences of view. In practice, of course, the federal government has in the past sought the unanimous consent of the provinces before seeking amendments that have affected the distribution of powers.

A second and perhaps preferable alternative would be to include in the action a provision that could lead to the establishment of a permanent and more flexible amending procedure. That could be done by detailing such a procedure in our Joint Address and having it included in the British legislation as an enabling provision that would come into effect when and only when it had received the formal approval of the legislatures of all the provinces. The obvious amending procedure to set forth would be the one agreed to at Victoria in application to those parts of our constitution not now amendable in Canada (Part I of the attached "Draft Proclamation"). This could be with or without modification respecting the four western provinces. (On this last point, the federal government would be quite prepared to accept the proposed modification and it is my understanding that the other provinces would equally agree if the western provinces can arrive at agreement.)

If we took the above step, we would achieve forthwith half of our objective of last April—"patriation"—and we would establish a process by which the other half—the amending procedure—would become effective as and when the provincial legislatures individually signify their agreement. Over a period of time, which I hope would not be long, we would establish the total capacity to amend our constitution under what is clearly the best and most acceptable procedure that has been worked out in nearly fifty years of effort, since the original federal-provincial conference on this subject in 1927. Until full agreement and implementation had been achieved, any constitutional changes that might be needed, and which did not come under Section 91(1) or Section 92(1) or which could not otherwise be effected in Canada could be made subject to unanimous consent. This would impose an interim rigidity for such very rare requirements for amendment, but, as I have said, the practice has, in any event, been to secure unanimous consent before making amendments that have affected the distribution of powers.

A third and more extensive possibility still, would be to include, in the "patriation" action, the entirety of the "Draft Proclamation" I am enclosing. In other words the British Parliament, in terminating its capacity to legislate for Canada, could provide that all of the substance of Parts I to VI would come into effect in Canada and would have full legal force when, and only when, the entirety of those Parts have been approved by the legislatures of all the provinces. At that point, we would have, not only "patriation" and the amending procedure, but also the other provisions that have developed out of the discussions thus far. Here again, of course, until all the Provinces had approved the entire Draft Proclamation, any constitutional change which did not come under Section 91(1) or Section 92(1) would be subject to unanimous consent.

As you can see, there are several possibilities as to the course of action now to take. So far as the federal government is concerned, our much preferred course would be to act in unison with all the provinces. "Patriation" is such a historic milestone that it would be ideal if all Premiers would associate themselves with it.

But if unanimity does not appear possible, the federal government will have to decide whether it will recommend to Parliament that a Joint Address be passed seeking "patriation" of the B.N.A. Act. A question for decision then will be what to add to that action. We are inclined to think that it should, at the minimum, be the amending procedure agreed to at Victoria by all the provinces, with or without modification respecting the western provinces, and subject to the condition about coming into force only when approved by the legislatures of all the provinces as explained above.

The implications of the different possibilities are complex, and you will undoubtedly want to consider them with care. To facilitate consideration, Mr. Robertson would be glad to come to see you, at a convenient time, for such discussions as you might wish to have. When opportunity offers at an early meeting, we might also discuss the matter together. . . .

Sincerely,
P. E. Trudeau (Signature)

FORM FOR A PROCLAMATION OF THE GOVERNOR GENERAL

DRAFT

CONFIDENTIAL

November 10th, 1975.

Whereas it is fitting that it should be possible to amend the Constitution of Canada in all respects by action of the appropriate instrumentalities of government in Canada acting separately or in concert as may best suit the matter in question;

And whereas it is desirable to make more specific provision respecting the constitutional status of the English and French languages in Canada and to ensure that changes in the Constitution, interpretation of its provisions or action by the Parliament or Government of Canada should not endanger the continuation and full development of the French language and the culture based thereon;

And whereas it is desirable that the Parliament and Government of Canada and the Legislatures and Governments of the Provinces act effectively to promote equality of opportunity and an acceptable level of public services among the different regions of Canada;

Therefore it is desirable to establish among other things:

(a) A method for the amendment in Canada of those parts of the Constitution of general interest and concern that cannot now be amended in Canada in which the consent will be required of the Legislatures of Provinces representative of both the official language groups of Canada as well as of the Legislatures of Provinces in all of the geographical regions of Canada;

(b) means by which Provinces can participate in the selection of persons to be appointed to the Supreme Court of Canada; and

(c) principles to guide the Parliament of Canada in the exercise of powers allotted to it under the Constitution of Canada and to guide the Government of Canada in the exercise of powers conferred upon it by the Constitution of Canada and by laws enacted by the Parliament of Canada;

Now therefore We . . . do proclaim as follows:

Part I: Amendments to the Constitution

[Six of the seven Articles in Part I are identical to Articles in the Canadian Constitutional Charter, 1971, (the "Victoria Charter"), except for the numbering. Articles 1-4 in Part I are identical to Articles 49-52 respectively in the Canadian Constitutional Charter, *supra*, p. 28. Articles 5 and 6 are identical to Articles 56 and 57 respectively, *ibid*. Article 7 is an addition.]

Art. 7. The enactments set out in the Schedule shall continue as law in Canada and as such shall, together with this Proclamation and any Proclamation subsequently issued under this Part, collectively be known as the Constitution of Canada, and amendments thereto shall henceforth be made only according to the authority contained therein.

Part II: Supreme Court of Canada

[There are 22 Articles in Part II, numbered 8-29. Articles 8-28 are identical to Articles 22-42, except for the numbering, in the Canadian Constitutional Charter, *supra*, pp. 24-27. Article 29 is identical to Article 61 in the Charter.]

Part III: Language Rights

[Articles 35 and 36 in Part III are identical to Articles 16 and 17 respectively in the Canadian Constitutional Charter, *supra*, p. 24. The other Articles in this Part, *infra*, differ from the corresponding Articles in the Charter in that they omit the Charter's references to their applicability to the provinces.]

Art. 30. English and French are the official languages of Canada, but no provision in this Part shall derogate from any right, privilege, or obligation existing under any other provision of the Constitution.

Art. 31. A person has the right to use English and French in the debates of the Parliament of Canada.

Art. 32. The statutes and the records and journals of the Parliament of Canada shall be printed and published in English and French; and both versions of such statutes are authoritative.

Art. 33. A person has the right to use English and French in giving evidence before, or in any pleading or process in the Supreme Court of Canada and any courts established by the Parliament of Canada, and to require that all documents and judgments issuing from such courts be in English or French.

Art. 34. An individual has the right to the use of the official language of his choice in communications between him and the head or central office of every department and agency of the Government of Canada.

Art. 37. In addition to the rights provided by this Part, the Parliament of Canada may, within its legislative jurisdiction, provide for more extensive use of English and French.

Part IV: Protection of the French Language and Culture

Art. 38. The Parliament of Canada, in the exercise of powers allotted to it under the Constitution of Canada, and the Government of Canada, in the exercise of powers conferred upon it by the Constitution of Canada and by laws enacted by the Parliament of Canada, shall be guided by, among other considerations for the welfare and advantage of the people of Canada, the knowledge that a fundamental purpose underlying the federation of Canada is to ensure the preservation and the full development of the French language and the culture based on it and neither the Parliament nor the Government of Canada, in the exercise of their respective powers, shall act in a manner that will adversely affect the preservation and development of the French language and the culture based on it.

Part V: Regional Disparities

[The one Article in this Part, numbered 39, is almost identical to Articles 46 and 47 in the Canadian Constitutional Charter, *supra*, pp. 27-28.]

Part VI: Federal-Provincial Agreements

Art. 40(1) In order to ensure a greater harmony of action by governments, and especially in order to reduce the possibility of action that could adversely affect the preservation and development in Canada of the French language and the culture based on it, the Government of Canada and the Governments of the Provinces or of any one or more of the Provinces may, within the limits of the powers otherwise accorded to each of them respectively by law, enter into agreements with one another concerning the manner of exercise of such powers, particularly in the fields of immigration, communications and social policy.

(2) Nothing in this Article shall be held to limit or restrict any authority conferred either before or after the coming into force of this Proclamation upon the Government of Canada or the Government of a Province to enter into agreements within the limits of the powers otherwise accorded to it by law.

SCHEDULE

[This Schedule lists the same Enactments as the Canadian Constitutional Charter, *supra*, pp. 30-32.]

[Prime Minister Trudeau's proposals were discussed by the provincial premiers during 1976. The Premiers' Conferences held in Edmonton and Toronto during the summer and fall failed to produce agreement among the provinces. The premiers of Alberta and British Columbia insisted on the inclusion in any amendment formula of the right of each of their provinces to have a veto over any proposed amendment of the B.N.A. Act.]

FIVE RECENT CANADIAN PARLIAMENTARY AMENDMENTS OF THE B.N.A. ACT*

Paul Fox

Amendment (No. 2) 1949 of the British North America Act conferred on the Canadian Parliament the power to amend "the Constitution of Canada" in certain respects. Under this power, which became Section 91(1) of the B.N.A. Act, the Canadian Parliament has enacted five amendments which may be summarized as follows:

1952—c.15, cited as the *B.N.A. Act, 1952*, which provided for the readjustment of representation in the House of Commons.

1965—c.4, cited as the *B.N.A. Act, 1965*, which provided for the retirement of certain senators at 75 years of age (incumbents opting for retirement and subsequent newly appointed senators).

1974-75-76—c.13, cited as the *B.N.A. Act (No. 2, 1974)*, which again provided for an adjustment of representation in the House of Commons.

---

* From information provided by the courtesy of Mr. T. B. Smith, Departmental General Counsel, and Acting Director, Constitutional, Administrative and International Law Section, Department of Justice, Ottawa, March 9, 1976.

1974-75-76—c.28, cited as the *B.N.A. Act, 1975*, which confirmed the representation in the House of Commons of one member of Parliament from the Yukon Territory and increased the representation in the Commons of the Northwest Territories to two members.

1974-75-76—c.53, cited as the *B.N.A. Act (No. 2), 1975*, which increased the number of senators by adding two, one each for the Yukon and Northwest Territories.

(There was no *B.N.A. Act (No. 1), 1974*, since the Bill originally submitted under this designation ultimately became *B.N.A. Act (No. 2), 1975*.)

From 1949 to March 9, 1976, there were three additional amendments passed by the United Kingdom Parliament. The *British North America Act, 1960, 9 Eliz. II, c.2 (U.K.)* repealed the existing Section 99 of the B.N.A. Act and substituted a new Section 99 which altered the tenure of judges of provincial superior courts from life to 75 years of age. The *British North America Act, 1951, 14-15 Geo. VI, c.32 (U.K.)* added Section 94A to the B.N.A. Act, enabling the Parliament of Canada to make laws in relation to old age pensions in Canada. The *British North America Act, 1964, 12-13 Eliz. II, c.73 (U.K.)* altered the foregoing amendment to permit the Parliament of Canada to make laws in relation to old age pensions and supplementary benefits, including survivors' and disability benefits irrespective of age. Both amendments specified that no such law shall affect the operation of any law present or future of a provincial legislature in relation to such matters.

THE OFFICIAL LANGUAGES ACT—
EQUAL STATUS FOR FRENCH AND ENGLISH*

Bilingual Districts Advisory Board

Introduction

1. The Official Languages Act was passed by Parliament and assented to in July 1969. It came into force in September of the same year. The passage of the Act marked the culmination of an intensive discussion and examination of the benefit of giving statutory recognition to the existence in Canada of two official languages, English and French.

2. In any country in which more than one language is commonly spoken, it is necessary to determine the official status of the languages used. While many languages are spoken in Canada, English and French are the languages of the two founding peoples who, in fact, constitute the two largest groups of citizens. According to the census of 1971, Canadians of English mother tongue amounted to 12,973,810 persons or 60.2 per cent of the total population of 21,568,310 while Canadians of French

* From *Report of the Bilingual Districts Advisory Board, October, 1975*, Ottawa, Information Canada, 1975. Reproduced by permission of the Minister of Supply and Services Canada.

mother tongue constituted 5,793,650 individuals or 26.9 per cent of the population; the remaining 2,800,850 Canadians, or 13.0 per cent, were of other mother tongue. In 1967, after an extended and thorough investigation of the subject, the Royal Commission on Bilingualism and Biculturalism recommended in its final report that the federal government should declare two languages official in Canada, English and French. Parliament accepted this advice and two years later passed the Official Languages Act.

3. Section 2 of the Act declares that "The English and French languages are the official languages of Canada for all purposes of the Parliament and Government of Canada, and possess and enjoy equality of status and equal rights and privileges as to their use in all the institutions of the Parliament and Government of Canada."

4. The statute contains a number of provisions to assist in the implemention of the intent of this declaration. Some clauses in the Act require the publication in both languages of statutory and other instruments, others place certain obligations upon federal departments and agencies to provide their services in both languages, others create the position of Commissioner of Official Languages to oversee the enforcement of the Act, and still others provide for the creation of bilingual districts. . . .

5. There are seven sections in the Act devoted to the establishment and functioning of bilingual districts and the role to be played in their creation by a Bilingual Districts Advisory Board. The relevant sections of the Act are numbers 12 to 18. . . .

The Purpose of Bilingual Districts

6. According to the Act, a bilingual district is to be an area in which both of the official languages are spoken as a mother tongue by persons residing in the locality and in which the number of individuals belonging to the official language minority amounts to at least ten per cent of the total population of the area. When a bilingual district is proclaimed, the federal government is required to communicate with the public and to provide its services in both official languages at each of its principal offices in every department, agency, and judicial, quasi-judicial or administrative body or Crown corporation in the bilingual district.

7. Although the purpose of bilingual districts thus appears to be simple and clear, we have encountered so much confusion in the public's mind on this point that we would like to emphasize the basic intention by reiterating it. The objective of creating a bilingual district is to require the federal government to provide its services in both languages.

8. However, it should be clearly understood that the existence of a bilingual district will not oblige the public to become bilingual. Far from it. In fact, just the opposite is true. A bilingual district can protect unilingualism by ensuring that an individual who speaks only English or only French can communicate with the federal government in his or her own language. The bilingual requirement that is imposed by a district does not fall upon the public but upon the government.

9. It should be added that the obligation incurred by the federal

government does not mean that all of its civil servants must be, or must become, bilingual. Only those employees dealing with the public under the circumstances described above would be expected to be bilingual.

10. It is also worth observing that nothing in the Official Languages Act, whether it be the clauses in the statute establishing English and French as the official languages of Canada or any other section providing for the implementation of this declaration, derogates in any way from the privileges enjoyed by any additional language. Section 38 of the Act expressly forbids the diminution of any legal or customary rights or privileges possessed or acquired by any additional language before or after the Act came into force.

11. The objective of the Act was summarized cogently in 1969 by the then Secretary of State, the Honourable Gérard Pelletier, when he remarked during a discussion of the Official Languages Bill in the House of Commons on May 16 on that year, "The purpose of the present bill is not to regulate the language which citizens must speak, but to ensure they may address the federal government agencies in the official language of their choice."

●　　　●　　　●

31. . . . While the intent of the Act and the meaning of most of its sections are very clear, some clauses are rather difficult to interpret precisely. Section 2 of the Act, for example, appears to state the intent of the legislation very explicitly. It declares that English and French are the official languages of Canada in regard to all the functions of the Parliament and government of Canada and that the two languages are to have equal status, rights, and privileges in their use in all federal institutions.

Some Qualifications

32. Yet, despite the apparent clarity of this statement, some of the sections which implement it qualify the generality of the declaration. Sections 3, 4, 5, 6, and 7, for instance, require equal treatment for French and English in the publication of federal public notices, rules, orders, regulations, by-laws, proclamations, and advertisements, and in the final decisions and judgments of judicial or quasi-judicial bodies, but these sections also attach some conditions to the requirement to publish some of these items simultaneously in both languages.

33. Furthermore, while Section 9 obliges the federal government to provide certain services in both languages in the National Capital Region, in bilingual districts, and on occasion elsewhere, the section qualifies this requirement in several ways which will be elaborated below. Section 10 provides for bilingual services to the travelling public, but only where there is significant and regular demand. Section 11 requires the use of the two languages in courts and judicial proceedings, but again subject to certain conditions, including in some instances the concurrence of enabling provincial legislation governing some courts. Likewise, Section 39

and 40 also specify certain qualifications. Finally, while Sections 12, 13 and 14 lay down the procedures for creating bilingual districts, the clauses make the proclamation of districts discretionary, not obligatory.

34. It would be misleading to convey the impression that every section of the Act attaches qualifications to the general declaration of the equal status of French and English. To take two examples in which this is not the case, Section 8, for instance, makes the construction of enactments in English and French equally authentic while Sections 19 to 34 establish the office of the Commissioner of Official Languages who is to enforce the Act and to ensure the recognition of the status of each of the two languages.

35. But the specification, in the clauses noted previously, of certain restraints in the provision of bilingual services by federal institutions does imply that the equality of the two languages referred to in Section 2 is not applicable universally throughout Canada in all federal agencies. The same inference can be drawn from the Act's provision for the establishment of bilingual districts themselves since the latter are to be selected areas within Canada in which the federal government is obliged to offer its services in both languages.

36. Thus, it is apparent that the Act does not envisage the provision of bilingual services by federal institutions everywhere in Canada and that to the extent that this limitation prevails, the principle of the equality of status of the two official languages is not fulfilled. However, a reading of the clauses of the Act which prescribe exceptions to the principle of equality reveals that the limitations are dictated by common sense and practicality. For example, the Act states, as noted already, that under certain circumstances bilingual services need not be provided where there is insufficient demand. Such a case might arise in a unilingual area in Canada in which almost all of the residents belong by mother tongue to one or the other of the two official language groups.

Basic Principle Clear

37. The Board did not need much time to decide that the utilization of common sense and practicality in the implementation of the principle of the Act did not nullify the basic principle itself, namely, the intent to give equality of status to the two official languages. We believed that the intent of the legislation is . . . apparent. . . .

BIBLIOGRAPHY

Constitution

Bissonnette, B., *Essai sur la constitution du Canada*, Montréal, Editions du jour, 1963.

Bohemier, A., *Faillite en droit constitutionnel Canadien*, Montréal, Les Presses de l'Université de Montréal, 1972.

Brossard, J., *L'immigration: Les droits et pouvoirs du Canada et du Québec*, Montréal, Les Presses de l'Université de Montréal, 1967.

Cairns, A. C., "The Living Canadian Constitution," *Q.Q*, Vol. LXXVII, No. 4, 1970.

The Canada Committee, *Declaration by English and French-Speaking Canadians*, Montreal, 1966.

Driedger, E. A., *A Consolidation of the British North America Acts 1867 to 1975*, Ottawa, Minister of Supply and Services, 1975.

Faribault, M., and Fowler, R., *Ten to One, the Confederation Wager*, Toronto, McClelland and Stewart, 1965.

Forsey, E. A., *Freedom and Order: Collected Essays*, Carleton Library No. 73, Toronto, McClelland and Stewart, 1974.

Gibson, D., "Constitutional Jurisdiction over Environmental Management in Canada," *University of Toronto Law Journal*, Vol. 23, 1973.

Kwavnick, D., *The Tremblay Report*, Carleton Library No. 64, Toronto, McClelland and Stewart, 1973.

La Forest, G. V., "Delegation of Legislative Power in Canada," *McGill Law Journal*, Vol. 21, No. 1, Spring, 1975.

La Forest, G. V., *Disallowance and Reservation of Provincial Legislation*, Ottawa, Department of Justice, 1955.

La Forest, G. V., *Natural Resources and Public Property Under the Canadian Constitution*, Toronto, University of Toronto Press, 1969.

Lajoie, A., *La pouvoir déclaratoire du Parlement*, Montréal, Les Presses de l'Université de Montréal, 1969.

La Société St. Jean Baptiste de Montréal, *Le Fédéralisme, l'acte de l'amérique du nord britannique et les Canadiens francais*, Mémoire au comité parlementaire de la constitution du gouvernement du Québec, Montréal, Les éditions de l'agence Duvernay, 1964.

Laskin, B., *Canadian Constitutional Law: Cases, Text, and Notes on Distribution of Legislative Power*, Toronto, Carswell, 3rd. ed., 1969.

Lederman, W. R. (ed.), *The Courts and the Canadian Constitution*, Carleton Library No. 16, Toronto, McClelland and Stewart, 1964.

Lyon, J. N., and Atkey, R. G., *Canadian Constitutional Law in a Modern Perspective*, Toronto, University of Toronto Press, 1970.

O'Hearn, P. J. T., *Peace, Order and Good Government: A New Constitution for Canada*, Toronto, Macmillan, 1964.

Pepin, G., *Les Tribunaux Administratifs et La Constitution: Etude des articles 96 à 101 de l'A.A.N.B.*, Montréal, Les Presses de l'Université de Montréal, 1969.

Russell, P. H., (ed.), *Leading Constitutional Decisions*, Carleton Library No. 23, Toronto, McClelland and Stewart, rev. ed., 1973.

Stanley, G. F. G., *A Short History of the Canadian Constitution*, Toronto, Ryerson, 1969.

Tremblay, A., *Les compétences législatives au Canada et les pouvoirs provinciaux en matière de propriété et de droits civils*, Ottawa, Edition de l'Université, 1967.

Federal Problems

Aitchison, J. H., "Interprovincial Co-operation in Canada," in Aitchison, J. H., (ed.), *The Political Process in Canada*, Toronto, University of Toronto Press, 1963.

Albrecht-Carrie, R., "The Canadian Dilemma", *Journal of Canadian Studies*, Vol. IX, No. 1, February, 1974.

Angers, F. A., "La phase du mouvement dans les relations fédérales-provinciales," *L'Action nationale*, Vol. LIV, novembre, 1964.

Black, E. R., *Divided Loyalties: Canadian Concepts of Federalism*, Montreal, McGill-Queen's University Press, 1975.

Black, E. R., and Cairns, A., "A Different Perspective on Canadian Federalism," *C.P.A.*, Vol. IX, No. 1, March, 1966.
Bonenfant, J. C., "Les projets théoriques du fédéralisme canadien," *Cahiers des dix*, Vol. 29, 1964.
Bonenfant, J. C., et Tremblay, J. N., "Le concept d'une nation canadienne est-il un concept équivoque?" *Culture*, Vol. XXV, No. 2, juin, 1964.
Breton, A., Breton, R., Bruneau, C., Gauthier, Y., Lalonde, M., Pinard, M., Trudeau, P. E., "Manifeste pour une politique fonctionnelle," *Cité libre*, Vol. XV, No. 67, mai, 1964. [English translation in *Canadian Forum*, Vol. XLIV, No. 520, May, 1964.]
Burns, R. M., "Uncertain Life of cooperative federalism", *Q.Q.*, Vol. 78, No. 4, Winter, 1971.
Burns, R. M., (ed.), *One Country or Two?*, London and Montreal, McGill-Queen's University Press, 1971.
Burton, T. L., *Natural Resources Policy in Canada: Issues and Perspectives*, Toronto, McClelland and Stewart, 1972.
Canada, *Dominion-Provincial and Interprovincial Conferences from 1887 to 1926*, Ottawa, Queen's Printer, 1951.
Canada, *Dominion-Provincial Conferences, 1927, 1935, 1941*, Ottawa, Queen's Printer, 1951.
Canada, *Dominion-Provincial Conference, (1945)*, Ottawa, Queen's Printer, 1946.
Canada, *Proceedings of the Federal-Provincial Conference, 1955*, Ottawa, Queen's Printer, 1955.
Canada, *Dominion-Provincial Conference, 1957*, Ottawa, Queen's Printer, 1958.
Canada, *Proceedings of the Federal-Provincial Conference, 1963*, Ottawa, Queen's Printer, 1964.
Caplan, N., "Some Factors Affecting the Resolution of a Federal-Provincial Conflict," *C.J.P.S.*, Vol. II, No. 2, June, 1969.
Cheffins, R. I., *The Constitutional Process in Canada*, Toronto, McGraw-Hill Ryerson, second ed., 1976.
Cohen, M., "The Judicial Process and National Policy—A Problem for Canadian Federalism" *McGill Law Journal*, Vol. 16, No. 2, 1970.
Cole, T., *The Canadian Bureaucracy and Federalism, 1947-65*, Denver, University of Denver, 1966.
Creighton, D. G., *The Road to Confederation: The Emergence of Canada, 1863-1867*, Toronto, Macmillan, 1964.
Crépeau, P. A., and Macpherson, C. B., (eds.), *The Future of Canadian Federalism; l'Avenir du fédéralisme canadien*, Toronto, University of Toronto Press, Montréal, Les Presses de l'Université de Montréal, 1965.
Croisat, M., "Planification et Fédéralisme," *C.P.A.*, Vol. XI, No. 3, Fall, 1968.
Dehem, R., *Planification économique et fédéralisme*, Montréal, Les Presses de l'Université Laval, 1968.
Dubuc, A., "Une interprétation économique de la constitution," *Socialisme 66, Revue du socialisme international et Québécois*, No. 7, janvier, 1966. [English translation in *Canadian Forum*, Vol. XLV, No. 542, March, 1966.]
Gallant, E., "The Machinery of Federal-Provincial Relations: I," and Burns, R. M., "The Machinery of Federal-Provincial Relations: II," *C.P.A.*, Vol. VIII, No. 4, December, 1965.
Gelinas, A., "Trois modes d'approche à la détermination de l'opportunité de la décentralisation de l'organisation politique principalement en système fédéral," *C.P.A.*, Vol. IX, No. 1, March, 1966.
Hawkins, G., (ed.), *Concepts of Federalism*, Proceedings of 34th Couchiching Conference, Toronto, Canadian Institute on Public Affairs, 1965.

Hawkins, G., (ed.), *The Idea of Maritime Union*, Report of a Conference sponsored by the Canadian Institute on Public Affairs and Mount Allison University, Saskville, N.B., 1965.

Hockin, T. A., *et al.*, *The Canadian Condominium: Domestic Issues External Policy*, Toronto, McClelland and Stewart, 1972.

Johnson, A. W., "The Dynamics of Federalism in Canada," *C.J.P.S.*, Vol. I, No. 1, March, 1968.

Kear, A. R., "Co-operative Federalism: A Study of the Federal-Provincial Continuing Committee on Fiscal and Economic Matters," *C.P.A.*, Vol. VI, No. 1, March, 1963.

Kwavnick, D., "Quebec and the Two Nations Theory: a Re-examination", *Q.Q.*, Vol. 81, No. 3, Autumn, 1974.

Lamontagne, M., *Le fédéralisme canadien*, Québec, Les presses universitaires Laval, 1954.

Leach, R. H., "Interprovincial Co-operation: Neglected Aspect of Canadian Federalism" *C.P.A.*, Vol. II, No. 2, June, 1959.

Leach, R. H., (ed.), *Contemporary Canada*, Toronto, University of Toronto Press, 1968.

Lederman, W. R., "The Concurrent Operation of Federal and Provincial Laws in Canada," *McGill Law Journal*, Vol. IX, 1963.

Lederman, W. R., "Unity and Diversity in Canadian Federalism: Ideals and Methods of Moderation," *Canadian Bar Review*, Vol. LIII, No. 3, September, 1975.

Leeson, H. A. and Vanderelst, W., (eds.), *External Affairs and Canadian Federalism: The History of a Dilemma*, Toronto and Montreal, Holt, Rinehart and Winston, 1973.

Livingston, W. S., *Federalism and Constitutional Change*, Oxford, Oxford University Press, 1963.

Lower, A. R. M., Scott, F. R., *et al.*, *Evolving Canadian Federalism*, Durham, Duke University Press, 1958.

McWhinney, E., *Comparative Federalism, States' Rights and National Power*, Toronto, University of Toronto Press, second ed., 1965.

May, R. J., "Decision-making and Stability in Federal Systems," *C.J.P.S.*, Vol. III, No. 1, March, 1970.

Meekison, J. P., (ed.), *Canadian Federalism: Myth or Reality*, Toronto, Methuen, second ed., 1971.

Ontario Advisory Committee on Confederation, *Background Papers and Reports*, Toronto, Queen's Printer, Vol. I, 1967; Vol. II, 1970.

Plumptre, A. F. W., "Regionalism and the Public Service," *C.P.A.*, Vol. VIII, No. 4, December, 1965.

Prévost, J.-P., *La crise du fédéralisme canadien*, Paris, Presses universitaires de France, 1972.

Riker, W. H., *Federalism: Origin, Operation, Significance*, Boston and Toronto, Little, Brown, 1964.

Russell, P., (ed.), *Nationalism in Canada*, Toronto, McGraw-Hill, 1966.

Ryerson, S. B., *Unequal Union*, Toronto, Progress, 1968.

Smiley, D. V., *The Rowell-Sirois Report*, Book, Carleton Library No. 5, Toronto, McClelland and Stewart, 1963.

Smiley, D. V., "Public Administration and Canadian Federalism," *C.P.A.*, Vol. VII, No. 3, September, 1964.

Smiley, D. V., "The Two Themes of Canadian Federalism" *C.J.E.P.S.*, Vol. XXXI, No. 1, February, 1965.

Smiley, D. V., *The Canadian Political Nationality*, Toronto, Methuen, 1967.

Smiley, D., *Canada in Question: Federalism in the 70's*, Toronto, McGraw-Hill Ryerson, second ed., 1976.
Soucy, E., "Confédération ou 'fédéralisme co-opératif'?" *L'Action nationale*, Vol. LIV, octobre, 1964.
Thorson, J. T., *Wanted: A Single Canada*, Toronto, McClelland and Stewart, 1973.
Trudeau, P. E., *Federalism and the French Canadians*, Toronto, Methuen, 1968.
Underhill, F. H., *The Image of Confederation*, Toronto, Canadian Broadcasting Corporation, 1964.
Veilleux, G., *Les rélations intergouvernementales au Canada 1867-1967: les mécanismes de coopération*, Montréal, Presses de l'Université du Québec, 1971.
Westmacott, M., "The National Transportation Act and Western Canada: a case study in cooperative federalism", *C.P.A.*, Vol. 16, No. 3, Fall, 1973.
Wheare, K. C., *Federal Government*, London, Oxford University Press, 4th ed., 1963.

Current Constitutional Documentation

Canada, *Constitutional Conference, Proceedings of First Meeting, February 5-7, 1968*, Ottawa, Queen's Printer, 1968.
Canada, *Constitutional Conference, Proceedings of Second Meeting, February 10-12, 1969*, Ottawa, Queen's Printer, 1969.
Canada, *Constitutional Conference, Proceedings of Third Meeting, December 8-10, 1969*, Ottawa, Queen's Printer, 1970.
Canada, *Constitutional Conference Proceedings, Victoria, B.C., June 14, 1971*, Ottawa, Information Canada, 1971.
Canada, (Benson, E. J.), *The Taxing Powers and the Constitution of Canada*, Ottawa, Queen's Printer, 1969.
Canada, (Lalonde, M.), *Working Paper on Social Security in Canada*, Ottawa, Information Canada, 1973.
Canada, (Martin, P.), *Federalism and International Relations*, Ottawa, Queen's Printer, 1968.
Canada, (Pearson, L. B.), *Federalism for the Future*, Ottawa, Queen's Printer, 1968.
Canada, (Sharp, M.), *Federalism and International Conferences on Education*, Ottawa, Queen's Printer, 1968.
Canada, Special Joint Committee of the Senate and the House of Commons on the Constitution of Canada, *Final Report*, Ottawa, Information Canada, 1972.
Canada, (Trudeau, P. E.), *A Canadian Charter of Human Rights*, Ottawa, Queen's Printer, 1968.
Canada, (Trudeau, P. E.), *Federal-Provincial Grants and the Spending Power of Parliament*, Ottawa, Queen's Printer, 1969.
Canada, (Trudeau, P. E.), *Income Security and Social Services*, Ottawa, Queen's Printer, 1969.
Canada, (Trudeau, P. E.), *The Constitution and the People of Canada*, Ottawa, Queen's Printer, 1969.
Canadian Intergovernmental Conference Secretariat, *The Constitutional Review, 1968-71, Secretary's Report*, Ottawa, Information Canada, 1974.

Bilingualism and Biculturalism

Albinski, H. S., "Politics and Biculturalism in Canada: The Flag Debate", *Australian Journal of Politics and History*, Vol. XIII, No. 2, August, 1967.
Bonenfant, J.-C. "Les études de la Commission royale d'enquête sur le bilinguisme et le biculturalisme", *C.J.P.S.*, Vol. IV, No. 3, September, 1971. Vol. V, No. 2, June, 1972 and No. 3, September, 1972; and Vol. VI, No. 1, March, 1973.

Canada, *A Preliminary Report of the Royal Commission on Bilingualism and Biculturalism*, Ottawa, Queen's Printer, 1965.

Canada, *Report of the Royal Commission on Bilingualism and Biculturalism*, Ottawa, Queen's Printer, Book I, *General Introduction and the Official Languages*, 1967; Book II, *Education*, 1968; Book III, *The Work World*, 2 vols., 1969; Book IV, *The Cultural Contributions of the Other Ethnic Groups*, 1970; Books V., VI, *Federal Capital, and Voluntary Associations*, 1 Vol., 1970.

Carson, J. J., "Bilingualism in the public service", *C.P.A.*, Vol. 15, No. 2, Summer, 1972.

Gibson, F. W., (Ed.), *Cabinet Formation and Bicultural Relations: Seven Case Studies*, Studies of the Royal Commission on Bilingualism and Biculturalism, No. 6, Ottawa, Queen's Printer, 1970.

Innis, H. R., *Bilingualism and Biculturalism*, (An abridged version of the Royal Commission Report), Toronto, McClelland and Stewart, 1973.

Joy, R., *Languages in Conflict: The Canadian Experience*, The Carleton Library No. 61, Toronto, McClelland and Stewart, 1972.

Lalande, G., *The Department of External Affairs and Biculturalism*, Studies of the Royal Commission of Bilingualism and Biculturalism, No. 3, Ottawa, Queen's Printer, 1969.

Paradis, J. B., "Language Rights in Multicultural States: A Comparative Study," *Canadian Bar Review*, Vol. XLVIII, No. 4, December, 1970.

Russell, P., *The Supreme Court of Canada as a Bilingual and Bicultural Institution*, Documents of the Royal Commission on Bilingualism and Biculturalism, No. 1, Ottawa, Queen's Printer, 1969.

Amending the Constitution

Alexander, E. R. "A Constitutional Strait Jacket for Canada," *Canadian Bar Review*, Vol. XLIII, No. 3, March, 1965.

Angers, F. A., "Le problème du rapatriement de la constitution," *L'Action nationale*, Vol. LIV, novembre, 1964.

Brady, A., "Constitutional Amendment and the federation" *C.J.E.P.S.*, Vol. XXIX, No. 4, November, 1963.

Canada, *The Constitutional Review, 1968-71*, Secretary's Report, Canadian Intergovernmental Conference Secretariat, Ottawa, Information Canada, 1974.

Cook, R., *Provincial Autonomy, Minority Rights and the Compact Theory, 1867-1921*, Studies of the Royal Commission on Bilingualism and Biculturalism, No. 4, Ottawa, Queen's Printer, 1969.

Favreau, G., *The Amendment of the Constitution of Canada*, Ottawa, Queen's Printer, 1965.

Gérin-Lajoie, P., *Constitutional Amendment in Canada*, Toronto, University of Toronto Press, 1950.

Laskin, B., "Amendment of the Constitution: Applying the Fulton-Favreau Formula," *McGill Law Journal*, Vol. XI, No. 1, January, 1965.

Marion, S., "Le pacte fédératif et les minorités françaises au Canada," *Cahiers des dix*, Vol. 29, 1964.

Miller, D. R., "The Canadian Constitutional Amendment Scheme", *C.J.P.S.*, Vol. VI, No. 1, March, 1973.

Morin, J. Y., "Le repatriement de la constitution," *Cité libre*, Vol. XVI, No. 2, décembre, 1964.

Stanley, G. F. G., "Act or Pact? Another Look at Confederation," *Canadian Historical Association Annual Report*, Ottawa, 1956.

Rowat, D. C., "Recent Developments in Canadian Federalism," *C.J.E.P.S.*, Vol. XVIII, No. 1, February, 1952.

3

FEDERALISM AND FINANCES

In the present edition this chapter has been enlarged and somewhat recast to emphasize the extent to which the operation of federalism in Canada is affected by the complexities of intergovernmental finances. The latter subject has become so intricate that the best this chapter can do is to discuss only its most salient features.

Professor Smiley's perceptive article is an excellent brief review of the major problems in contemporary Canadian federalism. Since he devotes considerable attention to the financial and economic aspects of federalism, his article is a very useful introduction to this chapter.

An extract from the 1976-77 edition of the Canadian Tax Foundation's annual publication, *The Nationald Finances*, explains the essential ingredients of the federal government's fiscal procedures. To assist students to grasp some of the details more readily, the editor has assembled a number of diagrams. They portray federal governmental expenditures and revenues for 1976-77 and two examples of provincial expenditures and revenues for the same fiscal year. The two budgets chosen as comparative examples are those of Ontario and British Columbia. A third set of diagrams, taken from *The Toronto Star*, shows the rapid increase in recent years in government spending, expressed as a percentage of every dollar of the gross national product.

An additional selection from *The National Finances, 1976-77* describes the complicated arrangements involved in current federal-provincial fiscal relations, transfers, and payments. The amounts concerned have become huge, totalling several billions of dollars annually. The details of these enormous payments are given in two tables drawn from the same source.

At a Federal-Provincial Conference of First Ministers held in June 1976, Prime Minister Trudeau proposed to the provinces a significant change in the method of financing three of the most expensive shared-cost programs—medicare, hospital insurance, and post-secondary education. Although reluctant and cautious, the provinces accepted the proposal and it is now part of the 1977-82 financial arrangements, as the relevant section drawn from *The National Finances* explains.

A number of items included in the comparable chapters in the third edition of *Politics: Canada* have been transferred to other chapters in this edition or omitted entirely. Thus, Prime Minister Trudeau's article "In Defence of Federalism" will now be found in Chapter 6 while a description of the Official Languages Act appears now in Chapter 2 above. The following articles have been omitted from this edition but they are located in the third edition at the pages noted: W. A. C. Bennett, "Objections to the Official Languages Act", pp. 68-69; Alexander Brady, "Contradictory Post-War Trends in Canadian Federalism", pp. 69-71; Jean-Luc Pepin, "Cooperative Federalism", pp. 71-77; P. E. Trudeau, "The Constitution and the People of Canada," pp. 77-80; Institute of Intergovernmental Relations, Queen's University, "Report on Intergovernmental Liaison on Fiscal and Economic Matters", pp. 81-83; P. E. Trudeau, "Federal-Provincial Grants and the Spending Power of Parliament", pp. 125-130; and P. E. Trudeau, "Income Security and Social Services", pp. 130-137.

There is a considerable growing literature on the subject of federal-provincial and provincial-municipal finances. Although the various governments generate most of the data and produce many position papers and some commentaries, the Canadian Tax Foundation continues to publish a great deal of very useful information. *Canadian Public Administration*, the quarterly journal of the Institute of Public Administration of Canada, and the new quarterly, *Canadian Public Policy*, are also important sources of commentary.

A reader should consult also two books in the McGraw-Hill Ryerson Series in Canadian Politics. Donald Smiley provides a masterly review of the fiscal and economic aspects of Canadian federalism in Chapter 5 of his book, *Canada in Question: Federalism in the Seventies*, Toronto, McGraw-Hill Ryerson, second edition, 1976, while Thomas Hockin gives a briefer account in *Government in Canada*, Toronto, McGraw-Hill Ryerson, 1976, Chapter 2.

The bibliography in this chapter has been confined almost exclusively to references dealing with federal-provincial-municipal finances. Items concerned with the following subjects have been transferred to the bibliography in Chapter 2 above: the constitution, federal problems, current constitutional documentation, and bilingualism and biculturalism.

THE STRUCTURAL PROBLEM OF
CANADIAN FEDERALISM*

Donald V. Smiley

• • •

In general terms, a federal system of government sustains and is sustained by geographically-based diversities. People in the states, regions or provinces have from the first to develop attitudes, traditions and interests both specific to these areas and significant for politics and government. The master-solution of federalism to the problem of territorial diversity is to confer jurisdiction over those matters where diversity is most profound and most divisive to state or provincial governments. However, in the interdependent circumstances of the contemporary world there can be no complete hiving off of such matters. What economists call 'spill-overs' of state or provincial policies are so ubiquitous that a matter of jurisdiction which concerns only the residents of particular regions will not be of crucial importance even to them. Enough integration on national lines to secure the continuing survival of the federation will eventually bring about demands that the national government take steps towards country-wide standards of services, taxation burdens and economic opportunities even where such actions involve federal involvement in matters within the constitutional jurisdiction of the states or provinces. There is another kind of conflict involving territorial particularisms which the federal division of powers is not able to resolve: those situations where the various states and regions impose contradictory demands upon the national government. In summary then, a constitutional division of powers between national and regional governments by itself cannot under modern circumstances resolve problems caused by geographical diversities. The stability of political systems is overwhelmingly a matter of the relation between the internal conflicts of these systems and their institutional capacity to give authoritative resolution to such conflicts. If conflicts are not numerous or profound the institutions and procedures for handling such differences need be neither elaborate nor effective. The opposite is of course true. Obviously too, the institutional structures condition the kinds of conflicts that arise for resolution and in turn are conditioned by these conflicts.

It is the argument of this paper that in the Canadian federal system territorial particularisms have come to find outlets almost exclusively through the provinces. This situation has come about largely as a result of the working of the institutions of the central government which from time to time operate so as to deny provincial and regional interests an effective share in central decision-making. Thus these interests turn to the provinces and continue to do so even after future circumstances provide them with more power in the central government. Canada is now experiencing

* From *Canadian Public Administration*, Vol. 14, No. 3, Fall, 1971. By permission.

a number of profound domestic conflicts where the contending forces follow territorial lines along with a relative institutional incapacity for giving authoritative resolution to these conflicts.

The Substance of the Present Conflicts

The major conflicts in Canadian politics along territorial lines are the following.

1. *Those related to interprovincial and interregional equalization by the federal government.* In recent years equalization has been extended much beyond the Rowell-Sirois recommendation that each province should have at its disposal adequate revenues to provide services at national average levels without imposing on its citizens taxation at rates above the national average. Equalization now involves a complex of federal and federal-provincial programs to encourage economic growth and enhance economic opportunities in the less favoured parts of Canada, particularly in Quebec and the Atlantic provinces.

2. *Those related to national economic policies.* The traditional economic cleavages between central Canada and the peripheral provinces to the east and west of the heartland remain, even though the peripheral economies—and in particular those of western Canada—have become more diversified. These continuing conflicts involve national trade, transportation and monetary policies as well as newer differences with respect to the development and sale of natural resources.

3. *Those relating to cultural duality in Canada.* The response of the provinces with English-speaking majorities to the French fact in Canada is most positive in those with large French-speaking minorities and least so where this minority is small. These differences are evident whether the claims of duality are expressed through recognition of the two official languages, some sort of special arrangement for Quebec or support for constitutional revision.

If we classify the interests and policies of the provinces toward each of these areas of conflict the result is something like that shown in Table I. In these terms, Quebec and the western provinces are ranged against each other on each of the axes of conflict. This conflict is more marked in the case of Alberta and British Columbia than in Saskatchewan or Manitoba. These two latter provinces are on the borderline between 'have' and 'have not' provinces and if favourable economic circumstances should push them toward the former category the country would be clearly divided on the issue of interprovincial equalization by the Ottawa River.

There appears to be an emergent conflict involving provincial and regional particularisms in respect to economic nationalism. Influences toward nationalism can be expected to be more insistent at the federal level than at the provincial. From about the mid-1950s onward the provincial governments have assumed major responsibilities for attracting foreign capital for development and have shown little concern whence such capital comes. It can be expected that economic nationalism will come to have influences on the politics and policies of some if not all of the provinces but it seems likely that these influences will be weaker at the provincial than at the federal level. More generally, it seems almost certain that the incidence of nationalistic sentiments and interests will vary significantly among the various provinces and regions.

TABLE I

	Contending Provinces		Provinces Whose Attitudes are Ambiguous
Interprovincial equalization	Quebec and the Atlantic provinces	Ontario Alberta BC	Saskatchewan Manitoba
National economic policies	Quebec Ontario	Atlantic and western provinces	
Cultural duality	Quebec Ontario New Brunswick	BC Alberta Saskatchewan Newfoundland	NS Manitoba PEI

Possible Procedures for Resolving Territorially-based Conflicts

There are several possible ways of resolving conflicts where the contending interests are limited to the various provinces or regions.

It seems unlikely that in the immediate future judicial review of the constitution will have more than a subsidiary role in giving authoritative resolution to the conflicting claims of territorial particularism. Significantly, the very great changes in English-French relations from 1960 onward have not been accompanied by any judicial decision which affected these relations in a crucial way, and successive Quebec governments have challenged the legitimacy of the Supreme Court of Canada in its present form as the final appellate court in constitutional matters. The various conflicts between Ottawa and the provinces over fiscal matters are inappropriate for judicial resolution. More generally, the delineation of federal and provincial legislative powers through judicial review relates for the most part to the regulatory activities of government and although these are of continuing importance they do not involve the most decisive of conflicts between the two levels.

A second device for resolving conflicts with a geographical base is through the party system, particularly in the relations between the federal and provincial wings of the two major parties. I can present here only in summary form the conclusions I have reached on this matter without giving the evidence for these conclusions. In general, there has been a long-term trend toward the mutual insulation of federal and provincial party systems. Although this matter is extraordinarily complex and has never been adequately analyzed on a country-wide scale, federal and provincial parties appear less electorally interdependent than in earlier periods of Canadian history. At the provincial level there are several parties which are exclusively or almost exclusively oriented toward provincial affairs (Parti Quebecois, Union Nationale, Social Credit in Alberta and British Columbia). At both levels there has been the development of extra-legislative party organizations involved both in leadership choice and increasingly in policy matters; such federal and provincial wings of the same party tend to be independent of one another. Career patterns of elected politicians have come to involve service at only one level more frequently than in earlier times. Increasingly, federal and provincial wings of the same party have financial resources at their disposal independent of the other level. In the two major parties, distinctive ideologies are not important integrative forces on federal-provincial lines. Thus intra-party interactions are not very effective in giving authoritative resolution to federal-provincial conflict.

The usual solution proposed for the problems of conflict between Ottawa and the provinces is more institutionalized collaboration between the executives of the two levels. There are two quite different possibilities here: they will be labelled 'functional federalism' and 'political federalism.'

Under functional federalism the major responsibilities for federal-provincial collaboration are given to officials of the two levels concerned with relatively specialized public activities. These activities are carred on with a relatively high degree of independence from control by officials and public agencies with more comprehensive concerns and tend to be regulated in accord with the perceptions, procedures and standards prevailing among specialists in these fields. The most characteristic device of functional federalism is the conditional grant arrangement.

Political federalism is characterized by a situation in which the most crucial of intergovernmental relations are those between political and bureaucratic officials with jurisdiction-wide concerns. In Canadian terms these may be departments of finance or specialized treasury agencies, first ministers and their staffs, agencies concerned specifically with constitutional reform or departments or sub-departmental agencies whose main or exclusive responsibilities are federal-provincial relations as such. Under contemporary circumstances there will be a great deal of interlevel collaboration between individuals and agencies with specialized concerns but under the political federalism alternative these are controlled in terms of more comprehensive policies and goals. As the most characteristic device of functional federalism is the conditional grant, so political federalism is manifested by the Federal-Provincial Conference of Prime Ministers and Premiers and by the departments, committees and agencies whose major or exclusive concerns are the government-wide management of relations between the two levels.

During the past decade Canada has passed from functional to political federalism, although great variations persist among the various jurisdictions as to the degree to which specific concerns are controlled in terms of broader goals. In, say, the mid-1950s the most important kinds of federal-provincial interactions were of two kinds. There was first an increasing number of collaborative schemes between agencies and officials with specialized concerns, often though by no means always within the framework of shared-cost arrangements. Then there was the periodic renegotiation of the tax agreements for the forthcoming five-year periods, a process involving in the first instance the treasury and finance departments but also inevitably the heads of government. Although agencies with government-wide concerns were never entirely without involvement in specific federal-provincial programs, there was relatively little integration between the two sorts of activities. Arrangements between Ottawa and the provinces related to specialized programs and services were for the most part devised and executed within the context of particularized problems. The tax agreements on the other hand were concluded in terms of considerations which in the main did not include individual services or facilities.

The coming to power of the Lesage government after the Quebec general election of June 1960 was crucial in the transition from functional to political federalism. For understandable reasons, successive Quebec administrations have been more suspicious of particularized federal-provincial interactions than have been other provinces, and in his speech to the November 1963 Conference of Prime Ministers and Premiers Mr. Lesage said 'The present policy of making decisions behind hermetically closed doors is no longer acceptable.' The new Quebec government established a Department of Federal-Provincial Relations in 1961. Apart from a few months after the coming to power of the Bourassa administration in 1970, the incumbent prime minister has always held this portfolio and the Department has played a central role in Quebec's relations with Ottawa, the other provinces and foreign countries. Thus particularized aspects of Quebec's relations within the federal system have been subordinated to the more comprehensive goal of defending and enlarging the province's range of autonomy. In Ontario there was the establishment during the 1960s of an impressive aggregation of bureaucratic talent and influence in federal-provincial relations within the Department of Treasury and Economics. So far as the other provinces are concerned there is with varying degrees a less complete integration of specific and comprehensive objectives than is the case with Ontario and Quebec. However, the trend toward political federalism continues. The increasing involvement of heads of government and their senior cabinet colleagues and advisors in federal-provincial relations, and the increasingly frequent meetings of prime ministers and premiers and of political and appointed members of treasury and finance departments all indicate the development of permanent institutional apparatus involving ministers and deputies where formerly such collaboration was at the middle levels of the federal and provincial bureaucracies. This general development toward subsuming even very particularized goals and activities under more comprehensive ones has been strengthened by the process of constitutional revision and review begun in February 1968. To take a crucial example of what has happened, conditional grants in the 1945-60 period were for the most part dealt with within the frame of reference of particular services. Now the exercise of the federal spending power on matters within provincial legislative jurisdiction is a subject of constitutional debate at the most fundamental level.

There are several consequences of the relative failure of federal-provincial interactions to give authoritative resolution to conflicts based on geographical particularisms. First, in some cases there is a stand-off where necessary public action is being frustrated. Effective policies in respect to many aspects of urban problems await federal-provincial agreement. . . .

Second, governments avoid collaboration by taking unilateral action with respect to matters where the interests of the other level are involved. Provinces take it for granted that it is appropriate without consulting Ottawa to devise and implement policies concerning, say, higher education or most aspects of natural resource development or the circumstances under which local governments may borrow on the capital market. In these circumstances as in others, important federal interests are directly or indirectly involved. However, it is equally easy to give examples of federal unilateralism—the decision about medical insurance in 1965, the 1966 policies providing for a new formula for federal assistance to post-secondary education, and more recently by federal legislation to deal with environmental pollution. In the constitutional field parliament has recently enacted important changes in the jurisdiction of the Supreme Court of Canada in a period where the role and function of the Court was a matter of discussion in the process of constitutional review.

Third, the provinces have successfully asserted their influence over matters which in the 1945-60 period were believed to be mainly or exclusively federal. Ottawa can be effective in regulating the general levels of income, prices and employment only with provincial collaboration, if at all. The federal tax system is now a matter for federal-provincial negotiation. Ottawa is on the defensive about the exercise of its spending power on matters within provincial jurisdiction. Broadcasting and some aspects of foreign affairs are the objective of provincial claims. At the Federal-Provincial Conference of 1963 Premier Lesage advanced his formulation of cooperative federalism. The first element was a fastidious respect by Ottawa for provincial jurisdiction. But because major federal policies in the economic field had a direct impact on provincial responsibilities, these matters should be regulated by joint federal-provincial institutions designed for that purpose. The institutionalization of collaborative procedures for designing national economic policies has not proceeded as the then Quebec premier wished, but the basic elements of his solution have in considerable part been achieved.

To an alarming extent, Canadian interests and attitudes which are territorially delimited have come to find an outlet exclusively through the provincial governments. This, I shall argue, has occurred largely because federal institutions have inadequately represented these particularisms. It has been too little stressed that during the first three years of the Quiet Revolution in Quebec there was in power in Ottawa a government less attuned to French-Canadian sensibilities than any other in Canadian history, with the exception of the administration emerging out of the conscription election of 1917. Similarly, the current regionalism in the prairie provinces can be explained partly by the relative lack of representation of the prairies in successive federal Liberal governments from 1963 onward.

The Confederation Settlement and its Passing

To repeat, in broad terms a federal system can deal with territorial particularisms by two kinds of procedures: (i) by conferring jurisdiction over several of the most crucial of these particularisms on the states or provinces, (ii) by securing for each of the major territorial interests a permanent influence on the decision-making processes of the central government. It is my argument that the Canadian system has come to rely too much on the first device and too little on the second.

The confederation settlement of 1864-67 contemplated a centralized federal system. But although this settlement provided for the dominance of the central government, it seems to have been taken for granted that the incidence of Dominion power would be localized. This condition has been attenuated. To trace the development away from localism in federal affairs would be to write the history of these institutions. However, it is perhaps useful to look at some important aspects of the federal government as it emerged at confederation in relation to where we are today.

The Senate. (*a*) At confederation. The composition of the upper legislature chamber was the most contentious issue resolved by the Fathers of Confederation. Further, it seems that these men believed in the crucial importance of this body in the working of the new institutions. Peter Waite has said,

> . . . most members of the Canadian Coalition government thought of federation largely in terms of the composition of the central legislature. In the lower house there would be 'rep by pop'; in the upper house there would be representation by territory. . . . Of course local powers would be given to local bodies, but that was taken as a matter presenting little difficulty. The basis of the federal principle lay in the central legislature and in the balance between the House of Commons on the one hand and the Senate on the other.

(*b*) Today. Whatever the usefulness of the contemporary Senate, it does not provide an effective outlet for interests which are localized.

The Parties in the House of Commons. (*a*) At confederation. It was not until the end of the nineteenth century that two cohesive national parties came into existence in Canada. As in the pre-confederation period, political parties in the House of Commons during the early days of the dominion were coalitions, often of a relatively loose nature, around political leaders, and many of these leaders themselves had a base of support which was exclusively regional.

(*b*) Today. It is unnecessary to emphasize the cohesiveness of political parties in the Canadian House of Commons, particularly in the case of the government party. Although there are countervailing influences at work to enhance the independence of private MPs, the more decisive developments have been in the other direction. So far as the government party is concerned, the dominance of the prime minister is strengthened by the circumstances that many MPs owe their election to his popularity, his powers of bringing about a dissolution and his control of preferments which members desire.

The Cabinet (a) At confederation. An historian [Jean Hamelin] has said of the first government of the dominion:

> It would have been wrong to suppose that Macdonald was leading a centralized party. He was rather the chief of a coalition of groups in which each obeyed a regional leader, rather than Macdonald himself. To keep the confidence of the majority, Macdonald knew that he must negotiate with these leaders. In this spirit the cabinet was to be, in a certain sense, a chamber of political compensation, where the provincial spokesmen traded their support in return for concessions to their regions.

(*b*) Today. Canadian prime ministers have come increasingly to dominate their cabinets. There have been many reasons for this which need only to be mentioned here—access to the media, the development of staff assistance in the prime minister's and Privy Council offices, the size of the cabinets and the complexity of issues which decrease the possibilities of genuinely collegial decisions and enhance the power of the head of government to impose his own solutions, the influence of the procedure by which leaders are chosen by party conventions. However, a crucial aspect of prime ministerial dominance is the relative decline in the position of cabinet ministers as representatives of provinces or regions, although the cabinet is usually constituted in terms of such representation. Since the departure of the late James G. Gardiner and of Jack Pickersgill it is difficult to think of any minister who has had an important base of provincial or regional political support independent of the head of government. Further, as Donald Gow has pointed out, ministers have virtually no staff involved with regions the ministers allegedly represent, and the departments are 'oriented to stress values associated with industrial and social structures and aggregates' rather than particular cultures and regions.

The federal bureaucracy. (*a*) At confederation. At the time of confederation, and for some decades after, the departments of government had a very high degree of autonomy in the recruitment of federal civil servants and positions were characteristically filled by political patronage. Thus to the extent that the cabinet included members of the various provinces and regions, the federal bureaucracy was in a broad sense representative of these localized sentiments and interests.

(*b*) Today. The establishment of the merit system in the Canadian public service, particularly with the reform measures of 1918, has had the effect of making the federal bureaucracy less representative in its composition. Current efforts of the federal government are to enhance the proportion of francophones at all levels. It is too early to assess the implications of this policy—and the related policy of increasing the number of anglophone civil servants who are bilingual—on the composition of the federal bureaucracy from various parts of English-speaking Canada. Up until the present, cultural and liguistic duality in the federal service has been explicitly concerned with two sorts of considerations: (i) the ability of citizens to deal with federal institutions in whichever of the official languages the citizen chooses, (ii) the ability of federal employees to advance their careers largely or exclusively in the official language milieu of choice. There has been little discussion of the federal bureaucracy as a locus of influence in which cultural and other territorially-based particularisms should be represented.

Broadly speaking, the party which forms the government has come increasingly to dominate parliament, and the prime minister, the government party. These developments have the effect of denying strong regional interests a permanent influence in national decision-making. Two other institutions work in the same direction.

1. The national party conventions. Since 1919 and 1927 respectively the Liberals and Conservatives have selected their leaders by national party conventions. In the 1960s the constitutions of these parties have provided for regular conventions even when the leadership was not at stake, although the role of these gatherings in forming or influencing party policy is still in process of evolution. The voting rules of leadership conventions, by which the leader is chosen by an absolute majority compiled through successive secret ballots, enormously enhance the power of individual delegates and decrease that of provincial leaders. Unlike an American convention, the winning of a national leadership is something other than building a coalition of support from regional chieftains.

2. The electoral system. Alan C. Cairns has demonstrated how the electoral system has both exacerbated sectionalism in Canadian politics and made sectional conflicts more difficult to resolve. [See Chapter 8.] From the point of view of my analysis, the crucial factor is that from time to time important regions are denied representation in the governing party, even while giving a significant proportion of the popular vote to this party. In general terms:

> The electoral system has made a major contribution to the identification of particular sections/provinces with particular parties. It has undervalued the partisan diversity within each section/province. By doing so it has rendered the parliamentary composition of each party less representative of the sectional interests in the political system than is the party electorate from which that representation is derived. The electoral system favours minor parties with concentrated sectional support, and discourages those with diffuse national support. The electoral system has consistently exaggerated the significance of cleavages demarcated by sectional/provincial boundaries and has thus tended to transform contests between parties into contests between sections/provinces.

But as the electoral system exacerbates sectionalism it makes such interests more difficult to reconcile through intra-party accommodation in the House of Commons. [To quote Cairns again:]

> The significance of the electoral system for party policy is due to its consistent failure to reflect with even rough accuracy the distribution of partisan support in the various sections/provinces of the country. By making the Conservatives far more of a British and Ontario-based party, the Liberals far more a French and Quebec party, the CCF far more a prairie and BC party, and even Social Credit far more of an Alberta party up until 1953, than the electoral support of these parties

'required,' they were deprived of intra-party spokesmen proportionate to their electoral support from the sections where they were relatively weak. The relative, or on occasion total, absence of such spokesmen for particular sectional communities seriously affects the image of the parties as national bodies, deprives the party concerned of articulate proponents of particular sectional interests in caucus and in the House, and, it can be deductively suggested, renders the members of the parliamentary party personally less sensitive to the interests of the unrepresented sections than they otherwise would be. As a result the general perspectives and policy orientations of a party are likely to be skewed in favour of those interests which, by virtue of strong parliamentary representation, can vigorously assert their claims.

A Brief Digression: the American Experience

If we compare the American and Canadian federal system it is immediately evident that the national government of the United States has a crucial range of powers and responsibilities which is withheld from its Canadian counterpart. Judicial interpretation of congressional power over interstate commerce has given the national authorities a kind of control over economic matters which the courts have denied parliament by restricting the meaning of trade and commerce. The Americans up to now have had no tradition of unconditional subsidies to the states, and conditional grants have tended to be more specific and to impose more restraints on the receiving governments than has been the case in Canada. Treaties concluded by the president and ratified by the US Senate are the 'supreme law of the land' and thus Congress has the power to override state jurisdiction in implementing such international arrangements; the Parliament of Canada acquires no powers it would not otherwise have by virtue of the executive concluding an international agreement. There has developed in the United States a pattern of direct federal-local relations which in Canada the sensibilities of the provinces have prevented. Control over the defence establishment is of course relatively more important in the United States than is the same function in Canada.

The American federal system is thus more highly centralized than the Canadian in the scope of powers wielded by the national government. However, the fragmented power system prevailing in Washington allows geographical particularisms to play a more important role than is the case in Ottawa. . . .

•   •   •

In general then, territorial particularisms are more effectively and continuously represented in the workings of the American national government than of the Canadian. It seems reasonable to conjecture that the scope of national power in the United States would be more limited than it is if there were a less fragmented power structure in Washington.

Conclusion and Recommendations

It may be that Canada is governable, if at all, only by adherence to John

C. Calhoun's principle of the concurrent majority which 'gives to each division or interest through its appropriate organ either a concurrent voice in making and executing the laws or a veto on their execution.' The concurrent majority principle might of course be embodied in the operation of federal-provincial relations and to some degree this has come to be so. However, as I have argued, Canada cannot be governed effectively by these means. To be realistic, the predisposition of British parliamentary institutions is against institutional restraints on the powers of government. Thus, although these institutions in Canada as elsewhere have proved very flexible, their thrust, in Calhoun's terms, is toward the rule of the numerical rather than the concurrent majority.

The following implications of my general argument are made in a very tentative way. 1. Any restructuring of federal institutions to give territorial particularisms a more effective outlet should recognize other diversities than those of Anglophone and Francophone. In the past decade the dominant currents of thought and policy in central Canada have emphasized cultural and linguistic duality to the neglect of other attitudes and interests which divide Canadians. The price of this neglect is the resurgence of regionalism in the western provinces. While such a formulation is inevitably somewhat arbitrary, it appears to me that a five-region division of Canada corresponds fairly closely with continuing territorial diversities which merit recognition as such in the institutions of the federal government.

2. Unless and until the government of Canada ceases to operate within British parliamentary traditions, the Senate can play only a restricted role in representing geographically delimited interests whatever changes are made in the way members of this body are appointed or in its functions. So long as the prime minister and his important ministers sit in the House of Commons and must retain the continuing support of a majority in that House to retain office, the Senate will remain in a secondary position.

3. A strong case can be made for the explicit recognition of representative bureaucracy in the federal government. Such an alternative does not imply that civil servants are primarily ambassadors of such territorial interests. W. R. Lederman has made an argument for regional quotas on the Supreme Court of Canada in terms which have direct relevance to the federal bureaucracy. Professor Lederman rejects in the name of the tradition of judicial independence that members of a final court of appeal are—or should be—the delegates of the government which appointed them. However, he asserts:

> The [regional] quotas are necessary and proper because Canada is a vast country differing in some critical ways region by region. There are common factors but there are unique ones too. If we ensure that judges are drawn from the various regions . . . we ensure that there is available within the Court collective experience and background knowledge of all parts of Canada. In judicial conferences and other contacts within the Court membership, the judges are able to inform and educate one another on essential facts and background from their respective parts of Canada.

4. In terms of Professor Gow's bold proposals, a strong case can be

made for a radical restructuring of the federal cabinet and departments of government to make these institutions more effectively representative of regional and cultural interests. One of his suggestions is that the cabinet should 'consist of ten to twelve ministers: five regional ministers and others drawn from External Affairs, Finance and a few other departments.' The regional minister's deputy 'would be a regional minister stationed in a central location within the area served by the minister. He would be the eyes and ears of the minister in the region reporting to him on any matter having to do with the coordination of the activities of the federal departments with one another, or with provincial or municipal departments.' Several of the departments with field staffs should have an assistant deputy minister stationed in each of the five regions of Canada. 'They would have coordinate standing with the most senior of existing assistant deputies. With such a status, it would be necessary that conflicts between a regional and functional or occupational point of view would be resolved at the level of the deputy minister and minister.'

5. Consideration should be given to the reform of the electoral system. In such a reform it seems to me that the first consideration should be to ensure that the regional composition of parties in the House of Commons conforms more closely to their respective regional strengths in popular votes than is the case under the existing electoral law.

6. In broader terms, the kinds of reforms I am suggesting are advanced by measures which attenuate the dominance of the prime minister over his own cabinet and caucus and of the governing party over the House of Commons. Thus an increase in the independence and effectiveness of parliamentary committees is to be welcomed. A case can be made for increasing the number of free votes in the House of Commons and for a rule by which a government would be required to resign only after defeat on an explicit vote of confidence. There should be a reversal of the current trend toward giving the majority in the House the power to determine the time allowed to debate particular measures. Some attenuation of the power of the prime minister to obtain a dissolution would be desirable. The effective and continuing representation of all important regional interests is clearly incompatible with the degree of dominance of the federal political system by the office of the prime minister that we are now experiencing.

The kinds of reforms I am suggesting would move our political institutions to be more like those of the United States. For this reason alone these recommendations might well be thought unworthy of consideration by Canadians. However, I have nowhere suggested an American-type separation of executive and legislative powers at the federal level. Responsible parliamentary government is a flexible instrument and, if I understand the circumstances of a century ago, the Fathers of Confederation believed it compatible with the highly localized incidence of federal power. It is perhaps more reasonable to argue that the present unsatisfactory results of federal-provincial interaction are at least as palatable as a constitutional system where many crucial political decisions are regulated by regional concurrent majorities at the federal level. On the other hand, the existing regime appears to me to be reducing the sphere in which the national government can act without provincial constraints to a dangerously restricted scope. If my argrument is even broadly accurate, the solution—if there is one—is to make federal institutions more effectively representative of territorially-based attitudes and interests.

[See also the article by Prime Minister Pierre E. Trudeau, "In Defence of Federalism," *infra*, Chapter 6.]

ESSENTIALS OF FEDERAL FINANCES*

Canadian Tax Foundation

. . . The vast phenomenon of the revenue and expenditure structure of the national government . . . is an operation involving outlays of over 42 billion dollars annually, a staff of employees running to several hundred thousands, and a range of activities which touches the life of nearly every Canadian citizen. Simply to maintain an organization of this size in being has profound effects on the financial system of the country, but in addition deliberate use is made of both the revenue and expenditure apparatus in order to exert an influence on the economy. . . .

Government by Legislation

One important fundamental is that almost every dollar of revenue raised or spent by governments under our democratic system has been previously authorized by laws passed by the elected representatives. The federal tax system, for example, is contained in four main statutes—the Income Tax Act, the Excise Tax Act, the Excise Act, and the Customs Tariff. These statues are enacted by Parliament and remain in force until amended. The statutory origins of the expenditure program are somewhat more involved. Various pieces of legislation (e.g., the Family Allowances Act) are passed by Parliament from time to time authorizing the expenditure of funds sufficient to carry out the purposes of the Acts. There are dozens of such predetermined forms of expenditure in the federal accounts; perhaps the best example of all is the interest on the national debt, which is a contractual obligation of the government. Each year, in addition, there are amounts to be spent on non-recurring programs or for purposes for which no previous statutory provision has been made. In order to maintain the rules of parliamentary control of annual outlays (principle of the budget), *all* amounts to be spent in the year are gathered together in one detailed presentation (the Estimates) and submitted to Parliament for approval.

The Estimates are referred to sixteen Standing Committees of the House of Commons, each specializing in a particular area. The Standing Committees are obliged by Parliamentary rules to report back to the

* From *The National Finances, 1976-77*, Toronto, Canadian Tax Foundation, 1977, Introduction. By permission.

House, normally by May 31. In addition, [under a new system adopted in 1975] the opposition may, during allotted days, bring forward selected items of estimates before a committee of the whole House for debate, possible amendment and eventual decision. The House grants approval by passing Appropriation Acts, providing the required funds for the government.

A Governor General's Warrant may be issued under section 21 of the Financial Administration Act when payment is urgently required for the public good. This section is applicable during any period when Parliament is prorogued or adjourned and when no appropriation is availabe for making payment. An Order in Council signed by the Governor General may permit the appropriation of moneys; such warrants may be issued only in the fiscal year for which the expenditure is required; they must be published in the *Canada Gazette* within 30 days of the date they are issued; a statement showing all warrants issued, with amounts, must be presented to Parliament by the Minister of Finance within 15 days after the commencement of the next ensuing session; and the Auditor General must include in his report every case where a special warrant has authorized the payment of money.

For both revenue and expenditure, the granting of approval by Parliament—that is, the enactment of a statute—is the end result of a rather involved procedure of submission for approval and subsequent accountability, the full details of which are not important for present purposes. However, certain documents, which emerge in the course of this procedure, contain much information. . . .

The Estimates

The main source of information on programs of expenditure for any prospective year is a large volume known as the Main Estimates. This document is a complete—or almost complete—statement, in detail, of the amounts of money required by the government to carry out its various activities during the coming year. It is divided into departments, and under each department details of proposed expenditures are given. These Main Estimates might be called Parliament's handbook to government activities. It is more than a handbook, however, because Parliament must authorize these expenditures by passing individually several hundred "votes" under which the total is classified. It does not always work out that the full amount of money appropriated by Parliament is spent during the year, but the shortfall is seldom very large. More commonly, it is necessary for the department to ask for more money from Parliament. Under-provisions or new expenditures frequently become known before the end of the session at which the Main Estimates have been introduced, and these are covered by the submission of Supplementary Estimates (A), (B), etc. Frequently also during the year, after Parliament has risen, additional expenditures must be made for unforeseen contingencies, and parliamentary approval for these is given by the passage of further Supplementary Estimates in the succeeding session.

Since the fiscal year is the twelve-month period commencing on April 1, the President of the Treasury Board will normally submit the Main

FEDERAL GOVERNMENT EXPENDITURES AND REVENUES, 1976-77 (estimates)

EXPENDITURES
(estimated total = $38.417 billion)
— by cents per dollar

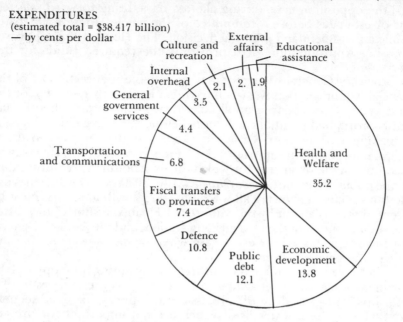

Data from Treasury Board, How Your Tax Dollar is Spent '76-'77, Ottawa, Information Canada, 1976. *Reproduced by permission of the Minister of Supply and Services Canada.*

REVENUES
(estimated total = $34.4 billion)
— by cents per dollar

Non-Resident Tax
Customs Duties
1.5
6.3
Other duties and Taxes
7.3
Non-tax Revenues
9.8
Personal Income Tax
46.6
Sales Tax
11.4
Corporation Income Tax
17.

Based on Budget Address by the Minister of Finance, House of Commons Debates, May 25, 1975, p. 13837. Reproduced by permission of the Minister of Supply and Services Canada.

PROVINCIAL EXPENDITURES AND REVENUES, 1976-77

EXAMPLE: ONTARIO BUDGET, 1976-77

EXPENDITURES
(estimated total = $12.5 billion)
— by cents per dollar

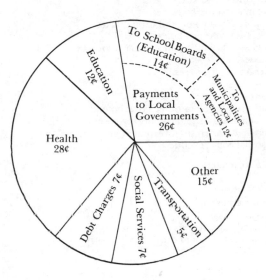

REVENUES
(estimated total = $11.27 billion)
— by cents per dollar

Data from the Ontario Budget, April 6, 1976

EXAMPLE: British Columbia Budget, 1976-77

Revenues	Estimates, 1976-77 (In thousands $)	Percentage
Property taxes	19,500	0.5
Sales and fuel taxes	948,400	26.4
Personal income taxes	815,900	22.7
Corporation income and capital taxes	286,000	7.9
Succession and gift taxes	26,000	0.7
Privileges, licences, and natural resources taxes and royalties	538,400	15.0
Sales and service fees	49,300	1.3
Court fees and fines	10,000	0.2
Interest	15,000	0.4
Contributions from other governments	33,750	0.9
Canada share of joint service programs	651,000	18.1
Contributions from government enterprises	168,000	4.6
Miscellaneous revenue	26,000	0.7
Total revenue	3,587,250	99.4
Expenditures		
Health and social services	1,548,341	42.8
Education	859,498	23.8
Highways and ferries	319,533	8.9
Natural resources and primary industry	304,134	8.4
Other	583,739	16.1
Total expenditure	3,615,245	100.0

(From *British Columbia Budget, March, 1976*, pp. 31, 41.)

Estimates to Parliament in the preceding February or March so that they may be considered as time permits during the parliamentary session. The Main Estimates are therefore available as a source of information . . . in the spring of each year, but must be supplemented with other data which become available during the session. An important additional source in recent years has been the minutes of the standing committees discussing the Estimates of the individual departments. . . .

Budget Speech

In the parliamentary process the budget speech follows next after the Estimates. In fact it may follow at a very long interval, the time depending on the exigencies of the business of the House, the state of the economy and other factors. The traditional purpose of the budget speech is to review the general position of the government's accounts for the old year and to make proposals for the year ahead; to relate the expenditure program for the new year, as presented in the Estimates, to the expected revenues from existing tax sources; and to propose any changes in taxation deemed necessary. The budget speech, therefore, is of greatest interest in connection with revenues, since its main purpose is to formulate the tax changes required to support the expenditure program. . . .

In recent years, the government has departed from the earlier practice

**GOVERNMENT SPENDING AS A PERCENTAGE OF EVERY DOLLAR
SPENT IN CANADA (GNP)***

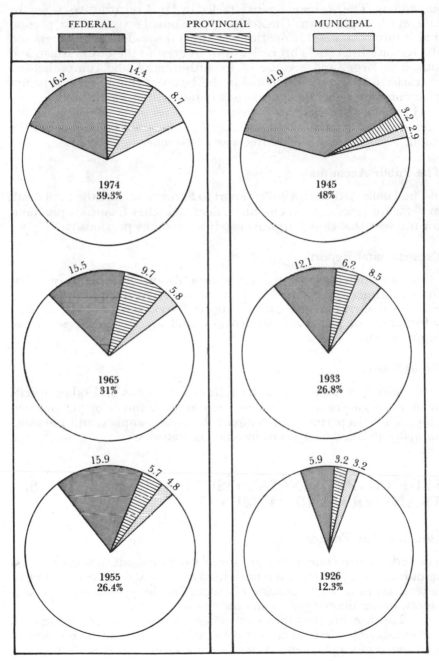

From The Toronto Star, *November 8, 1975. By permission.*

of including with the budget statement a review of the economy and a detailed preliminary statement of revenue and expenditure for the year just ending. The *Economic Review* is tabled in April, regardless of when the budget is brought down. The Review gives a broad review of past, present and future economic factors that will affect the outlook of business and the nation's finances. This review is of interest to the businessman and citizen at large, and because of its authoritative and comprehensive character is now very influential in the business community. It is supplemented by elaborate and up-to-date tables of economic data.

The detailed preliminary statement of revenue or expenditure has been dropped from the Budget Papers, but the publication date for the Public Accounts has been moved from December to October.

The Public Accounts

The Public Accounts, a bulky report to Parliament, give the final result in detail for revenues, expenditures, debt and other financial operations for the year that closed approximately six months previously.

Departmental Reports

In addition to the general financial compilations and reports issued by the Department of Finance, each operating department and most governmental agencies issue annual reports. These contain more detailed information on departmental activites, and are a valuable source of information. . . .

Other Sources

Statistics Canada prepares the National Accounts and other special analyses of government activities, such as the number of persons employed. The Department of National Revenue compiles, and publishes annually, detailed analyses of income tax statistics. . . .

FEDERAL-PROVINCIAL FISCAL ARRANGEMENTS, TRANSFERS, AND PAYMENTS*

Canadian Tax Foundation

The federal government now uses four basic methods to transfer fiscal resources to the provinces, territories and municipalities; the reduction of federal tax in order to provide tax room for the provinces, tax abatements, unconditional grants and conditional grants.

. . . The provinces levy their own personal income taxes, expressed as a percentage of the federal tax and collected by the federal government in all provinces except Quebec. Over the nine agreeing provinces, the rates

* From *The National Finances, 1976-77*, Toronto, Canadian Tax Foundation, 1977, Chapter 10. By permission. (Original Table numbers and references have been retained.)

range from 26.0% to 42.5% of federal tax, and they are expected to produce $4.2 billion in 1976-77. We have estimated that a further $4.2 billion will be collected in Quebec, including $1 billion attributable to the special federal abatement of 24% basic federal tax granted in compensation for opting out (see below). Provincial corporation income taxes, which are designed to take up, or, in some cases, to exceed the federal abatement, are expected to yield $746.4 million in the eight provinces that have a collection agreement with Ottawa. Ontario and Quebec collections are estimated at $3.2 billion.

Unconditional payments to the provinces, municipalities and territories are expected to total $3.2 billion in 1976-77. The unconditional grants to the provinces are principally equalization payments under the Federal-Provincial Fiscal Arrangements Act, statutory subsidies, and income tax on certain public utilities. Payments to the territories cover the deficiency on ordinary account, capital needs and amortization of debt. The general payments to municipalities take the form of grants in lieu of taxes on federal property.

The federal government also makes conditional payments or grants-in-aid to the other levels of government for specific purposes such as hospital insurance, medicare, welfare assistance and regional development. These conditional grants are not described in this chapter but are covered under the sections dealing with the subjects to which they apply. However, in order to provide a comprehensive view of federal assistance to other levels of government, a summary table showing both unconditional and conditional payments is included at the end of the chapter. The arrangements under which a province can opt out of certain conditional grant programs and receive tax abatements or cash compensation in lieu of grants are also described in this chapter. The cash transfers with respect to post-secondary education are shown as unconditional grants in the summary table, although they are classified in the functional analysis as "education" expenditures.

Federal-Provincial Fiscal Arrangements

A complete history of federal-provincial fiscal arrangements is availabe in the 1966 Foundation publication entitled *The Financing of Canadian Federation: the first hundred years*. This can be supplemented by an article in the *Canadian Tax Journal* entitled "Federal-Provincial Fiscal Relations: the Last Six years and the Next Five," (Vol. XX, No. 4, 1972, p. 349). . . .

● ● ●

1972 to 1977

In three major federal-provincial conferences, the eleven governments worked out revisions to the tax collection agreements, post-secondary education assistance, and equalization and stablization programs. These consultations resulted in the introduction in the House of Commons of Bill C-8, the Federal-Provincial Fiscal Arrangements Act, 1972. This was amended in 1973 by Bill C-233 and in 1975 by Bill C-57. Part I of the Act extended the 1967 equalization system for the five-year period 1972-77. Although basically unchanged, the formula was expanded to take into account 19 provincial revenue sources, the three added revenue sources being health insurance premiums (based on the weighted number of taxable income tax returns), race track taxes (based on amounts wagered at pari-mutuel tracks), and the provincial share of income tax on power utilities (based on actual federal payments to the provinces). The 1973 amendment added municipal taxes imposed for local school purposes.

In 1975, the Act was modified to redefine oil and natural gas revenues into items 11, 12, 13, 14 and 16 and a distinction made between "basic" and "additional" revenues from those sources. "Basic" revenue was defined as the actual revenues in 1973-74, adjusted for volume increases; these revenues are to be equalized in full. "Additional" revenues, the difference between actual and "basic" revenues, are to be equalized only to the extent of one-third. This change affects the years 1974-75 to 1976-77 inclusive. . . .

Equalization [and stabilization]
The present equalization system contains 23 different provincial revenue sources. . . .

Part II of the 1972 Act provided that a stablization payment will be made to ensure that any province whose total revenue falls below that of the previous year (assuming no provincial tax changes) will have that shortfall made up by the federal government.

Part III of the Act extended the tax collection agreements and provided additional flexibility for provincial action. Alberta, Manitoba and Ontario are able, under the new legislation and federal agreements, to provide an individual income tax credit (through the federal tax collection machinery) for residential property tax paid. Since the federal government withdrew from the estate and gift tax fields, most provinces moved in to fill the gap. The Atlantic provinces, Manitoba and Saskatchewan were thus permitted under this Act to empower the federal government to collect their succession duties for three years. The federal government will also collect gift taxes for these provinces, British Columbia and Ontario for the same period. A collection fee of 3% will be imposed for the collection of provincial succession duties.

Part IV of the Act provided a guarantee that for five years the provinces will not suffer a loss of income tax revenue as a result of adopting income tax Acts modelled on the new federal Act, provided that their rates are equivalent to those levied under the old Act. . . .

Opting-Out Arrangements

1972
Bill C-8 also extended the period of interim arrangements to March 31, 1977 and adjusted the compensating abatements as follows:

Hospital Insurance	16% of federal individual income tax
Special Welfare (including blind and disabled persons' allowances and CAP)	5% of federal individual income tax

The 3% abatement for Youth Allowances continues. . . .

Statutory Subsidies

The statutory subsidies paid to the provinces are traditional payments granted under the British North America Acts, 1867 to 1952, and other statutory authority. They include allowances for government, for population, interest on debt allowances and special grants.

1977 to 1982

Federal-provincial negotiations carried on during 1976 resulted, on December 14, in agreement by the First Ministers on the general outline of a system to replace the arrangements that were to expire March 31, 1977. In brief, the collection agreements and the equalization system are to continue relatively unchanged, but the revenue guarantee is replaced by a 1 percentage point abatement of federal individual income tax, plus the equivalent in cash. Medicare, hospital insurance and post-secondary education are to be financed by a 12.5% abatement of federal individual income tax, a 1 percentage point abatement of corporation income tax and unconditional cash grants.

Federal Payments to the Provinces—$2,933 million

As shown in Table 10-1, equalization payments to the provinces for 1976-77 have been estimated by the Department of Finance at $2,127.4 million. Adjustment payments to Quebec made under the provisions of the opting-out agreements are estimated at $383.3 million, offset by recoveries related to Youth Allowances of $130.7 million. Statutory subsidies are estimated at $33.9 million and the payment of 95% of the income tax on certain public utilities, at $36.3 million. It is expected that payments under the revenue guarantee section of the Federal-Provincial Arrangements Act, will amount to $360.2 million. Payments under Part V of the Act, are estimated at $15.6 million and payments to provinces in lieu of provincially imposed property taxes are expected to amount to $3.4 million in the current year.

•　　•　　•

Total Federal Payments to Other Governments

Although this chapter is primarily concerned with general or unconditional payments to the provinces, municipalities and territories, it is useful to see the whole picture of federal payments, both unconditional and conditional, to other levels of government. Conditional payments are those grants earmarked for specific purposes.

Table 10-3 summarizes both conditional and unconditional grants for fiscal years ending March 31, 1967 and 1974 to 1977. The figures for 1977 are estimates only. The table indicates that grants to all levels of government have risen from $1.7 billion in 1966-67 to an estimated $6.7 billion in 1974-75. Complete data for conditional grants for the last two years shown in the table are not available.

TABLE 10-1

Estimated Payments to the Provinces under the Federal-Provincial Arrangements Act for the Fiscal Year 1976-77
(all dollar figures in thousands)

Payments	Nfld.	P.E.I.	N.S.	N.B.	Que.	Ont.	Man.	Sask.	Alta.	B.C.	Total
1. Equalization	234,534	57,406	300,095	231,770	1,142,890	—	165,204	85,547	—	—	2,217,446
2. Individual income tax collected[a]	93,917	16,247	167,585	130,079	—	2,278,104	280,902	205,500	358,012	704,957	4,235,303
3. Corporation income tax collected[a]	23,027	3,078	36,478	26,447	—	—	79,676	53,765	264,181	259,738	746,390
4. Share of income tax on certain public utilities	1,854	482	—	—	2,947	10,130	835	46	17,993	2,011	36,298
5. Statutory subsidies	9,708	659	2,174	1,774	4,484	5,504	2,176	2,111	3,214	2,117	33,921
6. Adjustments for prior years	273	22	-497	-305	-2,297	-3,373	294	-340	1,954	—	-4,899
7. Opting out compensation	—	—	—	—	252,603	—	—	—	—	—	252,603
8. Payments under Part IV	7,885	1,785	12,020	11,460	77,670	155,395	21,915	15,120	33,215	23,715	360,180
9. Payments under Part V[b]	105	10	358	266	3,385	6,185	868	454	1,845	2,080	15,556
10. Total Payments[c]	371,303	79,689	518,213	401,491	1,481,052	2,451,945	551,870	362,203	680,414	994,618	7,892,798
Post-Secondary Education											
11. Value of tax abatements included in above, line (2) and (3)											
12. 4.357% of individual income tax	9,980	1,966	18,965	13,936	186,406	327,290	28,797	25,652	61,168	97,508	771,668
13. 1% of corporate income tax base	1,645	308	3,040	2,645	35,872	71,933	6,129	4,480	24,016	17,983	168,051
14. Additional cash transfer[d]	4,757	1,059	17,591	6,287	297,278	150,866	15,385	11,331	30,277	3,169	538,000
15. Total value of post-secondary education assistance	16,382	3,333	39,596	22,868	519,556	550,089	50,311	41,463	115,461	118,660	1,477,719
16. Individual income tax—rate %	41.0	36.0	38.5	41.5	34.0[e]	30.5	42.5	40.0	26.0	31.5	
Net amount	93,917	16,247	167,585	130,079	1,461,650	2,278,104	280,902	205,500	358,012	704,957	5,696,953
17. Corporation income tax—rate %	14	10	12	10	12	12	13	12	11	12-15	
Net amount	23,027	3,078	36,478	26,447	435,991	874,290	79,676	53,765	264,181	259,738	2,056,671
18. Rebates, credits and reductions											
— Personal income tax	—	—	—	2,696	—	491,000	67,000	30,000	23,000	15,000	628,696
— Corporate income tax	—	—	—	—	—	—	—	10,000	—	9,000	19,000

[a]Including post-secondary education abatement.   [b]Payment to provinces of 20% of the special 15% tax on special distributions of corporation income surplus built up prior to January 1, 1972 and paid out subsequently.   [c]Individual provincial totals incomplete because no breakdown available of prior years' adjustment payments.   [d]Considered an expenditure on education.   [e]Estimated equivalent. Quebec tax structure differs from the federal.

Source: Department of Finance; Estimates.

TABLE 10-3

Summary of Federal Contributions to the Provinces, Municipalities and Territories
Fiscal Years ending March 31, 1967 and 1974 to 1977
($ million)

	1967[a]	1974[a]	1975[a]	1976[b]	1977[c]
A *Payments to Provinces*					
Unconditional Grants					
Equalization and stabilization .	312.4	1,463.4	2,287.0	1,956.4	2,217.4
Share of federal estate tax[d] ...	44.9	.1	3.7	—	—
Adjustment for prior years ...	28.2	—	—	−1.1	−4.9
Atlantic provinces grants	35.0	—	—	—	—
Established programs (Interim Arrangements)	57.6	206.5	176.4	204.2[e]	252.6[e]
Share of income tax on certain public utilities	6.0	25.9	26.7	31.8	36.3
Statutory subsidies	31.6	33.8	33.8	33.8	33.9
Post-secondary education payments	—	485.1	503.6	535.0	538.0
Grants in lieu of provincial property tax	—	3.0	3.2	—	—
Payments under Part IV	—	—	—	460.5	360.2
Payments under Part V	—	—	—	14.0	15.6
Payments under *Oil Export Tax Act*	—	143.3	111.1	.2	—
Total unconditional grants	515.5	2,361.7	3,145.3	3,234.9	3,449.2
Conditional Grants					
Hospital insurance	396.3	1,062.2	1,303.4	1,704.0	2,023.5
Medicare	—	676.2	760.8	793.8	956.7
Other health	52.0	39.1	44.2		
Welfare	193.4	525.8	732.0		
Education	238.2	99.0	103.4		
Transportation	104.6	47.1	40.3		
Natural resources and regional development	39.9	222.3	188.9		
Other	79.1	25.7	135.2		
Total conditional grants	1,103.5	2,697.4	3,308.1	4,045.0	n/a
Total Payments to Provinces	1,619.0	5,059.1	6,453.4	7,279.9	n/a
B *Payments to Municipalities*					
Unconditional grants	39.0	63.9	69.5	79.4	90.6
Conditional grants	70.4	101.0	75.4	n/a	n/a
Total Payments to Municipalities	109.4	164.9	144.9	n/a	n/a
C *Payments to Territories*					
Statutory subsidies	6.3	85.3	95.3	145.1	197.6
Conditional	2.7	10.8	16.6	13.8	n/a
Total Payments to Territories	9.1	96.1	112.1	158.9	n/a
Total Federal Payments	1,737.5	5,320.1	6,710.5		

[a] Statistics Canada, *Federal Government Finance*. [b] Public Accounts and the Department of Finance. [c] The Department of Finance and Estimates for 1976-77. [d] Included in "Equalization and Stabilization" for years 1975-76 and 1976-77. [e] Payments reduced by amounts recoverable under *Federal-provincial Fiscal Revisions Act*, 1964, *Youth Allowances Act;* in 1975-76, $114.7 million; in 1976-77, an estimated $130.7 million.

BIBLIOGRAPHY

Bastien, R., "La structure fiscale du fédéralisme canadien: 1945-73", *C.P.A.*, Vol. 17, No. 1, Spring, 1974.

Benson, E. J., *The Taxing Powers and the Constitution of Canada*, Ottawa, Queen's Printer, 1969.

Birch, A. H., *Federalism, Finance, and Social Legislation in Canada, Australia, and the United States*, Oxford, Clarendon Press, 1955.

Bird, R. M., *The Growth of Government Spending in Canada*, Toronto, Canadian Tax Foundation, Paper No. 51, 1970.

Breton, A., "A Theory of Government Grants," *C.J.E.P.S.*, Vol. XXXI, No. 2, May, 1965. (See also "Notes," *ibid.*, Vol. XXXII, No. 2, May, 1966; Breton, A., "A Theory of the Demand for Public Goods," *ibid.*, Vol. XXXII, No. 4, November 1966, and "Notes," *ibid.*, Vol. XXXIII, No. 1, February, 1967.)

Burns, R. M., "Federal Provincial relations: the problem of fiscal adjustment", *Canadian Tax Journal*, Vol. 20, No. 3, May-June, 1972.

Canada, Minister of Finance, *Report of the Tax Structure Committee to the Federal-Provincial Conference of Prime Ministers and Premiers*, Ottawa, February 16-17, 1970.

Canada, *Dominion-Provincial Conference on Reconstruction; Submission and Plenary Conference Discussion*, Ottawa, King's Printer, 1946.

Canada, *Report of the Royal Commission on Dominion-Provincial Relations* [Rowell-Sirois Report]; *Book I, Canada: 1867-1939*; *Book II, Recommendations*; *Book III; Documentation*; Ottawa, King's Printer, 1940, 3 vols. (Reprinted in one volume, 1954.) Also Appendices 1-8.

Canada, *Report of the Royal Commission on Taxation*, [Carter Commission], Ottawa, Queen's Printer, 1966, 6 vols. (See also the Commission's individual research studies, Nos. 1-30, especially No. 23, J. H. Lynn, *Federal-Provincial Relations*, Ottawa, Queen's Printer, 1967.)

Canadian Tax Foundation, *Provincial and Municipal Finances*, 1975, Toronto, Canadian Tax Foundation, 1975.

Clark, D. H., *Fiscal Need and Revenue Equalization Grants*, Canadian Tax Papers No. 49, Toronto, Canadian Tax Foundation, 1969.

Dehem, R., and Wolfe, J. N., "The Principles of Federal Finance and the Canadian Case," *C.J.E.P.S.*, Vol. XXI, No. 1, February, 1955.

Dupré, J. S., "Tax-Powers vs Spending Responsibilities: An Historical Analysis of Federal-Provincial Finance," in Rotstein, A., (ed.), *The Prospect of Change*, Toronto, McGraw-Hill, 1965.

Dupré, J. S., "'Contracting out': A Funny Thing Happened on the Way to the Centennial," *Report of the Proceedings of the Eighteenth Annual Tax Conference*, Toronto, Canadian Tax Foundation, 1965.

Dupré, J. S., *Intergovernmental Finance in Ontario: A Provincial-Local Perspective*, Toronto, Queen's Printer, Ontario, 1968.

Dupré, J. S., *Federalism and Policy Development: The Case of Adult Occupational Training in Ontario*, Toronto, University of Toronto Press, 1973.

Graham, J. F., Johnson, A. W., Andrews, J. F., *Inter-Goverment Fiscal Relationships*, Canadian Tax Paper No. 40, Toronto, Canadian Tax Foundation, December, 1964.

Head, J. G., "Evolution of Canadian Tax Reform," *Dalhousie Law Review*, Vol. I, No. 1, September, 1973.

Johnson, J. A., "Provincial-Municipal Intergovernmental Fiscal Relations," *C.P.A.*, Vol. XXI, No. 2, Summer, 1969.

La Forest, G. V., *The Allocation of Taxing Powers Under the Canadian Constitution*, Toronto, Canadian Tax Foundation, 1967.

Mackintosh, W. A., *The Economic Background of Dominion-Provincial Relations*, Toronto, McClelland and Stewart, 1964.

MacNaughton, C., *Ontario's Proposals for Fiscal Policy Co-ordination in Canada*, Budget Papers, Toronto, Department of Treasury and Economics, 1970.

May, R., *Federalism and Fiscal Adjustment*, Ottawa, Queen's Printer, 1968.

Moore, A. M., Perry, J. H., and Beach, D. I., *The Financing of Canadian Federation: The First Hundred Years*, Canadian Tax Paper No. 43, Toronto, Canadian Tax Foundation, 1966.

Nowlan, D. M., "Centrifugally Speaking: Some Economics of Canadian Federalism," in Lloyd, T., and McLeod, J. T., (eds.), *Agenda 1970*, Toronto, University of Toronto Press, 1968.

Oats, W. E., *Fiscal Federalism*, Don Mills, Ontario, Harcourt Brace Jovanovich, 1972.

Ontario, Department of Treasury and Economics, *Intergovernmental Policy Co-ordination and Finance*, Staff Papers, Toronto, 1970.

Ontario, *Report of the Committee on Taxation* [Smith Committee], Toronto, Queen's Printer, 1967, 3 vols.

Perry, J. H., *Taxation in Canada*, Toronto, University of Toronto Press, 3rd ed., rev., 1961.

Perry, J. H., *Taxes, Tariffs, and Subsidies; A History of Canadian Fiscal Development*, Toronto, University of Toronto Press, 1955, 2 vols.

Perry, D. B., "Federal-provincial fiscal relations: the last six years and the next five", *Canadian Tax Journal*, Vol. 20, No. 4, July-August, 1972.

Quebec, *Report of the Royal Commission on Taxation* [Bélanger Report], Quebec, Queen's Printer, 1965.

Robinson, A. J., and Cutt, J., (eds.), *Public Finance in Canada: Selected Readings*, 2nd ed., (Chapter III), Toronto, Methuen, 1973.

Simeon, R., *Federal-Provincial Diplomacy: The Making of Recent Policy in Canada*, Toronto, University of Toronto Press, 1972.

Smiley, D. V., "The Rowell-Sirois Report, Provincial Autonomy, and Post-War Canadian Federalism," *C.J.E.PS.*, Vol. XXVIII, No. 1, February, 1962.

Smiley, D. V., *Conditional Grants and Canadian Federalism*, Canadian Tax Paper No. 32, Toronto, Canadian Tax Foundation, 1962.

Smiley, D. V., "Block Grants to the Provinces: A Realistic Alternative?" *Report of the Proceedings of the Eighteenth Annual Tax Conference*, Canadian Tax Foundation, Toronto, 1965.

Smiley, D. V., *Constitutional Adaptation and Canadian Federalism Since 1945*, Document 4 of the Royal Commission on Bilingualism and Biculturalism, Ottawa, Queen's Printer, 1970.

Smiley, D. V., and Burns, R. M., "Canadian Federalism and the Spending Power: Is Constitutional Restriction Necessary?" *Canadian Tax Journal*, Vol. XVII, No. 6, November-December, 1969.

Smiley, D. V., *Canada in Question, Federalism in the Seventies*, Toronto, McGraw-Hill Ryerson, second ed., 1976.

Strick, J. C., "Conditional grants and provincial government budgeting", *C.P.A.*, Vol. 14, No. 2, Summer, 1971.

Trudeau, P. E., *Federal-Provincial Grants and the Spending Power of Parliament*, Ottawa, Queen's Printer, 1969.

Trudeau, P. E., *Income Security and Social Services*, Ottawa, Queen's Printer, 1969.

4

REGIONALISM

The subject of regionalism in Canada has attracted increasing attention in the past few years. While the major focus has been upon regionalism within Canada, some provinces have moved in the direction of creating regions within their borders for administrative purposes. Ontario, for example, has established a number of different regions for different functions, such as regional municipal governments and ten intra-provincial economic regions.

Professor David Bell's article on "Regionalism in the Canadian Community" which inaugurates this chapter reviews both the national and provincial implications of regionalism. It summarizes admirably some of the major problems.

The emergence of this new interest in regionalism has not altered the traditional tendency of Canadians to think of regionalism in terms of a province or a group of provinces. As Professor Hodgetts remarks in his article noted in the bibliography, when Canadians talk about regions in Canada, they still are inclinded to think of "the regions" as the Atlantic provinces, the Prairies, British Columbia, Quebec, and Ontario. Thus, while new experiments with different regions have been under way lately, there is still considerable interest in the hoary argument about the advisability of amalgamating the Atlantic provinces into one government and the Prairie provinces into another consolidated government. This idea has always had a special appeal for Central Canadians but what is now apparent is that at least some residents in each of these two regions have begun to consider it seriously also. This chapter contains a submission to the commission from the Atlantic Provinces Economic Council (APEC) arguing in favour of amalgamation. In the west a conference was held in Lethbridge, Alberta, in 1970 to consider the pros and cons of the union of the Prairie provinces. Professor Norman Ward's devastating critique of prairie union presented at this conference is reproduced here. The problem of regional economic disparities in the Altantic provinces is explained well by Douglas Fullerton's article which concludes this chapter.

The third edition of *Politics: Canada* contained a number of additional items pertaining to regionalism which have been omitted from this edition. The page references to these selections in the third edition are as follows: Professor J. E. Hodgetts, "How Applicable is Regionalism in the Canadian Federal Systems?", pp. 94-99; Professor John F. Graham, "Should the Atlantic Provinces Unite?", pp. 99-104; Premier W. A. C. Bennett, "Let's Have Five Provinces", pp. 108-109; Hon. James Richardson, "Amalgamating the Prairie Provinces Has Great Advantages", pp. 109-112; and Premier Harry Strom, "Alberta Has Other Ideas", pp. 112-113.

A good deal of literature, including a number of valuable, commissioned, specialized studies, has been stimulated by this new interest in regionalism. Since it is too voluminous to be noted item by item in the bibliography appended to this chapter, students seeking further references should consult both federal and provincial sources. The bibliography in this chapter does refer, however, to many of the more general articles and books on regionalism that have appeared recently.

The bibliography is divided into three sections: regionalism, provinces and territories, and municipalities.

REGIONALISM IN THE CANADIAN COMMUNITY*

David V. J. Bell

The Two Faces of Regionalism

. . . "Regionalism in Canada," with its connotations of tension and conflict, seems antithetical to the notion of "the Canadian community," which connotes harmony and consensus. But regionalism, like drama, has two faces. Negative regionalism, to be sure, displays the frown of conflict and disintegration, manifested when one region is pitted against another, or against the national government. Positive regionalism, however, features the smile of co-operation and integration, the joining together of people living in a given territory to form a new political entity. In this sense, regionalism refers not to the opposite of community, but to the existence of community at a sub-national level.

This essay examines Canadian regionalism in both its positive and negative aspects. . . . Quebec regionalism has not been examined [here]. . . .The focus on negative regionalism is really equivalent to the study of provincialism; while the assessment of positive regionalism amounts to an evaluation of inter-provincialism. The latter concern will direct our attention to the Prairies and the Maritimes, which at present are

* Published here originally from an essay written in 1971 by the author who is Associate Professor of Political Science, York University. By permission of the author.

the only conceivable settings for "positive regionalism." After exploring the relationship between regionalism and federalism, the essay concludes with a brief, tentative speculation about the future of Canadian regionalism.

Negative Regionalism in Canada: Challenges to Community

The history of negative regionalism in Canada predates Confederation itself. In 1784, New Brunswick broke away from Nova Scotia in response to the regional aspirations of the newly arrived loyalist settlers. Similarly, Upper Canada was carved out of the enormous territory of Quebec in 1791. The failure to include Prince Edward Island within Confederation in 1867, and the Manitoba Rebellions led by Louis Riel, both represent regional challenges to national solidarity in Canada. Indeed, at some point in Canadian history, virtually every conceivable region has violently or peacefully asserted its autonomy vis-à-vis the larger entity.

Essentially, negative regionalism is simply a form of political cleavage with a territorial basis, best understood in the context of a general theory of political cleavages. . . .

Regional cleavages can interact with a variety of other political cleavages. It is widely believed among social scientists that conflict is positively correlated with the number and importance of reinforcing cleavages in a society. To the extent that this view is correct, it allows us to predict whether regional cleavages are likely to lead to low conflict or to relatively high conflict. The crucial consideration is the number of *other* cleavages that reinforce the regional one. Clearly, the least explosive combination includes a territorial or regional cleavage that is *not* reinforced by class, racial or religious-linguistic division; while the most explosive situation arises where *all* cleavages reinforce the territorial one. A hypothetical example of such a situation would feature a geographically concentrated racial minority, practising a different religion from the rest of society, all of whose members belonged to one social class. Perhaps the closest real world case exists in South Africa.

The situation in Canada is difficult to pinpoint. There is little doubt that economic, linguistic, and ethnic differences do reinforce regional cleavages *to a certain extent*. Economically, there is a fairly recognizable distinction between the "have" provinces (Ontario, British Columbia and to a lesser degree the Prairie Provinces), and the "have not" (all of the Atlantic Provinces and Quebec). Ironically, this line coincides exactly with the eastern boundary of Ontario. Linguistically, of course, the first fact of Canadian politics is the regional concentration of the French minority, . . . [although] a significant portion of this minority is found in regions other than Quebec. A classic, if somewhat overstated, assessment of this cleavage was written nearly forty years ago by A. R. M. Lower. . . .

> The French-English cleavage is the greatest factor in Canadian life, not only because it is a racial and linguistic cleavage, but because it coincides with an economic cleavage, a legal cleavage, a cultural cleavage, a religious cleavage, and a philosophical cleavage.

Ethnically, Canadian regions display distinct patterns. The often celebrated "mosaic" truly exists only in the Prairies, while other regions are
composed largely of members of the French or British "charter groups."
The percentage of non-British/French population in the Provinces
ranges from a low of less than four per cent in Prince Edward Island to a
high of over 53 per cent in Saskatchewan. . . .

Beyond these (and similar) crude estimates, precise measures of the
degree of reinforcing cleavages in Canadian society have never been
developed. . . .

Even multiple reinforcing cleavages do not produce the conflict characteristic of negative regionalism automatically. Besides the objective
existence of cleavage, conflict presupposes subjective awareness of the
cleavages and the *interpretation of the cleavage as an "unjust" one*. The suffix
of the term implies that like other "isms," regionalism contains a strong
subjective component. It is impossible to discuss regionalism in a political
context without considerable attention to the beliefs, values, and attitudes
of the inhabitants of the "region." Only when this subjective factor is
present does a region take on political (as opposed to economic or geographical) significance. Indeed, perceptions are probably more important than the objective situation in determining the nature and extent of
conflict. Do the inhabitants of a given region (a) perceive themselves as
possessing a regional identity? (b) believe that their region is the object of
"unjust" discrimination? If so, negative regionalism is likely to occur in the
form of inter-regional or regional-national conflict.

Taking these questions separately, it is generally agreed that regional
identities have been much stronger in Canada than say in the United
States. Again precise measures are lacking, but stimulating speculations
are not. J. M. S. Careless . . . observes that

> Regional, ethnic and class identities have all tended to fit together more
> than to develop national identification in Canada. The ultimate conclu-
> sion, indeed, might seem to be that the true theme of the country's
> history in the twentieth century is not national building but region
> building.

Part of the explanation for the existence and virility of this aspect of
regionalism can be traced to the traditional absence of any effective
national alternative to regional identity. Even today, the character of
Canadian national identity remains confused and uncertain, a reflection
of at least three factors: the French-English cleavage; the fact that nearly
one-third of Canada's population is composed of members of ethnic
groups other than the "charter" British and French minorities; and the
ambiguous psychological consequences of the Loyalist tradition in
Canada.

Throughout Canadian history, repeated efforts have been made to
discover or invent a national identity capable of integrating these diverse
elements. . . .

One significant obstacle to "the transfer of loyalty from the region to
the nation" is the persistence of feelings of regional injustice. Examples
could be culled from virtually every region in the country, but for the

purpose of illustration it is perhaps sufficient to draw on the experience of the Maritimes and the Prairies. Probably because compared to Ontario and British Columbia these have been among the disadvantaged provinces economically, one finds almost endemic to politics in these areas a profound sense of regional injustice and exploitation. But "Prairie injustice" has non-economic roots as well. Westerners, for example, still resent the fact that the Eastern provinces created Confederation, while the Western provinces were creatures of it. One noted Westerner went so far as to suggest that, "In some respects, the Prairie Provinces were conceived as a sort of colony of Central Canada." . . .

The image of the West as an exploited colony is still a vivid one. The only available survey data touching on the issue, gathered by David K. Elton in Alberta during 1968, support the hypothesis of widespread alienation in Western Canada. Sixty-one per cent of his respondents agreed that "the Eastern Canadians receive more benefits than do Western Canadians from being part of the Dominion of Canada" . . . . Despite these rather high feelings of perceived injustice, at present less than ten per cent of Albertans seem interested in radical movements such as annexation or secession. By the same token, few are genuinely interested in Prairie union as a solution to the problems that lie behind negative regionalism. Again, Elton's survey showed only 23 per cent agreement with the idea that "the three Western provinces should join together and form one large province." Even a relatively high degree of negative regionalism apparently does not guarantee the basis for positive regionalism. As far as the idea of regional integration is concerned, "hating Toronto," to paraphrase humorist Eric Nicol, "is not enough."

Distrust of "Upper Canadians" enjoys an even longer tradition in the Maritimes. George Rawlyk illustrates convincingly his assertion that "Since 1867, two important ingredients in Nova Scotian regionalism have been an often profound dislike of Upper Canada and 'Upper Canadians' and also a basic distrust of Confederation itself." These negative attitudes, Rawlyk continues, almost amount to a "paranoid style," which he defines as a tendency to ascribe to Ottawa and Toronto all blame for Nova Scotia's economic and social decline. . . . Even today, Maritime alienation is remarkably strong. An opinion survey of all three provinces, conducted in connection with the Deutsch Commission investigations, showed that a higher proportion (40 per cent as compared with 33 per cent) of Maritimers felt they had "most in common" with Maine rather than Ontario! A whopping 25 per cent declared that they "would be in favour of political union with the United States"; and fully 63 per cent favoured closer economic ties with their Southern neighbours. By contrast, David Elton's survey of Albertan opinion turned up only five per cent support for Western separatism.

Positive Regionalism in Canada: The Extension of Community

The other face of regionalism, its positive side, involves the attainment of regional integration. In studying integration, it is important to distinguish the integration of people into a community directly as individuals, from the integration of existing communities into a larger whole. The former is largely a social phenomenon, probably understood as well (or as poorly) by humanists as by social scientists. The latter is largely a political phenomenon,". . . a set of political decisions made by those who have the authority to commit their communities to collective action." Despite the elitist connotations of this approach, the focus on political decision-making as the crux of integration is particularly appropriate to the analysis of positive regionalism. For regional integration in Canada, at least as we have defined it, is equivalent to the amalgamation of two or more semi-sovereign provinces. . . .

Analysts as diverse as civil servants and geographers commonly divide Canada into five "regions." Three of the five regions, Ontario, Quebec, and B.C., coincide with existing provincial boundaries. The other two, the Maritimes and the Prairies, do not. "Regional integration" usually refers to the idea of union among two or more of the provinces in the latter category. At an earlier stage in Canadian history, the phrase might have connoted Upper and Lower Canada. No one seriously proposes this notion nowadays. By contrast, the "idea of Maritime Union" was the theme of an important Conference held at Mount Allison University in 1965; the question "One Prairie Province?" was discussed at an even larger conference held at the University of Lethbridge in 1970. A few weeks after the Maritime Union conference, the governments of Nova Scotia and New Brunswick established a commission to investigate "the advantages and disadvantages of a union . . ." In 1968 (after the characteristic lapse of three years) P.E.I. joined in sponsoring this project. What are the prospects for regional integration in these two areas?

Obstacles to Western unification are as numerous as they are difficult. In a brilliant, thorough analysis, Norman Ward virtually buried the idea of "one prairie province" under an avalanche of hypothetical problems. . . . [See Ward's article, below.]

But do his points apply as well to the idea of Maritime union? The members of the Royal Commission headed by John J. Deutsch to examine the feasibility of just such a union felt that the potential benefits of union far outweighed the expected costs. Their *Report*, finally completed in 1970, strongly recommended that amalgamation take place according to a suggested timetable covering five to ten years.

Several factors might account for the more optimistic conclusions reached by the Commission. In the first place, the idea of Maritime union predates its Prairie equivalent (which Ward dates from 1925) by over a century, going back at least as far as 1808 (see Beck, 1969). A much smaller area than the Prairies (less than one-third its size), the Maritimes are considerably more disadvantaged. . . . Perhaps these considerations alone account for the far greater degree of inter-provincial co-operation currently taking place in the Maritime provinces. A thorough inventory turned up 181 organizations (probably about four times the number that exist in the Prairies) whose activities range from academic to agricultural pursuits.

A number of these inter-provincial organizations have been assisted or created by the Federal Government itself! In fact in 1969, the Government set up a Department of Regional Economic Expansion whose explicit purpose is to foster co-operation in economic development at the regional level, especially in the poor regions of the country (including all of the Atlantic provinces and certain areas of the West). . . .

In line with this philosophy, the new Department has taken control of many of the "ad hoc" federal agencies and policies (including the Atlantic Development Board, the Agricultural Rehabilitation and Development Agency [ARDA], and the "Cape Breton Development Corporation") set up since World War II to deal with regional disparities in income, unemployment rates, etc., that resulted from Canada's uneven economic development. These policies, a Government study concluded in 1968, had managed only to prevent further widening of inter-regional gaps. Much greater effort would be needed, the report continued, to *reduce* regional inequalities. So far, like its predecessors, the Department has confined its activity to economic measures, shying away from such political issues as regional amalgamation of two or more provinces. Nevertheless, the political relevance of reducing regional economic inequality in Canada need not be laboured. Much of the support for negative regionalism stems from economic grievances; much of the incentive for positive regionalism grows out the search for solutions to regional economic problems.

Indeed, the single most significant consideration that lay behind the Deutsch Commission's recommendations was undoubtedly the nature and scope of the economic and social problems that the Maritimes shared jointly. According to the *Report* (pp. 30-31):

> What is needed is the ability to develop and to carry out plans, policies, and programs on a regional basis. The economies of the Maritime Provinces are individually too small and too inter-dependent for the effective planning and execution of development programs in the fact of present-day social and technological trends.

Reviewing the alternative courses of action available to the Maritimes, the Commission found that, despite the possibility for achieving some of the necessary objectives through "informal co-operation," a much higher and more formalized level of co-operation would be necessary. Though to be sure, a great deal might be accomplished through the setting up of *ad hoc* agencies to implement specific programmes, such a practice would result in additional burdens of administrative and overhead costs, while failing to provide the executive authority capable of carrying out these policies. The only way to avoid these disadvantages, they concluded, would be through a full political union rather than a lower level administrative or economic union.

According to the opinion survey conducted in connection with the *Report*, there is already much support for these recommendations. Sixty-four per cent of the respondents surveyed indicated that they would vote in favour of "complete union into a single province." More significantly, perhaps, opinion was approximately evenly divided in all three provinces, a situation precisely the opposite of that which exists in the Prairies. The vast majority of the respondents felt that Maritime union would bring more industry to the Maritimes, provide more jobs, make possible the greater development of natural resources, and also improve governmental efficiency. These expectations may or may not be correct. The important consideration *politically* is that they exist and are widely held.

So persuasive were the Commission's findings, that the three Maritime Provincial premiers moved quickly to follow the timetable set out for them. By the fall of 1971, they were already one year ahead of the suggested schedule in a number of important areas. It seems that the future of regional integration in the Maritimes is quite promising. Whether amalgamation of the three provinces will provide the solutions to the Maritimes' critical problems, of course, remains to be seen. Only when the time comes for action, rather than talk, will the movement toward Atlantic Union meet its crucial test. . . .

What is the relationship between negative regionalism and positive regionalism? A comprehensive answer to this question would fill many volumes. Several fascinating insights emerge, however, from a consideration of the paradoxical effect upon regionalism of federalism.

Regionalism and Federalism

Federalism (i.e., the existence of separate sub-national political units which are theoretically autonomous in at least one important sphere) is in theory an important facilitator of regionalism for the following reasons:

1. Federalism provides an explicit reminder to the citizen of a dual political status and identity. Indeed, citizens of the United States are legally referred to as citizens of the State wherein they reside. Canadian practice tends not to make explicit this dual citizenship notion, referring instead to "citizens" of Canada and "residents" of the provinces, although Quebec is becoming an obvious exception.

2. The existence of the provincial governments provides a career structure for politicians whose chief responsibility is to a sub-national community. Moreover the nature of the general relationship between sub-national and national political units almost automatically invites the provincial politician to appeal to localistic sentiments by attributing all evils and unpleasantness to the "tyrannical domination" of the national government, thereby exacerbating negative regionalism. Such "projection" of blame occurs in virtually any system/sub-system political arrangement regardless of level, considerations of nationality, class, etc. . . .

3. Provincial political authorities, like their national political counterparts (though usually to a lesser degree) are able to regulate social processes such as transportation, communications, and economics to encourage the development of sub-national socio-economic systems. Thus indirectly, federalism contributes to the strengthening of the "structural underpinnings" of provincialism. This influence even extends in Canada and elsewhere to the important spheres of education, where emphasis on provincial rather than national concerns can have lasting effects on the cognitive aspect of community. Through manipulation of the education process, young people may be inculcated with a provincial rather than a national identity.

4. Though in the U.S. few states are large enough to constitute poten-

tially self-sustaining eco-political systems, Canadian provinces often do approximate self-contained systems, or do so in combination with two or three other provinces. Thus in Canada geography reinforces regionalism in a simpler and more direct way than in other countries such as the U.S. ("The South," for example, comprises at least 13 separate states.)

While contributing to the centrifugal forces associated with negative regionalism, federalism in some ways provides an ideal solution for resolving or minimizing potentially disintegrative conflicts inherent in regional differences. If a society is deeply divided at the mass level on religious, social or other grounds, separation of the various sub-cultures into reasonably autonomous regions permits the functioning of a system of "consociational democracy" in which the political elites display towards each other the "sense of community" lacking in the society at large. Precisely this function is served by the federal system in Canada.

The conditions under which such a scheme can remain operable for Canada are outlined succinctly by S. J. R. Noel:

> . . . the lack of a pan-Canadian identity combined with strong regional sub-cultures is not necessarily a dysfunctional feature . . . as long as *within each sub-culture demands are effectively articulated through its political elite* . . . [and provided that there does *not* emerge] "within any one of the provinces an elite who . . . are unwilling to provide 'overarching co-operation at the elite level . . . .'" (Emphasis added.)

Though on several occasions in Canadian history, regional discontent (especially in the West) has given birth to political movements, none of these has seriously challenged the integrity of the nation. The Progressives in the "twenties" were quickly absorbed by the Liberal Party. The CCF/NDP almost from its inception embraced national aspirations which precluded its remaining a party with a purely regional outlook. Social Credit followed a similar path, though with less success. In the past, without exception, political movements which started out deeply committed to regional or provincial objectives either collapsed before ever challenging the federal government, or themselves became involved in the national political process.

The "nationalization" of political *groups* originally regional in orientation operates on the individual level as well, as Noel observes:

> Time after time, provincial politicians with no more attachment to the federal system than the mass of their constituents become transformed in Ottawa into cabinet ministers intent on making the system work.

This is not to say that Ottawa is untouched by regional influences. Regional considerations play a large role in determining selection of cabinet ministers, for example. But the Canadian political system probably allows less scope nationally for regional factors than, say, the American. Party discipline all but prevents American style regional "bloc-voting" in the lower House; while in the weak Canadian Senate, regional representation is minimal, with approximately one-half of the seats reserved for the central regions of Ontario and Quebec. (For a more thorough comparison, see Hodgetts, 1966, p. 9.) Ironically, under the present electoral rules, political unification in either the Maritimes or the West would further *reduce* the representation of these regions in Parliament! [See Ward.] Furthermore, while *conceivably* strengthening the Maritimes or Western voice in some Ottawa circles, amalgamation would *definitely* reduce regional representation in such crucial gatherings as Dominion-Provincial Conferences.

Another obvious point, too often underemphasized or overlooked entirely, is the fact that political unification is "bad business" for the provincial politicians and civil servants who must ultimately take the decisions to amalgamate. Not only does unification eliminate many lower-level elite positions (e.g., MPP or MLA), but it also cuts the number of high level posts (premier, cabinet minister, deputy minister, etc.) by about two-thirds. A professional politician or bureaucrat is as unlikely as anyone else to embrace fondly the opportunity of reducing his occupational life chances. . . .

In short, federalism in Canada has had a paradoxically ambivalent effect on regionalism. Though a contributing factor to "negative regionalism," especially at the popular level, the federal system fosters nationalism among the political elites through myriad subtle mechanisms and adjustments. Yet federalism tends to discourage regional integration because such a move would eliminate or reduce career opportunities for the political elite.

Conclusion: The Future of Regionalism in Canada

It is possible to discern two trends, operating simultaneously but in opposite directions, to shape the future of regionalism in Canada and elsewhere. One trend sees the extension beyond existing political boundaries of problems (such as economic development and the protection of the environment) the effective solution of which requires greater co-operation among political leaders whose current orientation tends to be narrowly local. The other trend involves a growing concern for preserving local autonomy in the fact of a sprawling, faceless bureaucracy that seems to grow like topsy. Tension between these two trends makes it difficult, if not impossible, to predict the future of regionalism. Projecting the first trend leads one to predict the increasing amalgamation of smaller political units into larger entities. In Canada this would mean a reduction in the number of provinces from ten to, say, five and perhaps even fewer. Projecting the second trend, however, leads one to expect increased momentum of the centrifugal forces that drive smaller units farther and farther away from co-operation. In Canada this could conceivably mean the breakup of the Confederation into ten (or more!) independent nations.

Perhaps the truth lies somewhere in between these two projections: *ad hoc* agencies for regional co-operation will probably continue to develop in response to specific problems that are regional in nature. Where local governments are unable to reach agreement on dealing with these issues, it is quite conceivable that the national government will intercede to encourage (or perhaps to coerce) the "necessary" degree of co-operation. At the same time, however, the progress toward actual political amalgamation will encounter many obstacles, as the molasses-like movement toward political union in Europe clearly shows. The prospects for Maritime Union seem high, but probably not as high as the Deutsch Commissioners would like us to believe. The likelihood of one Prairie Province is almost non-existent. In other words, [former B.C. Premier] W. A. C. Bennett's plan for five Canadian provinces is unlikely to materialize, though the present number may be reduced from ten to seven or eight.

All of this assumes stability of the status quo with regard to Quebec. It is, of course, tempting to back away quietly from the painful task of discussing regionalism in a Quebec-less Canada, imagining such an enterprise "unthinkable," or a likely cause of "future shock.". . . Indeed, procrastination is particularly encouraged by the tendency to treat the Quebec case as *sui generis*, thereby blinding ourselves to an otherwise unmistakable observation about the *general* malaise of Canadian federalism today. As our analysis indicates, negative regionalism is not limited to Quebec but rather is widespread throughout the country. Moreover it lies behind much of the sentiment in favour of regional integration. Not only, however, is the achievement of regional union unlikely to take place (for the reasons outlined above), but consequences of unification if it did occur are also totally unknown and (at present) unknowable. Perhaps Atlantic Union is the solution to the incredible regional disparities in Canada (which, as Merrill, 1968, reports are much worse than those in the United States). But perhaps not! Then what?

If negative regionalism is to lead to anything other than increasing frustration and anger, fresh thinking must be brought to bear on this problem, which, despite the particular sensitivity of its Quebec manifestation, is truly national in scope. Conceivably, the Department of Regional Economic Expansion might become the vehicle for an entirely new policy. It is too soon yet to tell, though early indications suggest that the Department has merely brought together under one administration the old policies which were clearly shown to be unsatisfactory. For example, no attempt has been made, as far as I know, to decentralize regional planning from Ottawa to the affected regions themselves. A major defect of the earlier policies lives on.

We find ourselves behaving exactly the way De Tocqueville described the Americans, "infinitely varying the consequences of known principles and . . . seeking for new consequences rather than . . . seeking for new principles." If ever Canada needed creative political imagination—and the bold leadership capable of implementing new ideas—the time is now. How have other nations acted to overcome negative regionalism? A number of models should be examined, including the interesting Yugoslavian attempt to confront similar problems by loosening their federation and giving greater autonomy to regional governments. This, according to Paul Fox (1969) and several other political scientists, is precisely what is happening in Canada on a *de facto* basis as a result of many factors, including changes in the relative significance of the responsibilities accorded the provinces under the B.N.A. Act. Fox points out, for example, that provincial expenditures in Ontario increased "more than 1300 per cent between 1947 and 1967." I am not suggesting, therefore, that Canadian federal-provincial relations are static; but that we have paid too little attention to the normative problem of what political arrangements will best serve Canada's social goals. Whatever approach is followed, the new policies must embrace broad concerns that go beyond the narrow horizons of economic planning.

The future of the Canadian community hinges in large part on how the political elites respond to the challenges posed by regionalism.

ARGUMENTS FOR MARITIME UNION*

APEC

A few days ago the Atlantic Provinces Economic Council presented its Submission to the Maritime Union Study, In it APEC states that it "fully endorses not only the concept of Maritime Union but also wishes to express deep concern that a single Maritime Province be created as the result of a political union of the provinces."

•   •   •

Three basis arguments for political union of the Maritime Provinces are set forth in the APEC submission. All evolve from fundmental economic reasoning. One is that the reasons for separation of the Maritime Provinces in the nineteenth century now appear to be reasons for union. Another is the increased quality and quantity of services which a single Maritime Province, having one administrative, judicial and economic framework, could provide from the limited provincial government revenues available to the three provinces. Still another basic reason for Maritime Union, the Council contends, is the psychological impact it would likely have on the population of the region.

The acceptance of Union as an instrument for guiding the future should also motivate the region towards acceptance of still other changes—in a rapidly changing world—an attitude and condition regarded by many as a prerequisite for economic growth and development.

(1) If we look at the reasons for the separation of the Maritime Provinces into three separate entities, the state of the economy and the socio-political feeling at that time, a strong argument evolves for union of the provinces at this time. Although Prince Edward Island has always been a separate province since its creation in 1769, the province of New Brunswick was not established until 1784. What is now New Brunswick

---

* From the *APEC Newsletter*, Vol. 13, No. 3, April, 1969. By permission. For the full text of the submission, see Atlantic Provinces Economic Council, *Submission to the Maritime Union Study*, Halifax, April, 1969, mimeographed.

was originally part of Nova Scotia under British rule but due to numerous pressures at the end of the American Revolution, Nova Scotia was partitioned off at the isthmus so that the peninsula and the mainland became separate provinces.

Although political and social pressures influenced the British to create the province of New Brunswick, the basic underlying reason which gave rise to the move was the existing state of communications. The political motive was to create small enough units so that the British would not receive the harassment they had recently experienced from the Thirteen States. The social problem was that the primarily Loyalist population in New Brunswick feared being governed from Halifax which was both remote and peopled with what they felt were "Republican sympathizers." There was also the problem of geographical, cultural and occupational diversity both between and within the provinces.

The basic reason for separation, however, was that of communications, both in the plain old-fashioned connotation of the word—that of getting from point A to point B—and in the sense of the spread of information and ideas. Today, with relatively good transportation systems and the rapidity of such forms of transporation as air travel; the predominance of radios, televisions and newspapers; and a highly educated public, the population is not only more mobile but much better informed than at any time in the history of the region. Thus, since there has been such a dramatic change in the economy of the region and in life in general, and since the reasons for separation now seem so archaic, it would seem that Maritime Union is the logical step to be taken in an age where a total systems approach is the order of the day.

(2) The Council feels that much of the rationale for Maritime Union is economic in nature. Although Maritime Union is often endorsed on the understanding that the implementation of administrative, judicial and economic co-ordination will ultimately lead to political union, the Council contends that although some informal institutional arrangements may be made towards the creation of a union, the presence and rigidity of present institutions in the region can only be overcome through complete Maritime political union.

. . . APEC believes that the Maritime Provinces are facing a threat today, more serious than in the history of the region.

> The threat, as we see it, is both internal and external. Internally, it is the rapidly rising demand for services in the three provinces and the resultant increases in provincial government expenditures, while increases in revenues needed to pay for these services fail to keep pace. Externally, the threat is that if the three provincial governments do not strive to act, together, through union, to increase the level of efficiency (in the pure economic sense of the word—of producing the optimum output at minimum cost) and the quality of services offered, demands for federal funds to cover increased costs in these provincial responsibilities could lead to the provincial governments finding themselves in the unenviable position of becoming mere "colonies" of Ottawa.

One example which shows quite clearly the opportunity for increased efficiency in the region is the excessive number of departmental employees in the three provinces relative to population as compared to other Canadian provinces.

For instance, in 1967, there were 24,106 persons employed in departments of the three provincial governments to cater to a population of 1,486,000. This represents a ratio of one employee per 61.6 of population. These ratios in the three provinces were: Prince Edward Island, 1:50.0; Nova Socita, 1:56.1 and New Brunswick, 1:73.6. The ratio for the nation excluding British Columbia, and the Atlantic Provinces on the other hand, was 1:106.1 with ratios ranging from 1:71.4 in Alberta to the 1:117.1 in Quebec and 1:114.9 in Ontario. In fact, for the figures available, the ratios for all of the other provinces are higher than those in the Atlantic Provinces with the exception of Alberta's, which was lower than that of New Brunswick.

This, of course, has important implications in dollars and cents terms. If the ratio in the Maritime Provinces (1:61.6) had been the same as that for the rest of Canada, (1:106.1), only 14,006 would have been employed, instead of the actual 24,106. An increase in productivity in this one aspect of government activity would have meant a gross payroll (if paid the Maritime Provinces' average of $3,743) of approximately $52 million in 1967. This increased efficiency then would have been worth almost $38 million—a relative saving of over 40 percent. It must be pointed out that it would probably be unrealistic to expect the ratio to approach that of the nation as a whole, at the present economic state of the region because of the unique factors which characterize it. This is particularly relevant when our smaller total population and our relatively larger rural populations are considered. These and other factors pose a problem since the economics of scale in the provision of public services cannot be called into play. However, even though the suggested savings figure may be high, there is another significant factor. Salary scales for civil servants could be upgraded and greater challenge offered to attract a larger proportion of more highly qualified personnel.

In its Submission APEC analyzes the revenue and expenditure figures of the Maritime Provinces and the rest of the Canadian provinces for the period 1953-67. The figures used are net figures since these are the closest approximations available on which to make comparisons both on a province-to-province and a year-to-year basis.

This analysis reveals that not only has the composition of each side of the provincial financial accounts changed, but also that growth in some segments far outdistanced that in others over the 1953-67 period. Another observation is that although there are some similarities between all the Canadian provinces on one hand, and the Maritime Provinces on the other, in the direction of changes in components, there are some very marked differences in the magnitude of the changes.

Looking first at total net general revenue, it becomes evident that the revenue of all provinces combined has grown at a faster rate than it has for any of the Maritime Provinces. While the rate for All Provinces was 11.6 percent per year, the rates of the three Maritime Provinces were 10.9 percent, 9.3 percent and 8.4 percent for Prince Edward Island, Nova

Scotia and New Brunswick, respectively, for the period. Although there is a significant difference between the rates of increase of All Provinces and the Maritime Provinces in total net general revenue, a more significant difference exists in the composition of the aggregate in the region as opposed to the other provinces.

The most striking aspect of the components which combine to make up total net general revenue is the conspicuousness of the amount and growth of revenue received from the other governments by the provincial governments in the region. Firstly, revenue from other governments has increased at more than twice the yearly rate for All Provinces in each of the Maritime Provinces—by 7.9 percent in Prince Edward Island and New Brunswick, and 7.2 percent in Nova Scotia, compared to 3.6 percent in All Provinces. Secondly, the proportion of total net general revenue received from other governments (almost exclusively the federal government) has remained consistently much higher in the Maritime Provinces than for All Provinces, and the gap is widening. Whereas the proportion received by the Maritime Provinces was almost double that of All Provinces in the early 1950s, it is now almost four times as high, at a level approaching 40 percent as opposed to about 10 percent.

The dominance of revenue received from other governments in the Maritime Provinces has, of course, repercussions on the relative size of revenues received by the provincial governments from other sources. For instance, total Tax Revenue for All Provinces increased from 38.7 percent of total net general revenue in 1953 to 68.0 percent in 1967. For the Maritime Provinces it increased from 27.7 percent to 44.3 percent. Both Tax Revenue and Non-Tax Revenue increased at substantially higher annual rates in All Provinces than in any of the three Maritime Provinces.

Looking at provincial expenditures, total net general expenditures of All Provinces increased at an average rate of 12.5 percent per year compared to the lower rates in the Maritime Provinces—Prince Edward Island, 11.1 percent; Nova Scotia, 10.3 percent; and New Brunswick, 8.9 percent. Putting both net general revenue and net general expenditures together, the most obvious conclusion that can be drawn is that spending seems to be growing faster than revenues, not only in the Maritime Provinces, but, also, in most of the other provinces as well. Over the 1953-67 period, the average yearly rates of increase in spending were greater than in revenue for all the entities considered: 12.5 percent as opposed to 11.6 percent for All Provinces, 11.1 percent versus 10.9 percent for Prince Edward Island (inflated by the heavy increase in revenue at the end of the period), 10.3 percent versus 9.3 percent for Nova Scotia, and 8.9 percent versus 8.4 percent for New Brunswick.

Since the tables used were adjusted for comparability, it is probably safe to say that the differences are of a greater magnitude than reflected in the annual rates of increase, even when it is realized that the rates are compounded for every year from 1953 to 1967.

Comparison of the figures for Gross Provincial, Regional and National Products with the respective net general expenditure figures reveals a general movement across the nation towards spending a larger proportion of output. Not only have provincial government expenditures in the Maritime Provinces exceeded increases in output, but also Maritime Provinces' governments continue to spend a significantly higher proportion of output than do All Provinces.

APEC's Submission emphasizes the importance of the increased efficiency which could come about as the result of political union of the three Maritime Provinces.

> Surely, three provinces with combined populations of only 1,486,000 do not require three departments of agriculture, fisheries, forestry, health and welfare, etc. In fact, the population after union, would probably be significantly less than three-quarters of Metropolitan Toronto or Montreal. For instance, in 1966, the total population of the Maritime Provinces was equivalent to about 68 percent of the population of Metropolitan Toronto (2,159,000) and approximately 60 percent of the population of Metropolitan Montreal (2,437,000). With the implementation of political union for the Maritime Provinces, at least some of the economies of scale may come into play.

Not only would political union with the resultant accompanying administrative, judicial and economic unions mean dollars and cents savings for government in the region, but it could also lead to an increase in the quality of services.

(3) The Submission also stresses the value of political union of the Maritime Provinces to the industrial and overall economic development of the region. It points out that the establishment of priorities and the successful implementation of policy can only be achieved by changing the institutions which have been built up to deal with industrial development. Since their establishment, many of them in the last decade, duplication and rivalry have occurred not only between provinces but within provinces as well. . . . It would seem then that it is the institutional framework within which each development and planning agency is set—that of individual provinces—that needs to be abolished before complete co-ordination and co-operation can be achieved. Maritime Union seems to be the most logical answer. . . . By concentrating growth at growth points, the spin-off to the rest of the Maritimes could lead to a faster sustained rate of growth for the entire region.

•   •   •

ONE PRAIRIE PROVINCE: HISTORICAL AND POLITICAL PERSPECTIVES*

Norman Ward

The union of the three Prairie provinces into one seems so obviously to offer a solution to some of the problems of a chronically vulnerable area that it is hardly surprising that unification is a recurring theme in western Canadian history. To that, it may fairly be added that some of the propos-

* From Elton, D.K., ed., *One Prairie Province? Conference and Selected Papers*, Lethbridge, Lethbridge Herald, 1970. By permission.

als have been such as to lead one to suspect that if the Prairies had been a political unit from the start, somebody would always have been insisting that, in order to focus local attention more closely on local difficulties, the province ought to be divided. The Prairies are so accustomed to change and experiment in public affairs that change as an end in itself appears to exercise a considerable appeal.

It would be unfair, however, to dismiss all unification schemes as examples of restlessness. The Prairies' common resources base; their shared problems of exporting, at the mercy of world markets, raw materials that do not lend themselves to fancy packaging or any other kind of differentiation that might help them sell; and their consistent victimization (as they see it) at the hands of absentee merchants, bankers and manufacturers who produce the machinery, canned goods and mortgages so indispensable to life on the plains; all these provide good reasons for huddling together in search of a comfort that no outside element is likely to supply. If in union lies strength, One Prairie Province suggests not only larger muscles in grappling with the rest of the world, but a healthy loss of weight as overlapping layers of political and bureaucratic fat are reduced. And with rapid developments in communication and transportation, the larger unit is generally attractive, for if largeness works for hospital and school districts, why not for provinces? A brief visit to the uninhabitable parts of any North American metropolis might of course raise some doubts as to whether largeness of itself brings virtue; but in our drearier cities one of the facts of life rests on the absence of space—and space is one thing the Prairies still have.

They had it in the beginning in such abundance, indeed, that sheer size was one of the chief reasons why three provinces were established in the first place. The Prairies, Prime Minister Sir Wilfrid Laurier said in 1905, were "altogether too large an area to be made into one single province according to the size of the other provinces.". . .

There is a history of suggestions for Prairie union, and it is varied and long; not so long, to be sure, as Maritime union, whose historian has traced it back to 1806, and subtitled his work "A Study in Frustration." The internal pressures towards Prairie union, as with the Maritimes, commonly coincide with perceived pressures from outside the region; and the striking similarities between Prairie and Maritime union, based as they are on a common search for an antidote to central Canadian influence and a remedy for the ailment now called alienation, suggest that the two may be worthy of joint study as a phenomenon associated with a twentieth century form of colonialism that can exist among political units that are theoretically equal in law and constitution but not in economics. . . .

To begin with, one cannot contemplate Prairie union without almost being overwhelmed by the sheer magnitude of the task. With one single major exception—the absence of a dichotomy separating English-speaking from French-speaking—the unification of the Prairies is by almost any measurable standard an incomparably larger union than was Confederation itself; and it is important to remember that Confederation was possible partly because the Fathers could settle many vexing problems by assigning to the provinces, as separate entitites, many subjects of legislation which in a unified Prairie will have to be consolidated. The combined area of the Prairie provinces is now three-quarters that of the modern area of the four provinces created in 1867; but both Ontario and Quebec are now at least twice the size they were in 1867. A far higher proportion of the Prairie area is privately owned than is the case to this day in Ontario and Quebec, holding promise of an almost infinite complexity if property and civil rights are to be unified under one set of laws. The population of the Prairies is roughly comparable to the Canada of 1867; but the population of 1867 demanded from its Dominion and provincial governments combined services costing, in round figures, twenty million dollars. The combined budgets of the three Prairie provinces alone in 1970 are almost exactly a hundred times greater, at two billion. The total number of public servants in both Dominion and provincial jurisdictions in 1867 is difficult to determine with precision, but seven thousand would be a generous estimate; the Prairie Provinces today employ seventy thousand. The variety and quality of the services offered today by the Prairies' modern governments is vastly greater than the simple activity of 1867. On the eve of Confederation for example, the combined provinces of Nova Scotia, New Brunswick and Canada were spending annually $2.6 million on transportation, including roads and bridges; Saskatchewan alone in 1969 was spending twenty-five times as much on highways. The original provinces in 1866 spent 9½ per cent of their budgets on education, and less than 5 per cent on public welfare; today they spend roughly one-third on education, and another third on health and welfare. I am not suggesting that the massive nature of these changes means that unification of the Prairie provinces is impossible; I am suggesting that the enterprise would require a colossal amount of political and administrative energy, at a time when the same skills might be better utilized elsewhere. After 1867, the relatively simple adjustment of governmental accounts, and the sorting out of public works and their related debts, nonetheless took several years.

Quantity alone is a misleading indicator of the kinds of adjustments that would be necessary for Prairie unification. Property and civil rights; health, welfare and labor legislation; and local electoral laws, are all under provincial jurisdiction in Canada, and the three Prairie provinces have all read differing meanings into them. Alberta has pioneered among the three with a provincial ombudsman, and Manitoba with an independent commission for drawing constituency boundaries; the Saskatchewan legislature has repeatedly rejected both these developments. Saskatchewan pioneered with hospitalization and medicare, and political rights for civil servants, and all of these have come more slowly to Alberta and Manitoba. Utilities that are under public enterprises in Saskatchewan and Manitoba, are private in Alberta. Saskatchewan has compulsory public automobile insurance, but the other two provinces do not. Legal minimum wages are different in the provinces, and so are provisions for separate schools. All three Prairie provinces experimented with dropping the voting age before the Dominion got around to it, but not simultaneously, and not to the same level.

These examples (and there are dozens more) support two separate propositions: if, as is commonly asserted, one of the great advantages of federalism is that it permits widespread local experimentation in public policy, the reduction of three active laboratories to one would mean a serious loss to both the region and the country; and the differing kinds of experimentation that the three have indulged in denotes that the provinces are politically a lot more different than a superficial look at their common economic problems might suggest. (And even economically, it may be added parenthetically, the provinces are more different than they appear). The first of these propositions, given the known facts of prairie history, hardly needs demonstration. The second leads one to ponder why Alberta's reaction to the modern period was to turn to Social Credit, Saskatchewan's to the Co-operative Commonwealth Foundation, and Manitoba's to a long run of coalition governments that did not include either Social Credit or the C.C.F. Alberta has never had a Conservative government, but it has had the United Farmers of Alberta and Social Credit. In Saskatchewan, Conservative MLAs are generally even scarcer than they have been in Alberta, but Saskatchewan did have one Conservative administration, but never more than a handful of Social Crediters in the legislature. Manitoba, though given to coalitions in the past, is the only one of the three to have had fairly conventional periods of history with alternating Liberal and Conservative governments, but it has recently turned to the New Democratic Party. The parliamentary tradition itself varies among the Prairie provinces, for both C.C.F. and Liberal governments in Saskatchewan, for example, have had to be tolerant of large robust oppositions of a kind that have at times virtually disappeared from the other two.

The party history of the provinces is such as to make one wonder if a single Prairie legislature would ever know anything but minority governments. . . . The most strongly entrenched party in one province was by far the weakest in the other two, while the Conservatives, now [1970] in power in none of the three, had a good deal more electoral support than Social Credit. The Liberals, on the other hand, who in 1966-67 were in power in one province and formed the official opposition in one other, would, on an even distribution of that vote over our single-member constituencies, form the government of One Prairie Province. A similar test of the elections of 1959-60 provides a roughly similar result, with the parties in the same order but a little more closely bunched.

Exercises such as these are only exercises; but they do emphasize that, barring coalition or minority governments, a unified Prairie province would mean that three differing administrations would be reduced to one, an inevitable step away from diversity towards uniformity. All the Prairie minority groups whatever their language, would similarly find themselves reduced from three governments to one more scattered group doing the same with one government, but one now larger and that much more remote. Unless the single province's legislature was to be as large as the current three together, provincial constituencies will have to be larger too; and since one of the great advantages that provincial parties on the Prairies have over their federal counterparts is the relative proximity of the elected provincial member to his constituents, at least some of that would be lost in union. Further, unless a drastic change occurs in the patterns of population growth on the Prairies, within a single province, seats in the assembly would inevitably gravitate from east to west, away from Saskatchewan and Manitoba, in that order, and towards Alberta. I think to put all this in a single sentence, that unification of the Prairie provinces would for a long time impose severe strains on representative democracy on the plains, with an accompanying loss of attention to local particularities. Federalism, as one wise Canadian scholar has observed, is probably the best known method of applying democracy to huge areas.

Yet even in the existing Prairies the benefits of representative democracy have not penetrated very convincingly into the provinces' northern halves. The large proportions of those populations that are uniformly poor, unorganized, and Indian or Metis, have been known about for years; yet even in Saskatchewan, the alleged socialism of the C.C.F. seemed peculiarly reserved for citizens of European descent, and it is only within the past year that a special service to take utilities into the north was organized under the province's public power corporation. In 1969 the first wholly Indian community to have gas piped to it was added to the corporation's books. If one takes into account the whole range of labor, education, health and welfare policies under provincial control, and the differing impacts of these on the northern and southern halves of the provinces, it is difficult to conclude from the record that the northern halves are likely to be better off under one government. I do not mean to suggest that nothing has been done, or that there are not sincere and able men concerned about the Prairies' northern poor. What I am saying is that the people of the north have enough difficulty now under the governments they have: how much better off will they be if the government is made that much larger and more remote, and preoccupied for years with fitting together the political and administrative jigsaw puzzles that unification will make of the south?

The north's problems are partly economic, of course, which serves to remind us that many political problems are inseparable from economics. Let me cite two that seem to be of almost pressing relevance where One Prairie Province is concerned. . . . It is inconceivable that the Dominion should take over the current debts of the Prairie provinces, totalling (in the last year for which official statistics are readily available) nearly one billion dollars in direct debt, and an additional nine hundred and fifty million of additional obligations, mostly guarantees on bonds and debentures . . . . This total burden is unevenly distributed: in the year cited, the direct per capita debt in Alberta was $27, that in Saskatchewan $587; the per capita indirect debt in Alberta was $349, in Saskatchewan $38. If in that year the provinces had had to meet all their obligations, the per capita burden would have been $805 in Manitoba, $625 in Saskatchewan, and $376 in Alberta. Manifestly, any consolidation of those debts would have involved a considerable transfer of burdens to the taxpayers of what is now Alberta.

Statistics are notoriously unreliable, of course, and taking one recent isolated year from a sequence does not permit one to come to precise conclusions; the point is that large variations, in matters of fundamental importance to politics, do exist among the Prairie provinces, and the story is much the same no matter what yardstick one uses. If one takes public school enrolment for the latest year for which official figures are available, and divides it into the total income of school boards, the boards in Manitoba spent $311 for each pupil, in Saskatchewan $363, and in Alberta $399; Alberta school boards, that is, spent over 20 per cent more on each pupil than Manitoba. The differences do not end there: Manitoba boards in that year received 59 per cent of their total income from local taxation, Saskatchewan 55 per cent, and Alberta 51 per cent. The boards' relative net bonded indebtedness showed a different picture: in Saskatchewan the boards' debts totalled 68 per cent of one year's revenue, in Alberta 108 per cent. Teachers' salaries also reveal major variations, with Alberta paying the largest annual average by a considerable margin.

Here again, these figures are not to be taken as gospel: what is significant about them is the consistent pattern of variation revealed, suggesting the scope of what would be involved in unification. In a united province all services provided by the single government will have to be levelled out, for it is hardly reasonable to expect Manitoba and Saskatchewan to accept membership in it as permanent poor relations. The pattern also indicates that in financial terms the burden will be largely Alberta's unless, as appears improbable, the taxpayers of Alberta are prepared to have all services levelled downwards in each individual instance to whichever of the three provinces has been spending the least.

These generalizations are sound of internal adjustments, and they are also relevant to an important external circumstance: under existing Dominion-provincial financial relations, Manitoba is a regular "have not" province, and Saskatchewan has just reentered that category after having briefly escaped from it. As have-nots, Manitoba and Saskatchewan together receive in federal subsidies, distinct from shared-cost programs, about fifty million dollars a year more than Alberta. Whether or not One Prairie Province would be a have or have-not province rests on a calculation I do not have the information to make; but whether it qualifies or not, Alberta is sufficiently wealthier than Manitoba and Saskatchewan that the creation of One Prairie Province would unquestionably shift a major financial burden from Ottawa to Alberta. If, indeed, a united Prairie province qualified as a "have" province, that whole fifty million—or whatever it might be—would have to be found within the province; and if it could be found within Manitoba and Saskatchewan, they would not be qualifying for the subsidies now. The alternative, of course, would be to eliminate the governmental services the money pays for.

And if One Prairie Province now is going to cost Alberta taxpayers a great deal, it must be added that a different kind of burden will rest on Manitoba and Saskatchewan. In a general sense, since Canada is internally what is generally called a free trade area, nobody on the Prairie will gain access to any new markets merely by the elimination of two artificial boundaries. But in a particular sense, the inevitable shifting of both political and economic weight westward within a single province has important implications for the central and eastern section: in a word, they may well find in significant aspects of their politics that they have merely exchanged Toronto for Edmonton or Calgary.

This westward gravitation is nowwhere more apparent than in the certain fate of Prairie seats in Parliament if one province is formed. It is often said that one good reason for merging the provinces is that it will give muscle to our parliamentary representation by providing one bloc of western seats, and one legitimate comment on that is that it will be muscle in grave danger of immediate atrophy. To begin with, given the Prairies' demonstrated political proclivities, there is no reason whatever to assume that the federal western members will act any more as a bloc than they usually do now. Secondly, even if they do, but are on the Opposition side in the Commons (another familiar pattern) a western bloc of members may not be in a position to do the west much good. Thirdly, acting as a bloc would in any event stimulate the formation of other blocs, and the two central provinces between them have one hundred and sixty-two seats to the Prairies' forty-five. And in One Prairie Province, those forty-five would be a lot less secure than they are now.

That conclusion rests on two separate bases: the Prairie's changing share of Canada's population, and the rules governing the distribution of seats in the House of Commons. At the moment, because of both population and the rules, Alberta has nineteen seats and Manitoba and Saskatchewan thirteen each. Under the same two factors Prairie representation in the Commons after the census of 1971 will, on the basis of population projections of the Dominion Bureau of Statistics, drop to forty-three; but if the provinces should be united by 1971 their representation will drop to forty-two, and could legally drop to thirty-nine. By 1981, if present trends continue and the rules for sharing seats remain the same, a united Prairie province could legally drop six more seats.

The reason for this is that one of the rules governing the distribution of seats says that no province, at any one redistribution, can lose more than fifteen per cent of the number of seats to which it was entitled at the last redistribution. Once a province's representation drops to thirteen, it can drop only one seat at the next redistribution, because two seats would be more than fifteen per cent. Saskatchewan has already been saved once by the 15 per cent rule, and under present projections will be saved one seat in 1971; Manitoba will probably not need the rule in 1971, but it will in 1981. The Prairies, in short, need the protection of the rule, but its protection would become all but meaningless under a united province.

That observation receives added point from another calculation: no province can have fewer seats in the Commons than it has senators, and as a result the three Maritime provinces, which have unusually large quotas of senators in relation to their size, will get six extra seats in 1971. Unlike seats added to the House of Commons under the 15 per cent rule, seats saved by the senatorial floor come out of a fixed basis provincial membership of 261, and therefore the extra Maritime seats come at the expense of the other provinces. It is virtually certain that in 1971 two of the Maritimes' bonus of six will come at the expense of the Prairies: Alberta will stay at 19 instead of going up to 20, and Saskatchewan would drop to 11, except that under the 15 per cent rule it will stay at 12. Saskatchewan loses two seats under the first calculation under the rules in the British North America Act, but gets one back under the next. With all these special protections for provinces whose populations are becoming smaller fractions of the Dominion total, it is important to note that by 1971 one M.P. in Prince Edward Island will represent 27,500 people, in New Brunswick 62,300, and in Nova Scotia 76,500; but the comparable Manitoba figure is 81,500, Saskatchewan's is 79,000, and Alberta's is 83,400. All these averages are based on projections which the 1971 census may to some extent upset; but there can be little doubt that for the next census or two the three provinces will have a strong case to make about their parliamentary representation which they will lose automatically once united. [See Chapter 9 for new arrangements.]

The same argument, in a different way, has strength in connection with Dominion-provincial conferences, which are obviously playing an increasingly important part in Canadian politics. If the Maritime provinces unite (and they have shown few signs of hustling into that) One Prairie Province would have one seat out of seven at the conferences: if the Maritimes do not unite, one seat out of nine. Given the small size of the conferences, and the forceful nature of most of our premiers, it is difficult to accept unquestioningly the view that the Prairie would be better off with those odds than they are now with three voices out of eleven. It is impossible to guess how Prairie representation in the federal cabinet might be affected by union, but if prairie seats in the Commons drop sharply, the present boundaries are a better safeguard for three prairie ministers than a united province would offer.

Since so much of this paper has been negative comment on One Prairie Province, I should like to conclude it by suggesting that most of the benefits of union, without its birth pangs and fitful childhood, could be achieved through devices such as the Prairie Economic Council, which has already effected a major agreement over water resources. All three provinces have common law systems; and all three have demonstrated an impressive capacity for co-operation in the past: Prairie highways, for example, do not end abruptly at provincial boundaries, but run straight into other highways. There is no need to multiply examples; but there may be a need to emphasize that increasing co-operative ventures among the provinces may in the long run be cheaper, both in monetary and non-monetary terms, than union.

No doubt there is now some wasteful duplication of political and administrative facilities that might conceivably be eliminated through union; although offhand I cannot recall a single example of a government growing smaller because of major reorganization. Size of itself seems to create new demands for research and the seeking of new ways to keep competent staff employed. The prime costs of modern government, in any event, are largely substantive rather than administrative: if one could reduce to zero the administrative costs of a provincial department of eduction, for example, the entire cost of maintaining and manning the school system would remain. If one could eliminate entirely the indemnities of legislative members and cabinet ministers, the resultant reduction in provincial budgets would be almost imperceptible. The machinery of government, although it has grown astoundingly in recent decades, has long since ceased to be the main cause of public expenditure: it's the machinery's end products—highways, university and school systems, hospital, health and welfare benefits—that really cost money, and there is no reason to suppose that Prairie union would reduce the demand for any of those.

Still the Prairies' political record is such as to indicate that if the prairie citizens want union, they will get it. After all, as a disgruntled champion of Maritime union, after speaking well of the benefits to be gained from that, said over sixty years ago: "We cannot do it while separated. We are ignored by the Dominion Government; the West gets whatever it asks for. . ."

REGIONAL ECONOMIC DISPARITIES:
THE PROBLEM—AND SOME SOLUTIONS*

Douglas Fullerton

"The only real problem facing the federal government is that the eastern third of Canada is going down the drain, and no one seems able to do much about it." My French-Canadian friend spoke bitterly. Even if he over-stated things a bit, there is no doubt that he touched on a problem which, despite massive intervention by governments, shows signs of getting worse rather than better.

All parts of Canada have their pockets of poverty. But the four Atlantic provinces and to a lesser extent Quebec have lagged behind the rest of the country for a long time, and show few signs of closing the gap between themselves and the other five provinces.

How many people are we talking about? The Atlantic provinces have 2.2 million, close to 10 per cent of Canada's 23 million. Quebec has 6.2 million, or 27 per cent.

How far are they behind? One measure is the rate of unemployment. [The mid-May 1976 figures show that unemployment is almost three times higher in some Atlantic provinces than in the prairies, as the accompanying graphic illustrates.]

Another index is the level of federal equalization payments to the provinces; these payments are designed "to ensure that every province can provide an adequate level of public services to its population without resort to rates of taxation that are above the national average." [The accompanying graphic shows that some provinces do not qualify for any equalization grants at all while the needy eastern provinces receive grants amounting to as much as $444 per capita in P.E.I.]

One could go on citing figures to prove the point—such as per capita income in 1974. [As the table indicates, per capita incomes in Canada ranged from an average of $5,559 in Ontario to $3,274 in P.E.I.] But they understate the true disparity.

* From *The Toronto Star*, June 12, 1976. By Permission.

UNEMPLOYMENT
RATE BY PROVINCE (MID-MAY, 1976)

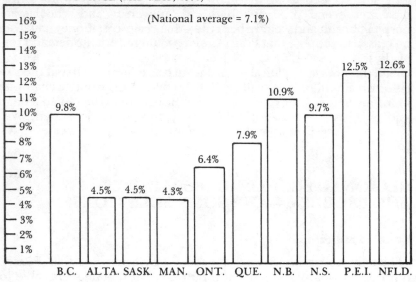

(National average = 7.1%)

B.C. 9.8% | ALTA. 4.5% | SASK. 4.5% | MAN. 4.3% | ONT. 6.4% | QUE. 7.9% | N.B. 10.9% | N.S. 9.7% | P.E.I. 12.5% | NFLD. 12.6%

EQUALIZATION PAYMENTS
ESTIMATED PER CAPITA BY PROVINCE (1976-77)

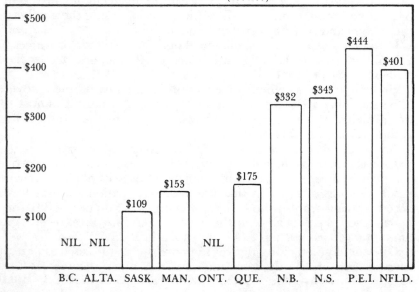

B.C. NIL | ALTA. NIL | SASK. $109 | MAN. $153 | ONT. NIL | QUE. $175 | N.B. $332 | N.S. $343 | P.E.I. $444 | NFLD. $401

From The Toronto Star, *June 12, 1976. By permission.*

Distribution of Average per Capita Income in Canada, 1974, by Province in Order of Magnitude

Province	Per capita average	Percentage of national average
Ontario	$5,559	112
British Columbia	5,374	108
Alberta	5,066	102
Manitoba	4,733	95
Saskatchewan	4,702	95
Quebec	4,504	91
Nova Scotia	3,990	80
New Brunswick	3,702	75
Newfoundland	3,319	67
Prince Edward Island	3,274	66
National average	4,966	100

The eastern provinces have been the beneficiaries not only of federal equalization grants, but of high average transfer payments to individuals, notably from welfare and unemployment insurance. Thus, in terms of Canadian output, the contribution of the five provinces is in varying degree lower even than the income figures suggest.

Is Quebec properly classed in the same group as the four Atlantic provinces? Montreal, after all, has a momentum of its own. Yet Montreal has been losing ground steadily to Toronto, and its health is still largely dependent on the rest of Quebec. And certainly that part of Quebec east of Montreal resembles the Atlantic provinces in many respects.

The economy which developed in eastern Canada was based largely on the small family farm, on lumbering and on inshore fishing, and on such older and labor intensive industries as textiles and footwear. Except in Montreal, this way of life remained surprisingly unchanged until World War II, but was badly hit by the changes which followed it: the movement off the farms, the decline of fishing, and the redirection of growth to newer and more technologically advanced industries, and to plants closer to main North American markets, the centre of which was gradually moving westwards.

Industrial growth in the Atlantic provinces was further prejudiced by a lack both of cheap energy supplies and of the natural resources on which so much of Canada's early postwar growth was based.

No New Blood

The migration itself has had an impact on the collective character of those who remained. Those best fitted and most inclined to move tended to be drawn from the ranks of the brightest, the best educated and the most adventurous. Little new blood came in. As a result the innate cautiousness of a people with close ties to the land and to the sea was reinforced, and the willingness to take entrepreneurial risks declined.

Until recent years, the closed nature of many of the societies—the French Canadians within their parish, family circle and language, the descendants of Scottish immigrants clinging to the Gaelic and to their clans, the particular isolation of the islands—provided fertile soil for the development of a society reluctant to accept change and unable to adapt to it readily.

The cumulative effect of these forces was concealed for a long time by isolation and by underemployment in farming and fishing. But during the past two decades a whole series of events has occurred to bring about rapid change—the declining role of the family farm and of fishing as a source of employment, the opening up of the eastern provinces to tourism, television and its show window of material delights, the welfare state with all its benefits, and the efforts of governments to bring renewed growth.

Adjustment to this change has been difficult for everyone in the region, but particularly for the labor force. The practical skills learned in the woods, on the farm, or in commercial fishing, are useful, notably in such trades as motor mechanics and construction. What is lacking is experience with the discipline of the regular 8-to-5 jobs in factory, building site or office, day in, day out.

Thus, despite the unemployment in the Atlantic provinces, labor productivity in many industries has been found to be substantially lower than in central Canada.

Some of the productivity gap has been due to poor management and organization, and to the scarcity of certain skills in the labor force, but labor intransigence has been damaging. Industrial Cape Breton has had unions for a century, and a long history of labor troubles; the time lost from strikes has been high, as is time off for casual vacations.

Possible Solutions

What could bring about a revitalization of eastern Canada? These are some courses of action which have been tried, or could be.

1. Lower the Wages.

A lower level of wages has always been important in inducing industrial migration; this has been one of the few weapons available to the poorer countries. For a long time, wages in Quebec and the Atlantic provinces were appreciably below those in Ontario; in some industries a gap remains. But union bargaining on a national basis, the pervasive effects of federal government pay settlements, and the increased union activity in the eastern region (notably in the public service unions) have largely eliminated the appeal of wage differentials as a stimulus for industry to shift to the east.

2. Move the People Out.

This is the oldest solution in history for depressed areas: Compel or persuade people to move out. We Canadians have done a bit of experimenting with grants to enable the unemployed to move to jobs in other regions, but it is a policy which has never been pushed too hard. One reason is that it is regarded as bad politics: "Depopulation" has odious overtones, and no politician likes to see his political base eroded by migration.

Some economists argue that, even if a particular area is overpopulated in terms of available jobs, a declining population tends to generate further economic weakness. A stable or growing population provides a stimulus to industry to remain and to expand.

Nevertheless, bringing jobs to the people has much more political sex appeal than bringing people to the jobs.

3. Build Public Works.

Roads, bridges, post offices, military establishments, and docks and wharves are traditional projects to create jobs in depressed areas: More recently we have seen massive federal spending in the Atlantic provinces on power projects, on the Trans-Canada Highway, and on city services such as sewers.

In Quebec, federal spending has taken similar directions, and the provincial government of Robert Bourassa has used capital spending (James Bay, highways) as the main weapon in the attack on unemployment.

The danger is that projects may be built which are not needed, or are build more as monuments than as useful contributions to society. The Olympic stadium of Montreal Mayor Jean Drapeau falls into this category. But, on balance, the approach is certainly one of the most useful yet devised for job-creation.

4. Offer Grants to Industry.

Analagous in some respects to public works are the federal and provincial efforts to use incentive grants to lure industry to a particular area. This is a fairly recent innovation (the federal Department of Regional Economic Expansion is only seven years old), but the sums laid out by governments over the past decade have been massive. If the programs have met with some success, such as the Michelin plants in Nova Scotia, the record is marred by resounding failures. The Come by Chance refinery, the Glace Bay heavy water plant, Clairtone and Bricklin have all made many headlines in our papers, but there are a host of others.

Considering the large number of dollars that have been poured in, why haven't we succeeded in creating more jobs?

—Politicians, and particularly provincial premiers, tend to like spectacular projects which attract publicity. These of course tend to have more risks attached, and the penalties are greater.

—Politicians may be naive. By nature they are salesmen, the people most susceptible to the wiles of other salesmen and con-artists.

—Administrators of provincial and federal grants programs may lack experience—and may be reluctant to let failing businesses die.

—The projects themselves often are bad: The deals the poorer provinces are offered have usually been well shopped across the country, and have failed to meet the normal standards of the marketplace. For instance, Quebec turned down Malcom Bricklin's auto-plant scheme before New Brunswick took it up.

—The labor force is likely to be lacking the skills and experience to build the plants economically, or to service them efficiently.

—The basic facts of economics are at work: If the location had been a good one the plant would have been put there in the first place, without subsidies.

Location grants and subsidies do have some place in the array of instruments to deal with unemployment. But as a large scale panacea they have failed.

5. *Give Them Money.*

When all else fails, the usual prescription for the poor or for a depressed area is to give the people money. Federal equalization payments to the five eastern provinces are expected to reach nearly $2 billion in 1976-77, or close to $250 per capita. But of equal importance these days are the personal transfers of unemployment insurance and welfare. As areas of greatest unemployment and poverty, the eastern provinces naturally attract a disproportionate share of federal disbursements.

Quite a case can be made for arguing that this approach—perhaps extended to become a guaranteed annual wage—may be the best solution. No money wasted on industry grants or government make-work projects; just the cash in the people's hands and their spending of it will generate employment.

But what about the long-term consequences? One great danger is that a proud, independent and self-reliant people, accustomed to hard work in the fields and forests and their fishing boats, will develop into a sub-nation of government wards, ready to take all they can get in welfare, unemployment insurance or subsidies.

How Long?

My concern is not only for the recipients of federal bounty. How long will the rest of Canada accept the fact that a large part of eastern Canada remains on a more or less permanent dole?

We've bought some time, but what next? My French-Canadian friend suggests that separation from Canada may be the only way to provide the necessary jolt to Quebecers, to make them pull themselves up by their own bootstraps. His is a radical solution, of course, and his views are influenced by non-economic concerns, such as survival of language and culture.

But what about separation of the Atlantic provinces, a not unlikely prospect if Quebec were to go its own way, and if the western five provinces decide the welfare burden of the Atlantic provinces is no longer worth carrying? The jolt would be tremendous and would likely lead to chaos and total breakdown, so complete is the current dependence of these provinces on money from Upper Canada.

Is this "thinking the unthinkable"? I'm not so certain as I was a few years ago that it could not happen, the result of the failure of the mixture of policies to work. I've even begun to wonder if such a denouement, harsh and draconian though it might be, is not the only way the Atlantic provinces will ever again get back on their own feet.

A gloomy prospect to be sure, but what is there to be optimistic about?

BIBLIOGRAPHY

Regionalism

Beck, J. M., *The History of Maritime Union: A Study in Frustration*, Federicton, Maritime Union Study, 1969.

Brewis, T. N., Paquet, G., "Regional Development in Canada: An Exploratory Essay," *C.P.A.*, Vol, XI, No. 2, Summer, 1968.

Brewis, T. N., *Regional Economic Policies in Canada*, Toronto, Macmillan, 1969.

Cameron, D. M., "Regional Integration in the Maritime Provinces", *C.J.P.S.*, Vol. IV, No. 1, March, 1971.

Campbell, A. B., Regan, G. A., and Hatfield, R. B., "The move toward Maritime integration and the role of the Council of Maritime Premiers", *C.P.A.*, Vol. 15, No. 4, Winter, 1972.

Card, B. Y., (ed.), *Perspectives on Regions and Regionalism*, Edmonton, University of Alberta Bookstore, 1969.

Chi, N. H., "Regression model of regionalism: a critique", with reply by W. P. Irvine, *C.J.P.S.*, Vol. V, No. 2, June, 1972.

Dehem, R., *et al.*, "Concepts of Regional Planning." *C.P.A.*, Vol. IX, No. 2, June, 1966.

Elton, D. K., (ed.), *One Prairie Province? Conference and Selected Papers*, Lethbridge, Lethbridge Herald, 1970.

Fergusson, C. B., "Maritime Union," *Q.Q.*, Vol. LXXVII, No. 2, Summer, 1970.

Fox, Paul, "Regionalism and Confederation," in Wade, M., *infra*.

Gertler, L. O., *Regional Planning in Canada*, Montreal, Harvest House, 1972.

Governments of New Brunswick, Nova Scotia, P.E.I., *The Report On Maritime Union*, Fredericton, 1970.

Hanson, E. J., "The Future of Western Canada: Economic, Social and Political," *C.P.A.*, Vol. 18, No. 1, Spring, 1975.

Hebal, J. J., "Approaches to Regional and Metropolitan Governments in the United States and Canada," *C.P.A.*, Vol. X, No. 2, June, 1967.

Helliwell, J., "National Fiscal and Monetary Policies: A Regional Interpretation", *BC Studies*, No. 13, Spring, 1972.

Hockin, T. A., *et al.*, *The Canadian Condominium*, Toronto, McClelland and Stewart, 1972.

Hodgetts, J. E., "Regional Interests in a Federal Structure," *C.J.E.P.S.*, Vol. XXXII, No. 1, February, 1966.

Howland, R. D., *Some Regional Aspects of Canada's Economic Development*, Ottawa, Queen's Printer, 1957.

Husband, D. D., "National versus regional growth: some issues", *C.P.A.*, Vol. 14, No. 4, Winter, 1971.

Irvine, W. P., "Assessing the Regional Effects in Data Analysis", *C.J.P.S.*, Vol. IV, No. 1, March, 1971.

Krueger, R. R., Sargent, F. O., de Vos, A., and Pearson, N., (eds.), *Regional and Resource Planning in Canada*, Rev. ed., Toronto, Holt, Rinehart and Winston, 1970.

Lajoie, A., *Les Structures Administratives Régionales: Déconcentration et Décentralisation au Québec*, Montréal, Les Presses de l'Université de Montreal, 1968.

Manzer, R., *Canada—A Socio-Political Report*, Toronto, McGraw-Hill Ryerson, 1974.

Merrill, G., "Regionalism and Nationalism" in Warkentin, J., (ed.), *Canada: A Geographical Interpretation*, Toronto, Methuen, 1968.

Mathias, P., *Forced Growth*, Toronto, James, Lewis and Samuel, 1971.

Neill, R. F., "National policy and regional development: a footnote to the Deutsch Report On Maritime Union", *Journal of Canadian Studies*, Vol. IX, No. 2, May, 1974.

Noel, S. J. R., "Consociational Democracy and Canadian Federalism," *C.J.P.S.* Vol. IV, No. 1, March, 1971.

Quesnel-Ouellet, L., "Régionalisation et conscience politique régionale: la communauté urbaine de Québec", *C.J.P.S.*, Vol. IV, No. 2, June, 1971.

Spelt, J., *Urban Development in South-Central Ontario*, Carleton Library 57, Toronto, McClelland and Stewart, 1972.

Wade, M., (ed.), *Regionalism in the Canadian Community, 1867-1967*, Toronto, University of Toronto Press, 1969.

Whalen, H., "Public Policy and Regional Development: The Experience of the Atlantic Provinces," in Rotstein, A. (ed.), *The Prospect of Change: Prosposals for Canada's Future*, Toronto, McGraw-Hill, 1965.

Provinces and Territories

Beck, J. M., *The Government of Nova Scotia*, Toronto, University of Toronto Press, 1957.

Bellamy, D. J.; Pammett, J. H.; Rowat, D. C., *The Provincial Political Systems: Comparative Essays*, Agincourt, Methuen, 1976.

Canada, *Report of the Advisory Commission on the Development of Government in the Northwest Territories*, [Carrothers' Report], Ottawa, Queen's Printer, 1966.

Donnelly, M. S., *The Government of Manitoba*, Toronto, University of Toronto Press, 1963.

Fleck, J. D., "Restructuring the Ontario Government", *C.P.A.*, Vol. 16, No. 1, Spring, 1973.

Krueger, R. R., "The Provincial-Municipal Government Revolution in New Brunswick," *C.P.A.*, Vol. XIII, No. 1, Spring, 1970.

Lajoie, A., *Les Structures Administratives Régionales: Déconcentration et Décentralisation au Québec*, Montréal, Les Presses de l'Université de Montréal, 1968.

Lotz, J., *Northern Realities*, Toronto, New Press, 1970.

MacDonald, D. C., (ed.), *Government and Politics of Ontario*, Toronto, Macmillan, 1975.

MacKinnon, F., *The Government of Prince Edward Island*, Toronto, University of Toronto Press, 1951.

Mayo, H. B., "Newfoundland's Entry into the Dominion," *C.J.E.P.S.*, Vol. XV, No. 4, November, 1949.

Neary, P., (ed.), *The Political Economy of Newfoundland, 1929-1972*, Toronto, Copp Clark, 1973.

Rea, K. J., *The Political Economy of the Canadian North*, Toronto, University of Toronto Press, 1968.

Richmond, D. R., *The Economic Transformation of Ontario: 1945-73*, Toronto, Ontario Economic Council, 1974.

Rohmer, R., *The Green North*, Toronto, Maclean-Hunter, 1970.

Tindal, C. R., "Regional development in Ontario", *C.P.A.*, Vol. 16, No. 1, Spring, 1973.

Zaslow, M., "Recent Constitutional Developments in Canada's Northern Territories." *C.P.A.*, Vol. X, Nov. 2, June, 1967.

Municipalities

Axworthy, J., (ed.), *The Future City*, [Government in Winnipeg], Winnipeg, Institute of Urban Studies, University of Winnipeg, 1971.

Baine, R. P., and McMurray, A. L., *Toronto, An Urban Study*, Toronto, Clarke, Irwin, 1970.

Baine, R. P., *Calgary: An Urban Study*, Toronto, Clarke, Irwin, 1973.

Bernard, A., Léveillé, J., and Lord, G., *Profile: Edmonton* (Political and Administrative Structures of the Metropolitan region), Ottawa, Information Canada, 1974; *Profile: Montreal*, 1974; *Profile: Ottawa-Hull*, 1975, *Profile: Hamilton-Wentworth*, 1975; *Profile: Quebec*, 1975.

Crawford, K. G., *Canadian Municipal Government*, Toronto, University of Toronto Press, 1954.

Feldman, L. D., and Goldrick, M. D., (eds.), *Politics and Government of Urban Canada*, Agincourt, Ontario, Methuen, 3rd ed., 1976.

Hardwick, W. G., *Vancouver*, Don Mills, Ontario, Collier-Macmillan, 1974.

Hebal, J. J., "Approaches to Regional and Metropolitan Governments in the United States and Canada", *C.P.A.*, Vol. X, No. 2, June, 1967.

Kaplan, H., "Politics and Policy-Making in Metropolitan Toronto," *C.J.E.P.S.*, Vol. XXXI, No. 4, November, 1965.

Kaplan, H., *Urban Political Systems: A Functional Analysis of Metropolitan Toronto*, Toronto, Copp Clark, 1967.

Lithwick, N. H., and Paquet, G., (eds.), *Urban Studies: A Canadian Perspective*, Toronto, Methuen, 1968.

Massam, B. H., "Local Government in the Montreal Area", *C.J.P.S.*, Vol. VI, No. 2, June, 1973.

McRae, K. D., *The Federal Capital: Government Institutions*, Studies of the Royal Commission on Bilingualism and Biculturalism, No. 1, Ottawa, Queen's Printer, 1969.

Nader, G. A., *Cities of Canada*, Vol. I, *Theoretical, Historial and Planning Perspectives*; Vol. II, *Profiles of Fifteen Metropolitan Centres*, Toronto, Macmillan, 1976.

O'Brien, A., "Local Government Priorities for the Eighties," *C.P.A.*, Vol. 19, No. 1, Spring, 1976.

Plunkett, J. T., *Urban Canada and its Government: A Study of Municipal Organization*, Toronto, Macmillan, 1968.

Quesnel-Ouellet, L., "Changement dans les structures municipales", *C.J.P.S.*, Vol. VI, No. 2, June, 1973.

Robinson, A. J., and Cutt, J., (eds.), *Public Finance in Canada: Selected Readings*, (Chapter V), Toronto, Methuen, second ed., 1973.

Rose, A., *Governing Metropolitan Toronto: A Social and Political Analysis, 1953-1971*, Los Angeles, University of California Press, 1972.

Ross, R. K., *Local Government in Ontario*, Toronto, Canada Law, second ed., 1962.

Rowat, D. C., *The Canadian Municipal System: Essays on the Improvement of Local Government*, Carleton Library No. 48, Toronto, McClelland and Stewart, 1969.

Rowat, D. C., "The Problems of Governing Federal Capitals," *C.J.P.S.*, Vol. I, No. 3, September, 1968.

Rowat, D. C., *The Government of Federal Capitals*, Toronto, University of Toronto Press, 1973.

Rowat, D. C., *Your Local Government: A Sketch of the Municipal System in Canada*, Toronto, Macmillan, second ed., 1975.

Spelt, J., *Toronto*, Don Mills, Ontario, Collier-Macmillan, 1973.

Stein, L. A., "The Municipal Power to Zone in Canada and the United States: A Comparative Study", *The Canadian Bar Review*, Vol. XLIX, No. 4, December, 1971.

Tennant, P., and Zirnhelt, D., "The Emergence of Metropolitan Government in Greater Vancouver", *BC Studies*, No. 15, Autumn, 1972.

Tennant, P., and Zirnhelt, D., "Metropolitan government in Vancouver: the strategy of gentle imposition", *C.P.A.*, Vol. 16, No. 1, Spring, 1973.

Trevor, P., (ed.), *Regional Government in Ontario*, Don Mills, Ontario Science Research Associates, 1971.

Whalen H. J., *The Development of Local Government in New Brunswick*, Fredericton, 1964.

Young, D. A., "Canadian Local Government Development: Some Aspects of the Commissioner and City Manager Forms of Administration," *C.P.A.*, Vol. IX, No. 1, March, 1966.

5

ENGLISH CANADA AND NATIONALISM

Nationalism has become much more vociferous in both English Canada and Quebec in the past 15 years. Despite the growing threat of separatism in Quebec, the change is more remarkable in English Canada. Thus, while Quebec has had a long tradition of French-Canadian nationalism and has produced a continual flow of literature on the subject, English Canadians have not displayed as much interest in Canadian nationalism until recently.

Some French Canadians are inclined to take the lack of English-Canadian nationalist literature as proof of the non-existence of a significant English-Canadian national spirit. That such an assumption is unwarranted is obvious from the facts of Canadian history which have amply demonstrated that many English-speaking Canadians have devoted themselves to building a Canadian nation with its own distinctive characteristics.

For the most part, however, these efforts have been defensive rather than aggressive. In the first half of our national existence they were directed in the main towards emancipating Canada from its colonial position within the British Empire. That goal was attained by the achievement of Dominion status in 1931. More recently, English-Canadian nationalists have found themselves engaged in a second phase of defensive action, this time directed against the absorption of Canada by an omnipresent and almost overwhelming American culture, which is both national and continental. As the political power of the United States has waxed mightily in the post-war period and the pull of North American economic continentalism has grown more pronounced, English-speaking nationalism has become increasingly strident. Its substance, however, is usually negative rather than positive, long in criticism and short in the development of any theory of Canadian nationalism, unless it is Marxist. The country still awaits the birth of a doctrine of Canadian nationalism, although there are those such as Prime Minister Trudeau and Professor Ramsay Cook who believe that such an event should be aborted.

Professor Gad Horowitz's article in this chapter deplores this fear of nationalism and makes the case for a necessary and salutary Canadian nationalism. Professor Charles Taylor's essay develops the argument further in one of the best-reasoned justifications of Canadian nationalism. A major flaw in this philosophy is underlined in a passage from Professor John Porter's well-known book on Canadian society. For further arguments pro and con Canadian nationalism, a reader should consult the bibliography, whose length indicates the mounting interest in the subject. One of the most useful sources on this topic is *Nationalism in Canada*, a book of essays edited by Professor Peter Russell.

A selection from one of the essays in this book concludes this chapter and leads into the next. In his article "The National Outlook of English-speaking Canadians", Professor Kenneth McNaught explains the nature of English-Canadian nationalism, particularly for the benefit of French Canadians.

ON THE FEAR OF NATIONALISM*

Gad Horowitz

Canada is, and has always been, a relatively stable and peaceful society. Our political tradition, in its substantive content and even more in its rhetoric, has emphasized above all, the themes of moderation. The tradition may have served us well in the past, but it must now be transcended if Canada is to survive. Let us not mince words; survival is the issue. The fear of political annexation is not realistic: but the prospect of total economic and cultural integration into American society, is real and immediate.

Our political and intellectual elites, true to the Canadian tradition, are moderately concerned about the impending demise of their country, and moderately determined to do something to prevent that demise, on condition that whatever is done, be moderately done. This moderation will be the death of us. One of the sources of contemporary moderation is a genteel fear of nationalism that pervades the English-Canadian establishment. The continentalist elements of establishment use this fear of nationalism cynically, in the interest of greater American nationalism of which we are a part. . . .

There are . . . elements of the establishment which are not continentalist, which might be prepared to do something if it were not for their genuine fear of nationalism. Americanization, they would agree, is an evil which we ought to avoid if we can, but nationalism is an even greater evil—it is the malevolent force which has bathed the world in blood.

The moderate view is that Canadian nationalism would be more harm-

* From *Canadian Dimension*, Vol. IV, No. 4, May-June, 1967. By permission.

ful to Canada and to the world than the Americanization of Canada. This view is false because it is based on a model of nationalism which is not applicable to Canada. The nationalism that has bathed the world in blood, is not the nationalism that seeks to prevent the integration of Canada into American society.

There are, to begin with, crucial distinctions to be made among the nationalism of expansionist great powers, the nationalism of small states struggling to preserve some degree of independence and the nationalism of colonized people seeking self-determination. The first of these is never justifiable. The other two, nearly always are. Canadian nationalism is clearly that of the small state: our relationship with the United States is analagous to the relationship of Finland with the Soviet Union. The Americans and the Soviets need not fear conquest by the Canadians and the Finns. The Canadians and the Finns are no threat to their great neighbours. The shedding of blood is simply not in this picture. Second of all, there is a difference between the nationalism that disrupts established states and the nationalism that preserves or consolidates existing states. Examples of the disruptive type are the nationalisms that destroyed the Austro-Hungarian Empire and the nationalisms that today threaten to destroy and dismember India and Nigeria. These nationalisms, though they are often justifiable reactions to alien domination, are usually accompanied by bitter chauvinistic hatred of neighbouring peoples and often result in the shedding of blood. The mutually antagonistic chauvinism of English and French Canada, are potentially analogous to those of Austro-Hungary, India and Nigeria. The intra-Canadian nationalist extremisms which threaten to tear this country apart are correctly feared, not only by our moderates, but by all Canadians with the exception of a fringe of separatists and a fringe of Orangemen. But the Pan-Canadian nationalism which seeks to preserve a Canadian state in some form, and to prevent the digestion of both English- and French-Canadian societies by the United States, is an entirely different matter.

Canada exists. The nationalism that preserves its existence is not disruptive.

Third, there is a difference between racist nationalism and other types of nationalism. This is a distinction which should require no elaboration. Canadian nationalism has nothing to do with race, nothing to do with blood and soil. . . .

Finally, there is a difference between what might be called doctrinal and non-doctrinal nationalism. A doctrinal nationalism perceives the nation as the embodiment of a specific set of values, such as Communism, Liberalism, Catholicism and fascism. This leads it to relate to the outside world in a paranoid manner. The values incarnated in the nation may be viewed as the unique possession of the nation—a treasured possession, which can only be tarnished and mutilated by contact with the outside world. If this is the case, the nation will be isolationist—in a sense, it will turn in on itself and shun the outside influences as a potential corruptor. Another possibility for doctrinal nationalism is the view that the nations have universal unique validity, and that the nation has a special mission to impose these values on the rest of the world by force, by persuasion, or by forceful persuasion. This is the messianic subtype of doctrinal nationalism.

Within its own borders, doctrinal nationalism imposes a rigid ideological conformity. The only legitimate ideology is the national ideology. Adherents of other ideologies are, at best, barely tolerated deviates and at worst, witches to be burned at the stake. I have of course, been describing the nationalism of the United States. The doctrine of its nationalism is liberalism, individualism, "democratic capitalism." To adhere to a different ideology is to be un-American, a deviate or a witch. . . .

Canadian nationalism cannot be doctrinal. On the contrary, its purpose must be to preserve on the northern half of this continent, a society which does not share the liberal conformitarianism, the isolationism and the messianism of the United States.

What is the doctrine of Canadian nationalism? The moderates cannot answer this question, because there is no such doctrine. There is no unique set of Canadian values which is to be preserved from corruption by outsiders and/or imposed on them by forceful persuasion. Certainly Canadian nationalists are anxious to diminish the economic and cultural influence of the United States in Canada—not in order to preserve some unique set of Canadian national values, but in order to preserve the possibility of building, in this country, a society which is better than the Great Society. It needn't be uniquely Canadian as long as it isn't a copy of the United States. It could be anything. It could be a replica of Sweden, or if you like, of North Korea, Albania or Ireland, or Spain or Yugoslavia, or Cambodia, or all of them. The point is not to preserve all aspects of Canadian society which differentiate it from the American, simply because they are uniquely ours, but to preserve those distinctive aspects of Canadian society which make it better than American society and above all, Canada's freedom of action to become something—who knows what it will be—different from Flint, Michigan. If the United States were Utopia, I would not be a Canadian nationalist; but the United States is not Utopia. . . .

Canadian nationalism is not "anti-Americanism" necessarily in a sense of hatred of all things American just because they're American. There is much we can learn from the United States, . . . but it should be intended learning for our purposes, not automatic imitation, not unconscious absorption.

The problem of Americanization can be faced without chauvinism, but also without a fake, self-effacing, embarrassed cosmopolitanism. It can be faced; without building Chinese walls, without "restricting the free flow of ideas." It can be faced positively, by taking control of our economy into our own hands and, this is just as important, releasing our production and distribution of ideas from a dam of market forces, by assigning a very high priority to the subsidization of Canadian cultural production of all sorts, on a scale very much larger than anything contemplated at the moment. By cultural production, I mean not only the arts, but anything that can be published or broadcast. The use of the state for nation building purposes is not a new idea in Canada. We need a National policy not of cultural tariffs and taxes, but of cultural bounties and subsidies.

The purpose of Canadian nationalism is not to close Canada to the world, but to open Canada to the world by keeping out the United States. The fears of our moderates are entirely groundless.

•   •   •

NATIONALISM AND INDEPENDENCE, AN ECONOMIC PROBLEM*

Charles Taylor

It is distressing to see how Canada is facing the fateful set of choices which are now opening. It seems almost as though many Canadians are bent on not facing the issues which demand an answer. . . .

The confusion is at its thickest when it comes to Canadian nationalism, and particularly nationalism in its relation to economics. In this domain there is a widespread attitude (in English Canada) that nationalism is something wrong, passé and irrational, which Canada must grow out of, and therefore the less said about it the better, and a commonplace idea that, if we do after all want to go in for it in a big way, it will cost us a large part of our present standard of living.

•   •   •

Common Purposes

. . . Are there common purposes, big and prepossessing enough to justify our common existence, or should we face the fact that Canada is not worth it, and wind it up? (meaning, I guess, break up into constituent parts, some of which join the U.S.A.) Both alternatives need much more serious examination than they have received.

As far as the first is concerned, I believe that there are such common purposes, and without claiming to express them definitively, I think they can be described in three main categories. First, Canada's vocation is to develop the five great regions as full-scale societies. . . .

This need not mean flying in the face of objective economic cost factors in order to pay for a country. The way an economy would develop without government intervention is not necessarily any more "natural" or "economic" than the way it develops if planned. Planned development can turn the tide in an underdeveloped region without increasing, often decreasing, the cost to the nation as a whole. Indeed the principal aim of uniting these diverse regions into one body politic can only be their combined development. If we let this drop, or pursue it half-heartedly, as has been the case for the last century, then there is good reason to ask why Canada should exist. But combined development does constitute a goal which would mean a fuller and more prosperous life for the vast majority of Canadians. . . .

. . .We have somehow to develop a mode of existence where different

* From *Canadian Dimension*, Vol. IV, No. 4, May-June, 1967. By permission.

cultures can grow and be fully themselves without paying the price of isolation, while helping, that is, to enrich each other. We have to develop a society in which diversity is welcomed as richness and not feared as the prelude to division. . . .

Thirdly, once we exist as a country, we cannot avoid our obligation to play a role on the international scene. Without launching into illusions of grandeur bred by our exceptional position immediately after the last war, we can nevertheless see a certain strategic role in the attempt to preserve peace for a middle power, rich, relatively trusted in all parts of the world, although white, and relatively free from deep involvement in the multiple mutual hatreds which crisscross the globe.

This statement of aims is very summary and imperfect. But any discussion of Canadian nationalism cannot be carried on properly unless these, or similar cards, are laid on the table. Since Canadian nationalism can only be prospective, we have to be able to express, even somewhat inarticulately, what our purposes are. But for those who are unconvinced by this three-fold purpose, or who are unmoved by it, let us examine the alternative.

Sometimes people speak of "joining the U.S.A.," as though this was a real option for Canada. But it could never be the object of a common decision by Canadians, as, for instance, we could decide one day to amend the constitution. Parts of what is now Canada could join the U.S.A. only if the country broke up, perhaps partly in disagreement over this. It is hardly likely that nationalism, for instance, in French Canada could ever be overcome to the point where Quebec would consent to be part of a fifty-first state, thus brusquely drawing a line under 350 years' history.

Secondly, it is not all that likely that the Americans would be eager to have us. The days of manifest destiny are past, or perhaps this policy has taken more subtle forms. It can, of course, be interesting to the U.S.A. to control Canadian policy more closely; but is it not much more valuable to them to have as a neighbour a middle power, with all the trappings of independence, which keeps its own intractable internal problems to itself and nevertheless does what it is told?

We should not assume that a viable alternative to refloating Canada is annexation. It may just be break up, or short of this, a kind of twilight zone of fictitious independence, more and more under remote control from Washington. Indeed, we are already entering a twilight zone of this kind.

When seen in this light, the alternative to a viable Canadian nationalism can hardly be called attractive. Canadians would be reduced to the status of very second class citizens. We would have to follow policies made in Washington without even the opportunity which anyone has living south of the border to influence these policies by our votes. . . .

Paralytic Continentalism

The alternative to Canadian nationalism is not a far-seeing policy of rational welfare on an international basis, but instead a gradual slide into satellite status, which will make it more and more difficult to solve even our problems of economic development with the full measure of freedom we require. The alternative is a policy of paralytic continentalism. And the tragedy is that that policy is being followed today, unavowedly, by the Liberal government.

Only the indescribable mixture of confusion and hypocrisy which is so characteristic of Canadian politics at the federal level can hide this fact from the general view. Beating back the vain attempt of Walter Gordon to give its policy a nationalist direction, the federal Liberal Party has consistently slid down the path of piecemeal, muddled integration. . . .

Whether consciously or not, this party is plainly oriented toward the continentalism of an increasingly paralytic kind. Since there are signs that this policy is approved of by the overwhelming majority of Canada's business elite, it is not surprising that it should be the policy of their major political instrument. But what is surprising, and symptomatic of Canada's sorry plight, is that all this should happen in a half-light of semi-consciousness, that the Liberal party can still pose as a party seriously interested in remaking Canada as an independent power, that all these measures are adopted under absurdly euphemistic titles, which hide their real import. . . .

But all this wouldn't work if there weren't a half-conscious connivance on the part of important sections of the electorate. Obviously, many Canadian electors do not want to face the choices. They prefer the hypocritical phraseology, because it hides the stark choice, whose implications are somewhat frightening. There is clearly in Canada a widespread lack of confidence, a sense of inferiority vis-a-vis the U.S.A., a failure of nerve. Again and again, in the course of a political campaign, one finds electors who say: that would be wonderful, but would the Americans let us do it? For these people and many others, the limits of possibility are drawn much more narrowly than they are in fact. They feel beaten in advance. The political activity of the Liberal party both feeds this mood and profits from it. . . .

Nub Is Economic

The nub of the question is in the end economic. One of the underpinnings of paralytic continentalism is the commonplace idea mentioned at the beginning of this paper, that our choice lies between economic nationalism and a high standard of living. Once again, as in the attitude toward nationalism in general, the possibilities open to us are arbitrarily reduced to two, of which one is so plainly unacceptable that it forces us to the other. . . .

Very often the question is posed in terms of the inflow of foreign capital, the lever by which the foreign take-over of the Canadian economy has occurred. The choice then seems to be: either we own our own economy but do without foreign capital, or we grow rich faster at the expense of foreign take-over. But this stark alternative ignores many crucial questions; for instance, what form does the capital inflow take, loan capital, or direct investment? The difference is important for future control; what kind of economy is being built by this inflow? This is perhaps the most crucial question of all.

Or else nationalism is seen in traditional terms, as the erection of higher tariff barriers, as a kind of super "National Policy." It is not hard to show the ill-effects of a policy of this kind. Indeed, the "satellitization" we now suffer is in part conditioned by the National Policy. But to pretend that the only alternative to paralytic continentalism is a desperate grab at autarchy is absurd.

The real choice lies elsewhere. The political economy of independence concerns principally a nation's foreign trade position, in this day and age at least. This is more important than who owns its industry, although it is evident that this later factor can itself affect the foreign trade position (and in all likelihood does in our case, to a significant extent). . . . Canada's lack of independence from the U.S.A. springs in large part from the fact that most of our trade is with our neighbours to the South and that we are in deep and chronic deficit with them. This means that the extent to which they can hurt us, while hurting themselves relatively little, is at a maximum. Fortunately, a reduction in their Canadian trade, although far from disastrous for the U.S. as a whole, would hurt certain sectional interests who therefore constitute a standing lobby in Washington against such measures. Canada is very fortunate that the U.S.A. is not a monolithic society and that the vast engine of government can still be immobilized by lobbies. Otherwise, we would have suffered a grisly fate long ago.

The major problem of Canadian independence is therefore the problem of developing a more favourable balance of trade, which in turn is the problem of developing a more competitive economy. How does this dovetail with our other, domestic economic objectives? One of our most pressing problems, as revealed by the reports of the Economic Council of Canada, is the development of our economy to give jobs to our rapidly growing labour force. In the opinion of the Economic Council this will require greater diversification into secondary industry. If we want to pursue the objective of combined development of the different regions of Canada—and it will become more and more difficult to justify the country's existence if we don't—we must also try to bring about a wider geographical spread of this new secondary industry. But this industry has to be competitive internationally. We cannot increase Canadian employment in secondary industry simply by raising the tariff barrier; or rather we solve the problem in this way only at the cost of a depressed standard of living—if even this solution is possible for a country like Canada in an era of lowering trade barriers.

Thus both the needs of national independence and those of our own basic economic objectives require the development of an economy with a greater component of secondary industry, and which is more competitive internationally—not only vis-a-vis the U.S.A., but in the Atlantic and also the world arena. What then is the relation of foreign economic penetration to these objectives?

The relation is basically threefold. First, the growth of foreign, principally U.S., direct investment in Canada means a high, growing and never ending service of this borrowing in the form of dividends. Of course, Canada has something to show for these payments, namely the plant or whatever built by direct investment. But to build the same plant on loan capital which is paid off over a period of years and then becomes Canadian owned is much less costly in the long run to the balance of payments. Loan capital is therefore preferable to direct investment from the point of view of the above objectives.

Second, foreign direct investment has largely taken a form which has given a certain shape to the Canadian economy. In its secondary sector it is to a significant degree an economy of subsidiaries and branch plants of large international (mostly American) companies. This has two very important effects. First, our economy is very much influenced by the policy of large international companies toward their branch plants, in the fields of exports, research and development, sales and purchases between units of a given international company, and so on. Moreover, certain evidence presented recently by Eric Kierans seems to show that this influence has been very negative in certain aspects and threatens to become more so.

It would appear that for a great many international corporations the role of a foreign subsidiary is principally to increase the market for the parent corporation. The foreign subsidiary therefore plays an important role in buying components from the parent, paying consultant fees, etc., to it, and in so doing, augmenting the profit of the parent company and helping it to amortize its capital. It is not so important that it make profits on its own and remit revenue in the form of dividends. The interest of the subsidiary for the parent is that it allows it to penetrate a foreign market; where the profit is taken, at the level of the subsidiary or at the centre, is secondary; many, perhaps most, corporations prefer to take it at the centre.

It is clear that this practice is bad for the host country. For the policy puts a premium on the subsidiary's buying from the parent, i.e., on increasing the host country's imports and thus depressing its balance of trade. Some such factor seems to be operating in the trade between Canada and the U.S.A. . . .

How much does this adverse balance reflect a natural superiority of the American parent as a supplier? Very little, it would appear, for the policy of buying from the parent is very price-resistant. And one can easily understand why, for a component bought even at a higher price from the parent factory means a greater profit to the corporation as a whole, which profit is taken at the centre, at the expense of the periphery. Thus a study of the National Industrial Conference Board showed that Canadian industry had much higher material costs than U.S. industry. . . .

This is one way, then, in which the "branch plant economy" does not serve the objectives outlined above. But in another, perhaps more serious way, it leads to a structure of the Canadian economy which is in the long run not going to be internationally competitive. It is not just that units of production which are tied to the purchase of high-cost components from parent companies are not likely to be very export competitive. What is at stake is the shape of our economy.

The joint result of our tariff policy and foreign investment has been the placing in Canada of a large number of relatively small-scale units of production, as each major company tries to secure its share of the market.

This result, of course, sins against the principle of achieving economies by large-scale operations; but this does not deter the large corporation for whom the marginal investment pays off in market penetration. The global result, however, is that Canada has an economy which in some sectors is made up of a large number of small productive units, more than a country of our size would warrant. . . .

In a sense, the Canadian economy must be unique in the world, for it is to some extent a miniature of the American economy. Now the Americans can afford to enter every field of economic endeavour and set up three or more corporations in oligopolistic competition. But this is an absurdity for a country the size of Canada. The only way that a country our size can survive economically is to specialize and achieve pre-eminence in a limited series of lines, as successful small European countries have done. We have only managed to set up this crazy patchwork quilt because of the economics of the international corporation which makes a high-cost additional outlet an interesting proposition.

Many Canadians are satisfied that the accident of geographic location and the tariff has induced American industry to set up this patchwork quilt which we could never have afforded on our own. But this is a very short-sighted attitude. For apart from the disadvantages to our balance of payments resulting from the policy of these corporations, this type of economy does not provide us with the basis for the rapid development toward competitiveness which we are going to need. Branch plant industry tends to be high cost; more, by its marginal nature it tends to be less resistant to the pressures of economic recession. . . .

But the most serious drawback is that there is no basis for dynamism. The new developments of research, the initiative which profits by them, the ability to re-adapt and break out in new fields, very little of that is resident in the branch plant economy; it belongs to the centre. The Canadian patchwork quilt, the miniature of the American economy is an expensive present; it deprives us of the basis of autonomous re-adaptation toward greater competitiveness. It is a mechanism whereby the capital accumulated through sales in Canada and all the leverage that that implies for research and innovation goes to centres of decision outside the country, for whom our problems and objectives must be of very secondary concern. It is also a mechanism whereby those Canadians who can make a contribution in research and innovation are attracted irresistibly in large numbers south of the border. Whereas what Canada needs is to achieve greater competitiveness by concentrated efforts in research and development which will give us pre-eminence in a limited number of fields, the branch plant economy offers us the uncertain status of marginal off-shoots of a larger economy whose major levers of adaptation lie forever beyond our reach. It does not seem the part of wisdom to entrust our entire future to a structure of this kind.

Defensive Action

If we want to achieve our objectives of combined development toward a more diversified and competitive economy, and thus ensure Canadians a rising standard of living and maintain our independence, we have to take action in the three domains outlined above in which the growth of foreign ownership and the branch plant economy represents a danger to us.

1. We have to try to reduce the proportion of direct equity investment in Canada's borrowing abroad. This will mean, of course, less investment made by foreign enterprise, and more initiative from inside Canada which, however, will make appeal to outside loan capital, or perhaps even enter into partnership with outside investors. The consequent reduction in the proportion of new investment accounted for by direct foreign investment, mostly of large international companies, will not be a bad thing in itself, as will be seen below, as well as improving the future pattern of our foreign indebtedness.

2. We need a brace of measures to ensure that the affiliates of international corporations which are and remain here behave in a way more consonant with Canadian interests. That these companies are capable of adapting their policies in a significant way if they feel the political pressure to do so is shown by their recent behaviour in a number of fields. . . .

The measures will have to include the proposal put forward by Eric Kierans, and recently echoed by Walter Gordon (*A Choice for Canada*, p. 110), to amend the Companies Act so as to force disclosure of the dealings between affiliates and their foreign parents. When we reflect that an essential element of the pressure that the U.S. government exerts on its international corporations to obey its guidelines is the requirement that they make regular reports on their foreign payments transactions, we can see how totally defenceless we have left ourselves in the past. If public disclosure and censure is not enough, tougher measures will have to be taken. But we must ensure that foreign subsidiaries do their part to maintain our balance of payments, and above all that they supply themselves in Canada when cost is no greater.

3. But these measures will be far from sufficient if the pattern of our economy itself as it develops under the impetus of branch plant investment remains the same. Here we have to supply a missing factor. Our historical situation made it inevitable that we have recourse for our development to foreign capital. But the shape that this foreign investment has taken was determined in part by ourselves: first, by our tariff policy, which made it an interesting proposition to set up a branch plant here, but second by a lack of indigenous entrepreneurship. The Canadian economy is increasingly being designed by outsiders because it is not being designed by Canadians. If we are going to alter the pattern of our economy toward a more competitive diversified economy, we have to supply that entrepreneurial element. This is also an essential part of the goal described above: if we are to rely more on loan capital, there has to be the Canadian initiative in making the investment for which the foreign loan is required, instead of leaving both initiative and financing to outsiders.

But both because of the inadequacy of Canadian private entrepreneurship and because of social objectives that our development must meet (particularly that of combined regional development), it is clear that this entrepreneurial element will have to be public; it will have to be supplied by government planning. This means something much more ambitious than a Canadian Development Corporation, genre Walter Gordon. This latter proposal would simply allow Canadian private capital to do on a slightly larger scale what they are already doing. What we need on the other hand is the kind of planning which will invest heavily in research and feasibility studies, which will be able to devise new favourable fields of investment for Canada and determine what is required to maintain our competitive advantage, and then will go out and find the investment funds required. A Canada Development Corporation under public control, as a lever in the hands of a planning authority, would play a valuable—indeed indispensable—role in this. But this is a far cry from the Gordon proposal. What we need in short is to design our own economy; and we can only do this through our governments (the provinces must also do their part). This is the crucial measure.

What then of the pre-occupation with foreign ownership per se?—this is in my opinion not a major problem. Its effects, as we have seen, are partially bad, but the way to tackle the problem is along the line of these ill effects. That the above policies would result in a reduction in the proportion of the Canadian economy owned by foreigners is, however, clear. The attempt to reduce foreign direct investment would, if successful, slow down the growth of foreign ownership; the new rules governing the behavior of foreign subsidiaries might discourage some further investment in this field. And if planned development took place in the context of a phased multilateral reduction of tariff barriers—which should be one of the prime aims of our policy—the interest in branch plant investment would be further reduced. But the major factor tending to reverse the trend towards greater foreign ownership would be a growing element of Canadian entrepreneurship which would flow from government planning. Foreign ownership grows because investment opportunities are met by foreign entrepreneurs, and because many Canadians firms are themselves integrated into foreign units by take-over. The only way to reverse this trend effectively is to increase the component of Canadian entrepreneurship in the economy.

But although the inseparable result of the above policies would be to reverse the proportion of foreign ownership, it would divert us from our main task to make foreign overnship a preoccupation in itself. There may be a case for legislation against foreign take-over in certain sensitive areas, but the attempt to "buy back" foreign owned industry is fundamentally misguided. For instance the aim of Walter Gordon to see Canadians given the opening to take minority holdings in foreign corporations runs counter to our main objectives. Gordon renews his plea for this kind of investment in his recent book (*A Choice for Canada*, pp. 98-100). But the argument remains very unconvincing. It is unlikely that minority holdings by (patriotic?) Canadian investors will have very much effect on the behaviour of international corporations; not half so much as government arm-twisting will, in any case. And since it will need a substantial amount of government arm-twisting to induce international corporations to depart from their usual policy of 100% ownership, we may as well save our elbow grease for our principal objective. If we really want to gain control over policy through the stock market, it would be much more sensible to invest a concentrated block in the parent company in the U.S.A.; but that is another type of adventure.

The decisive objection, however, against the policy of buying minority holdings in foreign corporations is that it would mean immobilizing scarce investment resources in the present inadequate structure of the economy. It would mean investing in the branch plant economy, when what we need is to get away from it. Gordon's answer to this is that there is a need, given the present financial set-up, for investment opportunities of this kind. But that means simply that, assuming the continued lack of Canadian entrepreneurship (i.e., planning), the best investment opportunities in Canada are foreign-held corporations. Insurance companies and other like institutions would therefore like in. But the aim of our policy is not to make things easier for the Canadian investor, but to change the pattern of the Canadian economy. A substantial proportion of those funds which insurance companies now invest should be mobilized in a Canada Development Corporation of the kind described above. . . .

It should be clear that the alternative to paralytic continentalism is not some irrational grasping at autarchy in the form of higher tariff barriers or an expulsion of foreign capital. The nub of the alternative is a policy of public Canadian entrepreneurship, and the policy would involve a drive to lower tariff barriers. The aim would be to escape the exceptional and abnormal reliance of our economy on the branch plant. What then sows confusion about this alternative, and what makes it possible for Liberal politicians to drag across the stage the ghouls and hobgoblins of autarchic stagnation? What, in short, lies behind the failure of nerve so characteristic of large sections of the electorate today?

Problem is Political

The problem is political. For the alternative I have been trying to outline to be a reality and a source of hope for large numbers of Canadians, it would have to appear as a live political option. But for this, in turn, this policy must find a constituency within the Canadian electorate which can be organized around it. And this is the source of the trouble. The normal constituency for this alternative has not yet crystallized; indeed, it has been a largely passive component of the Canadian political scene in the past.

Canada, to a greater extent than other comparable countries, has been under political leadership close to the financial and business elite. This group has had a decisive voice in both the traditional parties which have succeeded each other in office. . . .

Now this elite presided in a sense at the birth of the country. It was largely their ambition toward cross-continent development in rivalry to the U.S.A. which powered Confederation and helped shape the economic development of the new state. The crucial political fact underlying the present dominance of paralytic continentalism is that this same social group has over the decades come to accommodate itself to continental integration. The successors to the entrepreneurs of British North

America, the builders of trans-continental railroads, are the managers of branch plants and those who service them in one way or another. This drift toward integration lies behind the slowly growing hegemony of continentalism in the old political parties. . . .

The alternative policy is only possible if a new political alliance can be formed to take power at the federal level for the first time without the business elite as its vital centre. Because of the nature of the objectives which are the basis of the alternative—planned development of all regions—this alliance could only be founded on the natural political constituency of reform. In any country this includes middle and lower income groups, but in Canada reform has shown a potentially wide appeal among the people of less advantaged regions and among those who do not belong to the ethnic and confessional group which has virtually monopolized the key posts in the economy and to a significant degree in government as well.

•   •   •

This has a direct repercussion on Canadian unity. To achieve this by elite brokerage is no longer enough; it has to become real at the base of the political society as well. Unless the association with English Canada comes to have more significance—and value—for the averge Quebecer than it has today, the future of Canada is bleak indeed. And the same could undoubtedly be said for the average English-Canadian in relation to French Canada. . . .

Biculturalism and hence the Canadian future require a widespread sense of the value of the Canadian union among non-elites. It requires, therefore, in the same way as a viable Canadian nationalism, a break with elite politics and the creation of an alliance across the regions of the groups which have been kept under greater or lesser degrees of political tutelage in the past. The problems of unity and nationalism are therefore inextricably intertwined, and both are linked to a polarization of Canadian politics along socio-economic lines.

The alternatives before Canada: nationalism or continentalism, are therefore far from being as simple as they may first appear. Nor does this question constitute an isolated one. It enters into the heart of our political life as a nation and touches on a set of choices which may set the mould of our politics for generations. In a short space of time we must choose between the continental drift of the elites, and the building of a new political alliance. This implies obviously, too, a political choice in the direct partisan sense. For the building of this alliance is already being attempted by the New Democratic Party.

NATIONAL UNITY: CANADA'S POLITICAL OBSESSION*

John Porter

Canada has no resounding charter myth proclaiming a utopia against which, periodically, progress can be measured. At the most, national goals and dominant values seem to be expressed in geographical terms such as "from sea to sea," rather than in social terms such as "all men are created equal," or "liberty, fraternity, and equality." In the United States there is a utopian image which slowly over time bends intractable social patterns in the direction of equality, but a Canadian counterpart of this image is difficult to find.

•   •   •

It would probably be safe to say that Canada has never had a political system with this dynamic policy [emerging from the polarization of the right and the left, such as is found in Talcott Parsons' analysis of the American political dynamic or in British experience or in Marxism]. Its two major political parties do not focus to the right and the left. In the sense that both are closely linked with corporate enterprise the dominant focus has been to the right. One of the reasons why this condition has prevailed is that Canada lacks clearly articulated major goals and values stemming from some charter instrument which emphasizes progress and equality. If there is a major goal of Canadian society it can best be described as an integrative goal. The maintenance of national unity has over-ridden any other goals there might have been, and has prevented a polarizing, within the political system, of conservative and progressive forces. It has never occurred to any Canadian commentators that national unity might in fact be achieved by such polarization. Rather a dissociative federalism is raised to the level of a quasi-religious political dogma, and polarization to right and left in Canadian politics is regarded as disruptive. Consequently the main focus of Canadian politics has been to the right and the maintenance of the *status quo*. The reason that the Liberal party in Canada was in office so many years until 1957 was not because it was a progressive party, but because it served Canada's major goal of national unity.

The major themes in Canadian political thought emphasize those characteristics, mainly regional and provincial loyalties, which divide the Canadian population. Consequently integration and national unity must be a constantly reiterated goal to counter such divisive sentiments. The dialogue is between unity and discord rather than progressive and conservative forces. The question which arises is whether the discord-unity dialogue has any real meaning in the lives of Canadians, or whether it has become, in the middle of the twentieth century, a political technique of conservatism. Canada must be one of the few major industrial societies in

* Reprinted from *The Vertical Mosaic* by John Porter, by permission of the author and of the University of Toronto Press. © University of Toronto Press, 1973.

which the right and left polarization has become deflected into disputes over regionalism and national unity.

Canada's major political and intellectual obsession, national unity, has had its effect on the careers of men who take on political roles. It has put a premium on the type of man whom we shall label the administrative politician and has discounted the professional political career in which creative politicians can assume leadership roles. Creative politics at the national level has not been known in Canada since before World War I when the westward thrust to Canada's empire was still a major national goal. Since the empire of the west was secured national goals of development have not been known. . . .

THE NATIONAL OUTLOOK OF ENGLISH-SPEAKING CANADIANS*

Kenneth McNaught

Two Founding Races?

Probably because the alternative is so clumsy, the terms "English-Canadian" or "English" are used interchangeably in Quebec to signify those people in the rest of Canada who do not speak French or who are not of French descent. Yet these terms are wildly misleading. They imply the existence in Canada of only two races, and thus that any revision of Confederation must be based upon a dialogue or bargaining process between these two races. Each term also carries the suggestion that the words "Canada" and "Canadian" have come to mean "English Canada" and "English Canadian." Thus the problem in Quebec eyes concerns the relations between the "two nations"; and it is a striking fact that "nation" and "race" are virtually interchangeable terms in Quebec. . . .

Having established that Canada is composed of two races (or nations, or cultures), the argument goes on to say that only the French nation is really conscious of its own identity and destiny and that without Quebec Canada would become balkanized. The "English" race or culture is so amorphous that it depends upon the French-Canadian nation to keep it from falling into the arms of the United States or from breaking up into regional fragments. At the same time, it is this enfeebled English-Canadian race which has triumphantly imposed its image on Canada and made necessary the French-Canadian revolution. Strange argument. . . .

The most striking facts about the English-speaking view of Canada are that it rejects racial nationalism and is the product of a deep commitment to slowly evolved historical tradition. . . .

•   •   •

At the time of Confederation, indeed, all the supporters of the movement, French- and English-speaking alike, talked of the founding of a

* From Peter Russell, (ed.), *Nationalism in Canada*, Toronto, McGraw-Hill Company of Canada Ltd., 1966. By permission of the author and publisher.

new nationality. No amount of quibbling about the different meanings attached by "English" and "French" to the word "nation" can obscure the fact that in the 1860s a political nationality was being founded. The debate and conferences leave absolutely no room for doubt on the matter. Nor is there room to doubt that English-speaking Canadians, then and even more now, thought of Canadian nationality as something that included people of French, British and other origins and which would move steadily toward its own sense of identity. That identity was not to be homogeneous in the American sense, but diverse. It would, and has guaranteed to various minorities (especially the French-speaking minority) particular rights with respect to language, religion, land-holding, military service, hunting and fishing.

Yet, while local differences of culture and law were to be guaranteed (especially in Quebec), there was never any question of an "equality of two founding races." The "races" were, in fact, not equal. A central purpose of Confederation was to recognize this fact and to avoid the frictions which the "two nations" idea had created during the unhappy political evolution under the 1841 Act of Union.

In order to maintain minority rights within Quebec and the other provinces, without at the same time permitting Quebec to become a state within a state, the predominance of Ottawa and the rights of the Canadian majority there (however it might be composed) had to be accepted. . . .

Any survey of Canadian political history reveals that the idea of two "founding races" (each with the expectation of its own developing nationality) has been and must be destructive of the idea of Canada. . . .

Pragmatism and "The Compact"

A large part of contemporary Quebec's distrust of "English Canadians" stems from a fixed belief that they are inveterate centralizers. In fact, of course, centralization has never been a fixed goal of English-speaking Canadians. At the time of Confederation Macdonald encountered stiff opposition to an overblown central government from the Maritime Provinces and, in some respects, from the Grit elements within the coalition government of the united province of Canada. Indeed, it was one measure of his pragmatism and of his faith in the idea of a political nationality that he abandoned his preferred goal of legislative union as opposed to a federal pattern of government. Again, the great political-legal battles of the 1880s and '90s between Mowat and Macdonald, the "better terms" campaign in the Maritimes with its peak in the secession resolutions presented by W. S. Fielding in Nova Scotia, and the near-rebellion in Manitoba over the C.P.R. monopoly, all attest to a jealous regard for provincial rights on the part of a majority of English-speaking Canadians.

It is certainly true that English-speaking Canadians have also frequently turned to the central government for the fulfillment of some of their aspirations. But very often this has been for the protection of regional rights or opportunities. In the struggle over Manitoba Schools, for example, the division of Canadian opinion was not simply Quebec against the rest. A very large number of English-speaking Canadians believed that the remedial power of the federal government should be used to sustain minority rights within a province. Furthermore, in many of the instances of apparent English-speaking Canadian support for centralization, a major purpose has been that of using the economic powers of Ottawa to equalize provincial opportunities—not for the purpose of producing a bland national conformity but for the purpose of preserving viable provincial or regional differences of culture. This has been illustrated particularly in the various phases of the Maritimes Rights movement and in the western Progressive movement.

The point is that English-speaking Canadians have always seen the Canadian political state as one in which there is a necessarily shifting balance between the central and provincial powers. Their willingness today to undertake a major redressing of that balance is simply one of many historical examples of a continuing process. Nor is the process always dictated by reasons of ideology or politics. Frequently it has had a strong material basis. In the 1880s, the 1920s and the 1960s, the almost independent prosperity of Ontario and British Columbia has been a considerable factor in these provinces' ready acceptance of "co-operative federalism."

Yet despite the cyclical provincial-rightism of English-speaking Canadians, there is an equally consistent reassertion of the validity of the nation, and it is this that seems most to irritate the *nationalistes* of Quebec. It does so because they vastly underrate the complexity and change in the idea itself. . . . Much of the reason for this change—an acceptance of multi-racialism, or multi-culturalism—is to be found in the confidence produced by the simple fact of Canadian survival. And since that survival has clearly depended upon a flexible response to regionalism, racial feeling and religious differences, tradition has planted firmly in the minds of English-speaking Canadians the idea that their national loyalty is to national diversity. Unhappily this seems trite only to English-speaking Canadians.

Quebec's Complaints

Quebec, despite these facts of the English-speaking Canadian development, still charges that in the past English-speaking Canadians have broken "the compact"—by refusing to honour the guarantees to the French language in Manitoba, by refusing to extend language privileges to French-Canadian minorities in other provinces, by imposing conscription for overseas service in the interests of British imperialism and by excluding French Canadians from a fair share of the senior positions in the federal civil service. Less convincingly, but with even greater heat, Quebec charges that the English-speaking power élite has used its combined political-economic domination to exclude Quebeckers from managerial and ownership status in the province's industry. The result of this arrogant domination, argue the Quebeckers, was to render their province a "reservation" or "colony" to be exploited by the English-Canadian and American capital, which adroitly financed such unsavoury politicians as Maurice Duplessis and used demagogic pseudo-nationalism as a blind behind which to extend their economic control. The answer to such colonialism was, of course, revolution.

Again we find inconsistency in the Quebec argument. . . .From declaring that the Quiet Revolution is justified because "English Canada" broke the compact, the ideological directors of Quebec pass to the assertion that the original agreement never was good enough. Now it is not enough merely to undo the grievances within the original framework. It is necessary to break the structure altogether and establish two racial states. . . .

In dealing with this nimble logic English-speaking Canadians are both baffled and resentful. But to say that they have not drawn up any thin red line of verbal battle, that they have generally preferred the familiar paths of compromise and conciliation, is not to say that they have no convictions. I have already noted that the English-speaking Canadians have a very definite concept of Canada—an historic amalgam of the original and undoubted purposes of Confederation plus modifications enjoined by the facts of immigration and growth. Reluctance to contend directly with the ever more extreme racial nationalism of Quebec (except by way of concession) is also explained by a compound of causes.

First, strangely, is acceptance of much of the case put forward by Quebec. Most English-speaking Canadians agree that there has been injustice along the way. In the Manitoba schools question, that injustice was a specific and unconstitutional denial to French Canadians of rights and expectations spelled out in 1867 and 1870. In the case of conscription in 1917 there was extremely bad political management of the policy itself, and Quebec opinion was still further inflamed by the contemporaneous and deliberate prohibition by Manitoba and Ontario of teaching in the French language in public schools. There has also been admitted injustice in the appointments policy in the federal civil service—not unconstitutional injustice, but human and political injustice. On all these counts English-speaking Canadians feel guilty. . . .

The Present Condition

. . . Most Canadians sympathize entirely with the feeling of exclusion which is the basis of the Quiet Revolution's triumph. Indeed, most English-speaking Canadians who have followed Quebec affairs (and there are many more such people than Quebeckers care to admit) admire the new and forthright willingness to use the government of Quebec to achieve collective purposes: to broaden the base of social welfare and to halt the takover by American capital. But these are purposes which are agreeable to most Canadians, and they are repelled by the new Quebec insistence that such goals can be achieved only through virtually independent "provincial states." That insistence is bound to render difficult or impossible the achievement of similar goals at the national level since it will rob Ottawa of the essential powers of economic planning—indeed it has already placed grave impediments in the path of such planning.

But guilt-feelings and admiration for the new positive approach to the use of government are only half of the explanation of the English-speaking Canadian reluctance to spell out its mounting resistance to racial nationalism and to a new straightjacket constitution. The non-French Canadians know that they have attained a genuine sense of Canadian independence and that the growth of this feeling is not the result of logic-chopping and perpetual rewriting of constitutional formulae. It is the result of deep belief in growth by precedent and the converse suspicion that it is dangerous to commit to words the inner nature of human or social relationships. Since these two facts of feeling and philosophy lie at the heart of the matter, they are worth a further word.

First, independence. Since the enunciation in the 1860s of a new nationality, and despite the chronic outcropping of British loyalties, English-speaking Canadians have moved steadily towards independence. From one precedent to another down to the separate declaration of war in 1939 and the notably "un-British" stand taken at the time of the Suez crisis [in 1956] they gradually severed the constitutional and, to a considerable extent, the emotional ties with the "mother country." Not infrequently, as the career of Mackenzie King amply demonstrates, this process was hastened by an almost too sensitive recognition of Quebec's anti-British creed. Even with respect to the Commonwealth, as opposed to specifically British interest, it would take exceptional daring to assert that the English-speaking majority does not place its primary loyalty with the United Nations or with Canada itself before its concern for things British. The plain fact is that non-French Canada has experienced a sense of independence extending much further beyond the constitutional aspect than has Quebec. It is not without reason that some English-speaking Canadians begin to suspect Quebec of frailty in its protestations of independent goals. . . .

Canadians of British descent have always regarded the political process as essentially pragmatic-experimental. They have shied away from detailed and comprehensive definitions of political and social relationships, preferring to see change come by the establishment of precedents which then become the justification of future decisions. That is why they have continued to hold to the English common law, and that is why civil liberties in English-speaking Canada have been more carefully cherished than they have in Quebec. This is why, too, they adjust more easily to multi-racial nationality than does Quebec. A broadening of rights by precedent—such as the instituting of simultaneous translation in Parliament, the proliferation of dominion-provincial consultations, revision of the appointments policy in the federal civil service and crown corporations, or such other possibilities as special Supreme Court panels of judges trained in the Quebec Civil Code to hear cases arising under that Code—it is this method of change that appeals to English-speaking Canadians.

By contrast, French Canadians prefer to systematize and codify the law, the constitution and, indeed, a broad range of social relationships. Because of these philosophic characteristics and a natural proclivity to verbalization, French Canadians mistake the nearly silent and the usually flexible English-speaking attitude as an absence of conviction or determination. No misunderstanding could have more disastrous and predictable consequences. The point has been well taken by some of the very originators of the Quiet Revolution—by those, in particular, who saw that revolution not only as a movement for social justice but also for the liberalization of Quebec. Of these, Pierre-Elliott Trudeau is perhaps the outstanding example. . . .

BIBLIOGRAPHY

English Canada and Canadian Nationalism

Axline, A., Hyndman, J. E., Lyon, P., and Molot, M., (eds.), *Continental Community? Independence and Integration in North America*, Toronto, McClelland and Stewart, 1974.

Baldwin, D. A., and Smallwood, F., eds., *Canadian-American Relations: The Politics and Economics of Interdependence*, Hannover, N. H., Dartmouth College, 1967.

Berger, C., (ed.), *Imperialism and Nationalism, 1884-1914*, Toronto, Copp Clark, 1969.

Brady, A., "The Meaning of Canadian Nationalism," *International Journal*, Vol. XIX, No. 2, Summer, 1964.

Cairns, A., "Political Science in Canada and the Americanization Issue," *C.J.P.S.*, Vol. VIII, No. 2, June, 1975.

Canada, *Foreign Ownership and the Structure of Canadian Industry* [Watkins Report], Ottawa, Queen's Printer, 1968.

Canada, *Report of the Royal Commission on National Development in the Arts, Letters, and Sciences* [Massey Report], Ottawa, Queen's Printer, 1951.

Canadian-American Committee, *The New Environment for Canadian-American Relations*, Montreal, Private Planning Association of Canada, 1972.

Clark, S. D., "Canada and the American Value System," in *The Developing Canadian Community*, Toronto, University of Toronto Press, 2nd ed., 1968.

Clarkson, S., (ed.), *An Independent Foreign Policy for Canada?*, Toronto, McClelland and Stewart, 1968.

Cook, R., *The Maple Leaf Forever: Essays in Nationalism and Politics in Canada*, Toronto, Macmillan, 1971.

Cook, R., and McNaught, K., *Canada and the U.S.A.*, Toronto, Clarke, Irwin, 1963.

Cook, T., "The Canadian conservative tradition: an historical perspective," *Journal of Canadian Studies*, Vol. VIII, No. 4, November, 1973.

Cross, M. S., (ed.), *The Frontier Thesis and the Canadas: The Debate on the Impact of the Canadian Environment*, Toronto, Copp Clark, 1970.

Dickey, J. S., (ed.), *The United States and Canada*, Englewood Cliffs, N.J., Prentice-Hall, 1964.

Editorial Committee, "A Citizen's Guide to the Herb Gray Report," *The Canadian Forum*, Volume, LI, No. 611, December, 1971.

Federal-Provincial Committee on the Foreign Ownership of Land, *Report to the First Ministers*, Canadian Intergovernmental Conference Secretariat, Ottawa, Information Canada, 1975.

Fox, A. B., Hero, A. O., and Nye, J. S., (eds.), "Canada & the U.S. Trans-national and Trans-governmental Relations", *International Organization*, Vol. 28, No. 4, 1974.

Gagne, W., *Nationalism, Technology, and the Future of Canada*, Macmillan, Toronto, 1976.

Godfrey, D., and Watkins, M., (eds.), *Gordon to Watkins to You*, Toronto, New Press, 1970.

Gordon, W., *Storm Signals: New Economic Policies for Canada*, Toronto, McClelland and Stewart, 1975.

Gordon, W., *A Choice for Canada*, Toronto, McClelland and Stewart, 1966.

Grant, G., *Lament for a Nation: The Defeat of Canadian Nationalism*, Toronto, McClelland and Stewart, 1965.

Gray, Herbert E., *Foreign direct investment in Canada*, Ottawa, Government of Canada, 1972

Hardin, H., *A Nation Unaware: The Canadian Economic Culture*, Vancouver, J. J. Douglas, 1974.

Harvey, T. G., and Harvey, S., *Political Culture in a Canadian Community*, Toronto, Copp Clark, 1973.

Heisey, A., *The Great Canadian Stampede: The Rush to Economic Nationalism*, Toronto, Griffin House, 1973.

Johnstone, J. C., *Young People's Images of Canadian Society*, Studies of the Royal Commission on Bilingualism and Biculturalism, No. 2, Ottawa, Queen's Printer, 1969.

Kruhlak, O., Schultz, R., and Pobihushchy, S. I., (eds.), *The Canadian Political Process: A Reader*, Toronto, Holt, Rinehart and Winston, rev. ed., 1973, (see articles by Lipset, Truman, Clark, and Johnstone).

Laxer, R. M., Canada Ltd., *The Political Economy of Dependence*, Toronto, McClelland and Stewart, 1973.

Levin, M., and Sylvester, C., *Foreign Ownership*, Toronto, Musson, 1972.

Levitt, K., *Silent Surrender*, Toronto, Macmillan, 1970.

Lipset, S. M., *Revolution and Counter-Revolution*, New York, Basic Books, 1968, chapter 2, "The United States and Canada."

Lloyd, T., and McLeod, J. T., *Agenda 70: Proposals for a Creative Politics*, Toronto, University of Toronto Press, 1968.

Lumsden, I., (ed.), *Close the 49th Parallel, etc.: The Americanization of Canada*, Toronto, University of Toronto Press, 1970.

McCaffrey, G., (ed.), *The U.S. and Us*, Proceedings of the 37th Couchiching Conference, Toronto, Canadian Institute on Public Affairs, 1969.

McKillop, A. B., "Nationalism, Identity and Canadian Intellectual History", *Q.Q.*, Vol. 81, No. 4, Winter, 1974.

Mathews, R. D. "The U.S. and Canadian intellectual history", *Journal of Canadian Studies*, Vol. VI, No. 4, November, 1971.

Morchain, J., (ed.), *Sharing a Continent: An Introduction to Canadian-American Relations*, Toronto, McGraw-Hill Ryerson, 1973.

Morton, W. L., *The Canadian Identity*, Toronto, Madison, 1961.

Newman, P. C., *Home Country*, Toronto, McClelland and Stewart, 1973.

Pope, W. H., *The Elephant and the Mouse*, Toronto/Montreal, McClelland and Stewart, 1971.

Preston, R. A., (ed.), *The Influence of the United States on Canadian Development: Eleven Case Studies*, Durham, N.C., Duke University Press, 1972.

Purdy, A., (ed.), *The New Romans: Candid Canadian Opinions of the U.S.*, Edmonton, Hurtig, 1968.

Redekop, J., "A Reinterpretation of Canadian-American Relations," *C.J.P.S.*, Vol. IX, No. 2, June, 1976.

Redekop, J., (ed.), *The Star-Spangled Beaver*, Toronto, Peter Martin, 1971.

Roblin, D., "A new national policy and Canadian nationalism", *C.P.A.*, Vol. 16, No. 4, Winter, 1973.

Rotstein, A., *The Precarious Homestead: Essays on Economics, Technology and Nationalism*, Toronto, New Press, 1973.

Rotstein, A. and Lax, G., (eds.), *Getting It Back: A Program for Canadian Independence*, Toronto, Clarke, Irwin, 1974.

Rotstein, A., and Lax, G., (eds.), *Independence: The Canadian Challenge*, Toronto, McClelland and Stewart, 1972.

Russell, P., (ed.), *Nationalism in Canada*, Toronto, McGraw-Hill, 1966.

Safarian, A. E., *Foreign Ownership of Canadian Industry*, Toronto, McGraw-Hill, 1966.

Safarian, A. E., "Foreign investment in Canada: some myths", *Journal of Canadian Studies*, Vol. VI, No. 3, August, 1971.

Smiley, D. V., *The Canadian Political Nationality*, Toronto, Methuen, 1967.

Smiley, D. V., "The Federal Dimension of Canadian Economic Nationalism", *Dalhousie Law Review*, Vol. 1, No. 3, October, 1974.

Smiley, D. V., "Canada and the Quest for a National Policy," *C.J.P.S.*, Vol. VIII, No. 1, March, 1975.

Stevenson, G., "Foreign Direct Investment and the Provinces: A Study of Elite Attitudes", *C.J.P.S.*, Vol. VII, No. 4, December, 1974.

Swanson, R. F., *Canadian-American Summit Diplomacy, 1923-1973*, (speeches and documents), Carleton Library No. 81, Toronto, McClelland and Stewart, 1975.

Sykes, P., *Sellout: The Giveaway of Canada's Energy Resources*, Hurtig, Edmonton, 1973.

Symons, T. H. B., *To Know Ourselves: The Report of the Commission on Canadian Studies*, Vols. I and II, Ottawa, Association of Universities and Colleges of Canada, 1975.

Taylor, C., *Snow Job: Canada, the United States and Vietnam (1945-1973)*, Toronto, Anansi, 1974.

Teeple, G., (ed.), *Capitalism and the National Question in Canada*, Toronto, University of Toronto Press, 1972.

Tupper, S. R., and Bailey, D., *One Continent, Two Voices: The Future of Canada-United States Relations*, Toronto, Clarke, Irwin, 1967.

Wise, S. F., and Brown, R. C., *Canada Views the United States: Nineteenth Century Political Attitudes*, Toronto, Macmillan, 1967.

[See also Bibliography, "Social Issues," in Chapter 17, infra.]

6

FRENCH CANADA

There have been two facets to the problem of French Canada: the external, which concerns the place of French-speaking Canadians within Canada as a whole and their position and role within federal governmental institutions in particular, and the internal, which concerns the development of events inside the province of Quebec itself.

In the 1970s the crisis in the external dimension abated somewhat, or at least changed its nature. Adopting a number of the proposals contained in the final *Report of the Royal Commission on Bilingualism and Biculturalism* and in several of its associated research studies (for references to these, see especially the bibliography in Chapter 2), the Trudeau government attempted to provide greater opportunities for French-speaking Canadians both within Canada at large and in the federal government itself. (See, for example, the description in Chapter 2 of the statute establishing two official languages.) Prime Minister Trudeau also launched a process of wholesale constitutional review (see again Chapter 2) which was a response in part to Quebec's demands. While these moves succeeded in tempering the severity of some French-Canadian indignation, they provoked another problem, namely an English-Canadian backlash.

In the same decade the internal aspect of the problem became more serious. Stimulated by General de Gaulle's famous cry "Québec libre!" in Montreal in 1967, the separatist movement led by René Lévesque, a former Liberal cabinet minister, welded together the two small separatist parties that had acquired modest support in the provincial election of 1966. The new Parti Québécois which emerged in 1968 won 23 per cent of the popular vote in the provincial election in 1970, increased its support to more than 30 per cent in the 1973 election, and won power on November 15, 1976, having obtained approximately 40 per cent of the vote and 69 of the 110 seats.

This chapter concentrates on the Quebec scene. It begins with an edited version of a long interview with René Lévesque which conveys the tone and attitudes of the contemporary separatist movement in Quebec while selections from the 1975 program of the P.Q. give the major planks in its platform. A condensation of two articles by Harvey Shepherd wrestles with the much disputed question of whether Quebec would gain or lose financially from achieving independence. The excerpt from a speech by Prime Minister Trudeau counterbalances the separatist plea by giving a resounding defence of federalism while the editor's article discusses Quebec separatism as one illustration of Canadians' self-destructive death wish.

Mr. Dreifeld's excellent original article, which has been brought up to date for this edition, offers an account not available elsewhere of the complicated developments, twists and turns, and interrelations of recent nationalist and socialist factions in Quebec. A final table provides in a comparative form the results of the six most recent Quebec provincial elections. Since the table gives both the percentage of the popular vote won and the percentage and number of seats secured by each party, it is also useful as an illustration of the peculiar effects of our voting system. (See also in this connection both Professor Cairns' article in Chapter 8 and several items in Chapter 9.)

The bibliography is long but by no means exhaustive since the number of books and articles on the subject of Quebec is very extensive, especially in French, and keeps growing continually. The two Montreal daily newspapers, *Le Devoir* and *La Presse*, are undoubtedly the best sources of information and judicious commentary on the rapidly changing Quebec scene. For two years the Parti Québécois had its own daily newspaper, *Le Jour*, which gave the separatist point of view, but it went bankrupt in 1976 although it was later revived as a weekly.

RENE LEVESQUE TALKS ABOUT SEPARATISM—AND OTHER THINGS*

(From an interview with René Lévesque, the leader of the Parti Québécois, conducted by Greg-Michael Troy, editor, Medium II.)

Two Nations

Question: So, would you call Canada a nation?

Answer: . . . A nation just doesn't mean the state, however, in English it mostly is the state; in other words if you have a government you have a nation. So Canada is a nation by English definition only because it is political. In French, you have a second meaning, which is a more basic definition: people who have a common history, a common language, a sort of common community feeling of being an entity that wants to live together. Another example on an international level might be Scotland. I think Scotland is a nation. I think the Scottish people are beginning to come of the same opinion. They forgot it for awhile. The Basques are a

* From *Medium II*, student newspaper, Erindale College, University of Toronto, February 27, 1975. By permission.

nation both in France and Spain. The Slovaks are a nation. But the English definition of nation often means "there's the government, there's the nation." So I suppose on that basis, in English you would call Canada a nation. In French we wouldn't say "la nation canadienne" that easily.

Q: That sounds curiously a lot like what Chaput wrote about in his book: "Why I am a Separatist" . . . two nations within Canada.

A: That goes away back, I mean it's always been a sort of semantic defence for French Canadians, being a minority, being cooped up mostly in Quebec, at least the only place where we can make any decisions worthwhile. It's always been a sort of, I don't know, a bone of contention between the two groups because the moment we say that there are two nations "les deux nations" you've got a hell of a lot of good old Anglo-Saxon stock that get up and say "No. No, there's only one nation, one country." . . . one everything, but that's a lot of "crap". Eventually, if the Quebec people are a nation, that will be one particular problem they will have to face. If they want to be a nation both culturally and bureaucratically, that's something else again. But that's what we're working for. So in your sense, that there will be two nations, definitely, one with a Quebec government and the other with a government wherever you want to put it, Winnipeg or Toronto. Also, an association between two sovereign states, like the Common Market might be possible.

No Canadian Identity

Q: If Canada is two nations, loosely confederated under one flag, and the English nation has this growing trend towards nationalism, how does this affect the separatist movement or the Parti Quebecois?

A: Not much! Because Canadian nationalism is more or less a throw-back to John A. Macdonald except in modern costume. The Canadian federal state was set up, I think mostly, on the grounds of being scared of the United States. . . . Canadian nationalism is mostly the same thing today only under a different guise. American economic control doesn't seem to create the same kind of reaction in Quebec. We have had our own leftist groups, however, who would like to kick the Americans out, and even a few romantics tied into the image of the Che Guevara, but that was a few years back.

Q: It's died down now?

A: Yes, it has and in a way it's kind of sad because at least the kids were actively involved. Right now what you see is a sort of disinvolvement among the people between 18-22, the college age level. Thank God at the high school level—I'm speaking of Quebec—it seems to be picking up again; they're becoming curious about politics and seem to be a little less sub-cultural. But it's hard to gain people's interests because it's all par for the course now, and it will be until Quebec makes up its mind. It's all very classical, and being very classical is a problem. We in Quebec think of Canada as a very artificial creation conned upon our forefathers whom we now call the 'Fathers of Confederation', but who were really nothing but average politicians of the time who made money out of scandals like the Canadian Pacific. Confederation was conned upon people who were not consulted, because we were just colonies afraid of the American design for annexation. Canada never gelled into a real country, not even after a hundred years. . . . A Canadian is just someone who lives here. That's all. There's no national entity.

Q: . . . and the Parti Quebecois isn't asking the same question? Isn't searching for a national entity? Isn't frustrated with the same sort of results?

A: We don't have to go out and search to find it. Look, walk around the streets or walk somewhere where you will find French people of your generation and ask 10 of them, the first 10 you meet who are between 18-30, ask them "Are you a Canadian? A French-Canadian or a Quebecois?" 9 out of 10 of them don't need a philosophical discussion, 9 out of 10 will answer ". . . well what the hell, I'm Quebecois." That's the way they see themselves and that's basic.

Conditioned by Propaganda

Q: About as basic as a pair of Levi's pre-faded blue jeans, which are mass produced to meet the needs of a highly propagandized generation. Every young generation accepts what appears to be different, exciting. The emphasis is not on whether it is right or wrong, but rather on the social appeal. The Parti Quebecois is appealing to the new consciousness because you are different. . .

A: You are conditioned by social propaganda and Canadian propaganda. But what I mean is this: every god-damn thing in Canada that has real power—business, big-money, the Federal Government and presently the Quebec provincial government—are all extremely powerful propaganda tools. The C.B.C. is another example along with every other god-damn media who promote Canadian unity. Yet in spite of all that, the new generations in Quebec are growing up and calling themselves Quebecois.

Q: Granted, but what I'm basically asking is what makes your propaganda better than the Federal government's? As one gets older it becomes harder to distinguish one political party from the other . . . basically they're all structures with ravenous appetites for controlling people.

Parti Quebecois Different

A: Yes, that's a problem that nobody has solved yet, not in Mao's China or Ford's United States. Nobody has devised the perfect political system, not even the future system where people will participate (a lot of people use the word participation), in other words a system that allows people to be decision makers on all levels. I think, however, you have to drive towards that. The Parti Quebecois is doing so. We're the only party that I know of in North America that has had the idea and tries to implement it. For instance we're the only damn party I know of that has never taken a cent from any corporation and refuses to. One of our basic regulations states: people are voting, we're not a corporation and we're not a union either. In other words we're a party of and for the people. You can't create a revolution in people's minds. People change slowly, and that change becomes noticeable when people become more conscious of the fact that they hold the power. And that's the best thing we can hope for.

Q: A few years ago Vallieres wrote a book titled "Le Temps de Choisir" . . . in it Vallieres displayed a rather radically inclined Marxist temperament. I know he backs the Parti Quebecois. Do you support Vallieres' political and economic philosophies?

A: Take a guy who starts with a Marxist attitude and is honest about it. (We have a few in the party, a few of quality, but there are others who call themselves Marxists and don't know what they're talking about.) Vallieres is a very well structured guy and knows what he's talking about. He believes in it. Why the hell should we refuse him? He's working with the party. His Marxist ideas can be very stimulating, but the Party's platform and the Party's attitude doesn't go that far at all; so isn't that normal? I mean, for instance you have the waffle group of the NDP which are mostly wishy-washy people because they're tied to a machine. But there are people who are more radical and I hope to God we get more of them because we need them at least for now.

Bilingualism

Q: In Chaput's book, *Why I am a separatist*, he stated that the Quebecois fear bilingualism and that ". . . bilingualism is a meaningless word, a sin against nature." Would you agree with this?

A: NO! Consider bilingualism at the personal level. In other words a person living in Toronto is kind of cooped up and very narrow-minded. Canada is not that big an entity in the world if he only speaks English. The same would apply here. The more French Canadian kids become bilingual, or even trilingual, the better, because we're in a global village. The world is shrinking and we know damn well when the Arabs decide something about oil we're affected the next day. We should be open to the whole world. So bilingualism or trilingualism on a personal level is ideal. The Party pushes for better English teaching, but on the other hand, collectively, community-wise in Quebec, the basic official language and the language of promotion should be French. There's no contradiction in that.

French Survival

Q: When I lived in Montreal a couple of years ago I came to notice how critical the Quebecois are of themselves.

A: Yes, even in many ways they have complexes. I think every colony has that. You have inferiority complexes on the English-Canadian side facing the American border. What the hell.

Q: How has the French culture survived then? How do you explain the existence, the continued existence of loyalty towards the culture?

A: That's a hell of a good question because we're in a transition period. What kept the French culture going, at least the French language and some rather minor cultural achievements, was mostly the fact that we were a very rural society; basically, a peasant society tied to the church and tied to tradition. One saying we have held for generations in Quebec is "The language is the guardian of religion", in other words, the English were Protestants and the French were Catholics. That was more or less a rule of thumb. Plus we were a peasant rural-based social structure. Over a hundred years ago Montreal was mostly an English city, and even Quebec city which is 95 percent or more French was at least in good proportion English. That kept, basically like a museum piece, the French language and traditions going. Quebec's birth rate was extremely high as it is in peasant or underdeveloped societies, and that's what we were in many ways. Things are different now. Since the Second World War there has been a sort of acceleration of development in Quebec, notably in education (what was called the quiet revolution). The old fashioned traditional crutches just broke down. For example, the church is practically non-existent; certainly it is not a framing influence anyway. The same with rural life. The peasant-based society has practically disappeared. Quebec is a part of North America, which has changed more rapidly than any other place. From country people to city people. All the old traditional reasoning, the traditional vision of French cultural survival has broken down. What's going on now is a modernization, let's say a catching up process with ups and downs. We have a very fragile cultural identity now that we're not tied to religion, not tied to a traditional outlook or a country-based outlook of being homogenized by big cities. Out of all this is growing a new identity, a new cultural identity and this is what the PQ is working on. What we had before were people who called themselves French Canadians, but French Canadians were just another minority. Now the French people are becoming conscious that they themselves are really a national majority and that they better get themselves an institutional framework to replace what broke down 20 years ago.

Socialism Growing

Q: You've worked with the Liberal Party; you were a part of the Mouvement Souverainete Association; you've held some different and varying political views. Now as the leader of a very solid party—the Parti Quebecois—don't you fear having to cater to individual socialistic philosophies within the party? Won't this slow down the process of creating an institutional framework?

A: I don't see it that way, that we'll have to cater to socialists. "Creeping Socialism" is all over the place, it all depends on how you adapt to it. We're going to become more and more socialistic if we want to survive. That, in a sense, is world wide. . . .

After Victory

Q: How would you go about creating a central bank for Quebec?

A: Quebec is not completely underdeveloped. A central bank is not exactly like creating the world. You have for instance *"Les Caisses des peuples"* which has well over 3 billion dollars accumulated, a pension fund. It administrates open market operations and does it as well as anyone else.

We have competent people and the creation of a central bank is not the end of the world.

Q: All right, what if the Royal Bank with 12 billion dollars, the 8th or 9th largest bank in the world, were to withdraw all its capital from Quebec?

A: All *its* monies they can get out and the sooner the better. But Quebec money, Quebec owned assets, will they go out with that?

Q: The Royal Bank's Head Office is here in Montreal. Its accumulated assets are from across Canada, not just Quebec. What about loans, investments in Quebec corporations?

A: Loans will have to be honored and things like that, but look, why make it such a problem when it will only be a technical operation once we've made a political decision. The Government is set up in Quebec, a referendum is held, people say yes or no. . . . We want it or we want out, if we want out then Canada has a decision to make. Are they going to use the army, in other words, dishonor themselves? We're making a gamble that Canada can normally accept a political decision that will be very clear. Once that's made there'll be a transition period with problems—taxes become Quebec taxes, the banking system becomes a Quebec banking system, trust companies (if they are allowed to continue) will become Quebec based trust companies—and that's it. I mean it was done in Jamaica, it was done in Nigeria, it was done in Kenya, so why the hell shouldn't it be done in Quebec? There are at least a hundred different models over the last thirty years of countries doing it, so it's not the end of the world.

Q: You raised an interesting point about the Canadian Armed Forces and this is really the only firm control Trudeau has over Quebec.

A: There are basically two ways in changing political organizations, one is guns and the other is votes. If ever Canada should have the temptation against a clear decision in Quebec to use guns, then woe to Canada.

P.Q. Not Majority

Q: Vallieres said the majority of all the Quebecois are separatists. Is that true?

A: No. If Vallieres said that he meant deep down, past the frustrations every Quebecois has the old dream of independence. I would say even the most rabid Quebec federalist, if you were able to scratch down to his basic beliefs would say "oh well, maybe tomorrow, but we're not ready now, perhaps one day it should happen". I suppose on that basis of dreams 80 percent are separatists. If that's what Vallieres talks about he's right. If he's talking about nowadays—everybody knows we're not a majority, but we're growing.

Q: Disregarding fanciful philosophies, Mr. Levesque, and all the "open-eyed" dreams of the Parti Quebecois, what do you think your growth capacity is?

A: Look, I'll give you an example, suppose we win, it'll be a bare majority because it's hard to change institutions and it's hard to change a regime that's over a hundred years old, so we win with a 45-50 percent of the vote, then we form a government and there has to be negotiations and pressure and counter pressure and eventually a referendum on what people want. Eventually Quebec officially becomes a country, then it's not 50 percent but 80 percent of the Quebecois who will say, "... oh, it's not the end of the world, now it's done, now we believe in it because it answers an old normal dream," but in the meantime it's one hell of a job.

●　　　●　　　●

Peaceful Revolution

Q: Once you have raised the consciousness of the Quebec people to believe in "great expectations", what happens to the store clerk in Trois Rivières who you've turned into a violent revolutionary? How is he supposed to return to his old role? Or can he?

A: Firstly, a basic revolution doesn't mean you have to kill people, a revolution is simply a change that occurs within a hundred years, in other words a rather quick change is a revolution. It can be guns, it can be votes, but the real revolution is that people change their minds—their outlook towards something new. That's a revolution. You have cultural revolutions, you have political revolutions, and they can be tied together, in the sense that we want to change the basic political institutions, in the sense that we want to take the French culture from being just a "hanger on" in North America to becoming its own home and developing it as we think it should, in the sense that we want a society that would be a hell of a lot fairer than now. We want to have co-management of enterprise, in other words we want to see people who are the labor capital to have as much say as the people who are money capital. That's a long process; even unions don't know how to tackle that because they're used to fighting the boss. And all this means a sort of revolution. So in that sense we are making people revolutionaries.

A: Again, let's assume you're the leader of the first national Quebec government, what happens if you find you can't fill all the promises you've made and you can't adhere to all the philosophical principles you've set?

A: Well, supposing we win the next election and over a transition period the Parti Quebecois is in power and I'm there, all right, and four or five years later they kick us out, well, someone else takes over, what the hell.

Q: But in the meantime haven't you created a lot of problems, a lot of violence out of peace? i.e., the American Revolution of 1776 was started by a handful of revolutionaries, it wasn't supported by a majority at all.

A: But that was a civil war, I mean a war of Independence fought by the Americans to oust the British.

Verbal War

Q: Exactly, now instead of guns as weapons you're using words and ideologies as the weapons to free yourself from the colonial identity.

A: Yes, we're talking about wars; politics under a different guise, yes well it's always some sort of a war, but if you can keep it verbal it can kill less people won't it? But it's always war in a sense, yes you're right. Right now we're verbally warring against the Federal system and the Bourassa Liberals. I don't know of any other way of getting a result.

Q: Even verbal wars create some sort of violent reaction. Mr. Levesque, all you have to do is look at a map of Montreal, to see the first steps of a reaction; the English are segregated in areas like Hampstead and Notre Dame de Grace and the Quebecois in Montreal East, etc.

English and Immigrants

A: Out of 6 million people in Quebec only about 750,000 are English-speaking. Quebec is made up of many ethnic groups and we have finally come to the decision we weren't going to become one of them. Look, a Jewish family moves in, an Italian family moves in, a Greek family moves in and 9 out of 10 of them will join the English group, they assimilate themselves with the English while still maintaining their Jewish, Italian and Greek heritage, but they prefer to linguistically join the English group which immediately ties them to the English majority. In other words they're in Quebec as a sort of ghetto tied to Ottawa, Toronto, New York or simply to the English-speaking American continent. It's more productive, more profitable for them to do that. So when you see us, based on a French majority in Quebec, trying to yank Quebec out of Canada, well, the ethnic groups don't like it because it's pulling them out of a majority situation. So you say there's tension, bad feeling in some fields, well if these few hundreds of thousands of people don't like it, then they can get the hell out. If they want to live with us they'll share equal rights. We're not going to stop promoting our own nationalism just because some guys don't like it, the hell with that. There's bad feeling tied to that but we can't help it. There was more frustration and more god-damn exploitation for the French majority over generations by people who stepped on their heads and told them to speak "white" than you can imagine, but you weren't there. Now we're not even telling the English to speak French, we're even guaranteeing them schools if they want to stay here, but if they stay here they become a minority, an official, definite and final minority. If they don't like it when the day comes, then the hell with them. We're not going to go down the drain just because some Italian or English group doesn't want Quebec to make its own decision.

People are Learning

Q: The television behind you, Mr. Levesque, when the waiter saw you come in he switched the channel from an English station to a French station.

A: I didn't notice.

Q: Yes, but have you noticed that people, especially the Quebecois, are individualists out for themselves, perhaps for economic gain, who knows, but it appears to me that the movement you helped create promotes a communal identity "vive la nation de Quebéc," but in reality people are only interested in what they personally own.

A: I don't think we can change that, at least not in the foreseeable future. Everybody is going to keep on being number one, I guess, and out for himself. But, what is sinking in Quebec is that even if you are an individualist and you still call yourself a Quebecois or part of a French speaking group it is more profitable for you to be part of a dominant healthy society than to be a minority and considered inferior.

A lot of people are learning that.

A lot of people are learning.

THE PROGRAM OF THE PARTI QUEBECOIS*

Political Life in a Sovereign Quebec

. . . A nation is notably characterized by the homogeneity of the people living in the same territory. Now, four centuries of a common history have made Quebecers a NATION. Quebecers have an indisputable desire to live together and to preserve their own culture as it has been enriched by the contributions of each ethnic group which has chosen to live with us. We furthermore maintain to respect these cultural groups, to see them fully participate in the life of Quebec so that they may develop in complete freedom.

Meanwhile, Quebec does not yet have the political levers which will give it the means to guarantee its cultural and economic existence. In effect, the power is exercised at the federal parliament by a foreign majority, and with one government of eleven in the federal-provincial conferences, Quebec is always a minority in Canada. No people can run the risk of entrusting its destiny to others.

Quebecers have all the necessary human and material resources in order to assume their political independence, to conciliate that with an open, necessary interdependence with other nations. The real government of Quebec must therefore be in Quebec and it must be rid of all obstacles which inhibit its proper development. This is why the sovereignty of Quebec constitutes the base of the policies of the Parti Quebecois.

The Accession to Independence

In the program of the Parti Quebecois, the accession to independence is based on the right of self-rule, that is to say on the right of people to decide themselves, by democratic means, their own political regime.

In consequence, a government of the Parti Quebecois undertakes to:
1) Put the processes of accession to sovereignty into action immediately

---

* From *Summary of the Programme and the Statutes of the Parti Québécois*, May, 1975, provided by the P.Q. in 1976.

by proposing to the National Assembly, shortly after its election, a law authorizing a demand to Ottawa for the return of all powers to Quebec, with the exception of those which the two governments would like to give to a common organism, in order to develop an economic association.

2) In the case where it is necessary to unilaterally proceed, assume the exercise of all powers of a sovereign state, methodically, by assuring the approval of all Quebecers by a **referendum**.

3) Present a national constitution to the people.

4) Request the admission of Quebec into the United Nations and obtain the recognition of other nations.

The Political Regime: an Authentic Democracy

. . . a government of the Parti Quebecois undertakes to:

1—Present a **constitutional draft** comprising:

A—A declaration of the rights of man inspired by the Universal Declaration of the United Nations dedicated to:

1) the rights of the individual and his corporal safety;

2) equality before the law, the presumption of innocence, and a just procedure in penal matters;

3) the rights of liberty of thought, of opinion, and of religion;

4) the right to be informed;

5) the rights to work, to recreation, to health, to lodging and a satisfactory level of life;

6) the right to education;

7) the right to culture.

B—The institution of a republic with a presidential government.

C—The freedom for political parties to exercise their activities and to participate in electoral processes respecting the democratic principles.

D—Adopt a law concerning referendums, guaranteeing that any option offered will be clear and distinct, not ambiguous, permitting the expression of a **real choice**.

2—Recognize as Quebecers, at the moment of the declaration of independence, all Canadian citizens living in Quebec, including all New Canadians. In the case of landed immigrants, the processes of acquiring their Quebec citizenship will proceed normally under the Quebec rule, in the respect of their acquired rights in the immigration process.

3—Maintain the office of Ombudsman.

The Electoral System

With the coming of independence, the Parti Quebecois will institute a democratic system which will reflect the true desires of the people.

To do this, the actual electoral system, for the most part maintained in the present form, will be modified in order to improve the representation of the different recognized political formations and to remove the influence of certain **interest groups** who try to **usurp** and manipulate by means of contributions to electoral funds.

In consequence, a government of the Parti Quebecois undertakes to:

1) Maintain the actual manner of voting by adding a formula of partial proportional representation.

2) Equalize the electoral laws which regulate the national and local elections by using only one electoral office, one permanent electoral list; furnish a voter's card and establish voting bureaus in public places.

3) Assure the democratization of political parties by obliging the detailed publication of all their **expenses** and **all sources of income**, and by establishing public financing for essential services of research and documentation for the recognized parties.

Impartial and More Accessible Justice

Despite certain recent reforms, our judicial system is still characterized by its slowness, its inaccessibility, its ancient structures, the harsh nature of its punishments, and the lack of coordination and of specialization in its police forces. . . .

In consequence, a government of the Parti Quebecois undertakes to:

1) Place the judicial system above any suspicion:

    a) by expanding the administrative autonomy to the judicial power;

    b) by adapting a code of ethics for the magistrature which defines the rights and duties of judges, to provide for sanction of derogatory acts and determine the mechanism of the normal or premature retiring and that of dismissal of judges.

2) Facilitate the access to justice:

    a) by immediately transforming, in penal and criminal matters, the present regime of judicial aid to a free and universal service of judicial security . . . this service will be administered by a public organism and the lawyers in this employ will enjoy a professional freedom equal to their fellow lawyers in the private sector and will be salaried by the organism of the state; the right of the individual to choose his lawyer will be maintained and any person may, at his own cost, decide for the private sector.

    b) by a better geographical division of judicial services by decentralizing the public judicial services and favorizing a more equitable division of lawyers all over Quebec, to the needs of its prime expansion.

3) See that all citizens, by means of the public schools and mass methods of communication, are informed of their rights and informed concerning the laws which rule them.

Foreign Policies and Interdependence of the States

. . . a government of the Parti Quebecois undertakes to:

1) Promote the freedom of people and the respect of national characters at the same time of an international collaboration founded upon justice, progress and peace; reject all forms of new colonization in international relations; avoid being a party of guarantee for all regimes that do not respect the United Nations Charter of the Rights of Man.

2) Respect the principle of non-interference in the interior affairs of another State.

3) Establish cooperative ties and good relations with the international community.

4) Create a unit of research and supervision, pertaining to the National Assembly, which will oversee the elimination of political intervention by multi-national companies in Quebec.

Economic Life in a Sovereign Quebec

. . . a government of the Parti Quebecois undertakes to:
1) Bring back the principal centers of decision-making to Quebec by giving priority approval to public and cooperative enterprises.
2) Democratize the operation of the economy by favoring the collective bodies and by assuring the participation of the workers in decision-making operations.
3) Base the economic policies on human and social objectives, and, to do this, to establish an economic system which eliminates all forms of exploitation of the workers.
4) Assure each citizen a **guaranteed minimum wage**.
5) Work towards complete employment (0% unemployment).
6) Assure the distribution of information by making public the economic dossiers of the government and by requiring all incorporated enterprises and syndicate head offices to publish their financial statements.

Finances

. . . a government of the Parti Quebecois undertakes to:
1) Bring back to Quebec all taxes now received by Ottawa from the territory of Quebec and furnish the Quebec citizens all services (including benefits, such as the different allowances and pensions) which are now distributed by Ottawa.
2) Reduce gradually the differences of income by different ways, so that the graduated tax and its annual indexation to the cost of living, to protect the buying power of all consumers.
3) Exempt from all income tax those whose earnings do not exceed the guaranteed minimum salary, to insure an incentive to work.
4) Change the sales tax now applied at the manufacturer and consolidate it with the retail sales tax, in order to exempt **foodstuffs**, **medicines**, **rent** and essential services, but tax other services.
5) Abolish property taxes for school purposes and use in their stead regular income of the State, assuring equalization for less fortunate areas.

Businesses

. . . a government of the Parti Quebecois undertakes to:
1) Promote an unceasing growth of the public sector (State and mixed enterprises) in the areas where the impact will be important for the orientation of economic development.
2) Promote, by technical and financial aid, the development of cooperative businesses especially in the sectors concerning the welfare and consumers services.
3) Distribute public support in order to promote the growth of the

cooperative sector and the development of new and immediate avant-garde industries, of research, and of exporting capacities. If the business is not of a cooperative nature, to accord these grants, always making them public, in the form of contribution and voting shares.

4) Establish a code of investments listing the businesses in which the shares are held by non-residents, to gather within the framework of these rules the foreign participation in the economic development of Quebec . . .

5) Non-residents require the approval of the Quebec National Assembly in the case of all transactions which would have the effect of transferring a business to interests outside of Quebec.

6) Authorize the Society of Industrial Reorganization or any other organism created for this purpose to take to its accounts all profitable enterprises which close their doors or move out of Quebec. In addition, we will allow the workers to buy back the business . . .

Public Services

. . . a government of the Parti Quebecois undertakes to:

1) Spread free health services or other goods and services to all, so far as the cost can be lessened if it is assumed collectively.

2) Reorganize the area of transports by bringing together the railroads and by unifying the interior airlines and their extensions to the exterior, into two unified systems operated by two enterprises to be mainly public; by regulating navigation in the territorial waters of Quebec, by favorising [sic] the creation of a merchant fleet by re-grouping businesses and maintaining the navigability of the St. Lawrence year-around.

3) Reorganize the area of communications:

a) by creating a society of communications by regrouping, under mainly public control, the different networks of telecommunications (micro-waves, cable, satellites);

b) by extending a shared administration (governmental and cooperative) for cable diffusion enterprises to all the territory of Quebec.

4) Establish a general framework of regulations concerning energy, by specifying the roles of public enterprises which are the instruments of its realization;

a) to maintain for Hydro-Quebec the monopoly in the production and distribution of electricity.

b) to widen the scope of SOQUIP to make it one of the principal agents of petroleum exploration in Quebec as well as of importing, refining and the distribution of petroleum products.

c) to entrust the natural gas system to a mainly public society and to see to the expansion of this network.

Financial Institutions

. . . a government of the Parti Quebecois undertakes to:

1) Assure the democratization of the financial systems in making sure that the shares in financial institutions are primarily acquired by co-

operative institutions, public powers and the Quebec citizens.

2) Preserve the existence of financial institutions in a manner which assures the individual the control of his savings and the choice among different types of investments.

3) Create a central bank at the head of the Quebec financial system.

4) Expand the dimension of the **Caisse de Dépôt et de Placement**, by entrusting the handling of funds of all retirement funds in the public and para-public sectors. . . .

5) Complete the financial system of Quebec by public institutions specialized in the areas of farm and forest, of commercial fishing, hotel and tourism, exporting and importing, commercial and industrial expansion.

6) Abolish private small loans companies (so-called "finance"), forbid private financial societies . . .

7) Entrust the duty of consumer credit to public financial institutions and to cooperative financial movements . . .

8) Establish a public regime of automobile insurance which shall be complete and obligatory.

9) Assure, according to the need, by legislative means that the savings of Quebecers channelled into financial institutions are reinvested for the most part in Quebec.

Economic Development

. . . a government of the Parti Quebecois undertakes to:

1) Modernize and restructure the economy of Quebec by giving the necessary means of action. To accomplish this reorganization and this new start within a framework of a PLAN elaborated by representatives, of equal number, of workers and other parts of the population, of enterprises and public powers.

2) The PLAN will be elaborated as follows: the objectives of the PLAN will be determined beginning with the expressed needs of a multitude of local and sectorial planning committees, composed of representatives of all groups concerned and brought on afterwards to the council of l'OPQ (Office du Plan du Québec).

3) Respect and make respected the direct lines of the PLAN.

●   ●   ●

Foreign Economic Relations

. . . a government of the Parti Quebecois undertakes to:

1) Recognize the principle of free traffic of goods between the Quebec and Canadian markets: to this end, to renounce, with the reciprocity of the other party, the establishment of custom duties between the two, all by looking forward to a regime particularly concerning agricultural commodities.

2) Discuss and conclude, if that is the wish of the parties, a treaty of customs union.

3) Look forward to, together with all parties with which Quebec may be joined by treaty, the establishment of a larger area of free exchange.
4) Respect the "General Agreement of Tariffs and Trade" (GATT) foreseeing a freezing or reduction of customs fees and a renuniciation of their increase in a large number of lands.
5) Respect the rules of international law in the elaboration of our international economic policy.

Social Life in a Sovereign Quebec

. . . a government of the Parti Quebecois undertakes to:
1) Assure to all citizens, including older people, a **guaranteed minimum** wage which will be indexed to the cost of living and the growth of the national product at least twice a year.
2) Compensate the heads of families by establishing a sufficient family allowance system and by financially compensating the partner of the family who is in charge of the work of the home.
3) Recognize the contribution to society of the mother by the birth of her children by giving a benefit separate from the household income.
4) Enact a public network of free kindergartens and day-care centers devoted to the development of the child and run by professional family aides. The administration of these centers will be confided to the users and to the personnel. This network will be available to all without discrimination and may receive children of all groups. An adequate transportation service is also foreseen.
5) Develop the service of family helpers to satisfy basic domestic needs.

Working Conditions and Relations

. . . a government of the Parti Quebecois undertakes to:
1) Bring immediately (May 1, 1975) a minimum salary of $3.00 per hour in all regions of Quebec for all salary categories; and then, index this minimum rate to the rise of the cost of living and to the growth of the national product.
2) Assure a minimum period of four weeks vacation each year to each full-time employee, which may be taken consecutively if he so wishes.
3) Recognize the equality of men and women at work:
    a) by assuring to women, without discrimination, access to trades and professions, in the respect of the rule: "equal work, equal pay".
    b) by according to pregnant women a maternity-leave which, at her discretion, may last up to six months, during which she will receive benefits at least equal to the guaranteed minimum salary; at the end of the leave, the woman may take up her work without losing her acquired rights.
4) Permit the worker to retire at the age of 55.
5) Protect the health and life of the worker . . .
6) Guard that each worker, on prolonged unemployment or obliged to change his employ, will receive financial aid sufficient for his needs and those of his family during his recycling period.

. . . a government of the Parti Quebecois undertakes to:

1) Recognize syndicalism as a normal and indispensable element of economic, social and political life of Quebec.

2) Facilitate the regroupment of all employees in syndical organizations of their choice, by speeding up the procedures of accreditation.

3) Make the application of the Rand formula obligatory (to oblige the employer to withhold union dues from the time of the hiring of a new employee).

4) Impose severe sanctions on all employers or all syndical organizations who use forms of intimidation, physical violence, or discriminatory measures to prevent the employees from choosing their union, and, on the other hand, abolish shop unions, that is, not democratic and controlled by the employer.

5) Assure to all unions the possibility of requiring the respect of the democratic union, first in the interior of normal structures, and afterwards, by an efficient procedure of appeal.

6) Favorise [*sic*], in law and in fact, the development of democratic forms of growth in a manner in which the workers exercise a progressive partial or complete control on the functioning of their enterprise, by various formulas depending upon the sector.

7) Assure that a legal strike produces a halt to production of the unit concerned by negotiation.

●   ●   ●

Health

. . . It is therefore necessary for us to complete the scheme of health insurance to include all disciplines of medicine and surgery, even the other therapeutic disciplines which are legally recognized. It is also necessary to rationalize, democratize and improve the regional distribution of health establishments and social services, and the quality of these establishments and services.

Cultural and Ethnic Groups

The Language

. . . a government of the Parti Quebecois undertakes to:

1) Make French the only official language of Quebec in the manner which, after a maximum transition period of five years, French becomes the only language of the state.

2) Legislate that French effectively becomes the language of work and communications, notably between the personnel concerned by collective agreements and the management of business.

3) Guarantee to all Quebec workers, of all origins, the right to work in French.

4) Require that new immigrants register their children in public French-Language schools and that within five years of their arrival they

successfully pass an examination of the French language, which will also be one of the conditions for the obtaining of a permanent visa or of Quebec citizenship.

Education

. . . a government of the Parti Quebecois undertakes to:
1) Abolish the property taxes for school purposes and use regular income of the state for financement by assuring the equalization of less fortunate areas.
2) Reform the educational system so that it becomes a real tool of social advancement for the workers beginning with their experience.
3) Institute the obligatory teaching of Quebec history at the elementary and secondary levels in all learning institutions in Quebec.
4) Consider, as a priority, the training of teachers which will encourage a maximum professional competence and permanent recycling.
5) a) At the university and CEGEP level, assure the equal participation of students and teachers in the pedagogical decisions.

    b) Assure the participation of interested sectors of the work areas in order to know their needs and their problems in the matters of manpower.
6) Develop technical training, notably by the creation of technical universities or institutes of higher studies in order to assure the training of engineers and management specialized in secondary industries and the new, growing industries: to encourage the industries to give apprentice courses completing the professional training of the students.
7) Institute free education at all levels of teaching; to extend the obligatory school age to 18 years, and establish a coherent system of scholarships and grants.
8) Consecrate all monies now spent for elementary, secondary and university education to public institutions

•   •   •

The English-Speaking Minority in a Sovereign Quebec

. . . a government of the Parti Quebecois undertakes to:
1) Assure that at the first contact with the Bureau of Quebec Immigration in foreign countries, the future emigrant will be completely informed concerning the cultural, economic, and social policies of Quebec.
2) Guarantee to the English-speaking minority its own school institutions at all levels of learning within the following framework:

    a) The number of places will be fixed by a school board, in regards to the English-speaking population as determined in the primary general census.

    b) If, after a later census, the percentage is found to have decreased, the percentage of the budget of the Minister of Education devoted to the English-language school services will diminish in the same percentage.

    c) The English-language school institutions must furnish to their students an effective teaching of the French-language, respecting the norms established by the Ministry of Education.

3) Require that all the new immigrants of all origins send their children to French-language schools.

4) Assure that the public network and the private radio and television stations broadcast cultural programming addressed to all ethnic groups.

5) Require that new immigrants of all origins show a sufficient knowledge of the French language to obtain their Quebec citizenship.

•   •   •

THE BATTLE OF THE BALANCE SHEETS—HAS QUEBEC GAINED OR LOST MONEY?*

Paul Fox

April 6, 1977—With Ottawa's reply today to the P.Q. government's recent charge that Canada has drained $4.3 billion out of Quebec during 15 years, the battle of the balance sheets has begun.

Before the question of Quebec's separation is settled conclusively, we may expect to hear many more such claims and counter-claims. They are all part of the propaganda war being fought for Quebec's independence.

When Premier René Lévesque held a press conference after his government's presentation of the controversial report in the National Assembly on March 25, reporters were visibly impressed by the 222-page document.

Entitled "Economic Account of Quebec: Revenues and Expenditures: Annual Estimates, 1961-1975," the report swamped the press with a flood of figures and data. The journalists present were swept away. They did not stop to question the findings critically. As a matter of fact, most of them hardly looked at the report. What they quoted from most often was a statement read by Mr. Lévesque and a summary of the report presented by one of his ministers, both of which distorted the contents of the report.

The summary issued by Industry and Commerce Minister Rodrique Tremblay, former chairman of the Department of Economics at the University of Montreal, alleged that for 13 of the 15 years between 1961 and 1975 the federal government extracted much more money from Quebec than it returned to the province.

Citing the figures in the report that showed a federal "surplus" of $4.3 billion by 1975, Premier Lévesque claimed that allowing for inflation and translating the sum into 1975 dollars, the "deficit" would amount to $8.6 billion.

"In other words, the federal government bled the economy of Quebec for about half a billion dollars per year," the P.Q. leader said.

Premier Lévesque's lurid language and his magic method of multiplication indicate that the report is being used to reinforce the current prop-

* Prepared by the author in April, 1977.

aganda compaign to persuade Quebec's population to vote "yes" in the P.Q.'s promised future referendum on independence.

One of the key tables in the report asserts that the federal government garnered the following series of "surpluses" from Quebec:

Year:	Surplus (in millions):	Year	Surplus (in millions)
1961	$591	1968	$530
1962	588	1969	759
1963	588	1970	515
1964	720	1971	274
1965	686	1972	103
1966	764	1973	163
1967	595		

In the next two years the table acknowledges that the balance ran the other way. Quebec apparently acquired a "profit" of $542 million in 1974 and $2,021 million in 1975. However, Mr. Lévesque was quick to explain that this favourable balance was the result of Ottawa's oil-import subsidy and deficit spending.

When questioned by reporters, Mr. Tremblay admitted that the table of federal expenditures in his department's report did not include Ottawa's spending for the benefit of all Canadians. These items would include federal disbursements for defence, foreign aid, external affairs, the Bank of Canada, the department of finance, justice and other federal departments, except for salaries paid in Quebec or sums spent on the purchases of goods and services in the province.

Omissions like these reveal the confusion and propaganda in the way the report is used to give a one-sided picture. The statistics state only the fiscal relationships between the two governments—the gap between the federal taxes Quebecers pay and Ottawa's direct spending in the province.

But there is more to the story than that comparison. As even Mr. Tremblay allowed, his study was not "a complete balance sheet of federalism."

Every taxpayer in Canada has to pay for his share of the services he receives from Ottawa. The P.Q. argument implies either that Quebec residents should not have to pay for these benefits, or else that the services are worthless or unnecessary.

Since such services are essential in any developed country, they obviously are not without value. If Ottawa were not around to provide them, Quebec would have to pay for them.

Yet Mr. Tremblay did not include them in his reckoning. He said, "If the federal government spends $1 billion on foreign aid and it is not channelled through Quebec, that does not appear in the economic account."

The ministerial statements also ignored the "spin-off" effects from huge federal spending in the province. To take examples, dollars spent on defence installations in Quebec or the St. Lawrence Seaway or invested in regional economic expansion, circulate through the provincial economy like life-giving blood. They stimulate and sustain local businesses by being spent many times over on food, clothing, housing, entertainment, and many other consumer goods. It is very hard to measure the precise results of such expenditures on a province's economy, but when they amount to hundreds of millions of dollars a year, they are obviously of tremendous importance.

Ottawa's reply today to Quebec's assertions are contained in a 24-page analysis released by the federal Minister of Industry, Trade, and Commerce, Jean Chretien.

The federal document, "Preliminary Observations on the Economic Accounts of Quebec," claims that the Quebec study overestimated grossly the size of indirect taxes paid by Quebecers from 1961 to 1975 by $4.2 billion. This amount is almost exactly equal to the sum which Quebec says it lost to Ottawa.

Included in the $4.2 billion total are all sales taxes and excise duties collected in Quebec by the federal government when goods were imported into Quebec. But since many of these goods were ultimately consumed in other provinces, Ottawa argues that the taxes were actually passed on to those purchasers living outside of Quebec, and therefore not paid by Quebecers at all.

According to the federal paper, the Quebec report also underestimated expenditures in Quebec by federal crown corporations located there, such as Air Canada, Canadian National Railways, and the Canadian Broadcasting Corporation.

Pushing its analysis further, the Ottawa study says that federalism has benefitted Quebec rather than damaging it. The province's gross domestic product rose 4.5 per cent annually from 1961 to 1975 while in the same period real personal income increased by 5.4 per cent a year.

The report says, "from 1961 to 1975, total payments made by the federal government to individuals in Quebec rose from $973 million in 1975 dollars to $2,931 million." Ottawa's payments to the provincial government increased at the same time from $435 million to $2.2 billion.

A layman may be forgiven for wondering where the truth lies in this welter of statistics. As Mark Twain said, "There are lies, darn lies, and statistics." What is clear is that politicians will make maximum use out of whatever facts can be twisted to their advantage. The original Quebec report seems to have been a rather straightforward and qualified presentation of some of the facts in the case. It is the politicians who turned it into a battle of the balance sheets.

IN DEFENCE OF FEDERALISM*

Pierre-Elliott Trudeau

. . . Strictly from the point of view of economic objectives, the question is not to determine whether Quebec will govern itself by means of a sovereign state, or remain integrated with Canadian society, or will be joined to the United States. . . . What is important, in the last analysis, is for it to make sure that its *per capita* income will increase at the fastest possible speed; and, to achieve that, Quebec's economy must become extremely efficient, technologically advanced, fairly specialized, and capable of putting the best products at the best price on all the world's markets.

In fact, our province has too limited a population to support *alone* a modern industrial development, based on mass production and benefitting from the great economics of scale. By necessity, we have to depend on non-Quebec markets, and for that reason we have to be able to meet all competition.

In concrete terms that means that Quebec's economy must in no way be isolated, but rather integrated in a wider complex where we will find at the same time both markets and competitors.

Now it is very important to note that, whatever one says, most of the constitutional uproar at present in vogue in our province leans towards isolation. Thus some people are proposing to give the government of Quebec jurisdiction (more or less exclusive over) banks, immigration, the employment of labour, foreign trade, tariffs and customs, and many other things. This may be a praiseworthy goal—seizing one's economic destinies—but from all the evidence, it also indicates a desire to use legal instruments to protect our capital, our business men, and our higher ranks of management from foreign competition. That's a sure way to make our factors of production inefficient, and to ensure that our products will be rejected by foreign markets. Quebec will then have to require its consumers to "Buy at home" to dispose of its products, and finally it will be the workers and farmers who will have to pay the dearest for them (either in prices or in subsidies). This line of reasoning applies just as well to steel as to blueberries, and it's erroneous to think that working people have some long run advantage in being converted into a captive market.

•   •   •

In a general way, the present constitution gives to the provinces, hence to Quebec, wide jurisdiction over matters that will permit them to obtain the objectives [they want]. The provinces have complete jurisdiction over

* Translation by the editor of a portion of speech entitled "Le réalisme constitutionnel," given by the author to the founding Convention of the Quebec section of the Liberal Federation of Canada (QLF), in Quebec City, March 26, 1966. By permission of the author, who at the time of writing was the Member of Parliament for Mount Royal and a Parliamentary Secretary to the former Prime Minister Lester B. Pearson, and who is now the Prime Minister of Canada.

education, and it is above all by that means that labour and management can acquire the scientific and financial knowledge that will enable them to act efficiently in an industrial age. . . .

•   •   •

Welfare objectives sometimes conflict with economic objectives. . . . It would be too simple if one could merely say: welfare first, economics second. But one must be careful: scarcely any state can transgress with impunity the laws of economics and technology. Any state that would try to do it, for praiseworthy welfare objectives, would impoverish its economy and by the same act make the welfare goals unattainable. In fact, a determinedly progressive welfare policy can be devised and applied only if the economy is fundamentally sound. All social welfare measures, from children's allowances to old age pensions and forthcoming free education and health insurance, will be dead letters if the economic infrastructure is not capable of carrying the load and paying the cost of such programs. . . . In short, it is necessary to oppose the dislocation of the country because it would have the effect of weakening our economy and consequently of making it less able to pursue the welfare objectives and to pay for their cost.

Moreover, the Canadian constitution recognizes the widest provincial responsibility for social welfare matters. It allows each provincial government to apply in its own area the social philosophy that best suits its population. The diversity that results from this can provoke a healthy emulation among the provinces in the taxes and the benefits that will thus fall upon their respective taxpayers. Canadian federalism offers its citizens multiple choice, which adds to their democratic liberties. Within the whole Canadian economy, labour and capital will tend to move towards the mixture of fiscal burdens and social services that suit them best. Obviously, for reasons of language, the French-Canadian taxpayer will be relatively less mobile, but this is all the more reason for the Quebec government to choose with care and as democratically as possible its welfare and fiscal policies. . . .

•   •   •

. . . I would prefer to safeguard in every possible way the freedom and diversity that are offered by the decentralization of federalism. That is why I think it is urgent to negotiate agreements among provinces for the purpose of establishing at least in the large industrial provinces certain minimal standards of welfare legislation.

In this connection I can only see as incongruous and premature the preoccupation in certain quarters with constitutional reforms that would permit the provinces to conclude by themselves foreign treaties. As long as Quebec, for example, has not concluded with other Canadian provinces agreements on trade union legislation, is it very urgent, is it even economically wise to bind itself by conventions in respect to standards established in other countries? Moreover, Quebec is always invited to have representatives on Canadian delegations to the International Labour Organization, and our province has never grasped how to field a team that could ensure continued and serious participation.

In an analogous realm, the province just recently has been able to enter into certain agreements with France, without overstepping constitutional legality. I agree obviously with this sort of formal arrangement whereby Quebec can gain the greatest benefits; but I am not otherwise over-whelmed by "the image" that Quebec can project on the international stage. I think, for instance, that Quebec has better things to do than to appear at all the UNESCO meetings, while serious negotiations have not been undertaken with a neighbouring province relative to the education of the French-speaking minority there.

My second remark involves those provinces that are too poor to be able by themselves to reach minimal standards of social welfare. Under the existing constitution the central government can mitigate these inade-quacies by means of equalization payments, and this arrangement has to remain. From this point of view, I regret the last year between Quebec and Ottawa about the sharing of federal tax revenues. A theory of taxation that doesn't take into account the needs of the recipients, and which seems to claim that a given group of taxpayers must receive in return at least the equivalent of what it pays for taxes, repudiates the whole redistributive functions of taxation, and declares itself to be irrevocably reactionary.

My third remark concerns the concepts of planning and counter-cyclical policy which both involve a kind of intervention by the state in economic processes, on behalf of welfare goals like full employment and planned development. . . . Under the Canadian constitutional system both sorts of policies assume a certain collaboration between the central government and the provincial governments. The first is no doubt chiefly responsible for the overall economy, but its actions can't be effective if they are not coordinated with those of the second. . . This paper suggests, not constitutional changes, but a more systematic recourse to consultation and agreements between the federal and provincial authorities. . . .

[In regard to cultural aims] let us propound first that what creates vitality and value in a language is the quality of the group that speaks it. The question which arises then is whether the French-speaking people in Canada must concentrate their efforts on Quebec, or whether they should take the whole of Canada as the base of their operations.

In my opinion, they must do both, and I believe that for this purpose they couldn't find a better device than federalism.

For cultural values, in order to be disseminated fully, require a nice blend of protection and non-interference by the state. On one hand, the state has to ensure the protection of cultural values which without it would run the risk of being engulfed by a flood of dollars, but on the other hand, cultural values, even more than those based on economics, wither away quickly if they are removed from the test of competition.

That is why, in the matter of cultural aims, Canadian federalism is ideal. While requiring French Canadians, in the federal sector, to submit their way of doing things (and especially their political forms) to the test of competition, the federal system allows us at the same time to provide for ourselves in Quebec the form of government and the educational institutions that best suit our needs.

•   •   •

That is the reason that I am for federalism. . . . With the exception perhaps of marriage and of radio and television broadcasting, federal jurisdiction applies almost exclusively to those areas where the cultural aspect is reduced to a minimum. . . .

The provinces, on their side, have jurisdiction over all those matters that are purely local and private—over education, natural resources, property and civil rights, municipal institutions, highways, welfare and labour legislation, and the administration of justice. . . .

At one extreme, Quebec has to flee from the temptation of isolation, where one could certainly feel safe from all danger, but would also be barred from progress. At the other extreme, I would be opposed to Quebec taking its stand in a unitary Canadian state, or annihilating itself in a bigger American melting-pot. Nationalism for nationalism, I don't think that a kind of pan-Canadianism or a pan-Americanism is less imbued with chauvinism than the French-Canadian sort! . . .

I can only condemn as irresponsible those who would like to see our people invest undetermined amounts of money, time, and energy in a constitutional adventure that they have not yet been able to state precisely, but which would consist more or less vaguely in scuttling Canadian federalism in order to substitute for it hazy designs of sovereignty from which would emerge something like an independent Quebec, or associated states, or a particular status, or a Canadian common market, or a confederation of 10 states, or something else to be invented in the future—that is after political, economic, and social chaos will have been guaranteed.

Canadian federalism must evolve, of course. But it certainly has been evolving, very substantially, in the last hundred years without the constitution requiring wholesale changes. Periods of great decentralization have alternated with periods of intense centralization in the course of our history, that is, according to the conjunction of social and economic forces, external pressures, and the strength and astuteness of our politicians. Now if there is any immediate basic fact in politics—and at the same time a verifiable proposition in most industrial countries—it is that the state is obliged today to devote a continually increasing portion of its continually increasing budget to those areas which, in the Canadian constitution, fall under the jurisdiction of the provincial governments. In other words, Canadian federalism is evolving at present towards a period of great decentralization.

This reality becomes more obvious if one looks at the total of governmental expenditures apart from transfer payments between governments. . . . [See Chapter 3, Federalism and Finances.]

Thus, demographic, social and economic forces are in the process of transferring to provincial governments an enormous addition in power, without having to change a single comma in the constitution. The fact that some of our French-Canadian politicians and intellectuals have chosen this precise moment to demand imperatively that the country provide itself with a new constitution seems to us to be extraordinarily untimely. . . .

SEPARATISM—CANADA'S DEATH WISH*

Paul Fox

The first thing to be noted about Quebec's current separatist movement is that it is not new. It is no exaggeration to say that the history of Canada as a nation is the story of one long-running battle against divisive forces which would split it apart. In Freudian terms, Canada's attempts to fulfil its urge to national life have been accompanied by a contrary destructive death urge.

As a people we have had to fight not only against climate, which has kept us isolated in pockets (especially in winter), but against geography as well. The dividing lines in North America run north and south rather than east and west along the Canadian-American border.

With their backs against the Applachian mountain range, Maritimers have found traditionally that they have had far more in common—in trade, in industries, in outlook—with New Englanders than with "Upper Canadians", as they still call the residents of central Canada. The latter find that they look south for business and pleasure rather than east or west. Montrealers and Torontonians will visit New York, Lake Placid, Buffalo, or Detroit, often before they visit even each other, let alone Halifax, Calgary, or Vancouver. Prairie folk drift across a border created by men rather than by nature when they go to Chicago or the Midwest; and British Columbians, on the far side of the forbidding Rocky Mountains, feel much closer to the American Pacific states, as they are, than to the rest of Canada.

These natural obstacles have bred strong local sentiments in Canada, and it is against these tendencies that the nation has had to struggle ever since its birth on July 1, 1867.

Confederation brought together three scattered, undeveloped and under-populated British colonies, Nova Scotia, New Brunswick, and "Canada", as the union of what are now Ontario and Quebec was called. Though two other Atlantic colonies were included in preliminary consultations, they would not join in forming the new dominion. Prince Edward Island pursued its separate way for another six years and Newfoundland did not enter until 1949.

Meanwhile, many of the citizens in two of the three charter Confederation colonies wanted to withdraw. So serious was the opposition to union by the New Brunswick government that it had to be pushed out of office by the British governor, to make way for a more favourable government

* Revised in May, 1976, from an article which appeared originally in the *Family Herald*, March 15, 1962. By permission.

whose election was secured by financial contributions from Upper Canada. Nova Scotia was no more enthusiastic. Halifax celebrated Canada's first national birthday by draping its main street in black, and in the federal election which followed the province as a whole elected 18 out of 19 MPs pledged to repeal the act of union.

Out west, in what was to be Manitoba, Louis Riel led a rebellion against encroachment from Ottawa and set up a short-lived republic. Sixteen years later he made a second attempt in the North-West Rebellion. British Columbia entered as a province in 1871 but haggling over the terms of union and threats to secede continued for years.

Here were examples of genuine separatism, expressed in deeds, not just in words. And the spirit is not dead yet. A ludicrous illustration occurred a few years ago when a tiny municipality in Northern Ontario threatened to withdraw from the province if it did not get the road it wanted.

Thus separatism as a sentiment in Canada is common. It is the obvious form of protest of local groups which feel their interests are being threatened by the larger national entity. It is the outlet psychologically for the frustrations of a minority which recognizes rationally that it must buckle under to the majority but cannot accept the inevitability of it without a desperate kick, like a child lashing out against an overwhelming parent.

This is not said to deride the cause of separatism, merely to explain it. On a broader scale, many Canadians today express the same emotion in fighting off the encircling embrace of the United States.

French-Canadian separatism is accentuated by differences in language and religion. The Gallic tongue and Roman Catholic faith mark off French Canadians distinctively from the Anglo-Saxon Protestant majority. But these are only attributes of their fundamental differences, and despite all the hullabaloo to preserve them, they are not the cause of Quebec's separatism. The fight is nothing less than an endeavour to maintain a way of life which is 350 years old, a separate and distinctive French identity in a sea of North American Anglo-Saxonism.

The depth and intensity of this distinctive culture is what has made separatism in Quebec the prototype of such movements, and the most traditional, enduring, and serious of its kind. The nearest analogy that comes to mind is the successful persistence for centuries of the Jewish people in preserving their Hebraic separateness in a world full of Gentiles.

Separatism in Quebec therefore is not new. It is a theme which has often been voiced in French-Canadian history, especially at critical moments, such as 40 years ago by the Abbé Lionel Groulx and those who dreamed of an independent republic of "Laurentie". . . .

But it would be a mistake for English Canadians to dismiss the current song of protest as one more turn on the same old gramophone record. It is the old refrain, but something new has been added also—a modern, accelerated tempo.

A revolution has occurred in Quebec recently. In the last few years Quebec has commenced going through a transformation which is more significant and shattering than anything that has occurred in French Canada since the conquest.

Industrialization, urbanization, and modernization have arrived in French Canada with a bang. In the short space of a few years Quebec has entered into a transition that has taken half a century to run its course in other parts of Canada. For years these forces were blocked by the traditionalist patterns of thought of church and state. This Old Regime, as it might well be called, was personified by the late Premier Maurice Duplessis. With his death in 1959 and the fall of his Union Nationale party from power in the election of June, 1960, the dam burst. New ideas, new forces came surging to the surface. Most of these poured into courses more constructive than separatism, but the general spill-over of energy revived separatism in some quarters and gave it fresh grounds to feed upon.

Thus the present separatist movement in Quebec is old and new at the same time. . . .

If the separatists succeeded and Quebec split off from Canada, could it maintain itself for long as a progressive, dynamic national state? Is it not a backward step to split into a smaller unit? The trend of evolution is from the single cell to the multi-cellular. The path of economic and political development in the world is towards integration, not disintegration. Witness the growth of corporations, trading blocks, and regional groupings of nations in Europe and elsewhere. This does not mean that individuality is lost sight of. We do not necessarily all become identical because we become more interrelated. There is still room for diversity in unity—the two are not mutually exclusive. In fact, integration may promote individual development. Is the average modern Frenchman, German, and Englishman not a more developed and distinctive human creature living at a higher level in contemporary integrating Europe than his ancestor was in a more divided and primitive medieval Europe?

The challenge for French Canadians is to retain their distinctiveness while still remaining Canadians in an expanding world. It is a challenge that English Canadians also face in their relationship to the United States. The feat for French Canadians is admittedly more difficult and they are deserving of sympathy and assistance in their attempt to be themselves while moving ahead together. Many of the separatists' complaints against English Canadians are justified. But the solution is not to reverse the process of history. Should Ontario depart from Canada because Ontario pays more taxes into the federal treasury than other provinces? Should Anglo-Saxon Protestants in Montreal become separatists and withdraw from Quebec if French Canada becomes a separate state? Many of the Separatists' arguments can be turned against them. Separatists should remember that not all the penalties for bi-culturalism are paid by the minority; English Canadians as well as French Canadians make sacrifices in the interest of national unity. . . .

NATIONALISM AND SOCIALISM
IN FRENCH CANADA*

Juris Dreifelds

Quebec's political culture changed drastically in the 1960s. Socialism, which for a variety of reasons never received much support in Quebec, has become much more popular. Nationalism, which has been a recurring phenomenon in Quebec, has also grown more acute and changed some of its characteristics. There are probably many reasons for this trend. However, the first and major force that helped initiate and amplify the change was the extremely rapid dissolution of the power of the Roman Catholic Church which lost much of its relevance and hold especially in the urban areas and among the younger age groups. The erosion of its authority and status was hastened by the impingement of the state into traditionally church-controlled areas. This process, ironically, began under Maurice Duplessis in 1958 when a provincial Department of Welfare and Youth was created. This was followed in 1961 by a new government ministry of Cultural Affairs and by state involvement in hospitals. The greatest blow, however, came with the establishment of a secular Department of Education in 1964 which cut off the church from one of its main contacts with the population and from one of its major instruments of socialization.

The diminished relevance of organized religion can be gauged by several factors. The decrease in church attendance in Montreal has accelerated to the point that by 1973 only 12 per cent of those aged 18 to 35 practised their religion. Sunday church attendance in Metropolitan Montreal fell from 61.2 per cent in 1961 to 30 per cent in 1971. The number of theology students in the Grand Seminaire of Montreal has dropped dramatically from 270 in 1965 to 70 in 1969 and 42 in 1974. The reorientation of values has also penetrated the ranks of the ordained, especially the younger members. The diocese of Sherbrooke is a typical example of the change. From 1964 to 1974, 49 priests died, 47 were newly ordained but 45 abandoned their calling, with the result that the average age of the remainder has increased from 38.2 to 50.5 years.

This rapid decline of the Church and its loss of relevance especially among the young has created a crisis of identity and a need for a new belief system. Many French Canadians have now oriented their primary loyalty to the state of Quebec or to the "nation"; others have found a replacement of their world view in the all encompassing theories of Marxism and socialism. These new brands of metaphysics appear to engage many of the same emotions as religion in its initial stages. The ideology is crusading, relatively intolerant, and moral in outlook and tone.

Socialism

The political scene in certain areas of Quebec presents several left-

* Revised in 1974 by the author, who was a member of the Department of Politics, Brock University. By permission of the author.

inclining factors if viewed in terms of traditional political analysis. Seymour Martin Lipset and other political and sociological researchers have found that manual workers in one-industry towns exhibit high rates of communist support in most countries. One-industry towns, both in mining and lumbering, have become common in Quebec and although they have not shown traditionally any preference for left-wing parties, they now present a potential for radicalism since the ideological hold of the clergy has been rapidly dissipated. It could be that this void has been filled in part by the Social Credit party which has found its strongest support in such one-industry towns. Although Social Credit has been traditionally analyzed as a right-wing phenomenon and its anti-socialist rhetoric has been loud, it does incorporate a consciousness of many of the same frustrations which animate traditionally leftist groups.

Trade unions are one of the indicators of political change. Their history in Quebec reflects in part the general political atmosphere. In that province trade unions began under the auspices of the French-Canadian Roman Catholic Church and became defensive mechanisms against the incursions of "alien" international unions. The first national trade union federation in 1921 was named very appropriately the Confédération des Travailleurs Catholiques du Canada and its ideological orientation was predictably anti-socialist with overtones of corporatist French-Canadian nationalism. As long as it remained essentially a federation of localized craft unions it did not have to confront big business management with worker-oriented demands; however with the rapid increase of new industries generated by the war and with a new and young leadership it became even more dynamic. One of the most critical points in its development was the Asbestos Strike of 1949 which radicalized a large part of the membership and placed it in contact with more militant international unions. By 1960 the Church had also retreated in this area.

The new union, now called the Confédération des Syndicats Nationaux (C.S.N., or C.N.T.U. in English) evolved into a worker-oriented and more radical body. According to one commentator, A. J. Boudreau, "this union adopts the most anti-capitalist position in the North American continent". The leader of the Montreal section, Michel Chartrand, wants unions to eliminate "capitalist fascism" and replace it with socialism. Not all the members or leaders are that radical. In 1970 it was estimated that less than one-third of its members could be considered radical left. It appears, however, that the influence of the left wing has increased since then, because of militant labour confrontations, the arrest and imprisonment of their leader in 1972, and the founding of a break-away non-politicized union which has drawn many of those who once were a moderating influence.

The other two major labour organizations, the Quebec Federation of Labour (F.T.Q.) and the Quebec Education Federation (C.E.Q.) have also become more anti-system oriented. They have proffered manifestoes aiming at the replacement of the capitalist system and the creation of a socialist Quebec. This level of leftist consciousness is in part maintained through special labour newspapers, *Quebec Presse* and more recently *Le Travail*, as well as the widespread political action and propaganda cells called F.R.A.P. and C.A.P.

As the leadership itself readily admits, the rank-and-file members are much less politicized than the federation and local union organizers. Moreover, despite all the efforts to mount common front tactics against the system there are as yet many institutional antagonisms between the federations themselves which have pre-empted more ideological involvement and militancy.

The Church itself has lost its monolithicity [*sic*] on the question of socialism. If at one time it looked askance at parishioners who voted for such mildly socialistic parties as the N.D.P., now it apparently tolerates a wide divergence of views even within its own ranks. Thus, the periodical review *Maintenant*, which was founded by clerics and which still has several brothers on its staff, proposes socialism as the true answer for Quebec's problems. The Jesuit publication *Relations* has also opted for socialist measures. An editorial appearing in it in 1959 stated that "the nationalization of a certain number of large enterprises is necessary and inevitable."

There are many groups, especially among students and intellectuals, that have embraced extra-parliamentary left-wing activism. Their relative ideological intolerance and factionalism have led to a veritable kaleidoscope of changing organizations and publications.

Socialism, in effect, has become an acceptable part of the political culture of French Canadians. This does not mean that many people would opt for it in elections but it does mean that being a socialist will no longer put anybody outside the pale of French-Canadian society. This in itself is a giant gain for that ideology since its adherents can now engage in public discourse legitimately and be listened to without a priori rejection.

One of the ways that socialism has gained entry into French-Canadian society has been through the articulate stand on nationalism and "souveraineté" propounded by certain factions within the socialist group; for instance, P. Saucier wrote in *Maintenant* in 1967 that "the idea of socialism is gaining ground in combination with a very Quebecois oriented nationalism". People who would normally have discarded socialist arguments as heretical now approach them with less trepidation and even consider them as one alternative among many. Gilles Grégoire, who was deputy leader of the Social Credit and later Créditiste party, exemplifies this change of attitude. M. Grégoire is now a member of the Parti Québécois, but as early as November 1967 he stated: "I believe in strong intervention by the state. I believe that socialism has meaning in Quebec for the separatists today." His version of socialism, however, does not envisage full-scale nationalization until it becomes "relevant in the contemporary world." To him it implies, as he has stated later, "social security measures like Medicare and free education."

Nationalism

Although the decade of the 1960s is the only period in Quebec's history, with the possible exception of the revolt of 1837, in which there has been some resurgence of left-wing strength; nationalism, on the other hand, has historically found far more fertile ground. Far from being a very recent phenomenon like socialism, it has emerged as a strong force almost with cyclical regularity. Paradoxically, the periods between these cycles have been almost devoid of nationalist feelings.

The first nationalist period of this century developed during and after the Boer War from 1900 to about 1907 largely in reaction to a crusading British imperialism which had found strong resonance in anglophone Canada. Rather than fighting for a separate Quebec, the nationalists stressed developing Canadian interests and consciousness. At the same time there was a special concern for French Canada and a recognition of the differences between the two races which were seen as rooted primarily in genetic factors. Each race had a "voix de sang" and particular instincts and tendencies which gave it an indentifiable character. According to the chief moving force of this nationalist period, Henri Bourassa, the French race was naturally endowed with honour, probity, and perseverance. Moreover, it could boast of a certain intellectual superiority in contrast to the English who were instinctively good businessmen. Many of these ideas became common assumptions for generations of students who until recently accepted the debilitating argument that French Canadians were destined to be great thinkers rather than businessmen.

The second wave of nationalism was of a more radical nature. It followed the conscription crisis of 1917 and lasted until about 1924. It was initiated by the founding of *L'Action Française* in 1917. This nationalist review discussed French language rights as well as more theoretical and utopian concepts, such as the "revenge of the cradle" introduced by Father Louis Lalande. The guiding force of this entire nationalist period was Abbé Groulx, a historian who was one of the editors of its monthly voice, *L'Action Nationale*. Groulx felt that Confederation was destined to fail and that only the time of its death was as yet unclear. His creation of a new nationally oriented brand of history left its mark on future generations who were to rekindle French-Canadian nationalism. The anti-Confederation stand was later obviated by a seemingly increasing threat of Americanization—i.e. American economic imperialism, American films, and French-Canadian immigration to the U.S.A.

The third period, from 1933 to 1944, coincided with the years of the depression and the second conscription crisis. Its first overt expression was the nationalism of the student publication, *Quartier Latin*. Later, many nationalist groups emerged under the ideological direction of Paul Bouchard and his publication *La Nation*. There were also more militant youth groups such as Jeunesses Patriotes, Jeune-Canada, Front Corporatif, and Jeunesses Laurentiennes.

These various groups proposed several changes in the existing system. They criticized rural emigration and wanted to reinstitute a new policy of a "return to the land." They initiated certain economic campaigns, mostly to support small enterprises—e.g. "une campagne d'achat chez nous." They also wanted to eliminate foreign control from Quebec institutions, mainly through the establishment of corporatism. One of the main figures of nationalism in 1934, D. Dansereau, claimed that Confederation was only a transitory stage leading either to complete unitary consolidation or else to the creation of several new states. In 1935, the idealized state of an independent Laurentie was first presented. The war dampened the nationalist fervour somewhat but the conscription and referendum crises resulted in a nationalist political coalition—the Bloc Populaire party. It gained over 15 percent of the vote in the Quebec provincial election of 1944 and won four seats in the Legislative Assembly. Yet, because of its contradictory political tendencies of left and right, it collapsed quickly as a viable force.

Throughout these three periods of heightened nationalism there was a common belief that the Church formed an integral part of the French-Canadian nation. To be a nationalist then was tantamount to being a devout Catholic. Even before the turn of the century the Church had consolidated its position within the nationalist ideology of French Canada by standing out as the sole defender of "La Survivance." Its position was further strengthened when such men as Frechette and Abbé Casgrain grafted a universal religious mission to the calling of French Canada. Abbé Casgrain wrote that "French Canadians would lead back under the Aegis of Catholicism the errant peoples of the New World." Such messianic purposes managed to integrate admirably the sacred with the secular.

If this merging of French-Canadian nationalism with religion constituted the common bond throughout the past half century, it has become now the single great point of departure for modern nationalism in Quebec. At first it appeared that the trend of religiosity would continue when l'Action Laurentienne, the first separatist group in 1956, preached its great attachment to the Church. However, the trend of events has forced religion into a different position not attached to nationalism. It could also explain in part the fact that nationalism in Quebec today exhibits signs of various ideologies including socialism and Marxism.

Many students of French-Canadian nationalism before 1960 have tended to classify the ideology as a conservative, right-wing phenomenon. This description, however, was not universally true. Henri Bourassa, in the early 1900s, was one of the main champions against imperialism. Although he cannot be classified as a social radical, he did show some sympathy for the socialist C.C.F. party and for its leader, J. S. Woodsworth. The Bloc Populaire, founded in 1942 by Maxime Raymond, was also ambiguous in its political sentiments. It contained right-wing nationalists as well as left-wing elements.

But the political ideology of many nationalists was equally opposed to international socialism as well as to international monopolies. Even Duplessis was considered a reforming nationalist in his first years of political office. It is also true that many French-Canadian nationalists displayed certain sympathies for Mussolini and the Axis powers. But they did not approve of their external politics so much as of the idea of a charismatic leader. They saw the answer to their own divisions and to the creation of a unified collectivity in adoption of the "führerprinciple."

Nationalism and Socialism, 1950-1970

The new nationalism of the late fifties began as a movement closely parallel to that of the 1930s. In 1956, Raymond Barbeau, a young student, picked up the strands of nationalism which had been neglected for some years. He resurrected the idea of a republic of Laurentia in which religion would play an integral part. As he put it, "the Laurentian is above all a Christian." Gérard Gauthier, one of the editors of the first nationalist publication in this period, *La Laurentie*, again emphasized the stand against internationalism which was thought of as utopian and even "anti-human." Both international capitalism and international proletarian syndicalism were castigated for their disintegrative effects on morals, culture and religious sentiment. The French-Canadian nation was seen as a corporate whole united by the bonds of blood. Confederation was considered an impossible union of sovereign states acting against the best interests of French Canada. This nationalism was of a crusading type, not dependent on logical argument so much as on emotional appeal, intensity of feeling, belligerence, and mystification.

These nationalists seemed to glorify anti-democratic thought. Their ideal state would not be a parliamentary democracy but would be led by a "disciplined and energetic, coherent unity and comprehensive power." Classes would not be merged, yet there was to be a certain class mobility for children of workers and peasants who showed talent and aptitude for command posts. Social salvation was to come through hierarchic and stable organizations which had to be in conformity with ethnic, racial and national aspirations.

This wing of nationalism, organized into the Alliance Laurentienne, was the strongest faction of the separatist movement until 1961. It had youth sections, women's leagues and representatives in many parts of Quebec. Although its paid membership by 1961 amounted to only about 2,000, the publicity it received through its actions of defiance against the Queen and Confederation increased its stature in the separatist milieu. Raymond Barbeau's book, *J'ai choisi l'indépendance*, was widely read before Marcel Chaput's *Pourquoi je suis séparatiste* was even published.

Almost as fanatical, but stemming from the opposite extreme of the political spectrum, was the first truly socialist separatist party or faction. It did not have as many adherents as the Alliance, yet it was more articulate and seems to have had more people writing articles than did *La Laurentie*. It was the reassertion of the left-wing which had been found in milder form within the Bloc Populaire but which had been totally dissipated after the war. The leader of this movement, which was called Action Socialiste pour l'Indépendance du Québec, was Raoul Roy, a former communist and businessman. He edited the journal, *La Revue Socialiste*, which fought for "l'indépendance et la libération proletarienne nationale des Canadiens Français." The publication was also anti-internationalist and opposed the totalitarian version of communism in the Soviet Union. It did sympathize openly with Castro's Cuba, and the Cuban consul in Montreal, Carlos Herrerro, who helped the group organize and delivered speeches whenever necessary.

M. Roy's version of socialism was very intolerant of other brands of leftism in Canada, which were all called "pseudo-gauche" and were accused of living in a dream world of their own because they refused to admit the importance of national liberation. He was also wary of the other left parties because of their centralizing aspects. To him a leftist government in power seemed as much of a threat as a bourgeois type of government. He concluded that mere separatism was not as yet (in 1959) propitious because it would only throw Quebec under the increased domination of foreign monopolists and the old decadent and ultra-conservative Quebec bourgeoisie. His tactical solution was to fight a battle both against capitalist and nationalist exploitation.

The Rassemblement pour l'Indépendance Nationale (R.I.N.) was founded by André d'Allemagne, a young Montreal advertising copy-writer, on September 10, 1960. Together with Marcel Chaput and thirty other sympathizers, he worked out the fundamentals of its ideology. At first, it was meant to be only a non-political educational association which would propagate the idea of Quebec's separation and independence. However, by 1962 it had developed greater ambitions and it posited certain reforms which should accompany national independence.

The main outlines of the 1962 program contained in its publication, *L'Indépendance*, indicated the direction of its reforms. Thus, the sole language of the State of Quebec was to be French, schooling was to be free, and cooperatives were to be established both for producers and consumers. Moreover, it envisaged economic planning based on the interests of all the elements of the population. It recognized the need for foreign investments but the state was going to have greater powers of intervention in guiding this investment so that local capital could participate and local personnel could be employed.

When the R.I.N. became politicized, it suffered internal schisms and finally some factions broke away to form new groups. Marcel Rioux, after polling some of the R.I.N. supporters in 1966, found that there was a continual conflict between the pure nationalists and the socialist nationalists. In December 1962, Marcel Chaput, for example, decided to form his own faction after he was replaced as president of the R.I.N. by Guy Pouliot. Chaput's Parti Républicain du Québec was more right wing than the R.I.N. Paradoxically, this same P.R.Q. metamorphosed into another group which was again more leftist oriented. The R.I.N. also gave birth to the Rassemblement National (R.N.) which was created just before the 1966 Quebec election by dissident Créditistes and right-wing, middle class separatists who had walked out of the R.I.N. in 1964 because they opposed the party's "socialism."

To "true" socialists, such as those writing for *Parti Pris*, a radical journal founded by students at the University of Montreal in 1963, the R.I.N. and especially its leader, Pierre Bourgault, were an ideological enigma. In September 1967, they noted that Bourgault had declared his belief that if he lived in the United States he would be politically on the right. Yet, during the assembly of the R.I.N. after De Gaulle's famous pronouncement of "Québec libre!" in Montreal in 1967, Bourgault reaffirmed that French Canadians were fighting the same battle as the blacks of America. In the same year he criticized the "fascists of the left' within the R.I.N., but at different times Bourgault has stated that "to achieve independence we will have to pass through socialism."

The left faction of the R.I.N. finally did separate. Led by Mme Andrée Bertrand-Ferretti, it formed a new grouping, the Front de Libération Populaire (F.L.P.), in the spring of 1968 because it would not compromise with Bourgault's policy of rapprochement with René Lévesque's Mouvement Souveraineté Association (M.S.A.). Lévesque himself had once joined the R.I.N. but broke away after members of the R.I.N. indulged in street riots in Montreal.

Although the R.I.N. was the most successful of the separatist parties during the 1966 provincial election, achieving 5.5 percent of the vote compared to the R.N.'s 3.2 percent, if finally voted to disband and join Lévesque's Parti Québécois, founded in October 1968, because Lévesque was a "valuable instrument who can sell the separatist movement to a majority of Quebec voters." The R.I.N. members who voted to switch parties did so with the resolve that "we are joining the P.Q. without compromising our principles. We will be able to play the same role in that party that René Lévesque used to play in the Liberal Party."

Parti Québecois—Fusion of Socialism and Nationalism?

Whatever may have been the rationalization of the R.I.N. members in joining the new P.Q., the fundamentals and the direction of the latter party were set by the two founding groups: Lévesque's M.S.A. and Gilles Grégoire's R.N.

There was no question about the political sentiments of the Ralliement National, which were clearly right-wing. There was far more ambiguity about the M.S.A. and its relative position on the political spectrum. Several factors should be considered here. The focus of power within the M.S.A. lay in the hands of Lévesque's followers from the Liberal Party of Quebec. However, many of those forming the basic membership were certainly more radical and revolutionary, having come from quite leftist socialist groups. Yet as the leftists themselves openly acknowledged, their numbers were not great and their bargaining power in the M.S.A. was very limited. The R.I.N.'s influence in the M.S.A. was also limited because the R.I.N. refused to join as a constituent body and therefore its members who joined subsequently did so as individuals.

Having emerged from this sort of confused but predominantly cautious background, the Parti Québécois has not tended to favour radical socialist revolutionary measures. Its program, for example, parallels that of moderate social democratic parties in Europe with the inevitable projected increases in social welfare measures and greater attention to state planning and guidance in the economy. There seems to be a definite bias against cartels and conglomerates but at the same time there is an acceptance of the need for big industry and private capital. The program envisages a selective repatriation of the economy, requiring Quebec ownership in such fields as the media and primary steel production but allowing different levels of foreign investment in primarily non-strategic areas. The state is to play a greater role in the setting of the "rules of the game"; however, these are not to interfere with but rather help the development of the entire economy. Thus nationalization will be used only when it is found to be economically necessary although the state will become much more involved in the creation of new enterprises to provide leadership and equilibrium within important sectors of the economy. The P.Q. financial critic and member of the executive, G. Joron, claimed in 1973 that the P.Q. program was very clearly not socialist.

Judged by the political experience of other Canadians parties, party programs are not necessarily the only determinant of future tactics. Because they are trying to obtain political power, parties have to compromise to obtain the support of the majority of the electorate. One of the main reasons that the P.Q. will not move very much further left than the "Swedish type" of welfare statism lies in the social characteristics of those supporting independence. In its issue of November 2, 1963, *Maclean's* magazine published a very extensive analysis of separatism. The greatest percentage of support came from those in the higher income bracket and from those who had finished university or had special or technical training.

A study in 1971 by the P.Q. of its own membership again indicated a predominance of professionals (37.2 per cent), white collar employees (22.1 per cent), and students (14.9 per cent), but a relatively small group of blue collar workers and farmers (together 12.6 per cent). The middle class background of the P.Q. does not necessarily preclude individual radicalization but in general such groups are economic conservatives and provide the backbone of all free-enterprise parties. Moreover, the party itself is a delicately balanced movement and a compromise of a variety of ideological currents. Although there are elements, even within the leadership, that would favour a more socialistic position, the present overriding mood of pragmatism, both in terms of maintaining party unity and electoral support, argue against further radicalization. However, disillusionment with electoral politics could create pressures for a more ideological reassessment of goals.

In purely practical terms there is not much more to be gained on the left. During the first years of the party's existence there were many leftist groupings such as the Front de Libération Populaire (F.L.P.), the Union Générale des Etudiants de Québec (U.G.E.Q.), the Front de Libération du Quebec (F.L.Q.) and various journals such as *Quartier Latin*, *Socialisme*, and *Parti Pris* which did not support the Parti Québécois. But these groupings in their turn have been faced with the choice of pragmatism or ideological purity. The threat of cooptation within the deradicalizing mainstream of Quebec politics posed by joining the P.Q. has been offset in part by the fear of remaining out "in the cold" and continuing to be politically insignificant. No doubt many have been aware of the fate of such ex-radicals as Pierre Trudeau, Gérard Pelletier, Jean Marchand, Jean Luc Pepin and Jean Drapeau once they became recognized leaders within the confines of existing society. The "new" radicals are afraid that once they start to play the game, they too will inevitably have to accept the rules of that game. These rules are exactly what they want to change.

Conversion or acceptance of the Parti Québécois has not been uniform or sudden and the rationalizations and reasons for joining have been different. André Brochu, one of the founders of *Parti Pris*, eulogized the

P.Q. in April 1970 in poetic words: "Le Parti Québécois c'est la renaissance et la transformation en volonté d'action populaire, de ce que fût, pour nous, parti pris. C'est le parti du Québec, pris par tous les Québécois. C'est notre tranquillité, l'infini de nos patiences faits revolution." Brochu's letter in the press shows a very definite ideological evolution from an elitist revolutionary position several years ago to a more emotional and sentimental identification with all the streams of Quebec society. There is no trace left of the impatience and the ideological rigidity of former years. On the contrary, there seems to be a return to the veneration of a "chef" who has managed "to channel our most fundamental desires which in reality cannot be claimed by any single generation, any social milieu nor by any ideological sect or particular group."

Michel Chartrand had to retrace a more difficult path. He was for a long time one of the main bulwarks against separatism in the Quebec wing of the New Democratic Party. He attacked separatism as a smoke screen designed to cover the true lines of class conflict. He changed his mind, however, and successfully convinced the Montreal section of the C.S.N. to support the P.Q. during the 1970 elections.

It would seem that for labour leader Chartrand and many others, nationalism had been a negative ideology associated with reaction and the "exploiting classes". Now this nationalism, or rather "neonationalism" as they call it, is seen as a progressive force which can help to rectify many of the iniquities in Quebec society.

Two concepts above all seem to permeate the statements of many militant leftist ideologues who have reluctantly accepted the P.Q.: one of these is best summarized by the words "en attendant" and "faute de mieux" or "until something better comes along". Thus the cleric Louis O'Neil has attempted to justify his "uncomfortable position" as a P.Q. candidate in the 1973 election by pointing out that until the creation of a truly working class party, choices have to made. The second approach is to accept a sequential argument for the emancipation of the working class in Quebec. If Quebec workers are doubly exploited both as French Canadians and as labourers, then apparently the initial step to liberation has to be Quebec independence. Théo Gagné, militant socialist labour leader and former editor of *Socialisme*, has accepted a position on the executive of the P.Q. while openly acknowledging that independence is only a first step and that the party is merely a useful tool for reaching further objectives.

Probably the most spectacular advocate of this new concept of "historical stages" is the convert to the P.Q., Pierre Vallières, formerly one of the more committed and articulate representatives of the F.L.Q., the group involved in the October 1970 kidnapping of James Cross and the death of Pierre Laporte. Vallières, in his 1971 book *L'urgence de Choisir*, renounces everything that could impede national liberation, including terrorism and ideological purity which only lead to factionalism. The internal pressures for "urgent choices" exist because French Canadians are on the eve of a fatal third conquest (the second conquest apparently occurred in 1837-1838). There is no more time for limited gains in revolutionary conscience in view of the risk of collective suicide. Hence, he challenges the P.Q. left to "sacrifice ideological ping-pong for less sportive but more positive tasks."

His former comrade-in-arms, Charles Gagnon, and many other individual socialists, as well as the defunct journal *Socialisme Québécois* (last issue, Jan. 1972), have rejected Vallières' analysis and call for unity. Gilles Bourque has counter-attacked, claiming that the P.Q. is an elitist, unresponsive and middle-class dominated party which will use the state to further its own class interests. In fact "the leftist militant who joins the P.Q. hinders the organization of the working class and helps infiltrate bourgeois ideology among the workers."

Organized labour, one of the strongholds of socialist opinions, has not officially declared its support for the P.Q. but the reasons appear to be mainly tactical rather than ideological. Out of a total of 1000 delegates at the Quebec Federation of Labour convention in December 1973, 76 percent claimed to have voted P.Q. *Quebec Presse*, the labour newspaper which has several board directors from the party, including the recent convert Mme Andrée Bertrand-Ferretti, columnist, gave the party maximum coverage and support in the October 1973 elections.

There are certainly factions within the labour movement that have expressed disillusionment with the P.Q. Some labour political action committees (C.A.P.) have agitated for a new workers' party through their publication, *Mobilisation*. Several labour councils, including the large ones in Quebec City and Montreal, narrowly defeated resolutions in November 1973 calling for the creation of a new unequivocally worker-oriented party. However, the increased labour consciousness of the P.Q. leadership, as well as the combined action of many prominent P.Q. members and organized labour at the municipal political level in 1974, may cement solidarity and understanding.

There are still some small left "holdouts" whose effect is more symbolic than real. The Socialist, Trotskyite, and Communist Leagues, the emaciated version of *Quartier Latin* of the University of Montreal, and several ephemeral publications such as *Le Combat*, *La Lutte*, and others have as yet spurned the attractions of the P.Q. The N.D.P., which obtained about 12 percent of the total vote in 1965 but only six percent in 1972, has also remained officially aloof from the P.Q. although indicating its support for the social platform of that party. On the whole, however, it appears that the major part of the left has become absorbed by the Parti Québécois.

The "nationalists", or those who consider Quebec's sovereignty to be the major priority of politics, display a certain ambiguity towards socialism. A publication like *Action Nationale* has traditionally been accepted as representative of the "right side" of politics but some of its directors, such as Jean-Marc Leger, are associated with socialism. Its editor, Jean Genest, sees no evil in using the state to equalize the imbalance of ownership in the Quebec economy. In fact in the September 1972 edition he categorizes the P.Q. action program *Quand Nous Serons Vraiment Chez Nous* as a lucid and great work of intellectual emancipation. He explicitly rejects capitalism as a divisive evil but also praises the Parti Québécois' moderation and exclusion of doctrinaire socialism.

The economist Jacques Parizeau, who is one of the main intellectual bulwarks of the P.Q., does not shy away from contemplation of nationalization. His comparison of nationalization to the hammer of a carpenter, viewing it merely as a tool, would certainly not offend any socialist; yet he has been the main economic adviser to two Quebec governments and has advocated very orthodox methods for dealing with fiscal and economic problems. Gilles Grégoire's stand, as noted before, is also extremely ambiguous on the relationship of separatism to socialism.

One of the principal organizations providing continuity with the old-style nationalism of the nineteenth century, the Ligue d'Action Nationale under the leadership of Francois-Albert Angers, formally decided to support the P.Q. in October 1973.

There are nationalist-separatists who have been perturbed by the presence of radical socialists in the party ranks. Jean Genest finds no quarrel with the P.Q. program but he does feel concerned about the large contingent of socialist militants in the P.Q. ranks. Liberal M.N.A. Bona Arsenault finds very many appealing things about the P.Q. but would be horrified to be included in a group with people like Michel Chartrand. Camille Samson, now a Créditistes deputy, was at one time the chief founder of the separatist Rassemblement National and even ran as an R.N. candidate in Temiscamingue in 1966. His main reason for leaving the new coalition of Lévesque's M.S.A. and R.N. was the former's socialist membership and direction.

Moreover, there is a sizable group of people "favourable" to independence who in 1970 voted for the non-separatist parties. A study of the Montreal region in 1970 indicated 15.5 per cent of Liberal voters and 34.6 per cent of Union Nationale voters supported independence. It is difficult to determine, however, whether this factor reveals a non-acceptance of the Parti Québécois' program and membership or whether it is merely a reflection of habitual voting.

Finally, it should be made clear that the P.Q. has not received the support of all or even a majority of "nationalists". There are many nationalists who have not accepted the idea of separatism. A *Maclean's Magazine* poll published in November 2, 1963 found that only 13 per cent of French Canadians in Quebec were in favour of secession. A study carried out by a professional public opinion and research group in Montreal and published in the weekend magazine *Perspectives* on March 28, 1970, showed that seven years later there was still only the same percentage favouring separatism. In November 1974 a poll published in *La Presse* stated that 28 per cent of Quebec's voters favoured independence while 57.5 per cent were opposed.

Of greater significance for the P.Q. is the growth in the intensity and size of opposition to separatism. The Gallup Poll of April 17, 1971 found that 50 per cent of Quebeckers felt that Quebec should be held in Confederation by force even if the majority of its people want to separate. Only 30 per cent in Quebec felt that they should have a right to separate, in contrast with 40 per cent for Canada as a whole. There have been demands from some P.Q. members and even losing candidates that the separatist platform be abandoned. This, of course, has not yet become acceptable. However, in deference to political reality the fourth Party Congress of 1973 did support the idea of a special referendum on separatism to take place several years after a P.Q. victory, making it clear that a vote for the P.Q. was not an automatic vote for separatism.

René Lévesque has been the principal conciliator in holding the basically antagonistic factions together in one movement. He has also been the prime catalyst in overcoming many of the electoral obstacles. In 1963 when only 13 per cent of French Canadians in Quebec favoured separatism, 23 per cent claimed they would vote for a separatist party led by Lévesque. Pierre Bourgault, former president of the R.I.N., in an interview in *Quebec Presse*, December 9, 1973, characterized Lévesque as a genius, stating that "I personally believe, the Québécois do not vote for Lévesque because of what he has to say, but because they are in love with him."

No matter what the attraction of the P.Q., whether it be its social program, its stand on Quebec independence, or merely the appeal of Lévesque and the leadership generally, the committed membership has continued to grow from about 14,000 in 1968 to 87,000 in 1971 and 110,000 in 1973. The party has also received an increasing share of the total vote, 24 per cent in 1970 and 30 per cent in 1973. It would seem, however, that in view of the relative polarization of the 1973 election, the Parti Québécois has reached a plateau in its support, at least for the present. In the long run there are several factors working to its advantage, namely its appeal among the younger age groups and among the more educated. G. White, J. Millar, and W. Gagne found a linear relationship between education and preference for the P.Q. Thus only five per cent of those with some public school favoured the P.Q., but 21 per cent who had graduated from elementary school, 27 per cent with some high school, 35 per cent of those who had graduated from high school, and 46 per cent with university or technical education preferred the P.Q. A similarly linear relationship was found for age groups, with 50 per cent of those from 18 to 24 opting for the party but only 11 per cent in the 50-64 and 10 per cent in the over-65 age categories indicating any preference for the P.Q.

One of the Parti Québécois' main obstacles to winning an election is the almost automatic handicap of a 20 per cent anglophone vote. There is a danger that under such conditions many of those who have been coopted within the party may decide to either radicalize its orientation or go back into the streets for more direct action. There may also be a tendency to a loss of fervour and interest if the chances of winning are perceived to be non-existent or on the other hand inevitable.

The Parti Québécois has successfully assembled in one organization quite different and at times antagonistic factions which have in the past proven unblendable and fissiparous. The conditions at present favour a deradicalization of both tendencies for the sake of electoral politics and pragmatism. The institutionalization of the party with its concomitant vested interests and the consciousness of a common cause no doubt have helped in partly fusing the ideologically diverse membership. The creation of a party-oriented newspaper, *Le Jour*, will further help in stabilizing the stituation. However, Lévesque has claimed in March 1974 "by its nature the P.Q. is essentially a rassemblement [union or movement]. It will remain viable only so long as we maintain an equilibrium."

Conclusion

The common link between the nationalists and the socialist-nationalists is their view of the state and its function in French-Canadian society. Contrary to the right-wing conviction now popular in the U.S. that the state governs best which governs least and the equally strong stand against the expansion of government and bureaucracy, French Canadians have embraced a radically different trend. The state of Quebec has taken over many of the functions of the clergy in assuring "la survivance" and, as such, has been accorded much more confidence by both the left and the right. Professor Louis Sabourin, former dean of the Faculty of Social Sciences at the University of Ottawa, has noted this distinction: "In the past anti-statism was one of the dominant facts of political life. Today the situation has changed considerably. The French Canadians believe that only the State, which they can control, can assure their development in all areas."

This anti-statism of the past should not be taken as opposition to the idea of a strong state. French Canadians did not expect much previously from their provincial legislature and therefore their anti-statism was passive rather than active. For French-Canadian nationalists, however, the ideal of a powerful state is a recurring theme in the present century. Abbé Groulx did not pray for a charismatic wilful leader to lead a weak state. Neither was the idealized "Laurentie" a state where individual rights would flourish at the expense of collective rights. The state, whether the corporatist dream of the right or the instrument of nationalization of the left, has a unique and forceful position in French-Canadian nationalist ideology. It is only during the last decade that the idealized "state" has coincided with an actual "state".

The Parti Québécois may also differ from the nationalist movements of the past in not being as vulnerable to the disruption of periodicity, although Pierre Bourgault does not foresee an action of the P.Q. type continuing longer than twenty years. There will certainly be ebbs in the general enthusiasm for nationalism and even social reform. However, the institutionalization of the movement as well as the vested interests of many party members may preclude disintegration.

The "dialectic" between the nationalists and "socialists" is still continuing, although muted by the orientation to electoral politics. If the P.Q. were to take power or at least see the possibility of gaining power, its direction would be towards even greater moderation in both its nationalism and socialism. If, however, the P.Q. is denied any power, then the pressures for radicalization may well be increased. But in any case the end result will be far from socialism. Although Lenin utilized Marx's ambiguous legacy on nationalism for tactical reasons, he also stated that "there is not the slightest doubt that every nationalist movement can only be a bourgeois-democratic movement."

Quebec—Provincial Election Results, 1960-1976*

Year	Turnout Total %	Total Seats N	Total vote N	Liberal Vote %	Liberal Seats N	Liberal Seats %	Union Nationale Vote %	U.N. Seats N	U.N. Seats %	RIN / Parti Québécois Vote %	Seats N	Seats %	RN / Creditiste Vote %	Seats N	Seats %	Other Vote %	Other Seats N
1960	81.7	95	2,096,597	51.4	52	54.7	46.6	42	44.2							2.0	1
1962	79.6	95	2,136,781	56.4	63	66.3	42.1	31	32.6							1.4	1
1966	73.6	108	2,312,564	47.4	50	46.2	40.9	56	51.8	RIN 5.5	0		RN 3.2	0		3.1	2
1970	84.2	108	2,864,100	45.4	72	66.6	19.6	17	15.7	PQ 23	7	6.4	11.2	12	11.1	1.4	0
1973	80.5	110	2,970,978	54.8	102	92.7	4.9	0	0	30.2	6	5.4	9.7	2	1.8	—	0
1976	85.3	110	3,330,000	33.8	26	25	18.2	11	10	41.4	71	63	5	1	.9	2	1

* Compiled by the editor from preliminary returns reported in the press.
RIN is the abbreviation of le Rassemblement pour l'Indépendance Nationale, and RN for le Ralliement National.
(For more detailed and precise information, see Chapter 18.)

BIBLIOGRAPHY

(Also see the bibliographies for the Chapters on "Voting Behaviour" and "Political Parties".)

Allard, M., *The Last Chance, The Canadian Constitution and French Canadians*, Quebec, Editions Ferland, 1964.

d'Allemagne, A., *Le colonialisme au Québec*, Montréal, Editions Renaud et Bray, 1966.

Arès, R., *Nos grandes options politiques et constitutionnelles*, Montréal, Bellarmin, 1972.

Barbeau, R., *Le Québec, est-il une colonie?* Montréal, Editions de l'homme, 1962.

Bennett, A., *Quebec Labour Strikes*, Montreal, Black Rose, 1973.

Bergeron, G., *La Canada francais après deux siècles de patience*, Paris, Seuil, 1967.

Bergeron, G., *Du Duplessisme à Trudeau et Bourassa*, 1956-1971, Montréal, Editions Parti pris, 1971.

Bergeron, L., *The History of Quebec: A Patriot's Handbook*, Toronto, NC Press, 1971.

Bernard, A., *La Politique au Canada et au Québec*, Montréal, les Presses de l'Université du Québec, 1976.

Bernard, A., and Laforte, D., *La Législation électorale au Québec 1790-1967*, Montréal, Les Editions Sainte-Marie, 1969.

Boily, R., *Québec, 1940-1969, Bibliographie*, Montreal, Les Presses de l'Université de Montréal, 1971.

Bourgault, P., *Québec, Quitte ou Double*, Montréal, Ferron, 1970.

Brady, A., "Quebec and Canadian Federalism," *C.J.E.P.S.*, Vol. XXV, No. 3, August, 1959.

Brossard, J., *L'Accession à la Souveraineté et le Cas du Québec*, Montréal, les Presses de l'Université de Montréal, 1976.

Brichant, A., *Option Canada: The Economic Implications of Separatism for the Province of Quebec*, Montreal, The Canada Committee, 1968.

Burns, R. M., (ed.), *One Country or Two?*, London and Montreal, McGill-Queen's University Press, 1971.

Cameron, D., *Nationalism, Self-Determination, and the Quebec Question*, Toronto, Macmillan, 1974.

Canada, *A Preliminary Report of the Royal Commission on Bilingualism and Biculturalism*, Ottawa, Queen's Printer, 1965.

Canadian Broadcasting Corporation, *Quebec: Year Eight*, Glendon College Forum, Toronto, C.B.C., 1968.

Chaput, M., *Why I am a Separatist*, Toronto, Ryerson, 1962.

Chaput-Rolland, S., *My Country: Canada or Québec*, Toronto, Macmillan, 1966.

Chaput-Rolland, S., *Regards 1970-71: les heures sauvages*, Montreal, le Cercle du livre de France, 1972.

Chodos, R., and Auf der Maur, N., (eds.), *Quebec: A Chronicle 1968-1972*, Toronto, James, Lewis and Samuel, 1972.

Cook, R., *Canada and the French-Canadian Question*, Toronto, Macmillan, 1966.

Cook, R., (ed.), *French-Canadian Nationalism*, Toronto, Macmillan, 1969.

Corbett, E. M., *Quebec Confronts Canada*, Toronto, Copp Clark, 1967.

Cohen, R. I., *Quebec Votes*, Montreal, Saje Publications, 1965.

Cotnam, J., *Contemporary Quebec: An Analytical Bibliography*, Toronto, McClelland and Stewart, 1973.

Cuneo, C. J., and Curtis, J. E., "Quebec Separatism: An Analysis of Determinants with Social-Class levels", *The Canadian Review of Sociology and Anthropology*, Vol. II, No. 1, February, 1974.

DeBane, P., and Asselin, M., "Quebec's right to secede", (a minority report of the special Joint Committee of the Senate and House of Commons on the

Constitution), *The Canadian Forum*, Vol. LII, No. 616, May, 1972.

Dion, G., "Secularization in Quebec", *Journal of Canadian Studies*, Vol. III, No. 1, February, 1968.

Drache, D., (ed.), *Quebec: Only the Beginning*, Toronto, New Press, 1972.

Dumont, F., *La vigile du Québec, October 1970: l'impasse?*, Montréal, Editions Hurtubise, 1971. (English edition, Toronto, University of Toronto Press, 1974.)

Forsey, E., *Freedom and Order, Collected Essays*, Carleton Library No. 73, (Part IV), Toronto, McClelland and Stewart, 1974.

Garigue, P., *L'option politique du Canada francais*, Montréal, Editions du lévrier, 1963.

Garigue, P., *Bibliographie du Québec, 1955-1965*, Montréal, les Presses de l'Université de Montréal, 1967.

Gélinas, A., *Les Parlementaires et l'administration au Québec*, Montréal, Les Presses de l'Université Laval, 1969.

Gélinas, A., *Organismes autonomes et centraux de l'Administration Québécoise*, Montréal, les Presses d'UQAM, 1976.

Gellner, J., *Bayonets in the Streets, Urban Guerrillas at Home and Abroad*, Don Mills, Ontario, Collier-Macmillan, 1974.

Gold, G., and Tremblay, M.-A., *Communities and Culture in French Canada*, Toronto, Holt, Rinehart and Winston, 1973.

Gow, J. I., "Les Québécois, la guerre et la paix, 1945-60." *C.J.P.S.*, Vol. III, No. 1, March, 1970.

Guindon, H., "Social Unrest, Social Class, and Quebec's Bureaucratic Revolution." *Q.Q.*, Vol. LXXI, No. 2, Summer, 1964.

Groupe des Recherches Sociales, *Les électeurs Québécois*, Montréal, 1960.

Gzowski, P., "This is the True Strength of Separatism", *Maclean's*, Nov. 2, 1963.

Haggart, R., and Golden, A. E., *Rumours of War*, Toronto, New Press, 1971.

Hamilton, R., and Pinard, M., "The Bases of Parti Québécois Support in Recent Quebec Elections", *C.J.P.S.*, Vol. IX, No. 1, March, 1976.

Irvine, W. P., "Recruitment to Nationalism: New Politics or Normal Politics?", *C.J.P.S.*, Vol. V, No. 4, December, 1972.

Johnson, Daniel, *Egalité ou indépendance*, Les éditions renaissance, 1965.

Jones, R., *Community in Crisis: French Canadian Nationalism in Perspective*, Carleton Library, No. 59, Toronto, McClelland & Stewart, 1967.

Joy, R., *Languages in Conflict*, Carleton Library No. 61, Toronto, McClelland and Stewart, 1972.

Jutras, R., *Québec libre*, Montréal, Les éditions actualité, 1965.

Kwavnick, D., "The Roots of French-Canadian Discontent," *C.J.E.P.S.*, Vol. XXXI, No. 4, November 1965.

Kwavnick, D., "Quebec and the Two Nations Theory: A Re-examination", *Q.Q.*, Vol. 81, No. 3, Autumn, 1974.

Kwavnick, D., (ed.), *The Tremblay Report*, Carleton Library No. 64, Toronto, McClelland and Stewart, 1973.

Lacoursiere, J. and Huguet, H.-A., *Québec 72-73: Bilan*, Montréal, Editions fides, 1974.

Lamontagne, L., *Le Canada francais d'aujourd'hui*, Toronto, University of Toronto Press, 1970.

Larocque, A., *Défis au Parti Québécois*, Montréal, Editions du Jour, 1971.

La Terreur, M., *Les tribulations des Conservateurs au Québec, de Bennett à Diefenbaker*, Laval, Presses de l'Université Laval, 1973.

Laurin, C., *Ma traversée du Québec*, Montréal, Les éditions du jour, 1970.

Lemieux, V., *Le quotient politique vrai—le vote provincial et fédéral au Québec*, Laval, les presses de l'Université Laval, 1974.

Lemieux, V., *Parenté et politique: L'organisation sociale dans l'Ile d'Orléans*, Québec, Les Presses de l'Université Laval, 1971.

Lemieux, V., et Hudon, R., *Patronage et politique au Québec, 1944-1972*, Montréal, Boréal Express, 1975.

Lévesque, R., *Option Québec*, Montréal, Les éditions de l'homme, 1968. (English edition, Toronto, McClelland and Stewart, 1968.)

Lévesque, R., *La souveraineté et l'économie*, Montréal, Les éditions du jour, 1970.

Lévesque, R., *La solution: le programme du Parti Québécois*, Montréal, Les éditions du jour, 1970.

Macleod, A., "Nationalism and social class: the unresolved dilemma of the Quebec left", *Journal of Canadian Studies*, Vol. VIII, No. 4, November, 1973.

Marier, R., "Les objectifs sociaux du Québec," *C.P.A.*, Vol. XII, No. 2, Summer, 1969.

McRoberts, K., and Posgate, D., *Quebec: Social Change and Political Crisis*, Toronto, McClelland and Stewart, 1976.

Mellos, K., "Quantitative Comparison of Party Ideology", *C.J.P.S.*, Vol. III, No. 4, December, 1970.

Meyers, H. B., *The Quebec Revolution*, Montreal, Harvest House, 1964.

Meynaud, J., *Reflexions sur la politique au Quebec*, Montreal, Editions de Sainte-Marie, 1968.

Milner, S. H., and H., *The Decolonization of Quebec*, Toronto, McClelland and Stewart, 1973.

Monière, D., et Vachet, A., *Les idéologies au Québec*, (Bibliographie), Bibliothèque nationale du Québec, 1976.

Morf, G., *Terror in Quebec: Case Studies of the FLQ*, Toronto, Clarke Irwin, 1970.

Morin, C., *Quebec versus Ottawa: The Struggle for Self-government, 1960-72*, Toronto, University of Toronto, 1976.

Morin, C., *Le combat Québécois*, Montréal, Editions Boréal Express, 1973.

Morin, C., *Le pouvoir Québécois . . . en négotiation*, Montréal, Editions du Boréal Express, 1972.

Oliver, M., "Quebec and Canadian Democracy," *C.J.E.P.S.*, Vol. XXIII, No. 4, November, 1957.

Orban, E., *Le conseil législatif de Québec*, Montréal, Bellarmin, 1967.

Orban, E., "La fin du bicaméralisme au Québec," *C.J.P.S.*, Vol. II, No. 3, September, 1969.

Paré, G., *Au-delà du séparatisme*, Montréal, Collection les idées du jour, 1966.

Parti Pris, *Les Québécois*, Paris, Maspéro, 1967.

Pinard, M., *The Rise of a Third Party*, [Social Credit in Quebec], McGill-Queen's University Press, enlarged ed., 1975.

Québec, *Le rapport de la commission royale d'enquête sur l'enseignement*, (le rapport Parent), Québec, L'imprimeur de la rein, 1963-1966, 3 vols.

Québec, *Le rapport de la commission royale d'enquête sur la fiscalité*, (le rapport Bélanger), Québec, l'imprimeur de la reine, 1966.

Quebec, *Report of the Royal Commission of Inquiry on Constitutional Problems* (Tremblay Report), Quebec, 1956, 4 vols.

Raynauld, A., "Les implications économiques de l'option Québec," *Le Devoir*, 24 avril, 1970.

Reid, M., *The Shouting Signpainters: A Literary and Political Account of Quebec Revolutionary Nationalism*, Toronto, McClelland and Stewart, 1972.

Rioux, M., *Quebec in Question*, Toronto, James, Lewis and Samuel, 1971.

Rioux, M., and Martin, Y., *French Canadian Society*, Vol. I, Carleton Library, No. 18, Toronto, McClelland & Stewart, 1964.

Rotstein, A., (ed.), *Power Corrupted*, Toronto, New Press, 1971.

Roy. J.-L., "Dynamique du Nationalisme Québécois (1945-1970)", *Canadian Review of Studies in Nationalism*, Vol. 1, No. 1, Fall, 1973.

Scott, F., and Oliver, M., (eds.), *Quebec States her Case*, Toronto, Macmillan of Canada, 1964.

Séguin, M., "Genèse et historique de l'idée séparatiste au Canada français," *Laurentie*, No. 119, 1962.

Siegfried, A., *The Race Question in Canada*, Carleton Library No. 29, Toronto, McClelland and Stewart, 1966, (Reprint from 1906).

Sloan, T., *Quebec, The Not-So-Quiet Revolution*, Toronto, Ryerson, 1965.

La Société St. Jean Baptiste de Montréal, *Le fédéralisme, l'acte de l'amérique du nord britannique et les Canadiens français*, Mémoire au comité parlementaire de la constitution du gouvernement du Québec, Montréal, Les éditions de l'agence Duvernay, 1964.

Stein, M., *The Dynamics of Right-Wing Protest: Social Credit in Quebec*, Toronto, University of Toronto Press, 1973.

Stratford, P., (ed.), *Andre Laurendeau: Witness for Quebec, Essays*, Toronto, Macmillan, 1973.

Taylor, M. G., "Quebec medicare: policy formulation in conflict and crisis", *C.P.A.*, Vol. 15, No. 2, Summer, 1972.

Thomson, D., (ed.), *Quebec Society and Politics: Views from the Inside*, Toronto, McClelland and Stewart, 1973.

Treddenick, J. M., "Quebec and Canada: some economic aspects of independence", *Journal of Canadian Studies*, Vol. VIII, No. 4, November, 1973.

Troisième Congrès des Affaires Canadiennes, *Les nouveaux Québecois*, Québec, les Presses de l'Université Laval, 1964.

Trudeau, P. E., "Some Obstacles to Democracy in Quebec," *C.J.E.P.S.*, Vol. XXIV, No. 3, August, 1958.

Trudeau, P. E., *Federalism and the French Canadians*, Toronto, Macmillan, 1968.

Trudeau, P. E., (ed.), *The Asbestos Strike*, Toronto, James, Lewis and Samuel, 1974. (French version, Montréal, Les Editions du Jour, 1970.)

Vallières, P., *Choose!*, Toronto, New Press, 1972.

Vallières, P., *Nègres blancs d'Amérique*, Montréal, Editions Parti Pris, 1968. (English edition, Toronto, McClelland and Stewart, 1971.

Wade, M., (ed.), *Canadian Dualism: Studies of French-English Relations*, Toronto, University of Toronto Press, 1960.

Wade, M., *The French Canadians*, Vol. I, 1760-1911, Vol. II, 1912-1967, Toronto, Macmillan, 1970.

 II PROCESS

7

THE ROLE OF
PUBLIC OPINION

Many different forces shape public opinion. In recent years there has
been much discussion about whether public opinion polls influence how
citizens vote. Assuming the worst, several MPs have introduced private
members' bills into the House of Commons to ban the publication of
results of public opinion polls during election campaigns. However, the
House has not yet seen fit to follow the example of British Columbia and
some European countries and prohibit such publication. There has also
been concern about the increasing predilection of parties and candidates
to conduct private polls for their own advantage. Finally, there has been
debate about the methodology and accuracy of public opinion polls.

It is surprising that despite this concern very little that is definitive has
been written in Canada on the subject. Professor Hugh Whalen's article,
which he originally prepared for an earlier edition of this book and
which he has brought up to date and enlarged in this edition, stands as
the one major Canadian piece of literature on polling. It examines all of
these questions, concentrating in particular on the Gallup Poll in Canada
whose franchise is held by the Canadian Institute of Public Opinion.
References alluded to by Professor Whalen can be found in the bibliography at the end of the chapter. Richard Gwyn's amusing article relates
his experience in finally being interviewed by the Gallup Poll.

Pressure groups and lobbying in Canada have also attracted increased
attention lately. A new book in the McGraw-Hill Ryerson Series in
Canadian Politics has recently been published on this subject. Professor
Paul Pross's *Pressure Group Behaviour in Canadian Politics*, Toronto,
McGraw-Hill Ryerson, 1975, brings together a number of studies of
individual interest groups. Professor Robert Presthus's recent work in
the field and a number of additional articles and books also are listed in
the bibliography. The four-part article by Don McGillivray on "Lobbying
at Ottawa" which appeared in the third edition of *Politics: Canada*, pp.
163-172, has been replaced in this edition by Clive Baxter's article which
describes the rapid growth of lobbyists at Ottawa and their preference

for concentrating on civil servants and cabinet ministers. A list of prominent interest groups located in Ottawa is appended. W. D. H. Frechette's article explains the structure and operation of one such group, the Canadian Manufacturers' Association. Thus far, lobbyists at Ottawa have not been obliged to register, as they are required to do in Washington. However, the House of Commons has considered this possibility and on April 7, 1976, Conservative MP Walter Baker introduced Bill C-432, An Act to register lobbyists.

Students interested in how the media, politicians, and manipulators manufacture "pseudo-news" should consult Daniel J. Boorstin's classic book, *The Image: A Guide to Pseudo Events in America*, listed in the bibliography. Ron Haggart's article in this chapter gives some amusing and revealing illustrations. For an article showing how politicians make use of "trial balloons" to test public opinion, see the first edition of *Politics: Canada*, pp. 16-17.

The question of the relationship in Canada between the ownership of the media of communication and the influencing of public opinion, and in particular the dangers arising from the concentration of ownership of media, such as the existence of chains of newspapers, radio and television stations, has been thoroughly examined by Senator Keith Davey's Special Senate Committee on Mass Media. The committee published its three-volume study in 1970. This well-written and well-documented report is the basic work in the field. Volume I, *The Uncertain Mirror*, is descriptive while Volumes II and III provide the data. In 1976 the Report was being revised and updated. Some of the most important points dealt with in the Report are noted in David Surplis's article in this chapter, which is a revised version of his original contribution to the third edition of *Politics: Canada*. The list of Canada's major daily newspaper publishing groups with circulation figures has been brought up to date also.

Two proposals for improving the quality of the press appeared in the third edition of this book. Beland Honderich, pp. 186-192, urged the creation of self-governing press councils while Douglas Fisher, p. 192, suggested workers' control. Since 1972 press councils have been established in three provinces, Ontario, Quebec, and Alberta. Ron Lowman's article in this chapter describes briefly the work of the Ontario Press Council.

The bibliography contains references to recent Canadian literature on participatory democracy and the power structure as well as on polling, pressure groups, and the media.

THE PERILS OF POLLING*

Hugh Whalen

If the political significance of opinion survey research is to be understood, it must be viewed in its total social setting. For in most countries where it is now undertaken, opinion analysis is only incidentally concerned with the reporting of mass political views and voter intentions. During the last three decades, for better or for worse, attitude measurement and appraisal has become a potent force influencing the decisions taken by corporate leaders, media executives, politicians and civil servants. And in the social sciences attitude surveying is now a key instrument of inquiry. Much survey research is undertaken privately and concerns itself with consumer brand and design preferences, audience rating, market measurement, corporate image, and other commercial matters. The technical foundations which underlie much of this activity have only recently been developed by statisticians, computer technologists, and social scientists in endowed organizations, and government departments. As in most other fields, interdependence is everywhere apparent, and devices used successfully in one area have influenced developments in others.

Canadian government agencies, royal commissions, task forces and other policy-oriented bodies are now using survey research to a much greater extent than in the past. Professor Schindeler and Lanphier have noted the emergence of greater interdependence between social scientists and policy-makers as a result of this trend. Five years ago they indicated that of the 45 federal task forces then conducting investigations, fully 60 per cent were using survey techniques. Moreover, some 18 of those inquiries have been commissioned by either the Privy Council Office or the Office of the Prime Minister. Following is a short, illustrative list of the more significant national surveys conducted in recent years by public agencies: Statistics Canada (Labour Force, Consumer Price and other surveys); Royal Commission on Bilingualism and Biculturalism (27 studies); Task Force on Housing; Senate Committee on the Mass Media; Canadian Government Travel Bureau Survey; Armed Services (Recruiting and Collective Bargaining Surveys); Youth Culture study; Citizens' Groups study; Government Information study; and the national nutrition and immigration studies.

An interesting recent use of survey technique is evident in the presentation to the C.R.T.C. by the Canadian Broadcasting Corporation in connection with the renewal of its license. The Corporation commissioned a nation-wide attitude study whose results indicated that Canadians generally supported the public broadcasting system and its programs. It is worth observing, however, that the results of all publicly funded survey

* Revised in January, 1975 from an original article prepared in 1966 and published here with the permission of the author who is Research Professor of Political Science, Memorial University of Newfoundland. For sources alluded to in the article, see bibliography at end of the section.

research activity are not invariably made available to the public. Another fact worth emphasizing is that, apart from certain units like Statistics Canada, public agencies do not themselves normally undertake actual surveys. Most of this work is performed for them on contract by private survey organizations, many of whose clients also include political parties, party leadership contenders, provincial premiers, newspapers, magazines, the electronic media, and private associations or companies. It is my estimate that perhaps there are as many as thirty commercial organizations offering major survey services. Some Canadian political groups, on the other hand, have retained American polling firms, while at least one Canadian company has engaged in political survey activity in the United States.

There is little mystery why opinion surveying has appeared to attract more than its share of artful-dodgers and rain-makers. Since its inception in the 1930s, opinion analysis has seldom possessed validity or reliability in adequate amounts. Surveys are valid when they measure successfully those opinion characteristics they are intended to measure; they are reliable when they yield comparable results on different occasions. A perfect validity and reliability may indeed be impossible in practice; but it will not do to suggest, as some apologists of polling have done, that opinion research is scientific merely because it is now widely used. Yet it cannot be denied that much effort in recent years has been directed towards improving the quality of survey methods. What, it may then be asked, is the present state of the art, given its inauspicious beginnings?

Methodological Problems

Leading American pollers such as Gallup, Roper, and Harris, together with the more important survey research institutions, have experimented steadily with methods based upon statistical inference. The purpose of statistical inference is to estimate the unknown attributes of an entire population (or universe) from the known characteristics of a given sample thereof. Sample design is thus of key importance, for upon it depend the reliability measures of survey estimates. Various methods of sample estimation and selection can be used to indicate the risk factors associated with sampling error.

Critics of polling have frequently focused their attacks on the use of supposedly undersized samples. Such criticism may sometimes be valid; but often it rests on little rational foundation. Once certain minimum statistical requirements have been met, and a given order of sample error determined, the only justification for increasing sample size is to reduce still further the margin of estimated sample error. Typically, moreover, much greater percentage increases in sample size are required in order to produce small decreases in sample errors.

Let us assume that in a national probability sample of 100 Canadian voters, 40 percent of respondents indicate a preference for the candidate of Party A. It might be shown statistically that, with a confidence of 99 out of 100, the limits within which the total electorate actually preferred Party A would be from 28 to 52 percent. The error in this case is approximately plus or minus 12 percent in relation to the sample estimate of 40 percent. If the sample were increased to 200 voters, selected at random, the confidence limits might be reduced to, say, between 32 and 48 percent. The range of estimated error in this instance is 8 percentage points above or below the second sample estimate of 40 percent. The following table illustrates hypothetically the inverse relationship between sample size and the confidence limits for the entire electorate:

Sample Size	Percentage Confidence Limits
100	28 - 52
200	32 - 48
500	35 - 45
1,000	36 - 44
2,000	38 - 42
5,000	39 - 41

An absolutely correct size for a national opinion sample can never be established authoritatively. Decisions in this matter are bound to reflect accumulated polling experience, the individual poller's judgement, and the given survey's objectives. When surveys, for instance, are concerned strictly with aggregate national election forecasting, and when reliable results are not sought at the regional and provincial levels, it appears that small random samples of the electorate are usually adequate, given the tolerances in errors now accepted by pollers. But when accuracy at various subnational levels is required, when the margin of national survey error must be reduced, and even when elections turn out to be closely contested, larger samples are clearly needed. Herein lies the first of many dilemmas confronting the opinion analyst; for while the cost of polling varies directly with the size of sample, the precision of sample estimates increases only as the square root of the number of respondents interviewed.

A second feature of sample design relates to stratification. When selecting a national sample to measure voting intentions, for example, the various demographic categories of age, sex, rural or urban residence, and the occupation, income, education, religious and ethnic affiliation of the population must be given appropriate representation in the sample. To avoid bias, the sample must be constructed to include the proper proportion of each relevant category of the whole population.

Perhaps the most spectacular instance of sample bias in polling was recorded in the United States during the 1936 presidential election. On that occasion the *Literary Digest* poll, with a massive sample of 2.4 million mailed-in ballots, underestimated Roosevelt's victory by 19.3 percentage points, in large measure because a significant proportion of its respondents were persons listed in *Who's Who*. This polling failure illustrates the inadequacy of large but unrepresentative samples in election forecasting. Results of much greater accuracy have been obtained by the Gallup and other organizations using small stratified samples ranging from two to eight thousand respondents.

There are many different ways of selecting samples that are representative of the universe under study. In the formative years of polling the "quota-stratified" method of selection was widely used. But in recent years the selection of units for inclusion in opinion samples has come to depend increasingly on the principle of "known probability". A probability sample based on random selection is one in which all units of the universe being examined have an equal, and therefore a known, chance of being included. One method of random selection that has gained wide acceptance during the postwar period is "area-probability" sampling, which is described below. Some proponents of this method claim that when properly used it obviates the need for quota procedures since it automatically produces a suitably stratified national sample. Both methods are now generally combined in national opinion surveys.

Quota-stratified sampling involves essentially the following steps: (1) choice of those characteristics of the population to be sampled; (2) the determination of the proportions of the population having such characteristics; (3) the assigning of quotas to interviewers who, largely at their own discretion, select respondents in such a way that the sample is stratified in accordance with the proportions established in (2).

The classic quota method has two deficiencies. First, respondents tend to be selected by interviewers in a manner which prevents knowledge of the probabilities of selection. Thus, according to Hansen and Hauser in Katz's book, "Because the probabilities of inclusion in the [quota] sample of the various classes of elements are unknown, the estimates frequently made the sampling error of quota sample results, supposedly based on sampling theory, usually are erroneous". Second, the latitude given to interviewers may cause serious sample bias. The incorporation of random procedures within quotas has somewhat improved the method, but early surveys frequently underrepresented males, manual workers, and employed females who were not readily available for interview during working hours. Early quota samples for the same reason often gave undue weight to the opinions of middle and upper middle class strata.

The area-probability method of drawing an opinion sample includes the following steps: (1) choice of the characteristics of the population to be sampled; (2) in the case of a national sample, division of the country into classes of the appropriate *areal units*, usually of a politico-geographic nature (e.g., counties, rural municipalities, towns, cities), from which random selections are made; (3) the units so selected, in turn, are arbitrarily divided into smaller *area segments* (e.g., rural areas delineated by rail lines, roads, streams and powerlines; town and city blocks), from which further random selections are made; (4) the area segments so selected, in turn, contain *occupied dwelling units* (each consisting of one household), from which a number are selected by prescribed method; (5) the occupied dwelling units so selected, in turn, contains one or more *adults* (or eligible voters), from which a sample of one or more is drawn according to rule.

The first three steps in area-probability sampling are performed in the survey office using maps, aerial photographs, tables of random numbers, and other equipment. The last two steps, however, are undertaken by interviewers in accordance with strict rules intended to prevent subjective bias in selection. The strength of this method of drawing a sample stems from the nature of the selection process which is always verifiable in relation to some known probability, since every adult (or eligible voter) in the population can be associated with but one occupied dwelling unit which in turn can be associated with one, and only one, segment of land. The main practical difficulty with area sampling is its complexity and relative cost. While it does not require extensive pre-listing, it does normally demand greater administrative direction, more skilled interviewers, extensive travel, and time wastage due to "call backs" on respondents.

For these and other reasons most national opinion surveys now combine area-probability sampling with revised quota procedures. The various modes of combination are extremely complex. It seems clear, however, that in practice the pollers have not found methods of selection that guarantee a perfectly random choice of respondents. While progress has undoubtedly been made in that direction, it is known, for example, that interviewers err in applying the rules governing respondent selection and substitution, and that respondents who are to be chosen at random but who are difficult to locate are frequently excluded for budgetary reasons. As we shall see below, errors of this kind are not invariably self-cancelling.

Defects in selection or in size of samples are not the only sources of errors in forecasting. Actual interviewing may be ineffective, even when the respondent uses a secret ballot. Estimation of the proportion and characteristics of eligible voters who will not vote may be wide of the mark. Errors of a similar sort may occur when dealing with "leaning" voters, "undecided" voters, and with electors who refuse to communicate their intentions. Other errors may occur at the coding and data processing stages. Finally, many possibilities for miscalculation arise naturally in the interpretation of the processed data, including the corrections for trends and projects of forecast.

The last factor is of prime importance. Opinion surveys have sometimes failed to detect sharp movements of popular sentiment during the very last days of election campaigns. The classic instance was the American polling debacle of 1948. Gallup, Roper, and Crossley, along with other polling organizations, predicted a Republican victory but the Democratic candidate won 49.5 percent of the total vote. On the basis of only the ballots cast for the major parties, the following maximum (i.e., positive and negative) percentage point errors of forecast were recorded: Gallup, 9.4 percent; Crossley, 9.5 percent; and Roper, 19.5 percent.

Failure on this occasion to predict the election of President Truman caused gnashing of teeth and much explanation on the part of the polling fraternity, produced extreme joy and chagrin in the respective party camps, and stimulated the most elaborate inquiry of polling error ever undertaken. Sponsored by the Social Science Research Council, and weighing all the evidence—not merely the hypotheses suggested by the pollers, the media pundits and the politicians—the investigating committee reported that the failure was due in large part to important, late, unexpected, and undetected shifts of voter preference to the Democratic candidate. Sample errors of estimate were found to exist, but apparently they did not contribute significantly to the errors of forecast. Additional mistakes included a failure to predict the behaviour of an abnormally large group of undecided voters and an inadequate projection of voter turnout. For the most part, moreover, these errors were additive and did not cancel.

There are various measures of error associated with the sampling of total population characteristics. The poller, for instance, can calculate his chance "standard error" in relation to the number of respondents interviewed. Measures of this kind can be called *statistical errors*, since they emerge from the body of sampling theory and technique and were invented to deal with discrete objects exhibiting stability through time. Since pre-election attitudes in relation to the actual voting decision are often evanescent and imperfectly communicated even when the respondent uses a secret ballot, and since a significant part of the electorate (20-25 percent) never exercises the franchise, there is little necessary congruence between statistical error and what can be called the poller's *error of forecast*.

It appears that the limiting cases involving the relationship between the two kinds of error are these: (1) if the poller exercises correct judgment in appraising the many political, non-statistical variables affecting the election process, he may well achieve minimum forecast error even with substantial statistical error; (2) if, on the other hand, he deals inexpertly with political trends, he may obtain large forecast error even with minimum statistical error. Within these broad limits, of course, there is bound in practice to be much accidental cancellation of error.

Are the Polls Scientific?

In addition to the above factors, several other points should be noted before answering the question of whether or not the polls are "scientific". Clearly, the experimental work during the last three decades on opinion sampling has improved the quality of generalizations upon which pollers now base their projections of forecast. As compared with the pre-1948 period, for instance, there is now less tendency to assume that election campaigns do not influence voting intentions. Devices such as more extended interviewing and last-minute telegraphic probes have proved useful in the detection of late election trends. Improvements have also been introduced in areas not strictly related to statistical inference. The evaluations of "undecided" voter behaviour have improved, as have projections of the percentage of voter turnout at elections.

Yet, despite all these developments, V. O. Key's view is undoubtedly still true: "The sample survey is more useful as a means of identifying gross differences in the behaviour of voters and the correlates of these differences than in predicting the outcome of elections. Even with a purely random sample, the odds against predicting the winner when the division is near 50-50 are quite high, an inherent feature of the polls not well explained to the public by the polling organizations." Even Gallup concedes "that at some future date the 'polls will go wrong' again, especially in a close election." But as a justification of opinion surveying he adds that "no other method will be found—apart from sampling of the kind we do—which is more accurate."

There is, of course, little agreement on what constitutes accuracy of polling forecast. Ability to pick the winner is obviously the basic test. In this regard, even in some very close election contests, the polls have recently established a high degree of accuracy. The leading American polling organizations have predicted successfully the winners in nine of the last ten presidential elections. Their record in predicting the outcome of congressional and state elections, however, is much less outstanding. But in the American presidential race of 1960, for instance, Gallup forecast a Kennedy victory with 51 percent of the vote. When the more than 60 million ballots were cast, Kennedy received 50.2 percent as compared with Nixon's 49.8 percent. Using a national sample of approximately 8,000 respondents, Gallup's maximum error thus amounted to only 1.6 percentage points.

But in the last three British elections, on the other hand, there have been major polling errors. In 1970 all British polling organizations but one forecast incorrectly a Labour Party victory. One reputable polling unit even estimated that Wilson would obtain a 150-seat majority. Pre-election surveys also found that from a leadership standpoint the electors favoured Wilson over Heath, and that a very high voter turnout was probable. In the event, the Conservative Party under Heath obtained a 30-seat majority and voter turnout fell to 72 percent, the lowest election participation rate recorded since 1935.

In the British election held in February, 1974, another polling disaster must be reported. Prior to this election most surveys indicated a slight decline in Conservative support, a sharp growth in Liberal strength, but a narrow victory for Heath, who was almost universally supported by the mass media. The result, however, gave Labour 301 seats in the House of Commons, as against 296 for the Conservatives, 24 for the "fringe groups," and 14 for the Liberals. This polling error was publicly acknowledged by Lou Harris, who indicated the difficulties stemming from a constituency redistribution that produced 347 new seats out of 635.

In the election of October, 1974, the four major British polls were once again wide of the mark. The National Opinion Poll predicted a Labour lead of 14.5 percentage points over the Conservatives. Both Harris and the Opinion Research Centre gave Labour a 10 percentage point victory margin while Gallup forecast Labour would win by 5.5 percentage points. The actual results were 39.3 percent for Labour and 35.7 for the Conservatives, or a 3.6 percentage point victory for Labour. It is ironic that the N.O.P. had stated that even allowing for a maximum sampling error, Labour would still be about 8 percentage points in the lead. Certainly, recent British polls have amply confirmed Gallup's prediction, noted above, that "the polls will go wrong again".

Apart from accuracy in the prediction of the winning candidates or parties, polling success can be measured in terms of a correct forecasting of the distribution of the popular vote among contesting parties. In the latter case it is possible to distinguish forecast errors expressed in actual votes, in percentages, and in percentage points. These errors, in turn, may be totalled and expressed in simple or weighted averages. Let us assume the following election:

TABLE 1: Calculated Error of Polling Forecast: An Illustration

Forecast and Vote	Party A	Party B	Party C	Party D	Total
Poll forecast (in millions)	4.5	4.0	1.0	.5	10.0
Poll forecast (in percent)	45	40	10	5	100
Actual vote (in millions)	5.0	3.0	1.5	.5	10.0
Actual vote (in percent)	50	30	15	5	100
Error of Forecast					
Vote Error (million)	−.5	+1.0	−.5	0	±2.0
Percentage Error	−10	+33	−33	0	±76
Percentage Point Error	−5	+10	−5	0	±20

The total error of forecast in this illustration involves ±2 million votes out of a total of 10 million votes cast. The total *percentage error* (i.e., where the actual vote percentage is expressed as 100 and the forecast deviation is measured from the base) stands at ±76 percent. The total *percentage point* error (i.e., the total of the differences between the percentage forecast for each party and the percentage of actual votes cast for each party) is ±20 percent. When these cumulative errors are simply averaged among the four parties, percentage error is reduced to ±19 percent, while the percentage point error falls to ±5 percent.

The Gallup organization has always claimed that its final election forecasts are accurate only to within an average of four percentage points. An allowance for permitted error expressed in this way is, of course, thoroughly misleading; it permits substantial real forecast error while suggesting only minimal failure. But it also gives to polling organizations an important tactical advantage. When questioned about forecast errors, they can usually claim to be well within accepted limits. At that point the discussion tends to shift abruptly from the causes of forecast error to the public's error in appraising polling objectives and methods.

The committee which examined the American polling failure of 1948 made bold to say:

> Too many people had an exaggerated impression of the accuracy of the pre-election polls—in spite of the numerous statements, particularly by Gallup, that poll results were subject to average errors of 3 to 4 percentage points. Too many people seemed to feel that average error meant maximum error, and they did not realize that average error of 4 percentage points can produce errors of 8, 12 or more percentage points. Until readers and users of poll results understand these errors . . . there will continue to be adverse reactions. . . .

The Canadian Institue of Public Opinion (Gallup poll) has conducted eleven national pre-election polls since 1945. Since the Institute does not undertake to predict the number of parliamentary seats each party will win, it cannot be expected to name the winning candidate or party as in American presidential elections. It seeks rather to predict the distribution of the total vote among the contesting parties. The Institute's performance in eleven Canadian general elections is summarized in Table 2. (Unbracketed figures indicate the poll percentage error; bracketed figures indicate the poll percentage point error.)

TABLE 2: Calculated Error of C.I.P.O. Pre-Election Final Forecasts, 1945-1974

Election	Liberal		Progressive Conservative		CCF-NDP		Others	
1945	−5	(−2)	+6	(+2)	+9	(+1)	−6	(−1)
1949	−3	(−2)	+4	(+1)	+12	(+2)	−19	(−1)
1953	+2	(+1)	0	0	0	0	−9	(−1)
1957	+17	(+7)	−13	(−5)	−7	(−1)	−16	(−1)
1958	0	0	+4	(+2)	−16	(−2)	0	0
1962	−3	(−1)	+2	(+1)	−11	(−2)	+17	(+2)
1963	−2	(−1)	−2	(−1)	+6	(+1)	+6	(+1)
1965	+10	(+4)	−10	(−3)	0	0	−6	(−1)
1968	+4	(+2)	−6	(−2)	+6	(+1)	−14	(−1)
1972	0	0	−6	(−2)	+17	(+3)	−12	(−1)
1974	+2	(+1)	0	0	+7	(+1)	−25	(−2)
Total error	±48	(±21)	±53	(±19)	±91	(±14)	±130	(±12)
Average error	±4.4	(±1.9)	±4.8	(±1.7)	±8.3	(±1.3)	±11.8	(±1.1)

Sources: Vote allocations by party for the first five elections are as calculated by H. A. Scarrow, *Canada Votes*, New Orleans, 1962, pp. 118, 132, 146, 162, and 176. Subsequent election data were obtained from the Reports of the Chief Electoral Officer and from his preliminary results of valid votes cast by civilian and armed service electors in 1974. These figures were contrasted to the appropriate Gallup Poll final election party forecasts in order to obtain the differences set out above. (Unbracketed figures indicate the poll percentage error; bracketed figures indicate the poll percentage point error.)

In eleven federal elections in which the C.I.P.O. has made predictions about the percentage of votes to be cast for party categories, the Institute has correctly predicted the proportions in only seven of 44 instances. In the case of the two major parties, substantial forecast errors occurred in 1957 and in 1965. The Institute grossly overestimated Liberal strength in each case. In six instances, but notably in 1972, it also miscalculated CCF-NDP strength by substantial margins, but these errors were slight in relation to the total vote. Average percentage polling error in eleven elections was approximately the same for the two major parties, but inasmuch as the the publication of poll results has any real effect on the outcome of a Canadian election, the Conservatives were placed at a disadvantage in 1957 and 1965. Cumulative figures on polling error are set out in Table 3.

Various measures of the Institute's maximum and average forecast error are set out in the first four columns above (Table 3). Total percentage error in column 1 represents the sum of positive and negative percentage polling deviations measured from a 100 percent base of the actual vote proportions received by the four categories of parties. (Although not generally used in the analysis of polling accuracy, these aggregate percentage deviations are nevertheless the purest indicators of election forecasting performance. To illustrate, if it is projected that a given party is to receive 1 percent of the total vote and in fact it obtains only 0.5 percent of all votes cast, the percentage error is −50 while the percentage point error is only one-half of −1 percent.) In the elections of 1949 and 1962, when the Institute's maximum percentage point error was relatively small (6%), its cumulative percentage error of forecast was

TABLE 3: Measures of C.I.P.O. Cumulative Polling Error, Party Vote Plurality, and Electoral Participation Rates, 1945-1974

Election	Total Forecast Error		Unweighted Average Error	Vote Error (000's)	Winning Party Plurality (000's)	Voter Turn-out %
	%	Percentage Point				
1945	26	6	1.5	314.8	721.8	75
1949	38	6	1.5	350.9	1,161.4	74
1953	11	2	0.5	112.8	1,007.0	68
1957	53	14	3.5	964.8	129.8	74
1958	20	4	1.0	291.5	1,460.7	79
1962	33	6	1.5	466.4	7.8	80
1963	16	4	1.0	315.8	510.5	80
1965	26	8	2.0	616.9	599.6	75
1968	30	6	1.5	487.6	1,142.1	76
1972	35	6	1.5	576.5	334.7	77
1974	34	4	1.0	380.2	732.4	72
Average	29.3	6.0	1.5	443.5	709.8	75

Sources: Calculated from Table 2 and the Reports of the Chief Electoral Officer.

±38 and ±33 percent respectively, due to major miscalculations of the minor party vote. In the elections of 1957 and 1965, when the Institute's maximum percentage point error was very large (14% and 8%), its cumulative percentage error stood at ±53 and ±26 percent respectively. The latter figure is relatively small because of the polls' accuracy in predicting the minor party vote in 1965. In 1972 the total forecast error was ±35 percent and in 1974 ±34 percent, due largely to inaccuracies in its minor party projections.

It is clear from these comparisons that polling error expressed as an unweighted percentage point average—the measure used by all Gallup organizations—bears little relationship to actual polling competence. Such a measure is obtained by dividing total percentage point error by the number of categories of parties. Hence an average error of ±3.5 percent in 1957, while it remained well within the Institute's permissible error of ±4 percent, involved a total forecast error of 53 percent, or nearly one million votes when the Liberal and Progressive Conservative parties were separated by less than 130,000 votes. Similarly, an average polling error of only ±2 percent in 1965 involved a total forecast error of 26 percent, or almost 617,000 votes when the two major parties were separated by only 599,000 votes. Even when, as in 1962, average polling error was very low (±1.5%) the disparity between the error expressed in actual votes (466,000) and the leading party's plurality of 8,000 votes was spectacularly large.

Table 3 also indicates a somewhat uncertain relationship between polling accuracy and voter turnout in Canadian general elections. Assuming a minimal sampling error and a small proportion of "undecided" respondents, the error of polling forecasts ought to vary inversely with the size of voter participation. But in fact there appears to be little consistent correlation between these two variables. At the level of 74-75 percent turnout, for example, the following C.I.P.O. percentage point errors were recorded:

±6 (1945), ±6 (1949), ±8 (1965), and ±14 (1957). During the three elections when voter participation reached the peak of 79-80 percent, comparable errors ranged between ±4 and ±6 percent. When voter participation was at an all-time low of 68 percent in 1953, on the other hand, the Institute's error of forecast stood at its lowest point of only ±2 percentage points.

It would seem to be a reasonable conclusion that the Canadian Institute of Public Opinion has not achieved an outstanding record of accuracy in the prediction of Canadian election outcomes. On the basis of eleven election forecasts its average percentage error per election has been ±29.3, while its error in percentage points has averaged ±6.0. Moreover in the elections of 1957, 1962, 1965, and 1972, the latter error, expressed in votes, was greater than the leading party's vote plurality.

C.I.P.O. Polling Techniques

According to a newspaper article in the *Toronto Star* on November 8, 1961, the Canadian Institute of Public Opinion used at that time a force of 600 part-time interviewers to gather its findings. All the interviewers in Canada were women. An average study cost between $4,000 and $5,000. In its early years of sampling voters' opinions, the C.I.P.O. terminated its interviewing 10 days before an election, but after 1957 the date of final questioning was moved up to three or four days before polling day, in order to improve the accuracy of results. The normal sample of 690 persons per survey was also enlarged immediately before elections.

For its final pre-election surveys the C.I.P.O. has for some time drawn a national sample of rather less than 3,000 respondents. Of all the persons interviewed, some are not eligible to vote, some refuse to express their intentions, some are undecided at the time of interview, while a few always claim either to have no party preference or to favour some party other than the four major national parties. Of the 2,700 individuals interviewed prior to the 1962 election, for example, 510 (18.9%) for various reasons did not communicate a clear intention.

The standard question put to respondents is: "If a federal election were held today, which party's candidate do you think you would favour?" Respondents indicate their preferences by marking a "secret" ballot. When there is an expression of indecision, a further question is put: "Will you please mark the ballot to show the way you are leaning at the present time?" For survey purposes the "leaners" are assumed to have expressed adequately their party preferences.

As a general rule, moreover, the relatively large number of respondents unable to express their intentions clearly are presumed as a group to have the same preference characteristics as those who do mark their ballots. The adequacy of such procedures has often been questioned. In some countries behavioural regularities in this area have been observed. American Gallup poll officials claim that, within a two percent tolerance, their undecided voters tend to behave in the same way as voters who have expressed a clear intention, except, of course, in the 1964 presidential election where there is evidence to indicate that an unprecedented number of undecided voters actually cast ballots for Goldwater. An adequate understanding of similar phenomena is lacking in Canada.

In addition to the data on party preference, the Institute's interviewers in final election polls solicit opinions on various political questions and attempt to measure the intensity of voter interest in the campaign. Respondents are asked to rate their own interest in the pending election. From this latter information an attempt is made to project the rate of actual voter participation. With the possible exception of 1962 results, the projections of voter interest have appeared to parallel actual trends of turnout. For subsequent analysis of the correlates of voting preference, interviewers also obtain information on the age, sex, education, occupation, religion, mother tongue, and trade union characteristics of respondents. Finally, in each case socio-economic status is determined by the interviewer in accordance with a prescribed "home and standard of living" scale.

The Canadian Institute of Public Opinion purports to use area-probability sampling methods. But as in other countries a combined quota-area procedure is actually used. The rural component of the Canadian sample, in fact, is not based on area methods at all but rather on a crude geographic quota system which allows the interviewer much discretion in the choice of respondents. The urban part of the sample, however, incorporates some aspects of area-probability technique. The urban census tracts are first stratified in accordance with income and a random sample of units is chosen. From the tracts so selected a further sample of block units is chosen by random selection. Interviewers with given quotas, beginning at any convenient dwelling unit in the urban blocks, then proceed to interview a random selection of adults in every second dwelling. This process continues until all quotas are complete. When the field data are processed the sample is weighted for age by duplicating IBM cards for the age classes requiring greater representation. And the units thus added are assumed to have gross voting preferences similar to those actually interviewed.

A second limitation worth noting is that the Institute, apparently for budgetary reasons, restricts "call backs" on persons not directly available for interview. For this reason the sample is biased against men, employed adult females, and probably low income groups. "The effect of this [bias]", in the words of Professor R. R. Alford who has made extensive use of C.I.P.O. results, "is difficult to estimate".

Regenstreif Predictions

In addition to the forecasts of Canadian elections provided by the Institute, there are the newspaper-sponsored polling activities of Professor S. P. Regenstreif. This poller undertook his first national survey prior to the 1958 election, and during the next three elections his party seat predictions were widely publicized. His national polling record was as follows:

Certain characteristic features of this poll are apparent. First, Regenstreif has never succeeded in obtaining complete accuracy in his twelve

TABLE 4: Calculated Seat, Percentage, and Percentage Point Error of the Regenstreif Poll in Three General Elections, 1962-1965

Party	1962			1963			1965		
	Seat Error	% Error	% pt. Error	Seat Error	% Error	% pt. Error	Seat Error	% Error	% pt. Error
Liberal	− 5	− 5	− 2	− 7	− 5	− 3	+ 9	+ 7	+ 3
P.C.	−16	−14	− 6	−19	−20	− 7	−18	− 19	− 7
N.D.P.	− 3	−16	− 1	+ 4	+23	+ 2	− 4	− 19	− 2
S.C., etc.	− 6	−20	− 2	− 1	− 4	0*	− 9†	− 56	− 3
Total	−30	−55	−11	±31	±52	±12	±40	±101	±15
Doubtful	30 (11%)			23 (9%)			22 (8%)		

Sources: Calculated from S. P. Regenstreif, *The Diefenbaker Interlude*, p. xi. Seat prediction for 1965 as published in the *Winnipeg Free Press*, November 6, 1965.
* Less than 0.5%.   † Includes two elected Independent candidates.

attempts at predicting party seat distributions in the House of Commons. Second, in 10 of the party seat predictions he underestimated the number of members actually elected. In particular, he has consistently failed to predict accurately the electoral fortunes of the Progressive Conservative party. During the three elections under review that party returned 308 members to parliament, whereas Regenstreif's forecasts called for only 255. His total error in this regard stands at −17 percent. His miscalculations of total party seat distributions have ranged between 30 and 40 seats per election, or from 11 to 15 percent of all parliamentary seats. Regenstreif also designates a number of constituencies as being in doubt. In 1963 and 1965 the numbers left in doubt were 23 and 22 respectively, or slightly less than one-tenth of all constituencies.

These calculations, however, fail to convey the real limits of Regenstreif's polling errors. In spite of allowances for doubtful seats, he was prepared in all three elections to forecast which party would win a majority of seats, or which party would assume or retain office with minority status in parliament. As a justification for the use of his services in 1963 and 1965, the press frequently alluded to his earlier predictions that the Diefenbaker government would not obtain its majority in the election of 1962, and that the Social Credit party would emerge as a potent force in Quebec's federal ridings. The first of these forecasts was very accurate; the second was less accurate, since he had projected only 20 seats for the Caouette party when in fact it secured 26. Prior to the 1965 election, on the other hand, Regenstreif assigned 140 seats to the Liberals, 79 to the Progressive Conservatives, 17 to the N.D.P., and 7 to the Social Credit and *Créditiste* groups when in actual fact Mr. Pearson's government narrowly failed to get its majority and secured only 131 seats while the Progressive Conservatives elected 97 candidates. These errors of forecast had their source in a major underestimation of Mr. Diefenbaker's strength on the Prairies and in the Maritimes, and at least to some degree in a sanguine assumption of *Créditiste* decline in Quebec. The only element in his forecast sustained by the electoral decision was an increased support for the N.D.P.

In sharp contrast to his previous national polling efforts, Professor

Regenstreif's predictive performance in 1968 was extremely cautious. For the first time he did not assign a specific seat distribution to the contending parties but limited himself to a range of possible outcomes. The Liberals, he felt, could receive between 128 and 145 of the seats available. In the event, they obtained 155. The Progressive Conservatives were assigned victories in the range 75 to 93. They actually elected only 72 members. The N.D.P. potential was considered to be between 20 and 28 whereas they obtained 22. The *Créditistes* were thought capable of electing between 8 and 12 members when in fact they won 14. While conceding that all signs pointed to a Trudeau victory, Regenstreif said: "The Liberal potential straddles the majority line of 133 seats. The likelihood is that Trudeau will get it, provided most of the uncertainties are resolved in his favor. But political realities require a cautious analysis." (*Toronto Star*, June 22, 1968.) It is apparent that in spite of its more cautious approach the Regenstreif poll in 1968 continued to exhibit the weaknesses described above. In this case its projections failed to capture the magnitude of Mr. Trudeau's electoral sweep — a victory that produced a Liberal party plurality in excess of one million votes. At the same time, it seriously overestimated Progressive Conservative constituency potential. It is worth observing, finally, that the direction of poll forecast errors in 1968 is the reverse of those apparent in 1965.

In his first venture at public polling during a provincial election, Regenstreif's errors were even more substantial. His predictive performance during the Ontario election of 1963 is set out in Table 5.

TABLE 5: Calculated Seat, Percentage, and Percentage Point Error of the Regenstreif Poll in the Ontario Provincial Election, 1963

	Conservative	Liberal	N.D.P.	Total
Poll Forecasts (Seats)	56	35	5	96
Seats Won	77	24	7	108
Seat Error	−21	+11	− 2	±34
Percentage Error	−27.3	+46.0	−28.5	±101.8
Percentage Point Error	−19.4	+10.2	− 1.9	±31.5

Sources: *Toronto Daily Star*, September 23, 1963, p. 1; the *Canadian Parliamentary Guide, 1965*, Ottawa, 1965, p. 709.

Disregarding the 12 seats left in doubt, Regenstreif in this instance failed to forecast accurately 34 out of 96 constituency results. As with the federal polls he underestimated Conservative strength and overemphasized Liberal seat potential. But the margins of error in this poll were greater than in those examined above. Total percentage error due to seat misallocation, for example, exceeded ±100, while the maximum percentage point error exceeded ±31. If the 12 doubtful seats were added to those allocated in error, total failure of forecast extended to 46 of the 108 legislative contests. In the Ontario election of 1967, although he did engage in opinion sampling activity, Professor Regenstreif did not hazard a public prediction of party seat allocations.

Regenstreif's original method of polling requires brief comment. It is in no way related to the methods used by the Canadian Institute of Public Opinion. First, eleven main politico-geographic regions of Canada are chosen. The poller then visits each region and conducts interviews using a crude quota stratified in terms of income, residence (urban, suburban, and rural), religious affiliation, and ethnicity. Within these strata requirements the choice of actual respondents is supposedly made at random. Just how random selection is made in these conditions remains obscure. In comparison with other polling organizations, the Regenstreif sample is very small: 210 (1958), 375 (1962), 470 (1963).

Regenstreif's techniques of polling are not amenable to tests of statistical significance since, as he himself has said, he relies heavily on his own powers of judgment:

> ...most of the surveying done by me is based on what is known as 'judgment' sampling—in other words, the selection of the people to be interviewed was purely a matter of my own personal discretion—and there is no real way of statistically determining how representative of the general population my respondents are. Secondly, such efforts, ...are not 'scientific' because they are not really replicable by someone else, even if they were to operate on the same set of assumptions that I did. In this sense, this style of research is more in the category of 'art' than of 'science'.

Along with the much greater caution apparent in his polling activity since 1965, Regenstreif's projections in recent years have been based not only on his own personal interviews with voters but as well on the results of national pre-election surveys conducted by private opinion research groups.

Election Polls and the Mass Media

In recent provincial elections there has been a marked increase in polling activity sponsored by newspapers and undertaken by private survey organizations. In most cases an attempt is made to project proportional vote distributions rather than to forecast actual constituency outcomes. The preferred method involves the use of random provincial samples whose voting intentions are sought exclusively through telephone interviews. Some of these studies, notably those of the *Centre de Recherches sur l'Opinion Publique* conducted during the Quebec elections of 1970 and 1973, have succeeded in predicting election trends in a general manner, but have failed to attain high levels of accuracy. C.R.O.P. surveys in the first election projected the defeat of the Bertrand government, and in the second election correctly predicted the re-election of Premier Bourassa.

The C.R.O.P. poll, which uses a provincial sample in excess of one thousand respondents, was very inaccurate in 1970 when it recorded a total percentage point error of ±24. This margin of error was dramatically reduced in 1973 when it stood at ±8. In both cases, however, the poll understated Liberal strength and overstated the potential of the *Créditistes*. A feature of these polls is the very high proportion of the

TABLE 6: C.R.O.P. Pre-Election Polls: Quebec, 1970 and 1973

Party	1970			1973		
	Last Poll %	Actual Vote %	Error %	Last Poll %	Actual Vote %	Error %
Liberal	37	44	−7	50	54	−4
Parti Québécois	29	24	+5	30	30	0
Union Nationale	15	20	−5	6	5	+1
Créditistes	15	11	+4	14	11	+3
Others	4	1	+3	—	—	—

Source: Unofficial election and poll results as reported in the *Montreal Star*, *Toronto Star* and the Toronto *Globe and Mail*, 1970 and 1973.

sample that fails to communicate its voting intention. In the final poll before the 1973 election, for example, fully 29.4 per cent of the sample failed in this respect. In both elections, moreover, the Liberal party won heavy victories, capturing 72 of 108 seats in 1970 and 102 of 110 seats in 1973. The polling organization, in short, was not dealing in either case with a close election situation.

There is no agreement among the polling fraternity concerning the *bona fides* of telephone surveys. Some pollers reject them entirely on technical grounds; others believe that they should be supplemented with a sample which is extracted by personal interview; and a few hold that they are capable of achieving accurate projections. There is no doubt that they have been developed in response to the demands of the print media, since, if accurate, they can be regarded as "the ultimate scoop". They are also much less expensive to undertake than the conventional polling methods. But there is now sufficient evidence available to suggest their main technical shortcomings. First, the rate of outright refusals is very high, sometimes approaching 20 per cent. This result produces a major substitution problem. Second, the proportion failing to communicate a voting intention is, as we have seen, very large. And finally, there is no doubt that these surveys have a bias against rural, less educated and less wealthy individuals to a degree which it may be impossible to determine. These limitations reduce the probability that each voter in the provincial universe has an equal chance of being included in any given survey. Considering their recorded performance in both British Columbia and Quebec, we conclude that the media-sponsored polls have a growing, though still uncertain, reliability, particularly in close election races.

The Impact of Polling and its Future

Many commentators and not a few politicians have suggested that so far from having only a disinterested concern with the measurement of opinion and intention, polling activity itself exercises a powerful influence on the opinions and intentions that it seeks to measure. It is often held that during election campaigns, for instance, the publication of poll results tends to interfere with what ought to be the autonomous decision-making function of the electorate. Beyond these arguments there is the problem created for party leaders who must contend during the final stages of a campaign with unfavourable poll results. Three basic hypotheses have been suggested which attempt to connect the dissemination of poll results with actual voting behaviour. First, it has been argued that polls tend to foster a "bandwagon effect" in which voters decide to change their intentions in order to be on the winning side. Second, it is sometimes alleged that polls trigger an "underdog effect" and that weaker parties and candidates are the real beneficiaries. Third, there is what has recently been called the "withdrawal effect", when it is held that substantial numbers decide not to vote because polls indicate a foregone electoral result.

Pollers have done their best to refute each of these theories. Successive poll results in election campaigns clearly do not show that the strongest candidates tend systematically to become stronger or weaker as the first two hypotheses suggest they must. And with respect to the "withdrawal" thesis there is no clear evidence upon which to generalize. Some observers contend that this latter factor was at work in the British election of 1970, and that it explained the very low turnout of voters noted above which militated against the Labour Party's success. Others contend that if the participation rate had been higher, the trend toward the Conservative Party would have been even more pronounced. It has also been indicated, for instance, that in the 1964 American presidential election only one out of six hundred West Coast voters decided not to cast his ballot when he knew that Johnson had in fact achieved a landslide victory in the Eastern and Central States. The growing literature on voting behaviour in a large number of democratic states also fails to sustain these theories. That literature, indeed, suggests that the psychology of voting is infinitely complex, and certainly that its determinants include many factors other than those alleged above. In fact, it seems probable that as many as three-quarters of the voters in any election already have their minds made up when the first poll is reported, and that their predispositions are not altered during the campaign. Finally, there is good reason to believe that very little media information on poll results actually filters down to affect the voter's decisional calculus. On the other hand, notwithstanding the findings regarding the stability of mass voting intentions, there is little doubt that last minute campaign developments, such as the "economic scare" in Britain during the 1970 election, can alter the intentions of a sufficient, through small, proportion of voters to produce substantial polling error.

If there is no compelling reason to believe that polls systematically influence electoral behaviour in a manner which regularly affects voting outcomes, neither can it be established that in any give *close* election they have *not* influenced the result. But citizens in most democracies, generally speaking, appear to have great tolerance for the use or alleged misuse of polls by the media. And their tolerance, for that matter, seemingly extends to recorded polling errors. However, for obvious reasons some political leaders and activists have come to view the publication of re-election surveys with deep suspicion and even scorn. We recall, for instance, Mr. Diefenbaker's famous comment: "Every morning when I take my little dog, Happy, for a walk, I watch with great interest what he does to the poles." Two days before his government's defeat in 1970, Premier Bertrand, speaking on the C.B.C. French television network made the following remarks:

> I have had enough of these more-or-less falsified, or more-or-less truncated polls which are invading our newspapers with the precise purpose of demoralizing our supporters. Who is paying for these polls? In the newspaper *La Presse*, it is Power Corporation whose vice-president is Mr. Peter Nesbitt-Thompson, treasurer of the Liberal Party and whose board of directors includes the son of Mr. Paul Martin, a senator in Ottawa, and Mr. Simard, a cousin of Mr. Bourassa. In the *Gazette* it is the Southam Press group of Toronto, affiliated since the dawn of time with the Liberal Party. In the *Montreal Star*, it is the McConnell family devoted without limit to Liberal interests.

Before his retirement, the then national organizer of the Progressive Conservatives, Mr. Eddie Goodman, said in an interview (June 6, 1970): "The bad poll rating the Conservatives got in the 1965 election was wrong—but those polls cost us seven or eight seats. The whole course of Canadian history might have been changed if we had won those seats." In an inquiry conducted by a special committee of Quebec's National Assembly, evidence was presented that certain newspapers in the province had flagrantly misrepresented the results of some surveys taken in 1970. In a defensive action a group of nine Montreal polling organizations proposed to the committee, in lieu of an outright ban on polling activity such as exists in British Columbia, an elaborate set of rules to control media presentation of poll results. However, a prohibition on the distribution of poll results in Quebec was not introduced. At the federal level, on the other hand, the Barbeau Committee on Election Expenses in 1966 recommended that no poll results should be published during any pre-election period. A private member's bill providing for a similar prohibition was tabled in the House of Commons by Mr. Robert Coates barely a week after the Quebec election in 1970. None of these proposals has been acted upon. Indeed, except in British Columbia and France—the French Senate in 1972 prohibited public dissemination of poll results during elections to the National Assembly—restrictions on the publication of pre-election poll results in most democratic states have not been imposed.

A healthy popular scepticism toward polling, however, is required. For if people in large numbers come to regard the polls as a "sure bet" then the necessity for voting might itself be called into question. In this sense, the democratic process is strengthened by the failures of polling. James Reston of the *New York Times*, in his comments on the 1970 polling failure in Britain, summarized the position accurately:

> Accordingly, the joke is not on George Gallup and Lou Harris and the other pollsters but on the politicians. The pollsters are businessmen responding for a fee to an impossible public demand. The one thing the public seems to want to know about elections is precisely the thing nobody can be precise about: Who is going to win? And the politicians

have taken the pollsters' educated guess on this even more seriously than the pollsters have taken it themselves.

The threat of a prohibition of the publication of poll results, however, has clearly had a salutary effect. International and national associations of private polling agencies have begun formulating "codes of ethics" to guide their members on technical procedures and standards. There is evidence too that the Canadian media in general have tended to become increasingly cautious and circumspect in the presentation of election survey results. Much more technical explanation, for instance, now accompanies these surveys than was formerly the case.

The discussion in this article thus far has been centred on survey techniques and on the attempts of private polling and media organizations to predict election outcomes. But the increasing use of attitude surveys by government agencies, political leaders, political parties, party leadership candidates, and elected MPs undoubtedly has even greater implications for democratic practice. Senator Keith Davey, a leading exponent of the use of surveys in both governmental and political affairs, and a leader who has used them extensively in both his political and official capacities, put forward the following rationale in 1969:

> When one reflects upon it, any scientific measurement of public attitudes surely points the way to democracy. As society becomes more and more complicated, polling becomes an increasingly significant way of determing individual social and economic needs. Indeed, we may ultimately evolve into an even more direct form of computerized democracy. Until we do, the public-opinion study is surely a useful tool in the hands of those who seek to understand the nation and improve our government.

Any adequate examination of the meaning and consequences of this statement would require a volume of comment. We merely observe, however, that in Canada party leaders have used survey techniques with increasing frequency during the last decade. Beginning with the Quebec election of 1960 and the federal election of 1962, the Liberals have been most aggressive in this respect, often retaining prominent American pollsters. But the Conservatives and even, quite recently, the N.D.P., have commissioned national surveys for their private uses. Some provincial premiers (Thatcher, Bourassa, Smallwood, Davis and others) have made extensive use of polls. Before his defeat, Premier W. A. C. Bennett in B.C. used them effectively though his government banned media-sponsored poll results for public consumption. Increasingly, government parties use private polls to assist in decisions respecting the timing of elections and in formulating election strategies and tactics. Private polls were commissioned by some candidates at the 1968 federal Liberal leadership convention. The same party has used polls in connection with its policy conferences. The Conservative party of Ontario, on the other hand, now employs external and domestic polling organizations extensively. New techniques of motivational and mass-attitude analysis, such as those developed by Martin Goldfarb, are deployed at the national, provincial and constituency levels. Even children and young people are interviewed in order to obtain data on the political preferences and prejudices of their parents. These new departures involve not merely the expertise of conventional polling specialists but the services of sociologists and social psychologists as well. We may indeed soon be approaching the time when, as Davey has argued, social and political surveying has "become fundamental to the operation of all political parties and is often the most important guideline in the formulation of policy and strategy".

One, among the many, aspects of these developments which requires careful study is the degree to which they are likely to have an impact on inter-party competition. The newer survey methods are extremely costly. Parties in office, because of the resources at their disposal, may have an advantage in gaining access to the newer services. But a number of commentators have suggested, on the other hand, that party strategists rarely are able to make maximum use of survey results. There is too little time during election campaigns and there is continued scepticism among party leaders regarding their political efficacy. We also note that attitude surveys did not enable the Liberals to obtain parliamentary majorities in 1962, 1963, 1965 and 1972, nor did they enable Premiers Thatcher, Smallwood and Bennett to escape ultimate electoral defeat.

In any case, it seems clear that the techniques described above will continue to have a major impact on the political process. Regenstreif in a recent interview has accurately captured the central motivating force:

> The politician buys a pollster's services because he has a basic problem. If he doen't have some detached survey, he winds up talking to himself or to his "yes man" or to people whose interests are tied up in the campaign. A pollster can tell him what people are thinking about, what kind of reaction he's getting. Give him a chance to shape his image to evoke the best response. The man who runs a campaign without a pollster is courting defeat.

But the motivating influence itself suggests the consequence: an over-preoccupation with leadership image projection; an even greater personalization of a process already heavily personalized; a tendency for party leaders to dominate in elections and ultimately in decision-making; and an encouragement for leaders to negotiate or bargain with voters rather than to persuade them.

Our conclusion is that every failure of these survey techniques is a victory for democracy. Every technical failure, in a word, may be regarded as a signal to leaders that they ought not to take the voters for granted.

AT LAST—I AM INTERVIEWED FOR
A PUBLIC OPINION POLL*

Richard Gwyn

It was dark outside and the temperature was close to zero. So we opened the door as soon as the lady rang the bell. Then she sat down on the sofa in our living room and asked all these dumb questions about whether I preferred to take holidays in the United States or in Canada. The lady herself was bright and very nice. The reason she had to ask the dumb questions was because they were printed on her green interview forms.

It had finally happened. After years of writing about surveys and of analyzing them, I was being interviewed for one myself. The lady worked for *Canadian Facts*, which is a subsidiary of the Gallup Poll. She did eight interviews a night, which doesn't sound like much, but allow at least half an hour door-to-door and it adds up to four hours walking in the dark and cold.

The lady insisted on seeing the man of the house. My wife, later, complained this was sexism. Being a minor expert on these matters I was able to reassure her that surveys must be taken from a balanced sample and that the person interviewed before me must have been a woman. . . .

One interviewing technique intrigued me. The lady handed me a set of colored cards on which various salary levels were marked against different letters of the alphabet. Which letter, the lady asked delicately, corresponded to my total salary? Why not just ask for the actual amount? Only the lady interviewer and my wife were listening; my wife knew the answer and the lady knew the amounts that the letters corresponded to. Anyway, she was nice, so I solemnly said "J".

Then the lady got to the gut question: "If an election were held today, which political party would you vote for?" This was it, the most basic question of all, the quintessential question. Beside it, "Are you now or have you ever been a member of the Committee for an Independent Canada?"; "Do you support Women's Lib, and if not why are you such a pig?"; "Do you really think Sacha is such a great name for a boy?" all seem trivial and marginal to our continued existence as a nation.

"If an election were held today, which political party would you vote for," is where it's all at. Only 800 Canadians get asked that question each time, which gives each of us enormous power. Depending on our whims, the newspapers headline the results, Trudeau or Stanfield or Lewis goes into a deep depression or else elation, and an election is declared or postponed.

I thought of saying, "Well, you see I am a political columnist and am not allowed to have political preferences," but that seemed unutterably pompous, and meant the lady would have to go off to another house to make up her number. To say, "Don't know" would be to weasel out, and anyway would precipitate a whole lot of boring interpretive stories about how the undecided vote (it's small enough that one more would make a

* From *The Toronto Star*, January 17, 1974. By permission.

difference) had increased dramatically and how this meant Canadians were dithering about, unable to make up their mind, and so send Trudeau and Stanfield and Lewis simultaneously into a depression.

At last I blurted out a reply. It's a secret, of course. Not entirely, which is one interesting point about these surveys. The lady asked for my name, address and telephone number. This seemed to breach all the rules of privacy, but she explained that the reason was to allow Canadian Facts to phone some of her interviewees to make certain she hadn't cheated and filled in the answers herself while staying cosy in her home.

Canadian Facts loses money on its political questionnaire, but gets a whole lot of free publicity from it. The profits come from other questions that are "piggy-backed" onto this one, like the Canada-U.S. holiday survey. Also the last set of questions. "Have you," the lady asked, not looking at me and passing over another colored card with drug names on it, "ever itched and if so have you made use of any of the drugs listed on the card?"

She was much too polite to ask where I might have itched. I hadn't, anywhere, so the question was irrelevant and the interview was over. The issue that won't be resolved until all the survey results come out is whether Liberals or Conservatives itch more in the United States or Canada.

LOBBYING—OTTAWA'S FAST-GROWING BUSINESS*

Clive Baxter

OTTAWA—"People who really want to guide and influence government policy are wasting their time dealing with Members of Parliament, Senators, and usually even ministers.

"If you want results—rather than just the satisfaction of talking to the prominent—you deal with us, and at various levels."

That is how one senior civil servant put it to FP, talking about the question of how to deal with the ever-growing power of government. It is a view broadly supported by all the expert lobbyists in Ottawa, who, themselves, are fast forming a major, profitable—and controversial—industry. . . .

"Other backbenchers and Senators can try to arrange meetings between the top people and outsiders, and they can usually do it after some waiting. But it doesn't often produce results. To produce results you need to see the key planners, who may be way down in the system, and you have to see them early enough to push for changes in policy before it is politically embarrassing to make them."

To the outsider, looking for the right lobbyist is not an easy job. As a rough rule, if you come across a noisy, open contact who will work for you—you are wasting your time. The key insiders are quiet, are well known inside the government machine, but seldom, if ever, are visible to those on the outside.

A good example of just what is involved surrounds the two newest

* From The Financial Post, July 12, 1975. By permission.

—and among the better known—lobbyists, Simon Reisman, who has just retired as deputy minister of Finance, and Jim Grandy, who was deputy minister of Industry, Trade & Commerce.

They are setting up their new joint lobbyist operation, and it's widely expected that they will be very influential. But they will succeed only if they both operate so quietly and smoothly that no one else realizes whom they are working for.

One of their "competitors," a man who has been a highly successful lobbyist for some years now, puts it this way:

"First of all you have to keep a good lookout on what is going on, on how the government is thinking. That means knowing, and keeping in with, cabinet ministers and some senior civil servants. But that is only part of the craft.

"Really, most new ideas begin deep in the civil-service machine. The man in charge of some special office writes a memo suggesting a new policy on this or that. It works its way slowly up and up. At that stage civil servants are delighted, just delighted, to talk quietly to people like us, people representing this or that corporation or industry directly involved.

"That is the time to slip in good ideas. Later it oozes up to the politicians and becomes policy. By the time it is a government bill it is the very devil to change it. Then you have real trouble."

Of course, expense accounts are a great help around Ottawa. That is one area where visitor and lobbyist have a real advantage. The rules of the game are absolute: take a civil servant out to lunch and you pay. Except in very few jobs—almost always dealing with official visitors from other governments or abroad—there are no expense accounts available to civil servants, and the outsider or lobbyist is automatically expected to pick up all bills.

Another development on the Ottawa front in recent years has been the massive growth of trade, industry, medical, union, and educational association offices. (See list.) Many are big, most are growing, and the good ones have quite an impact at all levels.

Take, for instance, the Air Industries Association of Canada. It keeps a very close watch, from the ministers involved with aviation down to very junior civil servants. Its permanent president, David Mundy, was an assistant deputy minister himself before switching over, and it is his job to keep close contacts.

Other aviation companies use Mundy and the AIAC. But they also maintain their own offices in Ottawa with fairly senior executives, who make their own contacts. In addition to all that, when something big is going on—such as the current race to settle who will own de Havilland Canada and Canadair Ltd.—many of them also hire experienced lobbyists to work quietly for them behind the scenes.

The list of associations is long and, of course, the associations vary in size. Most of them clearly advocate and defend a certain point of view—for instance, the Canadian Ophthalmological Society is concerned with the problems and interests of eye specialists across the country.

Others, such as the Canada-Japan Trade Council, or the British Canadian Trade Association, are, in theory, simply in favor of trade growth between two particular nations. But they are, in fact, or at least in the eyes of the government, primarily concerned—pushing Japan's or Britain's case, or the case of whatever country is involved, when disputes arise.

For most civil servants, the associations almost all represent a chance to make contact with the outside world on a regular basis. Together with the quiet lobbyists, they provide news and ideas that isolated government men in Ottawa need. . . .

Certainly the list of government insiders moving to work with and for outsiders keeps growing. Military men—who retire on good salaries in their early to mid-fifties—show up all over the place. Admiral Harold Porter, for instance, now runs the Canadian Shipbuilding Association; General Bruce Macdonald heads the Canadian Chemical Producers Association; Air Commodore Gordon Diamond is de Havilland Canada's resident executive.

Léon Balcer, who was a minister in the Diefenbaker government, runs the Electronic Industries Association. David Golden was a deputy minister, then ran the Air Industries Association—was recalled to be deputy minister of the then-new Industry Department—and now is president of Telesat Ltd. . . .

While many in government welcome the information and viewpoints put forward by the associations—and the lobbyists see nothing at all wrong with the whole process—these activities do raise important questions.

If one company, one group, or one association has a particularly effective agent representing it around government, what does this do for democracy? Does the group that hired the best agent get the best results, even if it isn't the best and most deserving case? . . .

Yet the question remains, do the objectives of special interests with access where it matters really coincide with the interests of the public at large? Is the contribution of the lobbyist or association to the making of sensible legislation, as on many occasions must be the case, undercut at times by successful special pleading for very narrow objectives?

Although it can be a long process, the public can always get rid of politicians. But can the public get at the lobbyists?

[See also for Senators as lobbyists. J. McMenemy's article, *infra*, Chapter 14.]

Groups that push their point in Ottawa

Academy of Medicine
Agricultural Institute of Canada
Air Industries Association of Canada
Air Transport Association of Canada
Apparel Manufacturers Council of Canada
Army Navy & Air Force Veterans in Canada
   Inc.
Association Internationale Des Machinistes &
   Des Travailleurs de l'Aéroastronautique
Association Internationale Des Ouvriers &
   Plâtriers Et Finisseurs En Ciment

Association of Canadian Clubs
Association of Canadian Medical Colleges
Association of Consulting Engineers of Canada
Association of Postal Officials of Canada
Association of Translators & Interpreters of
   Ontario
Association of Universities and Colleges of
   Canada
Boy Scouts of Canada
Brewers Association of Canada
Canada-Japan Trade Council

Canada Jaycees
Canadian Aeronautics & Space Institute
Canadian Agricultural Chemicals Association
Canadian Air Traffic Control Association
Canadian Amateur Basketball Association
Canadian Amateur Football Association
Canadian Amateur Softball Association
Canadian Arthritis & Rheumatism Society
Canadian Association for Laboratory Animal
  Science
Canadian Association In Support of The
  Native Peoples
Canadian Association of Aerial Surveyors
Canadian Association of Broadcasters
Canadian Association of Chiefs of Police
Canadian Association of Equipment
  Distributors
Canadian Association of Medical Clinics
Canadian Association of Movers
Canadian Association of Optometrists
Canadian Association of Physicists
Canadian Association of Provincial Liquor
  Commissioners
Canadian Association of Social Workers
Canadian Association of University Teachers
Canadian Automobile Association
Canadian Bar Association
Canadian Broadcasting League
Canadian Cable Television Association
Canadian Cancer Society
Canadian Chamber of Shipping
Canadian Chemical Producers' Association
Canadian Construction Association
Canadian Council On 4-H Clubs
Canadian Council on Urban & Regional
  Research
Canadian Crafts Council
Canadian Federation of Agriculture
Canadian Federation of Business &
  Professional Womens Clubs
Canadian Federation of Civil Liberties &
  Human Rights Associations
Canadian Federation of Mayors &
  Municipalities
Canadian Feed Manufacturers Association
Canadian Field Hockey Council
Canadian Food Processor Association
Canadian Forestry Association
Canadian Foundation on Alcohol & Drug
  Dependencies
Canadian Gas Association
Canadian Grocery Bag Manufacturers
  Association
Canadian Hardwood Plywood Association
Canadian Home Economics Association
Canadian Home Manufacturers Association
Canadian Horticultural Council
Canadian Hunger Foundation
Canadian Institute of Food Science &
  Technology

Canadian Institute of Planners
Canadian Institute of Surveying
Canadian Institute of Timber Construction
Canadian Labor Congress
Canadian Lawn Tennis Association
Canadian Library Association
Canadian Lumbermen's Association
Canadian Manufacturers Association
Canadian Manufacturers of Chemical
  Specialties Association
Canadian Medical Association
Canadian Museums Association
Canadian National Millers Association
Canadian Nature Federation
Canadian Nursery Trades Association
Canadian Nurses' Association
Canadian Ophthalmological Society
Canadian Owners & Pilots Association
Canadian Postmasters Association
Canadian Psychiatric Association Journal
Canadian Public Health Association
Canadian Public Relations Society Inc.
Canadian Restaurant Association
Canadian Roofing Contractors Association
Canadian Seed Growers' Association
Canadian Shipbuilding & Ship Repairing
  Association
Canadian Society For Chemical Engineering
Canadian Society Of Radiological Technicians
Canadian Sporting Arms & Ammunitions
  Association
Canadian Standards Association
Canadian Teachers' Federation
Canadian Telecommunications Carriers
  Association
Canadian Testing Association
Canadian Track & Field Association
Canadian Trucking Association
Canadian Union of Public Employees
Canadian Veterinary Medical Association
Canadian Wildlife Federation
Canadian Wood Council
Canadian Youth Hostels Association
Care-Canada
Catholic Hospital Association of Canada
Chartered Institute of Secretaries
Chemical Institute of Canada
Dairy Farmers of Canada
Dominion Marine Association
Electrical Contractors Association of Ottawa
Electronic Industries Association of Canada
Employees Association of Computing Devices
Federated Women's Institutes of Canada
Graphic Arts Industries Association
Grocery Products Manufacturers of Canada
Industrial Accident Prevention Associations
Industrial Developers Association of Canada
Machinery & Equipment Manufacturers'
  Association of Canada
National Council of Canadian Labor

National Council of Women
National Dairy Council of Canada
National Union of Students
Navy League of Canada
Petroleum Association For Conservation of
    The Canadian Environment
Pharmaceutical Manufacturers Association of
    Canada
Professional Association of Foreign Service
    Officers

Professional Institute of The Public Service of
    Canada
RCAF Association
Roads & Transportation Association of Canada
Steel Castings Institute of Canada
The Mining Association of Canada
Travel Industry Association of Canada
Union of National Defence Employees

THE CMA—SPOKESMAN FOR INDUSTRY*

W. D. H. Frechette

The Canadian Manufacturers' Association is a non-profit, non-political organization supported and directed by its 7,300 members who manufacture every sort of industrial product in cities and towns all the way from St. John's, Newfoundland, to Victoria, B.C. We are just two years short of celebrating our hundredth birthday and growing more vigorous with the passage of time. Our member companies are both large and small, but obviously—with that many members—there is a preponderance of small ones. In fact, the great majority of our member companies employ less than 100 people. Yet our total membership is responsible for three-quarters of all the manufacturing production of Canada.

The main objective of the CMA is to encourage the pace of this country's industrialization. But that is far from all. We emphasize the greatest possible employment of Canadians and the maximum use of domestic materials. And side by side with the promotion of manufacturing we exist for the promotion of exports. We have, in other words, been propounding the "Buy, Make and Sell Canadian" philosophy in one way or another for over 60 years.

There are two ways we attempt to achieve our objective. The first is in the legislative field. As the recognized authoritative voice of the most important segment of the economy, the manufacturing industry, we are constantly appearing before all levels of government with submissions on legislation which affects manufacturers. Sometimes our briefs involve laws which we think should be placed on the statute books, sometimes laws that are already there. The second way we work toward our objective is in the area of consultation and individual service to our members through our head office departments and our division and branch offices across Canada. These services cover a wide field of subjects important to industry and over the years we like to think that we have developed them to a fine art.

Canada, for our purposes, is divided geographically into six Divisions, each under the supervision of a full-time manager, assisted by trained

* From an address delivered in January 1969, by the author, who is the General Secretary of the Canadian Manufacturers' Association. By permission.

staff. All CMA members are automatically members of the CMA Division in which their place of business is located. The Division is an integral part of the national organization, but has autonomy within its own field of activity. Similarly, most CMA members are now participants in one or other of the Association's 37 branches. Policies are established in a democratic way—by an appropriate committee. We have some 75 committees, on which over a thousand members serve voluntarily right across the country. . . .

Policies involving national matters—such things as unemployment insurance, trade and taxation—are established by a national standing committee, often advised by a subcommittee of top experts on the subject. They are presented for final ratification to the Executive Council, which is the overall governing body and which we call the parliament of Canadian industry. Policies on provincial or purely local matters are similarly formulated by division and branch committees. In this way, the thinking of the best brains in manufacturing industry is utilized to the utmost before policy is adopted.

At our head office in Toronto we have a variety of specialist departments which cover the fields of trade and tariffs, commercial intelligence, industrial relations, legislation, taxation, public relations, economic research and transportation. The consultative personalized services are of a kind to which a price tag may be more readily affixed than to the impersonal services of policing legislation and acting as advocate for the industry, although the latter are of at least equal importance.

Taking the two major areas of Association activity—those of establishing policies in relation to Government action, and those of service—it is appropriate to note that policies are established by Committees, composed of members; services to members are provided by the CMA staff complement of 114 people who man its nine offices across the country. Members of the staff are, of course, involved as well in the committee work as advisers and in carrying out the research on which committee decisions are made besides committing such decisions to the appropriate written words. [The CMA's total income in 1969 amounted to $941,000.]

By its very nature, an organization like CMA has little direct contact with any large proportion of the electorate. Its influence and effectiveness with governments are therefore dependent upon the objectivity and responsible character of its submissions. While its main focus is on the interests of its membership, it has to be well in tune with national goals and the public interest. This submissions range all the way from the presentation of formal briefs and the provision of written and oral evidence at public enquiries to informal discussion and day to day contacts at the more technical level.

The CMA's special contribution to the public policy-making process lies in its ability to foresee and to explain the practical impact on the manufacturing industries of a given line of government policy, a particular piece of legislation or the application of implementing regulations. In its absence, governments would be faced with the alternative of immense additions to their own information-gathering apparatus or resort to a lot of costly experimentation.

To illustrate the depth and variety of subject matters in the CMA hopper, perhaps it will suffice to mention some recent briefs:

— the British Columbia Division has recently submitted its views to the government on new legislation affecting collective bargaining in that province;

— the Newfoundland Branch has been engaged in discussions with the Provincial Government concerning its recent submission reviewing Workmen's Compensation laws and practice;

— the Quebec Division has been waging a prolonged battle against the St. Lawrence Seaway Authority proposal to cut off water service to industry along a part of the Lachine Canal;

— the Ontario Division, having submitted a detailed evaluation of the Rand Commission proposals on labour legislation, invited representatives of the news media to a no-holds-barred news conference at which the CMA position was fully explained and deeply explored;

— the national submission on combines, mergers, monopoly and restraint of trade was the subject of recent discussion with the Economic Council of Canada which has been assigned the task of an exhaustive review of legislation in this field.

Some mention, at least, should be made of the mammoth job of work done by the Tariff Committee in connection with Canada's new anti-dumping legislation and by the Taxation Committee on the Carter Commission's Report and subsequent proposals for tax reform. One further topic which was under examination for a good two years before our recent submission on the subject to the Prime Minister of Canada concerns the highly topical and controversial subject of wages and prices in the context of inflationary pressures. CMA tackled this subject early and in such a manner that our analysis was described by the Minister of Consumer and Corporate Affairs as "a splendid example of industry taking an initiative in the process of consultation which I and my colleagues have been striving for."

While in all these endeavours the CMA certainly concentrates its attention on the effects of public policy on manufacturers, we cannot be other than keenly aware of the views of other responsible organizations whose focus is on non-manufacturing sectors of the business community, to say nothing of our counterparts in other countries.

There is, in fact, a continuous flow of information between ourselves and, for example, The Canadian Chamber of Commerce and the Canadian Construction Association. The effect of these relationships is such that policy positions are harmonized to the fullest extent possible and in many cases become identical. A similarly valuable relationship is cultivated by the CMA through its periodic talks with, among others, representative Japanese organizations, with the U.S. National Association of Manufacturers and through its active participation in regional international business organizations covering the Americas, the North Atlantic and the Pacific Basin. The CMA's extensive international links and activities make a long story in themselves. . . .

THE BRILLIANT CAMPAIGN
TO MAKE PUBLIC OPINION*

Ron Haggart

At the end of last year, things were going rather badly for the Spadina Expressway project. The newspapers, reporting as usual the organized opinion of the community, were full of stories all blackly against another superhighway.

Controllers Won't Back Expressway, reported the Star. Planner Faces Opponents, said another headline. Chaos Feared if Expressways Slice Up Metro, said the Globe and Mail.

Meetings of 12 associations of taxpayers, and then of 85 associations, were reported under headlines like "Shame If It Carries" and "Spadina Results 'Bad As H-Bomb' ".

Suddenly, about the middle of January, the climate of public opinion radically changed. Citizens' associations and ratepayers groups, with all the fervor of an Algerian riot, appeared to be lining the streets, urging the reluctant politicans to hurry up with the Spadina highway.

This new public opinion was recorded in the Telegram of Jan. 12: "New life for the Spadina Expressway . . ." the paper reported, "emerged today with growing public support for the $67 million project. The expressway plan will be revived at Metro roads committee on Jan. 22 by ratepayer groups who are demanding that it be built immediately."

These demands from the citizens were heard at a number of meetings called by the roads committee of the Metropolitan council, and on Jan. 29 the extent of the swing in public opinion was recorded by The Star: "Champions of the Spadina combined expressway and rapid transit line," it reported, "outnumbered the opposition by better than three to one. . . ."

The single, most important hand behind this magical change in public opinion was a short, sharp bundle of hyperthyroid salesman's energy named Irving Paisley. He runs a prosperous insurance agency near Bathurst and Lawrence and is a councillor in North York.

"There is no doubt about it, that it was going the other way until I took over," Paisley has said of his success in this campaign.

Mr. Paisley's technique was to arrange for masses of approving briefs and statements to descend on the politicans who were making the decision.

Briefs from 25 ratepayer organizations, all enthusiastically in favour of the Spadina Expressway, were submitted to the Metropolitan roads committee.

Of these, Mr. Paisley himself wrote at least eight. He was the author of the briefs from the Winston Park Ratepayers' Association, the West Glen Ratepayers' Association, the Blackwood-Ranee Ratepayers' Association, the Joyce Park Ratepayers' Association, the Maple Leaf Ratepayers' Association, the Faywood Ratepayers, the Beverley Hills Ratepayers'

---

* From *Toronto Daily Star*, February 26, 1962. By permission of the publisher.

Association, the Danesbury Ratepayers, and the Hillmount-Viewmount Ratepayers' Association.

An example of Mr. Paisley's genius in the arts of creative public opinion was the brief in support of the Spadina Expressway submitted by the West Glen Ratepayers' Association.

Mr. Paisley describes this association as being "defunct." He went to see Mrs. Dorothy Somers, the secretary of the association, and she agreed that the Spadina Expressway was a good idea.

Mr. Paisley then phoned three members of the executive of the West Glen ratepayers and they, too, agreed with Mr. Paisley's enthusiastic support of the expressway. Mr. Paisley then wrote a brief which said ". . . I am instructed by the executive of the West Glen Ratepayers' Association to place on record its wholehearted support of construction of the Spadina Expressway." Then followed two pages of well-reasoned argument in favour of the highway.

The brief was signed by Mrs. Dorothy Somers, secretary. Curiously, Mrs. Somers' name was spelled incorrectly, appearing with two m's in this official communication from the West Glen ratepayers.

Another example was the brief from the Winston Park ratepayers. John O'Hagan, who lives on Winston Park Blvd. and publishes a paper in Woodbridge, is listed as president.

Mr. Paisley describes this organization as being "defunct."

Mr. Paisley visited Mr. O'Hagan at his home and got his agreement to the project, although Mr. O'Hagan told him he could not speak for the organization. Mr. Paisley went back to his insurance office on Bathurst St. and phoned a few members of the executive of this organization. Mr. Paisley then wrote the brief of the Winston Park ratepayers and took it back to Mr. O'Hagan for his signature.

The brief began: "I am instructed by the members of the Winston Park Ratepayers' Association to urge your committee . . ."

In this case, the members represented totalled approximately four.

In the case of the Hillmount-Viewmount Ratepayers' Association ("We endorse this project which should be put under way as quickly as possible"), Mr. Paisley telephoned the president, Albert Glazer, in hospital where Mr. Glazer was recovering from an operation, and repeated the creative process as before.

The brief from the Beverley Hills ratepayers, which was also written by Mr. Paisley, was signed "Isobel Walker, per." Nothing followed the "per," but that, too, was Mr. Paisley.

Twenty-five copies of each of the 25 briefs had to be submitted to the Metropolitan roads committee. Stencils for at least 10 of these were cut in Mr. Paisley's insurance office. He and his staff worked all one Saturday night until 1 o'clock in the morning turning out the material.

They were so overworked they had to send two of the briefs downtown to have the stencils typed by a friend of Mr. Paisley's. These two stencils (the ones from Winston Park and West Glen) were typed in the offices of Webb and Knapp, the land developers who are building the shopping plaza for Eaton's and Simpson's which will get its entrance from Highway 401 by way of the Spadina Expressway.

Almost all of the briefs from the 25 citizens' associations were mailed to the Metropolitan officials from Mr. Paisley's office, or dispatched downtown by taxicab from Mr. Paisley's office.

Mr. Paisley organized a car pool so that citizens could go down and hear the deliberations of the roads committee, and he wrote and mailed out to his constituents 9,076 copies of a leaflet supporting the Spadina Expressway.

He paid for the postage with a cheque for $136.29 drawn on the account of his insurance agency.

This brilliant campaign had the desired results. The Telegram reported on Feb. 5: "The ratepayers appeared to be evenly split, but growing support for the project was indicated as North York councillor Irving Paisley presented letters from 10 more groups in his township, representing 15,000 people."

And the [Toronto Daily] Star on Feb. 6 was able to report: ". . . a 3½-hour session which saw 36 briefs presented—28 of them in favour of the big transportation complex."

"I do have a knack for organization," Mr. Paisley says.

CONCENTRATION AND CONTROL IN CANADIAN MEDIA*

David Surplis

The Press

The first fact about news gathering and dissemination in Canada is that it is a business, a big business, based almost entirely on revenue from advertising. The amount of money required to start up a daily newspaper, that is the money needed to keep it going until circulation reaches the point where advertising revenue can generate a profit, is staggering. Although a few new dailies have succeeded in recent years (such as the Toronto *Sun* and Montreal's *Le Jour*), many more have failed. It would appear that only the larger publishing groups (they dislike the term "chains") can afford to expand their operations with any degree of confidence.

Actually, the number of daily newspapers in Canada has remained almost constant in recent years. The Audit Bureau of Circulations says 114 newspapers qualify as dailies in 1976; the figure was 113 in 1970. But as smaller, independent dailies flounder or are sold at a profit, they are frequently swallowed up by the larger groups. It is the number of owners of papers which is decreasing, not the number of papers. Three "chains" alone, Southam, F. P. Publications, and Thomson, own more than half of the dailies in Canada and their holdings continue to grow. The "big three" controlled 49 papers in 1970 and 58 by 1976.

* Revision in May, 1976, of an article published originally in the third edition of this book. By permission of the author.

As the Special Senate Committee on Mass Media (the Davey committee) found out, it is very difficult to prove the assertion that group ownership is bad per se but publishers admit that the tendency towards concentration concerns them. One man who should know more about this matter than anyone else was Canadian-born Lord Thomson of Fleet whose companies still control more than one hundred newspapers in various parts of the world. When asked why he purchased more and more newspapers, Lord Thomson replied that he bought them simply "to make more money" and that he made more money "to buy more newspapers." He often stated, however, that he had no desire to control the news and opinion carried in his papers.

The Davey committee heard statements on both sides of the argument over group ownership. The Senators were told that groups can provide the ability to improve coverage (by pooling resources, placing "chain" correspondents around the world, and providing long-term financial planning, for instance) but they were also warned that chain ownership could lead to editorial management, suppression of the news and other abuses. Large urban areas, such as Edmonton, Regina, Hamilton, London and Windsor, which are served by only one local daily newspaper, are often mentioned as potential sites for such abuse.

But the mass media field as a whole is quite competitive; no newspaper operates without competition from neighbouring dailies, radio or television. For example, on a typical day in January, 1976, Toronto and area residents got their news in a variety of ways: 440,000 listened to Torben Wittrup's most popular morning newscast on radio station CFRB; two and one-half million persons read one of Toronto's four daily newspapers (the Canadian Daily Newspaper Publishers Association estimates 2.5 readers for each newspaper printed, on average); and about 500,000 watched late newscasts on television. Moreover, these were not by any means the only news sources available to Torontonians. While there undoubtedly was overlapping for the sources given, the figures do show that there are alternatives available and that they are utilized by a great many people.

Overlapping Ownership

Of course, the beneficial results of such "competition" have to be questioned where the large groups may have an interest in all the major types of media in a given area, or where "competitors" may be relying on one another or a single wire service for much of their copy. Overlapping ownership has become more and more general as proprietors of one medium have sought to expand into the lucrative markets of the others. When John Bassett attempted to add cable television to his already wide media interests (a move disallowed by the Canadian Radio-Television Commission), he told the Davey committee that he believed it was a good way to make "lots of dough." Some indication of the extent to which one company has overlapping interests in Canadian media can be found in the example of Southam Press Limited.

Southam Press Limited

The interests of this large, public company extend far beyond the 14 daily newspapers listed in the accompanying table. Southam has a 49 percent interest in the Brandon *Sun*, 48 percent of the *Kitchener-Waterloo Record*, and owns the *Daily Oil Bulletin* of Calgary outright. Southam has a 50 percent interest in Pacific Press Limited (FP Publications holds the other 50 percent) which owns the Vancouver *Sun* and the Vancouver *Province* (Southam publishes the *Province* and FP publishes the *Sun*). The company also holds 50 percent of Southstar Publishers Ltd. (*Toronto Daily Star* has the other 50 percent) which publishes *Canadian Magazine*. Southam publishes the Financial Times of Canada, a burgeoning weekly financial newspaper, as well as 79 business and professional periodicals.

Southam has direct involvement in only one radio station but its interests are much wider by virtue of ownership of 30 percent of the voting and 38 percent of the non-voting shares of Selkirk Holdings Limited. In early 1976, Selkirk had 9 radio stations and 3 television stations in Alberta and British Columbia. The company had minority interest in three other television stations in British Columbia and three cablevision outlets across Canada.

The paradox with Southam is that the company has never founded a newspaper but has often been an innovator in the electronic media it subsequently sold to Selkirk. Southam executives state flatly that there is no interference by the parent company in the news and editorial affairs of its outlets.

Other Examples

Other examples of overlapping ownership could be given. There is the case in New Brunswick of the Irving family interests which control all of the province's five English-language daily newspapers, two radio stations and two television stations. Sale of the *Moncton Daily Times* and *Moncton Transcript* was ordered by the courts but the decision was reversed after an appeal. What is even more noteworthy about these holdings is the fact that Irving interests dominate the economic life of the province through ownership of vast resource, building and service industries.

Another giant in the media is Maclean-Hunter Ltd. of Toronto. Among the company's wide holdings are: six radio stations, one television station, 15 cablevision companies in Ontario, *Maclean's* magazine, four other wide-circulation magazines, the *Financial Post*, approximately 90 trade publications, and a magazine distribution company.

Another individual who has large holdings in the media is Paul Desmarais, the Montreal financier. Desmarais has personal interest in two radio stations and a television station. Through his ownership of Gelco Enterprises Ltd., Desmarais controls five newspapers including the influential *La Presse*. Gelco also has 53.1 percent of the immense holding company, Power Corp., which has wide interests in the Canadian economy.

It is obvious that control of the media is falling increasingly into fewer and fewer hands but whether this is altogether bad for the Canadian public has yet to be proven. There remains a great variety of sources of information and it would appear that profitable investment, rather than opinion management, is the prime goal of the owners.

Possible Improvements

The Davey committee made many recommendations on the strength of its exhaustive studies. Since ownership of the electronic media is carefully regulated by the CRTC, it was suggested that a similar body, a Canadian Press Ownership Board, be established. Such a board has not appeared, presumably because it is believed that anti-combines legislation can inhibit over-concentration of ownership.

With regard to content, the committee suggested the establishment of a national press council "to monitor the press the way the press monitors society." Three provincial councils are presently operating in Ontario, Quebec and Alberta but it is generally conceded that their effectiveness is only moderate since there is no compulsion to join them and their only weapon is suasion.

What is really required, to avoid arguments over the potential for abuse and the acceptable limits of government intervention, is some kind of institution to conduct long-range, continuing studies of all facets of the media. The Davey committee had significant influence, at least in awakening many people to the problems of the media, but its work has not been continued. Such an institution could be established by the media themselves with perhaps some assistance from government.

Publishers protest that the public must be satisfied or its members would not patronize their productions and the public have a vague notion of what they like. But there is confusion. Why, for instance, do Canadians howl when American TV channels are removed from basic cable service? Why do they continue to buy American periodicals while lamenting the absence of "quality" Canadian productions?

The plain fact is that not enough is known about the total picture. If the full impact of the media and the full role the media can play are not known, how can there be improvement? The establishment of an institution, sufficiently funded to provide the studies desperately needed, would be a welcome, and progressive, step.

Canada's Major Daily Newspaper Publishing Groups, 1975

Southam Press Limited (Public Company) 14 newspapers	Circulation*
The Vancouver Province	126,533
The Citizen (Prince George)	17,696
The Gazette (Montreal)	122,651
The Calgary Herald	116,071
The Edmonton Journal	153,061
The Medicine Hat News	10,315
The Winnipeg Tribune	69,223
North Bay Nugget	22,399
Owen Sound Sun-Times	17,137

The Spectator (Hamilton)	134,039
The Ottawa Citizen	95,136
Brantford Expositor	28,046
Windsor Star	82,726
The Star (Sault Ste. Marie)	22,518
Total Average Paid Circulation:	**1,017,551**

F. P. Publications (R. Howard Webster, R. S. Malone, et al.) 9 newspapers

The Daily Colonist/Victoria Daily Times	65,850
The Sun (Vancouver)	236,743
The Albertan (Calgary)	36,245
The Lethbridge Herald	23,240
Winnipeg Free Press	132,775
Ottawa Journal	79,924
The Globe and Mail (Toronto)	248,842
The Montreal Star	167,126
Total Average Paid Circulation:	**990,745**

Thomson Newspapers Ltd. (K. R. Thomson) 35 newspapers

British Columbia

Kamloops Daily Sentinel	6,328
Kelowna Daily Courier	9,440
Nanaimo Daily Free Press	10,411
Pentictón Herald	6,643
Vernon Daily News	6,057

Saskatchewan

Moose Jaw Times-Herald	8,033
Prince Albert Daily Herald	7,776

Ontario

Barrie Examiner	9,574
Belleville Intelligencer	17,558
Brampton Daily Times	8,638
Cambridge Daily Reporter	13,464
Chatham Daily News	14,419
Cornwall Standard-Freeholder	14,621
Guelph Mercury	17,242
Kirkland Lake Northern Daily News	5,382
Niagara Falls Review	19,872
Orillia Daily Packet and Times	8,117
Oshawa Times	24,453
Pembroke Observer	7,240
Peterborough Examiner	23,754
St. Thomas Times-Journal	11,155
Sarnia Observer	18,785
Sudbury Star	33,478
Thunder Bay Times-News/Chronicle-Journal	31,809
Timmins Daily Press	11,772
Welland Evening Tribune	17,432
Woodstock Daily Sentinel-Review	9,055

Nova Scotia

New Glasgow Evening News	9,708
Sydney Cape Breton Post	27,503
Truro News	5,820

Prince Edward Island

Charlottetown Guardian/The Evening Patriot	21,347

Newfoundland

Corner Brook Western Star	7,999
St. John's Evening Telegram	29,940
Total Average Paid Circulation:	**475,425**

Gelco Enterprises Ltd., Gesca Ltee. (Paul Desmarais) 5 newspapers

La Press, Montreal	173,780
La Tribune, Sherbrooke	37,234
Le Nouvelliste, Trois Rivières	48,448
La Voix de l'Est, Granby	8,720
Montréal Matin	115,781
Total Average Paid Circulation:	**383,963**

Irving Family 5 newspapers

The Daily Gleaner (Fredericton)	19,004
The Telegraph-Journal/Evening Times-Globe (St. John)	62,308
The Moncton Daily Times/Moncton Transcript	39,758
Total Average Paid Circulation:	121,070

Large Independents

Toronto Daily Star	521,399
Toronto Sun	123,062

* Circulation Source: Audit Bureau of Circulations, Publishers' Estimates for September 30, 1975.

GOT A GRIPE? TELL THE PRESS COUNCIL*

Ron Lowman

OTTAWA—A. Davidson Dunton has some simple advice for people who grumble about their newspaper: "Don't just talk about it; do something."

Dunton, the 62-year-old chairman of the Ontario Press Council, has no patience with people and organizations who constantly grouse about the sins of the press but take no action. He wants the public to send more and broader complaints to the council.

In its first 16 months of operation up to last Dec. 31, the council received 96 complaints against newspapers. In the first six months of this year there were 29 complaints.

Dunton wants . . . to increase the council's prestige and effectiveness by having more of the province's 45 daily newspapers join it. It also intends to offer membership to the 293 weekly newspapers in Ontario.

The present membership is eight, although among them they account for 55 percent of daily newspaper circulation in Ontario. The eight are the Ottawa Citizen, The Toronto Star, Hamilton Spectator, Brantford Expositor, Kitchener-Waterloo Record, London Free Press, Windsor Star and Owen Sound Sun-Times.

The council was formed by the newspapers to give the public a body to which complaints of unfair treatment can be brought if satisfaction cannot be obtained from an individual paper. It also hears complaints from newspapers against public boards and councils which interfere with the public's "right to know."

Its $50,000-a-year budget, which covers travelling and other expenses

* From *The Toronto Star*, August 5, 1974. By permission.

for members and complainants, is shared by member newspapers on the basis of their circulations.

The council's first annual report shows that of the 96 written complaints, 11 resulted in formal council decisions. Five were upheld, five rejected and an 11th was ruled identical with a previous case, in which The Star was rebuked for refusing to publish an ad for a homosexual publication.

The other 84 complaints were either settled between the parties, disallowed, weren't followed up by the complainants or were against papers that weren't council members.

A separate decision was on a complaint by a newspaper against a regional planning committee's decision to meet in secrecy. The newspaper, the Ottawa Citizen, was upheld.

Mayor Rene Piche of Kapuskasing was pleased with the council's ruling against the Canadian Magazine over an article which "misrepresented" the economic condition of his town.

Caroline Bell of Hagersville won a round with the Hamilton Spectator on behalf of the Hamilton Memorial Society. Mrs. Bell had complained that the newspaper discriminated against bereaved persons by refusing to allow such phrases as "in lieu of flowers," and "flowers gratefully declined" in paid death notices.

A court of appeal for people who feel they're not getting anywhere with their newspaper in a complaint, the council has a constitution which requires that its decisions—favorable or unfavorable—be published by the newspapers concerned.

The chairman is appointed by the member-newspapers, who also select 10 of their own editorial or business employees to serve on the council.

The other 10 members—among them a farmer, union leaders, a minister and a businesswoman—have nothing to do with newspapers and are appointed to represent the communities in which the newspapers are published. No council member who is a newspaper employee may be present when a complaint is being considered against his own journal.

•   •   •

[By March 1976 membership in the Ontario Press Council had grown to 11 newspapers, including two weeklies. The daily Sault Ste. Marie Star and the weekly Stittsville News joined in October 1975 and the weekly Port Elgin Reporter in March 1976.

Two additional provinces have press councils. Quebec's was formed in 1973 and Alberta's in 1972. The Alberta Council includes five of the province's seven daily newspapers.]

BIBLIOGRAPHY

Public Opinion

Albig, W., *Modern Public Opinion*, New York, McGraw-Hill, 1956.

Bellavance, M., and Gilbert, M., *L'Opinion publique et la crise d'octobre*, Montreal, Editions du Jour, 1971.

Bogart, L., *Silent Politics: Polls and the Awareness of Public Opinion*, New York, Wiley, 1972.

Christenson, R. M., and McWilliams, R. O., (eds.), *Voice of the People*, New York, McGraw-Hill, 1967.

Dion, L., "Democracy as Perceived by Public Opinion Analysts,' *C.J.E.P.S.*, Vol. XXVIII, No. 4, November, 1962.

Dion, L., "Régimes d'opinions publiques et systèmes idéologiques," *Ecrits du Canada Francais*, Vol. XII, 1962.

Fenton, J. M., *In Your Opinion*, Boston, Little, Brown, 1960.

Gallup, G., *A Guide to Public Opinion Polls*, Princeton, Princeton University Press, 1948, 2nd ed.

Gallup, G., and Rae, S. F., *The Pulse of Democracy: The Public Opinion Poll and How It Works*, New York, Simon and Schuster, 1940.

Hennessy, B. C., *Public Opinion*, Belmont, California, Wadsworth, 1965.

Katz, D., *et al.*, (eds.), *Public Opinion and Propaganda*, New York, Holt, Rinehart, and Winston, 1960.

Kish, L., *Survey Sampling*, New York, John Wiley, 1965.

Lane, R. E., and Sears, D. O., *Public Opinion*, Englewood Cliffs, N.J., Prentice-Hall, 1964.

Lippmann, W., *Public Opinion*, New York, Macmillan, 1960.

Lipset, S. M., "Polling and Science," *C.J.E.P.S.*, Vol. XV, No. 2, May, 1949, and *ibid.*, Vol. XVI, No. 3, August, 1950.

MacKenzie, R., "Quebec Results Spark Campaign to Curb Opinion Polls before Elections", *Toronto Daily Star*, May 25, 1970.

Maghami, F. G., "Political Knowledge among Youth: Some Notes on Public Opinion Formation", *C.J.P.S.*, Vol. VII, No. 2, June 1974.

Meir, N. C., and Saunders, H. W., (eds.), "The Polls and Public Opinion," *Iowa Conference on Attitude and Opinion Research, University of Iowa*, New York, Henry Holt, 1949.

Mosteller, F., *et al.*, in collaboration with Doob, L. W., *et al.*, *The Pre-Election Polls of 1948: Report of the Committee on Analysis of Pre-Election Polls and Forecasts*, Bulletin 60, New York, Social Science Research Council, 1949.

Qualter, T. H., "The Manipulation of Popular Impulse, Graham Wallas Revisited," *C.J.E.P.S.*, Vol. XXV, No. 2, May, 1959.

Qualter, T. H., *Propaganda and Psychological Warfare*, New York, Random House, 1962.

Regenstreif, S. P., *The Diefenbaker Interlude: Parties and Voting in Canada, An Interpretation*, Toronto, Longman, 1965.

Reston, J., "Lessons from the Polls' Defeat," *Montreal Star*, June 29, 1970.

Rogers, L., *The Pollsters, Public Opinion, Politics, and Democratic Leadership*, New York, Alfred A. Knopf, 1949.

Rolls, C. W., and Cantril, A. H., *Polls: Their Use and Misuse in Politics*, Basic Books, 1971.

Roper, E. B., *You and Your Leaders, Their Actions and Your Reactions*, New York, William Morrow, 1958.

Schindeler, F., and Lanphier, C., "Social Science Research and Participatory Democracy in Canada", *C.P.A.*, Vol. XII, No. 4, Winter, 1969.

Schneck, R., Russell, D., and Scott, K., "The Effects of Ruralism, Bureaucratic Structure, and Economic Role on Right-Wing Extremism", *C.J.P.S.*, Vol. VII, No. 1, March, 1974.

Schwartz, M., *Public Opinion and Canadian Identity*, Scarborough, Fitzhenry and Whiteside, 1967.

Sears, V., "Unrepentant Pollsters Dismiss U.K. Loss", *Toronto Daily Star*, June 27, 1970.

Zaritsky, J., "[Martin GoldFarb] A Man Who Sells Politicians like Tomatoes," *The Globe and Mail*, April 26, 1971.

Pressure Groups and Lobbying

Abella, I., (ed.), *On Strike*, Toronto, James, Lewis and Samuel, 1974.

Berry, G. R., "The oil lobby and the energy crisis", *C.P.A.*, Vol. 17, No. 4, Winter, 1974.

Blishen, B. R., *Doctors & Doctrines: The Ideology of Medical Care in Canada*, Toronto, University of Toronto Press, 1969.

Clark, S. D., *The Canadian Manufacturers' Association: A Study in Collective Bargaining and Political Pressure*, Toronto, University of Toronto Press, 1939.

Cooper, J., "The Struggle for Public Automobile Insurance", *Canadian Dimension*, Vol. 8, No. 4-5, January, 1972.

Dawson, H. H., "An Interest Group: The Canadian Federation of Agriculture," *C.P.A.*, Vol. III, No. 2, June, 1960.

Dawson, H. J., "The Consumers' Association of Canada," *C.P.A.*, Vol. VI, No. 1, March, 1963.

Dawson, H. J., "Relations between Farm Organizations and the Civil Service in Canada and Great Britain," *C.P.A.*, Vol. X, No. 4, December, 1967.

Dion, L., *Les groupes et le pouvoir politique aux États-Unis*, Québec, les presses de l'Université Laval, 1965.

Dion, L., *Le Bill 60 et la société québécoise*, Montréal, Ed. HMH, 1967.

Dion. L., "A la recherche d'une méthode d'analyse des partis et des groupes d'intérêt," *C.J.P.S.*, Vol. II, No. 1, March, 1969.

Dion, L., "Politique consultative et système politique," *C.J.P.S.*, Vol. II, No. 2, June, 1969.

Englemann, F. A., and Schwartz, M. A., *Political Parties and the Canadian Social Structure*, Toronto, Prentice-Hall, 1967.

Granatstein, G., *Marlborough Marathon: One Street Against a Developer*, Toronto, Hakkert and James, Lewis and Samuel, 1971

Horowitz, G., *Canadian Labour in Politics*, Toronto, University of Toronto Press, 1968.

"Inside the Ottawa Lobby", *Monetary Times*, July, 1968.

Jamieson, S., *Industrial Relations in Canada*, 2nd ed., Toronto, Macmillan, 1973.

Jamieson, S., *Times of Trouble: Labour Unrest and Industrial Conflict in Canada 1900-1966*, Ottawa, Task Force on Labour Relations, 1968.

Kwavnick, D., "Pressure Group Demands and the Struggle for Organizational Status: The Case of Organized Labour in Canada," *C.J.P.S.*, Vol. III, No. 1, March, 1970.

Kwavnick, D., *Organized Labour and Pressure Politics: The Canadian Labour Congress, 1956-1968*, London & Montreal, McGill-Queen's University Press, 1972.

Kwavnick, D., "Pressure-Group Demand and Organizational Objectives: The CNTU, the Lapalme Affaire, and National Bargaining Units", *C.J.P.S.*, Vol. VI, No. 4, December, 1973.

Lang, R., *The Politics of Drugs: a Comparative Pressure-Group Study of the Canadian*

Pharmaceutical Manufacturers Association and the Association of the British Pharmaceutical Industry (1930-1970), London, Saxon House, 1974.

Litvak, I. A., and Maule, C. J., "Interest-Group Tactics and the Politics of Foreign Investment: The Time-Reader's Digest Case Study", *C.J.P.S.*, Vol. VII, No. 4, December, 1974.

Manzer, R., "Selective Inducements and the Development of Pressure Groups: The Case of Canadian Teachers' Associations," *C.J.P.S.*, Vol. II, No. 1, March, 1969.

"People vs. Pollution," *Maclean's*, January, 1970.

Presthus, R., *Elites in the Policy Process*, Toronto, Macmillan, 1974.

Presthus, R., *Elite Accommodation in Canadian Politics*, Toronto, Macmillan, 1973.

Presthus, R., "Interest Groups and the Canadian Parliament: Activities, Interaction, Legitimacy, and Influence", *C.J.P.S.*, Vol. IV, No. 4, December, 1971.

Pross, A. P., "Canadian Pressure Groups in the 1970s: Their Role and Their Relations with the Public Service," *C.P.A.*, Vol. 18, No. 1, Spring, 1975.

Pross, A. P., (ed.), *Pressure Group Behaviour in Canadian Politics*, Toronto, McGraw-Hill Ryerson, 1975.

Tardif, G., *Police et politique au Québec*, Montreal, Les éditions de l'aurore, 1974.

Taylor, M. G., "The Role of the Medical Profession in the Formulation and Execution of Public Policy," *C.J.E.P.S.*, Vol. XXVI, No. 1, February, 1960.

Thorburn, H. G., "Pressure Groups in Canadian Politics: Recent Revisions of the Anti-Combines Legislation," *C.J.E.P.S.*, Vol. XXX, No. 2, May, 1964.

Woods, H. D., *Labour Policy in Canada*, Toronto, Macmillan, 1973.

Participatory Democracy

Budden, and Ernst, J., *The Movable Airport*, Toronto, Hakkert, 1973.

Carter, A., *Direct Action and Liberal Democracy*, Don Mills, Ontario, Musson, 1973.

Connor, D. M., *Citizens Participate—An Action Guide for Public Issues*, Oakville, Ontario, Development Press.

Draper, J. A., (ed.), *Citizen Participation in Canada*, Toronto, New Press, 1971.

Fraser, G., *Fighting Back: Urban Renewal in Trefann Court*, Toronto, Hakkert, 1972.

Greason, G. K., and King, R. C., *The Citizen and local government*, Rev. ed., Toronto, Macmillan, 1967.

Hill, D. M., *Participating in Local Affairs*, Pelican, Middlesex, England, Penguin, 1970.

Hunnius, G., *Participatory Democracy for Canada*, Montreal, Black Rose, 1971.

MacKinnon, F., *Postures and Politics: Some Observations on Participatory Democracy*, Toronto, University of Toronto Press, 1973.

Massey, H. J., *People or Planes*, Toronto, Copp Clark, 1972.

Massey, H., and Godfrey, C., *People and Places*, Toronto, Copp Clark, 1972.

New Brunswick, Participation and Development: The New Brunswick Task Force Report on Social Development and Social Welfare, Fredericton, Queen's Printer, 1971.

Pateman, C., *Participation and Democratic Theory*, Toronto, Macmillan, 1970.

Schindeler, F., and Lanphier, C., "Social Science Research and Participatory Democracy in Canada", *C.P.A.*, Vol. XII, No. 4, Winter, 1969.

Sproule-Jones, M., and Hart, K. D., "Political Participation", *C.J.P.S.*, Vol. VI, No. 2, June, 1973.

Stein, D. L., *Toronto For Sale*, Toronto, New Press, 1972.

Vrooman, P. C., "Power dilemma in citizen participation", *Canadian Welfare*, Vol. 48, No. 3, May-June, 1972.

Wilson, H. B., *Democracy and the Work Place*, Montreal, Black Rose, 1974.

The Power Structure

Black, E. R., "The fractured mosaic: John Porter Revisited", *C.P.A.*, Vol. 17, No. 4, Winter, 1974.

Bourassa, G., "Les élites politiques de Montréal: de l'aristocratic à la démocratie", *C.J.E.P.S.*, Vol. XXXI, No. 1, February, 1965.

Clement, W., *The Canadian Corporate Elite: An Analysis of Economic Power*, Carleton Library No. 89, Toronto, McClelland and Stewart, 1975.

Heap, J. L., (ed.), *Everybody's Canada: The Vertical Mosaic Reviewed and Reexamined*, Toronto, Burns and MacEachern, 1974.

McRae, K., (ed.), *Consociational Democracy*, Carleton Library, No. 79, Toronto, McClelland and Stewart, 1974.

Newman, Peter C., *The Canadian Establishment*, Toronto, McClelland and Stewart, 1975.

Park, L. and Park, F., *Anatomy of Big Business*, Toronto, James, Lewis and Samuel, 1973.

Porter, J., *The Vertical Mosaic: An Analysis of Social Class and Power in Canada*, Toronto, University of Toronto Press, 1965.

Presthus, R., *Elite Accommodation in Canadian Politics*, Toronto, Macmillan, 1973.

Presthus, R., *Elites in the Policy Process*, Toronto, Macmillan, 1974.

Roussopoulos, D., (ed.), *The Political Economy of the State—Canada/Quebec/USA*, Montreal, Black Rose, 1973.

Smith, D., and Tepperman, L., "Changes in the Canadian Business and Legal Elites, 1870-1970", *The Canadian Review of Sociology and Anthropology*, Vol. II, No. 2, May, 1974.

The Media

Adam, G. S., (ed.), *Journalism, Communication and the Law*, Toronto, Prentice-Hall, 1975.

Babe, R. E., "Public and private regulation of cable television: a case study of technological change and relative power", *C.P.A.*, Vol. 17, No. 2, Summer, 1974.

Boorstin, D. J., *The Image: A Guide to Pseudo-Events in America*, New York, Harper and Row, 1964.

Braddon, R., *Roy Thomson of Fleet Street*, London, Fontana Books, 1968.

Bruce, C., *News and the Southams*, Toronto, Macmillan, 1968.

Canada, *Report of the Royal Commission on Publications* (O'Leary Report), Ottawa, Queen's Printer, 1961.

Canada, Senate, *Report of the Special Senate Committee on Mass Media*, (Davey Report), 3 vols., Ottawa, Queen's Printer, 1970.

Canadian Facts Ltd., *Report of a Study of the Daily Newspaper in Canada and its Reading Public*, Toronto, 1962.

Chodos, R., and Murphy, R., (eds.), *Let Us Prey*, Toronto, James Lorimer, 1974.

Cook, R., *The Politics of John W. Dafoe and the Free Press*, Toronto, University of Toronto Press, 1963.

Donnelly, M., *Dafoe of the Free Press*, Toronto, Macmillan, 1968.

Eggleston, W., "The Press in Canada," *The Royal Commission on National Development in the Arts, Letters, and Sciences* (Massey Report), Ottawa, King's Printer, 1951.

Ferguson, G. V., and Underhill, F. H., *Press and Party in Canada: Issues of Freedom*, Toronto, Ryerson, 1955.

Gordon, D. R., *Language, Logic, and the Mass Media*, Toronto, Holt, Rinehart, Winston, 1966.

Gow, J. I., "Les Québécois, la guerre et la paix, 1945-1960," *C.J.P.S.*, Vol. III, No. 1, March, 1970.

Great Britain, *Report of the Royal Commission on the Press*, London, H. M. Stationery Office, 1949.

Great Britain, *Report of the Royal Commission on the Press*, 1961-1962, London, H. M. Stationery Office, 1962.

Hamlin, D. L. B., (ed.), *The Press and the Public*, Toronto, University of Toronto Press, 1962.

Harkness, R., *J. E. Atkinson of the Star*, Toronto, University of Toronto Press, 1963.

Hocking, W. E., *Freedom of the Press*, A Report from the Commission on Freedom of the Press, Chicago, University of Chicago Press, 1947.

Hunt, R., and Campbell, R., *K. C. Irving: The Art of the Industrialist*, Toronto, McClelland and Stewart, 1973.

Ickes, H. L., *Freedom of the Press To-day*, New York, Vanguard, 1941.

Irving, J. A., (ed.), *Mass Media in Canada*, Toronto, Ryerson, 1962.

Kesterton, W. H., *A History of Journalism in Canada*, Toronto, Carleton Library, McClelland and Stewart, 1967.

Levy, H. P., *The Press Council: History, Procedure and Cases*, Toronto, Macmillan, 1967.

Lindstrom, C. E., *The Fading American Newspaper*, Garden City, Doubleday, 1960.

McDayter, W., *A Media Mosaic: Canadian Communications Through A Critical Eye*, Toronto, Holt, Rinehart, and Winston, 1971.

McLuhan, M., *Understanding Media*, Toronto, Ryerson, 1940.

McNaught, C., *Canada Gets the News*, Toronto, Ryerson, 1940.

Peers, F., *The Politics of Canadian Broadcasting, 1920-1951*, Toronto, University of Toronto Press, 1969.

Qualter, T. H., and McKirdy, K. A., "The Press of Ontario and the Election," in Meisel, J., (ed.), *Papers on the 1962 Election*, Toronto, University of Toronto Press, 1964.

Robinson, G. J., and Theall, D. F., *Studies in Canadian Communications*, McGill University, 1975.

Royal Society of Canada, *Special Symposium on Communications into the Home*, Ottawa, 1972.

Singer, B. D., *Communications in Canadian Society*, Toronto, Copp Clark, second ed. rev., 1975.

Shea, A., *Broadcasting: The Canadian Way*, Montreal, Harvest House, 1963.

Weir, E. A., *The Struggle for National Broacasting in Canada*, Toronto, McClelland and Stewart, 1965.

Williams, F., *Dangerous Estate: The Anatomy of Newspapers*, London, Arrow Books, 1959.

Zolf, L., *Dance of the Dialectic*, Toronto, James, Lewis and Samuel, 1973.

8

POLITICAL PARTIES

More has been published on the subject of political parties than on almost any other aspect of Canadian politics, as the length of the bibliography in this section indicates. Two books which have recently been added to the McGraw-Hill Ryerson Series in Canadian Politics should be consulted in connection with this chapter. They are William Christian and Colin Campbell, *Political Parties and Ideologies in Canada: Liberals, Conservatives, Socialists, Nationalists*, Toronto, 1974, and Conrad Winn and John McMenemy, *Political Parties in Canada*, Toronto, 1976.

This chapter begins with an edited version of one of the most popular recent scholarly articles which deals with political parties: Alan Cairns' provocative analysis of "The Electoral System and the Party System in Canada."

The remainder of the chapter is devoted to explanations and critiques of the party system and to descriptions of the ideologies of our three principal federal parties. Professor McLeod's article summarizes the major interpretations of the Canadian party system while the essay by the editor sketches briefly the historical evolution and problems of our main parties. Flora MacDonald's reflective critique of our parties' performance which appeared in the third edition, pp. 227-230, has been omitted here. Mr. Roussopoulos, who is identified with the New Left, denounces the whole system as outmoded.

In the domain of ideology, Robert L. Stanfield, the recent leader of the federal Conservative party, gives his appreciation of the principles and philosophy of modern Canadian Conservatism while the late Prime Minister Lester B. Pearson does the same for Liberalism. Another former national party leader, David Lewis of the N.D.P., analyzes contemporary socialism. The N.D.P. Waffle Manifesto and David Lewis' reply to it, which appeared in the third edition, pp. 242-247, have been omitted.

Three charts indicate the constitutional organization of the Liberal, Conservative, and New Democratic parties.

The long bibliography is divided into four sections: parties and politics, political biographies, provincial politics and city politics.

THE ELECTORAL SYSTEM AND
THE PARTY SYSTEM IN CANADA, 1921-1965*

Alan C. Cairns

This paper investigates two common assumptions about the party system: (i) that the influence of the electoral system on the party system has been unimportant, or non-existent: and (ii) that the party system has been an important nationalizing agency with respect to the sectional cleavages widely held to constitute the most significant and enduring lines of division in the Canadian polity. Schattschneider, Lipset, Duverger, Key and others have cogently asserted the relevance of electoral systems for the understanding of party systems. Students of Canadian parties, however, have all but ignored the electoral system as an explanatory factor of any importance. The analysis to follow will suggest that the electoral system has played a major role in the evolution of Canadian parties, and that the claim that the party system has been an important instrument for integrating Canadians across sectional lines is highly suspect.

•   •   •

The Basic Defence of the System and its Actual Performance

If the electoral system is analyzed in terms of the basic virtue attributed to it, the creation of artificial legislative majorities to produce cabinet stability, its performance since 1921 has been only mediocre. Table 1 reveals the consistent tendency of the electoral system in every election from 1921 to 1965 to give the government party a greater percentage of seats than of votes. However, its contribution to one-party majorities was much less dramatic. Putting aside the two instances, 1940 and 1958, when

TABLE 1: Percentages of Votes and Seats for Government Party, 1921-1965

	% Votes	% Seats		% Votes	% Seats
1921	40.7	49.4(L)	1949	49.5	73.7(L)
1925†	39.8	40.4(L)	1953	48.9	64.5(L)
1926	46.1	52.2(L)	1957	38.9	42.3(C)
1930	48.7	55.9(C)	1958	53.6	78.5(C)
1935	44.9	70.6(L)	1962	37.3	43.8(C)
1940	51.5	73.9(L)	1963	41.7	48.7(L)
1945	41.1	51.0(L)	1965	40.2	49.4(L)

† In this election the Conservatives received both a higher percentage of votes, 46.5%, and of seats, 47.3%, than the Liberals. The Liberals, however, chose to meet Parliament, and with Progressive support they retained office for several months.
Note: The data for this and the following tables have been compiled from Howard A. Scarrow, *Canada Votes* (New Orleans, 1963), and from the *Report of the Chief Electoral Officer* for recent elections.

* From the *Canadian Journal of Political Science/Revue canadienne du Science politique*, Vol. I, No. 1, March/mars, 1968. By permission of the author and publisher.

a boost from the electoral system was unnecessary, it transformed a minority of votes into a majority of seats on only six of twelve occasions. It is possible that changes in the party system and/or in the distribution of party support will render this justification increasingly anachronistic in future years.

If the assessment of the electoral system is extended to include not only its contribution to one-party majorities, but its contribution to the maintenance of effective opposition, arbitrarily defined as at least one-third of House members, it appears in an even less satisfactory light. On four occasions, two of which occurred when the government party had slightly more than one-half of the votes, the opposition was reduced to numerical ineffectiveness. The coupling of these two criteria together creates a reasonable measure for the contribution of the electoral system to a working parliamentary system, which requires both a stable majority and an effective opposition. From this vantage point the electoral system has a failure rate of 71 percent, on ten of fourteen occasions.

● ● ●

The Effect on Major and Minor Parties

Table 2 indicates an important effect of the electoral system with its proof that discrimination for and against the parties does not become increasingly severe when the parties are ordered from most votes to least votes. Discrimination in favour of a party was most pronounced for the weakest party on seven occasions, and for the strongest party on seven occasions. In the four elections from 1921 to 1930 inclusive, with three party contestants, the second part was most hurt by the electoral system. In the five elections from 1935 to 1953 inclusive the electoral system again worked against the middle ranking parties and favoured the parties with the weakest and strongest voting support. In the five elections from 1957 to 1965 inclusive there has been a noticable tendency to benefit the first two parties, with the exception of the fourth party, Social Credit in 1957, at the expense of the smaller parties.

The explanation for the failure of the electoral system to act with Darwinian logic by consistently distributing its rewards to the large parties and its penalties to the small parties is relatively straightforward. The bias in favour of the strongest party reflects the likelihood that the large number of votes it has at its disposal will produce enough victories in individual constituencies to give it, on a percentage basis, a surplus of seats over votes. The fact that this surplus has occurred with only one exception, 1957, indicates the extreme unlikelihood of the strongest party having a distribution of partisan support capable of transforming the electoral system from an ally into a foe. The explanation for the favourable impact of the electoral system on the Progressives and Social Credit from 1921 to 1957 when they were the weakest parties is simply that they were sectional parties which concentrated their efforts in their areas of strength where the electoral system worked in their favour. Once the electoral system has rewarded the strongest party and a weak party with

TABLE 2: Bias of Electoral System in Translating Votes into Seats

Year	\- Rank order of parties in terms of percentages of vote -								
	1		2		3		4		5	
1921	Libs.	1.21	Cons.	0.70	Progs.	1.20				
1925	Cons.	1.017	Libs.	1.015	Progs.	1.09				
1926	Libs.	1.13	Cons.	0.82	Progs.	1.55				
1930	Cons.	1.15	Libs.	0.82	Progs.	1.53				
1935	Libs.	1.57	Cons.	0.55	CCF	0.33	Rec.	0.05	Socred	1.68
1940	Libs.	1.43	Cons.	0.53	CCF	0.39	Socred	1.52		
1945	Libs.	1.24	Cons.	1.00	CCF	0.73	Socred	1.29		
1949	Libs.	1.49	Cons.	0.53	CCF	0.37	Socred	1.03		
1953	Libs.	1.32	Cons.	0.62	CCF	0.77	Socred	1.06		
1957	Libs.	0.97	Cons.	1.087	CCF	0.88	Socred	1.091		
1958	Cons.	1.46	Libs.	0.55	CCF	0.32	Socred	0		
1962	Cons.	1.17	Libs.	1.01	NDP	0.53	Socred	0.97		
1963	Libs.	1.17	Cons.	1.09	NDP	0.49	Socred	0.76		
1965	Libs.	1.23	Cons.	1.13	NDP	0.44	Cred.	0.72	Socred	1.51

Independents and very small parties have been excluded from the table.

The measurement of discrimination employed in this table defines the relationship between the percentage of votes and the percentage of seats. The figure is devised by dividing the former into the latter. Thus 1 — (38% seats/38% votes), for example — represents a neutral effect for the electoral system. Any figure above 1 — (40% seats/20% votes) = 2.0, for example — indicates discrimination for the party. A figure below 1 — (20% seats/40% votes) = 0.5, for example — indicates discrimination against the party. For the purposes of the table the ranking of the parties as 1, 2, 3 . . . is based on their percentage of the vote, since to rank them in terms of seats would conceal the very bias it is sought to measure — namely the bias introduced by the intervening variable of the electoral system which constitutes the mechanism by which votes are translated into seats.

concentrated sectional strength there are not many more seats to go around. In this kind of party system, which Canada had from 1921 to Mr. Diefenbaker's breakthrough, serious discrimination against the second party in a three-party system and the second and third party in a four-party system is highly likely.

Table 3 reveals that the electoral system positively favours minor parties with sectional strongholds and discourages minor parties with diffuse support. The classic example of the latter phenomenon is provided by the Reconstruction party in the 1935 election. For its 8.7 percent of the vote it was rewarded with one seat, and promptly disappeared from the scene. Yet its electoral support was more than twice that of Social Credit which gained seventeen seats, and only marginally less than that of the CCF which gained seven seats. The case of the Reconstruction party provides dramatic illustration of the futility of party effort for a minor party which lacks a sectional stronghold. The treatment of the CCF/NDP by the electoral system is only slightly less revealing. This party with diffuse support which aspired to national and major party status never received as many seats as would have been "justified" by its voting support, and on six occasions out of ten received less than half the seats to which it was "entitled." The contrasting treatment of Social Credit and the Progressives, sectional minor parties, by the electoral system clearly reveals the

TABLE 3: Minor Parties: Percentages of Seats and Votes

	Progressives		Reconstruction		CCF/NDP		Soc. Credit		Créditiste	
	votes	seats	votes	seats	votes	seats	votes	seats	votes	seats
1921	23.1	27.7								
1925	9.0	9.8								
1926	5.3	8.2								
1930	3.2	4.9								
1935			8.7	0.4	8.9	2.9	4.1	6.9		
1940					8.5	3.3	2.7	4.1		
1945					15.6	11.4	4.1	5.3		
1949					13.4	5.0	3.7	3.8		
1953					11.3	8.7	5.4	5.7		
1957					10.7	9.4	6.6	7.2		
1958					9.5	3.0	2.6	—		
1962					13.5	7.2	11.7	11.3		
1963					13.1	6.4	11.9	9.1		
1965					17.9	7.9	3.7	1.9	4.7	3.4

bias of the electoral system in favour of concentrated support and against diffused support.

Distortion in Party Parliamentary Representation

No less important than the general differences in the way the electoral system rewards or punishes each individual party as such, is the manner in which it fashions particular patterns of sectional representation within the ranks of the parliamentary parties out of the varying distributions of electoral support they received. This sectional intra-party discrimination affects all parties. The electoral system consistently minimized the Ontario support of the Progressives which provided the party with 43.5 percent, 39.7 percent, and 29.4 percent of its total votes in the first three elections of the twenties. The party received only 36.9 percent, 8.3 percent, and 10 percent of its total seats from that province. Further, by its varying treatment of the party's electoral support from Manitoba, Saskatchewan, and Alberta it finally helped to reduce the Progressives to an Alberta party.

An analysis of CCF/NDP votes and seats clearly illustrates the manner in which the electoral system has distorted the parliamentary wing of the party. Table 4 reveals the extreme discrimination visited on Ontario supporters of the CCF from 1935 to 1957. With the exception of 1940, CCF Ontario voting support consistently constituted between 30 and 40 percent of total CCF voting support. Yet, the contribution of Ontario to CCF parliamentary representation was derisory. During the same period there was a marked overrepresentation of Saskatchewan in the CCF caucus. The 1945 election is indicative. The 260,000 votes from Ontario, 31.9 percent of the total CCF vote, produced no seats at all, while 167,000 supporters from Saskatchewan, 20.5 percent of the total party vote, were rewarded with eighteen seats, 64.3 perecent of total party seats. In these

TABLE 4: Percentages of Total CCF/NDP Strength, in Seats and Votes coming from Selected Provinces.

	N.S.	Que.	Ont.	Man.	Sask.	Alta.	B.C.
1935 votes	—	1.9	32.7	13.9	18.8	7.9	24.8
seats	—	—	—	28.6	28.6	—	42.9
1940 votes	4.5	1.9	15.6	15.6	27.0	8.9	26.2
seats	12.5	—	—	12.5	62.5	—	12.5
1945 votes	6.4	4.1	31.9	12.5	20.5	7.0	15.4
seats	3.6	—	—	17.9	64.3	—	14.3
1949 votes	4.3	2.3	39.2	10.6	19.5	4.0	18.6
seats	7.7	—	7.7	23.1	38.5	—	23.1
1953 votes	3.5	3.7	33.4	10.1	24.6	3.7	19.7
seats	4.3	—	4.3	13.0	47.8	—	30.4
1957 votes	2.4	4.5	38.7	11.6	19.8	3.8	18.6
seats	—	—	12.0	20.0	40.0	—	28.0
1958 votes	2.7	6.6	37.9	10.8	16.3	2.8	22.2
seats	—	—	37.5	—	12.5	—	50.0
1962 votes	3.8	8.9	44.0	7.4	9.0	4.1	20.4
seats	5.3	—	31.6	10.5	—	—	52.6
1963 votes	2.6	14.6	42.6	6.4	7.3	3.4	21.5
seats	—	—	35.3	11.8	—	—	52.9
1965 votes	2.8	17.7	43.0	6.6	7.6	3.2	17.3
seats	—	—	42.9	14.3	—	—	42.9

Note: Percententages of votes do not total 100 horizontally because the table does not include Newfoundland, Prince Edward Island, New Brunswick, or the territories where the CCF/NDP gained a few votes but no seats.

circumstances it was not surprising that observers were led to mislabel the CCF an agrarian party.

The major parties are not immune from the tendency of the electoral system to make the parliamentary parties grossly inaccurate reflections of the sectional distribution of party support. Table 5 makes it clear that the electoral system has been far from impartial in its treatment of Liberal and Conservative voting support from Ontario and Quebec. For fourteen consecutive elections covering nearly half a century there was a consistent and usually marked overrepresentation of Quebec in the parliamentary Liberal party and marked underrepresentation in the parliamentary Conservative party, with the exception of 1958. For ten consecutive elections from 1921 to 1957 Ontario was consistently and markedly over-represented in the parliamentary Conservative party, and for eleven consecutive elections from 1921 to 1958, there was consistent, but less marked, underrepresentation of Ontario in the parliamentary Liberal party. Thus the electoral system, by pulling the parliamentary Liberal party toward Quebec and the parliamentary Conservative party toward Ontario, made the sectional cleavages between the parties much more pronounced in Parliament than they were at the level of the electorate.

The way in which the electoral system affected the relationship of Quebec to the parliamentary wings of the two major parties is evident in the truly startling discrepancies between votes and seats for the two parties from that province. From 1921 to 1965 inclusive the Liberals gained 752 members from Quebec, and the Conservatives only 135. The

TABLE 5: Liberals and Conservatives: Percentages of Total Parliamentary Strength and Total Electoral Support from Quebec and Ontario

	Conservatives				Liberals			
	Ontario		Quebec		Ontario		Quebec	
	seats	votes	seats	votes	seats	votes	seats	votes
1921	74.0	47.1	—	15.5	18.1	26.6	56.0	43.8
1925	58.6	47.4	3.4	18.4	11.1	30.1	59.6	37.8
1926	58.2	44.9	4.4	18.7	20.3	31.7	46.9	33.4
1930	43.1	38.9	17.5	24.0	24.2	33.7	44.0	30.6
1935	62.5	43.1	12.5	24.7	32.4	34.4	31.8	31.5
1940	62.5	48.6	2.5	16.4	31.5	34.4	33.7	31.2
1945	71.6	52.7	3.0	8.3	27.2	34.6	42.4	33.3
1949	61.0	43.6	4.9	22.6	29.0	31.9	35.2	33.2
1953	64.7	44.2	7.8	26.0	29.8	32.6	38.6	34.2
1957	54.5	42.9	8.0	21.7	20.0	31.1	59.0	38.1
1958	32.2	36.2	24.0	25.7	30.6	33.3	51.0	37.8
1962	30.2	36.9	12.1	21.6	44.0	39.2	35.0	28.6
1963	28.4	37.8	8.4	16.0	40.3	39.1	36.4	29.3
1965	25.8	37.4	8.2	17.3	38.9	38.6	42.7	30.0

ratio of 5.6 Liberals to each Conservative in the House of Commons contrasts sharply with the 1.9 to 1 ratio of Liberals to Conservatives at the level of voters.

Given the recurrent problems concerning the status of Quebec in Canadian federalism and the consistent tension in French-English relations it is self-evident that the effects of the electoral system noted above can be appropriately described as divisive and detrimental to national unity. . . . The electoral system has placed serious barriers in the way of the Conservative party's attempts to gain parliamentary representation from a province where its own interests and those of national unity coincided on the desirability of making a major contender for public office as representative as possible. The frequent thesis that the association of the Conservatives with conscription in 1917 destroyed their prospects in Quebec only becomes meaningful when it is noted that a particular electoral system presided over that destruction.

The following basic effects of the electoral system have been noted. The electoral system has not been impartial in its translation of votes into seats. Its benefits have been disproportionately given to the strongest major party and a weak sectional party. The electoral system has made a major contribution to the identification of particular sections/provinces with particular parties. It has undervalued the partisan diversity within each section/province. By so doing it has rendered the parliamentary composition of each party less representative of the sectional interests in the political system than is the party electorate from which that representation is derived. The electoral system favours minor parties with concentrated sectional support, and discourages those with diffuse national support. The electoral system has consistently exaggerated the significance of cleavages demarcated by sectional/provincial boundaries and has thus tended to transform contests between parties into contests between sections/provinces. . . .

Party System as a Nationalizing Agency

. . . One of the most widespread interpretations of the party system claims that it, or at least the two major parties, functions as a great unifying or nationalizing agency. Canadian politics, it is emphasized, are politics of moderation, or brokerage politics, which minimize differences, restrain fissiparous tendencies, and thus over time help knit together the diverse interests of a polity weak in integration. It is noteworthy that this brokerage theory is almost exclusively applied to the reconciliation of sectional, racial, and religous divisions, the latter two frequently being regarded as simply more specific versions of the first with respect to French-English relations. The theory of brokerage politics thus assumes that the historically significant cleavages in Canada are sectional, reflecting the federal nature of Canadian society, or racial/religious, reflecting a continuation of the struggle which attracted Durham's attention in the mid-nineteenth century. Brokerage politics between classes is mentioned, if at all, as an afterthought.

The interpretation of the party system in terms of its fulfilment of a nationalizing function is virtually universal. Close scrutiny, however, indicates that this is at best questionable, and possibly invalid. It is difficult to determine the precise meaning of the argument that the party system has been a nationalizing agency, stressing what Canadians have in common, bringing together representatives of diverse interests to deliberate on government policies. In an important sense the argument is misleading in that it attributes to the party system what is simply inherent in a representative democracy which inevitably brings together Nova Scotians, Albertans, and Quebeckers to a common assemblage point, and because of the majoritarian necessities of the parliamentary system requires agreement among contending interests to accomplish anything at all. Or, to put it differently, the necessity for inter-group collaboration in any on-going political system makes it possible to claim of any party system compatible with the survival of the polity that it acts as a nationalizing agency. The extent to which any particular party system does so act is inescapably therefore a comparative question or a question of degree. In strict logic an evaluation of alternative types of party systems is required before a particular one can be accorded unreserved plaudits for the success with which it fulfils a nationalizing function.

. . . The basic approach of this paper is that the party system, importantly conditioned by the electoral system, exacerbates the very cleavages it is credited with healing. As a corollary it is suggested that the party system is not simply a reflection of sectionalism, but that sectionalism is also a reflection of the party system.

The electoral system has helped to foster a particular kind of political style by the special significance it accords to sectionalism. This is evident in party campaign strategy, in party policies, in intersectional differences in the nature and vigour of party activity, and in differences in the intra-party socialization experiences of parliamentary personnel of the various parties. As a consequence the electoral system has had an important effect on perceptions of the party system and, by extension, the political system itself. Sectionalism has been rendered highly visible because the electoral system makes it a fruitful basis on which to organize electoral support. Divisions cutting through sections, particularly those based on the class system, have been much less salient because the possibility of payoffs in terms of representation has been minimal.

Parties and Campaign Strategy

An initial perspective on the contribution of the parties to sectionalism is provided by some of the basic aspects of campaign strategy. Inadequate attention has been paid to the extent to which the campaign activities of the parties have exacerbated the hatreds, fears, and insecurities related to divisive sectional and ethnic cleavages.

The basic cleavage throughout Canadian history concerns Quebec, or more precisely that part of French Canada resident in Quebec, and its relationships with the rest of the country. The evidence suggests that elections have fed on racial fears and insecurities, rather than reduced them. The three post-war elections of 1921, 1925, and 1926 produced overwhelming Liberal majorities at the level of seats in Quebec, 65 out of 65 in 1921, 59 out of 65 in 1925, and 60 seats out of 65 in 1926. . . . In view of the ample evidence documented by Graham and Neatby of the extent to which the Liberal campaigns stirred up the animosities and insecurities of French Canada, it is difficult to assert that the party system performed a unifying role in a province where historic tensions were potentially divisive. The fact that the Liberals were able to "convince Quebec" that they were its only defenders and that their party contained members of both ethnic groups after the elections scarcely constitute refutation when attention is directed to the methods employed to achieve this end, and when it is noted that the election results led to the isolation of Canada's second great party from Quebec.

More recent indications of sectional aspects of campaign strategy with respect to Quebec help to verify the divisive nature of election campaigning. The well-known decision of the Conservative party in 1957, acting on Gordon Churchill's maxim to "reinforce success not failure," to reduce its Quebec efforts and concentrate on the possibilities of success in the remainder of the country provides an important indication of the significance of calculations of sectional pay-offs in dictating campaign strategy. The logic behind this policy was a direct consequence of the electoral system, for it was that system which dictated that increments of voting support from Quebec would produce less pay-off in representation than would equal increments elsewhere where the prospects of Conservative constituency victories were more promising. The electoral results were brilliantly successful from the viewpoint of the party, but less so from the perspective of Quebec which contributed only 8 percent of the new government's seats, and received only three cabinet ministers.

In these circumstances the election of 1958 was crucial in determining the nature and extent of French-Canadian participation in the new government, which obviously would be formed by the Conservatives. Group appeals were exploited by the bribe that Quebec would get many more cabinet seats if that province returned a larger number of Tory MPs. Party propaganda stimulated racial tensions and insecurities. . . .

The significance of Quebec representation in explaining the nature of the Canadian party system has often been noted. Meisel states that the federal politician is faced with the dilemma of ignoring the pleas of Quebec, in which case "he may lose the support of Canada's second largest province without the seats of which a Parliamentary majority is almost impossible. If he heeds the wishes of Quebec, he may be deprived of indispensable support elsewhere." Lipson describes Quebec as the "solid South" of Canada whose support has contributed at different times to the hegemony of both parties, a fact which is basic in explaining the strategy of opposition of the two major parties. An important point is made by Ward in his observation that Liberal dominance in Quebec contributes to "internal strains in other parties." He adds the fundamental point that it is the electoral system which "by throwing whole blocks of seats to one party" fosters for that party a "special role as protector of the minority," while other parties are baffled by their inability to make significant breakthroughs in representation. Prophetically, as it turned out, he noted the developing theory that opposition parties should attempt to construct parliamentary majorities without Quebec, thus facing French Canadians with the option of becoming an opposition minority or casting themselves loose from the Liberals.

Ward's analysis makes clear that the special electoral importance of Quebec and the resultant party strategies elicited by that fact are only meaningful in the context of an electoral system which operates on a "winner take all" basis, not only at the level of the constituency but, to a modified extent, at the level of the province as a whole. It is only at the level of seats, not votes that Quebec became a Liberal stronghold, a Canadian "solid South," and a one-party monopoly. The Canadian "solid South," like its American counterpart, is a contrivance of the electoral system, not an autonomous social fact which exists independent of it. . . .

Quebec constitutes the most striking example of the sectional nature of party strategy, electoral appeals, and electoral outcomes. It is, however, only a specific manifestation of the general principle that when the distribution of partisan support within a province or section is such that significant political pay-offs are likely to accrue to politicians who address themselves to the special needs of the area concerned, politicians will not fail to provide at least a partial response. The tendency of parties "to aim appeals at the nerve centers of particular provinces or regions, hoping thus to capture a bloc geographical vote," and to emphasize sectional appeals, are logical party responses within the Canadian electoral framework.

Electoral System and Party Policy

. . . The inquiry can be extended by noting that the electoral system affects party policies both directly and indirectly. The direct effect flows from the elementary consideration that each party devises policy in the light of a different set of sectional considerations. In theory, if the party is viewed strictly as a maximizing body pursuing representation, party sensitivity should be most highly developed in marginal situations where an appropriate policy initiative, a special organizational effort, or a liberal use of campaign funds might tip the balance of sectional representation to the side of the party. Unfortunately, sufficient evidence is not available to assert that this is a valid description of the import of sectional considerations on party strategies. The indirect effect of the electoral system is that it plays an important role in the determination of who the party policy makers will be.

The indirect effect presupposes the preeminence of the parliamentary party and its leaders in policy making. Acceptance of this presupposition requires a brief preliminary analysis of the nature of party organization, especially for the two major parties. The literature has been unanimous in referring to the organizational weakness of the Liberals and Conservatives. Some of the basic aspects and results of this will be summarily noted.

The extra-parliamentary structures of the two major parties have been extremely weak, lacking in continuity and without any disciplining power over the parliamentary party. The two major parties have been leader-dominated with membership playing a limited role in policy making and party financing. Although there are indications that the extra-parliamentary apparatus of the parties is growing in importance, it can be safely said that for the period under review both major parties have been essentially parliamentary parties. . . . Thus, the contribution of the electoral system to the determination of the parliamentary personnel of the party becomes, by logical extension, a contribution to the formation of party policies. Scarrow has asserted that "it is the makeup of the parliamentary party, including the proportional strength and bargaining position of the various parts, which is the most crucial factor in determining policy at any one time." While this hypothesis may require modification in particular cases, it is likely that historical research will confirm its general validity. For example, the antithetical attitudes of Conservatives and Liberals to conscription in both world wars were related not only to the electoral consequences of different choices, but also reflected the backgrounds and bias of the party personnel available to make such key decisions. . . .

The significance of the electoral system for party policy is due to its consistent failure to reflect with even rough accuracy the distribution of partisan support in the various sections/provinces of the country. By making the Conservatives far more a British and Ontario-based party, the Liberals far more a French and Quebec party, the CCF far more a prairie and BC party, and even Social Credit far more of an Alberta party up until 1953, than the electoral support of these parties "required," they were deprived of intra-party spokesmen proportionate to their electoral support from the sections where they were relatively weak. The relative, or on occasion total, absence of such spokesmen for particular sectional communities seriously affects the image of the parties as national bodies, deprives the party concerned of articulate proponents of particular sectional interests in caucus and in the House, and, it can be deductively suggested, renders the members of the parliamentary party personally less sensitive to the interests of the unrepresented sections than they otherwise would be. As a result the general perspectives and policy orientations of a party are likely to be skewed in favour of those interests which, by virtue of strong parliamentary representation, can vigorously assert their claims.

If a bias of this nature is consistently visited on a specific party over long periods of time, it will importantly condition the general orientation of the party and the political information and values of party MPs. It is in such ways that it can be argued that the effect of the electoral system is cumulative, creating conditions which aggravate the bias which it initially introduced into the party. To take the case of the Conservative party, the thesis is that not only does the electoral system make that party less French by depriving it of French representation as such, but also by the effect which that absence of French colleagues has on the possibility that its non-French members will shed their parochial perspectives through intra-party contacts with French co-workers in parliament. . . .

While a lengthy catalogue of explanations can be adduced to explain the divergent orientations of Liberals and Conservatives to Quebec and French Canada the electoral system must be given high priority as an influencing factor. A strong deductive case therefore can be made that the sectional bias in party representation engendered by the electoral system has had an important effect on the policies of specific parties and on policy differences between parties. Additionally, the electoral system has helped to determine the real or perceived sectional consequences of alternative party policy decisions. . . .

In some cases the sectional nature of party support requires politicians to make a cruel choice between sections, a choice recognized as involving the sacrifice of future representation from one section in order to retain it from another. This, it has been argued, was the Conservative dilemma in deciding whether or not Riel was to hang and in determining conscription policy in the First World War. Faced with a choice between Quebec and Ontario, in each case they chose Ontario. It should be noted that these either/or sectional choices occasionally thrown up in the political system are given exaggerated significance by an electoral system capable of transforming a moderate loss of votes in a section into almost total annihilation at the level of representation. If only votes were considered, the harshness of such decisions would be greatly mitigated, for decisions could be made on the basis of much less dramatic marginal assessments of the political consequences of alternative courses of action.

Electoral System and Perceptions of the Polity

A general point, easily overlooked because of its elementary nature, is that the electoral system has influenced perceptions of the political system. The sectional basis of party representation which the electoral system has stimulated has reduced the visibility of cleavages cutting through sections. . . .

. . . A hasty survey of political literature finds Quebec portrayed as "the solid Quebec of 1921," western Canada described as "once the fortress of protest movements," since transformed "into a Conservative stronghold," eastern Canada depicted in the 1925 election as having "punished King for his preoccupation with the prairies," and the Conservative party described in 1955 as "almost reduced into being an Ontario party," when in the previous election 55.8 percent of its voting support came from outside that province.

The use of sectional terminology in description easily shades off into highly suspect assumptions about the voting behaviour of the electorate within sections. One of the most frequent election interpretations attributes a monolithic quality to Quebec voters and then argues that they "have instinctively given the bulk of their support" to the government or it is claimed that the "the voters of Quebec traditionally seem to want the bulk of their representation . . . on the government side of the House. . . ." Several authors have specifically suggested that in 1958 Quebec, or the French Canadians, swung to Diefenbaker for this reason. . . . A recent analysis of New Brunswick politics argues that the strong tendency for MPs from that province to be on the government side of the House "must be" because "it seeks to gain what concessions it can by supporting the government and relying on its sense of gratitude."

The tendency of the electoral system to create sectional or provincial sweeps for one party at the level of representation is an important reason for these misinterpretations. Since similar explanations have become part of the folklore of Canadian politics it is useful to examine the extremely tenuous basis of logic on which they rest. Quebec will serve as a useful case study. The first point to note is the large percentage of the Quebec electorate which does not vote for the party which subsequently forms the government, a percentage varying from 29.8 percent in 1921 to 70.4 percent in 1962, and averaging 48 percent for the period 1921 to 1965 as a whole. In the second place any government party will tend to win most of the sections most of the time. That is what a government party is. While Quebec has shown an above average propensity to accord more than fifty percent of its representation to the government party (on eleven occasions out of fourteen, compared to an average of all sections of just under eight out of fourteen) this is partly because of the size of the contingent from Quebec and its frequent one-sided representation patterns. This means that to a large extent Quebec determines which party will be the government, rather than exhibiting a preference for being on the government or opposition side of the House. This can be tested by switching the representation which Quebec gave to the two main parties in each of the eleven elections in which Quebec backed the winner. The method is simply to transfer the number of seats Quebec accorded the winning party to the second main party, and transfer the latter's Quebec seats to the former. This calculation shows that had Quebec distributed its seats between the two main parties in a manner precisely the opposite to its actual performance it would have been on the winning side on seven out of eleven occasions anyway. It is thus more accurate to say that parties need Quebec in order to win than to say that Quebec displays a strong desire to be on the winning side.

One final indication of the logical deficiencies of the assumption that Quebec voters are motivated by a bandwagon psychology will suffice. The case of 1958 will serve as an example. In 1957 when there was no prediction of a Conservative victory, Quebec voters gave 31.1 percent of their voting support to the Conservative party. In 1958 that percentage jumped to 49.6 when predictions of a Conservative victory were nearly universal. On the reasonable assumption that most of the Conservative supporters in 1957 remained with the party in 1958, and on the further assumption, which is questionable, that all of the increment in Conservative support was due to a desire to be on the winning side, the explanation is potentially applicable to only one Quebec voter out of five.

In concluding this critical analysis of a segment of Canadian political folklore it is only necessary to state that the attribution of questionable motivations to Quebec or French Canada could easily have been avoided if attention had been concentrated on voting data rather than on the bias in representation caused by the single-member constituency system. The analysis of Canadian politics has been harmfully affected by a kind of mental shorthand which manifests itself in the acceptance of a political map of the country which identifies provinces or sections in terms of the end results of the political process, partisan representation. This perception is natural since elections occur only once every three or four years while the results are visible for the entire period between elections. Since sectional discrepancies between votes and seats are due to the electoral system it is evident that the latter has contributed to the formation of a set of seldom questioned perceptions which exaggerate the partisan significance of geographical boundaries.

Electoral System, Sectionalism, and Instability

Individuals can relate to the party system in several ways, but the two most fundamental are class and sectionalism. The two are antithetical, for one emphasizes the geography of residence, while the other stresses stratification distinctions for which residence is irrelevant. The frequently noted conservative tone which pervades Canadian politics is a consequence of the sectional nature of the party system. The emphasis on sectional divisions engendered by the electoral system has submerged class conflicts, and to the extent that our politics has been ameliorative it has been more concerned with the distribution of burdens and benefits between sections than between classes. The poverty of the Maritimes has occupied an honourable place in the foreground of public discussion. The diffuse poverty of the generally underprivileged has scarcely been noticed.

Such observations lend force to John Porter's thesis that Canadian parties have failed to harness the "conservative-progressive dynamic" related to the Canadian class system, and to his assertion that "to obscure social divisions through brokerage politics is to remove from the political system that element of dialectic which is the source of creative politics." The fact is, however, that given the historical (and existing) state of class polarization in Canada the electoral system has made sectionalism a more rewarding vehicle for amassing political support than class. The destructive impact of the electoral system on the CCF is highly indicative of this point. It is not that the single member constituency system discourages class based politics in any absolute sense, as the example of Britain shows, but that it discourages such politics when class identities are weak or submerged behind sectional identities.

This illustrates the general point that the differences in the institutional contexts of politics have important effects in determining which kinds of conflict become salient in the political system. The particular institutional context with which this paper is concerned, the electoral system, has clearly fostered a sectional party system in which party strategists have concentrated on winning sections over to their side. It has encouraged a politics of opportunism based on sectional appeals and conditioned by one party bastions where the opposition is tempted to give up the battle and pursue success in more promising areas.

A politics of sectionalism is a politics of instability for two reasons. In the first place it induces parties to pay attention to the realities of representation which filter through the electoral system, at the expense of the realities of partisan support at the level of the electorate. The self-interest which may induce a party to write off a section because its weak support there is discriminated against by the electoral system, may be exceedingly unfortunate for national unity. Imperfections in the political market render the likelihood of an invisible hand transforming the pursuit of party good into public good somewhat dubious.

Secondly, sectional politics is potentially far more disruptive to the polity than class politics. This is essentially because sectional politics has an inherent tendency to call into question the very nature of the political system and its legitimacy. Classes, unlike sections, cannot secede from the political system, and are consequently more prone to accept its legitimacy. The very nature of their spatial distribution not only inhibits their political organization but induces them to work through existing instrumentalities. With sections this is not the case.

Given the strong tendency to sectionalism found in the very nature of Canadian society the question can be raised as to the appropriateness of the existing electoral system. Duverger has pointed out that the single-member constituency system "accentuates the geographical localization of opinions: one might even say that it tends to transform a national opinion . . . into a local opinion by allowing it to be represented only in the sections of the country in which it is strongest." Proportional representation works in the opposite manner for "opinions strongly entrenched locally tend to be broadened on to the national plane by the possibility of being represented in districts where they are in a small minority." The political significance of these opposed tendencies "is clear: proportional representation tends to strengthen national unity (or, to be more precise, national uniformity); the simple majority system accentuates local differences. The consequences are fortunate or unfortunate according to the particular situation in each country."

Sectionalism and Discontinuities in
Party Representation

It might be argued that the appropriate question is not whether sectional (or other) interests are represented proportionately to their voting support in each party, but simply whether they are represented in the party system as a whole proportionately to their general electoral strength. This assertion, however, is overly simple and unconvincing.

An electoral system which exaggerates the role of specific sections in specific parties accentuates the importance of sectionalism itself. If sectionalism in its "raw" condition is already strong, its exaggeration may cause strains beyond the capacity of the polity to handle. By its stimulus to sectional cleavages the electoral system transforms the party struggle into a struggle between sections, raising the danger that "parties . . . cut off from gaining support among a major stratum . . . lose a major reason for compromise."

This instability is exacerbated by the fact that the electoral system facilitates sudden and drastic alterations in the basis of party parliamentary representation. Recent changes with respect to NDP representation from Saskatchewan, Social Credit representation from Quebec, and the startling change in the influence of the prairie contingent in the Conservative party, with its counterpart of virtually eliminating other parties from that section, constitute important illustrations. The experience of Social Credit since 1962 and more recent experience of the Conservative party reveal that such changes may be more than a party can successfully handle.

Sudden changes in sectional representation are most pronounced in the transition from being an opposition party to becoming the government party. As Underhill notes, it is generally impossible to have more than one party with significant representation from both French and English Canada at the same time. That party is invariably the government party. This has an important consequence which has been insufficiently noted. Not only are opposition parties often numerically weak and devoid of access to the expertise that would prepare them for the possibility of governing, but they are also far less national in composition than the government party. On the two occasions since the First World War when the Conservatives ousted Liberal governments, 1930 and 1957, their opposition experience cut them off from contact with Quebec at the parliamentary level. Even though the party was successful in making significant break-throughs in that province in 1930 and especially in 1958, it can be suggested that it had serious problems in digesting the sudden input of Quebec MPs, particularly in the latter year.

The transition from opposition to government therefore is a transition from being sectional to being national, not only in the tasks of government, but typically in the very composition of the party itself. The hypothesis that this discontinuity may have serious effects on the capacity of the party to govern is deserving of additional research. It is likely that such research will suggest a certain incongruity between the honorific status symbolically accorded Her Majesty's Loyal Opposition, and an electoral system which is likely to hamper the development in that party of those perspectives functional to successful governing.

The Electoral System as a Determinant of the Party System

Students of Canadian politics have been singularly unwilling to attribute any explanatory power to the electoral system as a determinant of the party system. Lipson has argued that it is not the electoral system which moulds the party system, but rather the reverse. Essentially his thesis is that parties select the type of electoral system more compatible with their own interest, which is self-perpetuation. He admits in passing that once selected the electoral system "produces a reciprocal effect upon the parties which brought it into being."

Lipson's interpretation is surely misleading and fallacious in its implication that because parties preside over the selection, modification, and replacement of particular institutions the subsequent feed-back of those institutions on the parties should not be regarded as causal. In the modern democratic party state, parties preside over the legal arrangements governing campaign expenses, eligibility of candidates, the rules establishing the determination of party winners and losers, the kinds of penalties, such as loss of deposits, which shall be visited on candidates with a low level of support, the rules establishing who may vote, and so on. Analysis is stifled if it is assumed that because these rules are made by parties the effect of the rules on the parties is in some sense to be regarded as derivative or of secondary interest or importance. Fundamentally the argument concerns the priority to be accorded the chicken or the egg. As such it can be pursued to an infinite regression, for it can be asserted that the parties which make a particular set of rules are themselves products of the rules which prevailed in the previous period, which in turn. . . . It might also be noted that parties which preside over particular changes in electoral arrangements may be mistaken in their predictions about the effect of the changes. It is clear that the introduction of the alternative ballot in British Columbia in 1952 misfired from the viewpoint of its sponsors, with dramatic effects on the nature of the provincial party system which subsequently developed.

The only reasonable perspective for the analyst to adopt is to accept the interdependence of electoral systems and party systems and then to investigate whatever aspects of that interdependence seems to provide useful clues for the understanding of the political system.

In a recent article Meisel explicitly agrees with Lipson, asserting that parties are products of societies rather than of differences between parliamentary or presidential systems, or of electoral laws. This argument is weakened by its assumption that society is something apart from the institutional arrangements of which it is composed. It is unclear in this dichotomy just what society is. While it may be possible at the moment when particular institutions are being established to regard them as separate from the society to which they are to be fitted, this is not so with long-established institutions which become part and parcel of the society itself. Livingston's argument that after a while it becomes impossible to make an analytic distinction between the instrumentalities of federalism and the federal nature of the society they were designed to preserve or express is correct and is of general validity. To say therefore that parties are products of societies is not to deny that they are products of institutions. The only defensible view is once again to accept the interdependence of political and other institutions which compose society and then to establish the nature of particular patterns of interdependence by research.

Confirmation of the view that electoral systems do have an effect on party systems is provided by logic. To assert that a particular electoral system does not have an effect on a particular party system is equivalent to saying that all conceivable electoral systems are perfectly compatible with the party system and that all conceivable party systems are compatible with that electoral system. This is surely impossible. Any one electoral system has the effect of inhibiting the development of the different party systems which some, but not necessarily all, different electoral systems would foster. To accept this is to accept that electoral systems and party systems are related.

Approaches to a Theory of the Party System

This paper has suggested that the electoral system has been an important factor in the evolution of the Canadian party system. Its influence is intimately tied up with the politics of sectionalism which it has stimulated. Sectionalism in the party system is unavoidable as long as there are significant differences between the distribution of party voter support in any one section and the distribution in the country as a whole. The electoral system, however, by the distortions it introduces as it transforms votes into seats produces an exaggerated sectionalism at the level of representation. In view of this, the basic theme of the paper in its simplest form, and somewhat crudely stated, is that statements about sectionalism in the national party system are in many cases, and at a deeper level, statements about the politics of the single-member constituency system.

The suggested impact of the electoral system on the party system is relevant to a general theory of the party system but should not be confused with such a general theory. The construction of the latter would have required analysis of the import for the party system of such factors as the federal system, the relationship of provincial party organizations to the national party, the nature of the class system, the underlying economic and cultural bases for sectionalism, a parliamentary system of the British type, and many others. For this discussion all these have been accepted as given. They have been mentioned, if at all, only indirectly. Their importance for a general theory is taken for granted, as are the interdependencies they have with each other and with the electoral system. It is evident, for example, that the underlying strength of sectional tendencies and the weakness of class identification are interrelated with each other and with the electoral system as explanations of sectionalism in Canadian politics. For any one of these to change will produce a change in the outcomes which their interactions generate. We are not therefore suggesting that sectional tendencies are exclusive products of the electoral system, but only that that system accords them an exaggerated significance.

Concentration on the electoral system represents an attempt to isolate one aspect of a complex series of interactions which is only imperfectly understood and in the present state of our knowledge cannot be handled simultaneously with precision. In such circumstances the development of more systematic comprehensive explanations will only result from a dialectic between research finding at levels varying from that of individual voters through middle-range studies, such as Alford's recent analysis of class and voting, to attempts, such as those by Scarrow and Meisel, to handle a complex range of phenomena in one framework.

We can conclude that the capacity of the party system to act as an integrating agency for the sectional communities of Canada is detrimentally affected by the electoral system. The politicians' problem of reconciling sectional particularisms is exacerbated by the system they must work through in their pursuit of power. From one perspective it can be argued that if parties succeed in overcoming sectional divisions they do so in defiance of the electoral system. Conversely, it can be claimed that if parties do not succeed this is because the electoral system has so biased the party system that it is inappropriate to call it a nationalizing agency. It is evident that not only has the electoral system given impetus to sectionalism in terms of party campaigns and policy, but by making all parties more sectional at the level of seats than of votes it complicates the ability of the parties to transcend sectionalism. At various times the electoral system has placed barriers in the way of Conservatives becoming sensitively aware of the special place of Quebec and French Canada in the Canadian polity, aided the Liberals in that task, inhibited the third parties in the country from becoming aware of the special needs and dispositions of sections other than those represented in the parliamentary party, and frequently inhibited the parliamentary personnel of the major parties from becoming attuned to the sentiments of the citizens of the prairies. The electoral system's support for the political idiosyncracies of Alberta for over two decades ill served the integration of that provincial community into the national political system at a time when it was most needed. In fact, the Alberta case merely illustrates the general proposition that the disintegrating effects of the electoral system are likely to be most pronounced where alienation from the larger political system is most profound. A particular orientation, therefore, has been imparted to Canadian politics which is not inherent in the very nature of the patterns of cleavage and consensus in the society, but results from their interplay with the electoral system.

The stimulation offered to sectional cleavages by the single-member constituency system has led several authors to query its appropriateness for national integration in certain circumstances. Lipset and Duverger have suggested that countries possessed of strong underlying tendencies to sectionalism may be better served by proportional representation which breaks up the monolithic nature of sectional representation stimulated by single-member constituency systems. Belgium is frequently cited as a country in which proportional representation has softened the conflict between the Flemish and the Walloons, and the United States as a country in which the single-member constituency system has heightened cleavages and tensions between north and south. Whatever its other merits, the single-member constituency system lacks the singular capacity of proportional representation to encourage all parties to search for votes in all sections of the country. Minorities within sections or provinces are not frozen out as they tend to be under the existing system. As a consequence sectional differences in party representation are minimized or, more accurately, given proportionate rather than exaggerated representation—a factor which encourages the parties to develop a national orientation.

EXPLANATIONS OF OUR PARTY SYSTEM*

John T. McLeod

[The] tedious similarity between [our] two major parties may be one reason for the difficulty of formulating any general theory explaining the Canadian party system. In the nineteenth century it was customary to interpret the two-party system in Macaulay's terms as the reflection of the division of mankind into those who exalt liberty above all else and those whose primary concern is social order. This "literary" theory was invoked by Laurier and given lip-service by Mackenzie King, but it is not taken seriously by contemporary scholars. It is also possible to regard our national parties as mere collections of interest groups in search of power, but the student will search in vain for any satisfactory interpretative theory suggesting how the vague "interests" are brought together or kept together, now by one party, now by another. In more fashionable terms of behaviourism and "images", Professor Mallory has attempted to explain the success or failure of Canada's major parties by stressing a leader's ability to capture the "national mood". Mallory argues that the important factor is "that at any given time only one party is in tune with a national mood—and that party is likely to stay in power until the mood changes and leaves it politically high and dry." However, Mallory fails to enlighten us as to how or why political moods change. Suggestive as the concept may be, it is not clear how "moods" may be created or identified, nor is it clear whether a leader creates the mood or whether the mood calls forth the leader.

How then do we make sense of the Canadian party system? Perhaps Mallory is most helpful when he gets down to fundamentals and insists

* From "Party Structure and Party Reform," in *The Prospect of Change: Proposals for Canada's Future*, edited by A. Rotstein, Toronto, McGraw-Hill of Canada, 1965. By permission of the author and publisher.

that "The most important thing about Canadian politics is that they are parochial rather than national." There persists a certain narrowness of viewpoint in the various sections of the Canadian population. The politics of each region tend to be rather introverted. Canada is composed of five major regions: the Maritimes, Quebec, Ontario, the Prairies, and British Columbia. Each of these regions possesses different political traditions and each contends with rather different social and economic problems. Our heterogeneous population is divided not only into segments of rural and urban, rich and poor, United Empire Loyalists and recent immigrants, but also and most important into a dualistic pattern of English and French. These cleavages make Canada an exceedingly difficult nation to govern. Democratic political parties attempt primarily to organize the population into majorities, but majorities are painfully difficult to attain when the electorate is so fragmented.

Faced with these difficulties, our major parties must inevitably be flexible and broadly inclusive if they are to be national. Above all, they must attempt to harmonize and conciliate the various conflicting interests of the society, and to do so they must emphasize the modest but essential virtues of moderation and compromise. In a nation lacking unity or cohesion, the national political party becomes the shock-absorber of domestic conflicts . . . the principal task of the national political party is to discover some means of bringing the various regions and interests closer together. . . .

Thus it is not surprising that our parties are constantly preoccupied with the search for simple common denominators of slogans and policies on which it may be possible to unite enough of the diverse elements of the population to win elections. . . . Issues for which no common denominator can be found tend to be evaded or solutions postponed.

. . . Intellectually tempting as it might be, further political polarization into radical and conservative camps seems to be a luxury which Canadians have been unable to afford. The chief function of the party in this country has always been to prevent new cleavages and to draw the divergent elements together into a majority by whatever means possible. . . .

All of this is readily understandable and familiar; however, it does not explain why a party may be more successful at one time than at another in working out broadly acceptable policies and controlling the seats of power. What more can be offered toward an explanation of the Canadian party system?

In the absence of a generally accepted theory of party operation, the most helpful informing hypothesis is that of Macpherson and Smiley who have set forth the concept of single party dominance. Macpherson's analysis of the rise of Social Credit in Alberta yields the suggestion that Alberta has never had an orthodox system of two evenly matched parties frequently alternating in office. Instead, Alberta reveals a pattern of one massive party completely overwhelming its opposition and remaining in power for a long period of uninterrupted years. This deviation from the two-party norm is what Macpherson has dubbed the "quasiparty system". Smiley takes American experience as his starting point and quotes Samuel Lubell to the effect that in American national politics the prolonged dominance of one party has been the usual state of affairs. . . . Smiley defines single party dominance as a system in which "one political party retains such overwhelming strength over a period of at least a decade that the major political issues of the community are fought out and the major conflicts of interest resolved within that party."

When the concept of a single party dominance is applied to the Canadian party system its relevance is at once apparent. Our politics since Confederation have normally been dominated by one broad middle-of-the-road party which has so effectively occupied the centre of the stage that the opposition has been squeezed off into the wings. There have been three major periods of such single party dominance in Canada. John A. Macdonald's Tories easily dominated our politics from 1867 until 1896, slipping from office only briefly in the aftermath of the Pacific Scandal. The Liberals under Laurier had things very much their own way from 1896 until 1911. After the interval of the coalition government of 1917, Mackenzie King and his hand-picked successor dominated our political life from 1921 until 1957 with only two short interruptions, and held office for one comfortably undisturbed period of 22 years. Altogether, these three leaders were in power for 56 of the 98 years since Confederation. We have not had frequent alternation between Liberal and Conservative governments, but long periods in which one party was clearly predominant.

Our experience at the provincial level also bears out the importance of the concept of single party dominance. Although the Maritime provinces for the most part seem closer to the classic pattern of the two-party system, most of the other provinces have demonstrated their adherence to the pattern examined by Macpherson and Smiley. Alberta never had a two-party system. The Liberals were in power there from 1905 to 1921 with only negligible Conservative opposition; the United Farmers of Alberta held sway from 1921 to 1935, and Social Credit has been so securely entrenched there ever since, that in the [1963] provincial election the opposition won only three of the sixty-three seats. In Saskatchewan the Liberals were the dominant party from 1905 to 1944, the Tories managing to win only one election during the whole period; after 1944 the CCF held power in the Wheat Province for twenty years. A series of non-partisan coalition governments in Manitoba during most of the 1922 to 1958 period kept that province in the quasi-party pattern, while [in 1976] in Ontario the Conservative party [had been in power thirty-three years continuously]. . . .

Inevitably, there is a high premium placed on artful leadership. In the absence of binding principles the leader of the party becomes the focal point of the member's loyalty. Personality rather than philosophy is the key to office. That leader succeeds who can best command the support of, and work out accommodations between, the most numerous interests. . . . A successful leader becomes the major symbol of his party; the party stands for what he stands for, and his pronouncements become party dogma. Whether it is Macdonald or Laurier, King or Diefenbaker, "The Chief" is the mainspring of the machine, and absolute power to formulate policy is concentrated in his hands. The most adroit conciliator will be longest in power.

If a party is to stay long in office its leadership must also reflect the duality of the Canadian nation. The most successful prime ministers have appeared to share their power with a lieutenant who represents the other major language group. An English-speaking leader must have an able French Canadian at his side; a French Catholic first minister must have a prominent English Protestant colleague. Macdonald leaned heavily on Cartier, Laurier on Fielding and Sifton, Mackenzie King on Lapointe and St. Laurent. The fundamental importance of this vestige of the pre-Confederation dual prime-ministership is emphasized by the failure of Borden, Meighen, or Diefenbaker to find such a lieutenant from Quebec. The inability of the Conservative party to win a parliamentary majority in any two successive elections in the twentieth century is often ascribed to this failure.

To become dominant, a national party must achieve a considerable degree of support from Quebec. The voters of Quebec traditionally seem to want the bulk of their representation at Ottawa on the government side of the House. This desire to find representation on Mr. Speaker's right is not peculiar to Quebec but appears to be shared by most of the major interest groups of the country. . . . Their desire for spokesmen in the cabinet helps to promote the "bandwagon" effect which broadens the support of the government party and strengthens single party dominance.

It follows that the cabinet of a dominant party includes a congeries of elements which have little in common except a willingness to support an attractive leader and an eagerness to have a voice in the councils of state. The wide divergences of opinion inside the governing party make conflict the rule rather than the exception within the cabinet. The major clashes of interest within the nation are likely to be expressed not between competing parties but inside the dominant party. . . . Argument between the parties on the floor of the House and on the hustings is superseded by argument behind the closed doors of cabinet and caucus; major issues are resolved mainly in secret, and the fruitfulness of open democratic debate to educate the voter is stultified. Elections do not often decide issues, and a danger arises of public apathy or contempt toward the ordinary democratic processes.

With the normal role of the opposition so greatly diminished, the minority party tends to be preoccupied with mere posturing and manoeuvering, attempting to splinter off dissident groups from the dominant party and waiting to exploit the inevitable schisms within the government ranks. An opposition leader will not usually try to compete with the governing party by emphasizing a sharply different approach to policy-making, but will concentrate on the omissions and shortcomings of cabinet policy in order to persuade groups supporting the dominant party that they would get a "better deal" if the ins and outs were reversed.

Moreover, when a transfer of power does take place, the new administration will alter the emphasis of government programs, but the basic orientation of policy will change very little. The new cabinet, like the old, will be concerned with placating the major interest groups, and one of the most important of these will still be corporate business. . . .

By definition, however, in a system of single party dominance, the ins and the outs do not exchange places very often, and a further character-istic of the system is that the opposition group will be very weak. The opposition may be weak numerically, as in the national parliament during 1958-62 or in Alberta since 1963, but, more often and more important, after a long period out of office, the opposition may be weak qualitatively. It will lack the practical experience of power which would enable it to probe and criticize the technicalities of government more effectively. A former minority party, when it does finally achieve power, may be so accustomed to negative opposition that it finds difficulty in formulating for itself constructive alternative policies. Like a nagging wife, it may know what it objects to but not what it wants. The traditional weakness of the opposition in Ottawa has been suggested as one of the reasons why most of the provincial governments are frequently controlled by the minority party or by third parties. The most effective opposition to the nationally dominant party then comes from the provincial capitals, and the device of federalism helps to redress the political imbalance.

Following a shift of power, a newly elected government may not be able to profit from the technical advice of the civil service if, over two decades or more, the senior civil servants have become intimately identified with the previously dominant party. This was apparent in Ottawa in 1957-58, and in Regina in 1964; in both cases the civil service had become closely linked with the government party over a long period of years and, through no necessary fault of its own, had become compromised in the eyes of the incoming administration. The complexity of modern govern-ment and the enormous technical demands on it make it imperative that a highly competent staff of civil service experts be built up, but when single party dominance has been the rule, a change of government may tend to destroy the top echelon of the old bureaucracy or at least make it less useful to the new cabinet. With a lack of experienced administrative advisors, the incoming government will have a harder time to find its feet, and new policy innovations are less likely to be attempted or to be success-ful.

The resulting stagnation of policy and the fact that most governments bog down in the middle of the road are reasons for the rise of third parties. Sameness of policy creates areas of discontent, and third parties appear as vehicles of protest against the inertia of single party dominance. Professor Pinard has argued that third parties arise not only where dissi-dent feelings against the majority party are strongest, but where the traditional minority party has become so weak as to be discounted as an effective means of expressing protest. The prolonged success of one party may so eviscerate the organization of its customary opponents that only a new party will be regarded as an effective alternative to the government.

The role of third parties in Canada has been not only to express sporadic electoral discontent but also to capture provincial governments, to formulate more concrete ideologies, and to seek a balance-of-power position in the national parliament at times of transition when no party has a clear majority. Most important, third parties like the CCF, and the Ginger Group before it, have served to popularize radical policy innovations and to push the government party off its conservative stance in the political dead-centre. The influence of third parties on policy has far exceeded their power as measured in numbers of seats won. The origins of such positive departures from the middle of the road as old age pensions, unemployment insurance, hospitalization insurance, and medicare can be attributed largely to the influence of third parties.

Why? There is no general agreement among scholars as to why this pattern of politics has been so prevalent in Canada. Although there is no one explanation which is entirely satisfactory, a number of hypotheses deserve consideration.

Macpherson's analysis of the quasi-party system in Alberta rests on the proposition that the conditions necessary for this pattern to emerge are a "quasi-colonial" economy and a "largely *petit-bourgeois*" class structure of independent agrarian producers. The argument is that Alberta's economy produces staples for distant markets, that the producers are dependent upon and united in their resentment of external capitalist interest, and that the independent small farmer gives the prairie society a virtual homogeneity of class consciousness. "The peculiarity of a society which is at once quasi-colonial and mainly *petit bourgeois* is that the conflict of class interest is not so much within the society as between that society and the forces of outside capital. . . ." Macpherson contends that as Canada's economy becomes increasingly dependent upon that of the United States, our position more closely approximates that of a quasi-colonial nation which is therefore likely to live under a quasi-party system.

Although Macpherson does not explain why the Alberta farmers turned to the political right under Social Credit while their neighbours in Saskatchewan veered to the left under the CCF, his book remains one of the most provocative pieces of social analysis published in Canada. We must weigh seriously the argument that the Canadian economy is a precarious one *vis-à-vis* the American industrial giant, and that single party dominance may be an expression of a Canadian will to bind our people more closely together and consolidate our politics in the face of external threats to our regional or national interest. Macpherson may exaggerate the importance of class as a factor in our politics, but at least it should be evident that the great bulk of our population regards itself as middle-class, that the predominant social ethos in Canada is a *bourgeois* ethos, that our major parties are principally middle-class parties financed by business, heavily influenced by the compact social elite, and led by middle-class men highly sensitive to commercial interests. If Canada does not possess class homogeneity, surely our closest approximation to a prevailing class consciousness is a middle-class consciousness. Can we seriously doubt that the relative absence of sharp class conflict in Canada is a primary factor in the existence of single party dominance?

Canada's preoccupation with the centrifugal forces of regional diversity and English-French duality may lead to a more orthodox interpretation which avoids emphasis on class. Political scientists are fond of referring to regional, economic, ethnic, and religious differences in the population as "structural cleavages". Professor Maurice Pinard has argued that "Such cleavages strongly alienate a region from one of the two major parties and tie it to a single party as the sole [principal?] defender of its interest, hence leading to one-party dominance." It may be possible for the bulk of the population to be persuaded at a given time that only one party possesses the requisite leadership to be able to form a strong majority government and act as the broker of interests, effectively smoothing over the structural cleavages. Many writers have also noted that the single-member simple-plurality electoral system amplifies the number of seats held by the winning party, reduces the seats held by the minority parties, and gives further institutional impetus to the system of single party dominance.

Whatever the reasons for the prevalence of the single party dominance pattern, some of the main implications and results of this phenomenon are apparent. It may be useful to review the most striking corollaries of the system.

First, there will be a deliberate avoidance of ideological issues by the national parties. This tends to render the parties more alike, to narrow the voter's range of choice between them, and to make our politics more gray and dull. Both parties will attempt to gain the dominant position by emphasizing their ability to include and conciliate most of the major contending interests in the nation, and to do so they will exalt pragmatism, compromise, and moderation. They will keep their "principles" as vague and nebulous as possible and avoid divisive philosophizing at all costs. . . . The parties compete not for the political right or left but for the centre. Their supreme role must be as unifying agents, and their chief method of operation must be compromise.

Periods of minority government in the twentieth century can be regarded as periods of transition during which no one party was able to achieve a position of national dominance. . . .

There are sound reasons to indicate that minority governments can provide effective administrations, but the old parties both laud "stable" majority government as infinitely preferable. The persistent re-appearance of minority governments since 1921 might suggest that coalition between a major and a minor party would prove attractive as a means of providing solid majority administrations, but Canada's parties have stoutly resisted coalition except at times of extreme crisis. We have had only two coalition governments in Canada, one at Confederation and one in 1917. Both worked; that is to say, both accomplished things and in neither case did the process of government break down. . . .

At present there appears no immediate prospect of national coalition government. Instead, the foregoing analysis suggests that we are in a period of transition in which neither party is yet able to attain a dominant position. It is a situation of great uncertainty, but one pregnant with possibilities, for transition periods such as this are times when new directions of policy may be sought and fundamental premises re-examined. . . .

POLITICS AND PARTIES IN CANADA*

Paul Fox

Canadian politics and political parties tend to be characterized by the word "moderate". Like Britain and the United States, to which Canadian political parties owe a good deal in formative influences, Canada is a predominantly middle class nation with middle class values. This is reflected in the fact that radical parties of either the right or the left are virtually non-existent and that those parties which do exist seek the golden mean in order to get the maximum number of votes.

This tends to diminish the differences between parties and to make them difficult to pinpoint. In some cases it is more a matter of history and traditional loyalty that distinguishes them rather than logic or the planks in their platforms. This is very apparent in comparing the two parties which have dominated Canadian politics since the country became a dominion in 1867, the Conservatives and the Liberals.

The Conservatives originated in Canada as the colonial equivalent of the British Tory Party. In pioneer days they were ardently loyal to the Crown and stood for the maintenance of the British connection. Under their first great leader, Sir John A. Macdonald, who was prime minister almost continuously from 1867 until his death in 1891, the party broadened its appeal by incorporating some of the opposing Liberals and by devising a "National Policy" which stressed the development of the country from sea to sea, the construction of transcontinental railways, and the fostering of industry and commerce by the adoption of relatively high tariffs.

These elements left their mark on the party for many years, so much so that it was stigmatized by farmers and French Canadians for decades. The farmers complained that it was the party of "big business", sacrificing the agrarian interests of the three wheat-growing prairie provinces to the financial and commercial demands of the large metropolitan centres (Toronto and Montreal) in the more populous and wealthier provinces of Ontario and Quebec. The French Canadians, Roman Catholic in faith and predominant in Quebec, were alienated by the militant Protestantism and pro-British sentiments of some of the leading Conservatives. When one Conservative government in the nineteenth century executed Louis Riel, a Roman Catholic rebel with French-Canadian blood in his veins, and another Conservative government rigorously implemented universal military conscription during World War I (which French Canadians considered to be a "British" war), the Conservative party went into an eclipse in Quebec from which, after four decades, it recovered in the elections of 1957 and 1958, but only spasmodically as it turned out.

In every general election from 1917 to 1957, with one exception, the Conservatives never won more than half a dozen seats in this French-Canadian province which, because of its size, has nearly one-quarter of the total number of seats in the House of Commons. Conservative weak-

* Revised in May, 1976.

ness in Quebec combined with meagre support in the western agrarian provinces explains to a large extent why the Tories went out of power nationally in 1921 and remained out, except for five years, until 1957.

The two elections within ten months in 1957 and 1958 brought about a striking change. In the former, the Conservatives under Mr. Diefenbaker secured nine seats out of 75 in Quebec. This provided a bridgehead for future operations. In the succeding election Mr. Diefenbaker won 50 Conservative seats in Quebec.

At the same time Mr. Diefenbaker, himself a western Canadian who had sat as a western M.P. for 18 years, was able to revive the cause of Conservatism in that part of the country by the sheer force of his own personality. . . .

The result of the election on 31 March 1958 was the most decisive victory in the history of Canadian federal government; the Conservatives were returned with 208 seats out of a total of 265. It was an astonishing revival for a party which had almost disintegrated during the long period of Liberal ascendancy.

Unfortunately for the party, its fortunes varied with its leader's. Mr. Diefenbaker's popularity and command of the situation waned almost as rapidly as they had waxed. The 1962 election returned the Conservatives to the status of a minority government, and the 1963 election found them defeated by the Liberals.

Like its British forbear, the Liberal party in Canada commenced as a reform movement. It was a fusion, after Confederation, of small-scale pioneer farmers of British stock and the more radical and progressive elements in the French-Canadian society known as "Rouges". The colours adopted by the party were red and white in contrast to the Conservatives' blue and white, a distinction that was quite valid. From its birth the Liberal party tended to be more egalitarian, proletarian, and nationalistic. With the advent to leadership of Sir Wilfrid Laurier, a Roman Catholic French Canadian from Quebec, the party became strongly bi-ethnic and succeeded in gaining power in 1896 and holding it till 1911. World War I and the conscription issue split its two wings apart; most French Canadians and Laurier opposed conscription, while many leading Anglo-Saxons abandoned Laurier and entered a wartime coalition government headed by the Conservatives.

From this crisis the party was rescued by the genius of William Lyon Mackenzie King, who, following his election as leader in 1919, set the Liberals on the path towards a broadly based middle-of-the-road social welfare state. By many artful compromises Mackenzie King kept himself and his party in power almost continuously from 1921 until his retirement in 1948, thereby establishing a personal record as the prime minister in Canada who had held office the longest, 21 years and five months.

He was succeeded by Louis St. Laurent, the second French Canadian (both Liberal) to be prime minister. Though Mr. St. Laurent tried to continue Mr. Mackenzie King's victorious tactics of maintaining the centre-of-the-road policy while moving forward, the process of aging had rendered the Liberal government less flexible and less dynamic, and in 1957, after 22 continuous years of power, during which it had won what appeared to be very comfortable electoral pluralities, the party was narrowly defeated by Mr. Diefenbaker's resuscitated Conservatives who secured 112 seats to the Liberals' 105. Mr. St. Laurent resigned as prime minister and subsequently retired as leader, being replaced by his former secretary of state for external affairs, Mr. Lester B. Pearson. But Mr. Pearson and his Liberals were no match for Prime Minister Diefenbaker's Conservatives, who in the 1958 election reduced the number of Liberal seats to 49.

Under Mr. Diefenbaker the Conservatives appeared to take over the mantle of the Liberals as the party of moderate reform and progress appealing to the diverse geographical, economic, religious, and ethnic groups in the country. However, the Liberals regained their ascendancy in 1963, winning a minority-government victory that they repeated in 1965, largely by appealing to the middle and upper middle class voters in large urban centres. The new Liberal leader chosen in 1968, Mr. Pierre Elliott Trudeau, was able to enhance this urban, middle-class support, and to win a majority government by combining it with his general personal appeal throughout the country. In 1972 Mr. Trudeau lost his majority and was reduced to leading a minority Liberal government. But in 1974 he regained his majority, winning 141 seats.

Additional proof of the middle-class nature of our politics is that there is no party in Canada on the extreme right wing and the party farthest to the left is virtually extinct. The Communist Party (formerly called the Labour Progressive Party) never had much success in Canada. It elected on only one occasion a federal member of Parliament and his career ended ignominiously in prison when he was convicted of conspiracy to turn over government secrets to Russia in wartime. This assisted in convincing most Canadian voters, if they needed further evidence, that the party was more interested in serving the Kremlin than the Canadian people, and subsequent events such as the Soviet restrictions on Jews and the repression of the Hungarian revolt created serious dissensions within its own ranks. Party membership has fallen to a few thousand and in the most recent federal election in 1974 only 69 Communist candidates were nominated, and together they received only 12,100 votes out of the 9,671,002 ballots cast, or approximately 0.13 percent. In the same election the Marxist-Leninist Party of Canada ran 102 candidates who won 16,261 votes, amounting to 0.17 percent of the total.

Further proof of the need to seek the middle of the road in Canadian politics is presented by the history of minor parties. Canada has had a number of these but as yet none has been strong enough to form a government at Ottawa. For the most part they have tended to be regional parties representing special interests, in particular western prairie farmers who have been prone to organize their own political movements in protest against the wealthier, more populous "east" (actually central Canada—Ontario and Quebec). Following the discontents of World War I the farmers created their own Progressive party which, at its zenith in 1921, sent 64 members to the House of Commons and acquired the balance of power. The party quickly dissolved, however, because of the centrifugal nature of its ultra-democratic organization and its lack of firm leadership. In 1935 the Social Credit party, which espoused unorthodox monetary doctrines and stirred up strong emotional and religious support, elected 17 members to Parliament from Alberta and Saskatchewan, but after reaching a high point of 19 in 1957 it was wiped out completely by the Conservative landslide in the following year. It gained great support in Quebec in 1962, electing 26 MPs from that province alone (for a total of 30) but subsequently the Quebec wing split away, electing nine *Ralliement des Créditistes* in 1965 to five for Social Credit. In 1968, the English-speaking Social Credit party was wiped out in Parliament, winning no seats at all, while the *Créditistes* continued with 14 seats. In 1972 they won 15; in 1974 only 11.

A party that attempted to fuse the agrarian interests of the west and the labour forces of the east was born during the depression of the 1930s with the cumbersome title of the Co-operative Commonwealth Federation. Dedicated to the principles of democratic socialism, it has tried to become the Canadian equivalent of the British Labour party but it has not had the success of its model. The number of seats it has won has fluctuated widely, from seven in its first trial in 1935 to 28 in 1945 and back to eight in 1958, though throughout the period its share of the popular vote varied between about eight and ten percent. After reorganizing itself as the New Democratic Party in 1961, its fortunes improved electorally. It won 22 seats in 1968, 31 in 1972, but only 11 in 1974.

The dilemma of the C.C.F.-N.D.P. is that it has been squeezed into an almost impossible position left-of-centre in politics in which it can scarcely find sufficient unique ground on which to make a stand. It fears moving left lest it be accused of being communist, which it abhors, and it cannot move right into the mixed field occupied by Conservatives and Liberals without losing the identity it desires as a working class party. While it is thus stuck on the horns of a dilemma, the Conservatives and Liberals have appropriated many of its social welfare planks. Its chief obstacle is the hard fact of Canadian middle class democracy; like all radical and sectional parties it can consider broadening its appeal only at the risk of losing its claim to existence. . . .

In the sphere of the provinces, each government, whatever its political stripe, finds that its most fruitful tactic is to set itself up as the defender of provincial rights against the central administration, particularly in the fields of taxation and finance. This has become so commonplace that some theorists have suggested that the real oppositon to the government of the day at Ottawa comes not in the traditional manner from the benches to the left of the Speaker in the House of Commons but from the provincial regimes, whether or not they are of the same political complexion as the federal government. This may or may not be true but it is undeniable that any provincial administration tends to make much more of an issue out of its wrangles with Ottawa than out of its own party ideology.

Dogma is either ignored or soft-pedalled and the provincial governments seek to become all things to all people—or at least to all voters. Like federal governments the provincial administrations move according to the inexorable fundamental law of Canadian politics towards the centre of the road, or perhaps it would be more precise to say they spread themselves all over the road. Whatever the official label of the party, whatever the planks in its platform before election, it tends to become moderate and eclectic when it obtains power. This has applied to radical parties like the United Farmers, Social Credit, and the C.C.F., but it also works in reverse sometimes with Conservatives and Liberals. Thus, a Conservative government in Ontario urged the public ownership of a natural gas pipeline and played a leading role in the achievement of national hospital insurance, while the C.C.F. government in Saskatchewan made a determined effort to attain more private capital investment in its natural resources. In Alberta, Social Credit, which drew its strength originally from rural farms, became the darling of business men. In Manitoba, the Roblin Conservative government was probably more progressive than the Liberal-Progressive government it replaced. Thus, the party names do not mean too much in Canada, both provincially and federally, and it is often difficult to establish differences clearly. . . .

THE SYSTEM IS OUTMODED— SAYS THE NEW LEFT*

Dimitrios Roussopoulos

Most people in Canada are fed up with "politics"—by which they mean the machinery of political decision-making. At the moment this feeling has no political expression, although anger, despair and frustration expresses itself in many acts of violence.

Our existing political institutions were developed at a time when a far less bureaucratized and centralized society existed. The party system in Canada, for instance, existed before universal suffrage; the parties represented special group interests in existence before the founding of Canada.

Power today is monopolized in immense bureaucracies which have become political institutions by virtue of the role they play in society. The power of the gigantic corporations is informal, to be sure, but there is little doubt that they have drawn off real power from our formal political institutions. Couple this development with the concentration of power at the top of the parliamentary pyramid, and both the legislature and the electorate are reduced to ritual.

This concentration of power, plus the new manipulative methods of conditioning public attitudes and motivation through the mass media, which celebrate the "values" of a society of compulsive consumption, raise in our minds a questioning of the value of the electoral and parliamentary system of representative democracy.

The issues that divided the political parties in this country are artificial—questions of *management* rather than *basic policy*. The important

* From the *Toronto Daily Star*, April 6, 1970. By permission.

questions of the day—the growth of liberal totalitarianism, the wasteland between people and government, the lack of quality in our lives and the purposelessness of our society, racialism, the arms race, Viet Nam and so on—are not usually put before the people.

Politicians and opinion makers exert strenuous efforts to fix our attention on ritual, in this case the casting of the vote. Voting, as a result, becomes an isolated, magical act set apart from the rest of life, and ceases to have any political or social meaning except as an instrument by which the status quo is conserved. Electoral pageantry serves the purpose of a circus—the beguilement of the populace. The voter is reduced to voting for dazzling smiles, clean teeth, smooth voices and firm handshakes.

If we could vote for those who really control the country—for example the directors of the Royal Bank of Canada, the governors of universities, social welfare agencies, industrial corporations and the shadows behind the ministries—then the trappings of liberal democracy would soon become transparent. The real power centres lie far beyond the people's influence at elections. They remain constant *whatever* party is "in power." So the only possible argument for participating in electoral politics, for voting during federal or provincial elections, is that marginal benefits may be gained.

This is obviously a serious conclusion to reach and to recommend—or at least to sanction—for it implies that the political parties, without exception, cannot operate within the province of deep political concern. This is not to say that "it makes no difference" who wins an election; it is rather to say that the "difference" is so slight or lies in such relatively trivial areas that one might very well bypass the area of electoral politics as being irrelevant to any fresh and profound issue of political circumstance.

To the New Left the elaborate procedures and structures of "representative" or parliamentary democracy (which is only one form), born in the 19th century and embroidered on since, stand as ossified caricatures. We live in a society where the majority of people passively consent to things being done in their name, a society of managed politics. The techniques of consultation are polished, but they remain techniques and should not be confused by anyone with participation.

Herbert Marcuse reformulated the libertarian insight that in our type of society any conventional opposition group inevitably assumes the values of the system it opposes and is eventually absorbed by it. In Canada as elsewhere this is the fate of socialists and social democrats.

The object of Canada's power elite and its supporting institutions is clear: It is to muffle real conflict; to dissolve it into a false political consensus; to build, not a participatory democracy where people have power to control a community of meaningful life and work, but a bogus conviviality between every social group. Consensus politics, essential to modern capitalism, is manipulative politics, the politics of man-management, and it is deeply undemocratic. Governments are still elected to be sure, MPs assert the supremacy of the House of Commons, but the real business of government is the management of consensus between the powerful and organized elites.

Consensus politics is not intended for any large-scale structural change.

It is the politics of pragmatism, of the successful manoeuvre within existing limits. Every administrative act is a kind of clever exercise in political public relations. Whether the manoeuvres are made by a Conservative, Liberal or New Democrat hardly matters, since they all accept the constraints of the *status quo*.

The product of this system is an increasing rationalization of the existing sources of power. The banks, corporations, the federations of industrialists, the trade union movement are all given a new and more formal role in the political structure. And to the extent that the "public interest" is defined as including these interests it also excludes what, on the other side, are called "sectional" or "local" interests—namely those of the poor, the low-paid and unorganized workers, youth in general and the backward regions. . . .

What we face is not simply a question of programs and ideologies; what we face primarily is a question of institutions. Certain institutions in our society will simply no longer yield fundamental social and political change.

Many people, along with the New Left, are concerned with such issues as: the boredom and conformity of life in the midst of a society of cybernetics; the human need for *creative* work; the continued existence of raw, naked exploitation at the work-place and at home; the power of the state over society, of centralized political entities over community, of the older generation over the younger, of bureaucracy over the individual, of parental authoritarianism over youthful spontaneity, of sexual, racial, cultural and imperialist privilege over the unfettered development of human personality.

At the same time, many of us believe that we have a qualitatively new order of possibilities—the possibility of a decolonialized Canada, of a free, non-repressive, decentralized society based on face-to-face democracy, community, spontaneity, and a new sense of human solidarity. This we believe amidst a technology so advanced that the burden of toil and material necessity could be removed from the shoulders of our people.

In the face of this kind of *revolutionary* change, electoral politics are meaningless, for elections are not won on these grounds; they are won amid tried formulas, old slogans and self-fulfilling prophecies. They are won by proposing changes of degree, not of kind; by working for adjustment not transformation.

So the New Left in this country, as in other industrial-technological societies, has concluded that there is no alternative but to withdraw our allegiance from the machines of electoralism, from the institutions of "representative" democracy, to forgo the magic rite of voting and to create instead an extra-parliamentary opposition.

The idea is to build a coalition of individuals and groups with a common critique of liberal democracy. The coalition will range from radicals to revolutionaires—from those who believe it still useful to support candidates who while campaigning will also criticize the inadequacies of the system of representation, to those who seek to encourage the development of new constituencies of the self-organized powerless, of producers who control what they produce, of people who control their environment and neighborhood *directly*. New forms of freedom need to be experimented with—workers' control, participatory democracy (which means control, not consultation), direct democracy—in a period where technology is laying the basis for a decentralized post-scarcity society. . . .

An extra-parliamentary opposition is primarily an act of negation. To paraphrase the philosopher Kolakowski, it is a wish to change existing reality. "But negation is not the opposite of construction—it is only the opposite of affirming existing conditions."

CONSERVATIVE PRINCIPLES AND PHILOSOPHY*

Robert L. Stanfield

Parties are Conciliators

. . . First, I would like to make a few comments on the role of political parties such as ours in Canada. Not only is it unnecessary for political parties to disagree about everything but some acceptance of common ground among the major parties is essential to an effective and stable democracy. For example, it is important to stability that all major parties agree on such matters as parliamentary responsible government and major aspects of our constitution.

I would like to emphasize too that in the British tradition political parties are not doctrinaire. . . . In our parliamentary tradition, which is substantially the British tradition, parties have a unifying role to play. . . . However, a truly national political party has a continuing role to try to pull things together: achieve a consensus, resolve conflicts, strengthen the fabric of society and work towards a feeling of harmony in the country. Success in this role is, I suggest, essential if a party is to maintain a strong position in this country. This role of a national political party, and success in this role, are particularly important in countries as vast and diverse as Canada and the United States.

It is partly because of this that I do not favour the [Senator Ernest] Manning thesis which urges polarization of political view points in this country. In Canada, a party such as ours has a harmonizing role to play, both horizontally in terms of resolving conflicts between regions, and vertically in terms of resolving conflicts between Canadians in different walks of life. It is not a matter of a national party being all things to all people—this would never work. But a national party should appeal to all parts of the country and to Canadians in all walks of life, if it is to serve this essential role, and if it is to remain strong.

Conservatives Stress Order

Turning now to the consideration of the Conservative Party as such,

* From a working paper presented to the federal Caucus of the Progressive Conservative Party by the National Leader, Nov. 14, 1974. By permission.

I would not wish to exaggerate the concern of British Conservatives through the years with principles or theory. After all, they were practising politicians for the most part, pragmatists dealing with problems, and of course, politicians seeking success. There are, however, some threads we can follow through the years. I am, of course, not suggesting that we in Canada should follow British principles or practices slavishly. Nor would I argue that our party in Canada has followed a consistent pattern. I believe it has frequently wandered far from the conservative tradition that I believe to be valuable, and conservative principles I accept.

British Conservative thinkers traditionally stressed the importance of order, not merely "law and order", but social order. This does not mean that they were opposed to freedom for the individual; far from it. They believe that a decent civilized life requires a framework of order.

Conservatives did not take that kind of order for granted. It seemed to them quite rare in the world and therefore quite precious. This is still the case. Conservatives attached importance to the economy and to enterprise and to property, but private enterprise was not the central principle of traditional British conservatism. Indeed the supreme importance of private enterprise and the undesirability of government initiative and interference was Liberal nineteenth century doctrine. It was inherited from Adam Smith and was given its boldest political statement by such Liberals as Cobden and Bright. It was they who preached the doctrine of the unseen hand with practically no reservation.

Restrictions on Private Enterprise and Government

The Conservative concept of order encouraged Conservative governments to impose restrictions on private enterprise where this was considered desirable. We all studied William Wilberforce and his factory legislation when we were in school. These were logical measures for Conservatives to adopt; to protect the weak against the excesses of private enterprise and greed. That is good traditional conservatism, fully consistent with traditional conservative principles. It is also good Conservatism not to push regulation too far—to undermine self-reliance.

Because of the central importance Conservatives attached to the concept of order they naturally favoured strong and effective government, but on the other hand they saw a limited or restricted role for government for several reasons. Because a highly centralized government is quite susceptible to arbitrary exercise of power and also to attack and revolution, Conservatives instinctively favoured a decentralization of power. National government had to be able to act in the national interest, but there had to be countervailing centres of power and influence. In the past, these might consist of church or the landed gentry or some other institution. Today in Canada, the provinces, trade unions, farm organizations, trade associations and the press would serve as examples. . . .

Man and the World Imperfect

Another reason why Conservatives traditionally saw a limited role for government was because Conservatives were far from being Utopians. They adopted basically a Judeo-Christian view of the world. . . . They certainly saw the world as a very imperfect place, capable of only limited improvement; and man as an imperfect being. They saw evil as an on-going force that would always be present in changing form. It would therefore not have surprised Edmund Burke that economic growth, and government policies associated with it, have created problems almost as severe as those that economic growth and government policies were supposed to overcome.

A third reason for Conservatives taking a limited view of the role of government was that men such as Edmund Burke regarded man's intelligence as quite limited. Burke was very much impressed by how little man understood what was going on around him. . . .

Burke questioned whether any one generation really had the intelligence to understand fully the reasons for existing institutions or to pass judgment on those institutions which were the product of the ages. Burke pushed this idea much too far, but Conservatives have traditionally recognized how limited human intelligence really is, and consequently have recognized that success in planning the lives of other people or the life of the nation is likely to be limited. Neither government nor its bureaucracy are as wise as they are apt to be believe. Humility is a valuable strain in Conservatism, provided it does not become an excuse for resisting change, accepting injustice or supporting vested interests. . . .

The National View

There is another important strain to traditional Conservatism. Conservatism is national in scope and purpose. This implies a strong feeling for the country, its institutions and its symbols; but also a feeling for all the country and for all the people in the country. The Conservative Party serves the whole country and all the people, not simply part of the country and certain categories of people. . . .

I suggest that it is in the Conservative tradition to expand the concept of order and give it a fully contemporary meaning. The concept of order always included some concept of security for the unfortunate, although the actual program may have been quite inadequate by our present day standards.

The concept of order certainly includes the preservation of our environment. And the concept of order, linked to Conservative concern for the country as a whole, certainly includes concern about poverty.

Social Goals

For a Conservative in the Conservative tradition which I have described, there is much more to national life than simply increasing the size of the gross national product. A Conservative naturally regards a healthy economy as of great importance, but increasing the size of the gross national product is not in itself a sufficient goal for a civilized nation, according to a Conservative. A healthy economy is obviously important, but a Conservative will be concerned about the effects of economic growth—what this does to our environment, what kind of living conditions it creates, what is its effect on the countryside, what is its effect on our cities; whether all parts of the nation benefit or only some parts of the nation, and whether a greater feeling of justice and fairness and self-fulfillment result from this growth, thereby strengthening the social order and improving the quality of national life.

. . . Any particular economic dogma is not a principle of our party, fond as most Conservatives may be of that particular dogma at any particular time.

At any given time our party is likely to contain those whose natural bent is reform and those whose natural bent is to stand pat or even to try to turn the clock back a bit. I think it is fair to say that Conservative statesmen we respect most were innovators. They did not change Conservative principles, but within those principles they faced and met the challenges of their time.

Traditional Liberalism started with the individual, emphasizing liberty of the individual and calling for a minimum of government interference with the individual. Conservatives, on the other hand, emphasized the nation, society, stability and order.

In this century, Liberals have resorted to the use of government more and more. Today big government and liberalism are synonymous in Canada. . . .

Some Conservatives want to move to the old individualistic position of nineteenth century Liberalism—enshrining private enterprise as the most fundamental principle of our party, and condemning all government interference. The Conservative tradition has been to interfere only where necessary, but to interfere where necessary to achieve social and national objectives. Conservatives favour incentives, where appropriate, rather than the big stick.

Of course, it has always been and remains important to Conservatives to encourage individual self-reliance; and certainly red tape and regulation have today gone too far, especially in the case of small business. Self-reliance and enterprise should be encouraged, but Conservatism does not place private enterprise in a central position around which everything else revolves.

Conservatism recognized the responsibility of government to restrain or influence individual action where this was in the interests of society. Whether a government should or should not intervene was always a question of judgment, of course, but the Conservative tradition recognized the role of government as the regulator of individual conduct in the interests of society. . . .

Reform and Justice

. . . I would not suggest that Conservatives have tried or would try to build a radically different society from that which they have known. But to reform and adapt existing institutions to meet changing conditions, and to work towards a more just and therefore a truly more stable society—this I suggest is in the best Conservative tradition. . . .

This is a period when true Conservative principles of order and stability should be most appealing. Principles of conservation and preservation are also high in the minds of many Canadians today, and a Conservative can very legitimately—and on sound historical ground—associate with these. Again I emphasize that these kinds of bedrock principles are national in scope and reflect an overriding concern for society at large.

Enterprise and initiative are obviously important; but will emphasis upon individual rights solve the great problems of the day: I mean the maintenance of acceptable stability—which includes price stability, acceptable employment, and an acceptable distribution of income. Would we achieve these goals today by a simple reliance on the free market, if we could achieve a free market?

It would certainly be appropriate for a Conservative to suggest that we must achieve some kind of order if we are to avoid chaos; an order which is stable, but not static; an order therefore which is reasonably acceptable and which among other things provides a framework in which enterprise can flourish. That would be in the Conservative tradition. . . .

LIBERALISM*

Lester B. Pearson

. . . The Liberal Party is the party of reform, of progress, of new ideas. The Conservative Party, by its very name, stresses conservation and caution. . . .

What, then, are the principles that have inspired and guided the Liberal Party in its service to the Canadian people? The fundamental principle of Liberalism, the foundation of its faith, is belief in the dignity and worth of the individual. The state is the creation of man, to protect and serve him; and not the reverse.

Liberalism, therefore, believes in man; and that it is the purpose of government to legislate for the liberation and development of human personality. This includes the negative requirement of removing anything that stands in the way of individual and collective progress.

The negative requirement is important. It involves removal and reform: clearing away and opening up, so that man can move forward and societies expand. The removal of restrictions that block the access to achievement: this is the very essence of Liberalism.

The Liberal Party, however, must also promote the positive purpose of ensuring that all citizens, without any discrimination, will be in a position to take advantage of the opportunities opened up; of the freedoms that have been won. . . . Liberalism is the political principle that gives purpose and reality to this kind of progress.

Liberalism stands for the middle way: the way of progress. It stands for

* From Introduction to J. W. Pickersgill, *The Liberal Party*, Toronto, McClelland and Stewart, 1962. By permission of the publisher.

moderation, tolerance, and the rejection of extreme courses, whether they express themselves in demands that the state should do everything for the individual, even if it means weakening and destroying him in the process, or in demands that the state should do nothing except hold the ring so that the fittest survive under the law of the jungle.

In other words, Liberalism accepts social security but rejects socialism; it accepts free enterprise but rejects economic anarchy; it accepts humanitarianism but rejects paternalism.

The Liberal Party is opposed to the shackling limitations of rigid political dogma, or authoritarianism of any kind, which is so often the prelude to oppression and exploitation. It fights against the abuse of power either by the state or by persons or groups within the state. . . .

Liberalism, also, while insisting on equality of opportunity, rejects any imposed equality which would discourage and destroy a man's initiative and enterprise. It sees no value in the equality, or conformity, which comes from lopping off the tallest ears of corn. It maintains, therefore, that originality and initiative should be encouraged, and that reward should be the result of effort. . . .

But how can freedom . . . be made meaningful in the face of today's industrial and economic pressures? Government must keep pace with the changing needs of the times and accept greater responsibilities than would have been acceptable to a Liberal a hundred years ago. That is why the Liberal Party favours social and economic planning which will stimulate and encourage private enterprise to operate more effectively for the benefit of all.

Liberalism must always remember that responsibility is the other side of freedom. . . .

In short, freedom and welfare must be kept in a healthy balance or there will be trouble. This essential balance can be achieved by applying to every proposal for further intervention by the state the question: will it truly benefit the individual; will it enlarge or restrict his opportunity for self-expression and development?

The Liberal purpose remains the creation of opportunity for men and women to become self-directing, responsible citizens. This means, as we have seen, the simultaneous pursuit of freedom and welfare. . . .

For the progress Canada has made, and will make, national unity has been essential. The necessity for doing everything possible to maintain and strengthen this unity has been the cornerstone of Liberal policy from the very beginning of its history. Moreover, Liberalism has understood that national unity must be based on two races, cultures, traditions, and languages; on a full and equal partnership of English- and French-speaking Canadians. . . .

Canada is a federal state in which the constitutional and historic rights of the provinces must be preserved. It is important also that the provinces must not be separated by economic inequality which would make national unity difficult, it not impossible. The Liberal Party, therefore, considers it a duty of the federal government to help equalize the distribution of income and wealth and development among the provinces. . . .

Constitution of the Liberal Party of Canada*

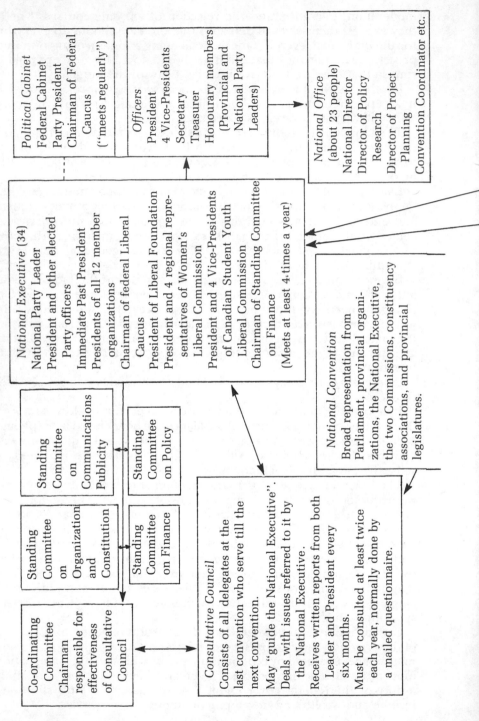

Political Cabinet
Federal Cabinet
Party President
Chairman of Federal Caucus
("meets regularly")

Officers
President
4 Vice-Presidents
Secretary
Treasurer
Honourary members (Provincial and National Party Leaders)

National Office (about 23 people)
National Director
Director of Policy Research
Director of Project Planning
Convention Coordinator etc.

National Executive (34)
National Party Leader
President and other elected Party officers
Immediate Past President
Presidents of all 12 member organizations
Chairman of federal Liberal Caucus
President of Liberal Foundation
President and 4 regional representatives of Women's Liberal Commission
President and 4 Vice-Presidents of Canadian Student Youth Liberal Commission
Chairman of Standing Committee on Finance
(Meets at least 4 times a year)

Standing Committee on Communications Publicity

Standing Committee on Policy

Standing Committee on Organization and Constitution

Standing Committee on Finance

Co-ordinating Committee Chairman responsible for effectiveness of Consultative Council

National Convention
Broad representation from Parliament, provincial organizations, the National Executive, the two Commissions, constituency associations, and provincial legislatures.

Consultative Council
Consists of all delegates at the last convention who serve till the next convention.
May "guide the National Executive".
Deals with issues referred to it by the National Executive.
Receives written reports from both Leader and President every six months.
Must be consulted at least twice each year, normally done by a mailed questionnaire.

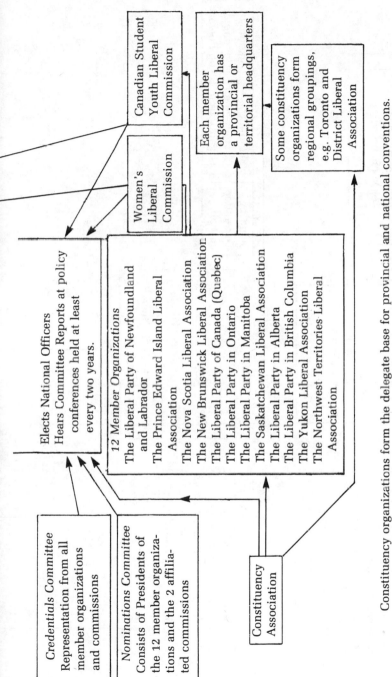

Canadian Student Youth Liberal Commission

Women's Liberal Commission

Each member organization has a provincial or territorial headquarters

Some constituency organizations form regional groupings, e.g. Toronto and District Liberal Association

Elects National Officers
Hears Committee Reports at policy conferences held at least every two years.

12 Member Organizations
The Liberal Party of Newfoundland and Labrador
The Prince Edward Island Liberal Association
The Nova Scotia Liberal Association
The New Brunswick Liberal Association
The Liberal Party of Canada (Quebec)
The Liberal Party in Ontario
The Liberal Party in Manitoba
The Saskatchewan Liberal Association
The Liberal Party in Alberta
The Liberal Party in British Columbia
The Yukon Liberal Association
The Northwest Territories Liberal Association

Credentials Committee
Representation from all member organizations and commissions

Nominations Committee
Consists of Presidents of the 12 member organizations and the 2 affiliated commissions

Constituency Association

Constituency organizations form the delegate base for provincial and national conventions.
Both the provincial and the federal constituency associations belong to the provincial organization.

* The chart is based on the party "constitution" as well as occasional organizational changes described in Liberal Party documents.
The arrows indicate the direction of the flow of personnel.

From C. Winn, J. McMenemy, *Political Parties in Canada*, Toronto, McGraw-Hill Ryerson, pp. 168-173. By permission.

Constitution of the Progressive Conservative Association of Canada*

National Headquarters
National Director
(appointed by
Steering Committee
on recommendation
of the national
leader)

*Steering Committee
of the Nat'l Exec.* (11)
Party Leader
Party President
3 Vice-Presidents
Secretary
Treasurer
Chairman of caucus
women and youth
executive members
(meets frequently)

National Executive (125)
Party Leader
Party President
Secretary
Treasurer
15 Vice-Presidents
Selected parliamentarians
National director and
others as ex-officio members
(meets at least once a year)

Standing
Committee
on Policy

Standing
Committee on
Organization

Standing
Committee
on Finance

Executive Committee (26)
Party Leader
Party President
Secretary
Treasurer
National Director
selected parliamentarians
Chairman of Committees on
finance and organization
(meets at least twice a year)

National
Executive
P.C. Women's
Assoc. of
Canada

National
Executive
P.C. Youth
Fed. of
Canada

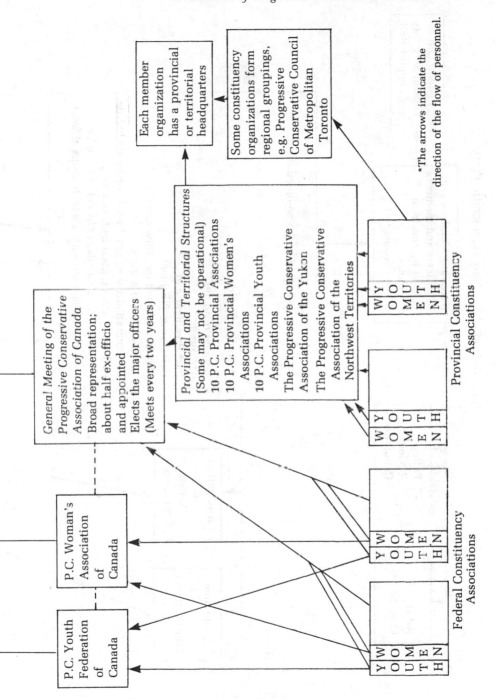

Each member organization has a provincial or territorial headquarters

Some constituency organizations form regional groupings, e.g. Progressive Conservative Council of Metropolitan Toronto

*The arrows indicate the direction of the flow of personnel.

Provincial and Territorial Structures
(Some may not be operational)
10 P.C. Provincial Associations
10 P.C. Provincial Women's Associations
10 P.C. Provincial Youth Associations
The Progressive Conservative Association of the Yukon
The Progressive Conservative Association of the Northwest Territories

General Meeting of the Progressive Conservative Association of Canada
Broad representation;
about half ex-officio and appointed
Elects the major officers
(Meets every two years)

P.C. Woman's Association of Canada

P.C. Youth Federation of Canada

Provincial Constituency Associations

Federal Constituency Associations

Constitution of the New Democratic Party*

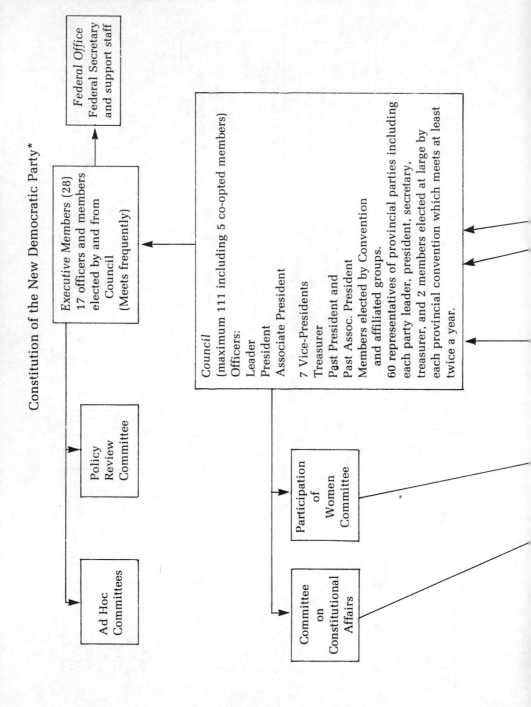

Federal Office
Federal Secretary
and support staff

Executive Members (28)
17 officers and members
elected by and from
Council
(Meets frequently)

Policy
Review
Committee

Ad Hoc
Committees

Council
(maximum 111 including 5 co-opted members)
Officers:
Leader
President
Associate President
7 Vice-Presidents
Treasurer
Past President and
Past Assoc. President
Members elected by Convention
and affiliated groups.
60 representatives of provincial parties including
each party leader, president, secretary,
treasurer, and 2 members elected at large by
each provincial convention which meets at least
twice a year.

Participation
of
Women
Committee

Committee
on
Constitutional
Affairs

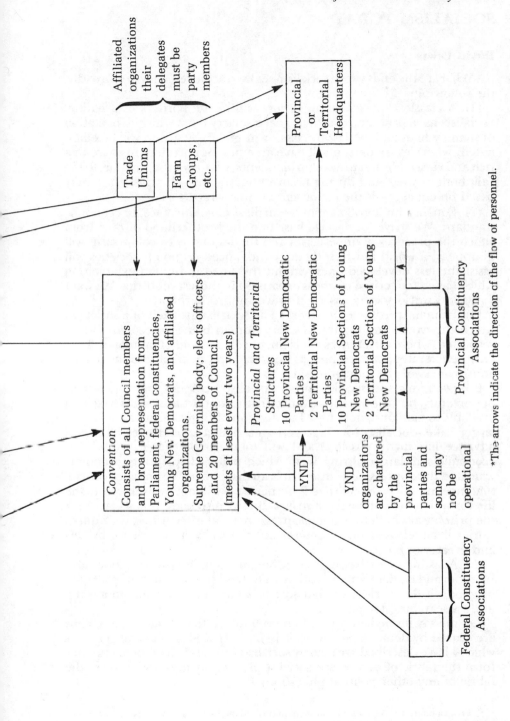

Affiliated organizations their delegates must be party members

Trade Unions

Farm Groups, etc.

Provincial or Territorial Headquarters

Convention
Consists of all Council members and broad representation from Parliament, federal constituencies, Young New Democrats, and affiliated organizations.
Supreme Governing body; elects officers and 20 members of Council (meets at least every two years)

Provincial and Territorial Structures
10 Provincial New Democratic Parties
2 Territorial New Democratic Parties
10 Provincial Sections of Young New Democrats
2 Territorial Sections of Young New Democrats

Provincial Constituency Associations

YND

YND organizations are chartered by the provincial parties and some may not be operational

Federal Constituency Associations

*The arrows indicate the direction of the flow of personnel.

SOCIALISM TODAY*

David Lewis

. . . What are the ends which socialism seeks to achieve? They are, broadly, the following:

(1) A classless or egalitarian society within the borders of a nation. Socialists have proclaimed as their goal a society from which exploitation of man by man and of class by class or of group by group will be eliminated; where every person will have an equal opportunity to share in a rich and varied life and to develop his talents, whatever they may be, to the full, both at work and during leisure hours. This—the classless society based on equality—is the major aim of democratic socialism.

(2) Equality among all nations, regardless of colour, race, or economic standard. We strive for a world based on the brotherhood of man from which the practices of imperialism and the ignominy of colonialism will disappear; a world in which the more advanced economic societies will assist the less developed ones without the price in human exploitation which has characterized overseas expansion in the last centuries. We want a classless world society based on universal brotherhood.

(3) Human freedom everywhere. The socialist dream is of a society in which the worth and dignity of every human being is recognized and respected, where differences of origin, of religion and of opinion will not only be tolerated, but accepted as desirable and necessary to the beauty and richness of the human mosaic.

(4) Economic and social security. Socialists seek not only equality of opportunity but a constant advance in the opportunities offered and available to mankind; not only a fair division of the cake, but a constantly larger cake. Socialists long ago recognized that modern technological advance has made possible, and will increasingly make possible, an economic standard of living from which material suffering, economic want and the oppression of insecurity can disappear. We know, of course, that meeting the economic needs of mankind will not by itself create the life for which the human spirit strives. But we also know that it can break the prison walls built by economic pressures and insecurities, the human spirit will be released and our moral and cultural values enriched by new and greater opportunities.

(5) A lasting peace based on freedom and equality within nations and freedom and equality among nations. This end is today shared by all men of goodwill the world over, but socialists have always been among the leaders searching for peace. . . .

Let me say immediately that I am well aware that some of these aims are shared by democratic non-socialists. . . . However, some of the aims which I have described are held by socialists only and all of them together form the fabric of democratic socialist philosophy and do not form the fabric of any other political philosophy.

* From a pamphlet *A Socialist Takes Stock*, published by the Ontario Woodsworth Memorial Foundation, Toronto, 1965. By permission of the author and publisher.

People who support the capitalist society as a desirable social system believe in a class society and not in a classless one; they believe in inequality and not in equality; they believe in the right of one nation to make profits at the expense of another, just as they believe in the right of one group within a nation to make profits at the expense of the rest; they believe in the right of the sons and daughters of the rich to have greater opportunities than those of the poor; and even as regards freedom they place the rights of property above those of human beings or, at least, on an equal footing. All these concepts the socialist passionately rejects.

At the other extreme, those who believe in the communist society reject in practice all of the aims of socialism, despite their deceitful words and slogans. In every communist land there has been established a new, but no less evil class society. The elite of the communist party, the membership of that party, the civil service in government as well as in the party, the secret police, and the army, form a class or classes which are the top of a social pyramid as clearly defined as the pyramid of wealth to which we are accustomed and, if anything, much more oppressive and evil in its consequences. It is unnecessary to remind you that the communist state stifles freedom and enthrones uniformity and conformity as the absolute duty of every citizen. Domination by the chief communist state over other nations and states, rather than equality among nations, has been the communist practice. . . .

•   •   •

What means has the socialist proposed for building the road to this [socialist] society? Briefly, they are, I think, the following:

(1) We must emphasize, first, the determination of the socialist to pursue at all times only democratic procedures and to base his actions on the consent of the people freely expressed. To use any form of dictatorship to achieve so-called desirable ends is a perversion of our basic ideas of freedom and will in practice also pervert the ends. . . .

(2) A constant and continuing improvement in the existing standards of living and in the social services provided by the state. . . .

(3) The third means which the socialist has proposed, and when he has had the chance, has used, is that of social planning. The socialist rejects the capitalist theory that an unregulated law of supply and demand should control the destinies of a society and its members. He believes that it is both necessary and possible for society collectively to plan at least its economic future and to regulate the production and distribution of goods and services so as to achieve an expanding economy of full employment and fair share for all members of society. . . .

(4) The fourth means which the socialist has proposed is that of public ownership, whether it be ownership by the state—federal, provincial or municipal—or ownership by a collectivity of citizens in the form of cooperatives, credit unions or the like. There are three main reasons behind the socialist belief in public ownership.

First and foremost, that the modern concentration of wealth and property places too much power, both economic and political, in the hands of too few people or, what is even worse, in the hands of giant corporations which, by their very nature, are without heart and without soul. . . .

Secondly, nationalization has been proposed by socialists because the job of social planning is made more difficult by the power of private corporations and would be made much easier by public ownership of the key levers in the economy.

Thirdly, the growth and power of private corporations have imposed on society a standard of values which perverts the best ideals of man. . . .

●   ●   ●

Among democratic socialists there is, and always has been, agreement about the ends. On the other hand, there is, always has been and probably always will be, disagreement about the means. . . .

Perhaps first among socialist controversies is the question of the extent to which the tool of public ownership can or should be used by socialists in modern society. . . .

Until fairly recently it had been accepted by most socialists as axiomatic that nationalization of industry would automatically bring with it greater social and political freedom and a release from the obstacles to the widest liberty which private economic power produces. . . .

The developments in the Soviet Union, in particular, and in other communist states as well, have completely shattered these assumptions and have shown them to have been and to be entirely false. In the communist societies all wealth, or almost all wealth, has been taken over by the state. But, instead of greater freedom, there is actually no freedom at all. . . .

Similarly, we have learned from the actions of the Soviet Union . . . that there are pressures toward aggression and war other than economic ones and that the lust for power and the zeal of fanaticism are at least as powerful forces endangering peace as economic competition and conflicts. . . .

Socialists can, therefore, no longer regard nationalization as an automatic panacea for all ills, but must regard it merely as one tool that is available in appropriate circumstances for the furtherance of socialist ends.

The experience of the Scandinavian countries, the history of the Roosevelt era in the United States and developments during the last war, have all shown that there are available in the modern economy tools of control and of planning which can be effectively applied without actually replacing private with public ownership in all spheres. . . . The use of fiscal and financial policies to influence the volume and direction of investments, to redistribute income, and to stimulate purchasing power, has been demonstrated as a practical tool for economic planning, at least in periods when there is no major depression. . . .

In all modern societies there is growing up a considerable body of social welfare legislation which produces what are known as "transfer payments." These—unemployment insurance benefits, old age pensions, family allowances, farm support payments and the like—provide a constant steam of purchasing power into the hands of large sections of the people. . . .

•　　　•　　　•

BIBLIOGRAPHY

Parties and Politics

(Also see the Bibliography for Chapter 10, Voting Behaviour.)

Abella, I. M.,*Nationalism, Communism, and Canadian Labour: The CIO, the Communist Party, and the Canadian Congress of Labour 1935-1956*, Toronto, University of Toronto Press, 1973.

Barr, J. J., *The Dynasty: The Rise and Fall of Social Credit in Alberta*, Toronto, McClelland and Stewart, 1974.

Buck, T., *Lenin and Canada*, Toronto, Progress Books, 1970.

Brown, P., Chodos, R., Murphy, R., *Winners, Losers: The 1976 Tory Leadership Convention*, Toronto, James Lorimer, 1976.

Canada,*Report of the Committee on Election Expenses*, Ottawa, Queen's Printer, 1966.

Caouette, R.,*Réal Caouette vous parle*, Montréal, Les éditions du Caroussel, 1962.

Caplan, G.,*The Dilemma of Canadian Socialism*, Toronto, McClelland and Stewart, 1973.

Carrigan, O., *Canadian Party Platforms: 1867-1968*, Toronto, Copp Clark, 1968.

Cherwinski, W. J., "Bibliographical Note: The Left in Canadian History, 1911-1969," *Journal of Canadian Studies*, Vol. IV, No. 4, November, 1969.

Christian, W., and Campbell, C., *Political Parties and Ideologies in Canada: liberals, conservatives, socialists, nationalists*, Toronto, McGraw-Hill Ryerson, 1974.

Clark, S. D.,*Movements of Political Protest in Canada, 1640-1840*, Toronto, University of Toronto Press, 1959.

Clark, S. D., and Price, R. G., *Recruitment and Leadership Selection in Canada*, Toronto, Holt, Rinehart and Winston, 1973.

Coates, R. C., *The Night of the Knives*, Fredericton, Brunswick Press, 1969.

Comeau, P. A., "La transformation du parti libéral Québécois," *C.J.E.P.S.*, Vol. XXXI, No. 3, August, 1965.

Cook R., (ed.), *Politics of Discontent*, (Essays on Aherhart, Pattulo, H. H. Stevens, George McCullagh), Canadian Historical Readings, Toronto, University of Toronto Press, 1967.

Cook, T., "The Canadian conservative tradition: an historical perspective", *Journal of Canadian Studies*, Vol. VIII, No. 4, November, 1973.

Courtney, J. C.,*The Selection of National Party Leaders in Canada*, Toronto, Macmillan, 1973.

Cross, M. S.,*The Decline and Fall of a Good Idea: CCF-NDP Manifestoes 1932 to 1969*, Toronto, New Hogtown Press, 1974.

Dawson, R. M., *The Conscription Crisis of 1944*, Toronto, University of Toronto Press, 1961.

Denman, N., *How to Organize an Election*, Montréal, Les éditions du jour, 1962.

Dimension Staff, *et al.*, "New Democratic Party: Essays", *Canadian Dimension*, Vol. 7, No. 8, April, 1971.

Dion, l'Abbé G., et O'Neill, L'Abbé L., *Le chrétien et les élections*, Montréal, Les éditions de l'homme, 8me éd., 1960.

Dion, L'Abbé G., et O'Neill, L'Abbé L., *Le chrétien en démocratie*, Montréal, Les éditions de l'homme, 1961.

Dion, L., "The Concept of Political Leadership," *C.J.P.S.*, Vol. I, No. 1, March, 1968.

Dion, L., "A la recherche d'une méthode d'analyse des partis et des groupes d'intérêt," *C.J.P.S.*, Vol. II, No. 1, March, 1969.

Dion. L., "Politique consultative et système politique," *C.J.P.S.*, Vol. II, No. 2, June, 1969.

Easton, D., "The Theoretical Relevance of Political Socialization," C.J.P.S., Vol. I, No. 2, June, 1968.

Elkins, D. J., "The Perceived Structure of the Canadian Party System", *C.J.P.S.*, Vol. VII, No. 3, September, 1974.

Engelmann, F. C., and Schwartz, M. A., *Canadian Political Parties: Origin, Character, Impact*, Toronto, Prentice-Hall, 1975.

Epstein, L., "A Comparative Study of Canadian Parties," *The American Political Science Review*, Vol. LVIII, No. 1, March, 1964.

Epstein, L. D., *Political Parties in Western Democracies*, New York, Praeger, 1967.

Farr, D. M. L., Moir, J. S., Mealing, S. R., *Two Democracies*, Toronto, Ryerson, 1963.

Finlay, J. L., *Social Credit: The English Origins*, London & Montreal, McGill-Queen's University Press, 1972.

Fox, Paul, "Early Socialism in Canada," in Aitchison, J. H., (ed.), *The Political Process in Canada*, Toronto, University of Toronto Press, 1963.

Gibbons, K. M., Rowat, D. C., *Political Corruption in Canada*, Toronto, Carleton Library No. 95, McClelland and Stewart, 1976.

Godfrey, D., and Watkins, M., (eds.), *Gordon to Watkins to You*, Toronto, New Press, 1970.

Granatstein, J. L., *The Politics of Survival: The Conservative Party of Canada, 1939-1945*, Toronto, University of Toronto Press, 1967.

Grant, G., *Lament for a Nation*, Toronto, McClelland and Stewart, Carleton Library Series No. 50, 1971.

Greenslade, J. G., (ed.), *Canadian Politics: Speeches by F. M. Watkins, Stanley Knowles, J. R. Mallory and H. D. Hicks*, Sackville, Mount Allison University Publication No. 4, 1959.

Gwyn, R., *The Shape of Scandal, A Study of a Government in Crisis*, Toronto, Clarke, Irwin, 1965.

Hamelin, M., (ed.), *The Political Ideas of the Prime Ministers of Canada*, George Vanier Lectures, No. 1, University of Ottawa, 1970.

Harbron, J. D., "The Conservative Party and National Unity," *Q.Q.*, Vol. LXIX, No. 3, Autumn, 1962.

Heasman, D. J., "Political Alignments in Canada: The Fragmentation of Canadian Politics," *Parliamentary affairs*, Vol. XVI, No. 4, Autumn, 1963 and Vol. XVII, No. 1, Winter, 1963-64.

Heasman, D. J., "Parliamentary Developments, The Politics of Canadian Nationhood," *Parliamentary Affairs*, Vol. XIX, No. 2, Spring, 1966.

Hogan, G., *The Conservative in Canada*, Toronto, McClelland and Stewart, 1963.

Horowitz, G., "Tories, Socialists and the Demise of Canada," *Canadian Dimension*, Vol. II, No. 4, May-June, 1965.

Horowitz, G., "Conservatism, Liberalism, and Socialism in Canada: an Interpretation," *C.J.E.P.S.*, Vol. XXXII, No. 2, May, 1966.

Horowitz, G., *Canadian Labour in Politics*, Toronto, University of Toronto Press, 1968.

Horowitz, G., "Toward the Democratic Class Struggle," in Lloyd, Trevor and McLeod, Jack, (eds.), *Agenda 1970*, Toronto, University of Toronto Press, 1968.

Hudon, R., "Pour une analyse politique du patronage", *C.J.P.S.*, Vol VII, No. 3, September, 1974.

Hunter, W. D. G., "The New Democratic Party: Antecedents, Policies, Prospects," *Q.Q.*, Vol. LXIX, No. 3, Autumn, 1962.

Irvine, W. P., "The 1972 Election: The Return of Minority Government," *Q.Q.*, Vol. LXXIX, No. 4, Winter, 1972.

Irving, J. A., *The Social Credit Movement in Alberta*, Toronto, University of Toronto Press, 1959.

Johnson, J., *The Party's Over*, Toronto, Longman, 1971.

Knowles, S., *The New Party*, Toronto, McClelland and Stewart, 1961.

Kornberg, K., Smith, J., and Bromley, D., "Some Differences in the Political Socialization Patterns of Canadian and American Party Officials: A Preliminary Report," *C.J.P.S.*, Vol. II, No. 1, March, 1969.

Kornberg, A., Smith, J., and Clarke, H., "Attributes of Ascribed Influence in Local Party Organizations in Canada and the United States", *C.J.P.S.*, Vol. V., No. 2, June, 1972.

Laponce, J. A., "Canadian Party Labels: An Essay in Semantics and Anthropology," *C.J.P.S.*, Vol. II, No. 2, June, 1969.

Laurendeau, A., *La crise de la conscription*, Montréal, Éditions du jour, 1962. (English edition, Toronto, McClelland and Stewart, 1962).

Lavau, G., "Partis et systèmes politiques: interactions et fonction," *C.J.P.S.*, Vol. II, No. 1, March, 1969.

Leduc, L., "Party Decision-making: Some Empirical Observations on the Leadership Selection Process", *C.J.P.S.*, Vol. IV, No. 1, March, 1971.

Lemieux, V., "Pour une science politique des partis", *C.J.P.S.*, Vol. V, No. 4, December, 1972.

Leslie, P. M., "The Role of Political Parties in Promoting the Interests of Ethnic Minorities," *C.J.P.S.*, Vol. II, No. 4, December, 1969.

Lipset, S. M., *Agrarian Socialism: The C.C.F. in Saskatchewan*, Anchor Books, 1968.

Lipset, S. M., *Political Man, The Social Bases of Politics*, New York, Doubleday, 1963.

MacDonald, J. and J., (eds.), *The Canadian Voter's Guidebook*, Don Mills, Ontario, Fitzhenry & Whiteside, 1972.

McGuigan, M., and Lloyd, T., *Liberalism and Socialism*, Toronto, Exchange for Political Ideas in Canada, 1964, [pamphlet].

McHenry, D. E., *The Third Force in Canada: The Cooperative Commonwealth Federation, 1932-1948*, Berkeley, University of California Press, 1950.

MacKinnon, F., *Postures and Politics*, Toronto, University of Toronto Press, 1973.

Macpherson, C. B., *Democracy in Alberta: The Theory and Practice of a Quasi-Party System*, Toronto, University of Toronto Press, 1953.

MacQuarrie, H., *The Conservative Party*, Toronto, McClelland and Stewart, 1965.

Manthorpe, J., *The Power and the Tories; Ontario's Politics—1943 to the Present*, Toronto, Macmillan, 1975.

Masters, D. D., *The Winnipeg General Strike*, Toronto, University of Toronto Press, 1973.

Meisel, J., *Working Papers on Canadian Politics*, Montreal, McGill-Queen's Press, second enlarged edition, 1975.

Meisel, J., "The Stalled Omnibus: Canadian Parties in the 1960s," *Social Research*, Vol. XXX, No. 3, Autumn, 1963.

Meisel, J., *Les transformations des partis politiques canadiens*, Cahiers de la Société canadienne de Science politique, no. 2, 1966.

Meisel, J., "Canadian Parties and Politics," in Leach, R. H., *Contemporary Canada*, Toronto, University of Toronto Press, 1968.

Meynaud, J., *Argent et politique*, Montréal, Le centre de documentation et de recherches politique, Collège Jean-de-Brébeuf, 1966.

Morley, J. T., "Comment: The 1974 Federal Election in British Columbia", *BC Studies*, No. 23, Fall, 1974.

Morrison, D. R., *The Politics of the Yukon Territory, 1898-1909*, Toronto, University of Toronto Press, 1968.

Morton, D., *With Your Help, An Election Manual*, Ottawa, New Democratic Party, 1966.

Morton, D., "The Effectiveness of Political Campaigning: The N.D.P. in the 1967 Ontario Election," *Journal of Canadian Studies*, Vol. IV, No. 3, August, 1969.

Morton, D., *The Dream of Power*, Toronto, Hakkert, 1974.

Morton, W. L., *The Progressive Party in Canada*, Toronto, University of Toronto Press, 1950.

Muller, S., "Federalism and the Party System in Canada", in Meekison, J. P., (ed.), *Canadian Federalism: Myth or Reality*, 2nd ed., Toronto, Methuen, 1971.

Murray, D., "The Ralliement des Créditistes in Parliament", *Journal of Canadian Studies*, Vol. VIII, No. 2, May, 1973.

Neatby, H. B., *The Politics of Chaos: Canada in the Thirties*, Toronto, Macmillan, 1972.

Neill, R. F., "Social Credit and National Policy in Canada," *Journal of Canadian Studies*, Vol. III, No. 1, February, 1968.

Neumann, S., *Modern Political Parties*, Chicago, University of Chicago Press, 1956.

Newman, P. C., *The Distemper of Our Times, Canadian Politics in Transition: 1963-1968*, Toronto, McClelland and Stewart, 1968.

Newman, P. C. and Fillmore, S., *Their Turn to Curtsy—Your Turn to Bow*, (Election Handbook), Toronto, Maclean-Hunter, 1972.

Nicholson, P., *Vision and Indecision: Diefenbaker and Pearson*, Don Mills, Longman, 1968.

Oliver, M., (ed.), *Social Purpose for Canada*, Toronto, University of Toronto Press, 1961.

Paltiel, K. Z., *Political Party Financing in Canada*, Toronto, McGraw-Hill, 1970.

Paltiel, K. Z., "Party and Candidate Expenditures in the Canadian General Election of 1972", *C.J.P.S.*, Vol. VII, No. 2, June, 1974.

Peacock, D., *Journey to Power: The Story of a Canadian Election, (1968)*, Toronto, Ryerson, 1968.

Peers, F. W., *The Politics of Canadian Broadcasting, 1920-51*, Toronto, University of Toronto Press, 1969.

Penner, N., *Winnipeg 1919*, Toronto, James, Lewis and Samuel, 1973.

Pickersgill, J. W., *The Liberal Party*, Toronto, McClelland and Stewart, 1962.

Pike, R., Zureik, E., *Political Socialization*, Vol. I, Carleton Library No. 84, Toronto, McClelland and Stewart, 1975; *Socialization, Social Stratification, Ethnicity*, Vol. II, Carleton Library No. 85, 1975.

Pinard, M., "Third Parties in Canada Revisited," *C.J.P.S.*, Vol. VI, No. 3, September, 1973.

Pinard, M., *The Rise of a Third Party: A Study in Crisis Politics*, McGill-Queen's Press, 1975.

Posner, M., "Canada's federal political parties: their ideologies and histories", *Canada and the World*, Vol. 38, No. 6, February, 1973.

Proulx, J., *Le panier de crabes*, Toronto, McClelland and Stewart, 1971.

Quinn, H. F., *The Union Nationale: A Study in Quebec Nationalism*, Toronto, University of Toronto Press, 1963.

Quinn, H. F., "The Role of the Liberal Party in Recent Canadian Politics," *Political Science Quarterly*, Vol. LXVIII, No. 3, September, 1953.

Regenstreif, P., "Note on the 'Alternation' of French and English Leaders in the Liberal Party of Canada," *C.J.P.S.*, Vol. II, No. 1, March, 1969.

Richardson, B. T., *Canada and Mr. Diefenbaker*, Toronto, McClelland and Stewart, 1962.

Robertson, H., *Reservations are for Indians*, Toronto, James, Lewis and Samuel, 1970.

Robin, M., *Radical Politics and Canadian Labour, 1880-1930*, Kingston, Queen's University, 1968.

Rodney, W., *Soldiers of the International: A History of the Communist Party of Canada, 1919-1929*, Toronto, University of Toronto Press, 1968.

Rose, W., *Social Credit Handbook*, Toronto, McClelland and Stewart, 1968.

Roussopoulus, D., (ed.), *The New Left in Canada*, Montreal, Our Generation Press, 1970.

Scarrow, H. A., "Distinguishing Between Political Parties—The Case of Canada," *Midwest Journal of Political Science*, Vol. IX, No. 1, February, 1965.

Schindeler, F., Lanphier, C. M., "Social Science Research and Participatory Democracy in Canada," *C.P.A.*, Vol. XII, No. 4, Winter, 1969.

Schultz, H. J., "The Social Credit Back-benchers' Revolt, 1937," *Canadian Historical Review*, Vol. XLI, No. 1, March, 1960.

Schwartz, M. A., *Politics and Territory: The Sociology of Regional Persistence in Canada*, Montreal, McGill-Queen's University Press, 1974.

Smiley, D. V., "The Two-Party System and One-Party Dominance in the Liberal Democratic State," *C.J.E.P.S.*, Vol. XXIV, No. 3, August, 1958.

Smiley, D. V., "The National Party Leadership Convention in Canada: A Preliminary Analysis," *C.J.P.S.*, Vol. I, No. 4, December, 1968.

Smith, D. E., *Prairie Liberalism: The Liberal Party in Saskatchewan, 1905-71*, Toronto, University of Toronto Press, 1975.

Stewart, W., *Divide and Con*, Toronto, New Press, 1973.

Stein, M. B., *The Dynamics of Right-Wing Protest: Social Credit in Quebec*, Toronto, University of Toronto Press, 1973.

Sullivan, M., *Mandate '68, The Year of Pierre Elliott Trudeau*, Toronto, Doubleday, 1968.

Taylor, Charles, *The Pattern of Politics*, Toronto, McClelland and Stewart, 1970.

Teeple, G., (ed), *Capitalism and the National Question in Canada*, Toronto, University of Toronto Press, 1972.

Thompson, R. N., *Canadians, It's Time You Knew*, n.p., The Aavangen Press, 1961.

Thompson, R. N., *Commonsense for Canadians: A Selection of Speeches*, Toronto, McClelland and Stewart, 1964.

Thorburn, H. G., (ed.), *Party Politics in Canada*, Scarborough, Ontario, Prentice-Hall, 1972.

Underhill, F. H., *Canadian Political Parties*, Canadian Historical Association Booklet No. 8, Ottawa, 1957.

Underhill, F. H., "The Revival of Conservatism in North America," *Transactions of the Royal Society of Canada*, Vol. LII, Series III, June, 1958.

Underhill, F. H., *In Search of Canadian Liberalism*, Toronto, Macmillan, 1960.

Vallières, P., "Le Parti Socialiste du Québec à l'heure de la révolution tranquille," *Cité libre*, Vol. XV, No. 1, janvier, 1964.

Ward, N., "Money and Politics: The Costs of Democracy in Canada", *C.J.P.S.*, Vol. V, No. 3, September, 1972.

Wearing, J., "Party Leadership and the 1966 Conventions," *Journal of Canadian Studies*, Vol. II, No. 1, February, 1967.

Wearing, J., "A Convention for Professionals: The PCs in Toronto," *Journal of Canadian Studies*, Vol. II, No. 4, November, 1967.

Wearing, J., "The Liberal Choice," *Journal of Canadian Studies*, Vol. III, No. 2, May, 1968.

Wearing, J., "The Trudeau Phenomenon," *C.J.P.S.*, Vol. II, No. 3, September 1969.

White, G., "One-Party Dominance and Third Parties", *C.J.P.S.*, Vol. VI, No. 3, September, 1973.

Williams, J. R., *The Conservative Party in Canada, 1920-1949*, Durham, Duke University Press, 1956.

Wilson, W. A., *The Trudeau Question, Election 1972*, Don Mills, Ontario, Paperjacks, 1972.

Winham, G. R., Cunningham, R. B., "Party Leader Images in the 1968 Federal Elections," *C.J.P.S.*, Vol. III, No. 1, March, 1970.

Winn, C., McMenemy, J., *Political Parties in Canada*, Toronto, McGraw-Hill Ryerson, 1976.

Young, W. D., *The Anatomy of a Party: The National C.C.F. 1932-61*, Toronto, University of Toronto Press, 1969.

Young, W. D., *Democracy and Discontent: Progressivism, Socialism and Social Credit in the Canadian West*, The Frontenac Library, Toronto, Ryerson, 1969.

Zakuta, L., *A Protest Movement Becalmed: A Study of Changes in the C.C.F.*, Toronto, University of Toronto Press, 1964.

Political Biographies

Barrette, A., *Mémoires*, Vol. I, Montréal, Librairie Beauchemin, 1966.

Beal, J. R., *The Pearson Phenomena*, Toronto, Longman, 1964.

Beck, J. M., *Joseph Howe, Voice of Nova Scotia*, Carleton Library, Toronto, McClelland and Stewart, 1964.

Benson, N. A., *None of It Came Easy: The Story of J. G. Gardiner*, Toronto, Burns and MacEachern, 1955.

Borden, H., (ed.), *Robert Laird Borden: His Memoirs*, Toronto, Macmillan, 1938, 2 vols.

Borden, R. L., *His Memoirs*, Carleton Library, Toronto, McClelland and Stewart, 1969, 2 vols.

Borden, R. L., (ed. by H. Borden), *Letters to Limbo*, Toronto, University of Toronto Press, 1971.

Bourassa, A., Bergevin, A., and Nish, C., (eds.), *Henri Bourassa, Biography, Bibliographical Index, and Index of Public Correspondence, 1895-1924*, Montreal, les Éditions de l'Action Nationale, 1966.

Bourassa, A., (ed.), *Henri Bourassa, Montréal*, les éditions de l'Action Nationale, 1966.

Bourassa, R., *Bourassa/Quebec!*, Montréal, Les Éditions de l'Homme, 1970.

Brown, R. C., *Robert Laird Borden; A Biography*, Vol. I. 1854-1914, Toronto, Macmillan, 1975.

Careless, J. M. S., *Brown of the Globe*, Vol. I, *The Voice of Upper Canada, 1818-1859*, Toronto, Macmillan, 1959; Vol. II, *Statesman of Confederation, 1860-1880*, Toronto, Macmillan, 1963.

Casgrain, T., *Une femme chez les hommes*, Montréal, Éditions du jour, 1972.

Chalout, R., *Mémoires politiques*, Toronto, McClelland and Stewart, 1969.

Chodos, R., *et al.*, "David [Lewis]: the centre of his party", *Last Post*, Vol. I, No. 7, April-May, 1971.

Creighton, D., *John A. Macdonald: The Young Politician*, Toronto, Macmillan, 1952; *The Old Chieftain*, Toronto, Macmillan, 1955.

Dafoe, J. W., *Laurier: A Study in Canadian Politics*, Carleton Library, Toronto, McClelland and Stewart, 1963.

Dawson, R. M., *William Lyon Mackenzie King: A Political Biography, 1874-1923*, Vol. I, Toronto, University of Toronto Press, 1958.

Dempson, P., *Assignment Ottawa*, Don Mills, General Publishing, 1968.

Donaldson, G., *Fifteen Men: Canada's Prime Ministers from Macdonald to Trudeau*, Toronto, Doubleday, 1969.

Drury, E. C., *Farmer Premier: The Memoirs of the Hon. E. C. Drury*, Toronto, McClelland and Stewart, 1966.
Ferns, H. S., and Ostry, B., *The Age of Mackenzie King: The Rise of the Leader*, London, Heinemann, 1955.
Graham, R., *Arthur Meighen*, Vol. I, *The Door of Opportunity*, Toronto, Clarke, Irwin, 1960; Vol. II, *And Fortune Fled*, Toronto, Clarke, Irwin, 1963; Vol. III, *No Surrender*, Toronto, Clarke, Irwin 1965.
Gwyn, R., *Smallwood: the unlikely revolutionary*, Rev. ed., Toronto, McClelland and Stewart, 1972.
Haliburton, E. D., *My years with Stanfield*, Windsor, N. S., Lancelot, 1972.
Heaps, L., *The Rebel in the House: The Life and Times of A. A. Heaps, M. P.*, London, England, Niccolo, 1970.
Hutchison, B., *The Incredible Canadian*, Toronto, Longman, Green, 1952.
Hutchison, B., *Mr. Prime Minister, 1867-1964*, Toronto, Longman, 1964.
Institut canadien des affaires publiques, *Nos hommes politiques*, Montréal, Éditions du jour, 1964.
Johnson, L. P. V. and MacNutt, O., *Aberhart of Alberta*, Edmonton, Institute of Applied Arts, 1970.
King, W. L. M., *Industry and Humanity*, Toronto, University of Toronto Press, 1973.
La Marsh, Judy, *Memoirs of A Bird in a Gilded Cage*, Toronto, McClelland and Stewart, 1969.
Lapalme, G. E., *Mémoires*, Vol. 1-3, Montréal, Leméac, 1969-73.
Laporte, P., *The True Face of Duplessis*, Montreal, Harvest House, 1960.
La Roque, H., *Camilien Houde, le p'tit gars de Ste. Marie*, Montréal, Les éditions de l'homme, 1961.
McGregor, F. A., *The Fall and Rise of Mackenzie King: 1911-1919*, Toronto, Macmillan, 1962.
MacInnis, G., *J. S. Woodsworth, A Man to Remember*, Toronto, Macmillan, 1953.
McKenty, N., *Mitch Hepburn*, Toronto, McClelland and Stewart, 1967.
McNaught, K., *A Prophet in Politics: A Biography of J. S. Woodsworth*, Toronto, University of Toronto Press, 1959.
Munro, J. A., and Inglis, A. I., (eds.), *Mike: The Memoirs of the Right Honorable B. Pearson, Vol. II, 1948-1957*, Toronto, University of Toronto Press, 1973.
Nadeau, J.-M., *Carnets politiques*, Montréal, Éditions Partis Pris, 1966.
Neatby, H. B., *William Lyon Mackenzie King, 1924-1932: The Lonely Heights*, Vol. II, Toronto, University of Toronto Press, 1963; Vol. III, 1932-39: *Prism of Unity*, 1976.
Neatby, H. B., *Laurier and a Liberal Quebec: A Study in Political Management*, Toronto, McClelland and Stewart, 1973.
Newman, P. C., *Renegade in Power: The Diefenbaker Years*, Carleton Library No. 70, Toronto, McClelland and Stewart, 1963.
Pearson, L. B., *Mike: The Memoirs of the Right Honourable Lester B. Pearson*, Vol. I, 1897-1948, Toronto, University of Toronto Press, 1972; Vol. II, 1948-1957, 1973; Vol. III, 1957-1968, 1975.
Pickersgill, J. W., *My Years with Louis St. Laurent*, Toronto, University of Toronto Press, 1975.
Pickersgill, J. W., *The Mackenzie King Record*, Toronto, University of Toronto Press, Vol. I, 1939-1944, 1960; with Forster, D., Vol. II, 1944-1945, 1968; Vol. III, 1945-1946, 1970; Vol. IV, 1947-1948, 1971.
Provencher, J., *René Lévesque, portrait d'un québécois*, Montréal, Éditions la presse, 1973. (English edition, Toronto, Gage, 1975.)
Roberts, L., *C. D.: The Life and Time of Clarence Decatur Howe*, Toronto, Clarke, Irwin, 1957.

Roberts, L., *The Chief: A Political Biography of Maurice Duplessis*, Toronto, Clarke, Irwin, 1963.

Rolph, W. K., *Henry Wise Wood of Alberta*, Toronto, University of Toronto Press, 1950.

Ryan, O., *Tim Buck: A Conscience For Canada*, Toronto, Progress Books, 1975.

Schull, J., *Laurier, The First Canadian*, Toronto, Macmillan, 1965.

Schultz, H. J., "Portrait of a Premier: William Aberhart," *Canadian Historical Review*, Vol. XXXV, No. 3, September, 1964.

Sévigny, P., *This Game of Politics*, Toronto, McClelland and Stewart, 1965.

Shaw, B., (ed.), *The Gospel According to Saint Pierre*, (Trudeau), Richmond Hill, Pocket Books, Simon and Schuster, 1969.

Sheppard, C.-A., *Dossier Wagner*, Montréal, Éditions du Jour, 1972.

Sherman, P., *Bennett*, [W.A.C.], Toronto, McClelland and Stewart, 1966.

Smallwood, J. R., *I Chose Canada*, [Memoirs], Toronto, Macmillan, 1973.

Smith, D., *Gentle Patriot—A Political Biography of Walter Gordon*, Edmonton, Hurtig, 1973.

Steeves, D. G., *The Compassionate Rebel: Ernest E. Winch and His Times*, Vancouver, Evergreen Press, 1960.

Stevens, G., *Stanfield*, Toronto, McClelland and Stewart, 1973.

Stewart, M., and French, D., *Ask No Quarter: A Biography of Agnes MacPhail*, Toronto, Longman, Green, 1959.

Stewart, W., *Shrug—Trudeau in Power*, Toronto, New Press, 1972.

Stinson, L., *Political Warriors: Recollections of a Social Democrat*, Winnipeg, Queenston House, 1975.

Thomson, D. C., *Alexander MacKenzie: Clear Grit*, Toronto, Macmillan, 1960.

Thomson, D. C., *Louis St. Laurent: Canadian*, Toronto, Macmillan, 1967.

Thordarson, B., *Lester Pearson, Diplomat and Politician*, Toronto, Oxford University Press, 1974.

Trudeau, P. E., *Conversation with Canadians*, Toronto, University of Toronto Press, 1972.

Van Dusen, T., *The Chief*, (Diefenbaker), Toronto, McGraw-Hill, 1968.

Wallace, W. S., *The Macmillan Dictionary of Canadian Biography*, Toronto, Macmillan, 1963, 3rd edition.

Ward, N., (ed.), *A Party Politician: The Memoirs of Chubby Power*, Toronto, Macmillan, 1966.

Watkins, E., *R. B. Bennett*, Toronto, Kingswood House, 1963.

Westell, A., *Paradox: Trudeau as Prime Minister*, Scarborough, Prentice-Hall, 1972.

Young, W. D., "M. J. Coldwell, the making of a Social Democrat", *Journal of Canadian Studies*, Vol. IX, No. 3, August, 1974.

Zink, L., *Trudeaucracy*, Toronto, Toronto Sun, 1972.

Zolf, L., *Dance of the Dialectic*, Toronto, James, Lewis and Samuel, 1973.

Provincial Politics

Aucoin, P., "The 1970 Nova Scotia provincial election", *Journal of Canadian Studies*, Vol. VII, No. 3, August, 1972.

Badgley, R. F., and Wolfe, S., *Doctors' Strike: Medical Care and Conflict in Saskatchewan*, Toronto, Macmillan, 1967.

Barr, J. J., *The Dynasty: The Rise and Fall of Social Credit in Alberta*, Toronto, McClelland and Stewart, 1974.

Beeching, W. C., and Lazarus, M., "Le socialisme en Saskatchewan—trop ou trop peu", *Socialisme 64, Revue du socialisme international et Québecois*, No. 2, Automne, 1964.

Black, E. R., "British Columbia: The Politics of Exploitation", in *Exploiting Our Economic Potential: Public Policy and the British Columbia Economy*, by R. Shearer, ed., Toronto, Holt, Rinehart and Winston, 1968.

Blais, A., "Third Parties in Canadian Provincial Politics", *C.J.P.S.*, Vol. VI, No. 3, September, 1973.

Caplan, G. L., *The Dilemma of Canadian Socialism: The CCF in Ontario*, Toronto, McClelland and Stewart, 1973.

Gagan, D. P., (ed.), *Prairie Perspectives*, Toronto and Montreal, Holt, Rinehart and Winston, 1970.

Grayson, J. P., and Grayson, L. M., "The Social Base of Interwar Political Unrest in Urban Alberta", *C.J.P.S.*, Vol. VII, No. 2, June, 1974.

Higginbotham, C. H., *Off the Record: The C.C.F. in Saskatchewan*, Toronto, McClelland and Stewart, 1968.

Hooke, A., *Thirty Plus Five: I Know, I Was There*, Edmonton, Institute of Applied Arts, 1971.

Irving, J. A., *The Social Credit Movement in Alberta*, Toronto, University of Toronto Press, 1959.

Jackman, S. W., *Portraits of the premiers: an informal history of British Columbia*, Sidney, B. C., Gray, 1969.

Knox, P., and Resnick, P., (eds.), *Essays in B.C. Political Economy*, Vancouver, New Star Books, 1974.

Leduc, L. Jr., and White, W. L., "The Role of Opposition in a One-Party Dominant System: The Case of Ontario", *C.J.P.S.*, Vol. VII, No. 1, March, 1974.

Lipset, S. M., *Agrarian Socialism: The Cooperative Commonwealth Federation in Saskatchewan*, New York, Anchor Books, Doubleday, 1968.

McCormack, A. R., "The Emergence of the Socialist Movement in British Columbia," (1880-1904), *BC Studies*, No. 21, Spring, 1974.

MacDonald, D. C., (ed.), *Government and Politics of Ontario*, Toronto, Macmillan, 1975.

McGeer, P. L., *Politics in Paradise*, Toronto, Peter Martin, 1972.

MacGregor, J. G., *A History of Alberta*, Edmonton, Hurtig, 1972.

Macpherson, C. B., *Democracy in Alberta: The Theory and Practice of a Quasi-Party System*, Toronto, University of Toronto Press, 1953.

Manthorpe, J., *The Power and the Tories*, Toronto, Macmillan, 1974.

Matthews, R., "Perspectives on recent Newfoundland politics", *Journal of Canadian Studies*, Vol. IX, No. 2, May, 1974.

Neary, P., (ed.), *The Political Economy of Newfoundland. 1929-1972*, Toronto, Copp Clark, 1973.

Neary, P., "Politics in Newfoundland: the end of the Smallwood era", *Journal of Canadian Studies*, Vol. VII, No. 1, February, 1972.

Neary, P., "Party Politics in Newfoundland: 1949-71: a survey and analysis," *Journal of Canadian Studies*, Vol. VI, No. 4, November, 1971.

Nelles, H. V., *The Politics of Development: Forests, Mines and Hydro-Electric Power in Ontario 1849-1941*, Toronto, Macmillan, 1974.

Nichols, H. E., *Alberta's Fight for Freedom*, (A History of Social Credit), n.p., 1963, 5 Vols.

Nixon, Robert, (ed.), *The Guelph Papers*, (Ontario Liberal Party Conference), Toronto, Peter Martin Associates, 1970.

Noel, S. J. R., *Politics in Newfoundland*, Toronto, University of Toronto Press, 1971.

Ontario Historical Society, *Profile of a Province, Studies in the history of Ontario*, Toronto, Ontario Historical Society, 1967.

Ormsby, M., *British Columbia: A History*, Toronto, Macmillan, 1958.

Parti Acadien, *Le Parti Acadien*, B. P. 354, Petit-Rocher, New Brunswick, 1972.

Peel, B. B., *A Bibliography of the Prairie Provinces to 1953*, Toronto, 1956.

Phillips, P. A., *No Power Greater: A Century of Labour in British Columbia*, Vancouver, Federation of Labour Borg Foundation, 1967.

Robin, M., (ed.), *Canadian Provincial Politics*, Scarborough, Ontario, Prentice-Hall, 1972.

Robin, M., "The Social Basis of Party Politics in British Columbia", *Q.Q.*, Vol. LXXII, No. 4, Winter, 1966.

Robin, M., *The Rush for Spoils: The Company Province, 1871-1933*, (British Columbia), Toronto, McClelland and Stewart, 1972.

Robin, M., *Pillars of Profit: The Company Province, 1934-1972*, (British Columbia), Toronto, McClelland and Stewart, 1973.

Rowat, D. C., (ed.), *Provincial Government and Politics: Comparative Essays*, 2nd ed., Ottawa, Carleton University, 1973.

Schultz, H. J., Ormsby, M. A., Wilbur, J. R. H., and Young, B. J., *Politics of Discontent*, Canadian Historical Readings, No. 4, Toronto, University of Toronto Press, 1967.

Sharp, P. F., *The Agrarian Revolt in Western Canada*, Minneapolis, University of Minnesota Press, 1948.

Simeon, R., and Elkins, D. J., "Regional Political Cultures in Canada", *C.J.P.S.*, Vol. VII, No. 3, September, 1974.

Sinclair, P. R., "The Saskatchewan C.C.F. and the Communist Party in the 1930's", *Saskatchewan History*, Vol. XXVI, No. 1, Winter, 1973.

Smith, D. E., "Interpreting prairie politics", *Journal of Canadian Politics*, Vol. VII, No. 4, November, 1972.

Smith, D. E., *Prairie Liberalism, The Liberal Party in Saskatchewan 1905-1971*, Toronto, University of Toronto Press, 1975.

Swainson, D., (ed.), *Historical Essays on the Prairie Provinces*, Carleton Library, No. 53, Toronto & Montreal, McClelland and Stewart, 1970.

Swainson, D., (ed.), *Oliver Mowat's Ontario*, Toronto, Macmillan, 1972.

Thomas, L. G., *The Liberal Party in Alberta: A History of Politics in the Province of Alberta, 1905-1921*, Toronto, University of Toronto Press, 1959.

Thorburn, H. G., *Politics in New Brunswick*, Toronto, University of Toronto Press, 1961.

Tyre, R., *Douglas in Saskatchewan: The Story of a Socialist Experiment*, Vancouver, Mitchell Press, 1962.

Walker, R. R., *Politicians of a pioneering province*, Vancouver, Mitchell, 1969.

Ward, N., and Spafford, D., (eds.), *Politics in Saskatchewan*, Toronto, Longman, 1968.

Whalen, H., "Social Credit Measures in Alberta", *C.J.E.P.S.*, Vol. XVIII, No. 4, November, 1952.

Wilson, J., "The Canadian Political Cultures: Towards a Redefinition of the Nature of the Canadian Political System", *C.J.P.S.*, Vol. VII, No. 3, September, 1974.

Young, W. D., *Democracy and Discontent: Progressivism, Socialism and Social Credit in the Canadian West*, The Frontenac Library, Toronto, Ryerson, 1969.

Zakuta, L., *A Protest Movement Becalmed*, (Ontario CCF), Toronto, University of Toronto Press, 1964.

City Politics

Barker, G., Penney, J., and Seccombe, W., "The Developers", *Canadian Dimension*, Vol. 9, Nos. 2 and 3, January, 1973.

Bettison, D. G., Kenward, J., and Taylor, L., *The Politics of Canadian urban development: the urban affairs of Alberta*, Edmonton, University of Alberta Press, 1973.

Caulfield, J., *The Tiny Perfect Mayor*, Toronto, James Lorimer, 1974.

Clarkson, S., "Barrier to Entry of Parties into Toronto's Civic Politics: Towards a Theory of Party Penetration", *C.J.P.S.*, Vol. IV, No. 2, June, 1971.

Clarkson, S., *City Lib: Parties and Reform*, Toronto, Hakkert, 1972.

Easton, R., and Tennant, R., "Vancouver Civic Party Leadership: Backgrounds, Attitudes, and Non-civic Party Affiliations", *BC Studies*, No. 2, Summer, 1969.

Feldman, L. D., and Goldrick, M. D., (eds.), *Politics and Government of Urban Canada*, 2nd ed., Agincourt, Ontario, Methuen, 1972.

Fraser, G., *Fighting Back: Urban Renewal in Trefann Court*, Toronto, Hakkert, 1972.

Granatstein, J., *Marlborough Marathon*, Toronto, Hakkert, 1971.

Granatstein, J. L., *et al.*, "Cityscape '72", *The Canadian Forum*, Vol. LII, No. 616, May, 1972.

Kay, B. J., "Voting Patterns in a Non-partisan Legislature: A Study of Toronto City Council," *C.J.P.S.*, Vol. IV, No. 2, June, 1971.

Lorimer, J., *The Real World of City Politics*, Toronto, James, Lewis and Samuel, 1970.

Lorimer, J., *A Citizen's Guide to City Politics*, Toronto, James, Lewis and Samuel, 1972.

Masson, J. K., *Emerging Party Politics in Urban Canada*, Toronto, McClelland and Stewart, 1972.

Maud, L. R., "The politics of local government progress", *C.P.A.*, Vol. 17, No. 3, Fall, 1974

Nowlan, D., and Nowlan, N., *The Bad Trip—The Untold Story of the Spadina Expressway*, Toronto, House of Anansi, 1970.

Phillips, N., *Mayor of all the People*, (Memoirs), Toronto, McClelland and Stewart, 1967.

Rose, A., *Governing Metropolitan Toronto: A Social and Political Analysis, 1953-1971*, Los Angeles, University of California Press, 1972.

Sewell, J., *Inside City Hall*, Toronto, Hakkert, 1971.

Sewell, J., *Up Against City Hall*, Toronto, James Lewis & Samuel, 1972.

Stein, D. L., *Toronto For Sale*, Toronto, New Press, 1972.

Vancouver Urban Research Group, *Forever Deceiving You—The Politics of Vancouver Development*, Vancouver, Vancouver Urban Research Group, 4632 West 11th St., 1972.

9

THE ELECTORAL PROCESS

The contents of this chapter have been altered considerably in this edition. Some items which appeared in the third edition have been omitted, the material carried over has been brought up to date, and new items have been added.

The changes arise in particular from the passage of a new federal Representation Act in 1974 and from the growth of legislation dealing with the financing of elections and parties.

The first item reproduces the Representation Act, 1974. It is accompanied by a table showing the changes in the distribution of seats in the House of Commons brought about by the new Act. In 1974 Ottawa and Ontario followed Quebec's example in 1963 and enacted laws controlling election expenditures and contributions to parties and candidates. All three statutes are in the same modern vein, seeking to make elections more democratic by curbing spending and broadening the base of election financing. The article by the editor explains the new federal legislation while the excerpt from an article by Daniel Stoffman shows the effects of Ontario's recent law. The material on Quebec's legislation has not been repeated in this edition but may be found in the third edition, pp. 264-266.

Two additions to this edition by Gerald Utting and Val Sears give a *realpolitik* account of how the professionals package and sell politicians.

Two articles from the previous edition have been carried over and brought up to date. The first describes the various steps involved in holding a federal election. It is followed by two tables; one shows the party standings in the House of Commons resulting from each of our federal general elections from 1867 to 1974 while the other gives the number of seats won and the percentage of votes gained by parties by provinces for the 1974 federal election compared to the 1972 election. For similar tables for the 1968 and 1965 elections, see the third edition, p. 259. In the next article the editor takes note of the discrepancy which usually occurs between the percentage of popular votes won and the percentage of seats gained by parties in order to assess the pros and cons of applying to Canada a modified form of the proportional representation system of voting. He has added as a postscript another proposal for altering the representation system which originally appeared in a different form in *The Toronto Star*, November 11, 1972.

The bibliography at the end of the chapter lists some of the relatively few works available on the electoral process. Particular note should be made of three books in the McGraw-Hill Ryerson Series in Canadian Politics which deal with the electoral process: T. H. Qualter, *The Election Process in Canada*; W. E. Lyons, *One Man, One Vote*; and K. Z. Paltiel, *Political Party Financing in Canada*; all were published in 1970.

NEW ARRANGEMENTS FOR REPRESENTATION IN THE HOUSE OF COMMONS*

23 Eliz. II, c.13

An act to provide for representation in the House of Commons, to establish electoral boundaries commissions and to remove the temporary suspension of the Electoral Boundaries Readjustment Act

[Assented to 20th December, 1974]

Her Majesty, by and with the advice and consent of the Senate and House of Commons of Canada, enacts as follows:

SHORT TITLE

1. This Act may be cited as the *Representation Act, 1974.*

Part I: British North America Act

2. Subsection 51(1) of the *British North America Act, 1867,* as enacted by the *British North America Act, 1952,* is repealed and the following substituted therefore:

"**51.** (1) The number of members of the House of Commons and the representation of the provinces therein shall upon the coming into force of this subsection and thereafter on the completion of each decennial census be readjusted by such authority, in such manner, and from such time as the Parliament of Canada from time to time provides, subject and according to the following Rules:

* From Vol. 1, No. 2, *Canada Gazette Part III*, Ottawa, 1974. Reproduced by permission of the Minister of Supply and Services Canada.

1. There shall be assigned to Quebec seventy-five members in the readjustment following the completion of the decennial census taken in the year 1971, and thereafter four additional members in each subsequent readjustment.

2. Subject to Rules 5(2) and (3), there shall be assigned to a large province a number of members equal to the number obtained by dividing the population of the large province by the electoral quotient of Quebec.

3. Subject to Rules 5(2) and (3), there shall be assigned to a small province a number of members equal to the number obtained by dividing

(a) the sum of the populations, determined according to the results of the penultimate decennial census, of the provinces (other than Quebec) having populations of less than one and a half million, determined according to the results of that census, by the sum of the numbers of members assigned to those provinces in the readjustment following the completion of that census; and

(b) the population of the small provinces by the quotient obtained under paragraph (a).

4. Subject to Rules 5(1)(a), (2) and (3), there shall be assigned to an intermediate province a number of members equal to the number obtained

(a) by dividing the sum of the populations of the provinces (other than Quebec) having populations of less than one and a half million by the sum of the numbers of members assigned to those provinces under any of Rules 3, 5(1)(b), (2) and (3);

(b) by dividing the population of the intermediate province by the quotient obtained under paragraph (a); and

(c) by adding to the number of members assigned to the intermediate province in the readjustment following the completion of the penultimate decennial census one-half of the difference resulting from the subtraction of that number from the quotient obtained under paragraph (b).

5. (1) On any readjustment,

(a) if no province (other than Quebec) has a population of less than one and a half million, Rule 4 shall not be applied and, subject to Rules 5(2) and (3), there shall be assigned to an intermediate province a number of members equal to the number obtained by dividing

(i) the sum of the populations, determined according to the results of the penultimate decennial census, of the provinces (other than Quebec) having populations of not less than one and a half million and not more than two and a half million, determined according to the results of that census, by the sum of the numbers of members assigned to those provinces in the readjustment following the completion of that census, and

(ii) the population of the intermediate province by the quotient obtained under subparagraph (i);

(b) if a province (other than Quebec) having a population of

(i) less than one and a half million, or

(ii) not less than one and a half million and not more than two and a half million

does not have a population greater than its population determined according to the results of the penultimate decennial census, it shall, subject to Rules 5(2) and (3), be assigned the number of members assigned to it in the readjustment following the completion of that census.

(2) On any readjustment,

(*a*) if, under any of Rules 2 to 5(1), the number of members to be assigned to a province (in this paragraph referred to as "the first province") is smaller than the number of members to be assigned to any other province not having a population greater than that of the first province, those Rules shall not be applied to the first province and it shall be assigned a number of members equal to the largest number of members to be assigned to any other province not having a population greater than that of the first province;

(*b*) if, under any of Rules 2 to 5(1)(*a*), the number of members to be assigned to a province is smaller than the number of members assigned to it in the readjustment following the completion of the penultimate decennial census, those Rules shall not be applied to it and it shall be assigned the latter number of members;

(*c*) if both paragraphs (*a*) and (*b*) apply to a province, it shall be assigned a number of members equal to the greater of the numbers produced under those paragraphs.

(3) On any readjustment,

(*a*) if the electoral quotient of a province (in this paragraph referred to as "the first province") obtained by dividing its population by the number of members to be assigned to it under any Rules 2 to 5(2) is greater than the electoral quotient of Quebec, those Rules shall not be applied to the first province and it shall be assigned a number of members equal to the number obtained by dividing its population by the electoral quotient of Quebec;

(*b*) if, as a result of the application of Rule 6(2)(*a*), the number of members assigned to a province under paragraph (*a*) equals the number of members to be assigned to it under any of Rules 2 to 5(2), it shall be assigned that number of members and paragraph (*a*) shall cease to apply to that province.

6. (1) In these Rules,

"electoral quotient" means, in respect of a province, the quotient obtained by dividing its population, determined according to the results of the then most recent decennial census, by the number of members to be assigned to it under any of Rules 1 to 5(3) in the readjustment following the completion of that census;

"intermediate province" means a province (other than Quebec) having a population greater than its population determined according to the results of the penultimate decennial census but not more than two and a half million and not less than one and a half million;

"large province" means a province (other than Quebec) having a population greater than two and a half million;

"penultimate decennial census" means the decennial census that preceded the then most recent decennial census;

"population" means, except where otherwise specified, the population determined according to the results of the then most recent decennial census;

"small province" means a province (other than Quebec) having a population greater than its population determined according to the results of the penultimate decennial census and less than one and a half million.

(2) For the purposes of these Rules,

(*a*) if any fraction less than one remains upon completion of the final calculation that produces the number of members to be assigned to a province, that number of members shall equal the number so produced disregarding the fraction;

(*b*) if more than one readjustment follows the completion of a decennial census, the most recent of those readjustments shall, upon taking effect, be deemed to be the only readjustment following the completion of that census;

(*c*) a readjustment shall not take effect until the termination of the then existing Parliament."

3. This part may be cited as the *British North America Act (No. 2), 1974*, and the *British North America Acts, 1867 to 1974* and this Part may be cited together as the *British North America Acts, 1867 to 1974-75*.

Part II: Electoral Boundaries Readjustment

4. Upon the commencement of this Act, sections 20 to 27 of the *Electoral Boundaries Readjustment Act* cease to be suspended and sections 5 to 7 of the *Electoral Boundaries Readjustment Suspension Act* are repealed.

5. (1) Upon the commencement of this Act, the *Electoral Boundaries Readjustment Act* shall be applied as if subsection 51(1) of the *British North America Act, 1867*, as amended by Part I of this Act, had been in force immediately following the decennial census of Canada taken in the year 1971, and electoral boundaries commissions shall be established and carry out their duties under the *Electoral Boundaries Readjustment Act* in all respects as though nothing had been done under that Act and no time had elapsed following the decennial census of Canada taken in the year 1971.

(2) Notwithstanding subsection (1), the certified return of the Chief Statistician of Canada referred to in section 11 of the *Electoral Boundaries Readjustment Act* and sent pursuant to that Act to the Secretary of State for Canada and the Representation Commissioner following the decennial census of Canada taken in the year 1971 shall be deemed to have been sent to, and to have been received on the day that this Act comes into force by, the Secretary of State of Canada and the Representation Commissioner for the purposes of applying that Act in accordance with subsection (1) of this section.

6. The number of members of the House of Commons and the representation of the provinces therein on the thirtieth day of December, 1974, remain unchanged until readjusted pursuant to subsection 51(1) of the *British North America Acts, 1867 to 1974*, as amended by the *British North America Act (No. 2), 1974*.

7. The President of the Privy Council shall,

(*a*) on the day not later than the twentieth sitting day of the House of Commons after the 30th day of June, 1979, if there is then an existing Parliament, or

Increase in Seats in House of Commons by Province, 1974-79

	1974	1975-79*
Ontario	88	95
Quebec	74	75
British Columbia	23	28
Alberta	19	21
Saskatchewan	13	14
Manitoba	13	14
Nova Scotia	11	11
New Brunswick	10	10
Newfoundland	7	7
Prince Edward Island	4	4
Northwest Territories	1	2**
Yukon	1	1
Total	264	282

* As determined by the application of the *Representation Act, 1974*, for which see the immediately preceding item.
** Increased by the *Northwest Territories Representation Act*, which is the short title of *An Act to increase the representation of the Northwest Territories in the House of Commons and to establish a commission to readjust the electoral boundaries of the Northwest Territories*, 23-23 Eliz. II, C.28, 1975.

(*b*) if there is not then an existing Parliament, on a day not later than the twenty-fifth sitting day of the House of Commons after Parliament has been summoned,
propose to the House of Commons that an order be made and referred to the appropriate committee of the House of Commons for the review by the committee of the Rules provided by subsection 51(1) of the *British North America Acts, 1867 to 1974*, as amended by the *British North America Act (No. 2), 1974*, and for the recommendations of such committee with respect to any amendments, alterations or modifications thereto that appear to the committee then to be necessary or desirable, and upon such order being referred to it the committee shall consider the matter of the order and report to the House its recommendations with respect thereto.

8. This Act shall come into force on the 31st day of December, 1974.

FEDERAL ELECTION EXPENSES ACT
AIDS PARTIES AND CAMPAIGN FINANCING

Paul Fox

After many years of discussion, Parliament has passed legislation which will provide financial assistance to political parties and candidates as well as putting limits on spending. The Election Expenses Act, which came into force on August 1, 1974 after the federal election of July 8, covers a number of aspects of financing:
— it creates a federal income tax credit system for individuals donating to parties or candidates;
— it requires the registration of political parties which wish to receive benefits under the Act;
— it limits the expenditures of parties and candidates in elections and defines election expenses;
— it requires disclosure of the names of donors of more than $100 to registered parties and candidates;
— it provides stiff penalties for infractions of the Act;
— it reimburses candidates for a portion of their campaign costs.

Tax Credits

The Income Tax Act will now permit a taxpayer to deduct from his federal income tax payable a portion of a political contribution that an individual makes to a registered political party or to a candidate. Contributions may be made annually to a political party or to a party or a candidate during an election. To be eligible for a tax credit, the contribution must be made only to a registered agent of a party or to an official agent of a candidate.

A tax credit is more than merely a deduction from taxable income since the credit is a direct reduction of the federal income tax payable in any given year on an individual's tax form. For instance, if a person must pay $100 in federal income tax in a certain year but has made a donation of $100 to a registered party or candidate, he would receive a tax credit of $75 and therefore have to pay only $25 in federal tax. Thus, by contributing to a party or candidate, the citizen "saves" paying a certain amount to the treasury. The anticipation is that this arrangement will broaden the basis of financing of the democratic process without costing the citizen very much.

The amount of the tax credit varies with the amount of the contribution up to a maximum credit of $500 in any one taxation year. Thus the tax credit will be:
— 75 per cent of a contribution up to $100;
— $75 plus 50 percent of a contribution of more than $100 but not more than $550;
— for donations of more than $550, the lesser of $300 plus 33$\frac{1}{3}$

percent of the amount by which the donation exceeds $550 or $500 for a contribution of $1150.

The following table gives a few examples:

Total Contributions	Tax Credit	Actual Cost to Contributor
$ 10	$ 7.50	$ 2.50
25	18.75	6.25
50	37.50	12.50
100	75.00	25.00
200	125.00	75.00
500	275.00	225.00
700	350.00	350.00
1000	450.00	550.00
1150	500.00	650.00
	(maximum)	

A taxpayer may contribute, of course, any amount he or she wishes to a party or parties or a candidate or candidates, but the maximum tax credit allowed in any one year for all donations is $500. Receipts for tax credit purposes can be issued only by a registered agent of a party or during an election also by an official agent of a candidate.

Donations may take the form of money or the provision of goods and services. The Canada Elections Act now requires political parties and candidates to list the "commercial value" of goods and services (other than volunteer labour) donated or provided as election expenses. The Act also defines "commercial value".

Registered Political Parties

A "registered political party" is defined in the Canada Elections Act as a political party which was either represented in the House of Commons on the day before the dissolution of Parliament immediately preceding the election, or 30 days before polling day had officially nominated candidates in at least 50 electoral districts in Canada.

The following political parties met these requirements at the election in July, 1974, and were qualified as registered political parties as of July 31, 1974:

Communist Party of Canada
Liberal Party of Canada
Marxist-Leninist Party of Canada
New Democratic Party
Progressive Conservative Party of Canada
The Social Credit Party of Canada.

Limitation of Election Expenses

The Election Expenses Act limits the amounts of money which political parties and candidates can spend in a federal election.

A party may not spend more than 30 cents for each elector registered on the preliminary voting lists in every constituency in which that party has an official candidate. Thus, if registered party A had 80 candidates running and each of the electoral districts of these candidates had 35,000 names on the preliminary voters' lists, the total amount that party A could spend would be $840,000 (i.e. 30 cents x 35,000 x 80).

A candidate also is limited in his election expenses. He or she may not spend more than the sum of $1 for each of the first 15,000 voters on the preliminary voting list, 50 cents for each of the next 10,000 voters, and 25 cents for each voter exceeding 25,000. Here are a few examples for constituencies with varying numbers of voters:

Constituency	A	B	C	D	E
No. of voters	15,000	25,000	50,000	60,000	75,000
Spending limit	$15,000	$20,000	$26,250	$28,750	$32,500

Definition of Election Expenses

Election expenses are strictly defined in the new Act. They include the "commercial value" of goods and services donated, except for volunteer labour. They also include the cost of media, time and space, personal labour, refreshments, etc. Any goods that are donated and have a commercial value (i.e. the equivalent purchase price) over $100 must be listed as election expenses.

Only registered parties, candidates and persons 'acting on their behalf can incur election expenses.

Disclosure

All registered political parties are required to file returns giving their election expenses and their annual receipts and expenses. Candidates must file returns covering the receipts and expenses of their election campaigns. Money that is given to candidates by their political party must be listed by the candidate as a contribution.

All contributions of more than $100 to registered parties and to candidates must be disclosed. The name of the individual or corporate donor must be given. No contributor can donate through a third party.

Each registered party and candidate must appoint an auditor who is required to report the receipts and expenses. All statements of contributions and expenditures by parties and candidates must be filed with the Chief Electoral Officer and become available for public inspection.

Stiff penalties are provided for an offence against the new Act. The maximum penalty for non-compliance is a fine of up to $25,000 and the possibility of a prison term for the official agent. A party can also be fined a maximum of $25,000.

Reimbursement of Candidates

If a candidate receives at least 15 percent of the valid votes cast in his or

her electoral district and has provided all the information required by the Act, he or she is entitled to a reimbursement from the Receiver General of Canada of an amount consisting of the following:
— a return of the $200 deposit required from a candidate;
— the cost of postage of a first class mailing to every voter on the preliminary voters' list;
— 8 cents for each of the first 25,000 voters on the preliminary list;
— 6 cents for each voter thereafter;
— in certain large ridings the actual value of a candidate's travelling expenses to a maximum of $3,000.

[For accounts of the first reports filed under the new Act, which give parties' receipts, expenditures, and names of donors for the year 1975, see three articles by Geoffrey Stevens in *The Globe and Mail*, January 10, February 10, and February 11, 1976.]

ONTARIO'S NEW LAW REVEALS DONORS AND EXPENDITURES*

Daniel Stoffman

The Progressive Conservative Party outspent the two opposition parties in all but three of the 29 ridings in Metro Toronto, according to financial statements filed by candidates in last September's provincial election.

But, proving that money doesn't always win, the Tories won only 12 of the 29 Metro seats.

The New Democratic Party, which led in Metro by winning 14 seats, outspent its opponents only in one riding, Yorkview, which was won by veteran MPP Fred Young.

The biggest spender among Metro candidates was a loser—Conservative Frank Vasilkioti who spent $53,768 trying to unseat Margaret Campbell of the Liberals in St. George. Campbell spent $21,705 while defeating Vasilkioti by 11,042 votes to 8,577.

An analysis of 38 ridings—the 29 in Metro and nine others adjacent to Metro—shows that the biggest spender won in 17 of them.

Canadidates' spending was made public for the first time in Ontario election history as part of the Election Finances Reform Act, passed last year before the Sept. 18 election in which the Conservatives lost their majority.

Name Donors

The act requires that candidates reveal how much they raised and spent and identify all donors who gave them more than $100. Donations from a single source are limited to $500 but there is no limit on the total amount a candidate may spend. . . .

* From *The Toronto Star*, March 20, 1976. By permission.

In addition to the candidates, the central party offices are also required to file statements.

The Conservatives spent $2.25 million in the campaign while the Liberals spent $864,000 and the New Democrats $469,000. These expenditures are in addition to the bills run up by the individual candidates and riding associations.

A maximum of $4,000 can be given to a party. Among those who gave that much to the Tories were Abbey Glen Property Corp., Acres Consulting Services Ltd., Addison on Bay Ltd., Algoma Steel Corp., Aluminum Co. of Canada Ltd., Ashland Oil Canada Ltd., Brascan Ltd., Bramalea Consolidated Developments, Bank of Montreal, Cadillac Fairview Corp., Canada Packers Ltd., Chrysler Canada Ltd., Comstock International Ltd., Campeau Corp., Denison Mines Ltd., Jannock Corp. Ltd., Merrill Lynch Royal Securities, Nesbitt Thompson and Co. Ltd., Noranda Mines Ltd., Ontario Chiropractic Association, Ontario Jockey Club, Pitts Engineering Construction, Steinbergs Ltd., Superior Sand and Gravel Ltd., and Union Gas Ltd.

Biggest donors listed by the NDP were the United Steelworkers of America, Textile Workers of America, United Auto Workers, Canadian Paper Workers. The Canadian head office of each union gave $2,000.

$2,000 Donors

The Liberals listed many $2,000 donors, including some of the same firms which gave large donations to the Tories. Top Liberal donors included Abbey Glen Property Corp., Abitibi Paper Co. Ltd., Aluminum Co. of Canada Ltd., A. E. Ames & Co. Ltd., Ashland Oil Canada Ltd., Brascan Ltd., Campeau Corp., Cadillac Fairview Corp. Ltd., Canada Packers Ltd., Chrysler Canada Ltd., Continental Can Co. of Canada Ltd., Dome Mines Ltd., Denison Mines Ltd., Domtar Ltd., T. Eaton Co. Ltd., Hawker Siddeley Canada Ltd., Hudson's Bay Co., International Nickel Co. of Canada Ltd., Jannock Corp. Ltd., A. E. LePage Ltd., Massey Ferguson Ltd., Mercantile Bank, Molson Cos., Noranda Mines Ltd., Olympia and York Ltd., Ontario Jockey Club, Pigott Construction Ltd., James Richardson and Sons Ltd., and Union Carbide Canada Ltd.

Under the Election Finances Act, a single donor can give $2,000 to a party during a given year and, in addition, $2,000 during a campaign period.

Although the Liberals listed their largest donations as $2,000, campaign chairman Bob Wright said last night that many of the same firms which gave a total of $4,000 to the Tories did the same for the Liberals. The $2,000 applying to the year as a whole was not listed in the Liberal submission, he said.

Two of the most expensive campaigns in Metro, on the basis of money spent compared to votes received, were those of defeated Tories Elio Madonia in Bellwoods and Joseph Marrese in Oakwood.

Finished Last

Marrese spent $36,858 and finished last with only 4,637 votes, an expenditure of $7.94 per vote.

Madonia spent $31,717 and also finished last, with only 3,234 votes, an expenditure of $9.80 per vote.

A case of massive outspending of opponents was that of Margaret Scrivener, who spent more than five times as much as each of her two major opponents. She defeated New Democrat Jim Lemon by 10,536 votes to 8,043.

Biggest spender among cabinet ministers was Attorney-General Roy McMurtry, whose Eglinton campaign cost $51,607. After Vasilkioti's, it was the second costliest campaign in Metro.

[Ontario's Election Finances Reform Act also established an election commission which uses public funds to reimburse candidates for campaign expenses. The subsidy provides 16 cents for each of the first 25,000 voters in each riding and 14 cents for each of the rest. A candidate has to receive at least 15 percent of the vote to be eligible for the subsidy.]

A "REALIST" TELLS HOW TO PACKAGE A POLITICIAN*

Gerald Utting

Some might call him refreshing in an age of ideology, where even elections to zoological society boards can be couched in the terms of class warfare. Others might call him an exponent of the Politics of Cynicism.

But Hal Evry, Los Angeles political campaign consultant, calls himself a realist. He believes would-be politicians should be aware that people are motivated only by three things: self-preservation, sex and the desire to make money. They neglect this basic fact to their peril, he told a group of politicians and public relations men at a recent seminar in Toronto. The audience paid $100 a head to hear him.

Evry has run campaigns for hundreds of aspirants to office in the United States, from constable in Cucamonga to governor in New Mexico. He's given political advice to such people as George Wallace. . . .

Evry told them what every politician and would-be politician doesn't want to hear—that his looks are more important than his opinions in winning the public, that it's usually better to be silent than silver-tongued, to avoid controversy because it's better to win than to be right.

Evry, who claims he can get almost anyone elected to office if his advice is followed, said eight out of 10 people don't like strangers they meet, including candidates, and insists nobody listens to speeches except a tiny minority of politically oriented people.

* From *The Toronto Star*, July 28, 1975. By permission.

Different Art

Essentially, Evry's message is that, while being an elected politician may be a skilled art for responsible and serious men and women, getting elected is quite a different art; that where an office-holder may need courage and integrity, a candidate needs to be recognized and liked.

Recognition and being liked, in Evry's book, depend not on the inner strengths of a man but on his marketability. A candidate is not too different to a can of shoe polish or a box of breakfast cereal in this light—he's something to be packaged and sold to the public by a professional ad-man who takes the trouble to do as much market research about how people vote as he would about people's preferences in the snap, crackle, pop market.

Since 1958, Evry's organization in Los Angeles has handled the campaigns of 350 candidates, half of them running for Congress. The rest have been candidates for state office, including would-be governors and county executives.

Some of the candidates he has handled: Sam Yorty, rambunctious ex-mayor of Los Angeles, a Republican; George Wallace, Democrat governor of Alabama and sometime hopeful for the U.S. presidency; Winthrop Rockefeller, former governor of Arkansas; Governor David Hall of Oklahoma, a Democrat; Senator Alan Cranston of California, a Democrat; and Senator Ted Stevens of Alaska, Republican.

"About 92 or 93 percent of our candidates have won," Evry told The Star. "The 7 or 8 percent who lost, in my estimation, did so because they didn't follow our advice; they felt they wouldn't stoop to hucksterism, or something like that, and they just wasted their money."

Evry's firm charges a basic fee of $5,000 a month for running a campaign for the U.S. Senate or a state governorship candidate, and $2,500 to $3,000 a month for a House of Representatives or local race. "Whatever else it's going to cost the candidate depends on how many voters he has to reach," said Evry. . . .

IQ Minimum

"I use two criteria: Does he have enough money to win or lose? And is he or she intelligent enough to do the work when elected? A person who has made enough money to be able to afford to run has passed one sort of test in society. And I insist that the candidate must take an IQ test, and prove he's got an IQ of at least 120, before I'll take him on."

Before asking what right someone has to run, he said, shouldn't concerned people be asking rather: Who should be allowed to vote?

"I don't think anyone should be allowed to vote unless they know what it is all about," he said. "But in my country, as in Canada, there are no standards for running and no standards for voting, not even literacy.

"We set standards for barbers and butchers in California, but not for voters and politicians. That doesn't seem right. I have my own standards in accepting clients, which is more than society does."

Every would-be politician, said Evry, claims he wants to serve his country or better his community. "You want to see some of the crazy people who say that to me." . . .

The first thing an aspiring politician must realize, Evry said, is that the incumbent he wants to unseat has everything going for him. "In the United States, 95 percent of incumbents are re-elected. Why? Recognition is with them, and the public relates recognition or notoriety with superiority. The public believes someone who has already been elected can do the job.

"What you have to do to overcome this is to act as if you were the incumbent. Make people think you are the incumbent rather than the guy himself.

"Get yourself a platform long before the election. Form your own groups with names that sound awfully official. Use words like Parliament, Mayor, Council . . . Form the Mayor's Purity Committee, say, with yourself as president. Make press statements. If the media don't report your meetings, take advertisements and report them yourself.

"All you need is a group of three or four people. Look at how Nelson Rockefeller formed his very own Commission on National Objectives before he got the vice-presidency. Everyone took it seriously."

Next, said Evry, you've got to find out what the potential voters are worrying about. "I send out researchers who ask, 'What's bugging you?' " The findings, he said, are often very different from the concerns that dominate the headlines and TV newscasts.

The candidate must also realize, Evry said, that most people don't give a hoot about elections. "In municipal elections about 70 percent don't even vote. The man who wins does it with about 15 percent of the potential voters." The important thing, he said, is to find out who votes and make sure they know your name and like your image.

The best way to do this, said Evry, is by putting most of your advertising into TV.

He said most campaign literature is simply thrown in the garbage, so if the candidate wants to pass brochures out they should be as cheap as possible.

Campaigning should be fun, "so if knocking on doors is your idea of fun, by all means do it, but it won't get any votes." . . .

After the candidate has established a platform, said Evry, he should keep his mouth shut during the actual campaign, relying instead on TV plugs, billboards ("high recognition factor"), sniping (the U.S. term for lawn signs) and gimmicks that enhance recognition but don't make enemies.

One of his best-known gimmicks was the one he used in the campaign of the late Ivy Baker Priest, a former U.S. federal treasurer, for the office of state treasurer in California. He got her to try to throw a silver dollar across the Sacramento River on George Washington's birthday, in imitation of Washington's feat in throwing a coin across the Rappahannock River. The silver dollar fell short into the river, and a carefully rehearsed Mrs. Priest told reporters: "That just goes to show a dollar doesn't go as far today as it used to." The picture was carried by newspapers all over California and right across the U.S.

Evry calls this "news that I make up—free advertising (except for my fee)—and it doesn't take much of the candidate's time."

The most effective way to get a vote, said Evry, is a personal letter from a respected friend urging the voter to back the candidate. The least effective is a bumper-sticker ("Your friends hate you for asking them to use stickers.").

He said candidates should try to associate themselves with respected symbols—pictures of Congress (or Parliament) on literature and letters, and in the U.S. pictures of George Washington, Thomas Jefferson and other historic figures.

His own firm's letterhead makes use of the ideas—it has a big color picture of the Capitol in Washington spread across it, even though the office address is in Los Angeles.

He said before candidates launch into a series of speeches and controversies, they should remember that Brazilian voters once elected a hippo to office and that Panamanians even voted for a can of shoe polish.

Say Nothing

Don't be drawn into issues promoted by the media, he said. "No newspaper can help you, but they can hurt you. Don't talk to reporters. Better not to say anything than be quoted as saying something you really didn't mean.

"Avoid issues. You're bound to alienate someone. There's no law saying you have to tell a reporter anything and no law saying you have to tell the voter anything."

Campaign literature should consist mainly of direct mail, Evry said. The latest idea is to totally avoid metered mail. "Use as many stamps as possible on a letter—don't use one where you could use 10, it looks more sincere and personal." Machine-written handwriting is good, he said, and a candidate can get supporters to give him lists of names for "Dear Friend" postcards that appear to have been written by a friend but are in fact manufactured by the campaign agency.

One of Evry's successful campaigns involved flooding a small district with 3 million signs saying just, "Three cheers for Milligan," an unknown who said nothing, made no speeches but romped into office over his more tasteful opponents. . . .

Evry thinks Canadian campaign techniques in general are so bad "it embarrasses me."

One Canadian who takes Hal Evry seriously is Ralph Bruce, a chiropractor turned campaign consultant who lives in Val d'Or, Quebec. He said that he was worried about crime in that mining community and decided to run for the city council. "I called Hall in Los Angeles and asked his advice. I followed it, and became the first English Canadian alderman elected in many years—and with a record majority." . . .

Bruce said the fee he aims at for a provincial riding is $4,000 and thinks a seat can be won for a total expenditure of $20,000 to $25,000. The candidate should start working on getting his image before the public a year in advance of the election, said Bruce, who was trained by Evry's organization in California. . . .

Can Canadians be sold politicians the way they are sold soap?

Same Here

Evry said: "People universally have the same interests. Canadians may think they are different to Californians, but really it's only the climate that's different.

"You can say the political system is different, that parties are different, but parties are people. There's no such thing as a party machine. The voters are people, and independent people.

"The swinging vote decides the election and the majority of people aren't going to be influenced by what the media think are the issues, they don't even bother to read the political reporting. In the last presidential election in the United States, more people watched Sandford and Son on TV than the election results. . . .

SELLING THE LEADERS*

Val Sears

Jerry Goodis was having a real fine day.

The man who gave you, adwise, Hush Puppies, Speedy Muffler King and Hiram Walker had a new client: the Prime Minister of Canada.

And here he was, down in Kensington Market with cameraman Dick Leiterman running hundreds of feet of great film through Dick's Arriflex as Pierre Elliott Trudeau went among The Ethnics.

"And you, sir," asked Jerry of a Portuguese gentleman after Trudeau had passed, "what do you think of the Prime Minister?"

"Wonderful man," said the Portuguese gentleman as Dick's camera whirred. "The Liberals allowed me into this country. I have made good here. And that Mr. Trudeau is a strong leader. This country needs a strong leader . . . just like they have in Russia."

Zap. Cut. Hold, it, Dick.

'Cut the Last Bit'

"Now," said Jerry Goodis, the other day, "we might—I'm not saying we will—but we just might cut out that last bit."

This is selling-of-a-prime-minister time. And the boys from the ad agencies are very sensitive about the handling of this new and exciting product—the 1974 federal election campaign.

There's Goodis, from Goodis Goldberg Soren Ltd.; Norm Atkins, from Camp Associates Advertising Ltd. for the Progressive Conservatives; and

* From *The Toronto Star*, May 31, 1974. By permission.

Manny Dunsky, whose Montreal-based agency turns up everywhere the New Democratic Party forms a government.

They are, naturally, twitchy about discussing details of their work. Atkins obviously has read *The Selling of The President*, a devastating book on the huckstering of President Richard Nixon, and now won't even talk to his shoeshine boy. Dunsky's office shifts inquiries to NDP party publicists in Ottawa. Jerry Grafstein, a Liberal lawyer who heads a témporary consortium of ad agencies, is somewhat more forthcoming.

He lets you know this much: "I like a juicy campaign—and this one's going to be juicy."

Sellers are There

But the salesmen are there all right. And you'd better believe what you see on the screen—on CBC free-time broadcasts and private network commercials—represent hundreds of hours of hard, sweaty image making.

There's big money as well. In the 1972 campaign, the Conservatives were estimated to have spent $960,000 on national broadcasting alone: the Liberals, $557,000 and the New Democrats, $163,000. . . .

Blue-ribbon Clients

But for the ad agencies, the Big Apple is still television, particularly the four hours of CBC free time that has been allotted to all four parties on the basis of Commons standings.

Jerry Goodis, whose book *Have I Ever Lied to You?*, and a stable of blue-ribbon clients, has made him the best known among the current political admen, is a dedicated Liberal.

He doesn't wince—as some of the others do—at the use of the word "selling" applied to politicians.

"Why is it immoral to sell a politician?" he wonders. "Everybody sells something. Sure you try to emphasize the candidates' strong points. Why not? When you're chasing a girl you don't tell her you've got bad breath." This is his first campaign.

"Mr. Trudeau is easy to film. In this campaign he's angry and excited. He's a man who's witty, charming, warm, full of humanity, and we're going to try and get that across on television." . . .

All three parties are leaning heavily in this campaign on a simulated news-documentary technique by using man-on-the-street interviews and campaign scenes carefully edited to create the best impression of the candidate.

John Griffin, a veteran news documentary cameraman who has filmed for all three parties and is currently working on the NDP campaign, says this technique makes him uneasy.

"People watching TV really don't distinguish between news and partisan political broadcasts done this way," he says. "Film lies all the time. We don't shoot empty chairs in a meeting hall, for instance. And you can manipulate film to do anything you want with it.

"Sometimes, though, I think the parties take people for fools. Do they really think Stanfield is so well liked, so pure? Everybody always claps for him, the halls are always full of wildly cheering people, the people interviewed on the street think he's great.

"We may have to film 100 people to get half a dozen who say what the party would like them to say." . . .

At a meeting of party communications chiefs from all provinces at the Hyatt Regency Hotel last week, there was almost solid agreement on one thing: Trudeau was the selling point.

Dave Harrison, a MacLaren's vice-president working for Red Leaf, said the provincial representatives wanted national party programming featuring Trudeau.

"When we aked them what they wanted to emphasize in local programming they said . . . more Trudeau," Harrison smiled.

The Conservatives have produced a detailed campaign manual to be distributed to all of their candidates under the title, Winning Ways. It contains everything a candidate may have wanted to know about campaigns but might be afraid to ask.

No Bare Legs

Such as: On television—"Get black or dark knee length socks. A show of bare leg on men is distasteful to viewers. Directors usually advise people who are a little chubby or tending to baldness to go light on sideburns."

On outdoor advertising: "It will make your campaign look big and powerful."

The Liberals prefer a much briefer graphics book and a series of educational sessions in which candidates and their managers are briefed on campaign techniques.

Certainly, after the debacle of the last campaign on the theme, The Land is Strong, the Liberals are exercising a great deal more political control over the admen.

Grafstein, a veteran Liberal backroom boy, now stands between the ad agency consortium and the party itself.

"There'll be no advertising man saying 'we can get this past those big dumb politicians this time,'" he says, "because one of the 'dumb' politicians is going to be right in the room.

John Thompson, a transportation executive who is the Conservatives' chief of operations (tour, advertising, transport) hopes to keep Conservative campaign plans secret—so the Liberals won't steal them.

"They're copying almost everything we did in the last campaign," Thompson says disgustedly, "but we're still ahead of them."

The New Democrats are running a co-ordinated national selling campaign except for Saskatchewan, where the provincial party has rejected Dunsky for its own agency, J. A. C. Struthers Associates.

"When you've elected as many NDP seats as we have," the Saskatchewan party told national headquarters, "then you can tell us how to run a campaign." . . .

ELECTING A CANADIAN GOVERNMENT*

One of the most important powers exercised by the prime minister is the right to ask that the Governor General dissolve Parliament and give orders that writs of election be issued. . . .

In this manner the machinery for conducting a general election in Canada is put in motion. On instructions from the Governor in Council (in other words, the cabinet) the Chief Electoral Officer, an independent official chosen by the House of Commons, issues the writs of election to the returning officer in each constituency or riding. These officers direct the preparation of voters' lists, appoint deputy returning officers for each polling subdivision in the constituency, receive nominations of candidates and provide for the printing of ballots.

The voters' lists are compiled by enumeration of the electors, which begins 49 days before the election. Enumerators [in twos], representing the two opposing political interests that received the highest numbers of votes in the constituency in the preceding election, make a door-to-door list of urban voters. (Only one enumerator is required in rural ridings.) Preliminary lists of electors are posted in public places, such as telephone poles, so that any voter may protest the inclusion or omission of any name. The official list of eligible urban voters must be compiled at least 42 days before the election date. Final revision of voters' lists must be completed 12 days before the election. . . .

The returning officer in every constituency designates the locations of the polling stations. In a recent election, the number of polling stations within each riding ranged from 27 to 458, and the number of voters who cast their ballots in each station was between 2 and 350. Each deputy returning officer and his poll clerk supervise the conduct of the polling on election day, under the scrutiny of two agents for each candidate. The Canada Elections Act requires a voter to fold the ballot paper as directed so that the initials on the back and the printed serial number on the back of the counterfoil can be seen without unfolding it, and hand it to the deputy returning officer, who ascertains, without unfolding it, that it is the same ballot paper as that delivered to the elector. If it is the same, the officer is required in full view of the elector and others present to remove and destroy the counterfoil and himself deposit the ballot in the box. After the poll is closed, the ballots are counted by the deputy returning officer in the presence of the poll clerk and party scrutineers, and the ballots, locked in the ballot box, are forwarded to the returning officer. Although the results of the election are usually made public on election night, the official addition of votes for all of the polling divisions in the constituency is made by the returning officer who subsequently issues a declaration of election in favour of the candidate who obtained a plurality; that is, more votes than any other candidate. (In case of a tie, the returning officer, who is not otherwise permitted to vote, may cast the deciding ballot.) This candidate will become the parliamentary representative for the constituency.

---

* Reprinted originally from the Bank of Montreal *Business Review*, May 29, 1962. By permission. Revised by the editor in March, 1976.

Canadian General Elections 1867-1974
Party Standings in House of Commons

Date of Election	Party Standing							Total
	Cons.	Lib.	Prog.	C.C.F.-N.D.P.	S.C.	S.C.R.	Other	Seats
August 7-September 20, 1867	101	80						181
July 20-September 3, 1872	103	97						200
January 22, 1874	73	133						206
September 17, 1878	142	64						206
June 20, 1882	139	71					1	211
February 22, 1887	126	89						215
March 5, 1891	121	94						215
June 23, 1896	88	118					7	213
November 7, 1900	80	133						213
November 3, 1904	75	138					1	214
October 26, 1908	85	135					1	221
September 21, 1911	134	87						221
December 17, 1917	153*	82						235
December 6, 1921	50	116	64				5	235
October 29, 1925	116	99	24				6	245
September 14, 1926	91	128	20				6	245
July 28, 1930	137	91	12				5	245
October 14, 1935	40	173		7	17		8	245
March 26, 1940	40	181		8	10		6	245
June 11, 1945	67	125		28	13		12	245
June 27, 1949	41	193		13	10		5	262
August 10, 1953	51	171		23	15		5	265
June 10, 1957	112	105		25	19		4	265
March 31, 1958	208	49		8				265
June 18, 1962 †	116	100		19	30			265
April 8, 1963	95	129		17	24			265
November 8, 1965	97	131		21	5	9	2	265
June 25, 1968	72	155		22		14	1	264
October 30, 1972	107	109		31	15		2	264
July 8, 1974	95	141		16	11		1	264

* Unionist.

† Figures include results of service vote and deferred election in Stormont held July 16, 1962. C.C.F. became N.D.P. July 31, 1961.

In federal elections in Canada the ballot bears in alphabetical order the names of the candidates in the constituency and their party affiliation if the party has met the requirements as a registered party. (A candidate may list also his address or occupation.) To qualify to be on a ballot, a party must register in advance with the Chief Electoral Officer and have members in the previous House of Commons or run at least 50 candidates in the current election.

When a person wishes to become a candidate for election to the House of Commons, he must take certain formal steps in order to have his name appear on the ballot. To assure his candidacy any elector (that is, a person 18 years of age or over who is a Canadian citizen and is not disqualified) must file nomination papers endorsed by 25 other electors and make a deposit of $200 with the returning officer for the constituency within the time prescribed in the Elections Act. It is possible for a candidate to seek

Results of Federal General Elections in 1974 and 1972

Seats Won by Parties by Province in 1974 (1972 results in brackets)[1]

Prov.	Lib.	P.C.	N.D.P.	S.C.	Ind.	Totals
Nfld.	4 (3)	3 (4)				7 (7)
P.E.I.	1 (1)	3 (3)				4 (4)
N.S.	2 (1)	8 (10)	1			11 (11)
N.B.	6 (5)	3 (5)			1	10 (10)
Que.	60 (56)	3 (2)		11 (15)	(1)	74 (74)
Ont.	55 (36)	25 (40)	8 (11)		(1)	88 (88)
Man.	2 (2)	9 (8)	2 (3)			13 (13)
Sask.	3 (1)	8 (7)	2 (5)			13 (13)
Alta.		19 (19)				19 (19)
B.C.	8 (4)	13 (8)	2 (11)			23 (23)
Yuk.		1 (1)				1 (1)
N.W.T.			1 (1)			1 (1)
Totals	141 (109)	95 (107)	16 (31)	11 (15)	1 (2)	264 (264)

Discrepancies Between Percentages of Seats Gained and Percentages of Valid Votes Won by Parties Nationally in 1974 (1972 Results in Brackets)

	Lib.	P.C.	N.D.P.	S.C.	Ind.
Seats[2]	53.4 (41.2)	35.9 (40.5)	6.0 (11.7)	4.1 (5.6)	0.3 (0.7)
Valid Votes[3]	43.1 (38.4)	35.4 (34.9)	15.4 (17.7)	5.0 (7.6)	0.4 (0.5)

[1] From *Report of the Chief Electoral Officer, 1974* and *Report of the Cheif Electoral Officer, 1972*.
[2] Calculated from data given in *ibid*.
[3] From *ibid*. Percentages do not total 100 since votes for other parties have been omitted.

election in a constituency in which he does not reside. The deposit of each candidate is refunded if he polls at least half the number of votes of the winning candidate; if less, the deposit is forfeited to the Crown. In a recent election such forfeitures totalled some $75,000.

•   •   •

The campaign which follows the announcement that an election will be held usually lasts for a month to six weeks. The facilities of air transport, television, and radio have done little to reduce the pressure on the contestants; on the contrary, they are subjected to increased demands for their presence. The leading members of the various parties are presented with schedules well nigh impossible to meet as they cross and re-cross the country, giving speeches, meeting thousands of people, making countless appearances on platforms and before the press, consulting with their campaign managers and advisers, and performing multitudinous other duties. All electioneering must end two days before election day.

In 1974 there were 13,620,353 Canadians registered as eligible voters. The turnout in the election was about 71 percent nationally, varying from a high of 80 percent in Prince Edward Island to a low of 57 percent in

Newfoundland. Electing one M.P. from each of 264 ridings, the voters were also indirectly choosing the prime minister and cabinet.

The leader of the party which has the largest number of its candidates elected to the House is traditionally invited by the Governor General to take office as prime minister and to form a government. Usually the party which forms the government has a majority of seats in the Commons. But in fact, as may be seen from the following table, there have been seven occasions, all in the last 55 years, in 1921, 1925, 1957, 1962, 1963, 1965, and 1972 when the party winning the largest number of seats still had less than half the total number in the House and therefore functioned as a minority government.

General elections must be held in Canada at least once in five years. During the 1974 election the Chief Electoral Officer's requirements for staff and supplies cost $29,132,896, compared with $20,435,278 in 1972. This was entirely apart from the costs incurred by the parties and candidates, which one authority has estimated to be $35 million in 1974. In that election Liberal national headquarters alone spent $5.5 million, the Conservative office $4.4 million, and the NDP $353,852. Declared Liberal candidates' expenditures amounted to an additional $4.9 million.

The most expensive campaign reported by a candidate was conducted by Stephen Roman, Conservative aspirant in York North. He spent $108,759—and lost.

THE PROS AND CONS OF P.R. FOR CANADA*

Paul Fox

Most voters would probably be quite shocked if they were told that they were seldom ruled by a majority, that there is every chance that a Canadian government will not likely represent a majority of the Canadian people, and that more people will probably vote against a government than for it.

Yet that has been the case in 15 out of the last 17 federal elections. Only twice since 1921 has the winning party got more than 50 percent of the popular vote (the Liberals won 51.5 percent in 1940 and Mr. Diefenbaker about 53.6 percent in 1958).

How do minority wins occur? The winner may get more votes than any of his several opponents, but he may not get more than 50 percent of the total. For example, in a certain Ontario riding recently the Liberal candidate received a vote of 14,035, the Progressive Conservative 11,155, the NDP 8,302, the Communist 1,413, and another candidate 307. The top man thus had 14,035 votes for him and a grand total of 21,177 against him.

When this sort of thing is repeated in constituency after constituency, a party may win an election by obtaining more seats than any other party or

---

* Reprinted originally from *The Financial Post*, August 8, 1953, with permission of the publisher. Revised in November, 1976.

all the other other parties combined and still not have had even half the citizens voting for it.

The appearance of important smaller parties, like the NDP and Social Credit, has had a lot to do with this sort of outcome. But the minor parties aren't the real cause of the weakness. The actual defect is in the election machinery. It works in such a way that the party that wins the election ordinarily gets far more seats in the House of Commons than its share of the popular vote entitles it to.

At the same time, the opposition parties usually get far fewer. In every election since 1896 the incoming government has ridden into power with more seats than its portion of the national vote gave it. Sometimes the discrepancies have been really shocking.

In 1930, when the Conservatives won, they polled 48 percent of the vote and secured 56 percent of the seats.

Five years later, after the 1935 election, the shoe was on the other foot. The Liberals won only 44.8 percent of the vote but got 70.6 percent of the seats. That left only a quarter of the desks in the Commons for all the other parties, which had got more than half of all the votes in the country. The result was that the Tories got about half as many seats as they might have expected from the vote, and the CCF got only about a third as many.

These figures also show how our election system multiplies slight shifts in voting at the polls into big landslides for the winner in terms of seats in parliament. In 1930, for example, the Conservatives increased the number of seats from 91 to 137. But there was no landslide in public opinion. The voting showed that they had won only 3.3 percentage points more of the votes.

Five years later the Liberals were swept back into power by something that looked more like an avalanche. They just about doubled the number of their seats, from 91 to 173. Almost a 100 percent increase in seats, but how much of an increase in popular vote? 80 percent? 50 percent? No, it was actually half a percentage point *less* than in 1930!

In Quebec's provincial election in 1976 in which the Parti Québécois won power, the P.Q. increased its vote by 30 percent but its number of seats increased by 1,000 percent.

Absurd results like these bring our present system of voting into question and raise the issue, what can be done to remedy such defects? The answer is: not much, so long as we retain our present election machinery which, in effect, maximizes the importance of the winning party's ballots and minimizes the value of the vote for the other parties.

Should we scrap our present system, then, and try something different? Few Canadians realize that we came close to doing this in the 'twenties.

In 1924, and again in 1925, the federal government introduced a bill to abolish our present method of election and to replace it by Alternative Voting. These bills were never passed. But about the same time, Manitoba and Alberta switched over to the new system, followed by British Columbia in 1952.

The big difference between Alternative or Preferential Voting and our present federal method is that the voter gets as many choices as there are candidates and marks his ballots in order of his preference: 1, 2, 3, 4, 5, and so on. When the polls close, the first choices for each candidate are counted, and if no one has a clear majority, the contestant with the fewest votes is dropped and the second choices on his ballots are distributed. If there's still no majority, the next lowest man is put out and his second choices on his ballots are distributed. And so it goes until someone finally gets a majority.

The great advantage to this method is, of course, that it ensures that the winner finally gets a majority and that nobody gets in by a plurality. But that's about all it does. It doesn't solve the problem of the wasted votes for the losing parties and it doesn't give the minorities any representation. It can also encourage a little skullduggery because by means of it two parties can cooperate at an election to knock out a third. (Party A and Party B pass the word along to their supporters to vote their own party first and the other party second, but under no circumstances to cast a ballot for Party C.) This is what happened in B.C. in 1952.

The truth is that no system of voting will guarantee equal weight to all votes and fair representation to minority groups so long as we stick to our present method of electing only one member of parliament from each constituency.

The big weakness of single-member districts is that only one man and one party can be chosen to represent all the voters living in that area.

This is unreal if there are many different points of view in the riding. The only sure way of giving them representation is to enlarge the constituency so that it has a number of seats and to fill these seats in proportion to the way the electorate votes.

This, in a nutshell, is the system of voting known as Proportional Representation. It had quite a vogue in Canada about 40 years ago when cities like Winnipeg, Calgary, Edmonton, and Vancouver adopted it, and it is still popular in some cities in the United States, Belgium, Holland, France, Italy, and Scandinavia. Israel and Australia have also introduced it.

There are about as many different systems of proportional representation as there are ideas about government. Somebody once counted 300 varieties, but they all work much the same way. Under the Hare System, which is probably the best known in Canada, electors go to the polls and vote for all candidates in order of preference. There will likely be a large number of candidates, at least as many as there are persons to be elected multiplied by the number of political parties, for each party will want to nominate a full slate. A minimum of five candidates is essential to make P.R. work well.

The quota necessary for election is figured out by dividing the number voting by the number of seats to be filled plus one, the one being added to reduce the quota a bit to allow for such contingencies as spoiled ballots.

The next step is to count the first choices for each candidate. Anyone who has secured the quota is declared elected. If he has more than the quota, his surplus is transferred to the second choices. If none of the hopefuls has a quota, or if too few have it, then the man with the least first choices is eliminated and the second preferences on his ballots are distributed as marked. If this is not enough, the next lowest candidate is put out and his second choices are allocated. This goes on until the required number of candidates reaches the quota.

The supporters of P.R. say it has been tried in Canada in cities like Winnipeg and that it has worked well. They argue that its greatest asset is that it eliminates the startling discrepancy between the popular vote for parties and the number of seats they win in the legislature.

Representation in parliament of political parties becomes identical to the proportion of votes they get at the polls: no more plurality wins, no more narrow-majority wins for one party in a lot of constituencies and a huge "wasted" vote for the other parties; no more over-representation of one party and under-representation of the others with a small knot of voters swinging an election one way or the other and converting a small shift in votes into a landslide in seats.

Instead, there would be an exact mathematical similarity between proportion of popular vote and proportion of seats and completely un-biased treatment for both minor and major parties. There would also be a seat for any minority that could muster a quota, and as many seats for the larger groups as would be proportional to their voting strength.

If P.R. is such a cure-all, why not adopt it in Canada?

Oddly enough, the best argument for it is also the best argument against it. The fact is that P.R. produces *too* accurate a rememblance between public opinion and representation in parliament.

If we used it across the country, it would be rare for a party to get a majority in the House of Commons, at least judging by the voting since 1921. This would change completely the basis of our system of cabinet government, which depends on the party in power having enough strength to get its legislative programme through parliament. A party without a majority would be forced to battle every proposal through the Commons, or to enter into a coalition with some other party or parties.

There are other arguments against P.R. A favourite is that it multiplies the number of parties because it gives them a better chance of securing representation in the legislature. This is not as true as most people think. In France and Belgium, for example, there are no more parties now than there were before P.R. was introduced.

But there is a danger in a country like Canada, which has strong regional feelings and interests, that P.R. might foster a large number of regional parties in the federal House. Even under the existing system, the tendency in that direction is strong. Another difficulty is that P.R. in-creases the size of constituencies in thinly populated areas to almost unreasonable dimensions. If P.R. were put into effect in Canada and no riding were to have less than five members, it might well be, for example, that the whole of Manitoba outside of Winnipeg and its suburbs would become one or two gigantic electoral districts. Candidates would have a tremendous and expensive task trying to campaign over such a huge area and the voters might never get a glimpse of their MPs.

Actually, none of the disadvantages of P.R. is really significant except the one overwhelming argument that if it were introduced all across Canada it would jeopardize our system of parliamentary government.

And that limitation is so serious that it makes it impossible to recommend the wholesale adoption of P.R. in this country.

Is there no solution then?

The remedy seems to be to mix the two systems together judiciously to get the good effects of each. This could be done quite easily. Our present system of voting could be left for large rural areas and most other places, while P.R. could be introduced in a few densely-populated urban centres. This was first suggested and debated in Parliament 50 years ago.

Vancouver, Toronto, and Montreal might be good places to start. An analysis of the election results in these three places shows a crying need for a fairer method of representation. . . .

Postscript—Another Proposal

Frustration was the word for the results of Canada's federal election on October 30, 1972. No party came out of the contest armed with enough of an edge to form a strong government. Liberals won 109 seats, Conservatives 107, New Democrats 31, Social Credit 15, and Independents 2.

Worse still, no party had sufficient seats in the different regions of Canada to give it credibility as a truly national party representing the whole of the country.

Liberal strength was concentrated in Quebec and Ontario. It was thin in the Atlantic provinces and almost non-existent in the West. The Liberals elected 56 of their 109 MPs from Quebec, 36 in Ontario, 10 in the Atlantic region, and only 7 from the 3 Prairie provinces, British Columbia, and the Yukon and Northwest Territories combined.

Conservative leanness was almost a mirror image of the Liberals. The Tories won 22 out of 32 possible seats in the East, 40 out of 88 in Ontario, and 43 out of 70 in the West. But Quebec was a disaster area. The Conservatives captured only 2 of the French-Canadian province's 74 seats.

If major paties were squeezed into grotesque shapes, the minor parties were even more distorted. The NDP's 31 seats were all drawn from only 4 provinces, chiefly from Ontario and B.C. with 11 each, 3 from Manitoba, 5 from Saskatchewan, and 1 from the Northwest Territories. Social Credit's 15 victories were all confined to Quebec. . . .

The truth is that in terms of the actual votes cast by Canadians our parties have much broader support across the country than the Oct. 30 results show.

What shrinks our parties into weird shapes is not the uneven pattern of voting across the country so much as the voting system itself.

In this election, for instance, the Conservatives won about 58 percent of the votes in Alberta but got 100 percent of the seats. The Liberals got 25 percent of the vote but no seats at all. Ditto for the NDP's 12 percent of the vote and Social Credit's 4 percent.

One way to overcome this grave weakness would be to alter the system so that each party would receive as many seats in a province as its percentage of the popular vote warranted.

Distribution of Seats in House of Commons After 1972 Election if Seats Allocated to Parties by Proportion of their Vote Within Each Province (Actual Number of Seats Won in Parentheses)

	Nfld.	P.E.I.	N.S.	N.B.	Que.	Ont.	Man.	Sask.	Alta.	B.C.	Y.-N.W.T.	Totals
Libs.	3 (3)	2 (1)	4 (1)	5 (5)	36 (56)	34 (36)	4 (2)	3 (1)	5 (0)	7 (4)	1 (0)	104 (109)
Cons.	4 (4)	2 (3)	6 (10)	5 (5)	13 (2)	35 (40)	5 (8)	5 (7)	11 (19)	8 (8)	1 (1)	95 (107)
N.D.P.			1 (0)		5 (0)	19 (11)	4 (3)	5 (5)	2 (0)	8 (11)	0 (1)	44 (31)
S.C.					18 (15)				1 (0)			19 (15)
Inds.					2 (1)	0 (1)						2 (2)
Totals	7	4	11	10	74	88	13	13	19	23	2	264

Using the Alberta case, the Conservatives would get 58 percent of the province's total of 19 seats, which would be 11 MPs. The Liberals would get 25 percent, that is 5 seats, the NDP 2 MPs, and Social Credit would get 1.

Applying the revised system in each province in the recent election would have produced much evener results across the country, as the table given here illustrates.

If it had been used, each of the two major parties would have ended up having significant representation in every province and the Yukon-Northwest Territories. Even the two minor parties would have obtained more widespread national representation.

The Liberals would not have been reduced to a corporal's guard in the West. They would have gotten 20 seats west of Ontario instead of 7.

The Tories would have profited by having their Quebec contingent raised to 13 MPs from 2. New Democrats could have extended their base to additional provinces by acquiring 1 MP from Nova Scotia, 5 from Quebec, and 2 from Alberta, plus increasing the number of their Ontario MPs from 11 to 19.

Even Social Credit would have benefitted by adding another 3 seats in Quebec and getting out of its ghetto there by receiving 1 seat in Alberta.

Overall our representative system would have been vastly improved by eliminating the regional bunching that occurred in this election. There would be less foundation to the charge that the Liberals do not represent the West, that the Tories are a washout in Quebec, that the NDP is not a national party, and that Social Credit is a dying force limited to Quebec.

The new system would not be a gimmick. Far from it. Instead it would make the House of Commons a much more accurate reflection of Canadian voters' actual decisions.

One problem that would have to be resolved is how to select the MPs to fill each party's quota of seats won in a province. For instance, which 11 of the Conservatives' 19 candidates in Alberta would get the nod for Ottawa? The simplest and fairest answer would be the 11 who won the biggest percentages of votes in their own riding. An alternative method that is used in some countries employing the List system of Proportional Representation is to let the parties rank their own candidates in advance and then take the first 11 on the tally, but that puts too much power in the hands of the party.

BIBLIOGRAPHY

Cairns, A. C., "The Electoral System and the Party System in Canada," *C.J.P.S.*, Vol. I, No. 1, March, 1968. (Reprinted in *Politics: Canada*, Chapter 8.)

Canada, *Report of the Committee on Election Expenses*, [Barbeau Committee], Ottawa, Queen's Printer, 1966, 2 volumes.

Daniels, S. R., *The Case for Electoral Reform*, London, Allen and Unwin, 1938.

Hermens, F. A., *Democracy or anarchy? A study of proportional representation*, Rev. ed., N.Y., Johnson Reprint Corp., 1972.

Horwill, G., *Proportional Representation; Its Dangers and Defects*, London, Allen and Unwin, 1925.

Humphreys, J. H., *Proportional Representation*, London, Methuen, 1911.

Lakeman, E., and Lambert, J. D., *Voting in Democracies*, London, Faber, 2nd edition, 1959.

Lakeman, E., *How Democracies Vote*, London, Faber, 1970.

Lightbody, J., "Swords and ploughshares: the election prerogative in Canada," *C.J.P.S.*, Vol. 5, No. 2, June, 1972.

Long, J. A., "Maldistribution in Western Provincial Legislatures: The Case of Alberta," *C.J.P.S.*, Vol. II, No. 3, September, 1969.

Lovink, J. A. A., "On Analysing the Impact of the Electoral System on the Party System in Canada", *C.J.P.S.*, Vol. III, No. 4, December, 1970.

Lyons, W. E., *One Man—One Vote*, Toronto, McGraw-Hill, 1970.

MacKenzie, W. J., *Free Elections*, London, Allen and Unwin, 1958.

Milnor, A., *Elections and Political Stability*, Boston, Little, Brown, 1969.

Ontario Commission on the Legislature, *Third Report*, September, 1974. [Re election financing.]

Paltiel, K., *Political Party Financing in Canada*, Toronto, McGraw-Hill, 1970.

Pasis, H. E., "The Inequality of Distribution in the Canadian Provincial Assemblies", *C.J.P.S.*, Vol. V, No. 3, September, 1972.

Qualter, T. H., "Representation by Population: A Comparative Study," *C.J.E.P.S.*, Vol. XXXIII, No. 2, May, 1967.

Qualter, T. H., "Seats and Votes: An Application of the Cube Law to the Canadian Electoral System," *C.J.P.S.*, Vol. I, No. 3, September, 1968.

Qualter, T. H., *The Election Process in Canada*, Toronto, McGraw-Hill, 1970.

Rae, D., *The Political Consequences of Electoral Laws*, New Haven, Yale, 1967.

Ross, J. F. S., *Elections and Electors*, London, Eyre & Spottiswoode, 1955.

Sancton, A., "The Latest Redistribution of the House of Commons", *C.J.P.S.*, Vol. VI, No. 1, March, 1973.

Sancton, A., "The Representation Act, 1974," *C.J.P.S.*, Vol. VIII, No. 3, September, 1975.

Schindeler, F., "One Man, One Vote: One Vote, One Value," *Journal of Canadian Studies*, Vol. III, No. 1, February, 1968.

Spafford, D., "The Electoral System of Canada", *A.P.S.R.*, Vol. LXIV, No. 1, March, 1970.

Stevens, G., "Electoral Systems," a four-part series, *The Globe and Mail*, August 6, 7, 8, 9, 1974.

Stevens, G., "Financing Election Campaigns", *The Globe and Mail*, Oct. 11, 12, 13, 1973; Nov. 9, 10, 1973; June 27, 28, 1974.

Stewart, W., *Divide and Con*, Toronto, New Press, 1973.

Ward, N., "A Century of Constituencies," *C.P.A.*, Vol. X, No. 1, March, 1967.

Ward, N., "The Representative System and the Calling of Elections", *C.J.P.S.*, Vol. VI, No. 4, December, 1973.

Wearing, J., "How to Predict Canadian Elections," *Canadian Commentator*, February, 1963.

10

VOTING BEHAVIOUR

Voting behaviour in Canada has attracted a great deal of interest and study in the past fifteen years, as the length of the bibliography at the end of this chapter indicates.

A number of items might have been reprinted here if space permitted. The two chosen deal with themes which currently are of concern. Both are by the same author.

John Wilson's provocative article, "The Canadian Political Cultures: Towards a Redefinition of the Nature of the Canadian Political System," tackles the popular contemporary question of the nature of Canadian political culture. Using voting behaviour data as well as other evidence, he argues that we should abandon the traditional notion of Canada as a country having two political cutures, English and French, and recognize instead that we probably have a number of different political cultures corresponding to provincial divisions or groups of provincial divisions.

The second article by John Wilson in this chapter is a classic in Canadian voting behaviour studies. "Politics and Social Class in Canada: The Case of Waterloo South" argues that class is finally becoming a significant voting factor in a country in which religion, ethnicity, and region have been dominant influences.

Professor Jerry Hough's article on the relationship between participation and voting turnout in Toronto's municipal election in 1969 has been omitted from this edition. It may be found in the third edition, pp. 284-296.

THE CANADIAN POLITICAL CULTURES: TOWARDS A REDEFINITION OF THE NATURE OF THE CANADIAN POLITICAL SYSTEM*

John Wilson

Although the character of political competition has changed radically in Canada in the years since Confederation, our perception of the nature of the national political system has hardly changed at all. Lord Durham's famous image of "two nations warring in the bosom of a single state" serves . . . to describe what is generally regarded as the most fundamental distinction in modern Canadian politics. . . . Few areas of Canadian society have escaped the impact of the differences between French and English Canada. . . . the distinctions are often held to be so great that it has become customary to think of Canada as having what the modern language of comparative political analysis would call two political cultures.

Such a conclusion is, on the face of things, so obvious that it barely seems worthwhile to challenge it. There is some ground, however, for supposing that the easy division of the country into French and English misses more subtle variations which with further examination may be shown to have some significance. No one would deny, for example, that there are important differences in political practice (to say nothing of historical experience)within English Canada, even if they do not always seem to match the grand contrast between the two founding cultures. Yet these differences have persisted over a long period of time, and while they might ordinarily be dismissed as little more than idiosyncratic variations in the "rules of the political game" from one part of English Canada to another, they may nonetheless reflect the existence of more profound differences in attitudes and orientations to the political system which rival in their magnitude the difference which is customarily perceived between French Canada and the result of the country taken as a whole. There is a possibility, in other words, that Canada contains more than two political cultures.

If it is granted, for a moment, that such differences can be shown to exist, it seems probable that they will be associated with individual provinces. That is not to suggest that each province is so different from all the others that there are 10 distinct political cultures in Canada—it may well be that several of them are so much alike in this respect that there is no point in making a distinction—but rather that each province constitutes, in effect, an independent political system and has on that account a political culture of its own.

•   •   •

* Abridged by the editor from the *Canadian Journal of Political Science/Revue canadienne de science politique*, Vol. VII, No. 3, September/septembre, 1974. The numbers of the Tables and Figures in the original have been retained in this extract. By permission.

TABLE I: As far as you are concerned personally which government is most important in affecting how you and your family get on? (horizontal percentages)*

Residents of	Federal	Provincial	Local	All combinations	None	Don't know	N
Newfoundland	38	38	8	4	—	12	48
Nova Scotia	40	29	16	5	—	10	116
New Brunswick	22	47	13	1	—	17	99
Quebec	28	44	12	4	1	11	754
Ontario	33	35	19	3	1	9	970
Manitoba	31	41	12	8	1	7	139
Saskatchewan	36	40	11	5	—	8	139
Alberta	34	40	15	4	1	6	235
British Columbia	28	47	20	3	—	2	250
Total	31	40	15	4	1	9	2767

* Data from the 1968 national election survey by Prof. John Meisel.

To all of this may be added the evidence which is presented in Table 1 that in almost every part of the country people regard their provincial government as more important than the federal government when it comes to dealing with issues which are crucial to their well-being, and the suggestion of at least one recent study that this tendency is likely to increase rather than decrease in the future. In short, there does not seem to be any compelling reason for not accepting the proposition that Canada is in reality a loose collection of 10 distinct political systems. By definition, therefore, we have at least 10 political cultures. But that is no more than a technical observation, based on the argument that every independent political system must have at least one political culture. On the face of things, the differences which are commonly acknowledged to exist within English Canada have nothing to do with differences in attitudes and orientations to the political system—they are almost entirely behavioural in character—and there is therefore still no ground for supposing that we have more than two *distinct* political cultures.

Such a judgment, however, overlooks what appears to be, on reflection, an important characteristic of many of the differences which the now-flourishing literature on regionalism in Canadian politics has identified. Whether it is significant variations in the relationship between social class and voting behaviour, or the persistence over time of different "climates of opinion," or even the frequently noticed differences in philosophy between parties bearing the same name but acting in different provincial systems, there is an unmistakable suggestion that the provinces are by no means all at the same stage of political development. Indeed, the moment the comparison between them is cast into this context a whole range of differences which had hitherto seemed to have no particular significance suddenly appear in a new light. . . .

The possibility that these differences may represent more fundamental kinds of distinctions arises, of course, from the fact that the concept of political cluture is itself usually presented in developmental terms. That is to say, where there are significant dissimilarities in the dominant political attitudes and orientations of different communities they are generally associated with considerable differences in the extent to which each has developed along a scale leading from a less advanced to a more advanced stage of political development. If, therefore, it can be established that only certain kinds of political institutions and behaviour are likely to occur at specific stages of political development, it follows that there is some possibility that the existence of a particular kind of behaviour may be taken as a signal to the existence of a particular political culture. That is not to say that there is a causal relationship between political behaviour and political culture, but rather that *both* are consequences of a more important underlying factor.

I take that factor to be the stage of economic development which the society in question has reached, and in particular the dominant economic and social relationships of the time. No doubt it would be necessary to undertake a much more sophisticated analysis to establish the point, but perhaps it will be sufficient for the immediate purpose to observe that it seems probable that the political institutions and processes which are appropriate for a society dominated by independent producers (whether large or small), who on that account may perceive themselves to be in control of their own destiny, are not likely to be appropriate for a society dominated by a large number of people who are dependent on someone else for their livelihood and who are not the least bit likely to so perceive themselves. It seems probable as well that attitudes and orientations to the political system will vary for similar reasons.

•   •   •

The history of Canadian party politics is well known. For roughly 50 years from Confederation to the end of the First World War the system was dominated without serious challenge by the Liberals and Conservatives. Since that time, beinning with the election of 1921, it has been necessary to describe the structure of Canadian party competition as, at the very least, that of a "two-plus" party system, while in more recent years it has frequently been argued that there are three "major" political parties in Canada. . . . In the modern era there has been a high degree of variation from one province to another in each federal party's rate of success.

The conventional wisdom has been to ascribe these differences to the obvious differences in economic well-being of different parts of Canada, or to speak of the growing regionalism of Canadian party politics. . . . . But if Canada is in fact composed of 10 distinct political systems it is entirely possible that a more accurate description of national party competition would recognize that there are provincially based cases of both two-party and three-party systems at the federal level, and that it is these differences which require explanation. To put the point in a deliberately oversimplified way it could be said that there is no national party system at all but rather a loose association of 10 distinct provincial systems which, because of wholly understandable variations in their patterns of behaviour, are bound to aggregate at any federal election to the peculiar hybrid which Canada appears to be.

Such a characterization of our circumstances disposes of the odd position which Canada is usually held to occupy in comparison to other systems in the literature on democratic party politics. By denying the existence of the national party system altogether, attention is focused on the behaviour of its regional components where, as might be expected if it is agreed that there are in fact 10 independent political systems in Canada, the pattern of party competition in both federal and provincial elections more closely resembles norms which have been drawn from the experience of other countries. That is to say, while there are several cases of multiparty systems most of the Canadian provinces are dominated at both levels by competition between two electorally strong parties.

● ● ●

. . . While two-party dominance may indeed be the hallmark of a stable political system, there are, far from the one to which the literature customarily refers, at least three analytically distinct types of two-party system. They have, of course, the usual attributes of all two-party systems but they appear to occur at different stages of a system's development and they may be distinguished precisely because they serve societies which are fundamentally different in their leading interests. For the moment we may call them Type 1, Type 2, and Type 3 two-party systems.

A Type 1 system is the kind which is usually found in preindustrial or beginning industrial society. It is dominated by two great parties of the left and the right whose ideological divisions are rooted in the circumstances of that kind of society. That is to say, while both of them may serve the interests of the owning class, one of them is likely to be a party of aristocracy—or of the landed gentry, or if one likes, simply an agricultural party—and the other is likely to be a party of the master manufacturers—a party of trade and commerce or, in a very narrow sense, a capitalist party. Apart from the policy differences which disagreement over the most important sector of the economy is likely to produce between them, the two parties may also be distinguished in terms of the social characteristics of their electoral support. Although very little is known about voting behaviour in this early period of the development of the British and American systems it seems probable that partisan division was also based on such religious or racial conflicts as may have existed in the two societies as well as on the obvious clash between rural and urban interests. Indeed the latter, which may be characterized as an economic dispute, was likely rather less important simply because the differences of opinion on which it was based were not as intense (being essentially an argument between owners of different kinds of resources) as were the apparently fundamental disagreements of, let us say, Catholic and Protestant. In any case, there is no hint in the preindustrial two-party system that political life turns upon questions of economic equality. Nor should there be, because the circumstances of preindustrial and even beginning industrial society are not such as to raise these issues.

Both the Type 2 and Type 3 two-party systems are more modern. What happens to the preindustrial party system is that as the structure of the society changes, that is to say, as it industrializes, so it becomes clear that the older party system is inadequate. With the development of industrial society a new interest appears which was not previously of any consequence—namely a wage-earning class—and as its cohesiveness grows through the organization of trade unions, cooperative societies, and the like it becomes necessary for the party system to adjust to accommodate its demands.

The Type 2 and Type 3 two-party systems arise out of the process of adjustment. Historically, the process appears to have taken the following form. When the new interest represented by the labouring class grows to the point where its demands constitute a threat to the older regime, there is first of all an attempt to co-opt it into the older structure. Generally speaking, the parties of the landed gentry have been more successful at this than others, since they were able to recognize the common interest which they shared with the new working class in being opposed to the excesses of unrestricted individualistic capitalism. But the combination cannot last for very long because the party of the landed gentry, given the nature of its perception of the most important issues, fairly quickly becomes irrelevant as the rate of industrialization increases, unless it can alter its thinking in a significant way. At this somewhat more advanced stage of the process the party of the master manufacturers may also be able temporarily to attract the support of certain sections of the working class, since it can claim a superior understanding to that of its opponents of the needs of the new society. In time, however, it must also adjust as its adherents come to terms with problems of that society which interfere in a fundamental way with principles they had earlier espoused. Issues such as state interference to provide for the education of the working class, or legislation to regulate the conditions of work in the factories, strike at the roots of laissez-faire liberalism. In fact, both of the older parties must adjust or face extinction.

Out of this period of adjustment two quite different kinds of two-party systems emerge. Either the new labour interest is successfully co-opted on a long-term basis by the accommodation of one or both of the older parties to its demands, or the least adjustable of the older parties is eliminated from serious contention in the system and replaced by a new party which is more easily able to meet the requirements of representation in a developed industrial society. Since it has been the more common amongst the Western nations we may characterize the latter outcome of the period of adjustment as a Type 2 two-party system, that is to say, one where elimination has occurred. The Type 3 two-party system is thus one where accommodation has occurred.

Both the Type 2 and Type 3 two-party systems are found, of course, in what we may call advanced industrial society. . . .

The conclusion of this much of the analysis seems inescapable. For the effect of the argument is to suggest that the four quite distinct kinds of party system which it is claimed can be found in the political history of the most prominent English-speaking nations correspond to three rather different points on a time scale of economic, social, and political development: preindustrial or beginning industrial society, industrializing society, and advanced industrial society. If this is so then it must also be the case that not only will there be important and perhaps fundamental differences between the dominant social and political institutions at different points on the scale—due to the very different needs and interests of the societies which each point represents—but the leading political beliefs and values at each point are likely to vary substantially as well. There can hardly be any doubt that this will be true of the first and third points—mid-twentieth-century America bears very little resemblance to the United States of the Civil War—even if it is less obviously certain to be the case with the second. In other words, if it is possible to argue with some degree of certainty, through an examination of the kind of development which has taken place in the party system, that different political communities are at different stages of political development, it is open to us to advance the hypothesis (I put it no higher than that) that they also have different political cultures. We may now turn to a more careful analysis of the Canadian case.

It has already been suggested . . . that treating Canada as a single unit . . . is highly misleading. It is not just that examples of provincially based two-party and three-party systems exist in different parts of the country in federal elections; in nearly every instance, as Table III demonstrates, the *same kind* of system (if not always the same leading participants) also exists at the provincial level. Only Quebec and to some extent Saskatchewan appear to be exceptions to this rule in the years since the end of the Second World War and here, of course, it is the intervention of parties in federal elections which have no comparable history of provincial activity during the period (Social Credit in Quebec and the Conservatives in Saskatchewan) which affects the relationship. Without that intervention it might very well be argued that both are cases of two-party systems, along with the very obvious examples of the four Atlantic provinces. These observations add considerable weight to the suggestion that it would be more accurate to view the Canadian system as simply a loose aggregation of 10 distinct provincial systems.

But the data in Table III are cast in the conventional mould of comparative analysis of party systems. They make no attempt to distinguish, in particular, between the character of the various two-party systems which are found in Canada, and because they are only averages over a relatively brief space of time they may hide important features of each system's development.

The modified histograms which are presented in Figures V and VI [omitted here] are much more useful in this respect. To begin with, they confirm the impression gained from the data in Table III that the same kind of party system exists in each province in both federal and provincial elections. However, while they also appear to settle the question of Saskatchewan (which seems in Figure VI [omitted here] to be a wholly conventional example of a Type 2 two-party system very similar to the British case) they do not provide an immediate explanation of the situation in Quebec and at the same time indicate that both Alberta and British Columbia may be special cases. No one familiar with the political history of these two provinces will find that very surprising. Ontario and Man-

TABLE III: Average Percentage Share of the Popular Vote Won by the Two Leading Parties in Federal and Provincial Elections in the Canadian Provinces held after 1945*

	Federal elections (1949-74)	Provincial elections (1947-74)
Prince Edward Island	97	99
New Brunswick	91	97
Newfoundland	96	96
Nova Scotia	92	93
Quebec	79	90
Saskatchewan	75	84
Ontario	82	78
Alberta	76	78
Manitoba	72	74
British Columbia	66	70

Sources: *Report of the Chief Electoral Officer* (or other official agency) for each jurisdiction for the years shown. For the 1974 federal general election results were obtained directly from the Canadian Press immediately following election day and are therefore to some extent incomplete.
* Elections held just at or near the end of the Second World War have been excluded because of the extent to which they appeared to be unrepresentative cases. Their inclusion, however, would not materially affect the data. In the table the provinces are ranked according to the two-party share of the vote in provincial elections.

itoba, on the other hand, are very clear cases of three-party systems (although the process of adjustment seems to have gone further in Manitoba) and there seems to be little doubt that the four Atlantic provinces should be classifed as Type 1 two-party systems. The implications of these findings are startling enough to require rather more detailed examination.

The idea that Saskatchewan is an advanced industrial society (because it appears to have a Type 2 two-party system) is, perhaps, a little difficult to accept. Yet when its electoral history is compared to that of the other provinces it is clear that only Saskatchewan has *passed through* a period of three-party activity of the kind which the British paradigm suggests is typical of the transformation from preindustrial or beginning industrial society to a more advanced stage of political development. Moreover, it is the only contemporary two-party system in the country where the contest is between an older party and the Canadian equivalent of the British Labour party—the NDP. The contrast between Saskatchewan and the other clear cases of two-party systems (in the Atlantic provinces) is in fact quite striking. Figure VII [omitted here] presents in graphic form the history of Saskatchewan's development alongside that of Nova Scotia, and the very obvious difference between the two should be enough to dismiss any significance which might be attached to the fact that in the 1970s they are both equally competitive systems. But if Saskatchewan has a Type 2 two-party system further investigation should show that its dominant political values are of a kind only appropriate in an advanced industrial society. How could this be the case in a province which, despite other changes, still has a larger proportion of its work force engaged in agriculture than has any other part of Canada?

The stress which has been laid on the idea that it is the development of industrial society as such which brings about the kinds of changes represented by the British paradigm disguises an important aspect of the analysis. What really matters, of course, where the evolution of new political values and different political institutions is concerned, is the *perception* that individuals have of their role in the system. An agricultural society where the independent producers who dominate it are genuinely independent (or can lead themselves to believe that they are) would therefore be expected to exhibit political behaviour of a kind which is typical of a preindustrial society. But where this is not the case, where, that is to say, there are only nominally independent producers who in fact perceive that they are inescapably dependent for their well-being on the will of others who are outside their control, it is entirely likely that an otherwise thoroughly agricultural society will behave very differently. There is a good deal of evidence to suggest that exactly these kinds of circumstances prevailed in Saskatchewan when the CCF first came to power, and that their impact has not been seriously diminished. For in fact the experience of Saskatchewan farmers in the 1930s—and especially that of wheat farmers—was of a degree of economic insecurity and uncertainty wholly beyond their capacity to control as individuals which was so debilitating in its effect upon their life chances that it may be compared to the early experience of the urban working class in Great Britain in the later part of the nineteenth century. But it was precisely that experience which led to the formation of the Labour party and to the demand for government action to mitigate the harsher evils of industrialization. It seems reasonable, therefore, to conclude that the modern party system which has grown in Saskatchewan from the effects of the depression on a wheat economy may be taken as evidence that it has reached a stage of political development analogous to that of modern Britain. This, in turn, suggests that further investigation might be expected to show that there exists in the province a collection of attitudes and orientations to the political system of a kind which is typical of a more advanced political system.

But it would be difficult to make the same claim for the Atlantic provinces. Figure VIII [omitted here] presents graphically the development of the provincial party systems in New Brunswick, Prince Edward Island, and Newfoundland, and while there are minor differences between them and Nova Scotia (such as the existence in the latter of the physically and culturally isolated mining communities of Cape Breton Island, which have from time to time exhibited the electoral behaviour at least of an industrial society) it is clear that none of them has ever experienced a degree of third-party activity even remotely comparable to that of Saskatchewan. Nor is there any reason to believe that they may be examples of a Type 3 two-party system where the established parties have accommodated themselves to the new kinds of demands which arise in an industrial society, for those kinds of pressures, if they have ever been present in Atlantic Canada, appear never to have constituted the threat to the system which they have elsewhere.

It is true, of course, that in both New Brunswick and Nova Scotia the farmers' movement enjoyed a brief moment of success immediately after the First World War, but in neither case was their intervention as dramatic as it was at about the same time in Ontario and the prairie provinces. Both groups disappeared almost as quickly as they had risen, less through any concessions which were made to them by the older parties than because the reason for their protest had little to do with the nature of the society. In Nova Scotia in particular, where there had been an attempt to produce the much more serious coalition of forces represented by the Farmer-Labour party (a union which in the 1930s was to become the basis for the development of the CCF in Saskatchewan), nothing could be accomplished because neither group perceived itself as sharing with the other a lasting grievance with the structure of the system. As a result, the movement quickly fell apart through internal bickering in much the same way that the Farmer-Labor government collapsed in Ontario in 1923. And unlike Ontario, support for the later development of the CCF and the NDP has never materialized in a serious way in Nova Scotia outside of Cape Breton Island.

In short, because they are all reasonably clear examples of what I have called a preindustrial or beginning industrial party system the four Atlantic provinces should be expected to exhibit—if the proper data were available—that set of attitudes and beliefs which are typical of underdeveloped political systems. It is possible that a further distinction could be made between Newfoundland on the one hand, where there is already some evidence to suggest that the dominant political attitudes are even less developed than this, and the three Maritime provinces on the other (although it seems likely that Prince Edward Island, given the almost "pure" state of its party system, will be closer to Newfoundland than to its immediate neighbours). But whether we attach names to these phenomena or not, there can hardly be any doubt that Saskatchewan is at the opposite end of a time scale of political development as compared to the Atlantic provinces, which is to say—if the significance I have attached to that scale is properly placed—that the two areas are likely to have radically different political cultures.

We come now to the three provinces which were earlier held to present a problem for the analysis, Quebec, Alberta, and British Columbia. As it happens, despite the many obvious differences which it has with the rest of Canada, Quebec is the least difficult of these cases. Inspection of her electoral history as recorded in Figure IX [omitted here] shows that so long as the Union Nationale is regarded as nothing more than the continuation of an older conservative tradition in the province (a proposition which would not now attract much dissent) Quebec has had more or less the same kind of two-party development—at least until the election of 1970—that has dominated in Atlantic Canada. The extraordinary bursts of activity by groups other than the two established parties, which appeared in the provincial histogram in Figure VI [omitted here], are now seen to be entirely due to intermittent success for a number of different nationalist groups of varying ideological character. And while it may be arguable that the circumstances which led to the demise of the Action Libérale Nationale in 1936 and the coming to power of Maurice Duplessis represent exactly the kind of accommodation which occurs in the emergence of a Type 3 two-party system, the record of the Duplessis governments from that time on surely demonstrates that Quebec remained locked in the grip of political values typical of preindustrial or beginning industrial society.

Of course industrial development occurred, but its political consequences never materialized either because the Church made sure through its control of the education system and the organization of Catholic trade unions, cooperatives, farmers' associations, and the like that disruptive tendencies would not get out of hand, or because the state itself suppressed them. Thus, "the potential for conflict was rarely given a chance of becoming activated, because, more than elsewhere, the choices open to the lower classes were dictated by established elites who were monolithic enough to render the appearance of reformist or radical alternatives most unlikely."

It is possible, however, that these circumstances are now changing. The result of the 1973 election suggests that the Parti Québécois is not simply a nationalist movement of the kind which has emerged from time to time in the past—no such group has ever increased its share of the vote in the election immediately following its first appearance—even if it does not yet seem to have the kind of support which would be expected if it were the harbinger of a new left-wing development in the province. Given the pattern of the change which occurred in the paradigm case of Great Britain (and the time which it took) it is a trifle premature to argue that the 1970 election in Quebec represents a period of transition (marked by a high degree of multiparty competition) and that with the 1973 result the province has now established a Type 2 two-party system. It nonetheless seems probable that Quebec has entered the transitional phase, which is to say that it has reached a stage of political development broadly analogous to that of Great Britain in the 1920s. In other words, further investigation might be expected to show that Quebec has a more advanced political culture than any of the Atlantic provinces, even if it falls short of the stage which Saskatchewan is said to have reached.

Alberta and British Columbia, on the other hand, are obviously a different matter. Were it not for the extraordinary size of the black areas in each of these cases in the modified histograms presented in Figures V and VI [omitted here], the movement over time in Alberta would suggest the presence there of a Type 3 two-party system (Social Credit and the Conservatives accounted between them for 87 per cent of the votes cast in the 1971 provincial election) while British Columbia would appear to be either still in the transitional phase or an example of yet another Type 2 two-party system. Although the extent of the support enjoyed by the two older parties varies substantially between federal and provincial elections in Alberta there appears to be a clear trend in the province towards a regeneration of that support after a long period of three-party activity. By contrast, the Liberals and the Conservatives do not seem to be recovering in British Columbia.

The reason for the size of the black areas in both cases is, of course, the presence of an abnormally high level of support (compared with the rest of Canada) for the Social Credit party. This suggests a need for a slight elaboration of the general theory of the development of party systems which will, perhaps, account for the activity of a party such as that which is represented by Social Credit and will at the same time enable us to make more sense of the Alberta and British Columbia systems.

There are several reasonably well-known facts of political life in the two provinces which, taken together, indicate the direction in which an explanation lies. The first is the extent to which the purpose of the Social Credit party has been to provide a bulwark against the development of socialism in Canada. While this aim was less stridently proclaimed in Alberta (no doubt because the threat was not as great) it always constituted the central theme of Premier Bennett's campaigns in British Columbia. In this connection it is important to recognize that although the idea of coalition against the CCF was considered in several other provinces (notably in Manitoba and Ontario) British Columbia presents the only open case in Canadian history of the Liberals and Conservatives joining forces to the extent that they became, in effect, one party. After the abortive election of 1941 had failed to reduce the socialist menace to the province the two parties began to work together in the legislature and in 1945 and 1949 actually ran a single coalition candidate in each constituency. These tactics, not surprisingly, substantially reduced the number of CCF MLAs, but had no impact on the level of the CCF vote. In fact, support rose for the party to very nearly 40 per cent in 1945, falling back to 35 per cent in 1949. Two things, however, are important about this period in British Columbia history. The first is that the coalition of the Liberals and the Conservatives effectively forced the BC electorate to abandon, for nearly a decade, such ties to one or the other of the older parties as they may have previously entertained, thus paving the way for the rise of the Social Credit party. The other, and perhaps more important, consequence of these events is that a strong sense of the importance of defeating the CCF must have been left in the minds of British Columbians by the behaviour of the older parties.

These observations suggest that the role of the Social Credit party, at least in British Columbia, was to act as a substitute for the original parties of the system when they proved incapable of doing the job which the conservative element in an industrial society is expected to do. In Alberta, on the other hand, the party came to power as a reaction against the bankruptcy not only of the original parties in the system (which had, in any case, been reduced by 1935 to mere shadows of their former strength) but also of the radical farmer alternative which had governed the province since 1921. In both systems, therefore, the left had been discredited either by its performance (the link between the UFA leadership and the CCF was well understood in 1935) or by the inordinate fear of what it might do which was generated by the behaviour of the older parties.

One other aspect of the more recent electoral history of the two provinces has a bearing here—the kinds of voting shift which occur between the parties between federal and provincial elections. The record of the earlier period in Alberta is uncertain (although the aggregate data are very suggestive: the Social Credit party never fared as well in federal elections as it did provincially and the beneficiary appears always to have been the older parties) but since 1957 the Conservative party has won the lion's share of flagging Social Credit strength at the federal level. In British Columbia as well, both the Liberals and Conservatives appear to gain in federal elections at Social Credit expense while the CCF/NDP vote has often been nearly identical between the two levels. And, of course, in the provincial system it was the Conservatives who were the main victims of the rise of Social Credit, just as it appears to have been a mild resurgence on their part which contributed to the defeat of the Bennett government in 1972.

These facts all suggest that there are other purposes to be served by new third parties than simply the representation of the interests of the working class. The general theory requires that as industrialization proceeds an adjustment in the older party must take place, but it is entirely possible that two quite different kinds of change may be necessary. Ordinarily, one of the two original parties at least is able to adjust to the new circumstances, but it is wholly consistent with the theory to suggest that where neither is able to do so there will be a need for *two* new parties. Since it is usually the rather different demands of the working class to which one or the other of the older parties cannot adjust (because the change that is required is simply not philosophically acceptable to the party's former understanding of things) it is generally the case that the new party which appears is oriented to labour. But it is equally possible that either one or both of the established parties cannot develop the flexibility which has become the hallmark of modern European conservatism, and that the middle class on that account is in danger of going without representation in the new society. In these circumstances we would expect a new party of the right to appear as well as a new party of the left. There would then follow the period of transition in which the nature of the new party system worked itself out and the result would still be either a Type 2 or a Type 3 two-party system, although the leading actors might not be the ones we would normally expect.

Still, their functions would be the same, and it is the recognition that this is likely to be the case which provides a solution to the problem presented in the first instance by Alberta and British Columbia. It seems to me probable that in both provinces dissatisfaction with the ability of either of the older parties to perform one of the principal functions of conservatism in an industrial society—namely, to counterbalance the strength of the left—is what led to the rise of Social Credit. . . .

The character of the Alberta and British Columbia systems becomes clear immediately. The former is, apparently, a case of a Type 3 two-party system, which is to say that it is at more or less the same stage of political development as Saskatchewan. Further investigation should therefore show that the Alberta and Saskatchewan political cultures are identical, even if the leading issues in the political life of the two provinces are not always going to be the same, and that both of them are rather more advanced in this respect than any other part of Canada. For the reconstitution of British Columbia history in Figure X [omitted here] shows that it is not a Type 2 two-party system at all but is instead still in the transitional stage.

That observation brings us to a brief examination of the clear three-party systems which exist in Canada. Figure XI [omitted here] presents graphically the history of the development of the system in British Columbia, Manitoba, and Ontario. Inspection of the BC graph demonstrates the extent to which the analysis which has just been completed provides an explanation of that province's situation. The relationship between the decline of the Conservative party and the success of Social Credit is very clear. What is perhaps more striking, however, is the broad similarity which exists between the pattern of all three systems. All of them, of course, are *industrializing* provinces. It is one of the great fallacies of eastern high school education that Manitoba is a prairie province like the others, yet there is no end of evidence to suggest otherwise. It is not simply that the province's life is dominated by the great metropolis of Winnipeg in a way that Alberta and Saskatchewan have not been dominated by their leading cities, but also that a good part of the Manitoba economy is taken up with primitive industry—forestry and mining—rather *like* British Columbia and Ontario, and *unlike* Alberta and Saskatchewan.

Three-party systems occur, according to the theory, only during the period of transformation in the political institutions and values of a society which is bound to take place as industrialization advances. We should therefore expect to find, with further investigation, that British Columbia, Manitoba, and Ontario all have similar political cultures and that these will bear traces of both the less-developed attitudes and orientations to the political system which the theory argues are associated with a Type 1 two-party system and the more advanced political values and beliefs which appear after the transition to a Type 2 or Type 3 two-party system.

That suggests that when the 10 provinces are considered together there is a possibility that there are at least three distinct political cultures in Canada because it appears to be the case that at least three rather different stages of political development can be identified as existing from one part of the country to another. Table IV summarizes the apparent implications of the analysis on the assumption that this is the case, but it is worth noticing that if the argument I have been making has any validity at all there are no less than two (although not the two which are commonly recognized) and perhaps as many as five distinct sets of attitudes and orientations to the political system now flourishing from coast to coast. If there are only two it seems probable that the kind of investigation which would be required to establish the fact would discover a distinction between five developed and five underdeveloped provincial systems, while the groups shown in Table IV could be expanded by putting Newfoundland and Quebec into individual categories of their own on the ground that each is too different from its neighbours to be lumped together with

TABLE IV: The Canadian Political Cultures in 1974

Underdeveloped	Transitional	Developed
Newfoundland	Quebec	Alberta
Prince Edward Island	Ontario	Saskatchewan
New Brunswick	Manitoba	
Nova Scotia	British Columbia	

them. But whatever number is finally agreed upon there can hardly be any doubt that our conventional image of a system based simply on conflict between French and English Canada is inadequate.

If differences at the level of the political culture of the kind I have suggested cannot, in the nature of the case, be shown to exist without a much more elaborate study, it is at least possible to pursue the idea of different degrees of political development. Given the character of the argument it is comparatively easy to define the nature of a number of other differences which ought to be associated with each stage in the process of change. In terms of the social structure, for example, there should be a less open stratification system in the less developed provinces, and while social classes will of course exist everywhere we would not expect to find them harnessed to the politics of the less developed systems in the way they are in an advanced industrial society such as Great Britain. Instead, we might expect to find that other social cleavages—such as religious affiliation and ethnic origin, which the earlier analysis has suggested are more meaningful political divisions in a preindustrial or beginning industrial society—are the major determinants not only of voting behaviour but of other aspects of electoral politics as well. I propose, however, to examine only two areas where certain kinds of findings could be taken as a demonstration of the existence of at least the different stages of development I have characterized for the Canadian provinces. Both are really variations of the same idea—that social class is a more important political cleavage in an advanced sytem while religious affiliation is more significant in an underdeveloped system—but the different illustrations of the proposition are, perhaps, intriguing.

The general relationship between the three variables of party support, social class, and religous affiliation which it is claimed exists in each of the four different kinds of party systems I have isolated is set out in the models presented in Figure XII. The society is assumed in each case to be equally split into two social classes (based on economic division) and two religious faiths, although there is a differing class composition as between the adherents of the religions of the kind which is generally found in the real world. In preindustrial or beginning industrial society religious affiliation is the main determinant of support for the different parties, and members of the two social classes appear to be equally distributed between them. In the period of adjustment represented by a three-party system the support bases are less clear. Two of the parties are differentiated along class lines, although not very strongly, and also, apparently, along religious lines. The other party, in the centre both literally and figuratively, seems to have no special support in any group. Finally, the customary pattern of an advanced industrial society where elimination has occurred in the party system (Type 2) shows two strongly class-based parties with religious affiliation being evidently irrelevant, while in a Type 3 system the parties differ in terms of both kinds of support, although neither is very marked, indicating the effect of accommodation.

The most obvious test which can be conducted within this framework is, of course, for the relationship between party support in the electorate and the two socioeconomic variables. The models in Figure XII suggest that a proper inquiry into this question requires a multivariate analysis, even though this will result in certain distributions being based on a very small number of cases—since the size of the sample from which the data are taken was comparatively small in certain provinces—and will force us to combine the Atlantic provinces into one unit. In order to avoid possible error due to the respondent's inability to recall correctly his last provincial vote we will use provincial party identification (as established by a series of questions in the 1968 national survey) as the indicator of partisan support. Those who said they did not belong to a social class as well as those who said they did were pressed to name the class in which they would place themselves, and it is the combination of these answers which is used as the measure of subjective social class in each province. Inspection of the results of this analysis as presented in Table V shows that there does appear to be some relation between the actual behaviour patterns of the provinces and what would be expected in each case on the basis of their supposed stages of political development.

It is quite clear, for example, that in both the Atlantic provinces and Quebec social class has virtually nothing to do with variations in partisanship, while religious affiliation appears to have a considerable impact. A measurement of the effect which each variable has on partisanship towards each of the parties (excluding the NDP and Social Credit in cases where their support is very small) is presented in Table VI, based on Coleman's method for calculating "effect parameters," along with a value which summarizes the effect of each variable for each province. These data indicate that among the provinces west of the Ottawa River the impact of social class and religious affiliations on partisanship is lowest in Alberta, as would be expected if it is an example of a Type 3 two-party system. It may be noticed as well that the effect of religious affiliation is lower than in any other part of the country, which suggests that Alberta is neither a transitional system nor a Type 1 two-party system. Both social class and religious affiliation have an effect in the other four systems, although there is no evidence that Saskatchewan differs from the so-called three-party systems in this respect. Although it is by no means conclusive, the evidence thus leans in the direction of support for the hypothesis that the various provinces are at the different stages of development which the analysis of party systems suggested.

Reliable data dealing with the actual voting behaviour in the provinces—as distinct from party identification—are less easy to find. Tables VII and VIII therefore present the results of two comprehensive surveys conducted in Ontario and Manitoba, showing the relative effect of ethnic

FIGURE XII: MODELS OF PARTY SUPPORT IN DIFFERENT PARTY SYSTEMS.

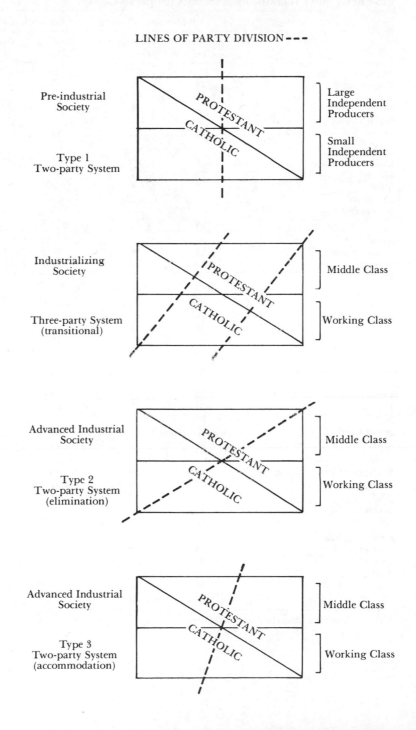

LINES OF PARTY DIVISION - - -

Pre-industrial Society

Type 1
Two-party System

PROTESTANT
CATHOLIC

Large Independent Producers

Small Independent Producers

Industrializing Society

Three-party System
(transitional)

PROTESTANT
CATHOLIC

Middle Class

Working Class

Advanced Industrial Society

Type 2
Two-party System
(elimination)

PROTESTANT
CATHOLIC

Middle Class

Working Class

Advanced Industrial Society

Type 3
Two-party System
(accommodation)

PROTESTANT
CATHOLIC

Middle Class

Working Class

TABLE V: The Relationship between Religious Affiliation, Social Class, and Provincial Party Identification in 1968 (in percentages)*

	Protestant		Roman Catholic	
	Middle class	Working class	Middle class	Working class
Atlantic provinces				
Conservative	48	55	35	37
Liberal	47	43	65	63
NDP	3	2	—	—
Social Credit	2	—	—	—
N	62	100	17	41
Quebec				
Union Nationale	18	15	33	36
Liberal	79	77	57	52
NDP	3	8	2	4
Créditiste	—	—	5	7
Nationalist	—	—	3	1
N	33	13	362	231
Ontario				
Conservative	51	39	25	10
Liberal	39	33	66	70
NDP	9	28	9	20
N	330	236	117	125
Manitoba				
Conservative	49	35	18	14
Liberal	34	41	59	67
NDP	12	24	23	19
Social Credit	5	—	—	—
N	41	34	17	21
Saskatchewan				
Conservative	32	23	33	30
Liberal	35	23	47	45
NDP	30	53	20	25
Social Credit	3	—	—	—
N	37	51	15	20
Alberta				
Conservative	41	34	25	35
Liberal	17	12	37	20
NDP	5	7	—	—
Social Credit	37	47	37	40
N	86	68	16	20
British Columbia				
Conservative	14	9	—	12
Liberal	37	26	73	41
NDP	10	25	—	18
Social Credit	39	40	27	29
N	104	69	11	17

* Data taken from the 1968 national survey.

TABLE VI: The Relative Effect of Religious Affiliation and Social Class on Provincial Party Identification*

	Effect of religion				Effect of class				Total effect of	
	Con	Lib	NDP	SC	Con	Lib	NDP	SC	Religion	Class
Atlantic Provinces	.16	.19			.04	.03			.18	.04
Quebec	.18	.23			†	.03			.21	.02
Ontario	.27	.32	.04		.14	.01	.15		.21	.10
Manitoba	.26	.26	.03		.09	.07	.04		.18	.07
Saskatchewan	.04	.17	.19		.06	.07	.14		.13	.09
Alberta	.08	.14		.04	.01	.11		.06	.09	.06
British Columbia	.05	.25	.08	.11	.03	.22	.17	.02	.12	.11

* The measures shown are Coleman's effect parameters for the data presented in Table v. Where no entry occurs, the level of support was too small for useful measurement.
† No effect.

origin, as well as religious affiliation and social class, on the vote. Table IX gives Coleman's effect parameters for the three independent variables, and it is clear that in both provinces they have a more or less equal impact on voting behaviour although for Liberal supporters the effect of social class is much less marked than it is with the Conservatives and the NDP. But these findings are exactly what we should expect with systems which are said to be in the transitional stage of development.

A second test of the theory examines the same set of relationships which the models in Figure XII assign to the different systems, but does so in a rather different way. If it is the case that the importance of religion vastly outweighs that of economic position in a preindustrial or beginning industrial society, we should expect that fact to be reflected in the characteristics of those who seek public office in the system, and we should equally expect alternative characteristics to be dominant amongst the same kinds of people in the more advanced systems. That is to say, if one's religion is, on the whole, the independent variable which determines one's party (as should be the case in the Type 1 two-party systems) rather than economic position, then the distribution of religious affiliations amongst each party's candidates should be radically different while their occupational backgrounds should be quite similar. The opposite should be the case in Type 2 two-party systems, and in Type 3 two-party systems there should be no recognizable differences between the parties on either of these variables. The candidates of parties in transitional systems, of course, should exhibit differences on both scores.

The difficulty with this test is the effective absence of reliable data. Entries in the *Canadian Parliamentary Guide*, while useful, are usually only for a little more than half of all the governing party's candidates, and their selection may very well have been biased by the existence of the characteristics we are looking for. In several provinces, however, the chief electoral officer's *Report* lists the occupations of all candidates and, from time to time, surveys of all candidates in a particular election have been conducted. There is therefore some opportunity to apply a test of this kind as a further check on the validity of the theory.

TABLE VII: The Relationship Between Ethnic Identification, Religious Affiliation, Social Class, and Voting Intention in Ontario in 1967 (in percentages)

| | English Canadian* | | | | Not English Canadian* | | | |
| | Protestant | | Roman Catholic | | Protestant | | Roman Catholic | |
	Middle class	Working class	Middle class	Working class	Middle class	Working class	Middle class	Working class
Conservative	56	51	18	16	40	6	27	24
Liberal	32	28	67	44	49	56	64	62
NDP	12	21	15	40	11	38	9	14
N	474	512	73	123	65	53	78	155

* Respondents were asked, "To what ethnic group do you consider that you belong: English Canadian, French Canadian, or another ethnic group?" Nearly two-fifths of the sample said they were "just Canadian" and these cases are not included in the table.

TABLE VIII: The Relationship Between Ethnic Origin, Religious Affiliation, Social Class, and Voting Intention in Manitoba in 1973 (in percentages)

| | British | | | | Non-British | | | |
| | Protestant | | Roman Catholic | | Protestant | | Roman Catholic | |
	Middle class	Working class	Middle class	Working class	Middle class	Working class	Middle class	Working class
Conservative	50	40	53	23	45	34	25	20
Liberal	24	12	20	33	18	15	25	18
NDP	23	48	27	44	33	49	48	60
SC and Others	3	—	—	—	4	2	2	2
N	176	121	16	16	138	111	79	96

TABLE IX: The Relative Effect of Ethnic Origin, Religious Affiliation, and Social Class on the Vote in Ontario and Manitoba*

	Conservative	Liberal	NDP	Total effect
Ontario				
Ethnic identification	.11	.15	.04	.10
Religious affiliation	.17	.18	.01	.12
Social class	.11	.05	.17	.11
Manitoba				
Ethnic origin	.10	.03	.12	.08
Religious affiliation	.12	.07	.06	.08
Social class	.14	.02	.17	.11

* The measures shown are Coleman's effect parameters for the data presented in Tables VII and VIII.

The data in Table X represent a selection from the more reliable sources for the sake of illustration, chosen primarily to give an example of each kind of system. It may be observed, however, that a thorough examination of the available data for all provinces, bearing in mind their limitations, confirms the impression created by Table X that on this count as well the developmental theory gains support. As should be expected, Conservative and Liberal MLAs in New Brunswick divide on religion and not on occupation, candidates for the three parties in Ontario exhibit differences on both variables, and in Saskatchewan occupation rather than religion constitutes the main difference in the backgrounds of members of the two parties—the more so if farmers are thought of as representing, in that province at least, a special kind of working-class movement.

The two tests which have been conducted are, of course, somewhat duplicative in character since they focus on the same set of relationships. But there is no reason why other areas which might be expected to reveal variations in behaviour and practice between the provinces that would reflect the different stages of political development I have hypothesized for them should not be examined. For the possibilities are almost endlessly intriguing. In Ontario, for example, until very recently the opposition was not permitted to question the ministry in an even remotely effective way in the legislature. In British Columbia, until the election of an NDP government there was no Hansard, although in the final years of the Bennett regime summaries of proceedings in the legislature were published. In the realm of party organization, as well, there are fascinating variations from coast to coast. During Mr. Smallwood's rule in Newfoundland nominating conventions were never held to choose provincial or federal Liberal candidates. Instead, the premier held a press conference and announced their names. Or there is the part which electoral and other forms of political corruption have played in Canadian politics. The extent to which patronage remains a crucial element in the political systems of some provinces is also suggestive.

All of these things in one way or another point to the existence of rather different political values in different parts of Canada, even if we can have

TABLE X: Religious Affiliation and Occupation of Provincial Candidates and Members of the Legislative Assembly—Selected Examples From New Brunswick, Ontario, and Saskatchewan (in percentages)

	New Brunswick				Ontario			Saskatchewan			
	Con	Con	Lib	Lib	Con	Lib	NDP	Lib	Lib	NDP	NDP
Election year	1967	1970	1970	1967	1967	1967	1967	1967	1971	1971	1967
Protestant	81	78	31	31	86	66	56	62	71	64	64
Catholic	19	22	69	69	12	30	18	35	29	24	24
Jewish	—	—	—	—	2	3	6	—	—	—	—
No information*	—	—	—	—	—	1	20	3	—	12	12
N	26	32	26	32	117	117	117	34	14	42	25
Unlisted cases	—	—	—	—	—	—	—	—	1	3	—

	New Brunswick		Ontario			Saskatchewan	
	Con	Lib	Con	Lib	NDP	Lib	NDP
Election year	1970	1970	1967	1967	1967	1964	1964
Professional	29	29	32	48	50	29	19
Commercial	53	59	53	35	11	34	12
Agricultural	9	3	10	10	9	33	49
Manual†	9	9	5	7	30	4	20
N	58	58	117	117	117	58	59

* Despite a full entry in the *Canadian Parliamentary Guide* no religious affiliation is given. In some cases this may mean that the member has no formal religious affiliation. In the Ontario cases the candidate reported that he had no religion.
† Includes trade union officials.

no way, given the data now available, of assessing the significance of those differences. If it is accepted, however, that the kinds of distinction which further investigation may discover are likely to be related to the developmental differences which the analysis of party systems suggests, there are a number of immediate consequences for our understanding of the capacity of the national political parties to perform the functions which many people have assigned to them. Whether it is argued that they should seek to eliminate the sectional differences of the past by abandoning the practice of brokerage politics (which it is said merely reinforces the traditional divisions of race, religion, and region) in favour of a more "creative politics" based on social class, or simply that the national party system must be able to foster the development of a national political culture, most observers have seen the Canadian party system as playing a critical role in the promotion of greater national unity.

But if the country is indeed divided in the way I have suggested —merely in terms of the extent to which different regions are at different stages of political development—the capacity of class politics to have the unifying effect which is claimed for it disappears. The likelihood of its success as an instrument for promoting greater national unity obviously depends upon all, or nearly all, parts of the country being in a condition which would permit them to respond to this kind of approach. If, however, the different stages of political development I have identified for the various provinces do, in fact, exist it is clear that any attempt by the national parties to appeal to Canadians on class lines will fall on deaf ears over a sufficiently large area of the nation to defeat the purpose. For if only *some* parts of Canada are ready for class politics, each party in order to contemplate national success will have to base its campaign elsewhere in the country on other perceptions of the most important divisions in the electorate. In other words, the practice of brokerage politics will have been preserved by the very behaviour which it is said is most likely to eliminate it.

That is the minimum consequence if the developmental theory of the nature of the Canadian political system is correct. If, however, it is found that the different stages of development which have been identified are sufficiently far apart to be associated with radically different political cultures—if, that is to say, there are in fact different perceptions of what is right and wrong in politics depending upon where one happens to be in Canada—it is difficult to see how any formulation of the task could leave it to the national party system to be an agent for the creation of a national political culture. If the language of politics varies in this fundamental way from region to region, our national leaders will be incapable of speaking to the nation collectively except in times of crisis.

We must therefore either abandon the search for national unity altogether or redefine its meaning in a way which recognizes that our "limited identities" constitute the essence of what it is to be Canadian. If we can accomplish that, and yet remain a nation, we will have taught the world a lesson it sorely needs to learn.

POLITICS AND SOCIAL CLASS IN CANADA: THE CASE OF WATERLOO SOUTH*

John Wilson

●   ●   ●

. . . There is . . . some evidence to suggest that social class may be becoming a more important influence in the electoral behaviour of certain parts of the country than has been the case in the past. An analysis of the result of the federal by-election held in the autumn of 1964 in the southwestern Ontario riding of Waterloo South may throw further light on the kinds of changes which appear to be taking place in Canada.

One of the most obvious consequences of the brokerage doctrine [of parties] is the greater propensity of the party organizations to stress the characteristics of their candidates rather than the party program or the interests of the electorate which a party might seek to serve. If, as the theory requires, a major national party has to behave as a department store—putting everything on sale because it cannot be sure which "line" will "go best" with its customers—then it is only a short step to the belief that it will gain as much through the smile of the counter clerk as it will through the quality of its merchandise.

On the face of things the Waterloo South by-election was typical in this respect of the practice throughout Canada. Each of the three parties nominated candidates who were thought to have a special claim on the loyalties of the electorate. Moreover, when the New Democrat won —breaking a Conservative hold on the constituency which went back almost without interruption to the First World War—it was widely claimed that his special qualities had been the principal cause of his victory, that the circumstances of the by-election were in any case unique, and that Mr. Saltsman would not be able to hold the riding in a general election. Not only does this explanation have very little to do with the more deeply rooted attachments to party which have been found to exist in most other democratic countries, it is not even necessarily internally consistent. If Mr. Saltsman did have a special personal drawing power there would be no reason to suppose that he could not continue to win in Waterloo South in general elections irrespective of the cause of his first victory.

It is, however, comparatively easy to show that such an explanation leaves too much unaccounted for to be acceptable. What was ignored by the analysts was the fact that the same Max Saltsman—in the provincial election only fourteen months earlier—had given the poorest performance of any NDP or CCF candidate in Waterloo South since before the Second World War. Yet he had been living in the constituency for nearly seventeen years. It hardly seems likely that his personal following could

---

* From the *Canadian Journal of Political Science/Revue canadienne de Science politique*, Vol. I, No. 3, September/septembre, 1968. By permission of the author and publisher.

TABLE: I Recent Federal Results in Waterloo South

	1962	1963	1964	1965	1968
Conservatives	Chaplin 10,448	Chaplin 10,143	Chaplin* 9,086	Chaplin* 8,609	O'Brian 9,993
Liberals	Shaver 6,759	Shaver 7,387	Stewart 4,563	Menary 4,758	Epp 7,121
New Democrats	Stewart 6,889	Stewart 7,105	Saltsman 11,856	Saltsman 12,465	Saltsman 10,622
Social Credit	Fast 486	Bezan 328			Gervais 114
Total	24,582	24,963	25,505	25,832	27,850

* A son of the member whose death caused the 1964 by-election.
Source: Report of the Chief Electoral Officer for Canada and for 1968 the preliminary recapitulation provided by the Returning Officer for Waterloo.

have mushroomed almost overnight to the extent required to win the by-election.

There were other peculiarities in the result which suggested that it was not to be explained in terms of the candidate's characteristics alone. One of the most intriguing aspects of the campaign was the fact that the Liberal candidate had run as a New Democrat in the two previous federal elections. Although he believed that by switching to the Liberals he could unite the progressive vote in the riding and thereby defeat the Conservatives, the immediate effect of his candidacy was merely to divide the local Liberal association so badly that its ability to mount a campaign at all was in serious doubt. In these circumstances it would not be expected that Liberal supporters who wished to protest the adoption of a former New Democrat as their candidate would do so by voting for the NDP. Yet, on the face of it, that is what happened.

If the votes cast for each party are compared with those for 1963 (see Table I) it appears that the result depended on the defection of roughly a thousand Conservatives and nearly three times that number of Liberals—all to the NDP. In fact, however, the shifts which took place were rather more complex than that. The data in Table II [see original article] show that although a somewhat larger *proportion* of 1963 Liberals switched to the NDP, because there were originally many more Conservatives in the riding the latter made a greater contribution to the NDP victory in absolute terms. The fact that the change which occurred was primarily the result of the defection of former Conservatives raises intriguing questions about the sources of party support in southwestern Ontario. And when it is remembered that Mr. Saltsman maintained his position in the succeeding general election of 1965 (and with somewhat less support in 1968) it seems likely that a more profound change—based, perhaps, on the identification of the parties with specific interests in the electorate—took place in Waterloo South.

Religious Affiliation, Ethnic Origin and the Vote

The idea that certain sociological factors may have some influence on

TABLE III: Federal Electoral Behaviour of Roman Catholics in Selected Areas (horizontal percentages)

Year	Area	CON	LIB	NDP	SC	n
1963	National	19	52	9	20	930
1953	Kingston	2	95	3	*	89
1962	St. John's	53	47	*	*	128
1962	Hamilton	15	78	7	†	91
1963	Sudbury	16	70	11	3	295
1964	Saskatoon	23	60	17	*	203
1964	Waterloo South	14	34	52	*	91

* No candidate.
† Social Credit and Conservative votes combined.
Sources for the data from other studies presented in TABLE III are, respectively: Peter Regenstreif, *The Diefenbaker Interlude: Parties and Voting in Canada* (Toronto, 1965), 104, calculated from CIPO data in Table IX; John Meisel, "Religious Affiliation and Electoral Behaviour: A Case Study," *Canadian Journal of Economics and Political Science*, 22, no. 4 (Nov. 1956), 486, calculated from Table II; George Perlin, "St. John's West," in Meisel, ed., *Papers on the 1962 Election*, 10, calculated from Table I; Grace M. Anderson, "Voting Behaviour and the Ethnic-Religious Variable: A Study of a Federal Election in Hamilton, Ontario," *Canadian Journal of Economics and Political Science*, 32, no. 1 (Feb. 1966), 30, calculated from Table I; J. E. Havel, *Politics in Sudbury* (Sudbury, 1966), 65, calculated from Table 36; and John C. Courtney and David E. Smith, "Voting in a Provincial General Election and a Federal By-election: A Constituency Study of Saskatoon City," *Canadian Journal of Economics and Political Science*, 32, no. 3 (Aug. 1966), 349, calculated from Table X.

the pattern of our voting is given recognition in all the major studies of Canadian electoral behaviour, whether at the constituency, regional, or national level. In these analyses two main observations have been made: first, that the intensity of the influence exercised by any one factor will vary from area to area throughout the country, and second, that whatever the strength of the factor which seems most prominently at work the influence of social class has very little to do with it. Instead, as has already been suggested, the system encourages electors to distinguish between themselves on the basis of their religious affiliation or their ethnic origin, or collectively as residents of a particular region. While such differentiation suggests that the practice of brokerage is not entirely successful it is nonetheless the case that these factors generally cut across class lines and thereby eliminate the possibility that the nation will fall apart in class war.

It has become a commonplace of political analysis in Canada that of the influences affecting our electoral behaviour the most significant for many years has been religious affiliation. And few studies which have tested the relationship have failed to find a very strong connection between professing the Roman Catholic faith and a preference for the Liberal party. Table III brings together from a number of recent studies evidence which shows how consistently the connection has been found in most parts of the country. The strength of the relationship is, of course, not absolutely uniform, and Perlin's Newfoundland data as well as those for Waterloo South show that it is not even necessarily the case that the Liberals will be the leading party amongst Roman Catholics everywhere in Canada. But such regional variation as may occur does not affect the possibility that religious affiliation will still be found to be the most important single

TABLE IV: Some Religious Groups Were More Likely to Change Than Others (percentages)

Religious affiliation	Switched to the NDP	All voters
Anglican	42	23
Baptist	9	7
Lutheran	15	10
Presbyterian	3	14
Roman Catholic	24	18
United Church	2	18
Other	5	10
N	103	504

influence on the way Canadians vote. It may be that the party preference of Roman Catholics is simply a product of the local circumstances in which they find themselves, but it may also be that the fact that an elector adheres to that faith remains the principal element in the choice he makes on election day. In St. John's that tends to make him a Conservative, in Kingston and Sudbury and in other places it tends to make him a Liberal, and in Waterloo South it apparently tends to make him a New Democrat.

In fact, however, before the 1964 by-election the Liberals *were* the dominant party amongst Roman Catholics in the riding, [the percentage distribution among the 75 Roman Catholics in the sample who remembered how they had voted in 1963 was Conservative 29, Liberal 52, and NDP 19], and the magnitude of the shift to the NDP in this group suggests that something other than religious affiliation may have been the principal motivating factor. If this were the case we might expect to find a general shift in all religious groups. Table IV makes it clear not only that this did not happen, but that these were very marked differences in the propensity of particular groups to change the pattern of their vote. Anglicans, Lutherans, and Roman Catholics appeared much more likely to change than others, while adherents of the United Church seemed hardly inclined to change at all. Thus, while the distribution does not conform to the national pattern, it may still be the case that an association exists between religious affiliation and the vote sufficient to account for the behaviour of the riding.

In fact there are important differences in party strength in each of the larger religious faiths in Waterloo South. Even though they do not dominate, Table V shows that the Liberals do find greater support amongst Roman Catholics than in any other group. It can be seen as well that the Conservatives appear to be especially dependent upon Anglicans and Baptists for their position in the riding, while the NDP draws disproportionate support from Presbyterians. But while the existence of a general connection between religious affiliation and the vote can easily be shown, that factor alone by no means explains the behaviour of all electors. A closer examination of Table V suggests that since the level of the NDP vote does not vary as sharply from group to group as is the case with the other parties, religious affiliation plays a much smaller part in explaining its strength. In fact, if an association is sought between either seven or

TABLE V: Religious Affiliation and the Vote in 1964 (percentages)

	Anglican	Baptist	Lutheran	Presby-terian	Roman Catholic	United Church	Other	All voters
Conservatives	48	45	40	35	14	37	34	36
Liberals	5	10	18	9	34	21	16	16
New Democrats	47	45	42	56	52	42	50	48
N	118	33	50	71	91	91	50	504

three religious groups and a hypothetical two-party vote (Conservatives and Liberals together, and the NDP) no relationship is found to exist at all. Obviously, therefore, religious affiliation only helps to account for the difference between the level of the Conservative and Liberal vote in Waterloo South; it tells us nothing about the NDP.

It is possible, however, since the same kinds of links between religious affiliation and voting are not found in all parts of Canada, that the variation is due not just to local circumstances but to other factors being more important as determinants of electoral behaviour. The religion to which a person adheres is so very often a function of his ethnic origin that it may be the case that the apparent connection between the Liberal party and adherents of the Roman Catholic faith in some parts of the country is in reality an association between that party and the dominant ethnic group in such areas. It has been suggested, for example, that the strong relationship between being Catholic and voting Liberal in Sudbury is probably only a reflection of the more important link between the French minority in that city and the national Liberal party viewed as the special agent of French minority in that city and the national Liberal party viewed as the special agent of French interests in Canada. If this kind of association were the dominant one we would of course expect to find differences in the intensity of the Catholic-Liberal relationship from region to region depending upon the proportionate strength of particular ethnic groups.

In Waterloo county, of course, a large part of the population is of German origin. While the south riding is by no means as notable in this respect as Kitchener and other areas to the north, it may still be the case that ethnic origin has a more fundamental influence on the vote than does religious affiliation, and that it goes farther in accounting for the support of all three parties. Table VI shows that there are substantial differences in Liberal and Conservative strength among the groups examined but that, again, the level of the NDP vote seems unaffected by such considerations. A general association between ethnic origin and the vote clearly exists irrespective of the group combinations used, but, as with religious affiliation, no association can be found at all when the Liberal and Conservative vote is combined and contrasted to that of the NDP.

The fact that religious affiliation and ethnic origin are differentiating influences only between Conservatives and Liberals means that by themselves these factors give a rather inadequate explanation of the voting pattern in Waterloo South. If the NDP were an unimportant element in the riding this would perhaps be of less significance, although to the

TABLE VI: Ethnic Origin and the Vote in 1964 (percentages)

	English	Irish	Scots	German	Other	All voters
Conservatives	43	43	31	32	27	36
Liberals	8	14	16	20	30	16
New Democrats	49	43	53	48	43	48
N	185	44	89	103	83	504

extent that a thorough description of Canadian electoral behaviour is being sought it should be a matter of some concern when the traditional explanations cannot account for any part of that behaviour, however small. In any case it seems probable that our concern with the differences which have been with us since the beginning—together with the fact that it is generally possible to find some sort of relationship between religious affiliation, ethnic origin and the vote—has served to disguise a development of recent years that needs to be made more explicit.

Social Class and the Vote

It has already been suggested that since religious affiliation and electoral behaviour do not necessarily show the same kind of relationship in all parts of Canada, the varying level of the association may be the consequence of local circumstances. It may also be the case that other, more permanent, societal conditions which vary from one part of the country to another are the real cause of the differential influence which the traditional elements of race, religion, and region have been found to have. Thus, to take one example, the apparently increasing regionalization of Canadian electoral preference, to which Professor Meisel has drawn attention, may in fact be no more than an expression of the comparatively *unequal* growth of urbanization and industrialization in different parts of the country. A comprehensive national study might very well find that these factors are the most fundamental influence at work in our system. It might also find that the older patterns of voting are able to maintain themselves only in areas unaffected by the pressures of an increasingly complex economy, while in Canada's major industrial centres what appears to be a continuing relationship between religious affiliation, or ethnic origin, and the vote is in reality only a reflection of the more permanent influences which city life tends to promote. To put the matter in another way, it may merely be the case that Roman Catholics in some areas do not vote for the Conservative party because as a general rule Roman Catholics are not as well off as some other religious groups.

The extent to which significant differences in wealth between various religious groups exist in Canada is unclear, but it is a fact that in Waterloo South there are important distinctions to be made between the kinds of people who are adherents of each of the larger faiths. Table VII shows how very sharp those distinctions may be. In fact there appears to be a broad connection between the relative class composition of the riding's religious groups and their propensity to shift to the NDP. It was noticed

TABLE VII: There Are Sharp Occupational Class Differences Between Religions (percentages)

	Anglican	Baptist	Lutheran	Presbyterian	Roman Catholic	United Church	Other	Whole sample
Non-manual workers	42	37	29	42	26	52	32	38
Manual workers	58	63	71	58	74	48	68	62
N	130	40	59	84	110	118	65	606

earlier (in Table IV) that Anglicans, Lutherans, and Roman Catholics were the most likely to change their vote and adherents of the United Church were hardly inclined to change at all. It can now be seen that the Lutheran and Catholic groups tend to be substantially more working class in composition than the others, while the United Church is much more heavily middle class in composition than is the riding as a whole. Nothing approaching the same degree of distinction on an occupational class basis can be found among ethnic groups, although this appears to be mainly a consequence of the dominantly British character of the constituency. However that may be, the differential class composition of the leading religious groups—taken together with their varying propensity towards changing their voting pattern between 1963 and 1964—suggests that social class may have more to do with the vote in Waterloo South than any other single variable.

The fact is that while the NDP attracted broadly the same level of support among all religious and ethnic groups, the class composition of its vote makes it clear that it may be characterized—in Waterloo South—as a working class party. That it also polls a respectable share of the lower middle class vote does not necessarily detract from this interpretation of the data in Table VIII. Such evidence as is available in other English-speaking countries where social class is thought to be the prime determinant of electoral choice suggests that strong support in the lower middle class is not at all uncommon with labour-oriented parties. Nor is the NDP's superior strength among skilled and semi-skilled workers—compared to unskilled workers—necessarily unique: the same phenomenon has been found in both Germany and Sweden. On the other hand, Table VIII shows that the Conservatives and the Liberals are both more heavily dependent upon middle class support than would be expected if social class were of no consequence at all as an influence on the vote.

TABLE VIII: Social Class and the Vote in 1964 (percentages)

	Middle class		Working class		
	Upper middle	Lower middle	Skilled and semi-skilled	Unskilled	All voters
Conservatives	55	45	27	31	36
Liberals	21	20	13	17	16
New Democrats	24	35	60	52	48
N	66	135	261	42	504

TABLE IX: Social Class and the Vote in 1963 and 1964 (percentages)

	1963 federal election*			1964 by-election		
	Middle class	Working class	All voters	Middle class	Working class	All voters
Conservatives	64	46	53	48	28	36
Liberals	29	25	27	21	13	16
New Democrats	7	29	20	31	59	48
N	177	254	431	201	303	504

* Excluding five Social Credit voters.

Of course, in a riding where three-fifths of the electorate is to be found in the working class any party which is to be successful will have to attract a large proportion of the labour vote. That such drawing power on the part of the Conservatives was an important element in their earlier victories in Waterloo South is made clear by the comparative data for 1963 and 1964 in Table IX. Although it is obvious that an association between class and the vote exists in both elections, the fact that NDP strength in 1963 fell considerably short of dominating the riding suggests that the role played by social class before the by-election was a comparatively minor one. This is not to claim that the changes which occurred were necessarily due to an increase in class-voting. But when a party whose main appeal is to the working class is conspicuously unsuccessful in one election and then manages to capture the constituency in another (while the association between class and the vote is maintained) the very least that may be said is that there appears to have been an increased willingness on the part of the electorate to accept it on the terms on which it offers itself. If that is the case it may be said that social class has become a more important influence.

That acceptance does not, however, mean that individual electors necessarily actively think of themselves as members of distinct social classes. While an association can also be found between self-assigned class and the vote, there is a marked disparity between the subjective and objective assignments of class status, especially in the middle class. This suggests that the kind of association which exists is more probably based on a broad recognition of economic interests rather than on any more doctrinaire view of the matter. That this is the case appears to be confirmed by the data in Table X. Within each objective class the pattern of the vote is not altered at all by variations in the subjective status of respondents. Clearly what counts is where a person finds himself in the social hierarchy whatever label he attaches to the position.

The proposition that social class is now the most important influence on the vote in Waterloo South is further supported by the fact that an association between the two variables can be found irrespective of the manner in which the data are organized. It will be recalled that while religious affiliation and ethnic origin both appeared to affect the three-party vote, when an association between them and a hypothetical two-party vote (Conservatives and Liberals, and the NDP) was sought none

TABLE X: Objective Social Class Is More Important Than Subjective Social Class (percentages)

	Objective middle class		Objective working class	
	Subjective middle	Subjective working	Subjective middle	Subjective working
Conservatives	48	47	29	27
Liberals	21	21	10	13
New Democrats	31	32	61	60
N*	105	92	48	246

* Only 491 cases are included because 13 respondents did not know their subjective social class.

could be found to exist. But between social class and the same two-party vote there continues to be a relationship every bit as significant as that found when the three parties are treated as separate entities. It therefore seems probable that the influence of class gives a more all-inclusive explanation of the electoral behaviour of the riding than any other single variable.

The Relative Importance of Religious Affiliation, Ethnic Origin, and Social Class

Examination of the apparent effect of individual variables on the vote leaves a good deal to be desired. It is obvious that the three influences which have been discussed each have some part to play in determining the pattern of the vote in Waterloo South, but what is most needed is a method of assessing their relative importance.

Considerable support for the interpretation of the riding's behaviour which has been developed so far may be found when the data relating to religious affiliation, ethnic origin, and social class are organized in a multivariate table. When this is done for the 1964 data (Table XI) it can easily be seen that the variation in the level of the NDP vote continues to be a function of social class regardless of religious or ethnic pressures. There appears also to be an influence due to class in the Liberal and Conservative vote, but it is much less precise and evidently interfered with by the effect of religious affiliation and ethnic origin. In order to assess the change which has taken place in the riding the data for the 1963 election are organized in the same fashion in Table XII. But apart from the fact that there are substantially different levels of support for all three parties it can be seen that the direction of the relationship observed in Table XI remains the same.

Using Coleman's method of calculating "effect parameters" for each dichotomized variable it is possible to measure the importance of each of the three independent attributes in relation to the others as factors affecting each party's vote. The result of these calculations for both elections is presented in summary form in Table XIII, together with a statement in each case of the probability that the observed effect could have occurred by chance. A number of conclusions necessarily follow from this analysis.

TABLE XI: The Effect of Religious Affiliation, Ethnic Origin, and Social Class in 1964 (percentages)

| | Principal Protestant faiths* | | | | Roman Catholics | | | |
| | British | | Non-British | | British | | Non-British | |
	Middle class	Working class	Middle class	Working class	Middle class	Working class	Middle class	Working class
Conservatives	53	33	46	40	55	13	15	5
Liberals	14	7	27	7	27	17	69	34
New Democrats	33	61	27	53	18	70	15	61
N†	115	151	44	53	11	23	13	44

* Anglican, Baptist, Lutheran, Presbyterian, and United Church.
† Only 454 cases are included because of the exclusion of 50 adherents of other religions.
Note: Percentages do not always add to 100 because of rounding.

TABLE XII: The Effect of Religious Affiliation, Ethnic Origin, and Social Class in 1963 (percentages)

| | Principal Protestant faiths* | | | | Roman Catholics | | | |
| | British | | Non-British | | British | | Non-British | |
	Middle class	Working class	Middle class	Working class	Middle class	Working class	Middle class	Working class
Conservatives	71	50	67	59	64	38	23	13
Liberals	24	14	25	19	27	48	69	57
New Democrats	5	36	6	22	9	14	8	30
N†	105	131	36	46	11	21	13	30

* Anglican, Baptist, Lutheran, Presbyterian, and United Church.
† Only 393 cases are included because of the exclusion of 43 adherents of other religions.
Note: Percentages do not always add to 100 because of rounding and the Social Credit vote, which is not shown.

First, roughly half of the variation in the 1964 vote for each party is accounted for by the three factors of religious affiliation, ethnic origin, and social class acting together. Clearly these are the most influential sociological determinants of the vote in Waterloo South. However, while religious affiliation has the strongest effect on both the Liberal and Conservative vote, the influence of social class is nearly as powerful as, and in the case of the Conservatives is more important than, the effect of ethnic origin. But since class is the only significant influence among the three factors in the NDP vote it follows that it explains more of the variation in the riding's electoral behaviour than either of the other two elements considered.

The effect parameters for 1963 show that this was not the case before the by-election. For each party in that year the effect of class was less important than in 1964, and the over-all influence of the variable fell considerably short of that of religious affiliation. In the case of the NDP the difference between the two elections in the effect of class is particu-

TABLE XIII: Effect Parameters

	Effect parameters			Significance		
	CON	LIB	NDP	CON	LIB	NDP
1964						
Religious affiliation	.21	.23	.03	<.001	<.001	>.30
Ethnic origin	.12	.18	.06	<.018	<.001	>.10
Social class	.20	.18	.38	<.001	<.001	<.001
r	.06	−.04	.19			
s	.41	.45	.34			
1963						
Religious affiliation	.27	.30	.02	<.001	<.001	>.30
Ethnic origin	.15	.14	.01	<.009	<.013	>.40
Social class	.16	.02	.18	<.006	>.35	<.001
r	.19	.12	.06			
s	.23	.42	.73			

The values associated with each variable in Table XIII are estimates of the effect of each upon the vote of the party in question. These are calculated in each case by averaging the percentage differences in each pair of controlled comparisons shown in Tables XI and XII. The two values r and s represent the total effect of what Coleman calls, "random shocks"—r in the direction of the behaviour being examined (i.e., voting for a particular party) and s in the opposite direction (i.e., not voting for that party). In the case of each party all five values aggregate to unity, indicating that all influences have been accounted for even though all are not identified. The probability that the observed effect could have occurred by chance is tested by estimating the variance of each effect parameter, finding the standardized normal deviate, and consulting tables of the standardized cumulative normal distribution. For examples of these particular calculations see Coleman, *Introduction to Mathematical Sociology*, 205-7.

larly striking. It is also worth noticing in this instance that nearly three-quarters of the variation in the party's 1963 vote is apparently due to factors which promote support for the other parties—measured by the effect of random shocks. What this analysis suggests is that the weakness of the NDP before the by-election stemmed from its apparent irrelevance to the principal concerns of the electorate in Waterloo South. That does not necessarily mean that individual voters did not regard their social status as a relevant electoral consideration; it may be that they did not see the NDP as a party capable of serving that interest. If that was so, what was required to develop the necessary identification was an opportunity for the party to spend as much time as possible with every voter. The by-election offered just such an opportunity by allowing the party to concentrate its resources in one place, and the evidence is that they were used to maximum advantage. Whether or not this resulted in an active identification between working class voters and the NDP cannot be precisely determined from the data available, but it does seem strongly suggested by the differential effect of class on the party's vote between 1963 and 1964.

Such an interpretation obviously depends upon the questionable assumption that a substantial section of the working class in the riding had—for reasons associated with their economic position—been voting Conservative before the by-election, since (as was seen at the outset) the NDP victory depended heavily upon defections from the Tory party. But in Waterloo South there are excellent reasons for supposing that a connection between the Conservative party and organized labour has existed for quite a long time. So much attention has been paid to its almost unbroken record of Conservative victories in federal elections since 1921 that it is often forgotten that the riding not only returned a Labour member to Queen's Park after the First World War but that it continued to return the same man long after the Farmer-Labour government collapsed in 1923. That Karl Homuth's following was not an entirely personal one is shown by the fact of his defeat in 1934. But what is most striking is that the same Karl Homuth went over to the Conservatives in the early 1930s and sat as the federal member for Waterloo South from 1938 until his death in 1951. His long association with the riding must have helped to promote a belief in at least the national Conservative party's sympathy for the aims of labour. . . .

But whatever the historical source of the connection between the working class and the Conservative party in Ontario it is clear that in many areas of the province—especially in dominantly British ridings where the effect of ethnic or religious "cross-pressure" is less significant—the level of the party's support is being sharply reduced by the success of the NDP. And since the Conservative party's appeal to the worker has always been couched in the terms required by the brokerage theory the growth of a sentiment favouring an openly labour-oriented party suggests the growth of a class politics. It is possible, therefore, that the behaviour of Waterloo South is typical of what is happening in Ontario.

A Class Politics for Canada?

The extent to which the evidence of the by-election affects a general account of the role of social class in the Canadian political system is necessarily uncertain. While it seems clear that the NDP has established a hold on the riding which must depend upon the effect of influences more permanent than the attractiveness of its current candidate, the area is by no means a microcosm of the nation. On the other hand, there are many constituencies throughout Canada with social structures similar to that of Waterloo South where the growth of urbanizatin and industrialization has created conditions in which a class politics might be expected to flourish. As more and more of our people move to the cities the traditional influences of religious affiliation and ethnic origin are likely to become less important in the face of the pressures of an increasingly complex technological society. Nor is there any reason to suppose that the affluence which accompanies this development will result in a decline in the willingness of people to distinguish between themselves on the basis of social class. Lost in any of our sprawling metropolitan areas, the one link which the voter has with those around him is his occupation and the social status which it gives him in combination with related attributes such as income and education.

These considerations all point to a greater potential role for class as a determinant of Canadian electoral behaviour in the future. Whether any of our parties will actively seek to harness that potential remains to be seen, for the electoral success which the practice of brokerage has won for the Liberals, and to a lesser extent for the Conservatives, makes the full acceptance of a different style of political behaviour comparatively unattractive even to the NDP. But the price which the nation pays for that kind of success may well prove to be too great. Gad Horowitz has put the case very simply that a greater influence for social class is necessary in Canadian politics: "The promotion of dissensus on class issues is a way of mitigating dissensus on many non-class issues." While the evidence of Waterloo South is that social class *can* become the principal influence in our electoral behaviour, it remains the case that a substantial proportion of the electorate continues to divide itself on the basis of religious affiliation and ethnic origin. But since these people tend also to be rather more middle class it may be argued that we are approaching the stage—in southwestern Ontario at least—where the middle class persists in dividing itself along racial and religious lines in support of the two older parties at the same time as the working class is turning in increasing numbers to the New Democrats.

This growth in strength is, however, generally not sufficient to permit the NDP to make significant constituency gains, for although it is the leading party in most areas of working class concentration throughout the country its share of the labour vote remains substantially lower than that of social democratic parties in other parliamentary systems cast in the British mould. Its success therefore frequently depends upon the Liberals and the Conservatives dividing the rest of the vote, simply because there are comparatively few constituencies in Canada which are sufficiently working class in character to guarantee an NDP victory on that basis alone. On the other hand, since there is no prospect of a marriage of convenience between the two older parties, and since their division of the vote tends in many cases to be based on their promotion of those racial, religious, and regional differences which have been with us since the beginning, it may be said that if the NDP is allowed to become a major party in the House of Commons it will be because the traditional brokers of the Canadian political system were unable to rid themselves of the doctrine handed down from their fathers. But in that case, if Professor Horowitz' account of the matter is correct, national unity will have been preserved in spite of our traditional political practice rather than because of it.

BIBLIOGRAPHY

Alford, R. R., *Party and Society: The Anglo-American Democracies*, Chicago, Rand McNally, 1963.

Anderson, G. M., "Voting Behaviour and the Ethnic-Religious Variable: A Study of a Federal Election in Hamilton, Ontario," *C.J.E.P.S.*, Vol. XXXII, No. 1, February, 1966.

Beck, J. M., "Quebec and the Canadian Elections of 1958," *Parliamentary Affairs*, Vol. XII, No. 1, 1959.

Beck, J. M., "The Election of 1963 and National Unity," *Dalhousie Review*, Vol. XLIII, No. 2, Summer, 1963.

Beck, J. M., "The Electoral Behaviour of Nova Scotia in 1965," *Dalhousie Review*, Vol. XLVI, No. 1, Spring, 1966.
Beck, J. M., and Dooley, D. J., "Party Images in Canada," *Q.Q.*, Vol. LXVII, No. 3, Autumn, 1960.
Beck, J. M., *Pendulum of Power: Canada's Federal Elections*, Toronto, Prentice-Hall, 1968.
Blake, D. E., "Another Look at Social Credit and the British Columbia Electorate," *BC Studies*, No. 12, Winter, 1971-72.
Blake, D. E., "The Measurement of Regionalism in Canadian Voting Patterns", *C.J.P.S.*, Vol. V, No. 1, March, 1972.
Canada, *Report of the Chief Electoral Officer, Twenty-Ninth General Election, 1972*. Ottawa, Information Canada, 1973.
Casstevens, T. W., and Denham, W. A., "Turnover and Tenure in the Canadian House of Commons, 1867-1968", *C.J.P.S.*, Vol. III, No. 4, December, 1970.
Cohen, R. I., *Quebec Votes*, Montreal, Saje Publications, 1965.
Copes, P., "The Fisherman's Vote in Newfoundland", *C.J.P.S.*, Vol. III, No. 4, December, 1970.
Courtney, J. C., (ed.), *Voting in Canada*, Toronto, Prentice-Hall, 1967.
Courtney, J. C., and Smith, D. E., "Voting in a Provincial General Election and a Federal By-Election: A Constituency Study of Saskatoon City," *C.J.E.P.S.*, Vol. XXXII, No. 3, August, 1966.
Cunningham, R., "The Impact of the Local Candidate in Canadian Federal Elections", *C.J.P.S.*, Vol. IV, No. 2, June, 1971.
Curtis, J., Lambert, R., "Voting, Election Interest, and Age: National Findings for English and French Canadians," *C.J.P.S.*, Vol IX, No. 2, June, 1976.
Davis, M., "Ballot Behaviour in Halifax Revisited," *C.J.E.P.S.*, Vol. XXX, No. 4, November, 1964.
Davis, M., "A Last Look at Ballot Behaviour in the Dual Constituency of Halifax," *C.J.E.P.S.*, Vol. XXXII, No. 3, August, 1966.
Dean, E. P., "How Canada Has Voted: 1867 to 1945," *Canadian Historical Review*, Vol. XXX, No. 3, September, 1949.
Eldersveld, S., *Political Parties: A Behavioural Analysis*, Chicago, Rand McNally, 1964.
Elkins, D., and Blake, D., "Voting Research in Canada," *C.J.P.S.*, Vol. VIII, No. 2, June, 1975.
Engelmann, F. G., "Membership Participation in Policy-Making in the C.C.F.," *C.J.E.P.S.*, Vol. XXII, No. 2, May, 1956.
Engelmann, F. G., and Gilsdorf, R. R., "Recent Behavioural Political Science in Canada: An Assessment of Voting Behaviour Studies," Address to the 38th Annual Meeting of the Canadian Political Science Association, Sherbrooke, P.Q., June 8, 1966.
Eulau, H., *The Behavioural Persuasion in Politics*, New York, Random House, 1963.
Filley, W. O., "Social Structure and Canadian Political Parties: The Quebec Case," *Western Political Quarterly*, Vol. IX, No. 4, December, 1956.
Fox, P. W., "A Study of One Constituency in the Canadian Federal Election of 1957," *C.J.E.P.S.*, Vol. XXIV, No. 2, May, 1958.
Fox, P. W., "Canada's Most Decisive Federal Election," *Parliamentary Affairs*, Vol. XI, No. 3, Summer, 1958.
Gagne, W., and Regenstreif, P., "Some Aspects of New Democratic Party Urban Support in 1965," *C.J.E.P.S.*, Vol. XXXIII, No. 4, November, 1967.
Gilsdorf, R. R., "Cognitive and Motivational Sources of Voter Susceptibility to Influence", *C.J.P.S.*, Vol. VI, No. 4, December, 1973.
Granatstein, J. C., "The Armed Forces Vote in Canadian General Elections, 1940-1968," *Journal of Canadian Studies*, Vol. IV, No. 1, February, 1969.

Grayson, J. P., "Social Positions and Interest Recognition", *C.J.P.S.*, Vol. VI, No. 1, March, 1973.

Grossman, L. A. "'Safe' Seats: The Rural-Urban Pattern in Ontario," *C.J.E.P.S.*, Vol. XXIX, No. 3, August, 1963.

Hahn, H., "Voting in Canadian Communities: A Taxonomy of Referendum Issues," *C.J.P.S.*, Vol. I, No. 4, December, 1968.

Hamilton, R., Pinard, M., "The Bases of Parti Québécois Support in Recent Quebec Elections," *C.J.P.S.*, Vol. IX, No. 1, March, 1976.

Hamilton, R., Pinard, M., "Separation and Polarization of the Quebec Electorate: the 1973 Provincial Election," *C.J.P.S.*, Vol. X, No. 2, June, 1977.

Havel, J. E., *Les citoyens de Sudbury et la politique*, Sudbury, Laurentian University Press, 1966.

Hoffman, D., "Intra-Party Democracy: A Case Study," *C.J.E.P.S.*, Vol. XXVII, No. 2, May, 1961.

Irvine, W. P., "Canadian Partisan Identity," *C.J.P.S.*, Vol. VII, No. 3, September, 1974.

Jacek, H. J., "Party Loyalty and Electoral Volatility." *C.J.P.S.*, Vol. VIII, No. 1, March, 1975.

Jacek, H. J., McDonough, J., Shimizu, R., Smith, P., "Social Articulation and Aggregation in Political Party Organizations," *C.J.P.S.*, Vol. VIII, No. 2, June, 1975.

Jenson, J., "Party Loyalty in Canada," *C.J.P.S.*, Vol. VIII, No. 4, December, 1975.

Jenson, J., "Party Strategy and Party Identification," *C.J.P.S.*, Vol. IX, No. 1, March, 1976.

Jewett, P., "Voting in the 1960 Federal By-Elections at Peterborough and Niagara Falls: Who Voted New Party and Why?" *C.J.E.P.S.*, Vol. XXVIII, No. 1, February, 1962.

Kamin, L. J., "Ethnic and Party Affiliations of Candidates as Determinants of Voting," *Canadian Journal of Psychology*, Vol. XII, No. 4, December, 1958.

Kim, K. W., "The Limits of Behavioural Explanation in Politics." *C.J.E.P.S.*, Vol. XXXI, No. 3, August, 1965.

Koenig, D. J., *et al.*, "The Year that British Columbia Went NDP: NDP Voter Support Pre- and Post-1972," *BC Studies*, No. 24, Winter, 1974-5.

Land, B., *Eglinton, The Election Study of a Federal Constituency*, Toronto, Peter Martin Associates, 1965.

Laponce, J. A., *People vs. Politics, A Study of Opinions, Attitudes, and Perceptions in Vancouver-Burrard*, 1963-1965, Toronto University of Toronto Press, 1969.

Laponce, J. A., "Post-dicting electoral cleavages in Canadian federal elections, 1949-68: material for a footnote," *C.J.P.S.*, Vol. 5, No. 2, June, 1972.

Leduc, L., "Political Behaviour and the Issue of Majority Government in Two Federal Elections," *C.J.P.S.*, Vol. X, No. 2, June, 1977.

Leduc, L., Clarke, H., Jenson, J., Pammett, J., "A National Sample Design," *C.J.P.S.*, Vol. VII, No. 4, December, 1974.

Lemieux, V., "Les dimensions sociologiques du vote créditiste au Québec," *Recherches Sociographiques*, Vol. VI, No. 2, May-August, 1965.

Lemieux, V., "L'analyse hiérarchique des résultats électoraux," *C.J.P.S.*, Vol. I, No. 1, March, 1968.

Lemieux, V., "La composition des préférences partisanes," *C.J.P.S.*, Vol. II, No. 4, December, 1969.

Lemieux, V., (ed.), *Quatre élections provinciales au Québec*, Québec, les presses de l'Université Laval, 1969.

Lemieux, V., Gilbert, M., and Blais, A., *Une élection réalignment; l'élection général du 29 avril 1970 du Québec*, Montréal, Éditions du jour, 1970.

Long, J. A., and Slemko, B., "The Recruitment of Local Decision-Makers in Five

Canadian Cities: Some Preliminary Findings", *C.J.P.S.*, Vol. VII, No. 3, September, 1974.

Lovink, J. A. A., "Is Canadian Politics too Competitive?", *C.J.P.S.*, Vol. VI, No. 3, September, 1973.

MacDonald, K. J., "Sources of Electoral Support for Provincial Political Parties in Urban British Columbia", *BC Studies*, No. 15, Autumn, 1972.

Meisel, J., "Religious Affiliation and Electoral Behaviour," *C.J.E.P.S.*, Vol. XXII, No. 4, November, 1956.

Meisel, J., *The 1957 Canadian General Election*, Toronto, University of Toronto Press, 1962.

Meisel, J., "Political Culture and the Politics of Culture," *C.J.P.S.*, Vol. VII, No. 4, December, 1974.

Meisel, John (ed.), *Papers on the 1962 Election*, Toronto, University of Toronto Press, 1964.

Meisel, J., *Working Papers on Canadian Politics*, Montreal & London, McGill-Queen's University Press, 2nd enlarged ed., 1975.

Morley, J. T., "Comment: The 1974 Federal Election in British Columbia", *BC Studies*, No. 23, Fall, 1974.

Morrison, K. L., "The Businessman Voter in Thunder Bay", *C.J.P.S.*, Vol. VI, No. 2, June, 1973.

Morton, D., "The Effectiveness of Political Campaigning: The N.D.P. in the 1967 Ontario Election", *Journal of Canadian Studies*, Vol. IV, No. 3, August, 1969.

Palda, K. R., "Does Advertising Influence Votes? An Analysis of the 1966 and 1970 Quebec Elections", *C.J.P.S.*, Vol. VI, No. 4, December, 1973.

Pammett, J., Leduc, L., Jenson, J., Clarke, H., "The Perception and Impact of Issues in the 1974 Federal Election," *C.J.P.S.*, Vol. X, No. 1, March, 1977.

Penniman, M. R., (ed.), *Canada at the Polls: The General Election of 1974*, Washington, American Enterprise Institute, 1975.

Philpotts, G., "Vote trading, welfare, and uncertainty", *C.J.E.*, Vol. 5, No. 3, August, 1972.

Pinard, M., "One-Party Dominance and Third Parties," *C.J.E.P.S.*, Vol. XXXIII, No. 3, August, 1967.

Regenstreif, P., "The Canadian General Election of 1958," *Western Political Quarterly*, Vol. XIII, No. 2, June, 1960.

Regenstreif, P., "Some Aspects of National Party Support in Canada," *C.J.E.P.S.*, Vol. XIX, No. 1, February, 1963.

Regenstreif, P., *The Diefenbaker Interlude: Parties and Voting in Canada, An Interpretation*, Toronto, Longman, 1965.

Richert, J. P., "Political Socialization in Quebec", *C.J.P.S.*, Vol. VI, No. 2, June, 1973.

Robin, M., "The Social Basis of Party Politics in British Columbia," *Q.Q.*, Vol. LXXII, No. 4, Winter, 1966.

Rothney, G. O., "Denominational Basis of Representation in the Newfoundland Assembly, 1919-1962," *C.J.E.P.S.*, Vol. XXVII, No. 4, November, 1962.

Ruff, N. J., "Party Detachment and Voting Patterns in a Provincial Two-Member Constituency: Victoria 1972", *BC Studies*, No. 23, Fall, 1974.

Scarrow, H. A., "Federal-Provincial Voting Patterns in Canada," *C.J.E.P.S.*, Vol. XXVI, No. 2, May, 1960.

Scarrow, H. A., "By-Elections and Public Opinion in Canada," *Public Opinion Quarterly*, Vol. XXV, Spring, 1961.

Scarrow, H. A., "Patterns of Voter Turnout in Canada," *Midwest Journal of Political Science*, Vol. V, No. 4, 1961.

Scarrow, H. A., "Voting Patterns and the New Party," *Political Science*, Vol. XIV, No. 1, March, 1962.

Scarrow, H. A., *How Canada Votes, A Handbook of Federal and Provincial Election Data*, New Orleans, Hauser Press, 1962.

Schindeler, F., and Hoffman, D., "Theological and Political Conservatism," *C.J.P.S.*, Vol. I, No. 4, December, 1968.

Schwartz, M., "Canadian Voting Behaviour", in R. Rose, (ed.), *Electoral Behaviour: A Comparative Handbook*, New York, Free Press, 1974.

Simeon, R., and Elkins, D., "Regional Political Cultures," *C.J.P.S.*, Vol. VII, No. 3, September, 1974.

Simmons, J. W., "Voting Behaviour and Socio-Economic Characteristics: The Middlesex East Federal Election, 1965," *C.J.E.P.S.*, Vol. XXXIII, No. 3, August, 1967.

Smith, D. E., "A Comparison of Prairie Political Developments in Saskatchewan and Alberta", *Journal of Canadian Studies*, Vol. IV, No. 1, February, 1969.

Sniderman, P. M., Forbes, H. D., and Melzer, I., "Party Loyalty and Electoral Volatility: A Study of the Canadian Party System", *C.J.P.S.*, Vol. VII, No. 2, June, 1974.

Sproule-Jones, M., "Social Credit and the British Columbia Electorate", *BC Studies*, No. 11, Fall, 1971, and No. 12, Winter, 1971-72.

Ulmer, S., (ed.), *Introductory Readings in Political Behaviour*, Chicago, Rand McNally, 1961.

Van Loon, R., "Political Participation in Canada: The 1965 Election", *C.J.P.S.*, Vol. III, No. 3, September, 1970.

Warburton, T. R., "Religious and Social Influences in Voting in Greater Victoria", *BC Studies*, No. 10, Summer, 1971.

Wilson, J., "The Myth of Candidate Partisanship: the Case of Waterloo South," *Journal of Canadian Studies*, Vol. III, No. 4, November, 1968.

Winn, C., and McMenemy, J., "Political Alignment in a Polarized City: Electoral Cleavages in Kitchener, Ontario", *C.J.P.S.*, Vol. VI, No. 2, June, 1973.

Wiseman, N., and Taylor, K. W., "Ethnic vs Class Voting: The Case of Winnipeg, 1945", *C.J.P.S.*, Vol. II, No. 2, June, 1974.

Woodward, C. A., *A History of New Brunswick Provincial Election Campaigns and Platforms, 1866-1974*, Toronto, Micromedia, 1976.

Wrong, D. H., "Ontario Provincial Elections, 1934-1955," *C.J.E.P.S.*, Vol. XXIII, No. 3, August, 1957.

Young, W. D., "The Peterborough Election: The Success of a Party Image," *Dalhousie Review*, Vol. XL, No. 4, Winter, 1961.

Zakuta, L., "Membership in a Becalmed Protest Movement," *C.J.E.P.S.*, Vol. XXIV, No. 2, May, 1958.

11

THE EXECUTIVE PROCESS: THE CROWN

The argument over whether to continue the monarchy in Canada has recurred fitfully but fairly often in recent years. Canadians thus far have avoided trying to resolve the question conclusively. The recommendation on the subject presented by the Special Joint Committee of the Senate and of the House of Commons on the Constitution of Canada illustrates the attitude of many Canadians. The Committee's *Final Report* in 1972 said, "Because of the state of divided opinion in Canada, the Committee does not recommend any change in the monarchical system at the present time" (p.29). There have been some changes, however, in the use of traditional royal nomenclature in Quebec and to a lesser extent at Ottawa. Thus, for example, the designation "Queen's Printer" has been abandoned in both jurisdictions while Quebec has also altered the name of the provincial legislature to "the National Assembly" and "the Speech from the Throne" to the "inaugural address".

Professor Frank MacKinnon has become one of the leading academic defenders of the monarchy. (For his recent book, see the bibliography.) The extract in this chapter from an article by him gives the gist of his arguments in favour of retaining the Canadian monarchy. Peter Dempson's article points out that whatever the merits of the monarchy, the continuation of the crown in Canada seems to be endangered by creeping republicanism.

Almost all of the monarch's remaining powers in Canada were transferred to the governor general by the revised Letters Patent issued in 1947. The relevant section of the Letters Patent conferring these powers was published in the third edition of *Politics: Canada*, pp. 307-309.

The present chapter contains Senator Eugene Forsey's description of the 1926 constitutional crisis in Canada, taken from his classic study of the royal power of dissolution of Parliament. Professor James Mallory's article dealing with the lieutenant-governor's choice of a successor to Premier Duplessis in Quebec may be found in the third edition of this book, pp. 314-318. The most recent case of a lieutenant-governor reserving a bill, which occurred in Saskatchewan in 1961, is discussed in the portion of another article by Professor Mallory which is reproduced in this chapter.

A final item explains the recent history of the award of honours in Canada, including the introduction of an exclusively Canadian honours system in 1967.

Some of the relatively few recent books and articles dealing with the governor general and the lieutenant-governors in Canada are cited in the bibliography at the end of the chapter.

THE VALUE OF THE MONARCHY*

Frank MacKinnon

A constitutional monarch protects democracy from some peculiarities of political power. It has been retained in our system because it works. Other reasons, such as nostalgic recollections of the past and sentimental ties with Britain, are secondary—to some, irrelevant—and should not obscure basic facts of government. One of these facts is a tendency of man, whether deep-sea diver or astronaut on the one hand or politician on the other, to suffer from the "bends" during rapid rises from one level of pressure and atmosphere to another.

History clearly indicates how common and serious are the "bends" in government. Even small rises from private citizen to mayor may bring on giddiness while major ascents from backbencher to minister or from minister to head of government can cause acute distress of the equilibrium. Constitutions have prescribed various remedies. Complicated procedures select those who are to make the political climb; ascent by stages is sometimes provided—perhaps by planned pauses in the back benches or the opposition; control of those on high is arranged through established contacts with those below; and, most difficult of all, some arrangement must be made to end the stay in political orbit of those who have been there long enough and can not or will not come back by themselves. A sure cure has not yet been devised, however, and the "bends" remain a major occupational hazard of rulers, which some overcome for varying periods and to which others fall quick and tragic victims.

To relieve this difficulty at the heights of political power is the main purpose of the constitutional monarchy. Some human being must be at the summit of government, and much depends on his stability. Unfortunately great talent, public acclaim and hero worship, and even assumptions of "divine right" have not been reliable stabilizers when the head of state wields power. We therefore place two persons at the top: one is at the very summit and he stays there permanently and is accustomed to living at

* From *The Dalhousie Review*, Vol. 49, No. 2, Summer, 1969, by permission of the author and publisher.

that level; the other is temporary and he is made to understand that his status is sponsored and may be ended at any time.

The monarch holds power in the state on behalf of the people, and he or she is the personal symbol of authority which man finds necessary in every system. Heredity makes his tenure unquestioned and ensures a rigid training for the job. Pomp and ceremony attract respect and provide the show which people always expect from heads of state. But the monarch is not allowed to wield the power of head of state by himself; the pomp and ceremony are all that he can manage safely at his level and he must wield the power only on the advice of others.

These others are the sovereign's ministers, especially the prime minister, who is the head of government. A prime minister is almost at the summit but not quite, and that difference is crucial to democracy. He is given no power whatever; he advises the Crown on the exercise of the Crown's power; and that difference is also crucial to democracy. He has no pomp of his own, so that he knows that he is not an indispensable symbol. He is a trustee into whose hands is placed the exercise of power but not power itself.

This separation of pomp and power at the top took centuries to develop and was the result of the mistakes of many sovereigns and ministers. Other arrangements for such separation in other systems did not go so far as the British, who make the monarch so colourful and the prime minister so powerful and responsible an adviser that each, regardless of the personalities concerned, knows his place. . . .

The monarchy therefore serves democracy. It keeps the ministers in second place as servants of the state—electable, responsible, accountable, criticizable, and defeatable—a position necessary to the operation of parliamentary government. The people and their parliament can control the head of government because he cannot identify himself with the state or confuse loyalty to himself with allegiance to the state and criticism with treason. He is discouraged from the common tendency of officials, whether elected or not, to regard and make themselves indispensable, to entrench themselves in expanding power structures, to resent accountability and criticism, and to scoff at the effects of prolonged tenure of office or advancing years. Moreover, such control avoids the charges of treason, executions, assassinations, revolutions, and miscellaneous other expensive upheavals which so often accompany attempts to control and change governments that take themselves too seriously.

The democratic sensibilities of some people are disturbed by the idea of an élite, a symbol, an official who is neither elected nor chosen by someone who is elected. They err if they think the withdrawal of monarchy will remove such elements from government. These elements are characteristic of government itself, whatever its form, and are simply transferred to other institutions when a monarchy disappears. Whatever their system, men will have élites and symbols. Heads of government, elected or not, will take to themselves if they can the prestige and power of monarchs, disguised perhaps, but with the same basic elements; they find them a natural and necessary feature of government authority. The existence of a monarchy protects the prime minister from such temptations. . . .

Monarchal phenomena are common in other activities of society. The cult of the celebrity is as dominant in our day as it ever was in history. How often is "I touched him" heard in a screaming crowd! The élite in athletics have always been admired and well paid. Universities feature academic ceremonial. There are many resemblances between churches and royal courts—the raiment, titles, powers of clergy, even the throne, tiara, and crown. And in the smallest communities the dignities and regalia of fraternal and religious lodges are reminiscent of the potentates and knights of old. These are such natural and acceptable phenomena that it is not difficult to understand government officials taking advantage of them. Man has found, however, that in government it is hard to criticize and advise a tremendous swell in robes or uniform who also has power, a retinue, and a palace. Our system discourages these things as much as possible for working politicians, but, since they are inevitable anyway, they are placed with the Crown, partly to provide a good show, mainly to strengthen the democratic state.

All systems, including democracy, contain the means for their own destruction. It is in time of crisis, when some serious and unexpected dislocation takes place for which there is no normal remedy, that systems break down for good. . . . Parliamentary government presupposes change as required; but such change means orderly alteration of power, not conditions of general panic and destruction. When an electoral system is stalemated, when a parliament breaks down, when a prime minister dies in office and there is no obvious successor, when a leader becomes very ill or insane and everyone knows it but himself and the public—these are among the times when political paralysis is brought on by shock and uncertainty. In such circumstances a constitutional monarch provides a symbol of continuity, order, and authority. He cannot, of course, step in and take over; he can only encourage others and sponsor the search for an orderly solution of the difficulties. He is above suspicion and can command confidence because of his prestige, because he is above politics and ambition for personal aggrandizement, and because he does not exericise power on his own initiative. Even in such modest periods of upheaval as elections, he represents the state as a whole while the parties involved, including the government, can oppose each other to even the most vituperative extremes—a process which should never be taken for granted. No political leader can be a symbol of the whole state either in crisis or in elections; nor should he be in a parliamentary democracy. That is the job of a monarch.

There are other purposes of the monarchy: the encouragement of dignity and respect for government, the example of a royal family, the colour of pageantry, the sponsorship of good works and the inevitable social activities of government; the source of honours and awards; a continuing focus of loyalty and emotion; a unifying force among a people; and, in our monarchy, a headship for a family of nations, the Commonwealth. Each of these functions has its own merits and weaknesses. Whether or not we approve of any or all of them, we must remember that none is irrelevant or disposable: each one crops up in some form in every system of government. When a monarchy disappears, other institutions soon take them on. Then trouble begins because of the transfer of such functions to the power structure. Officials and political parties from right to left have found many ways of using them to protect themselves and their powers and prestige from the legitimate operation of democracy. They are in safer hands, and are more effective, with the Crown.

An elected non-political president is often used as an alternative to a monarch. His main problem, aside from the temporary and relatively uninteresting and colourless character of his office, is the ease with which he can be overshadowed by the prime minister and, worse, the ease with which he can compete with the prime minister. Everyone concerned knows exactly where the monarch and his advisers stand in relation to one another and to the people. This arrangement, as already noted, is not so clear in a republic because two elected heads can get in each other's way and trespass on each other's powers.

An elected political president wielding power directly is a completely different institution at the head of a different system of government. He could not function in the parliamentary system as we know it. As every American president has testified, this kind of official also finds burdensome the combination of head of government and head of state.

Which is the "best" system? No one knows; some people tend to think their own is "best" whatever it is; others tend to admire any system other than their own; some are more concerned with the kind of system they have than with how it works. Two things, however, are clear; that systems are not automatically transferable from one place to another—too much depends on the environment; and that any system must allow, not only for logical forms and cherished principles, but also for peculiarities of human nature in government, particularly the hierarchal "bends."

Canadians have retained the Crown as represented by the Sovereign, the Governor-General, and the Lieutenant-Governors. All the reasons for the Crown have applied in both federal and provincial governments, and, on the whole, the relations between the Crown and the Ministers have worked extremely well. The twelve incumbents together cost a little more than two cents per citizen per year. By no stretch of the imagination can the Governors-General or the Lieutenant-Governors be considered to have played any significant role in actual government in our time, or to have obstructed or overshadowed their Premiers. Their job has been to occupy the top levels in their respective jurisdictions and to handle the decorative and emergency functions, while leaving the Prime Ministers and Premiers to handle the powers of government without actually possessing them, and to be electable, responsible, accountable, criticizable, and removable. The Governors-General and the Lieutenant-Governors are something more than constitutional presidents; they have Sovereign's auspices to signify authority, to enhance their prestige, and to clearly mark the line between pomp and power.

Over the years, Canada's eleven heads of government have been a mixed lot. Some have been everything democratic theory describes, real leaders of a parliamentary system. Some have been virtual dictators; some could control their legislatures personally with an iron hand; some had delusions of grandeur; some would do with their constitutions exactly what they could get away with. Some, on the other hand, have been weak, indecisive, ineffective, or inadequate to the demands of high office. The offices of Prime Minister and Premier, like any office, are only partially what the constitution says they are; they are in large measure what the talents and personalities of the incumbents make them. To all of them, the fact that they were elected gave them a mandate. It did not ensure good government, but it did make them responsible and disposable. The existence of the Crown made sure that they stayed that way. . . .

Those who worry about the monarchy sometimes doubt the relevance in Canada of the Sovereign herself because she is Queen of several countries. Such a situation is common in Canada; many citizens owe allegiance to outside heads of their businesses, churches, unions, international political parties, and other groups. Nevertheless, a shared head of state is controversial. We need to remember that under our constitution the Sovereign is a part of Parliament and is the formal, ultimate source of political power, and the law sets out the facts of power with clarity for all to see and recognize as authentic. Governments in Canada may have quarrelled over which may do what, but power to govern has itself been unassailable and unquestioned from colonial times to the present. This stability of law is by no means universal around the world in an age when constitutions have been unusually short-lived and unreliable and when human rights have enjoyed only modest protection. Governments and their supporters come and go, but the Canadian people know that their rights and the powers of their state enjoy a solid, recognized base and the validations of centuries of usage. The sovereign is the legal expression and permanent non-partisan symbol of that fact.

Canadians may some day have their own resident sovereign. Perhaps, when the Queen's reign ends, Prince Charles could become King of the rest of the Commonwealth while Prince Andrew moved to Ottawa to found a purely Canadian dynasty while continuing the stable heritage of constitutional power. Whatever happens, vague or emotional platitudes about monarchal and democratic theory and principle are unrealistic unless considered with the actual practical operation of government and the political performance of men. When the monarchy makes the constitution work as a plan for humans as distinct from a paper declaration, however grand, then it should be recognized as a bulwark of democracy and of the rights Canadians want to enjoy under their parliamentary system.

WE'RE ON THE ROAD TO REPUBLICANISM*

Peter Dempson

Whither the monarchy in Canada? The question of the future of the monarchy was resurrected again last September by State Secretary

---

* From *The Telegram*, Toronto, December, 4, 1969. Reprinted by permission of *The Toronto Sun Publishing Limited*.

Gerard Pelletier who, when visiting London, casually predicted that Canada would evolve into a republic in one or two generations. But it soon became apparent he was speaking only for himself.

Prime Minister Pierre Trudeau was quick to issue a mild rebuke to Mr. Pelletier, pointing out that the Crown was still a vital part of the Canadian constitution and would continue to be. . . .

Many Canadians—mainly those under 30—have come to the conclusion, however, that the monarchy is outdated, and that Canada would be better off as a republic. This was pointed up in a poll taken for the Canada 70 series, published by The Telegram.

More than half of the Canadians polled in the study outside of Quebec were either loyal or indifferent to the monarchy. In Quebec, 90 percent expressed the view that the monarchy had outlived its usefulness.

Prince Philip, who isn't one to back away from a contentious issue, was asked when he visited Ottawa what he thought the future of the monarchy in Canada was. He promptly replied that it was a matter for Canadians themselves to decide.

"The monarchy exists in Canada for historical reasons," he said, adding that it was considered to be a benefit to the nation. "But if Canadians feel the monarchy has no further role to play in Canada, then for goodness sake, let's end the thing on amicable terms without having a row about it."

The Prince said flatly that the royal couple didn't make periodic trips to Canada "for our health, so to speak. We can think of other ways of enjoying ourselves.". . .

Along with other family benefits, Prince Philip gets £40,000 ($104,000) a year from the British Parliament. . . .

The Queen draws an allowance of $1.3 million a year from the state. It has remained unchanged since she ascended the throne in 1952. Although one of the richest women in the world, she spends more than that amount to meet the demands made on her. She makes up the difference by dipping into her private income, mostly the revenues of real estate.

The Queen is responsible for paying 300 fulltime employees, from the lord chamberlain to the housemaids. A new government employment tax also comes out of her allowance. . . .

Canadian taxpayers bear none of the direct costs of the monarchy in Britain. Canadians, however, contribute to the institution through the upkeep of Crown representatives in Canada—the Governor General and the 10 lieutenant governors of the provinces

Many Canadians are convinced that eventually the monarchy will disappear in Canada and be replaced by a republican form of government, patterned, perhaps, after India or some other Commonwealth countries. But this isn't likely to happen in the foreseeable future.

The ties with Britain remain strong, even though more than half of Canada's population is now of other than Anglo-Saxon descent. . . .

Still, even if a majority of Canadians now favor stripping the trappings of royalty from the constitution, it would be exceedingly difficult to do. Any change in the British North America Act must have the consent of all provinces, hence any provincial government could veto abolition of the monarchy at the outset.

Should Canada become a republic in time, however, it's likely it would retain the parliamentary system of government, modelled on British precedents. It would be necessary, of course, to have a non-partisan head of state on the analogy of the modern Crown. The Governor General would probably be replaced by a president and the lieutenant-governors by governors.

The new system, to be successful, should stem from the constitutional expression that modern monarchs and their viceroys have been stripped of all political power. But in a republic this might be difficult. An elected president could defy Parliament, as Charles de Gaulle did on more than on occasion.

The last two Governments have been whittling away at the monarchy, like tidal waves lashing a rugged shore. Royal Mail on post boxes has become Canada Mail. The royal insignia on buildings and documents has been replaced by the Canadian coat-of-arms. . . .

Eugene Forsey, of Ottawa, long regarded as one of Canada's outstanding constitutional experts, has branded these moves as "creeping republicanism." But whether creeping, crawling or bounding, nothing could be plainer or more flagrant than what is happening.

It almost makes a mockery of what Queen Elizabeth said in the fall of 1957 when she opened Parliament and greeted senators and MPs as ". . . your Queen—together we constitute the Parliament of Canada."

It's obvious that those words have now been largely forgotten, despite the reassurances by the Prime Minister that the monarchy still has a vital role to play in Canada.

WAS THE GOVERNOR GENERAL'S REFUSAL CONSTITUTIONAL?*

Eugene A. Forsey

In the Canadian Parliament of 1921-5, the Liberal party, under Mr. Mackenzie King, had 117 members, the Conservatives 50, Progressives, Labour and Independents 68. For most purposes, however, the Liberal Government enjoyed the support of a majority of the Progressives, so that it was able to carry on for four years without serious difficulty. By September 5, 1925, Mr. King had become convinced of the necessity of seeking at the polls a clear working majority over all other parties. He accordingly advised and secured dissolution. The election was held October 29. It returned 101 Liberals, 116 Conservatives and 28 Progressives, Labour members and Independents. The Prime Minister and eight other Ministers lost their seats.

On November 5, a month and two days before the new Parliament's legal existence could begin, the Prime Minister issued a statement asserting that three courses were open to him: to resign at once, to meet the new

* From *The Royal Power of Dissolution of Parliament in the British Commonwealth*, Toronto, Oxford University Press, 1943, pp. 131-140. By permission of the author and publisher.

House of Commons, or to advise "an immediate dissolution". He had decided to meet the new House, at the earliest practicable moment.

This proved to be January 7, 1926. From then till the House adjourned, March 2, to allow the Prime Minister to find a seat in a by-election, and again from March 15, when the sittings resumed, till June 25, the Conservatives made repeated efforts to defeat the Government, but without success. The Government's majorities were: 3, 10, 10, 1, 7, 8, 11, 13, 6, 9, 13, 13, 15, 1, 6, 8. On June 18, a committee appointed to investigate alleged scandals in the Customs Department presented its report. The Conservatives were not satisfied with the report, and one of them, Mr. H. H. Stevens, on June 22, moved an amendment which, among other things, described the conduct of "the Prime Minister and the government" as "wholly indefensible" and the "conduct of the present Minister of Customs in the case of Moses Aziz" as "utterly unjustifiable". On June 23, Mr. Woodsworth (Labour) moved what Keith calls a "non-partisan" sub-amendment which would have struck out the condemnation of the Prime Minister, the Government, and the Minister of Customs, and added a condemnation of various persons on both sides of politics and in the Civil Service and provided for a judicial commission to continue the investigation. The Government accepted this sub-amendment; the Conservatives opposed it. On June 25 it was defeated by a majority of two. Mr. Fansher (Progressive) then moved a second sub-amendment, which would have left in the Stevens amendment the condemnation of the Prime Minister, the Government and the Minister of Customs, and added Mr. Woodsworth's proposed condemnation of other persons, and provision for a judicial commission. The Speaker ruled this out of order. His ruling was challenged, and overruled by a majority of two. A motion to adjourn the debate, supported by the Government, was lost by one; somewhat later, at 5:15 a.m., Saturday, June 26, a second motion to adjourn the debate, also supported by the Government, carried by one. The Fansher sub-amendment had meanwhile been carried without a division, but the Stevens amendment had not been voted on.

During the week-end Mr. King asked for dissolution. The Governor General, Lord Byng, refused. Mr. King thereupon resigned. He announced his resignation to the House, Monday, June 28, saying that he believed that "under British practice" he was "entitled" to a dissolution. He declared that there was "no Prime Minister", "no Government"; declined to take part in a conference on the means of winding up the session; and moved that the House adjourn, which it did, at 2:15 p.m. The Governor General at once sent for Mr. Meighen, and asked him "if he could command a majority in the House to get the work of the session concluded in orderly manner." Mr. Meighen replied that he could, having received informal promises from a number of the Progressives to the effect that they would vote with the Conservatives to get these all-important Bills through, pass Supply, and prorogue. The Governor General then requested Mr. Meighen to form a government, and in the evening he undertook to do so. Next day, during a conference of the Progressives, the Governor General sent for the Progressive leader, Mr. Forke. The Progressives thereupon drew up and gave to Mr. Forke "a confidential memorandum for his guidance". . . . The memorandum was as follows:

> That we assist the new administration in completing the business of the session. That we are in agreement on the necessity of continuing the investigation into the customs and excise department by a judicial commission. . . . That no dissolution should take place until the . . . commission has finished its investigation . . . and that Parliament be summoned to deal with the reports.

Mr. Meighen had accepted office as Prime Minister, but the formation of his Cabinet presented unusual difficulties. Mr. King and his colleagues had not followed the customary practice of holding office till their successors were appointed. They had left the Crown without a ministry, the country without a government, an action which appears to be without precedent in the history of the Empire. Mr. King had refused to engage in a conference on the question of finishing the session's business. The session was almost at an end; but Supply had not been voted; bills to amend the Special War Revenue Act and the Canada Evidence Act, thirteen divorce bills and eight other private bills had passed both Houses and awaited the royal assent. The important Long Term Farm Mortgage Credit Bill was still before the Senate. Under the law as it then stood, if Mr. Meighen formed a government in the ordinary way, every one of the 15 or so ministers with portfolio from the Commons, upon accepting office, would automatically have vacated his seat. This would have left the Conservatives and Liberals about equal. The government would have had to seek an adjournment or prorogation of about six weeks to allow time for ministerial by-election. [Later, the Act of 1931, 21-22 George V, c. 52, did away with the necessity for such by-elections.] Mr. King's attitude on the question of a conference suggests that he might have opposed an adjournment. . . . If he had opposed adjournment, it is by no means impossible that, with the Conservative strength reduced by 15 or 16, he could have carried with him enough Progressives to succeed. Mr. Meighen might have got prorogation for six weeks. But either adjournment or prorogation would have involved a long delay, highly inconvenient to the members of Parliament, especially the farmer members at that time of year; prorogation would have killed the Long Term Farm Mortgage Credit Bill, the Montreal Harbour Commission Loan Bill and two private bills; and either adjournment or prorogation would have involved carrying on for six weeks without Supply, which would have been possible but not desirable.

Mr. Meighen therefore announced that, to bring the session to an end promptly, he had "decided to constitute . . . a temporary Ministry . . . of seven members, who would be sworn in without portfolio, and . . . would have responsibility as acting Ministers of the several departments." After prorogation, he would "immediately address himself to the task of constituting a Government in the method established by custom. The present plan is merely to meet an unusual if not unprecedented situation."

The new Government met the House June 29, and proceeded to deal with the business on the Order Paper. The first main item was of course the still unfinished debate on the Stevens amendment. Mr. Rinfret, Liberal, now moved a fresh sub-amendment, which the Speaker declared to be in order. Mr. Geary, Conservative, challenged the Speaker's ruling, which was sustained by a majority of one. On a vote on the sub-amendment itself, the new Government received a majority of 12. A further new sub-amendment was then carried by agreement, the Stevens amendment so amended was carried by a majority of 10, and the report of the Committee, as amended, was also carried by 10.

On June 30, the Liberal Opposition moved a vote of want of confidence in the new Government on the ground of its fiscal policy. This was defeated by a majority of seven.

Mr. King followed this up in Committee of Supply by an elaborate cross-examination of the Ministers, designed to show that they were not validly appointed and were therefore not ministers at all. Mr. Lapointe, Liberal ex-Minister of Justice, then raised a question of privilege; that the acting ministers of departments, having really (so he alleged) accepted offices of profit under the Crown, had vacated their seats and had no right to appear in the House. These two propositions, as Mr. Bury, Conservative M.P. for Edmonton East pointed out, are of course mutually exclusive. If the acting ministers of departments were really *Ministers* of departments, there could be no question of the validity of their appointments; if they had not been validly appointed, and were not ministers of departments, then they had not vacated their seats. The two propositions, however, were ingeniously combined in a motion of Mr. Robb, Liberal ex-Minister of Finance:

> That the actions in this House of the Honourable Members who have acted as Ministers of the Crown since the 29th of June, 1926, namely the Honourable Members for West York, Fort William, Vancouver Centre, Argenteuil, Wellington South, and the Honourable senior Member for Halifax, are a violation and an infringment of the privileges of this House for the following reasons:—That the said Honourable gentlemen have no rights to sit in this House and should have vacated their seats therein if they legally hold office as administrators of the various departments, assigned to them by Order-in-Council; that if they do not hold such office legally, they have no right to control the business of Government in this House and ask for supply for the Departments of which they state they are acting Ministers.

After debate, this motion was put. Mr. Meighen's seat was of course vacant, which reduced the Conservative strength by one. Mr. Bird, Progressive member for Nelson, broke his pair and voted with the Liberals. As a result, the Government was defeated by one vote. The House then adjourned. Next day, July 2, before it could meet again, Mr. Meighen advised the Governor General to dissolve Parliament. Lord Byng accepted the advice, and Parliament was accordingly dissolved, without prorogation and without royal assent being given to any of the bills which were awaiting it.

These events raised no fewer than eight constitutional questions.

1. Was Lord Byng's refusal of dissolution to Mr. King constitutional in the light of the circumstances as they stood on the morning of June 28?

2. Did the constitutionality of that refusal depend on Mr. Meighen's actually being able to carry on with the existing House of Commons?

3. Did the constitutionality of the refusal depend on the constitutionality of the government of ministers without portfolio?

4. Was the Government constitutional?

5. Was the grant of dissolution to Mr. Meighen constitutional?

6. Was the constitutionality of refusing dissolution to Mr. King on June 28 affected by the grant of dissolution to Mr. Meighen on July 2?

7. Was the manner of dissolution of July 2 constitutional?

8. Did Lord Byng's action relegate Canada to a status inferior to that of Great Britain?

THE LIEUTENANT-GOVERNOR'S DISCRETIONARY POWERS: THE RESERVATION OF BILL 56 IN SASKATCHEWAN*

J. R. Mallory

Before proroguing the legislative session on April 8, 1961, the Lieutenant-Governor of Saskatchewan, Frank L. Bastedo, intimated that he was reserving Bill 56 for the signification of the pleasure of the Governor General. This bill, entitled "An Act to Provide for the Alteration of Certain Mineral Contracts," would have given to the lieutenant-governor in council the power to modify existing mineral contracts, and contained the provision that it would expire on December 31, 1961. After prorogation Mr. Bastedo issued a statement to the press, which said in part, "this is a very important bill affecting hundreds of mineral contracts. It raises implications which throw grave doubts of the legislation being in the public interest. There is grave doubt as to its validity." These doubts were not shared by his constitutional advisers, who informed him that in their view the bill was within the powers of the legislature and advised him to assent to it.

The royal veto—even a suspensive veto, which is what in effect reservation is—is deemed to be dead in most jurisdictions where the British cabinet system operates. No British sovereign since Queen Anne has refused to give assent to a bill, and the exercise of the power to reserve or withhold assent is generally regarded as a relic of colonial thraldom which disappeared when the fetters of Downing Street control were removed. How then can it continue to exist in a Canadian province?

Under the powers conferred upon him by section 90 of the British North America Act, a lieutenant-governor may do one of three things with a bill which has passed through all its stages in the legislature and is presented to him for royal assent so that it is transformed into an Act of the legislature: he may signify that he assents to the bill in the Queen's name; he may withhold his assent; or he may reserve the bill so that it may

* From *The Canadian Journal of Economics and Political Science*, Vol. XXVII, No. 4, November, 1961. By permission of the author and publisher.

be considered by the governor general. The first of these three courses is the normal one, and requires no comment. The second is a simple veto; the bill is dead and can be revived only by introducing it again into the legislature, passing it through all its stages, and presenting it again for assent at a subsequent session of the legislature. The third is not a withholding of assent (that is, there is no veto), but the decision as to whether assent will be given or withheld is passed back to the governor general, acting on the advice of his ministers in Ottawa.

Seventy bills have been reserved by lieutenant-governors since Confederation. However, fifty-nine of these were reserved before 1900, most of them in the early days of provincial government. Since 1920 there have been four: three in Alberta in 1937, and the one here considered. The use of these wide discretionary powers of the lieutenant-governor was characteristic of the period of almost colonial status of the provinces (particularly the western provinces) in relation to the dominion. The revival of the power in Alberta in 1937 caused general surprise. It had become widely believed that the power had become constitutionally obsolete in the same way that the position of the governor general as an imperial officer had disappeared as a result of the achievement of Canadian autonomy. So general was the uncertainty that the federal government referred the whole question of the scope and validity of the powers of disallowance, reservation, and withholding assent to the Supreme Court in the autumn of 1937.

The Supreme Court had no difficulty in finding that these powers continued to subsist, unaffected by changes in constitutional conventions, and the powers were equally valid, whether the legislation was *intra vires* the provincial legislature or not, and that the only limitations on the discretion of the lieutenant-governor were instructions from the governor general.

While the power of the lieutenant-governor is unrestricted in law, it was intended to operate as one of the means by which the federal government could intervene in a province to prevent the enactment of legislation which threatened some wider interest which required protection in the national interest. In other words, the reservation of bills was intended to be a power exercised by the lieutenant-governor acting in his capacity as a Dominion officer. . . .

Sir John A. Macdonald, when minister of justice, caused a minute of council to be adopted in Ottawa in 1882 and communicated to lieutenant-governors in order to make clear to them that they should exercise their powers of reservation only when instructed to do so. "It is only in a case of extreme necessity that a Lieutenant-Governor should without such instructions exercise his discretion as a Dominion Officer in reserving a bill. In fact, with the facility of communication between the Dominion and provincial governments, such a necessity can seldom if ever arise."

In other words, a lieutenant-governor who reserves a bill on his own authority is acting within the scope of his legal powers, but not within the spirit of the constitution.

Was Mr. Bastedo acting, directly or indirectly, on instruction from Ottawa? The present instructions of lieutenant-governors do not specify any classes of bills which may, or should be reserved. Prime Minister Diefenbaker, when asked in the House of Commons on April 10 whether the bill had been reserved, replied:

> ... The first information the government received on this matter was on Saturday, when the lieutenant governor telephoned the under secretary of state that he had reserved a bill of the Saskatchewan legislature for the signification of the Governor General's pleasure. ... We have no other information on the matter. There was no consultation in advance in any way, and any action in this regard would be taken by the lieutenant governor himself.

Two days later, in answer to another question in the House, the Prime Minister made a further statement in which he said:

> ... The reservation by lieutenant governors have [*sic*] been generally accepted as dependent on a request from the governor in council. There was no discussion in this regard, as I have already pointed out. We had no knowledge of the action to be taken by the lieutenant governor. However, the action was taken, and as yet the reasons which the lieutenant governor is required to transmit to the Governor General for the course he followed have not come to hand. As soon as they do the governor in council will take such action as is deemed proper, with full regard to the fact that this government has consistently taken the attitude that if legislation is within the legislative competence of the provinces, except constitutionally in extra-ordinary circumstances there should be no interference with provincial jurisdiction.

Finally, on May 5th, Mr. Diefenbaker tabled in the House the order in council "in which His Excellency the Governor General by and with the advice of Her Majesty the Queen's privy council for Canada declares his assent to Bill No. 56 of the legislature of Saskatchewan passed during the present year and which was reserved by the lieutenant governor of Saskatchewan for the signification of the pleasure of the Governor General in accordance with the terms of the British North America Act." The order in council dealt with the two grounds upon which the Lieutenant-Governor had acted noting that in the opinion of the Minister of Justice the bill was *intra vires* the Saskatchewan legislature, and that "the expression 'conflict with national policy or interest' does not relate solely to a difference of principle or point of view, but must include matters of practical or physical effect, and that in this sense the bill is not in conflict with national policy or interest."

In his statement to the House, the Prime Minister reminded members that the Lieutenant-Governor's action had not been preceded by consultation with the federal government. "I have no hesitation in saying," he said, "that had there been such consultation my colleagues and I would have recommended to the Governor General that the lieutenant governor be instructed not to reserve the bill."

He referred to Macdonald's minute of council of 1882 and noted that "in view of the development of communications since" there should be ample opportunity for consultation before reservation. He then said, "I should point out that while no formal instructions have yet been given to lieutenant governors [never] to reserve a bill unless upon specific instructions, my colleagues and I are now considering whether such formal instructions, should be given." Unfortunately, the *Hansard* reporters omitted that "never," here inserted in brackets, which was in the typewritten text of the Prime Minister's statement. The instructions to lieutenant-governors referred to above seem, however, not to have been issued.

Mr. Bastedo seems to have felt impelled to reserve the bill for two reasons: he thought, contrary to the advice of his own Attorney-General and cabinet, that it was *ultra vires*, and he doubted if the bill was in the public interest. The federal government was unable to subscribe to either of these views. However, even had the Lieutenant-Governor been right, there are other remedies in the constitution which are less reminiscent of the prerogative powers of the Crown as they existed in the days of the Stuart kings. The proper body to decide the question of *vires* is the courts, and there can be little doubt that the interests adversely affected by the bill are able to afford recourse to litigation. Should the bill be regarded as gravely affecting the public interest of the country, then the responsibility for disallowing it—after due deliberation—rested on the federal government. Instead they were dragged into the issue without being given any choice in the matter.

The action of Mr. Bastedo furnishes sufficient reason, if any more is needed, for removing the power of reservation from the constitution. The Lieutenant-Governor acted with complete legality, but his action was wholly alien to the spirit of the constitution. A peculiarity of the British constitutional system is that behaviour which may be legally correct can nevertheless be wholly unconstitutional. This is particularly true in the realm of the prerogative, where wide discretionary powers exist but are in fact strictly confined by a number of conventions of the constitution which Dicey defined as "rules for determining the mode in which the discretionary powers of the Crown (or of the Ministers as servants of the Crown) ought to be exercised."

In Canada, we cannot safely assume that even lieutenant-governors have read Dicey or understand the constitution. In this matter it has now become necessary to bring the law of the constitution closer to political and constitutional realities. . . .

Reservation has one particularly objectionable feature, in that it contains within it a sort of "pocket veto." The federal government is not obliged to do anything at all about a reserved bill. If no action is taken at all, then the bill has been effectively vetoed. Since the bill under consideration would expire in any event on December 31, 1961, inaction would have destroyed its effect completely. Such a course of action would be interference with provincial jurisdiction. As long as the disallowance power remains in existence, reservation is in any event an unnecessary prop to the federal power. The continuance of reservation merely makes it possible for the federal government to be involved by inadvertence in local issues in which it may have no direct interest.

THE AWARD OF HONOURS IN CANADA

Paul Fox

From Confederation to the end of the first world war it was customary for some hereditary honours such as knighthoods and companionships in orders of chivalry to be awarded to Canadians. However, during the prime ministership of the Rt. Hon. Robert L. Borden, the House of Commons passed a resolution on May 22, 1919, requesting His Majesty to refrain from granting titular honours to Canadians thereafter. Prime Minister R. B. Bennett's government reversed this policy in 1933 by recommending a number of such awards. Although some honours of this kind were conferred on Canadians in 1934 and 1935, the policy was reversed again when Prime Minister W. L. Mackenzie King took office in the latter year. No titles have been awarded since then.

In 1967 Canada established its own honours system when the Order of Canada was introduced. In 1972 this honours system was amplified by the creation of the Order of Military Merit. To recognize bravery, a Medal of Courage was included in the Order of Canada in 1967. However, no awards of the medal were made and subsequently it was replaced by a series of three decorations.

The Order of Canada, which originally provided for two levels of membership, has had three categories since 1972: Companion (CC), Officer (OC), and Member (CM). The Order of Military Merit has three levels of membership also: Commander (CMM), Officer (OMM), and Member (MMM). The three decorations for bravery are: the Cross of Valour (CV), the Star of Courage (SC), and the Medal of Bravery (MB). A member of an Order or a person receiving a decoration for bravery is entitled to place the appropriate initials after his or her name.

BIBLIOGRAPHY

Lieutenant-Governor
Forsey, E. A., "The Extension of the Life of Legislatures," *C.J.E.P.S.*, Vol. XXVI, No. 4, November, 1960.
Hendry, J. McL., *Memorandum of the Office of Lieutenant-Governor of a Province: Its Constitutional Character and Functions*, Ottawa, Department of Justice, 1955.
La Forest, G. V., *Disallowance and Reservation of Provincial Legislation*, Ottawa, Department of Justice, 1955.
McGregor, D. A., *They Gave Royal Assent: The Lieutenant-Governors of British Columbia*, Vancouver, Mitchell Press, 1967.
Mallory, J. R., "Disallowance and the National Interest: The Alberta Social Credit Leglisation of 1937," *C.J.E.P.S.*, Vol. XIV, No. 3, August, 1948.
Mallory, J. R., *Social Credit and the Federal Power in Canada*, Toronto, University of Toronto Press, 1954.
Mallory, J. R., "The Lieutenant-Governor as a Dominion Officer: The Reservation of the Three Alberta Bills in 1937," *C.J.E.P.S.*, Vol. XIV, No. 4, November, 1948.

Saywell, J. T., *The Office of Lieutenant-Governor*, Toronto, University of Toronto Press, 1957.

Governor General

Cobham Viscount, "The Governor General's Constitutional Role," *Political Science*, Vol. XV, No. 2, September, 1963.

Forsey, E. A., *Freedom and Order: Collected Essays*, Carleton Library No. 73, Toronto, McClelland and Stewart, 1974.

Franck, T., "The Governor General and the Head of State Functions," *Canadian Bar Review*, Vol. XXXII, No. 10, December, 1954.

Graham, Roger, (ed.), *The King-Byng Affair, 1926: A Question of Responsible Government*, Toronto, Copp Clark, 1967.

Kennedy, W. P. M., "The Office of Governor General of Canada," *Canadian Bar Review*, Vol. XXXI, No. 9, November, 1953.

MacKinnon, Frank, *The Crown in Canada*, Calgary, Glenbow-Alberta Institute, McClelland and Stewart West, 1976.

Mallory, J. R., "Canada's Role in the Appointment of the Governor General," *C.J.E.P.S.*, Vol. XXVI, No. 1, February, 1960.

Mallory, J. R., "Seals and Symbols: From Substance to Form in Commonwealth Equality," *C.J.E.P.S.*, Vol. XXII, No. 3, August, 1956.

Mallory, J. R., "The Election and the Constitution," *Q.Q.*, Vol. LXIV, No. 4, Winter, 1957.

McWhinney, E., Mallory, J. R., Forsey, E. A., "Prerogative Powers of the Head of State (The Queen or Governor General)," *Canadian Bar Review*, Vol. XXXV, Numbers 1, 2, 3, January, February, March, 1957.

Morton, W. L., "Meaning of Monarchy in Confederation," *Royal Society of Canada, Transactions*, Fourth Series, Vol. I, 1963.

Saywell, J. T., "The Crown and the Politicians: The Canadian Succession Question, 1891-1896," *Canadian Historical Review*, Vol. XXXVII, No. 4, December 1956.

Stanley, G. F. G., "A 'Constitutional Crisis' in British Columbia," *C.J.E.P.S.*, Vol. XXI, No. 3, August, 1955.

Willis-O'Connor, H., *Inside Government House*, Toronto, Ryerson Press, 1954.

12

THE EXECUTIVE PROCESS: CABINET, PCO, PM, PMO

Since Mr. Trudeau became prime minister, probably no aspect of federal government has provoked more interest and discussion than the development of the instruments of central executive power: the role of the prime minister and the cabinet, the privy council office (PCO), and the prime minister's office (PMO). The celebrated article by Professor Denis Smith which criticizes the trend, "President and Parliament: The Transformation of Parliamentary Government in Canada", will be found in the next chapter.

The present chapter reproduces in abridged form much of the most significant recent literature on federal executive institutions. Gordon Robertson's definitive article on "The Changing Role of the Privy Council Office" commences this chapter. The two charts which follow depict the alteration in the structure of the PCO that was introduced in 1975 and the revised cabinet committee system that was inaugurated by Prime Minister Trudeau.

Marc Lalonde's paper on "The Changing Role of the Prime Minister's Office" has been edited and retitled to retain his description of the contemporary role and activities of the Canadian prime minister, but the section of his paper which dealt with the PMO has been omitted and replaced by a more recent account written by Thomas d'Aquino. The latter is supplemented by two charts. The first shows the actual organization of the PMO in May, 1976, while the second depicts the restructuring that Mr. d'Aquino proposes. Details of the size and costs of the PMO and PCO are provided in a brief account by the editor.

The articles by Professors Alan Alexander and Denis Stairs on parliamentary secretaries which appeared in the third edition, pp. 350 to 358, have been replaced in this edition by Kenneth Tilley's original essay on ministerial executive staffs, a subject on which very little has been written.

The editor's article on the representative nature of Canadian cabinets has been brought up to date in this edition. It shows that the considerations governing the selection of Canadian cabinet ministers apparently change very little from government to government. Since the ambition of individuals to get into the cabinet also seems to be persistent, it is useful to repeat as an example Sir George Foster's revealing account of his attempt to make it to the top. A final item compiled by the editor gives the current salaries and allowances of federal ministers and parliamentary secretaries. For an explanation of the Treasury Board, see the article by A. W. Johnson in Chapter 15.

The bibliography is divided into two sections. The first gives references to recent works on the privy council, the cabinet, and the prime minister, while the second deals with the political process and policy-making.

THE CHANGING ROLE OF THE PRIVY COUNCIL OFFICE*

Gordon Robertson

[In his article "Mackenzie King and the Cabinet Secretariat," *C.P.A.*, Vol. 10, No. 3, September, 1967] Arnold Heeney gave a survey of the changes that had overtaken the Privy Council Office when Mackenzie King, faced by the pressures the second world war brought to the cabinet, decided that Canada had to do what Britain had done in 1914: establish a Cabinet Secretariat. . . .

However accidental some of the results may have been in relation to Mr. King's initial expectations, the Cabinet Secretariat was grafted onto the Privy Council Office, which had discharged largely formal and legalistic functions since Confederation, and the entire nature of the Office changed. With it gradually changed the operation of cabinet government in Canada.

•   •   •

The Development of the Cabinet Committee System

. . . [In 1940 the cabinet had] no agenda, no secretariat, no official present at meetings to record what went on, no minute of decisions taken, and no system to communicate the decisions to the departments responsible to implement them. Subjects to be discussed at each meeting were settled by the prime minister with no advance notice to ministers. As ministers had no notice of what was going to come up, they were normally quite unprepared for the discussion or for the decisions expected of

* From *Canadian Public Administration*, Vol. 14, No. 4, Winter, 1971. By permission. Mr. Robertson was Clerk of the Privy Council and Secretary to the Cabinet at the time of writing.

them. . . . After a meeting few knew precisely what had been decided; there could be no confidence that all relevant information had been available or considered; and the accurate transmission of decisions, if it occurred at all, was a happy accident.

By March of 1940, "conditions of government had become such that sheer necessity compelled the introduction of systematic procedures for the conduct of ministerial business". Ten cabinet committees had been set up in December 1939, each one theoretically responsible for an aspect of wartime operation. In actual fact, of these ten only the War Committee of the cabinet had any continuing and active existence early in the war. It was for that committee that the small initial Cabinet Secretariat worked. There, the procedures for agendas, documents and the recording of decisions were developed. At the end of the war, it had become apparent that having cabinet committees, served by a secretariat, was an enormous advantage. A number of new committees were established and the secretariat was permitted to begin to serve the cabinet itself. . . .

A third stage in the development of the cabinet committee system began with a re-organization instituted by Mr. Pearson and announced on January 20th, 1964. . . . Nine cabinet committees were established. Rather than being oriented toward specific ad hoc problems or operations, they were for the first time directed toward defined areas of the total governmental process.

A change in procedure was also initiated. Previously things had gone to the cabinet first and had been referred by it to cabinet committees when special consideration and report were required. The new procedure provided that matters requiring cabinet decision in most cases be first brought to the appropriate standing committee by the minister concerned. The committee thus became a normal and formal part of the decision-making process: a stage before consideration in the cabinet itself. In addition to the nine committees listed in Mr. Pearson's announcement, there was a tenth—the Treasury Board—which has functioned since 1867. It was established by statute; at that time it was regarded as a committee to aid the Minister of Finance; and was scarcely recognized as a committee of cabinet at all. It continued its powerful and quasi-independent existence; setting administrative standards in departments, improving management in the public service, dealing with contracts, departmental programs and estimates and the expenditures of government in general.

The system established by Mr. Pearson in 1964 lasted throughout his regime. The only important change was the addition in January, 1968, of a Cabinet Committee on Priorities and Planning. The government found itself in recurring financial difficulties and crises and it became apparent there was serious need of a systematic assessment of overall priorities of expenditure with a view to better long-term planning. . . .

When Mr. Trudeau became prime minister, one of his earliest actions, announced on April 30th, 1968, was a modification of the cabinet committee system. He said: "I have revised the system of Cabinet committees to reduce the number of committees and to provide for a regularity in their meetings."

While the establishment of regular times each week for the meeting of each of the standing committees of the cabinet may seem a small change, experience has demonstrated that it produced the major improvement that it was designed to achieve. Ministers are overwhelmed by the obligations, engagements and pressures that throng upon them. Time is committed weeks and even months in advance. With no regular schedule for the meetings of their committees, attendance was poor and spasmodic. Continuing attention to areas of policy by the committee members was impossible. With regular meetings over the entire year, it became possible to have systematic and orderly consideration of problems for submission to the cabinet.

The second important change in 1968 was to give the committees the power, not simply to recommend courses of action to the cabinet, but to take specific decisions. The main object was to remove as many questions as possible from the over-burdened cabinet. It was recognized, however, that there would have to be some means by which ministers who were not on a cabinet committee, or who did not attend a meeting, could re-open discussion or could register a view that differed from the decision of the committee. Without such a capacity, they could not reasonably be expected to assume their share of collective responsibility for policy. Two provisions were made: one was that all ministers, whether members of a committee or not, would receive agendas and documents. They would then know the questions to be discussed and decide whether they had an important interest or view. They could attend any meeting they wished to attend, with the exception of the Cabinet Committee on Priorities and Planning which the prime minister wanted to keep relatively small. The second provision was that decisions of the committees would not become effective simply by reason of such decision. They would be listed on an annex to the cabinet agenda for its next meeting. Any minister could notify the deputy secretary to the cabinet before the meeting of the cabinet that he wished to have any particular committee decision discussed. However, if no such notice were given, items on the annex were to be taken as approved by the cabinet and became its own decisions. At that point they were operative and became part of government policy.

Of the standing cabinet committees that now exist, five deal with areas of government activity: External Policy and Defence, Economic Policy, Social Policy, Science, Culture and Information, and Government Operations. Four are co-ordinating committees: Priorities and Planning, Treasury Board, Legislation and House Planning, and Federal-Provincial Relations. In addition, the Special Committee of the cabinet handles regulations and other proposed Orders in Council that do not require the attention of the full cabinet. Other special committees deal, at irregular intervals as required, with questions relating to security and intelligence, the public service, and a few other matters. From time to time special problems assume an importance that requires ad hoc committees that are abandoned when a satisfactory solution is reached.

One result of the changes introduced in 1968 was to increase greatly the number of cabinet committee meetings. The other was to reduce equally sharply the number of meetings of the cabinet. A statistical comparison of several recent years is of interest:

	July 1, 1966 to June 30, 1967.	July 1, 1968 to June 30, 1969.	July 1, 1969 to June 30, 1970.	July 1, 1970 to June 30, 1971.
Number of Cabinet Documents	780	1287	1307	1367
Number of Cabinet Meetings	139	72	78	75
Number of Cabinet Committee Meetings	120	317	310	311

The number of cabinet documents indicated for the last three years has to be adjusted since about one-third are reports by the cabinet committees on their recommendations or decisions on the substantive documents considered. Excluding such committee reports, the number of cabinet documents has averaged 818 for the last three years against about 700 for 1966-67 on a similarly adjusted basis. The interesting thing is that, as compared with the situation before the revisions in the system were made in 1968, cabinet is dealing with a larger volume of business but taking only half as many cabinet meetings to do it. The number of cabinet committee meetings has more than doubled and, according to our calculations in the Privy Council Office, the number of "minister-hours" devoted to the total executive function has remained about the same as in 1966-67. The difference is in the more probing, searching and formative nature of discussion that the committees permit, with both ministers and officials present. . . .

Organization of the Privy Council Office

Making the cabinet and cabinet committee system work effectively has involved a substantial development of the Cabinet Secretariat begun in 1940. Heeney records that there were ten officers in 1945. In 1971 there are 55 officers engaged in work relating to the secretariat proper, and there were 13 officers providing the key services in relation to cabinet documents, Orders in Council and administrative and financial services. There is, of course, in addition the normal complement of clerical and secretarial staff. But it is not a large office to attempt the tasks that are involved in relation to the entire range of government activities.

●   ●   ●

[For more recent figures on the size and cost of the PCO, see the accompanying article by Paul Fox. For a more recent organizational structure, see the accompanying chart of the PCO.]

Each secretariat is responsible for moving forward, to and through the cabinet, the proposals that must be considered and decided in relation to the "operations" of government coming within its area of responsibility. The [operations] division services a number of other special and ad hoc cabinet committees with assistance from the other divisions, and has the primary responsibility of providing service to the cabinet itself.

The other main divisions of the Office are responsible for the co-ordinating committees of the cabinet other than the Treasury Board, which continues to be served by a separate department of government under its own minister, the President of the Treasury Board. The Secretary and Deputy Secretaries of the Board maintain close collaboration with the Secretary of the Cabinet and the several Deputy and Assistant Secretaries. In the Privy Council Office the Plans Division services the Cabinet Committee on Priorities and Planning as well as the Cabinet Committee on Legislation and House Planning. The Federal-Provincial Affairs Division has a general responsibility for federal relations with the provinces, including constitutional questions, and serves the co-ordinating committee where policies on matters affecting the provinces are considered. It is, significantly, two of these co-ordinating committees that are chaired by the prime minister: the Cabinet Committee on Priorites and Planning and the Cabinet Commitee on Federal-Provincial Relations. All other standing committees are chaired by designated ministers and are not attended by the prime minister unless some quite unusual circumstance makes it desirable.

The scope of the Cabinet Committee on Priorities and Planning is now more inclusive than the mainly financial aspects of policy toward which it was directed in 1968. It gives special attention to the broad objectives of the government and to major questions of policy having long-term implications. It is in that committee that the basic decisions on objectives and strategies are taken, for recommendation to the cabinet. A very important aspect of these is, of course, deciding the general priorities of the government for the allocation of financial resources and in the policy discussion of other cabinet committees the determination of such priorities is obviously related to and conditioned by the decisions as to policies and strategies. The priorities are set in broad terms: objectives to be achieved, the amount of effort and resource to be directed toward each, the increase or decrease in the emphasis to be accorded to general areas of government action. It is on the basis of such broad decisions that the Treasury Board determines in detail the funds to be made available for specific programs administered by the various departments and fixes the personnel establishment to be allocated to them.

Despite its key role, it is quite wrong, as some have done, to call the present Cabinet Commitee on Priorities and Planning an "inner cabinet". Like other committees, its decisions or recommendations go to the cabinet for confirmation or for debate and final decision. They have no status without that confirmation. Moreover the committee is intended to deal with matters of long-term and broad scope. It is not a committee intended to cover any and all areas of government action or to take quick decision on urgent matters.

Federal-Provincial Relations

It may seem curious that in a federal state, where relations with the provinces are now so important, it was not until Mr. Pearson's changes of 1964 that a concerted effort was made to achieve real co-ordination of them within the government of Canada. It was, perhaps, because the activities of government hitherto had been more limited in scope and tended more readily to stay within allocated heads of federal or of provincial jurisdiction. Close and frequent relations were less necessary than they are now and they did not, in fact, exist as we now know them. Co-ordination poses a problem. Relations with the provinces may be and for some years now have been in respect of virtually any subject-matter of government. To assign them to a single minister would create difficulty in defining his responsibilities of a "horizontal" character as distinct from those of his colleagues under whom the various subjects fall. The Privy Council Office and the Department of Finance, which had a specialized group dealing with federal-provincial fiscal policy and economic relations, did try before 1964 to achieve some co-ordination but, in general, each department conducted such relations as there were in its own areas of responsibility. It became clear that this was not adequate. Programs that were logical and reasonable in relation to one aspect of government—health, transport, agriculture, or whatever it might be—often involved principles that were at conflict with those that had to be applied or developed for other areas or for general application. Action in one program area might unconsciously but fundamentally affect policy or action in another without the responsible federal department—or any minister—realizing it. After 1964, the task of co-ordination was placed more specifically with officers working as part of the general cabinet secretariat and in 1968 a special division was established headed by the deputy secretary to the cabinet.

The Federal-Provincial Affairs Division, in developing a uniform and consistent policy in relations with the provinces, maintains liaison with government departments and tries, within the limits of its resources, to keep contact with the provinces as well. It co-ordinates preparations for major federal-provincial conferences and for constitutional review meetings.

It has become a common theme of public comment that federal-provincial relations should be more constant and intimate, and that this would remove the disagreements that have been, and continue to be, a feature of our national life. I must confess to a certain scepticism. At times one could be led to wonder whether it is not the very plethora of meetings that has provided the occasions for the disagreements and for the wide reporting of them. . . . The following table indicates the number of formal committees as of June, 1970 that meet at the ministerial or deputy ministerial level:

Federal and all provinces	28
Federal and all Provinces plus outside groups	9
Federal-Provincial-Municipal	2
Interprovincial, federal representatives as observers	12
Federal and provincial— regional representatives	6
Total	57

On the same date the total number of multilateral committees and sub-committees involving officials was 260. There were another 150 bilaterial committees of the same type. Whatever the source of problems may be, it is not the lack of meetings to talk about them.

Cabinet Government—Some Modern Aspects

The organization and the activities of cabinet committees and of the cabinet secretariat are directed to one essential purpose: the more effective operation of our cabinet system, in which a collective executive decides the objectives, policies and programs of government and in which its members take a joint responsibility for the result. From the nature of our executive, so different from that in countries like the United States where it is a single person, there flow a number of implications and consequences. The first and most obvious is that each member of the executive must know what is involved in the policy and program decisions for which he shares responsibility, whether they are his direct concern or that of a colleague. The second is that each must have an opportunity to participate in those decisions. Participation is at its most rudimentary if it is simply to approve or disapprove a fully developed proposal. To be real and substantial it should involve awareness of problems and relevant considerations and discussion of lines of solution at a stage early enough that a minister can share in shaping the final result. Either to accept or to reject a finished product may be totally unsatisfactory and, indeed, the wrong decision so far as the government as a whole is concerned: some unknown and unconsidered alternative might have been the preferred and much better course if participation could have been effected at an earlier stage.

The cabinet before 1940 failed adequately to meet either of these needs for a collective executive. . . . It was a system in which each minister had his own empire, big or small. He and his officials worked out a policy and program that seemed sensible for it. The prime minister, within the limits of his information and knowledge, had a general influence and control. The rest of the cabinet "participated" at the final stage, with a "yes" or a "no", or with limited modifications on the edges of a developed proposal. . . .

Discussions now on broad policy and general priorities mean that all ministers have an opportunity to share in giving shape to government in general and to the areas of policy for which others of their colleagues are directly responsible.

The second feature of today's system has already been pointed out. In all but the most exceptional circumstances, matters go to a cabinet committee *first* before coming to the cabinet. The essential officials of all interested departments are normally present. . . . Ministers talk to other deputies than their own, and deputies to other ministers. Advice is less monolithic and discussions are much more real. Frequently the result is to refer a matter back to officials or to the originating department for further work or for development of a different proposal. At the very least, significant modifications may be suggested in the report to the cabinet for further discussion and final decision.

The positive results of the new system are many. Ministers have the opportunity to learn more of what their colleagues are doing and to be better informed about all aspects of government activities than under the previous methods. Policies and programs are related more consciously and more constantly to the totality of problems and less to partial or sectional aspects. Ministers have more influence on the shape of policy as a whole and on its development and officials have proportionately less than they used to. This judgment is at variance with the conventional wisdom but, after thirty years in the operation of government, more than half of it at the centre, I feel confident it is correct. Finally, there is a more planned attempt to assess in advance the probable nature of developments of broad national and social moment before they arrive as immediate problems for urgent action. Such things rarely fall within the boundaries established for administrative convenience and when plans were confined within these tidy limits, some quite major questions remained neglected. Obviously the success of such efforts is only partial, but they do constitute important gains. They have, however, had their price.

One price is in the ministerial time: the rarest of government commodities. Better understanding and analysis of complex interrelated problems and policies take time. Discussion that leads to mature decision-making takes time. All this time, and the energy that is expended in the decision-making process, is subtracted from the finite capacity and endurance of the minister. If a minister works a five-day week of eleven hours a day, plus a good part of each week-end, what competition is there for those hours? Attendance in the House, executive work in his department, constituency business, general work for the party, general work for the government; consultation with businessmen, representatives of public organizations and others to keep him informed and to learn their views; ceremonial duties, travel to and from the constituency, travel to and from departmental assignments away from Ottawa; personal business; and finally, as part of the collective executive, reading cabinet documents, attending cabinet committees and attending cabinet. To do these last three thoroughly in the face of all of the other demands is almost impossible. Something must suffer if more time goes into the process of executive decision. It is quite possible that the improvements in the cabinet system may have been at too high a cost in the time ministers can devote to the total political role that they fill. The right balance will never be final or certain: it will change with prime ministers, governments and the stages in their four or five year life cycles.

. . . Ministers now, in many cases, have to give up some share of their authority and control to other ministers if the totality of policies is to be co-ordinated. . . . Another resentment which ministers must feel is that caused by the ubiquity of officials, including Privy Council officers. . . .

The relationships between ministers and officials are seen in interesting and sensitive focus at cabinet committee meetings. Ministers in general carry the discussion but officials participate actively, especially on factual and operational aspects. They are conscious that policy decision, and therefore the main aspects of policy assessment, are for ministers. There are, however, occasions when a deputy must objectively review the full policy and public implications of proposed action. There are times when the responsible minister lets the deputy explain: there are equally times when the deputy remains silent while the minister explains. Both normally participate in active discussion. It is a blending of roles that requires mutual confidence and an awareness of their differences. . . .

During policy discussion there comes a time when the ministers must be alone. Candour is required. There must be no restraints on frank talk. This occurs at cabinet where the ultimate decision is taken. The ministers are responsible. It is their government. There must be no inhibition caused by the presence of an advocate official. He advises, he has full opportunity to be heard in the appropriate forum, but the cabinet decides. Not the senior officials or any group of them.

Our decision-making process differs from that in Britain in several respects. One is in the degree to which ministers and officials are brought together in meetings. The British depend on inter-departmental committees of officials for the preliminary analysis and for the development of policy recommendations. There are cabinet committees, but none are attended by both ministers and officials. . . . Canadian ministers prefer to hear at first hand the differing views of senior officials. . . . Inter-departmental committees may have to be relied on rather more in future but the valuable blend of ministers and officials at committees will undoubtedly be retained.

The changes in the operation of our cabinet, and the advantages I have suggested for the system today, do not mean that those governing today are somehow possessed of greater wisdom than those who did so under other arrangements. It is rather that the conditions and the problems are very different, mainly in complexity and in scale. The change in thirty-odd years from a country relying essentially on a few primary products to an advanced, technological society is manifest. That alone would be a significant development. Equally complex and difficult for government has been the increased expectation that the state should achieve a more rapid growth and more equitable distribution of both means and products so a better share in the good life can be obtained by the greatest number. Social policies and social programs are complex and difficult in themselves: the added dimension of integration with provincial policies and programs multiplies the difficulties. New problems are added as personal and social expectations reach higher and higher. New policies must be devised to meet the relentless growth of the large urban areas. Other contributions to complexity are added continually: the revolution of rising expectations; ceaseless innovation and technological change; increasing mobility of people and rapidly changing social and moral values; feelings of alienation and disorientation; the demand for better protection of the consumer—and dozens of others: new, demanding, urgent.

Governing Canada has some special complications: the fact of our bilingual national character, our multicultural nature; our sheer size; the regional differences in economic growth and prosperity; the geographic, economic and cultural bonds that fuse us to the United States of America while we struggle to be different. All of these social, economic, physical, psychic and systemic factors and forces produce stress. Much of the task of regulating these stresses and strains, assuaging the pain and balancing the growth, falls upon the federal government. . . .

On Planning

The principal planning objective of the past three years has been to increase the time available between the perception of a problem by ministers and the necessity of action with regard to it. . . .

What is urgent will always clamour for attention and probably get it. What is important must receive attention well in advance and be given lots of time for organization for action. . . .

A good deal is being written about "normative planning" and what is taken by some to be the converse, "incrementalism". Considerable improvement has been made in the Privy Council Office in the last four years in methods of analysis, using general systems theory and to some extent general communications theory. Understanding the governmental system and the social system better, due to the insights of these theories, is one thing, but successful application of the theories by the central executive in a rational, creative way is another. The policy sciences taken together constitute a frontier field, and applying policy science to cabinet government is still a frontier effort. From our experience it might be said that "top down" policy determination works part of the time, "bottom up" policy determination works much of the time, and that, despite all efforts, many government decisions will continue to be in response to problems arriving at a different time and in a different form than was anticipated. The process of integrated planning has, however, made great strides in the last few years at all levels of the government. . . .

Cabinet, Prime Minister and Departments

In the complex operation of the cabinet system, with ministers together deciding the policies and the strategies of government, it is obvious that the role of the prime minister is crucial. He alone of the cabinet is responsible for no one aspect of government. He alone looks constantly at the total picture. He it is who has chosen his colleagues; he is recognized by the country and by Parliament as the person generally responsible for the success or failure of government in meeting the problems of the state. Within the cabinet he must be the master of his administration but he must recognize its collective nature and avoid autocracy. Where necessary he must change the functions of his colleagues and, when necessary, invite or require a departure. He is the only one with the authority to police and to change the boundaries between them. The many-sided role of the prime minister is nowhere more difficult or more demanding of a sensitive balance of intellectual and human qualities than when he is chairman of the collective executive. Assisting the prime minister in ensuring a coherence of policy and giving support in the total process of decision-making are two of the main functions of the Privy Council Office.

As a department provides its minister with analysis, advice and recommendations on the objectives of the department, so the Privy Council Office gives the prime minister information, analysis and advice on the totality of policies. The probability of a coherence of policy is thus enhanced.

It will be readily apparent that the information, analysis and advice for the prime minister ties in completely with the broader function of the Privy Council Office in servicing the entire system of cabinet and cabinet committees which I have described. Programs and policy proposals come to the Office as submissions to the cabinet and are immediately circulated to all ministers. At the same time they are allocated to one or another of the cabinet committees. The appropriate secretariat picks it up at that point. If more information is needed, that is secured. If it has aspects that relate to another committee or secretariat, there is consultation to see how best to cover all aspects for consideration. When the matter goes to the committee, the secretariat records the discussion, prepares the minutes, and draws up the report of decision or recommendation to go on to the cabinet. All of this provides the information for a briefing document to the Prime Minister covering all essential aspects of every question on each cabinet agenda. It provides too the basis for the information system of the Office on the operations of government as a whole.

When decisions are taken by the cabinet, or when committee recommendations or decisions are confirmed, the next stage in the Privy Council Office function is to inform departments and agencies with speed and precision so that action may flow. This may be done orally if the need for speed is great, but the standard procedure is communication by a "Record of Decision" within twenty-four hours. Orders in Council may or may not be involved: usually not. It is only when a formal, legal instrument is required that they enter the picture.

This, in essence, is the role of the Privy Council Office: one of information, co-ordination, follow-up and support provided to the prime minister and the cabinet as a whole with, as a vital aspect, constant relations with all departments of the government. It is a role that is replete with possibilities for misunderstanding, bruised feelings and grievances, and it has been necessary to develop principles to avoid them as much as possible. I might mention a few.

The first is the "stay-off-the-field" principle. The Privy Council Office operates no programs and administers no projects except those which are related to its own housekeeping. Administration and action are with the departments. . . . The Privy Council office remains aware and is frequently informed or consulted, but enters the game only if inter-agency operation is required where a "neutral" can provide a co-ordinating service, or where there is a requirement for counsel and assistance that can only be provided by those with a general view.

With regard to planning as we define it, a similar principle applies. . . . departments are left to act and to be guided by the principles laid down. This does not however, mean that the roles are carried through in isolation. One of the benefits of the central planning process, with a longer look ahead and a broader look around, has been to help departments to anticipate new needs and new developments. . . .

The second principle, that supports the first, is that "Plans works through Operations". The Operational Division and the Federal-Provincial Affairs Division have the major portion of the workload relating to the various secretariats and cabinet committees. The Plans Division does not have a parallel structure covering the various areas of government activity but works through the other divisions, using their expertise, their contacts and their channels of communication. Thus planning is not divorced from operational insight and a duplication of contact with departments and agencies is avoided as much as possible.

A third principle is that there are virtually no officers making a career within the Privy Council Office. . . . There can be no tendency to usurp the authority and the control which belongs to ministers and to the prime minister. Recognizing the fact of human frailty, it is unwise to permit too long a time in the sensitive work of the Privy Council Office. Conscious identification with a particular line and the wish to see action follow a course one believes to be wise, are subtle forces that can limit usefulness in this peculiar organization.

The term of appointment is purposely kept short: three to five years with personnel on loan from all departments. Vigour and integrity are maintained, but an elite with any sense of separateness or difference is not permitted to form. Privy Council Office service is part of broader career development. . . .

Principle four is that the Privy Council Office is deliberately kept small. By recruiting versatile officers who work hard *not* to be encumbered by program responsibility, a large staff is avoided. . . .

One other matter that must be referred to is the relationship between the Privy Council Office and the Prime Minister's Office. It is one that calls for the greatest harmony. Given the prime minister's functions as leader of a political party, leader of the government in the House of Commons, and chairman of the cabinet, the prime minister's own staff are constantly securing information, analyzing and recommending on matters that relate to policies and objectives of the government. The Prime Minister's Office is partisan, politically oriented, yet operationally sensitive. The Privy Council Office is non-partisan, operationally oriented yet politically sensitive. . . .

Obviously each office requires a knowledge of the areas of action of the other and the actions of the two must, to the extent that they affect the total policy or action of the government, be consistent. To aid in information and coherence two sets of meetings with the prime minister involving both offices have been established. The first, a daily meeting, with two officers from the Privy Council Office and two from the Prime Minister's Office, has been a constant base for co-ordination for many years. It started with one officer from each place and, as life became more complex and difficult, became the two from each that now attend. It deals with the day-to-day flow of affairs that the prime minister must know, consider, prepare for or decide. The second meeting is on planning, and occurs once a week with an additional person from each office who has responsibility in the longer term development and direction of policy. . . .

Of Politics and Public Service

Finally, a word about politics and liberty. The popular will is expressed through politics. Ideology, technology and bureaucracy have to be restrained so that politics may rule, otherwise theories, inventions and organizatons would smother life. The elected respresentative of the people, who makes a trade of politics but who makes no claim to total knowledge or wisdom, must be provided with optimum liberty to decide what set of relationships ought to prevail which, stabilized at a chosen level, constitute the goals of government. Providing this liberty to the politicians is exceedingly difficult. From the standpoint of the cabinet minister, the complications start with the catalogue of complexities of existing policies, programs and activities. To ensure that responsible politicians and not civil servants have the final say, the cabinet has the responsibility of decision. For what it does, it is responsible to Parliament. It would be entirely unrealistic to expect the larger body of politicians to be quiescent and, in fact, our democratic system would be failing if they were. Thus the desired freedom of ministers to consider and to decide is conditioned by a torrent of observations, questions, and advice all proclaimed publicly from committees of the House of Commons and Senate, backbenchers of all parties and from party conventions.

Further constraints on freedom and decision come from the fact of instant communications. Opinions and reactions, relevant or irrelevant, tumble in without ceasing. . . . There is an unrecognized inconsistency in the demand for both speed and participation in difficult decisions on complex issues.

Conscious of the catalogue of complexities in the society which they have been elected to regulate, surrounded by the reality of the existing amalgam of policy, programs and activities; sensitive to the clamour of friendly and unfriendly voices and often urged to act boldly but with due regard, in the light of all considerations but at once, cabinet ministers can only feel more captive than free. The staff of the Privy Council Office have as their duty to provide whatever aid and assistance they can to permit individual and collective judgment to prevail in the cabinet chamber and, through its wise application, sound policy to emerge to meet the problems of the present and the future. . . .

Privy Council Office and Federal Provincial Relations Office
TBS Chart 27 January, 1975

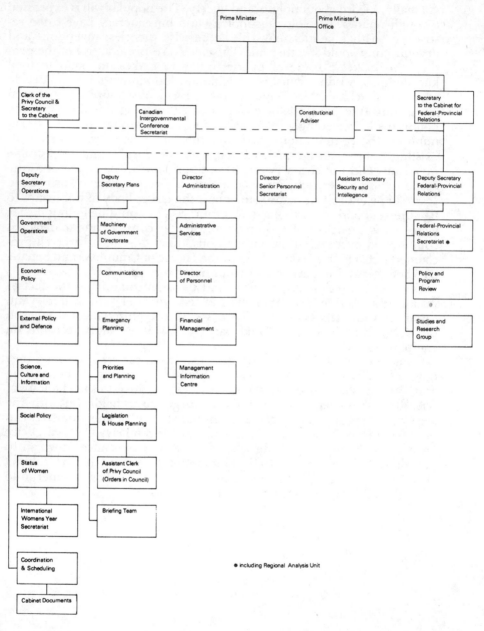

TBS Chart 27, January, 1975. Reproduced by permission of the Minister of Supply and Services Canada.

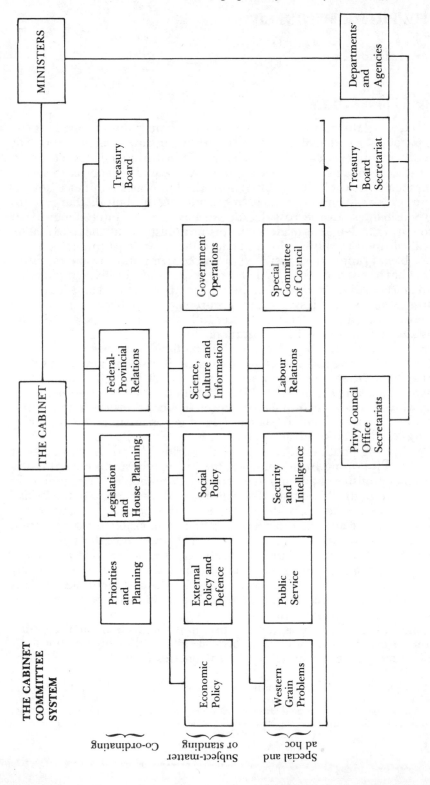

THE CABINET COMMITTEE SYSTEM

MINISTERS

THE CABINET

Treasury Board

Priorities and Planning

Legislation and House Planning

Federal-Provincial Relations

Economic Policy

External Policy and Defence

Social Policy

Science, Culture and Information

Government Operations

Western Grain Problems

Public Service

Security and Intelligence

Labour Relations

Special Committee of Council

Departments and Agencies

Treasury Board Secretariat

Privy Council Office Secretariats

Co-ordinating

Subject-matter or standing

Special and ad hoc

Courtesy of P.M.O. May, 1976.

THE PRIME MINISTER*

Marc Lalonde

History of the Office

In analyzing the role and function of the prime minister, one must be suspicious of a text book approach. A purely constitutional description of his office would reveal that it has changed little during the past century in Canada. A constitutional analysis, however, would be subject to severe limitations. It would inevitably ignore the "pith and substance" of his office which can only be revealed by considering the daily discharge of his responsibilities. In the past decade we have seen a multi-dimensional growth of the demands made on the prime minister in all the roles that he is called upon to fulfil. I do not believe that new constitutional powers have been granted to or assumed by the contemporary prime minister. What has happened instead is that greater demands for his accountability and participation made by ministers, members of parliament, public administrators, the press, pressure groups and the public in general have required the Canadian prime minister fully to assume the powers that he has always had under the constitution.

For some time, many concerned Canadians have been wondering whether the Canadian Parliamentary system is evolving into a presidential system. When asked about this, it is only half jokingly that I usually answer by asking the question, "Why should the Canadian prime minister, who occupies one of the most powerful elected offices in the world, seek to implement a congressional style of government and accept in so doing a reduction of his powers?"

Within the political framework of the British North America Act of 1867 and following British practice, the prime minister is recognized as the chief minister of a committee known as "the cabinet". The cabinet in turn is part of the Privy Council established under section 11 of the British North America Act. Considering the extensive power exercised by the prime minister and the cabinet, it is rather remarkable that the written constitution nowhere mentions the office of prime minister nor specifically the institution of cabinet. Though power is not explicitly vested in the prime minister and cabinet by the law, they exercise it formally through some other body in accordance with the custom of the constitution. The vital aspects of prime ministerial and cabinet power rest, therefore, on constitutional conventions.

Some idea of the basis for the pre-eminent position of the prime minister can be gleaned from an official statement of his functions. . . .

The most recent minute of Council on this subject is P.C. 3374 of

---

* Adapted by the editor from an article by Marc Lalonde, former Principal Secretary to the Prime Minister, which appeared under the title "The Changing Role of the Prime Minister's Office" in *Canadian Public Administration*, Vol. 14, No. 4, Winter, 1971. By permission of the author and the Institute of Public Administration of Canada.

October 25, 1935, which reads as follows:

> The Committee of the Privy Council on the recommendation of the Right Honourable W. L. Mackenzie King, the Prime Minister, submit the following Memorandum regarding certain of the functions of the Prime Minister,
>
> 1. A Meeting of a Committee of the Privy Council is at the call of the Prime Minister and, in his absence, of that of the senior Privy Councillor, if the President of the Council be absent;
>
> 2. A quorum of the Council being four, no submission, for approval to the Governor General, can be made with a less number than the quorum;
>
> 3. A Minister cannot make recommendations to Council affecting the discipline of the Department of another Minister;
>
> 4. The following recommendations are the special prerogative of the Prime Minister:
>
> Dissolution and Convocation of Parliament:
>
> Appointment of
> Privy Councillors;
> Cabinet Ministers;
> Lieutenant-Governors;
> (including leave of absence to same);
> Provincial Administrators;
> Speaker of the Senate;
> Chief Justices of all Courts;
> Senators;
> Sub-Committees of Council;
> Treasury Board;
> Committee of Internal Economy,
> House of Commons;
> Deputy Heads of Departments;
> Librarians of Parliament;
> Crown Appointments in both Houses
> of Parliament;
> Governor General's Secretary's Staff;
> Recommendations in any Department. . . .

While this official statement is useful, it is far from complete. To gain a fuller understanding of the extent of the prime minister's power, it is necessary to examine the fundamental political reality upon which his position rests. He is chosen by a popular convention of a major party; he ordinarily commands substantial and deeply rooted support amongst the electorate; he is the directing force in both cabinet and Parliament; he has a key role in the Commons, answers many questions there, and takes the lead in explaining and defending his government's policies and activities; he must be consulted on important decisions by all cabinet ministers; to a large extent he prescribes the functions of his colleagues and he can, if necessary, advise the Governor General to dismiss a minister; he recommends most important appointments to the cabinet; he has a special responsibility for external affairs; and he has the important prerogative of advising the Governor General when Parliament should be dissolved.

The powers of the prime minister are, therefore, potentially enormous.

How they are wielded, however, depends in large measure on his personality and on his interpretation of his leadership role. In the words of Lord Oxford and Asquith, "The office is what its holder chooses and is able to make of it".

Prime Minister and Parliament

. . . The traditional duties of the prime minister in the House of Commons have changed very little in the past century. When in the House of Commons, he is inevitably the chief spokesman for the Chamber. He is the dominant figure, and his position and responsibilities are recognized by the House as a whole.

A great deal has been said and written lately concerning the contemporary role of the Canadian Parliament. It has been suggested by some that the present prime minister has purposely attempted to downgrade the power and effectiveness of Parliament. This suggestion is quite untenable. The prime minister considered the parliamentary reforms of 1968 essential if that body was to meet the heavy burden of modern legislative needs. . . .

These reforms have unquestionably increased the effectiveness of Parliament. One thing they have not done, however, is reduce the burden of the prime minister's parliamentary duties. Not only has he carried on all his traditional parliamentary duties but the elaboration and adoption of these various reforms have required increased personal attention and leadership on his part.

Among those traditional duties is participation in Question Period, undoubtedly one of the institutions most cherished by the Members of the House. . . . Whereas cabinet ministers are frequently called upon to answer questions that touch their respective departments, the prime minister, on the other hand, is expected to answer questions which involve general issues or the interrelationships of the various departments. Attendance by ministers during question period has changed with the introduction in 1968 of the rota system. This innovation frees ministers from attendance in the House for two days of each week, but it also ensures the representation of each government department by its ministers or his parliamentary secretary three days out of five. As for the prime minister, he attends question period on a daily basis and when necessary replies on behalf of his absent ministers.

A vitally important aspect of the prime minister's parliamentary responsibilities concerns his relationship with the government caucus. Every Wednesday morning, unless he is out of Ottawa, he meets with the members of the caucus to hear their questions and opinions and to offer answers and guidance in reply. This weekly meeting with caucus is by no means the only contact between the prime minister and Liberal Members. On the occasion of his daily presence in the House, they have another opportunity to raise various questions with him. . . .

Finally, the prime minister, like all other Members, represents a particular electoral riding and, as such, he has a direct responsibility to his constituents. . . .

Prime Minister and Cabinet

... For a time it was popular to refer to the prime minister as *primus inter pares* or as *inter stellas luna minores*. Both interpretations do not do justice to his office. He cannot be first among equals because in a political sense no individual is his equal. It would be wrong, however, to assume that the prime minister stands in a position of unquestionable supremacy over his colleagues in the cabinet. Unlike the President of the United States, the prime minister is not in a positon of strength superior to that of the total cabinet. Members of the Canadian cabinet are responsible to the House of Commons; and while they acknowledge the leadership of the prime minister, and will in fact usually bow to his decisions, they have important political and administrative responsibilities which they must discharge independently of the prime minister. It must also be remembered that ministers who are dissatisfied with their leader retain the weapon of resignation—they can resign of their own free will, and if enough ministers were to resign, a prime minister would face serious difficulties.

One of the most important factors distinguishing the prime minister from his cabinet colleagues is the manner in which he obtains and relinquishes his office. He is requested by the Governor General to form a government, while he himself issues the invitation to all other members. Whenever the prime minister vacates his office, the act normally carries with it the resignation of all those who compose the government; but whenever any other member leaves, the tenure of the remainder is undisturbed.

The powers of the prime minister in cabinet derive from his positon as chairman. He controls the agenda and is the principal guiding force in helping the cabinet arrive at decisions. He is both co-ordinator and arbitrator of the executive decision-making process; he is concerned with the total activity of the government and is principally responsible for its policies, style and thrust; he oversees the operation of his colleagues' departments and ensures that harmonious relations exist between his ministers. Supported by the doctrine of cabinet solidarity, his task is to crystallize the collective point of view and to infuse into cabinet decision-making a sense of direction, coherence, efficacy and unity.

The relationship of the prime minister to the various committees of cabinet is most important. He is responsible for appointing members to the nine standing committees. He also chairs a number of committees: Security and Intelligence; Public Service; Federal-Provincial Relations; and Priorities and Planning. ... Functioning at the level of Federal-Provincial Conferences, a growing number of which involve him directly, he acts as convenor and chairman, negotiator and arbitrator. The constitutional review process in particular has demanded considerable amounts of the prime minister's time and energy. As chairman of the Priorities and Planning Committee, he concerns himself with the setting of government priorities, planning for the orderly development of integrated policy, and evaluating on-going programs.

Any discussion of the prime minister's executive duties should include some mention of his control over the power of appointment. . . . The great majority of public servants are now appointed by the Public Service Commission. Nonetheless, with the growth in the number of governmental departments and agencies, a large number of senior appointments are still made by Order-in-Council. Approxiamately four hundred appointments are made every year by cabinet. While the initiative for recommendations to cabinet for a large number of them lies with individual ministers, the prime minister must ensure that such recommendations carry the assent of his colleagues and have been the subject of adequate investigation. In addition, many appointments are presented to cabinet upon the initiative of the prime minister himself. . . .

Some appointments are a mere formality, others require the prime minister's involvement in numerous hours of consultations and discussions. For instance, a cabinet shuffle is likely to involve individual discussions with most members of the cabinet or appointments of deputy ministers might require consultations with ministers concerned as well as with senior officials. . . .

Prime Minister and the Party

The prime minister is the leader of his party and is ultimately responsible for its direction. To remain in office he must be master of his party and enjoy its confidence and support. In this respect, the relationship of prime minister and his party has changed little in the last century. What has changed, however, is the role of the party itself as a political instrument and as a vehicle of citizen involvement. Parties are being subjected to a technocratic and professional transformation. More important, citizens are seeking greater involvement in influencing party decisions. . . .

The democratization of the Liberal party has affected the position of the prime minister in some additional ways. The constitution of the party now requires the leader formally to "account" to the membership of the party at its bi-annual National Policy Convention and to submit to a "leadership convention ballot" at the first national meeting of the party following a general election. . . .

A new and important way of ensuring some kind of accountability to the Liberal party and insuring that it receives the information and support it requires, is the special meetings of cabinet ministers with party officials sometimes referred to as "political cabinet". These meetings take place about every two months and are organized by the P.M.O. In addition to the ministers, the chairman of the parliamentary caucus and the president of the Liberal party attend. The purpose of these meetings is to review the current political situation, to set overall political goals and priorities and to outline political strategy.

An additional method of maintaining liaison between the prime minister and the cabinet, on the one hand, and the extra-parliamentary party, on the other hand, is the various Provincial Advisory Groups sometimes referred to as "troikas". Each Advisory Group is composed of a minister from that province, the chairman of the Federal Liberal caucus from that province, and the chairman or representative of the Liberal party organization for that province. They meet from time to time to discuss a variety of subjects ranging from the consideration of government decisions affecting the region to the evaluation of political strategy. . . .

Prime Minister and the Public

. . . Changes in the nature of the body politic have had a profound effect upon relations between the public and the executive, and in particular between the public and the prime minister. The present prime minister came to office at a time when the movement for "direct" or "populist" democracy was gaining momentum across the country. . . .

This new style of politics has required heads of government to make themselves more available to more and more people. Direct communication between the public and the prime minister has required him to devote an increasing amount of time to the media and to travel outside of Ottawa. . . .

But a voice on radio, a TV image or a press report, however faithful, do not sufficiently satisfy the public's desire for communication. Canadian voters also wish face to face contact with their political leaders, and more particularly with the prime minister.

One interesting indication of the public's demand on the prime minister's time can be seen from the number of invitations which he receives. In the twelve month period following July 1, 1970, the prime minister received over 3,000 invitations to attend specific functions. In addition he receives, every week, a number of requests from special interests groups desirous of presenting him with their briefs. . . .

It is interesting to note some specific examples of how the prime minister's time is allocated. A recent staff review revealed that his time in Ottawa is divided roughly between 11 or 12 hours per week of cabinet activities, including meetings with individual ministers and cabinet committees; approximately 11 hours of House of Commons activities, including caucus; and approximately 20 hours of miscellaneous activities, including working lunches, meetings with officials, special conferences, meetings with private organizations and citizens. This analysis does not, of course, reveal the full extent of the prime minister's time commitments. To this must be added frequent week-end travel outside of Ottawa on official business as well as numerous hours of study and reading of documents and briefing notes for all activities in which he is involved. . . .

Conclusions

My conclusions . . . stem from my observations of the evolution and possible future development of the office of prime minister.

(i) The prime minister will continue to maintain his pre-eminent position in the governmental apparatus because of the continuing and pressing need for centralized planning, co-ordination and control. His pre-eminence should not compromise the authority of Parliament. So long as the prime minister remains responsible to the House of Commons, the advent of a *de facto* presidency is impossible.

(ii) The pre-eminent position of the prime minister as a national leader
is likely to continue as well. Politics in democratic countries has tended to
become more personalized and this phenomenon has unquestionably
taken root in Canada.

(iii) The prime minister's contacts with the public will continue to
expand because of the changing nature of public needs, expectations and
demands. As a consequence, his symbolic, motivational and pedagogic
roles will inevitably increase in importance.

(iv) The prime minister's power and influence is unlikely to emasculate
the role of the cabinet or Parliament. The growing demands of the body
politic have brought to all these bodies an increase in work, responsibility,
power and influence.

(v) If future prime ministers are to meet their expanded responsibilities, they will have to maintain in their service a personal staff of
adequate proportions. The alternatives are quite unpalatable—
assumption of these functions by the administration or by the extra-
parliamentary party.

THE PRIME MINISTER'S OFFICE:
CATALYST OR CABAL?*

Thomas D'Aquino

•   •   •

The Development of the Office

In the Beginning

The Prime Minister's Office began to attract particular attention in
Canada in the sixties when it assumed a character and proportions quite
unlike any in the past. The growth of the Office up until the government
of Lester Pearson had been gradual. Sir John A. Macdonald and his early
successors managed with several secretaries. R. B. Bennett had a staff of
twelve, and William Lyon Mackenzie King had a staff of thirty. Surprisingly, Louis St-Laurent and John Diefenbaker did not increase the
number of their staffs above thirty. Under Lester Pearson, however, the
Office staff reached a total of forty, and under Pierre Trudeau, the
number more than doubled to ninety-one.

During this evolution, staff nomenclature changed. The traditional
and understated title of 'secretary' gave way to others such as executive
and special assistant, program and press secretary, regional adviser, and
research assistant. Staff functions changed too. Once-simple housekeeping duties now include appointments and press relations, speechwriting

* From Canadian Public Administration, Vol. 17, No. 1, Spring, 1974. By permission of the
author and the Institute of Public Administration of Canada.

and strategic planning, regional travel and Order-in-Council appointments. All have become the concern of a Prime Minister's Office organized in hierarchical fashion under the watchful eye of a chief-of-staff—the Prime Minister's Principal Secretary.

A Departure From the Past—The Trudeau Rationale

The Prime Minister's Office did not assume a clear identity of its own until Trudeau became Prime Minister in 1968. Before that time, and particularly during the governments of Mackenzie King, Pearson, and Diefenbaker, the Prime Minister's Office had its share of individuals who were colourful and indeed influential. But the Office, in an institutional sense, never assumed the importance it was to have in the period following 1968.

Pierre Trudeau purposely set out to build an Office different in style and function from the Offices of the past. With his approval, a detailed organization was set up, wide-ranging responsibilities were created and allocated, and lines of authority and access were designed. 'From the outset Mr. Trudeau was determined to achieve two principal objectives: exercise a great degree of collective political control over a large and complex government apparatus; and respond more effectively to the increased demands upon Parliament, government and himself by a more active and interested public.'

Pierre Trudeau's rationale for changing the nature and scope of his Office was a timely response to a serious dilemma faced by political leaders at the federal level in Canada. Prime Ministers had long since become the victims of bigness—the number and complexity of decisions facing them had become staggering; the size and activity of the government bureaucracy they headed had increased enormously; the demands of national leadership, Parliament, cabinet committees, constituency, party, public consultation, federal-provincial relations, foreign affairs, and ceremonial duties had become virtually impossible to cope with in the absence of organized assistance. By enlarging and reorganizing his Office the Prime Minister sought to strengthen his personal ability to oversee and to direct the administrative and political machinery which he heads.

The Critics Attack

Reaction to the Prime Minister's moves was predictable. Some public servants feared that the interposition of dozens of 'political appointees' at Prime Ministerial level would interfere with traditional links between the chief executive and the public service. Members of Parliament on both sides of the House openly questioned whether their historically recognized representative roles would be undermined by an Office seeking to establish its own contacts with the electorate. Some cabinet ministers feared that Prime Ministerial assistants might supplant their position as the Prime Minister's chief political advisers, and that this latter-day praetorian guard might even become overseers and evaluators of ministerial activity. Liberal Party spokesmen warned against any curtailment of the party's traditional role by the activity of the Prime Minister's Office. Constitutionalists argued that the growth of the Office was a *de facto* move towards a presidential style of leadership and that Parliament would be downgraded as a result. And journalists, wary of any move that would concentrate greater power in the Prime Minister's hands, attacked the Prime Minister's moves with sometimes scorching cynicism. All the critics feared, in effect, that by strengthening his personal Office the Prime Minister would become more independent of Parliament and more isolated from the principal actors on the political stage.

The Myth of Supergroup

More than five years have passed since the Prime Minister's Office assumed a different role and meaning within the Canadian political system. Some of the fears were from time to time given momentary substance (often exacerbated by exaggerated journalistic commentary about the almost limitless power of 'supergroup'). But, in the final analysis, changes in the Prime Minister's Office have had less impact than is generally believed. . . .

Limitations

The Prime Minister's Office today, as in the past, operates within certain constraints. A former Principal Secretary outlined some of these by saying what the Office is not. 'It is not a "mini-cabinet"; it is not directly or indirectly a decision-making body at all; members of the staff have no special powers nor any special authority except that vested in them by the Prime Minister; they are all in a "staff" and not a "line" situation; and they are answerable to the Prime Minister for their conduct and activities in the same way as Ministerial staff are answerable to their respective Ministers.'

There are additional constraints which he did not mention. The first and most obvious is that the Office is by no means exclusive in providing advisory and non-advisory support to the Prime Minister. Cabinet colleagues, members of Parliament, party officials, and private individuals assist the Prime Minister in a wide variety of ways.

The second is that only a few members of the Prime Minister's personal staff are engaged in substantive advisory activity, and direct and frequent access to their chief is limited largely to these individuals. An Office staff which exceeds ninety suggests that the Prime Minister has surrounded himself with a formidable array of advisers, indeed that he has created his own 'department.' But of this number, over seventy function in secretarial and principally non-advisory roles. The Correspondence Division alone, greatly enlarged to handle a sharp increase in the volume of mail received by the Prime Minister, accounts for over forty people.

The third constraint is the limited resources available to the senior members of the Office staff. Each is deeply involved in his or her specific area of responsibility and each operates almost entirely without the assistance of research or planning personnel. There is, in other words, a very limited 'second layer' capability within the Office, and this has obvious implications. One is that the present advisory capability must operate on a largely *ad hoc* trouble-shooting basis. Another is that this advisory capability cannot normally generate policy initiatives or in-depth policy analysis. . . .

Key Changes

In spite of the constraints outlined above, several important developments in the Office during the past five years constitute a break with the past and have potentially significant implications for the future.

The Principal Secretary

One of the most important of these developments was the appointment by the Prime Minister in 1968 of a Principal Secretary from outside the public service. Principal Secretaries had been appointed from time to time in the past in Canada, but traditionally they were members of the public service and as such had no overt political role whatsoever. . . .

With the appointment of Marc Lalonde, an 'outsider,' as Principal Secretary in 1968, and the establishment of new terms of reference for the post, a new focus of power and influence emerged within the Prime Minister's circle of key advisers. Although it can be argued that Tom Kent's advisory role under Pearson from 1963 to 1965 was a precursor to this development, Trudeau's decision to invest his Principal Secretary with formal political and administrative responsibilities of considerable magnitude was an unprecedented step. He is the Prime Minister's chief of staff and 'main political advisor.' As such he has virtually uninhibited access to the Prime Minister, senior officials, and members of the Office staff; he attends cabinet meetings with the Prime Minister's approval; he attends or is represented at weekly meetings of the Privy Council Office senior staff; he ensures that the Prime Minister's Office maintains close liaison with the Privy Council Office and with the extra-parliamentary party; he oversees the activities of the Prime Minister's personal staff; and from time to time he offers the Prime Minister advice on Policy issues. . . .

The Program Secretary

The appointment by the Prime Minister in 1968 of a Program Secretary was another important development in the evolution of the Office. He is charged with the primary responsibility of 'ensuring that the Government and the extra-parliamentary party have and maintain a comprehensive and coherent program.' In conjunction with this duty this in-house philosopher and one-man think tank devoted a great deal of his time during the first Trudeau government to bridging the gap between politicians and administrators on policy matters. From him the Prime Minister regularly received assessments of the Government's over-all performance measured against its basic political philosophy and goals, and advice on the development of long-term policy choices and political strategy. . . .

The work of Trudeau's first Program Secretary had an impact on the way the staff perceived its function and on the thinking of the Prime

Minister himself. An appreciation of norms and value-oriented politics was fostered in an environment in which brokerage politics had always been acceptable as the rule. Emphasis was placed on problem-avoidance as much as on problem-solving, and scientifically based political analysis came to supplement raw political intuition.

Senior Appointments

A third significant change in the Prime Minister's Office was in the area of senior appointments. In 1969 a division was created in the Office to assist the Prime Minister and the Cabinet with part-time Order-in-Council appointments to boards and commissions. The actual selection of candidates remains the prerogative of ministers, but the Nominations Division ensures that candidates are of a high quality, and that adequate information about them is available to Ministers, and that full consultation among Ministers precedes a decision.

In regard to full-time appointments—Deputy Ministers, heads of crown corporations, and members of full-time boards, for example—the Nominations Division plays a much more limited role, and on a more irregular basis, even though the Prime Minister's prerogative in this area has long been recognized as one of his most important political powers. Since 1968, regular meetings of the Prime Minister, his Principal Secretary, and the Secretary to the Cabinet have taken place to discuss these appointments. The involvement of public servants in this process is dominant for it is the Privy Council Office and not the Prime Minister's Office which usually prepares the memorandum which serves as a basis for discussion. The advisory input of the Nominations Division is limited to the occasional identification and assessment of candidates from outside government.

This new kind of involvement of the Prime Minister's Office in senior appointments, although limited and especially so in the case of full-time appointments, is significant and beneficial because it constitutes a move away from patronage. . . .

Regional Desks

. . . After the general election in October 1972, . . . the Regional Desks, which had played an active role in the day-to-day conduct of the campaign, were among the targets of criticism. They were later officially disbanded, though with a reduced profile the function continues to exist. . . .

External Affairs

. . . The Prime Minister long has had a special role in the conduct of foreign policy and, in the past, has relied almost exclusively on the advice of the Department of External Affairs.

The allocation of special advisory responsibilities in this area to a member of his personal staff, Ivan Head, was a shift away from this traditional pattern. A Legislative Assistant in 1968, and later a Special Assistant (Research), Head has carried out a series of missions to foreign countries on the Prime Minister's behalf (e.g. Lagos, Washington, Moscow, Commonwealth countries), has had significant influence on a number of key foreign-policy issues (e.g. 1969 NATO decision), and has offered the Prime Minister a wide range of advice on the general conduct of foreign affairs. To many observes of the Ottawa scene Head appears to be the Prime Minister's 'number one foreign-policy adviser.' . . .

Some Thoughts About the Future of the Office

Crossroads and Challenges

The Prime Minister's Office has reached a particularly significant stage in its development. The needs and attitudes of the present Prime Minister and his successors will determine whether the Office reverts to its pre-1968 form—a handful of assistants, informally organized, in essentially a service role—or remains as it is—several dozen assistants in a combined service/trouble-shooting role, with a limited policy capability, and a formal chain of command. Or, indeed, the Office may become an even more effective vehicle of political management and policy advice for the Prime Minister. This latter possibility is worth examining.

At least two fundamental issues are involved. First, have cabinet government and the *primus inter pares* doctrine been transcended by 'Prime Ministerial Government?' Have unique and final responsibilities for the conduct of government devolved upon the Prime Minister so as to make him more than equal to his Cabinet colleagues? It is assumed in this paper that the answer to these questions is a qualified yes. The Prime Minister cannot act independently of the Cabinet for the Cabinet remains the sole source of political authority, and any Prime Minister who were to ignore this fact 'could rapidly come to grief.' Yet the Prime Minister is very much the leader and as such has a status and a number of important responsibilities which no Cabinet Minister has. It follows that he should have staff services adequate for the exercise of these responsibilities.

Secondly, can the political leadership of the Canadian government afford to depend as heavily as it has in the past on the public service for policy advice? It is suggested in this paper that the answer to this question is no. The public service consists largely of career-minded, professionally oriented specialists who, for all their knowledge, skills, and great integrity, sometimes lack flexibility, breadth of understanding, and of course, political sensitivity. . . . The need for these qualities can be met by supplementing public service advice from various outside sources; in particular, a bolstered policy-capability in the Prime Minister's Office would supply the strong political perspective so essential to a well-balanced advisory service.

A Management Role

If a case can be made for the Office having a strong management role it is because the Prime Minister has a unique position at the centre of the political and administrative machinery of government. As the elected leader of his party he is its political head and is ultimately responsible for the direction of its policies and initiatives. As chairman of the Cabinet he is the principal guiding force in helping it to arrive at decisions. He is both co-ordinator and arbitrator of the executive decision-making process, and it is through him and his Cabinet colleagues collectively that political control is exercised over the totality of government activity. The knowledgeable and effective performance of these pre-eminent duties has many facets and requires various kinds of help.

Political Machinery

Managing the political machinery of government is not an easy task. The Prime Minister has important relationships with Parliament, with individual Members of Parliament, with ministers and with the executives of the extra-parliamentary party. These relationships must be carefully nurtured and here the Prime Minister's Office can play an important part.

First, the Prime Minister should be aware of the significant political activities of his colleagues—a notable speech, a program in trouble, an important party meeting, a regional flare-up. The Prime Minister's Office could perform a highly constructive information-gathering function in such cases as these. By receiving a systematic 'current political issues' briefing from his staff he would be better prepared to take the initiative on any political issue.

Secondly, there are occasions when it would be beneficial, and prevent duplicated effort, if the Prime Minister shared the results of his staff's political research and fact-finding with his colleagues, particularly when the issues involved are of major or national significance. Someone on the Prime Minister's staff should be available to carry on this information-sharing service and maintain, in so doing, close contact with ministers' offices, the caucus research group and party headquarters. . . .

Thirdly, the Prime Minister should ensure that when he and his colleagues speak publicly they agree in their interpretation and explanation of government policies and programs. Here the Prime Minister's Office can assist by working closely with ministers' offices in co-ordinating major government announcements, in preparing important policy statements and speeches, and in planning communications strategies. . . .

Administrative Machinery

. . . The Prime Minister occupies a position at the top of a huge pyramid formed by an immense bureaucracy with numerous departments and levels of decision-making. Although the federal bureaucracy has earned a reputation as one of the world's finest public service organizations, it is not meant to control itself. It is meant to respond to political direction, for government activity is supposed to reflect the will of the Canadian people through their elected representatives. . . .

The successful exercise of political control over the administrative machinery of government requires first, that public servants acknowledge and understand the philosophy, objectives, and aspirations of the government; secondly, that government departments generate programs and policies reflecting the substance of this over-all direction; thirdly, that there be accountability to the Prime Minister and ministers for the competence, sensitivity, and speed with which the administrative machinery works. In attempting to exercise this breadth of political control, the Prime Minister and ministers must rely on well-organized political support systems that will assist them in communicating political objectives to the public service, in assessing the political implications of on-going programs and policies, and in ensuring that a sufficient degree of accountability exists. Here again, although the Office of the Prime Minister (and the office of each minister) could play a vital role and is very concerned about these needs, the assistance it provides is regrettably limited.

So the Prime Minister is faced with inadequate resources to manage either the political machinery he heads, or the administrative machinery he ought to control. Improvement of the situation would not require the addition of dozens of assistants to the Prime Minister's staff. Two senior officers forming a Management Co-ordination Group would improve the present situation: one responsible for research (information-gathering and sharing), co-ordination and communications in relation to the political machinery of government; the other identical responsibilities in relation to the administrative machinery. Reporting to the Prime Minister through the Principal Secretary, these officers would have a strictly staff function. They could work closely with all key individuals and organizations involved in high level political and administrative operations with the over-all objective of assisting the Prime Minister in his management role (see Appendix, Proposed Model of PMO).

A Policy Role

Constitutionally, the Prime Minister and his Cabinet colleagues are collectively responsible to an elected Parliament for new and on-going policies and programs. But within the executive structure the Prime Minister occupies the most prominent position, and in the policy area he is regarded as the prime mover.

To what extent the Prime Minister's Office should become involved in this policy function is a subject of potential controversy. Historically, its involvement has always been of a very limited nature. This should not surprise anyone; for in the past, the Prime Minister's staff has performed mainly a service function. . . .

But in the systematic initiation of policy, in its development, its analysis, and its assessment the Prime Minister's Office is overshadowed by the work of three bodies in particular: the Privy Council Office, Treasury Board, and the Department of Finance. Of the three, the Privy Council Office has the key role. Because of its position at the apex of administrative activity it can maintain an overview of total government operations. . . .

In the policy field the Prime Minister's Office is obviously no match for the Privy Council Office with its formidable array of talent and resources.

Nor has it tried to be. . . . A good case can be made for expanding this capability so that the Prime Minister will have benefit of a perspective he cannot get from the Privy Council Office, namely, systematic and in-depth political advice in the formulation of all policies and programs, comprehensive political assessment of them, and a continual flow of fresh ideas for long-term planning purposes. As a result, the Prime Minister would be better appraised of the views of politicians and citizens and so feel more confident in initiating and developing new programs and policies, and in guiding on-going ones. And politically oriented contributions towards long-term thinking from his own Office would encourage greater realism and sensitivity when determining political strategy. . . .

The upgrading of the policy capability of the Prime Minister's Office could be achieved by introducing perhaps six additional officers and altering the existing organization (see Appendix, Proposed Model of PMO). A fundamental step would be the creation of a Policy and Program Review Group composed of four officers, each responsibile for one major operational area of government: economic policy; external policy and defence; science, culture, and information; and social policy. Reporting to the Prime Minister through the Program Secretary and Principal Secretary, these officers would have a strictly staff function and assume responsibility for providing political advice in relation to their respective operational area, and for providing political assessments of on-going policies and programs in their area. They would liaise closely with their counterparts in the Operations Division of the Privy Council Office but in no way encroach upon their activity. And they would maintain constant contact with Ministers' Offices, the caucus, and the executive of the extra-parliamentary party.

Their activity should be complemented by a Planning Group composed of two officers responsible for generating ideas on, and making contributions towards, long-range political strategy. These officers too would report to the Prime Minister through the Program Secretary and Principal Secretary. Functioning in a staff capacity, they would liaise closely with their counterparts in the Plan Division of the Privy Council Office, and with Ministers' Offices, the caucus, and the executive of the extra-parliamentary party. . . .

It would be especially beneficial if, as in the United Kingdom, the Prime Minister shared the output of these special policy resources with the Cabinet. However, ministers would be even better off if they expanded the capability of their own offices to advise them on policy in their particular area of responsibility. Some ministers feel this need, but progress in this direction has been very limited.

A Service Role

By far the overriding reason for the expansion of the Prime Minister's Office between 1968 and 1973 has been a very practical one: the need for the Prime Minister to respond to greatly increased demands upon his time. . . . A substantial and effective service capability has been developed in the Prime Minister's Office to meet these escalating demands.

Though it might be argued that this service capability has reached optimum size and effectiveness for the time being, suggestions that it is unnecessarily large and elaborate fail to appreciate either the magnitude of the Prime Minister's over-all responsibilities, or the variety and number of tasks he is called upon to perform on a daily basis. . . .

The Prime Minister and His Advisers

There is remarkably little in the way of well established precedents or guidelines in Canada concerning the appointment, conduct, organization, or role of the Prime Minister's staff. Equally little has been written about this subject. Part of the reason is that Prime Ministers and their assistants come and go,. and each Prime Minister's Office tends to be fashioned to suit the needs of the incumbent. Continuity in an institutional sense has never been considered very important.

Staff Appointment
Staff members, other than public servants seconded to the Office, are usually appointed by Order-in-Council and hold their positions at the will of the Prime Minister and as long as the Prime Minister remains in office. Historically, and following the British example, most of the Prime Minister's staff were seconded from the public service. During the fifties and sixties this practice was eroded with the introduction of individuals other than public servants into senior positions. In 1968 the balance shifted decisively with virtually all senior appointments being accepted by 'outsiders.' This shift had an unmistakable impact on the Office because 'outsiders' tended to view time spent in the Prime Minister's Office not as an integral part of an on-going governmental career, but as worthwhile 'time-out' from other endeavours. They were drawn to the Prime Minister's Office in most instances by strong feelings of loyalty and allegiance to the Prime Minister himself. Entering the Office free of bureaucratic affiliations gave them an independence of style and thinking that otherwise would have been difficult to come by.

But, during the period 1968 to 1973, loyalty certainly has not been the principal criterion considered by the Prime Minister and his Principal Secretary when making appointments. The particular knowledge and skills possessed by an individual are paramount, while representation from the various regions of Canada is considered important, a balance of anglophones and francophones is considered mandatory, and women have been consciously recruited. Lawyers, businessmen, journalists, academics, and former public servants have been prominent among the appointees. . . .

Staff Conduct
When, in the sixties, the Prime Minister and ministers began introducing an increasing number of individuals from outside the public service to their personal staffs, a problem emerged which before that time had

received little attention. Many of these personal appointees did not have the same attitude towards government as their counterparts in the public service. Nor did they work within the same constraints. A high level of integrity, an aloofness from day-to-day politics, a total detachment from partisanship, a high degree of professionalism—these were qualities, inherited from the British practice, that ministerial and Prime Ministerial secretaries seconded from the public service were expected to have. The personal appointees, on the other hand, while expected to be individuals of integrity, were obviously much more directly involved in day-to-day politics, vigorously partisan in most instances, and well versed in the art of political gamesmanship.

. . . Prime Minister Pearson established what is in effect a code of conduct applicable today to both ministerial and Prime Ministerial staff. 'It is by no means sufficient for a person in the office of a Minister—or in any other position of responsibility in the public service—to act within the law. That goes without saying. Much more is required. There is an obligation not simply to observe the law but to act in a manner so scrupulous that it will bear the closest public scrutiny. The conduct of public business must be beyond question in terms of moral standards, objectivity and equality of treatment.'

Staff/Prime Minister Relations

In the past the Prime Minister's relationship with his personal staff was very close. Few in number, they enjoyed a great deal of personal contact with the Prime Minister and worked largely under his personal direction. With the enlargement of the staff in 1968 this became impossible. Inevitably, a degree of institutionalization occurred and a hierarchy of command was established. . . .

It is difficult to describe in any detail the relationships between the Prime Minister and individual members of his staff. Ever changing interpersonal dynamics and the emergence of special relationships often render organization charts and published terms of reference obsolete. Some members of the staff may, from time to time, and for perfectly legitimate reasons, exert unusually strong influence within the Office. But integrity, discretion, and low profile are unfailingly accepted as essential prerequisites to effective service, and rightly so. . . .

In the technical terms of management theory, the individual staff member's role usually is assumed to fall clearly on the staff side of the familiar 'staff/line' distinction. To a management theorist this means he provides information, formulates possible courses of action, co-ordinates decisions, and reports on results. In fact the staff/line distinction becomes somewhat blurred in the Prime Minister's Office because staff members do at times exercise authority. They work as extensions of the Prime Minister's persona, controlling or influencing activities in the Prime Minister's name and to the extent that the Prime Minister allows them to do so. What is essential is that staff members do not act without authority. . . .

If the work of his staff is to be of positive value to the Prime Minister it must be executed with a high sense of responsibility and a great deal of discipline. As a gatherer of information a staff member must ensure that his data base is as wide and as accurate as possible. As a formulator of possible courses of action he must ensure that each course is fully documented and free of his personal bias. As a co-ordinator of decisions he must resist the temptation to try to take the decisions himself. As a reporter on results he must take great pains to deliver his findings as fairly and as objectively as possible. And he must have the courage to be frank with the Prime Minister when withholding unpleasant information or advice would seem to be the easier alternative. Particularly important, he must know when to relinquish his role as intermediary between others and the Prime Minister, and ensure that individuals and groups that have legitimate rights of access to him are not inhibited or obstructed. These desiderata, because of pressures of time, circumstance, or personality, are not always met; but they are acknowledged and felt to be essential.

Catalyst or Cabal?

... Since members of the Prime Minister's staff are not directly accountable to Parliament or to the electors, they must be accountable to the Prime Minister. For this reason it is a wise Prime Minister who takes an active part in the selection of all but the more junior members of his staff instead of leaving the task entirely to his trusted lieutenant. In the final instance it is the Prime Minister and not the Principal Secretary who must bear the responsibility for the actions of his staff.

There are other possible safeguards against the Prime Minister's Office becoming a dangerous clique. One is the attachment of a time limit to senior appointments (subject to renewal of course). ... Another is the institutionalization of senior functions to guarantee their continuity, and to ensure that they be understood. A clearly defined organization, carefully explained terms of reference, meticulously constructed relationships with individuals and organizations outside the Office, a rejection of unnecessary secrecy—all would assist the Office in fostering a spirit of co-operation and trust among those who have dealings with it, in establishing its legitimacy as a constructive political institution, in satisfying its raison d'être: service to the Prime Minister.

The strongest safeguard of all is reliance by the Prime Minister on the time-honoured technique of balancing access to himself among a number of individuals and advisory groups. What this means, in effect, is that the advisory function should be divided in a balanced way among spokesmen from his personal staff, the Cabinet, the public service, members of Parliament, the party, and from important segments of the community at large. The Prime Minister, and not members of his personal staff, must retain primary responsibility for managing this process. ... The Prime Minister should be, in other words, the arbitrator of the advisory process that serves him.

Has the growth of the Prime Minister's Office during the past five years been desirable? On balance, clearly yes; for without an expanded staff the Prime Minister simply could not respond effectivly to the immense and

PRIME MINISTER'S OFFICE

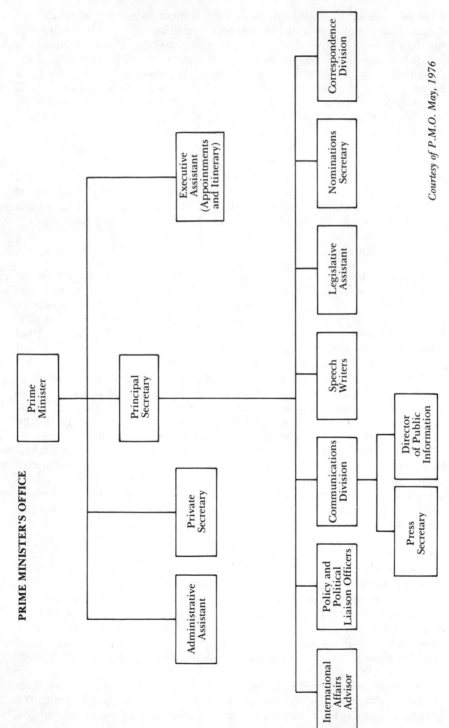

Courtesy of P.M.O. May, 1976

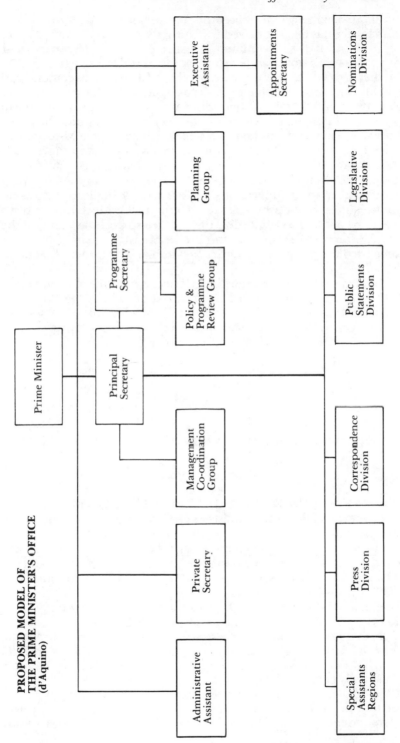

**PROPOSED MODEL OF
THE PRIME MINISTER'S OFFICE**
(d'Aquino)

multitudinous challenges of contemporary political leadership. Lester Pearson's Office has been criticized for being disorganized, even at times chaotic, in the face of the continual pressure of events. This particular criticism at least has not been levelled against Trudeau's Office. . . .

Is further growth of the Office desirable? In the management and policy fields, yes, provided that safeguards against the dangers inherent in growth exist, and that the Office adheres to a code of professionalism and integrity. Unlimited growth of the Office, however, would be counterproductive. It must be limited to a size which the Prime Minister can both effectively use and effectively control: growth must stop short of the admittedly ambiguous point where staff is needed to serve staff *per se* rather than the Prime Minister, where excessive levels in the hierarchy contribute to delays and duplication of effort, to inflexibility or confusion of responsibilities, or to problems of accountability. Moreover, growth must never be allowed to jeopardize the balance so necessary among the centres of influence surrounding the Prime Minister.

Is some further growth of the Office inevitable? The evidence seems to suggest so. . . .

The dangers of the Prime Minister's Office as cabal have been recognized. The advantages of the Office as catalyst must be recognized also. Every Prime Minister should have the benefit of a broadly experienced, mature, and politically sensitive staff which is honest in its approach to its tasks and respectful of the democratic process.

[For additional remarks on this subject, see Denis Smith, "Comments on 'The Prime Minister's Office: Catalyst or Cabal?'", *C.P.A.*, Vol. 17, No. 1, .Spring, 1974.]

SIZE AND COST OF PMO AND PCO

Paul Fox

According to a report by The Canadian Press published on May 21, 1975, the cost of operating the Prime Minister's Office was 40 times greater than 15 years previously.

The miscellaneous estimates committee of the House of Commons was told that the combined cost of running the Prime Minister's Office and the Privy Council Office had risen to about $19 million in 1975, in contrast to $514,000 in 1960-61.

Although a break-down of the figures was not given, the same report said that the staff of the offices had risen to 468 from 92.

A reply to question number 2984 tabled in the House on February 6, 1976, gave a break-down by individuals of the staffs of the PMO and PCO for 1975-76. The details can be compared to those for Prime Minister L. B. Pearson's period.

In 1975-76 there were in toto 90 members of the PMO in contrast to Mr. Pearson's 44 in 1967. Part of the increase was attributable to the growth in correspondence to Prime Minister Pierre Trudeau. In 1970 Anthony

Westell reported that Mr. Trudeau was receiving an average of 450 pieces of mail a day in comparison to 185 when Mr. Pearson was prime minister. During the Pearson period there were 21 employees in the correspondence section of the PMO. By 1973 Mr. Trudeau had 40. According to a report in *The Toronto Star* on June 7, 1976, Mr. Trudeau received more than 128,000 letters in the preceding year.

The return to the question in the Commons showed that in 1975-76 salaries in the PMO ranged from a bracket of $5,665 to $7,877 for a stenographer to $47,500-60,500 for the top official, the prime minister's Principal Secretary.

In 1975-76 the PCO had a total of 451 staff, including 125 executive officers. The salaries ranged from $7,136 to a bracket of $54,000-66,000 for the Clerk of the Privy Council who is also the Secretary to the Cabinet.

It should be noted that the PCO now has two secretaries to the cabinet. Following the appointment of Michael Pitfield to succeed Gordon Robertson as Clerk of the Privy Council and Secretary to the Cabinet in January, 1975, Mr. Robertson continued as a secretary to the cabinet in charge of federal-provincial relations and as an adviser on the appointment of other deputy ministers.

MINISTERIAL EXECUTIVE STAFFS*

Kenneth G. Tilley

> "... I have always considered ministerial staffs to be very mysterious, and best kept that way." (An anonymous executive assistant.)

Very little is known about ministerial executive staffs. Even the Prime Minister's Office does not seem to have a clear idea at any given time who is employed by which minister and in which position. Contact between the various ministers' offices is also virtually non-existent except in instances of personal friendships.

This study draws on several different sources of information, as well as the writer's personal experience as an executive aide to a minister in the federal government since 1972. The first source is a directive issued by the Prime Minister's Office in 1970, prepared by Thomas P. D'Aquino, a Special Assistant in that office, and entitled *Organization of Ministerial Offices—An Organizational Study of Ministerial Offices in Aid of Ministers and Staff*. It is the only significant published source of material on the subject which the writer could find. The other sources of information were interviews and a questionnaire. The author interviewed three persons associated with the federal government, a current minister, a recent former minister, and a deputy minister. In order to obtain some basic statistics about executive staffs, a questionnaire was drafted and sent in

---

* Written in March, 1973, and published here for the first time with permission of the author who was a postgraduate student in the Department of Political Economy, University of Toronto.

February 1973 to approximately 60 individuals out of a total of 77 executive officers serving the 29 ministers who, in addition to the prime minister, comprised the cabinet. Thirty-two responses were received.

The minister's personal staff originated with the creation of the office of private secretary (i.e. executive aide, not stenographer) who was appointed by the minister but paid out of public funds. From that beginning, ministers have continually sought to expand their staffs. Most ministers now have a number of aides who fall into various categories known as executive assistants, special assistants, administrative assistants, and research assistants. The title of the senior aide has been changed from "private secretary" to "executive assistant".

Until 1950, according to D'Aquino, ". . . the number of a minister's staff exempted from the provisions of the Civil Service Act was five: one secretary to the executive, two stenographers, one messenger, and the minister's private secretary". An Order-in-Council in 1950 raised the number of exempt positions to eight; an additional clerical position was added in 1955, and the term "special assistant" was first introduced in 1958. The 1962 Civil Service Act exempted all members of a minister's staff from the provisions of the Act and removed the previous limit of nine imposed by the Treasury Board. In 1973 the number of exempt positions varied from ministerial office to office but averaged approximately twelve persons.

Some basic statistics about the age, sex, education, position, length of service, and previous profession or occupation of executive staff can be gleaned from the responses to the questionnaire sent out by the writer.

The breakdown, by title of position, of those reporting was as follows: 37.5 percent were executive assistants, 56.3 percent were special assistants, and 6.3 percent were research assistants.

With 28 of the 32 respondents answering the age question, the age of executive staffers varied from 22 years to 62 years. The average age was 31.7 years, which seems rather young. A list of executive staffs published in 1973 by the Liberal Federation revealed that 10 out of the 77 assistants, or 12.9 percent, were females.

All of the respondents answered the question concerning education; 9.4 percent had achieved only high school graduation, 46.9 percent held a first degree, 31.3 percent a second degree, and 12.5 percent a third degree. Length of service as ministerial assistants ranged from a minimum of one month (which generally could be accounted for by the post-1972 election cabinet changes) to a maximum of 9 years. The average was 28.5 months or approximately 2.3 years of service.

The most common previous occupation listed by respondents was that of student, of whom there were five. There were also three former consultants, three executives, two lawyers, two special assistants, and two writers or film makers. Other occupations mentioned were research assistant, chartered accountant, engineer, educator, federal civil servant, "business", legal adviser, Member of Parliament, social worker, sales manager, clergyman, staff of the provincial Liberal party, financial analyst, Parliamentary Intern, and labour economist.

The P.M.O. directive states that "the size and effectiveness of a minister's staff and the degree of authority it possesses varies widely due to the highly personal nature of the relationship between the minister and his staff. A minister is responsible for choosing his staff and he decides what functions specific members of his staff will discharge. The qualifications of staff members are to be judged only by the minister . . .". Staff members are responsible only to their minister and owe him a personal allegiance. British Prime Minister Benjamin Disraeli went so far as to say in *Endymion* that "The relations between a minister and his secretary should be the finest that can subsist between two individuals".

One might wonder if this attitude has led to a considerable number of a minister's personal friends being appointed as his assistants. However, the answers to the questionnaire seem to indicate otherwise. Only 9 of the 31 assistants who answered this question (29 percent) said they were friends before they were hired, while 22 (or 71 percent) said they had had no previous personal contact with their minister. Of the 29 percent who were formerly personal friends of their minister, the minimum length of the friendship was 18 months and the maximum 120 months. The average was 50.9 months or approximately 4.3 years.

The minister and ex-minister whom the writer interviewed disagreed on whether or not they would prefer hiring a personal friend as an assistant. One felt that the factor of personal friendship was irrelevant unless the individual concerned possessed other qualities which the minister thought were important; "I don't think personal friendship is so important. . . . I think ability, compatibility is [*sic*] damned important."

The other felt that the term "friend" needed further defining but thought that it would be difficult for him ". . . to have as my right-hand man or woman someone whom I didn't know reasonably well, whom I've known for some time, at least well enough to feel that I have a fairly good understanding of the way he thinks and the way he works. . . ."

Another aspect of the question which may be important is whether or not executive staff members have ever held either elected office at some level of government, or party office. Surprisingly few had done so. Of the 32 individuals answering the questionnaire, only three (9.4 percent) said they had held elected office; 29 (90.6 percent) replied in the negative. Of the three who had held some elected office, two had been municipal representatives and one had been a Member of Parliament.

As for partisan office, the questionnaire results showed that 25 percent of the respondents had held some party office while 75 percent had not. Most of the former had held elected party office at the constituency level although there were several who had held provincial office and one who had held university office, while one was a past national office holder.

Both privy councillors were quite emphatic that staff members must be sympathetic to the government party. Both considered the job of a ministerial assistant to be highly political, requiring a high degree of partisan loyalty. One said that personal loyalty came first, but party loyalty a close second because ". . . a minister is part of a team which includes a whole caucus of party representatives, and the interests of the party are pretty crucial to any minister's decisions".

●   ●   ●

The P.M.O. directive breaks the duties of executive staffs into about half a dozen categories: time utilization, personal assistance to the minister, general administration, planning, research and public statements, liaison with Members of Parliament, and liaison with the public service.

The directive suggests that executive staff members will be involved in the preparation of daily, weekly, monthly and yearly planning of the minister's engagements and appointments, the useful allocation of the minister's time, the management of his travel requirements and itinerary, the handling of his social arrangements, the answering of his private and personal correspondence (e.g. to his constituency), control of the ministerial budget and administration of office personnel, collection of statistics on incoming mail and preparing reports from these statistics so that the minister may be regularly apprised of the volume, topics and origin of his correspondence, and maintaining supervision of the filing and records system.

In addition, the P.M.O. sees a role for executive staff in strategic political planning, political and policy research, and the planning and preparation of ministerial speeches, public statements, articles and messages. The directive attaches considerable importance to the staff's relationship to Members of Parliament and members of the public service. The main function outlined by the directive for a staff member vis-à-vis the M.P. is to provide information to him and keep him informed, wherever possible, of matters that will affect his constituency and his areas of interest. In regard to the public service, the minister's aides have a staff relationship to him and are to assist him, advise him, and execute his orders and provide a liaison between his office and the public service. The directive is careful to point out that the assistants themselves have no line authority or function in relation to their minister's department.

Both the minister and ex-minister who were interviewed felt very strongly that the prime function of an executive staff was political. One noted two functions: "One is service and the other is advisory. . . . I found the service function was a very important one. Organizing the minister's staff to perform that service was a very important role of the E. A. . . . Contact with the constituency I don't think can be performed by an administrative assistant [i.e. a civil servant] because you are there dealing with constituents. . . . I think that is one of the roles of the executive, the political staff."

The other believed that the essential purpose of a personal executive staff was to help the minister to look at questions in a broader way than he would if he were assisted only by the public service, because the civil servant has a departmental view and certain interests which naturally do not take into account the political implications in the broadest sense. He said, "I don't just mean party political, but the general interest of the country is not necessarily the same as the departmental interests. For instance, I always expect someone on my staff to be very critical, I don't mean in a destructive way, of what the public servants present so that I can see every aspect of the question, some of which may have been ignored or neglected by the public service, others of which might have been rejected and sorted out in the process of reaching me. . . ."

When asked specifically if there was a political input into departmental matters by the executive staff, both interviewees replied in the affirmative. One said, "I suppose it's all political in one sense. They have to look at everything from a political perspective as opposed to primarily a departmental or civil service perspective. . . . Otherwise, there wouldn't be any real purpose to having a personal staff. You could rely on the public service to be your staff. . . . It's the same kind of assessment as I might be making myself trying to take into account, the 'public interest', the total political assessment, including a party political assessment, an assessment of the interests of the government. But not an expert assessment, not one that demands the expertise of the public service."

The deputy minister who was interviewed saw the function of a ministerial staff as primarily a liaison between the deputy minister's office and the minister's office. He minimized the political input of the staff members. However, he did think that ministerial staffs were very, very useful: "A most obvious reason, I think, is that particularly in our system, ministers are extraordinarily tied-up. You have the minister in Parliament, . . . he can't be reached or contacted. He sits in cabinet, he can't be reached or contacted by his deputy minister or by his department. He sits in caucus, he can't be contacted. He has his constituency to worry about, he can't be contacted. The nature of his responsibilities in the Parliamentary system are so overwhelming and so arduous that it is often the case that ministers get a chance to focus only rarely on administrative responsibilities in terms of their portfolio. . . . So in many, many ways I think the only way that one can dialogue with a minister, get his response, find out what he thinks, is through a member of his personal staff who is with him all the time or is closely available to him in his outer office or on the plane."

When the executive staff members were asked how they envisaged their roles as ministerial assistants, they stressed two points. First, they felt it was their job to keep their minister aware of all potential and continuing problems and issues within his department and constituency and to bring these to his attention before they got out of hand. Second, they believed they were public relations persons for their minister, that they should keep his image before the public and try to insure that the image presented was as favourable as possible.

In addition, the respondents saw their function as one of handling routine inquiries and questions and generally administering the office in order to allow the minister to make the best use of his time for matters that were indeed important. Closely related to this duty was that of obtaining and preparing material in concise form for the minister.

Midway down the list of duties came one function which the writer thought would rank much higher, and which both the minister and former minister held to be the prime quality of a good staffer, the exercise of political judgment. However, the respondents indicated they were more interested in providing the minister with relevant information than in exercising political judgement. It is possible, of course, that they understood this function to be obvious and self-evident.

Other functions mentioned less frequently by the respondents were: enhancing the position of the minister without eclipsing him; acting as a sounding board for the minister's ideas; acting as a liaison between the minister and his colleagues, M.P.s, the media, constituents, and the department; "protecting" the minister, and "screening" those seeking access to the minister.

The comments of two assistants were contradictory. One considered his role to be that of a "surrogate M.P." or an "ombudsman", an extension of the minister. The other felt quite strongly that assistants were not employed to make a lot of decisions on the minister's behalf without advance consultations with him.

•   •   •

It is clear that there is a difference of opinion among the P.M.O., ministers, civil servants, and staff members themselves as to the nature of the functions and duties of ministerial aides. The variations, however, are probably not dysfunctional. Each minister must recruit and shape his staff to suit his particular needs. While ministerial staffs have no uniform structure, they apparently are essential and are here to stay. Their size has grown in the past 25 years from approximately five persons to an average of 12 persons, per minister, and they are likely to continue to expand.

[According to an editorial in *The Financial Post*, December 20/27, 1975, there were on the average 4.5 executive and special assistants per federal cabinet minister. Since the average salary of an executive or special assistant was about $25,000 a year, the total cost per minister was about $100,000 or $3 million for the entire cabinet. (The maximum allowable cost per minister is $130,000 per annum.) In one year the number of executive and special assistants had increased from 89 to 118.]

THE REPRESENTATIVE NATURE OF THE CANADIAN CABINET*

Paul Fox

Since the cabinet is the centre of power in the Canadian system of government, many different interest groups will seek to be represented in it. Provinces such as Quebec, for instance, will be much more concerned about protecting their minority position by means of representation in the cabinet than in the Senate, which was intended originally to be the organ for guaranteeing the provinces a voice at Ottawa. The same will hold true for minority religious and ethnic groups, or for occupational and professional organizations.

A prime minister will be prepared to listen to such pleas not only because he wishes to secure the allegiance of all these different factions but also because, by means of well-chosen cabinet ministers, he can establish across the country pillars of party strength responsible to him. In each

* From an article by the author which was revised in March, 1976.

province a federal cabinet minister may well be the chief power in the local party, the link between it and Ottawa, and the channel through which flows influence, patronage, and party loyalty.

Thus, by virtue of the federal and party systems in Canada, certain definite customs have grown up governing the construction of cabinets which no prime minister, whatever his party, would dare to flout. First, he must make sure that he has tried to give representation to each of the ten provinces (with the possible exception of the smallest, Prince Edward Island). The largest provinces of Ontario and Quebec will believe themselves entitled to more than one member, the quota having been raised progressively through the years to at last 10 each, while British Columbia, as third in order of size, will claim two or three seats. Even with these provinces there will be such strong feelings of parochial identity that eastern Quebec, including Quebec City, will have to receive recognition as well as western Quebec, including Montreal. The eastern townships in Quebec will also probably try to get representation. In Ontario it will be impossible to select all the ministers from the central area around Toronto, since eastern, western, and northern Ontario will expect representation too. Careful attention must also be given to achieving a proper distribution of posts amongst the religious faiths in the country. Protestants and Roman Catholics and perhaps others, will receive appointments in proportion to their numerical strength in the country. Catholic appointments will have to be subdivided between Anglo-Irish Roman Catholics and French Roman Catholics and Protestant appointments amongst the various Protestant churches, if possible in proportion to their sizes. Members of other faiths (such as Jews) will feel that they should be recognized as well. Moreover, some of these groups located in certain provinces will demand specific representation, for example, the English-speaking Protestants in Montreal and Roman Catholics in Ontario.

Various economic groups will also press their claims, often to particular portfolios. Prairie wheat farmers will expect the minister of agriculture to be chosen from amongst their numbers or, at least, from the west. The department of fisheries will have to go to someone from either the east or west coast. Business and financial circles will seek a minister of finance who is sympathetic to their views, trade unions a minister of labour who understands their problems, and veterans a minister of veterans' affairs who has been a serviceman and will listen to them.

Special interests will also make their voices heard. Women's associations may argue that there should be more women in the cabinet, young people's groups that there should be more youthful ministers, Indians that there should be an Indian member, and French-speaking Acadians that there ought to be an Acadian in the government.

The result is that every Canadian cabinet becomes highly federalized, a mirror of the various forces that compose the country. This is well illustrated by a comparative analysis of the Liberal government of Mr. St. Laurent at the beginning of 1957, the Conservative government of Mr. Diefenbaker which replaced it later that year, the Liberal government of Mr. Pearson that in turn succeeded it in 1963, and the Trudeau governments of June 10, 1970, and March, 1976.

The St. Laurent Liberal cabinet contained one member of parliament from every province except Prince Edward Island, which received a parliamentary assistant. British Columbia had two representatives in the cabinet, Ontario six, and Quebec five (formerly six, one was recently deceased). The Ontario members were apportioned judiciously in the ratio of two to northern Ontario, one to western, one to eastern and two to central Ontario. In Quebec three ministers were chosen from the province's eastern region in the neighbourhood of Quebec city and two from Montreal in the west.

There were 13 Protestants in the cabinet, of whom eight belonged to the largest Protestant denomination, the United Church, and two to each of the Anglican and Baptist churches, while one called himself simply a "Protestant." Of the six Roman Catholic ministers, four were primarily French-speaking , one was Anglo-Irish, and one was of English-speaking and French-speaking parentage. Ontario's group of six ministers was composed of four Protestants and two Catholics and Quebec's five included one representative of the Protestant English-speaking enclave in Montreal.

Occupationally, this cabinet contained nine lawyers (the most numerous occupational group in the Commons), one notary, three engineers, two former civil servants, one farmer, one educator, one medical doctor, and one businessman. The farmer was the minister of agriculture, the minister of fisheries was from the west coast, and the minister of trade and commerce was a prominent former businessman and engineer.

In addition, the group of 13 parliamentary assistants of the day showed much the same sort of proportional distribution in terms of geography, religious faith, and occupation.

The Conservative government that succeeded this Liberal administration illustrated that the same principles of federalism were at work. Every province received at least one seat in the new cabinet while Ontario was given seven members, Quebec three (later increased to five with one more "promised"), British Columbia three, Saskatchewan two, and Manitoba two. In these provinces with plural membership the appointments were distributed fairly equitably throughout each province.

There were 17 Protestants in the cabinet, their grouping by denominations corresponding exactly, by happy coincidence or design, to the order of size of the various Protestant faiths: six members of the United Church, five Anglicans, three Presbyterians, two Baptists, and one "Protestant". With later additions from Quebec, there were six Roman Catholics, four of whom were primarily French-speaking, and two of whom were Anglo-Irish. There was also one member of the Ukrainian Orthodox faith, who as a Ukrainian represented what was then the fourth largest ethnic group in Canada. He came from Ontario, while Quebec's contingent included one English-speaking Protestant from Montreal.

The Conservative cabinet contained nine lawyers, four educators, four businessmen, two chartered accountants, two farmers, and one army officer. The ministry of finance went to a member from Toronto, the department of agriculture to a member from Alberta, and the portfolio of fisheries to an MP from Prince Edward Island. A former army general with the Victoria Cross became minister of national defence. (The Liberals had also had a minister with the Victoria Cross. He had held the portfolio of veterans' affairs.)

The 13 parliamentary assistantships were also distributed amongst various provinces, faiths, and occupations.

The Liberal cabinet appointed by Mr. Pearson after his electoral victory in April, 1963 reflected the continuation of the representative principle. Its 26 members (the largest number to that date) contained 10 representatives of Ontario, eight of Quebec, two of British Columbia, and one of each of the other provinces except Saskatchewan, which had not seen fit to elect any Liberals to Parliament. The 10 Ontario appointments were distributed so that five went to central Ontario (including three to Toronto), three to northern Ontario, and one each to western and eastern Ontario. Eastern Quebec received only one minister but the Eastern Townships and the Anglo-Saxon bastion in Westmount were not overlooked.

The cabinet was balanced neatly with an even split between Protestants and Roman Catholics, 13 each. The Protestants included eight members of the United Church, three Presbyterians, one Anglican, and one "Protestant", while the Roman Catholics were subdivided into nine predominantly French-speaking members, three Anglo-Saxons, and one of mixed parentage.

Mr. Pearson's first cabinet contained 10 lawyers, six businessmen, four former civil servants, two ex-professors, two agriculturalists, and one economist. The ministries of finance and trade and commerce went to Toronto, justice to Quebec, northern affairs and forestry to British Columbia, fisheries to New Brunswick, veterans' affairs to a former prisoner-of-war, and agriculture to Alberta.

The 16 parliamentary secretaryships were distributed in such a way that they reflected the representative principle also. Ontario received six, Quebec five, British Columbia two, and Nova Scotia, New Brunswick, and Newfoundland one each. Nine of the secretaries were Protestants and seven Roman Catholics. Balance within the top echelon of departments was achieved by frequently appointing as a parliamentary secretary to a minister an MP of a different provincial and religious affiliation from the minister, for instance, an Ontario, English-speaking, Protestant secretary to a Quebec, French-speaking, Roman Catholic minister, or a Quebec, French-speaking, Roman Catholic secretary to an Ontario, English-speaking, Protestant minister.

When Mr. Trudeau became prime minister in April, 1968, it might have been expected that his more unconventional approach to politics would result in a major departure from observing the traditional representative principle in the Canadian cabinet. But an examination in detail of the appointments to his first cabinet as modified by later changes, reveals that there was no substantial alteration in adherence to the longstanding customs regarding representation in the cabinet.

The body continued to grow in size, acquiring 30 members in place of Mr. Pearson's 26 ministers and in sharp contrast to the 13 members with which Sir John A. Macdonald began in 1867. Ontario and Quebec still received the lion's share of nominations, the former obtaining 11 and the latter 10, but with the exception of British Columbia which captured three awards and Prince Edward Island which received none (having failed to elect any Liberals), the rest of the provinces each got one cabinet minister. In Ontario and Quebec the prizes were distributed throughout each province with reasonable judiciousness, although some Torontonians, including one leading newspaper, complained about the under-representation of Toronto in comparison to Montreal since after Paul Hellyer's resignation the score was only two to six. Perhaps because of such criticism, the prime minister promoted a parliamentary secretary from Toronto, Robert Stanbury, to cabinet rank shortly thereafter. This appointment brought the number of ministers without portfolio in Mr. Trudeau's government to the unusually large total of four, which did mark a minor departure from form.

Despite the fact that Prime Minister Trudeau implied he was putting more emphasis on quality than had some of his predecessors, his cabinet nevertheless emerged with much the same complexion in religious and occupational respects as prior administrations. It contained 15 Protestants, 14 Roman Catholics, and one Hebrew, the last being an innovation since the Hon. Herb Gray was the first Jew ever to be appointed to a Canadian cabinet. Occupationally, however, the familiar pattern was repeated with 11 lawyers leading the pack accompanied by eight businessmen, four academics, two agriculturalists and two labour figures, and one former civil servant, one journalist, and one chartered accountant. The average age of ministers was about 45 years, not all that much less than in previous governments.

In one respect Mr. Trudeau's cabinet did differ from its predecessors. While the prime minister did not increase the proportion of ministers of French mother tongue beyond the customary one-third of the total, he tried consciously to give a greater number of senior posts to French-speaking members, in keeping with his policy of fostering genuine equality between the two official language groups.

As for the 16 parliamentary secretaries appointed to the Trudeau ministry, their characteristics differed little from the traditional pattern of representing the various geographical, denominational, linguistic, and occupational components of Canadian federal politics.

Mr. Trudeau continued to observe traditional considerations when he reshuffled his cabinet after his victory in the general election of July 8, 1974. Including some subsequent changes, his 29-member cabinet displayed the following characteristics on March 10, 1976 (the date of revision of this article). There were 11 ministers from Quebec, 10 from Ontario, two from B.C., and one each from Saskatchewan, Manitoba, New Brunswick, Nova Scotia, P.E.I., and Newfoundland. In short, every province was represented except Alberta which had forestalled its elevation to the summit by electing nothing but Conservatives. In Ontario metropolitan Toronto and western Ontario each received four ministerial posts while northern and eastern Ontario got one each. Montreal received seven, eastern Quebec three, and western Quebec one.

Religious considerations were marvellously well balanced with 14 to Roman Catholics, and one to a Hebrew. The ethnic factor was obviously not overlooked since the ministerial roster included 17 Anglo-Saxons, eight French Canadians, three "others", and one half-and-half Anglo Saxon-French Canadian (the ideal combination, which happened to be the prime minister himself).

By occupation the 1976 cabinet contained nine lawyers, nine businessmen, four educators, two farmers, two journalists, one trade union official, one blue collar worker, and one civil servant. The average age of ministers rose to nearly 50 years, but remained within the recent customary span from 45 to 55 years.

Mr. Trudeau's appointment of 27 parliamentary secretaries indicated that similar representative considerations were at work. There were 10 each from Ontario and Quebec, two each from B.C. and Saskatchewan, and one from each of Nova Scotia, New Brunswick, and Newfoundland. The distribution of parliamentary secretaryships within regions of Ontario compensated for the unevenness of cabinet appointments within the province. Thus, northern Ontario received four parliamentary secretaries, eastern Ontario three, Toronto two, and western Ontario one. Sixteen of the secretaries were Roman Catholics, while 10 apparently were Protestants and one was Hebrew. There were seven lawyers, six businessmen, five educators, and an assortment of journalists, veterinarians, chiropractors, accountants, economists, medical doctors, and farmers. The average age was 40 years.

Finally, it is interesting to note that the principle of balance was carried over into the individual appointments of parliamentary secretaries to cabinet ministers. Hence, it was common to appoint a French-Canadian parliamentary secretary to an English-Canadian minister, and vice versa.

Such a striking similarity in the elements represented in five different cabinets is a good indication of the strength of the representative principle that lies behind cabinet-making in Canada. In addition to this, of course, a prime minister must consider the desire of friends and party supporters (for themselves or others), the claims of the "grand old men" of the party, who may have been ministers in previous regimes, and the need to blend into a harmonious team conflicting and antipathetic personalities and points of view. Thus, it is not surprising that one British prime minister said that the business of drawing up a cabinet "resembled nothing so much as the zoological gardens at feeding time." The wonder is that any cabinet contains as much ability as it does since capacity is frequently a minor consideration.

GETTING INTO THE CABINET*

Sir George Foster

[The scramble for a position in the cabinet which occurs when a new government is being formed is well illustrated by excerpts from the diary

---

* From W. S. Wallace, *The Memoirs of the Rt. Hon. Sir George Foster, P.C., G.C.M.G.*, Toronto, Macmillan, 1933, pp. 155-156, as corrected from the original diary in the National Archives, Ottawa. By permission of the Estate.

of Sir George Foster during the cabinet-making period that followed the Conservative victory in the 1911 election. Having served as minister of Finance in five previous Conserative administrations, Foster believed himself entitled to the same post again, and he did not hesitate to let the new prime minister, R. L. Borden, know. The anxieties of the aspirant, the pressures applied to the prime minister, and the inner forces at work are all clearly revealed in a few brief entries.]

Sept. 22. The govt. defeat is a decisive and general one. . . .

Sept. 23. General congratulations pour in from all sides. Left for Ottawa.

Sept. 24. At home in peace and quietness again. Borden came in at noon. Telephoned him, but he was being protected by wife—no communication.

Sept. 25. Now the cabinet-making begins, in the papers and in the clubs. B. keeps to his house and sees those he calls for. No communication.

Sept. 26. Taylor as a middleman suggests Ch. Tariff Comm., with $10,000, as a nice thing, I told him I was not out for office, and would accept none. No other communication.

Sept. 27. Certain parties are in tow. Perley appears to be the manager. Davis-Shaughnessy in evidence. Reporters (Hamilton) at old business. No communication.

Sept. 28. To-night Osler sees me. Financial interests opposed to my being F.M. Would relieve situation if I would remain out. *Globe* criticism feared. I told him plainly I would not commit suicide. No communication from Borden. Rogers says a portfolio, but not F.M. or Trade and Commerce, seat in Senate.

Sept. 29. The interests seem to be dominant, and Borden doesn't know his mind from day to day. I have advised my friends, and they are at work. No communication.

Sept. 30. To-night at 9 p.m. B. asks me to come up. He skated all around, and finally suggested Sec'y of State. I told him I wouldn't consider it. My old position was what I wanted.

Oct. 1. A quiet day, rest and reading. Hazen is here, and Rogers seems in charge. The Kemp Gooderham-McNab-Graham crowd make up the financial int.

Oct. 2. Fine. More people here. More excitement. Saw Hazen, McLeod, Crockett, Roach, etc. All are strong for me in old position. McGrath had peculiar conference.

Oct. 3. No further word from B. Letter from Clouston, and conference with Dobie. Financial interests not adverse. My friends are making things hot.

Oct. 4. More people. More wire-pulling. Deputations galore, and general suspense. B. seems helpless on the surf.

Oct. 5. Called by Chief, and offered Trade and Commerce. Ask why F.M. not given. Ans.: reasons of high politics. My capabilities, honesty and service fully recognized.

Oct. 6. A bothersome day. [Borden] backing and filling. Irresolute and fearful. He is an odd man.

Oct. 7. No word from Borden to-day. Saw Boyce and Smith, who are raging at the outsiders, especially White.

Oct. 8. The day fine. Rested without outside disturbance. . . .

Oct. 9. No announcement yet, and no word from Borden since Friday night. I hear Toronto is bombarding him. Hazen is here—what others I know not.

Oct. 10. This morning the announcement of new govt. The unseemly squabble is ended. Some weak links in the chain. There will be deep dissatisfaction with White. Sworn in at 11 a.m. except Burrell.

[Foster was appointed minister of trade and commerce.]

SALARIES AND ALLOWANCES OF FEDERAL MINISTERS AND PARLIAMENTARY SECRETARIES*

Paul Fox

Office	Salary	Sessional Allowance	Tax Free Allowance[1]	Total[2]
Prime Minister	$33,300	$24,000	$10,600	$67,900
Ministers in charge of Departments and Ministers of State	20,000	24,000	10,600	54,600
Parliamentary Secretaries	5,300	24,000	10,600	39,900

[1] The prime minister, ministers, and the leader of the official opposition in the House of Commons also receive automobile allowances of $2,000 per annum. The Speaker of the House of Commons and the Speaker of the Senate receive car allowances of $1,000 per annum.

[2] The total equivalent taxable incomes would be considerably larger because of the tax free allowance. The Act also provides for an annual increase in salaries and allowances based on increases in the Industrial Composite Index. Beginning January 1, 1976 the increase was to be 7 percent but in June, 1976 the House approved a government bill cancelling this increase for 1976.

[For MPs, Senators, and other officials of both Houses, see Chapter 13, Salaries and Allowances of MPs, Senators, and Officials, p. 449.]

* From *An Act to Amend the Senate and House of Commons Act, the Salaries Act and the Parliamentary Secretaries Act*, 23-24 Eliz.II, C.44, 1975, assented to May 8, 1975, but retroactive to July 8, 1974.

BIBLIOGRAPHY

The Executive Process: Cabinet

(Privy Council, Cabinet, Prime Minister)

Banks, M. A., "Privy Council, Cabinet, and Ministry in Britain and Canada: A Story of Confusion", *C.J.E.P.S.*, Vol. XXXI, No. 2, May, 1965. (See also "Comments", *ibid.*, Vol. XXXI, No. 4, November, 1965 and Vol. XXXII, No. 1, February, 1966.)

Berkeley, H., *The Power of the Prime Minister*, Toronto, Methuen, 1971.

Burke, Sister T. A., "Mackenzie and His Cabinet, 1873-1878", *Canadian Historical Review*, Vol. XLI, No. 2, June, 1960.

Courtney, J. C. "Prime Ministerial Character: An Examination of Mackenzie King's Political Leadership, *C.J.P.S.*, Vol. IX, No. 1, March, 1976. (Also *ibid.*, J. E. Esberey, "An Alternative View.")

D'Aquino, T. P., *Organization of Ministerial Offices—An Organizational Study of Ministerial Offices in Aid of Ministers and Staff*, Ottawa, Prime Minister's Office, 1970.

Dawson, R. M. *William Lyon Mackenzie King: A Political Biography*, Vol. 1, *1874-1923*, Toronto, University of Toronto Press, 1958, Chapter 13.

Donaldson, G., *Fifteen Men: Canada's Prime Ministers*, Toronto, Doubleday, 1969.

Fleck, J. D., "Reorganization of the Ontario Government", *C.P.A.*, Vol. 15, No. 2, Summer, 1972.

Fleck, J. D., "Restructuring the Ontario Government", *C.P.A.*, Vol. 16, No. 1, Spring, 1973.

Forsey, E. A., *Freedom and Order: Collected Essays*, Carleton Library, No. 73, McClelland and Steward, 1974.

Gibson, F. W., (ed.), *Cabinet Formation and Bicultural Relations: Seven Case Studies*, Studies of the Royal Commission on Bilingualism and Biculturalism, No. 6, Ottawa, Queen's Printer, 1970.

Halliday, W. E. D., "The Executive of the Government of Canada," *C.P.A.*, Vol. II, No. 4, December, 1959.

Halliday, W. E. D., "The Privy Council and Cabinet Secretariat in relation to the Development of Cabinet Government," *Canada Year Book, 1956*, Ottawa, Dominion Bureau of Statistics, 1956.

Hockin, T., (ed.), *Apex of Power: The Prime Minister and Political Leadership in Canada*, Scarborough, Ontario, Prentice-Hall, rev. ed., 1977.

Hutchinson, B., *Mr. Prime Minister, 1867-1964*, Toronto, Longmans, 1964.

Jones, G. W., "The Prime Minister's Powers," *Parliamentary Affairs*, Vol. 18, No. 2, Spring, 1965.

Lalonde, M., "The Changing Role of the Prime Minister's Office", *C.P.A.*, Vol. 14, No. 4, Winter, 1971.

MacQuarrie, H. N., "The Formation of Borden's First Cabinet," *C.J.E.P.S.*, Vol. XXIII, No. 1, February, 1957.

Mallory, J., "The Two Clerks: Parliamentary Discussion of the Role of the Privy Council Office, *C.J.P.S.*, Vol. X, No. 1, March, 1977.

Matheson, W. A., *The Prime Minister and the Cabinet*, Toronto, Methuen, 1976.

Morton, W. L. "The Formation of the First Federal Cabinet," *Canadian Historical Review*, Vol. XXXVI, No. 2, June, 1955.

O'Leary, D., "The Cabinet Revolt—How They Tried to Get Rid of Diefenbaker," *Canadian Commentator*, July-August, 1963.

Ondaatje, C., Swanson, D., *The Prime Ministers of Canada, 1867-1968: Macdonald to Trudeau*, Don Mills, General Publishing, 1967.

Bibliography 423

Pitfield, M., "The Shape of Government in the 1980's" *C.P.A.*, Vol. 19, No. 1, Spring, 1976.
Public Archives, *Guide to Canadian Ministries Since Confederation, July 1, 1867, January 1, 1957*, Ottawa, 1957; *Supplement, January 1, 1957-August 1, 1965*, Ottawa, 1966.
Punnett, R. M., *The Prime Minister and Canadian Politics*, Toronto, Macmillan, 1977.
Robertson, G., "The Canadian Parliament and Cabinet in the Face of Modern Demands," *C.P.A.*, Vol. 11, No. 3, Fall, 1968.
Sharp, M., "Decision-making in the Federal Cabinet," *C.P.A.*, Vol. 19, No. 1, Spring, 1976.
Ward, N., "The changing role of the Privy Council Office and the Prime Minister's Office: a commentary", *C.P.A.*, Vol. 15, No. 2, Summer, 1972.

The Political Process and Policy-Making

Albinski, H. S., *Canadian and Australian Politics in Comparative Perspective*, Toronto, Oxford University Press, 1973.
Auld, D. A. L., "Social welfare and decision-making in the public sector", *C.P.A.*, Vol. 16, No. 4, Winter, 1973.
Bourassa, G., "Les élites politiques de Montréal: de l'aristocratie à la démocratie," *C.J.E.P.S.*, Vol. XXXI, No. 1, February, 1965.
Bryden, K., *Old Age Pensions and Policy-Making in Canada*, London & Montreal, McGill-Queen's University Press, 1974.
Clement, W., *The Canadian Corporate Elite: An Analysis of Economic Power*, Carleton Library, No. 89, McClelland and Stewart, 1975.
Corbett, D., *Politics and the Airlines*, Toronto, University of Toronto, 1966.
Courtney, J. C., "In Defense of Royal Commissions," *C.P.A.*, Vol. 12, No.2, Summer, 1969. (See also same subject and policy-making, articles by H. R. Hanson and C. E. S. Walls, *C.P.A.*, Vol. 13, No. 3, Fall, 1969.)
Crispo, J. H. G., *International Unionism in Canada: A Canadian-American Experiment*, Toronto, McGraw-Hill, 1966.
Deutsch, J., "Governments and Their Advisors," *C.P.A.*, Vol. 16, No. 1, Spring, 1973.
Dobell, P. C., *Canada's Search for New Roles: Foreign Policy in the Trudeau Era*, Toronto, Oxford University Press, 1972.
Doern, G. B., "Recent Changes in the Philosophy of Policy-making in Canada", *C.J.P.S.*, Vol. IV, No. 2, June, 1971.
Doern, G. B., and Wilson, V. S., (eds.), *Issues in Canadian Public Policy*, Toronto, Macmillan, 1974.
Doern, G. B., and Aucoin, P. C., (eds.), *The Structures of Policy-Making in Canada*, Toronto, Macmillan, 1971.
Dupré, J. S., *et al.*, *Federalism and Policy Development: the Case of Adult Occupational Training in Ontario*, Toronto, University of Toronto Press, 1973.
Eayrs, J., *In Defence of Canada: Vol. I, From the Great War to the Great Depression, Vol. II, Appeasement and Rearmament; Vol. III, Peacemaking and Deferrence*, University of Toronto Press, 1961, 1965, and 1972 respectively.
Farrell, B., *The Making of Canadian Foreign Policy*, Toronto, Prentice-Hall, 1969.
Gallager, J. E., and Lambert, R. S., *Social Process & Institutions: Canadian Studies*, Toronto, Holt, Rinehart and Winston, 1971.
Green, L. C., "Canada's Indians: Federal Policy, International and Constitutional Law", *Ottawa Law Review*, Vol. 4, No. 1, Summer, 1970.
Hawkins, F., *Canada and Immigration: Public Policy and Public Concern*, London & Montreal, McGill-Queen's University Press, 1972.

Hockin, T. A., (ed.), *Apex of Power*, Scarborough, Prentice-Hall, rev. ed., 1977.

Mallory, J. R., *The Structure of Canadian Government*, Toronto, Macmillan, 1974.

Mann, W. E., (ed.), *Poverty and Social Policy in Canada*, Toronto, Copp Clark, 1970.

McMillan, C. J., "After the Gray Report: The Tortuous Evolution of Foreign Investment Policy," *McGill Law Journal*, Vol. 20, No. 2, 1974.

Miles, S. R., Cohen, S., and Koning, G., *Developing a Canadian Urban Policy: some problems and proposals*, Toronto, Intermet, 1973.

Mitchell, C. M., "The Rule of the Courts in Public Policy Making: A Personal View," *University of Toronto Faculty of Law Review*, Vol. 3, No. 1, Spring, 1975.

Newman, P. C., *The Canadian Establishment*, Toronto, McClelland and Stewart, Vol. I, 1975.

Peers, F. W., *The Politics of Canadian Broadcasting 1920-51*, Toronto, University of Toronto Press, 1966.

Pickersgill, J. W., "Bureaucrats and Politicians," *C.P.A.*. Vol. 15, No. 3, Fall, 1972.

Porter, J., *The Vertical Mosaic: An Analysis of Social Class and Power in Canada*, Toronto, University of Toronto Press, 1973.

Rowan, M., "A conceptual Framework for Government Policy-Making," *C.P.A.*, Vol. 13, No. 3, Fall, 1970.

Schindeler, F. F., *Responsible Government in Ontario*, Toronto, University of Toronto Press, 1969.

Shillington, C. H., *The Road to Medicare in Canada*, Toronto, Del Graphics, 1972.

Stewart, W., "The Powerful Ottawa Politicians You Don't Elect," (Executive Assistants to Ministers), *Canadian Weekly*, July 31, 1965.

Thordarson, B., *Trudeau and Foreign Policy: A Study in Decision-Making*, Toronto, Oxford University Press, 1972.

Warnock, J. W., *Partner to Behemoth*, [Military Policy], Toronto and Chicago, New Press, 1970.

13

THE LEGISLATIVE PROCESS: HOUSE OF COMMONS

In a cabinet-parliamentary system of government such as Canada enjoys the most persistent—and probably the most important—facet of the legislative process is the continual conflict between the executive and legislative branches of government. The battleground is the House of Commons. Ministers composing a government are seated on one side of the House, confronted across the aisle by an opposition containing elected representatives of the people who are bent on destroying the administration. The ingeniousness of this system of government is its adversarial nature. Thus conflict cannot be eliminated because it is an inherent ingredient.

In such a situation the power of each of the two contending sides, government and opposition, is all important. The balance of power between them will be affected greatly by the rules of the game, that is, by the procedures of the House of Commons which are embodied in the Standing Orders of the House. Hence, it is not surprising that the substance of this chapter remains much the same as it was in the previous editions of this book. The major issues which continue to be disputed are the powers of the executive, concentrated now in the prime minister, and the alteration or reform of House procedures. Most of the items in this chapter deal with these two subjects.

Professor Denis Smith's attack upon Prime Minister Trudeau's power, "President and Parliament: The Transformation of Parliamentary Government in Canada," launches the chapter. It is followed by Mark MacGuigan's article which describes the new rules of procedure that were introduced in the House in 1969. In his article which he has brought up to date, Mr. MacGuigan, who is a Liberal MP, also discusses the new committee system in the Commons and the role of backbenchers and the caucus. A graphic from the *Canada Year Book* illustrates how a bill passes through various stages to become a law in Parliament.

The next item is a thoughtful paper by the former Leader of the Government in the House and President of the Privy Council, the Hon.

Mitchell Sharp, proposing a number of changes in present House procedures.

Geoffrey Stevens' article provides a glimpse into the limited opportunity which individual MPs have to introduce their own legislation into the House. Two tables drawn up by the editor give the salaries and allowances of MPs, senators, House officials, and members of provincial legislatures. The subject of the ombudsman has been transferred in this edition to Chapter 15 where a new item on the ombudsman will be found.

The fairly lengthy bibliography lists a good deal of the most important current literature on Parliamentary procedure and the functioning of Parliament.

PRESIDENT AND PARLIAMENT: THE TRANSFORMATION OF PARLIAMENTARY GOVERNMENT IN CANADA*

Denis Smith

In the last five years, the Canadian House of Commons has gone through the first thorough and comprehensive reform of its procedures since 1867. The process of reform that was begun in 1964 came to a stormy climax with the adoption under closure of the Government's proposal for a regular time-limitation (or guillotine) rule. . . .

Members of the Canadian House of Commons have intermittently criticized aspects of the House's rules and practices since Confederation; and there have been desultory attempts to alter the rules in this century, especially in 1906, 1913, 1927, 1947, and 1955. . . .

The measures of reform adopted from time to time in this century have all tended to restrict unlimited debate in the House, by limiting acceptable motions and debatable motions (1906, 1913); by providing for the possibility of closure (1913); by limiting the length of speeches (1927, 1955, 1960); and by restricting the number of days devoted to major general debates on the Speech from the Throne, the Budget, and Supply (1955). But the most severe restrictive measure, the closure, has rarely been used, because of its clumsiness and the likelihood of public criticism; and the other measures have done little to make the House's operations more orderly or more subject to the efficient leadership of the Government. . . .

●　　　●　　　●

* Extract from a paper presented to the Progressive Conservative Party's Priorities for Canada Conference, Niagara Falls, Ontario, October 10, 1969. By permission of the author, who wishes to express gratitude to the Canada Council for a grant to assist research on the condition of Parliamentary government in Canada, of which the paper was a reflection.

Big government [has] overtaken both Cabinet and Parliament. In Canada as elsewhere in the industrialized world over the last half century, the size, responsibilities, and opportunities for initiative of the permanent administration have expanded enormously. While departments have multiplied and divided, while independent agencies and crown corporations have been born and grown prematurely into monsters, the instruments of Cabinet and Parliamentary control of the leviathan have remained negligible. . . .

What may be equally as important as the growing burdens of government is the mythology of Parliamentary government. For the mythology has disguised the reality. We are still bemused by the classic models of Parliamentary government presented with such grace and clarity by Walter Bagehot and John Stuart Mill to an English audience in the mid-nineteenth century. . . . We have, we are told, a system of responsible parliamentary government, in which the public elects individual Members to the House of Commons and the House of Commons, in turn, chooses a Government. Thereafter, while the Cabinet governs, the House holds it responsible for all the actions of the administration, and in the event of parliamentary disapproval, can overthrow the ministry, or force it to seek a fresh mandate from the electorate. The Prime Minister is chairman of the Cabinet; the public service is the loyal and anonymous servant of the Cabinet; the Cabinet is the servant of the House of Commons and only indirectly of the electorate. The theory puts the House of Commons close to the centre of the system, where it is meant to act as "the grand inquest of the nation," influencing, supervising and controlling the actions of the executive.

While the Canadian literature of politics points out that parliamentary control may not be quite up to the theory, the theory is maintained as the ideal. As a result, many of the real forces at work in Canadian politics are underrated or ignored. The tendency is, when describing forces and practices which contradict the model, to see them as aberrations pulling the system away from the Victorian ideal, but rarely as primary forces in their own right which may be basically shaping the system.

. . . But a point may come, in adding up the distortions and aberrations from the norm, when it becomes more comprehensible to abandon the original description and try to put together another one which accommodates the evidence more completely and satisfactorily. I think this point has been reached in understanding how the Canadian system works.

•   •   •

The best short reassessment of the British model—and now a familiar one—is Richard Crossman's introduction to the 1964 edition of Bagehot's *The English Constitution*. Here, Crossman argues that Bagehot's description of the Cabinet in Parliament was falsified soon after publication of *The English Constitution*. The emergence of highly disciplined mass parties took independent power from individual Members of Parliament; the immense new administrative bureaucracy took much ordinary

decision-making power away from ministers; and an organized secretariat for the Cabinet, and especially for the Prime Minister, gave the
Prime Minister the effective powers of a president. . . .

Does the story sound familiar in Canada? It does. The Canadian Prime
Minister, indeed, may be further along the road to being a presidential
leader than the British, for distinct Canadian reasons.

For one thing, the Canadian House of Commons has never possessed
the reserve of aristocratic prestige which once gave the British House of
Commons some leverage alongside or against the Prime Minister. For
most of its life the Canadian House has been a popular chamber, based on
wide popular suffrage; Canadian Prime Ministers have always made their
primary appeal for support not *in* the House of Commons, but outside, to
the electorate. . . .

The House of Commons is diminished in importance, as compared to
the British House in the period from 1832 to 1867, because it is the
electorate, not the House of Commons, which chooses and deposes Prime
Ministers. The essential influence upon government is the sovereign
public, not a sovereign Parliament. Prime Ministers keep their eyes upon
the Gallup Polls, and not normally upon readings of the House of Commons' temperature. And the public sees the Government as one man's
Government. This public assumption gives the Prime Minister great
power over his colleagues.

The fact is a commonplace in Canadian understanding, and yet it is not
satisfactorily integrated into the normal liberal model of the parliamentary constitution. We know that general elections are competitions between party leaders for the Prime Minister's office; we concentrate our
attention upon the leaders, and the parties encourage us to do so; we see
that Prime Ministers, once in office, exercise almost tyrannical power over
their ministers and backbenchers; Prime Ministers frequently ignore the
House of Commons, or treat it with disdain, unless they perceive that the
public is watching (which it only occasionally is); and our Prime Ministers
freely admit their own predominance over the House of Commons and
the necessity of it. . . .

These events [the return of Mackenzie King as Prime Minister after
Arthur Meighen in 1926 and the defeat of the Diefenbaker Government
in the House of 1963] illustrate Richard Crossman's claim that a Prime
Minister can no longer be replaced by public and constitutional means if
he does not wish to go. They illustrate more than that: given an alert
Prime Minister, it is virtually impossible to replace him even by "under-
cover intrigue and sudden unpredicted *coup d'état*." He has too many
weapons of influence and patronage in his hands, and his adversaries
have too few. He is virtually as immovable as an American President
during his term of office.

The five years of minority government under Mr. Pearson emphasized
the same point. Even without a majority in Parliament, a Canadian Prime
Minister is normally secure in office, and scarcely faces the danger of
defeat in the House, because one or another of the opposition parties is
almost certain to vote with the Government on any division to assure its
own survival. . . .

In both the United Kingdom and Canada, the Prime Minister gains his predominance over his colleagues and the House of Commons by winning general elections and exercising the power of dissolution at his own discretion. But in Canada the Prime Minister possesses still more authority granted him from outside Parliament which brings him closer to the American President. He is chosen by a popular convention. The Canadian conventions have increasingly come to duplicate the effects of the American presidential conventions. Under the open embrace of gavel-to-gavel television, the conventions have become as central a part of national political life as the campaigns, and perhaps more central, because of their concentrated drama and intense TV coverage. In the conventions the political process is almost entirely personalized, issues fade away, and the winner is the only one to walk away alive. . . . If anything has accelerated the trend to presidential politics in Canada, it has been the enthusiastic adoption of televised national leadership conventions. . . .

Set against the overwhelming power and public prestige of the Prime Minister are the traditional duties of the legislature. Even if one admits that the power of *overthrowing* governments has been surrendered, the House of Commons is supposed to retain the power and responsibility to provide a public forum of discussion on national issues, to scrutinize spending and legislation, and to safeguard the rights and freedoms of citizens by its vigilant criticism. These are worthy goals; but even *they* fade on closer examination. . . . In its less spectacular, day-to-day performances, the House of Commons normally, if grudgingly, does the work the Government directs it to do, and does so without making much critical impression on Government measures or on the public. This is so because the Government wishes it to be so, and because, until the December, 1968 reforms, the House was the victim of its own diffuse rules, which did not lend themselves to sharp, critical investigation of Government measures.

•   •   •

Conclusion

We seem to have created in Canada a presidential system without congressional advantages. Before the accession of Pierre Trudeau, our presidential system, however, was diffuse and ill-organized. But Pierre Trudeau is extraordinarily clear-headed and realistic about the sources of political power in Canada. On the one hand, he has recognized the immense power of initiative and guidance that exists in the federal bureaucracy; and he has seen that this great instrument of power lacked effective centralized political leadership. He has created that coordinated leadership by organizing around him a presidential office, and by bringing order and discipline to the Cabinet's operations. He has made brilliant use of the public opportunities of a party leader, in convention, in the general election, and in his continuing encounters outside Parliament. He has recognized that the public responds first to personalities, not to issues, and so he campaigns for the most generalized mandate. And now, finally, he has successfully altered the procedures of the House of Commons so that it may serve the legislative purposes of an efficient presidential administration.

In doing all these things he has taken advantage of trends and opportunities that already existed. *All* Prime Ministers have been moving —under pressure—in the same direction, but none so determinedly as Prime Minister Trudeau; he has taken the system further, faster, more self-consciously, than it would otherwise have gone. Are we now to be left with this completed edifice of presidential-parliamentary government, in which the House serves the minor purpose of making presidential programs law without much fuss?

Probably not, because the system still contains some fundamental inconsistencies. How clearly the Prime Minister and Members of Parliament see these inconsistencies, I cannot be sure; but they exist, and they will create difficulties. As we have seen, the changes in the rules and practices of the House have *not only* served the *Government's* purposes; they have also, in many ways, benefited individual Members and the opposition parties.

In the course of achieving rules of procedure much more tractable for the Government's purposes, the reforms and the reforming atmosphere have also created a more intractable *membership* of the House, with new and potentially powerful instruments of leverage *against* the Government in their hands. The opposition parties are better equipped by their research funds and their role in legislative committees to criticize the administration from a basis of knowledge. The restrictions of time allocation in the House give these parties an incentive to organize their attacks with more precision and directness than before. Government backbenchers, long silent and frustrated by party discipline, permitted only to express their opinions freely in secret caucus, have been given the taste of greater freedom in the new committees of the House. . . . For the moment, the Government may hold the reins tightly, but the pressures in the House are likely to mount.

One result may be that the Government will find itself more frequently embarrassed by independent backbenchers. They will probably continue to demand *their own* research assistance, and increasingly the rights to speak critically and to vote against Government measures: first in committee, and then, by extension, in the House. (But always more and more in public, where they can be heard.) The party discipline of the majority will be put under increasing strain, and the Opposition will take every chance to encourage the tension. If we have a President, they will be saying, in effect, then why shouldn't we also have an independent Congress?

The Government, in response to such pressures, may put on the screws in private, but it will have difficulty withdrawing the public machinery of criticism that it has now acquiesced in. The House will never agree to return to its fumbling and disorganized pattern of pre-1965. With the taste of influence, and facing a more efficient executive, it will be more inclined, not less, to be independent and sometimes intransigent. If we believe, as the parliamentary myth leads us to believe, in the virtues of *public* policy making and strong *public* criticism of Government, this will surely be a salutary development. The Prime Minister will be challenged by the kind of countervailing force that he believes in.

The other possible response of Governments may be to accept the logic of these Parliamentary pressures, and to move more surely to a system of congressional checks and balances. This would involve the granting of independent powers to Parliamentary committees to choose their own chairmen, hire their own substantial staffs, pursue their own independent investigations, initiate their own legislative proposals, and freely amend and reject the Government's measures. It would involve the provision of administrative assistance for MPs comparable to that available to Senators and Congressmen, and salaries matching their new responsibilities. It would involve, undoubtedly, the admission of television cameras to committees and to the House floor, to bring the House closer to the public. It would involve, finally, and probably gradually, the abandonment of the convention of confidence, so that Governments could expect to stay in office for full terms in spite of regular defeats in the House. . . .

BACKBENCHERS, THE NEW COMMITTEE SYSTEM, AND THE CAUCUS*

Mark MacGuigan

Backbenchers

Members of Parliament may walk the corridors of power but they do not yet have access to the executive suites where the important decisions of government are made. Ours is still an executive-run system in which the decisions that matter most are made, not by Parliament, nor even by the parliamentary caucus of the majority, but by cabinet ministers and senior government officials.

But the power of the decision-making elite is far from absolute. Backbenchers sometimes rebel, at least in the privacy of caucus, and they are not unacquainted with lesser ways of making ministers' lives uncomfortable. More important, the complexity of the whole governmental system defies absolute control by any man or any group, however highly placed. To some degree the system itself is the master, limiting the options of both government and caucus.

Perhaps this is because the system does not have a military-like chain of command. Rather it is a number of power centres: cabinet ministers (not necessarily themselves all working in tandem), the mandarins of the civil service, the managerial group in Crown corporations and agencies, and in a small way members of Parliament and senators. The system is not easily

* Revised in January, 1975 from a series of three articles written by Mark MacGuigan, Liberal Member of Parliament for Windsor-Walkerville, who was Chairman of the Special Committee of the House of Statutory Instruments. The articles were published in the *Windsor Star* on June 11, June 18, and July 2, 1969. By permission of the author and publisher.

put in motion, nor easily brought to a halt, by any power centre.

Certainly what most clearly stands out in the view from the back bench is the system itself—not the control of the cabinet, nor the daily conflict with the opposition, but the systematic mass which is not readily converted into energy. The legislative mills appear to grind slowly, and not always exceedingly fine. The executive appears to have many of the same matters continually under consideration, without coming to a conclusion. The administrative mechanism appears to proceed on its own, sometimes blunting the sharp points of legislation by overly rigid interpretation, sometimes filling in the gaps through exaggerated powers of regulation-making. The very complexity of the system keeps both MPs and ministers so occupied that they have little time for critical reflection. It might seem to be a gigantic conspiracy, if there were any conspirators, or at least any conspirators apart from everyone in the system. But it is not a conspiracy so much as a common plight.

How is change possible? Cabinet ministers have the power to accomplish a great deal but are harried by administrative, legislative, and political duties which leave them with little opportunity for anything beyond their daily round. Obviously the civil servants have little incentive to attempt to change the system. They are more comfortable in it than any other group, and, if their wishes do not always prevail, at least they are not often thwarted. The backbenchers have the will, but neither the power, nor the time, nor the organization to carry out the reform of the system.

The principal reason for hope has been the expressed determination to reform the system on the part of the one man with sufficient power to do it—the prime minister. In his years of office he has moved in many directions to change the system. In the House of Commons, for instance, the rules have been changed to allow Standing Committees to take over all the detailed work of scrutinizing estimates and of the clause-by-clause study of legislation which was formerly done in Committee of the Whole in the House. The establishment of a new Joint Standing Committee on Regulations and other Statutory Instruments to scrutinize all delegated legislation will in time probably considerably limit executive power.

On the administrative side the changes have been equally impressive. Although the details are shrouded in the secrecy characterizing all cabinet matters, important changes have been effected in cabinet procedures which have led to a more profitable use of cabinet time through a greater use of cabinet committees. In addition, a number of departments have been reorganized along more functional lines, and effective use has been made of ministers without portfolio in assisting more senior ministers. Ministers of State have been appointed for the first time. The institution of duty days for ministers' attendance during the oral question period has made available more ministerial time to enable ministers to master their departments, although this experiment had to be abandoned in the 29th Parliament because of the minority situation.

Perhaps the next important change has been in the position of backbenchers. The unchecked power of the executive was owing in no small measure to the inertia of backbenchers, which in turn resulted in large part from an excessive workload combined with inadequate facilities and assistance. In the 28th Parliament backbenchers were given second sec-retaries, second telephone lines, access to research assistance (given col-lectively to the parties), the right to exchange ten of their regular weekend flights home for trips elsewhere in Canada, and the right to send four householder mailings a year to their constituents, as well as increases in salaries and expense allowances. In the 29th Parliament MPs obtained the right to a riding office and secretary and additional office space in Ottawa plus greater access to governmental telephone lines. These factors, along with the minority situation and the election of an increased number of younger and more activist MPs led to greatly increased parliamentary activity, especially in committee, in the 29th Parliament.

The executive has not yet conceded the need for a more open govern-ment and, to judge from its slowness in announcing even major necessary decisions, has not yet made itself into a fully efficient organ of govern-ment. Parliament has not yet learned how to allocate its time wisely and parliamentarians do not yet act with sufficient freedom. The new scrutiny committee has only just begun to control the process of delegated legisla-tion. But great strides have been taken and the parliamentary system in Canada has probably never been healthier.

The New Committee System

It is probable that the principal motivating force in the Trudeau government's decision to establish the committee system as an integral part of the legislative process was to save parliamentary time. A legislative committee system can save time on bills or estimates because a number of committees meeting simultaneously can accomplish a great deal more than a single Committee of the Whole. Paradoxically they can also give a more detailed and penetrating scrutiny to legislation or estimates; the division of labour enables certain members to specialize and available time allows more leisure for pursuit of subtle points.

Under the new system of procedure which came into effect on January 14, 1969, the government undertook to send all bills to committee as a matter of course after second reading. Although the number of Standing Committees was increased to 18, the membership was reduced to 20 (with the exception of two committees of 30 members each). In a majority parliament the government takes one more than half of the places on each committee, and all committees except Public Accounts choose a govern-ment member as chairman. However, in the minority 29th Parliament the government and official opposition were each assigned an equal number of members (8), and the government's necessity to choose a chairman from its number reduced it to a clear minority status on every committee.

Most MPs belong to two committees. Committees usually meet on Tuesday and Thursday mornings and afternoons, with occasional night and Friday morning meetings. Each committee is assigned a clerk, and all committee proceedings are conducted and published in both official languages.

Since the establishment of the new system, there has been considerable controversy, both public and private, over the role of the government backbencher in it. While clearly the government foresaw that greater participation by its backbenchers would result from the changes, it perhaps did not realize how greatly a taste of freedom would affect its backbenchers.

There have always been two controls which kept the backbenchers in line. The positive one was that of advancement, which does not need to be explicit in order to be real; while "yes" men are not necessarily promoted, "no" men almost never are (and hence there have been very few of them). The negative factor was effective where a sufficiently large number of backbenchers was involved as to make individual reprisals impracticable. A government's most potent weapon is to threaten dissolution of Parliament and a general election. Although the crisis of February, 1968, which resulted from the government's defeat on third reading of a tax bill, finally made it clear that a government is not compelled to regard a defeat on a particular measure as a vote of non-confidence unless it chooses to do so, the government can always hold over the MPs' heads the threat that it will decide to interpret any adverse vote in the House that way.

The institution of the committee system completely removed the negative control over matters referred to committee, because a defeat for the government in a committee vote cannot even theoretically be considered a vote of non-confidence. It also lessened the effectiveness of the positive control, because most matters on which the government would be likely to be defeated in a committee by its own supporters (who, after all, accept the same basic philosophy) would usually be comparatively minor and therefore much less likely to prejudice a member's career.

The result of the new system was, therefore, predictable. In the 28th Parliament, Liberal members on several occasions themselves moved amendments to government bills, or voted in support of opposition motions or amendments. A notable instance occurred in the Justice Committee on March 25, 1969, when an amendment to the breathalyzer sections of the Omnibus Criminal Code Bill was proposed by a Liberal MP and, despite the opposition of the minister of justice, was carried, with five Liberals and four Conservatives outvoting two New Democrats and the four Liberal members who voted for the government version. In the 29th Parliament the government lost a number of committee votes by reason of opposition votes, but because of the atmosphere of partisanship that often prevailed on all sides normally received the support of its backbenchers. On the Justice Committee, however, during the consideration of the "Wiretap Bill", some government backbenchers showed considerable independence of mind.

The significance of additional freedom for government backbenchers on Standing Committees does not so much lie in the number of times they may actually reverse their own frontbenchers. Such occasions will undoubtedly remain rare. Rather what is important is that, once recognized as having this right, they can then effectively pressure ministers to make changes in legislation which they would not otherwise be likely to make but which do not actually impair the overall scheme of the legislation. There is no better example of a minister's accepting an unwanted change than in the case of the breathalyzer amendment. Despite the fact that he had the power to reverse the committee decision on report stage in the House when the committee reported the amended bill back to the House and the matter again became a question of confidence, the minister decided not to do so. No doubt ministers will have to learn to live with a good many such compromises in the future.

Whether or not the government yet accepts the fact, it made a fundamental change in our system when it introduced the legislative committee. In my view, the change is a major improvement, because it enables the individual member to make a more creative contribution to the law-making process. At the same time it produces better legislation, because it is the product of a broader decision-making group. The only loss is in the power of the executive.

Some older parliamentarians feel that private debate in caucus achieved the same effect of modifying Government proposals without the disadvantage of embarrassing the government, since it was removed from the ken of the outside world. But those who have sat in caucus know how easy it is for a government to manage caucus, and even to ignore its views on any particular matter, unless the caucus is almost unanimous and prepared to press a matter strongly. Whatever the merits of the older system, (and I do not think they are great), the government cannot now abolish the legislative committee because the new system is too much more efficient. And given the system, the new breed of backbenchers is not going to accept the role of mere ciphers in which the executive controls every parliamentary action.

. . . There are still too many committees and probably too many MPs on each committee. There are too few committee rooms, interpreters, transcribers, and clerks, and no experts to assist members in acquiring technical knowledge.

There is inadequate time allowed in the parliamentary schedule for meetings to take place. Committees have no budgets and no right to establish their own agendas. Finally, committee members have no guarantee of relative permanence of assignment and therefore have inadequate incentive to master particular fields of legislation. The legislative committee system has been well begun, but it will not achieve its great potential without time, money, and intelligent direction.

The Caucus

A caucus is a private meeting of the elected members of a political party for the purpose of exchanging views on the political question of the day. The word "caucus" probably comes from an Algonquin word, *kaw-kaw-was*, meaning to talk, and it first appeared in the English language in the early part of the eighteenth century as the name of a political club in Boston. . . .

The word made its first appearance in England in 1877 with a rather different meaning, when it was used by Joseph Chamberlain to describe a new system of party organization through constituency meetings which he was developing in Birmingham. Since Disraeli's colourful use of the term the next year to describe the Liberal political machine of the day, it has usually had in England the unflattering sense of a system of party organization with the sole purpose of election management. . . . The British political system still does not have a body which is equivalent to the Canadian understanding of a caucus. The 1922 Committee is the organized form of the backbench members of the Conservative Party in the House of Commons, but ministers do not attend its meetings unless specially summoned. The Parliamentary Labour Party more closely approximates a caucus since it theoretically includes the frontbenchers as well, but when the Labour party forms the government, the relationship between the ministry and the backbenchers tends to follow the Conservative pattern.

The common attendance of ministers and backbenchers which characterizes the caucus in Commonwealth countries other than Britain is probably a legacy of their colonial past in which all elected members worked together against the executive officials appointed by the Mother Country. As the first British colony to achieve self-government, Canada had to develop a system of party solidarity in Parliament without the assistance of parliamentary precedents from anywhere else. The Canadian party caucus is therefore a uniquely Canadian institution, though now paralleled by similar structures in other Commonwealth countries.

There is a basic difference between the role of the caucus in a party which forms the government and its place in a party which is in opposition, resulting from the fact that opposition parties do not have responsibility for the presentation of a legislative program. An opposition caucus may have internal difficulty in establishing a common position respecting government legislation, but there is no difference in the responsibility which its various members bear either in the House or in caucus (except the unique responsibility of the leader of the official opposition)—all are equal in status. But within the government caucus the members of the cabinet carry a special responsibility for the introduction of government legislation, and therefore have a special status within the caucus just as they do within the House. The principal focus within a government caucus is therefore always the relationship between the ministerial and non-ministerial members of the caucus.

Former Prime Minister Mackenzie King probably accurately expressed the general purpose of a government caucus when he said in the House in 1923 that it "is the means whereby a government can ascertain through its following what the views and opinions of the public as represented by their various constituencies may be . . . a means of discovering the will of the people through their representatives in a manner which cannot be done under the formal procedure which is required in this chamber." The government caucus exists for the purpose of consultation between ministers and backbenchers.

But to whose use is the consultation put? In other words, is the caucus a device by which the government controls its members or is it rather a means through which the backbenchers control the cabinet? The history of Canadian politics leaves little doubt that the government caucus is of greater utility to the ministry than to the members, and that it is, in effect, the chief instrument of government control of the House of Commons. Undoubtedly the years have seen a lessening in cabinet absolutism and a growth in caucus democracy, but even yet caucus control of cabinet is only weak and interstitial. A closer look at the operation of the government caucus at present will explain why.

The government caucus meeting usually runs from 10:30 to 12:15 on Wednesday mornings during a parliamentary session. Cabinet ministers are expected to attend and most backbenchers want to. The meeting opens with announcements of events or committee meetings, followed by reports from the regional caucuses (which have met earlier from 9:30 to 10:30). Sometimes these reports spark brief debates. Next there are reports from the House leader and from the Whip respecting the business of the House, which may provoke questions. Then, unless there is a special subject for discussion, the floor is thrown open for members to raise subjects of which they have given advance notice to the chairman.

On a typical morning the chairman will have had notice of perhaps six or eight subjects, on each of which there may be a number of speakers (without notice) depending on the degree of interest the subject arouses. If the subject concerns a particular cabinet minister, he may be one of the speakers. Even with the time limit of three minutes for each speaker except a minister, it may happen that only three or four subjects are reached before the chairman calls on the prime minister to reply at 12 o'clock. The prime minister normally takes about 15 or 20 minutes to comment on the views expressed earlier. When the prime minister has finished, the caucus immediately adjourns.

On rare occasions these regular weekly meetings are completely devoted to a single subject. Somewhat more often, a minister will give a report to the caucus on what he proposes to do with respect to some matter under his jurisdiction, though in very general terms, because our parliamentary tradition is that MPs other than ministers may not know the details of government legislation until a bill has obtained first reading in Parliament.

In addition to these meetings of the full caucus, there are also many meetings of caucus committees, all of which are of an ad hoc character even when they meet frequently. There is no established procedure and the chairman is usually whichever member happened to call the group together. Sometimes the minister whose departmental responsibility is related to the subject under discussion may attend, but often he will not. When a minister attends, he will listen to the views of backbenchers on policy which has not yet been announced, or, where a bill has already been presented, explain its terms to those present.

In such a situation there are obviously many factors working in favor of governmental control. The caucus is very loosely organized (its executive has only the power to recommend and seldom does even that), and consequently discussions in full caucus cover only a small part of the government's total legislative program. Many of the matters raised by members are either local in nature or trivial in character. No motions are put in caucus and no votes taken, and the government is therefore always free to interpret caucus opinion in its own way. There is no real dialogue with the prime minister since he always has the last word. Perhaps worst of all, most of the discussion is after the fact, when the government has already announced its policy, or at least made up its mind as to what it will do.

It is hardly surprising that most government MPs in the past have abandoned any attempt to work collectively through the caucus and have set about attempting to advance their ideas, and incidentally their careers, through individual action. If the individual member's influence comes solely from his own gifts of intellect, personality, and persuasion, and in no way stems from his status as a member of the caucus, then he will normally lack the incentive to participate seriously in the caucus.

The fact that the government caucus in the 28th Parliament was composed of members who, rather than devoting all their efforts to individual achievement, were determined to make the caucus work as a system, in conjunction with a prime minister who encouraged it to organize itself in such a way as to increase its influence and even its power, brought about a major strengthening of the caucus system.

However, the advance did not occur in a straight line. In the 28th Parliament the government agreed to present proposed bills or policy statements in outline to the caucus after they had been considered by the full cabinet. A half dozen standing caucus committees were established with permanent chairmen to which the proposed legislation or policy was referred. For a time these committees preempted national caucus time every second Wednesday morning.

This system quickly broke down because the simultaneity of the meetings both limited the number of the participants unduly and frustrated the many members with major interests in several fields. With the greatly reduced number of government members in the 29th Parliament, such a system was clearly inoperative from the outset. The new caucus structure substitutes a committee of the whole for the standing committees of caucus and two bilingual chairmen handle all the meetings.

Since the government commitment to consult with caucus in advance continues, the new system guarantees effective minimal consultation, especially in important matters, and when there is considerable back-bench disagreement with a government proposal, further meetings are scheduled until consensus is reached. Nevertheless the absence of set times for caucus committee meetings means that members cannot schedule their time in advance so as to be sure of participation, and the limited time available serves to sort out only the most blatant disagreements and not to allow consultation on the fine points. It is a rough-and-ready system which works but which does not provide full satisfaction to caucus members.

In sum, the cabinet guarantee of advance consultation of caucus has opened the possibility of a real, though partial, transfer of power. The failure of the government caucus to organize a fully effective consultative mechanism indicates that the opportunity has not yet been fully seized.

HOW A BILL BECOMES LAW IN PARLIAMENT*

Policy proposal
requiring legislation
(submitted to
Cabinet by a
Minister)

Consideration of
policy
in a subject–
matter committee
and decision
or recommendation

Cabinet
confirmation
of committee
decision

Responsible
Minister issues
drafting instructions
for legislation
to Department
of Justice

Cabinet
confirmation of
committee decision
and Prime Minister's
signature

Consideration
of draft Bill
by Cabinet
Committee on
Legislation and
House Planning

Draft Bill
prepared by
Department of
Justice and
approved by
responsible Minister

The Cabinet process

Parliament First
Reading in either
Senate or House of
Commons[1] (reading
of title and brief
explanation of Bill)

Parliament Second
Reading in same
House of Parliament
(debate and vote on
principle of Bill)

Consideration
by appropriate
Parliamentary
committee
(clause by clause
examination of Bill)

Introduction of
Bill into other
House of Parliament
and repetition of
the process

Parliament
Third Reading
and vote

Parliament
Report Stage
and vote on any
amendments prepared
by committee

The legislative process

The
Governor
General in
presence of Senate
and House of Commons
assents to Bill and
signs it into law

1. All money Bills must be introduced in the House of Commons.

*From *Canada Year Book, 1973,* p. 109. Reproduced by permission of
the Minister of Supply and Services Canada.*

AN OUTLINE FOR HOUSE OF COMMONS REFORM*

Mitchell Sharp

Any program of procedural reform in the House of Commons must be undertaken with a clear understanding of the rôle of the Commons within the democratic system.

There are two extreme assessments. On the one hand, there is the view of the House as a legislative mill, the prime purpose of which is to grind out bills that will solve all the problems of the day. On the other hand, there is the view of the commons essentially as a political forum in which the Government faces its critics and the parties face one another, incidentally producing legislation.

The reality is that the Commons must be able to produce legislation effectively, but it must also be able effectively to examine the financial and administrative affairs of the government and it must be a sufficiently credible body that the major political directions for the nation can be decided in its deliberations.

Few people seem to think that the Commons has been fulfilling this rôle. Ministers are impatient with long delays; private members—on both sides of the aisle—are frustrated by their apparent incapacity to affect policy; political reports give the Commons only passing attention; those few scholars who study Parliament invariably publish prescriptions for substantial reform.

Yet the pressure for legislation increases apace.

How does the Commons use its time?

In the present session of Parliament—up to the summer adjournment —the greatest proportion of time of the House of Commons was taken by matters other than Government business. About 45 per cent was taken by question period, private members' hours, questions of privilege, adjournment debates and so on.

Somewhat less than 40 per cent of the Commons' time was taken by consideration of the government bills. The remaining 15 or so per cent of the time was taken by consideration of other government motions or on the business of Supply, the approval of expenditures, (which takes place on days that are colloquially, but not completely accurately, called "opposition days").

These figures refer to the 182 sittings of the House itself. They do not include the 697 meetings of standing and special committees (a total of 1189 hours!). The use of time by committees is even more revealing of the importance of the non-legislative functions of Parliament. Only 28 per cent of the committees' time was used for legislation. Contrast this with 36 per cent of the time used by committees on financial business (estimates

* From a submission by the author, who was President of the Privy Council and Government House Leader, to the Standing Committee on Procedure and Organization, printed as Appendix "C" to the *Minutes of Proceedings and Evidence of the Standing Committee on Procedure and Organization*, November 20, 1975, pp. 9:27-9:36. Reproduced by permission of the Minister of Supply and Services Canada.

and public accounts) and an equal proportion of time used by committees in considering 21 various subject matters (e.g. egg marketing, immigration policy, procedural reform) referred to them by the House over the session.

One can see, then, that while legislation tends to be the principal public focus of Parliament, in fact it occupies a distinctly small proportion of the time of the House of Commons or of its committees.

The average number of government bills introduced for the last ten sessions of Parliament is about 61; by removing the four sessions in that period that were cut short by dissolutions, the average number of government bills introduced during sessions not interrupted for elections in the last decade is approximately 79. The build-up of legislation is amply demonstrated by the very much above average figures for the sessions that followed periods of particularly contentious Parliamentary partisanship: in the 1966-1967 session, 107 government bills were introduced and in the present session, to date, 89 government bills have been brought in.

On the average approximately 80 per cent of the government bills introduced in a session have been given Royal Assent during the session. This means that more than a dozen government bills are not completed each session. Some are stopped by political forces; some were so-called first reading bills, never intended to be proceeded with until a later session after the interested public had been able to comment; but most were merely victims of time. All of them were bills that were judged by the government to be needed. The Cabinet each year spends a great deal of time attempting to pare down the list of required legislation to a size that Parliament may be expected to digest, but every year a substantial proportion of the list is not passed.

As a legislator, the Commons cannot therefore be given high marks. As a scrutineer of administration and as a political forum it is felt to be inadequate. One cannot take time from one area of activity and apply it to another if one feels that both are unsatisfactory in operation. The conclusion is inevitable: either more time must be found or existing time must be put to better use.

For most members of the House there is already too little time to discharge their obligations to the House and to their constituents. For Ministers the situation is even worse. If anything, sittings of the House ought to be reduced.

One faces, then, the only viable option. The time of the House must be better organized.

The first step is obvious: any incentive to go slow must be eliminated. Members tend to drag their feet for three reasons. First, they tend to feel that their words alone have little effect on policy. By going slow and consuming more precious time they hope to attract more attention from the government. Second, members tend to put local views "on the record" to impress their electorates. Third, public opinion in Canada is slow to mobilize on a national basis except in the most dramatic circumstances. Members tend to go slow on certain bills so that there will be more reports over a long period and, hopefully, some public support will be found for their viewpoints.

A step toward removing the first incentive can be taken by Ministers. Governments often assume defensive postures by restricting information, by giving obscure or even evasive answers to questions and by being unresponsive to requests or points made in debate. Ministers who take the extra time with private members on both sides save time in the House. So do Ministers who respond to issues as they are raised and who react quickly to parliamentary developments.

Ministers and private members, however, are subject to all of the human frailties and one may safely assume that it will take more than an altruistic desire to improve the Commons to put more work into their parliamentary performances.

Happily, this incentive may be forthcoming, resulting from the Government's determination, announced in the Speech from the Throne in September, 1974, to have the House of Commons permit the radio and television broadcasting of its proceedings and of its committees' proceedings. With such a dramatic increase in the public's access to the Commons, the politicians will very quickly see the value of improved performance. One may well expect that speeches will become shorter, questions and answers more to the point.

One cannot expect complete broadcasting throughout Canada of the Parliamentary day—at least not immediately. Under these "electronic Hansard" conditions, one may expect that broadcasters are unlikely to use the "tub-thumper" speeches or the evasive non-answers. . . .

There is little of a formal nature that can be done to improve Question Period, which is in many ways the centre piece of the Commons. . . .

The rules regarding the length of speeches, however, will clearly have to be changed. At present, with certain exceptions provided for the Prime Minister and the Leader of the Opposition, for "set" debates such as on the Address, the Budget and Supply, etc., maximum length of speeches is 40 minutes. This is clearly too long under present circumstances and would be disastrous for broadcasting conditions. This maximum should be reduced by at least 50 per cent and perhaps, after the first round of speeches, by as much as 75 per cent. It may be that a system of progressive reductions of maximum limits by a set number of hours or days of debate could be developed. In any case, the limits must be reduced substantially.

While a reduction of the length of speeches would limit many debates, there remains the problem of planning the over-all business of the House. When members have less time to make their points and greater expectation for public attention (through broadcasting), they will require a more specific plan of business in order to prepare their intervention. With Governments facing an ever escalating demand for legislation, they will require a more specific idea of what kind of program they can reasonably expect to see passed in the time available.

For many years there have been limits in the rules on the length of the Address and the Budget debates. Limits were extended to Supply (i.e. the approval of expenditures) in 1968. It is generally accepted that, beyond these "set" debates, Governments have to take the responsibility for limiting deliberation.

The existing methods of limiting debate are intentionally cumbersome. Traditional "closure" requires a period of at least three days at second or third reading of a bill. It does not apply to Standing Committees and, as the St. Laurent Government discovered in 1956, it is a political disaster in a Committee of the Whole. At the Report Stage it would require a period of at least three days on every proposed amendment and there is no limit on the number of amendments that may be proposed at this stage.

The "time allocation" rules of 1969 are also difficult to apply. Standing Order 75A (agreement of all party representatives), because of the political realities of the relationships between parties' leaderships and caucuses, is almost tantamount to a special order by unanimous consent. Standing Order 75B (agreement of a majority of party representatives) has never been used. Standing Order 75C (unilateral allocation by the Government) has been used twice, under unusual circumstances. No party will agree to an allocation of time to a bill that it opposes and after more than six years it has never been possible to isolate only one party on the question of time. The Government is therefore in a position where it has two basic situations for limiting debate: when there is virtual unanimity or when there is complete disagreement with the opposition that has resulted in prolonged debate. Thus the existing rules are almost useless for planning purposes.

Since it is the Government's program, the Government must take the responsibility for taking steps to put it through Parliament. At the same time, the Commons must be in a position to resist arbitrary actions and to attempt to mobilize public opinion. In Canada, the principal battle on a bill has usually been fought at the second reading stage. This makes little sense since the second reading stage is really merely a motion to refer a bill to a committee. A delay at second reading not only creates log jams down the system, but it results in undue pressure on committees, when they get difficult bills, to proceed in a more hasty and more partisan manner, thereby detracting from the serious work of hearing representations and making amendments. The committee stage becomes a rather repetitive and boring (and unobserved) prelude for an equally repetitive and boring report stage, when the House is often asked to spend much time reconfirming the partisan positions taken in committee. Ironically, by the time the third reading stage is reached, i.e. the stage at which the House is asked *the* essential question, "Shall the bill pass?", opposition to a bill has usually worn itself out and, if there is any debate at this stage, it is a dreary dénouement. While the political effects of this system can be impressive, it usually does little to improve the bill and nothing to assist the overall legislative program. The system to be sought should be aimed at preserving the political potentials but, at the same time, increasing the likelihood of improving the legislation.

A suitable legislative process should be oriented to moving bills along toward the third reading stage rather than impeding their progress until that point. If there is to be a political pitched battle, it is most logically held at the third reading stage. At the second reading stage, debate should be of a preliminary nature. In committee and at report stage, consideration should be dispassionate and orderly. Supporters and opponents of a bill can plan their respective approaches to a bill and, in the earlier stages, lay the groundwork for any political pyrotechnics at third reading. A planned approach, of course, implies an orderly arrangement of time; supporters and opponents of a bill must have adequate time to prepare their cases, but this time must be so organized as to avoid impairing the entire program.

A Government should be prepared to make public virtually all of its planned program at the beginning of a session. Members cannot be expected to be able to make plans if they are not permitted to examine that for which they plan. The bills on the program should be introduced during the Address Debate. From this point forward, considerable consultation between parties will be necessary. . . .

As great a consensus as possible should be sought on the question of how much time would appear to be required. In the final decision, the Government must be prepared and empowered to take the responsibility. Since, inevitably, parties will differ on specific items, time should not be allocated to specific items at second reading stage or report stage, but packages of bills should be made. These would be groupings of bills of varying degrees of controversy. The Government could then, under a new rule, propose an allocation of a certain number of days to a specific package of bills. Notice of such an allocation motion should be required and a limited amount of time should be provided for debate and amendment. This would be required to reduce the temptation for a Government to propose to allocate too little time to too many bills or to too controversial a package. The principal discouragement to arbitrary action is exposure.

The bills within a package would be taken up in an order determined by negotiation. Any member who felt that too much time was being taken by an item could move the adjournment of the debate on that item and the House could determine the matter. In any case, at the close of the final day of an allocation (which might be prolonged if a log-jam developed) the questions would be put on all items in the package not then disposed of.

This system could be applied to the second reading and the report stage of bills. Committee stages, however, do not lend themselves to package allocations. If they are to be useful, however, they too must be planned and therefore they really must have specific amounts of time to deal with specific bills. Once more, considerable discussion of this matter must be undertaken between parties, but, once again, ultimately the Government must take the responsibility for allocations of time. Under a new rule, the Government could propose the allocation of a specific number of hours of the time of a specific committee to consideration of a specific bill. Perhaps several of these allocations could be put into a single motion. Once again provision for notice and limited debate would afford protection against arbitrary action. Once a committee knew how long it had, it could readily divide its time into periods for representations, for deliberations and for clause-by-clause decisions.

If the third reading stage is to be made the principal focus for political confrontation, the package-allocation system cannot apply to that stage. Each item will have to be considered separately at third reading stage.

Since third readings are likely to come just before long adjournments, Governments can postpone adjournments in order to accommodate prolonged third reading stage debates. Alternatively, they can take the political responsibility—and risk—of involving closure.

It is quite likely that as members become used to more careful planning of the legislative process more Commons time will become available for debates on more general policy questions. Under present conditions virtually the only time available for such debates comes during the Address Debate, which tends to be unfocussed, or on opposition motions on Supply Allotted Days, which tend to be unduly partisan debates because of the usual working of the motions. General policy debates can be immensely useful to members on both sides of the House, on both front benches and back benches. For Ministers there is the opportunity to air ideas, to test responses and to assess opinion. For opposition leaders there is the opportunity to develop public policy alternatives and to espouse their virtues. For backbenchers on both sides there is the rare opportunity to advance their personal views and to demonstrate their skills. Most important of all, for the public at large there is improved opportunity to be informed about and, ultimately, to participate in the development of policy.

Greater opportunity for general debate on policy formulation is desirable; so is improvement in the methods by which the Commons examines the administration of policy.

During the late 1960s and early 1970s the work of the Standing Committee on Public Accounts suffered from delays and partisanship. The Auditor General, however, now finds it possible to present his report by the required year end and the Committee, through diligence, has been able to clear its back-log. There is, however, still almost no consideration of the work of the Standing Committee on Public Accounts in the House itself. In the interests of sound administration it would be useful to set aside a few days each session—whether through Allotted Days or another device—to consider these matters.

Although a very substantial proportion of the time of the House and its committees is occupied by the business of Supply, (approving expenditures) there is perhaps no procedure that causes more frustration for members. The 25 Allotted Days are distributed into periods, five in the fall, seven in the winter and 13 in the spring. Since the present system was adopted at the end of 1969, few of these days have been used by the opposition to discuss directly financial matters. In the spring period especially, the Allotted Days tend to be dull and repetitive. Often members run out of subjects. In the present session, on an experimental basis, an attempt was made to discuss some estimates in a committee of the whole on some Allotted Days. This experiment was of mixed success. It may be that a redistribution of Allotted Days among the three periods would reduce the problems in the spring. Another possibility, if the package-allocation system of managing time were adopted, might be a more radical reform; namely, lifting appropriation bills from the Alloted Day cycle. This would have to be accompanied by a reduction in the number of Allotted Days, for the amount of time spent on appropriation bills—part of the business of Supply—would likely be substantial. This proposal would not only tend to change the tone of Allotted Days, it would also provide a more defined focus for the House on expenditure.

In the days when the greater part of legislation passed in a session was constituted by private bills (incorporating railways, canals, banks, etc.), the Government could afford to see a substantial part of the week committed to private members' business. Private bills, however, are now reduced to a handful each session. Most of the legislation now dealt with is of a general application and the Government sponsors virtually all of it. Private members' business is relegated to four one-hour periods [a week] in the first part of a session and two one-hour periods in the latter part.

Traditionally, the Government has paid little attention to private members' bills and motions. One-hour debates lend themselves to the practice of "talking out" and therefore become futile, boring and frustrating to all concerned. In recent sessions, some attempt has been made by the Government to consider the merits of private members' proposals and, in the past year, there has been a substantial increase in the number of private members' public bills passed. Nonetheless, the one-hour debates are often postponed and, even when they are held as scheduled, they do not readily accommodate themselves to reaching decisions.

It may be that the answer to this frustrating situation would be to return to the system of private members' days, rather than hours. A method could be provided for a member, with the concurrence of a specified number of others, to bring his proposal to a vote. Probably the British system of determining the order of private members' business is better than ours. In Canada, members submit proposed bills and motions at the beginning of a session and draws are held to determine the order of the bills and motions. This means that a member has little subsequent flexibility in what he presents to the House. Often, several months after the draw, a member has different priorities. In Britain, it is the members' names that are drawn and they determine what measure to bring forward much closer to the event.

The system of standing committees remains a problem to Government and private members alike. The tendency over the years has been to give the standing committees more and more responsibilities. Subject-matter investigations have become more frequent. Occasional consideration of bills and estimates in an advisory capacity has become regular consideration with full power to amend. There is no doubt that the Commons can perform its ever-increasing duties only through increased reliance on standing committees.

Unhappily, the present committee system puts extremely heavy burdens on members' time. The committees are sufficiently large and the membership of the House is sufficiently small, that many members serve on four or more committees. In the struggle to maintain quorums, whips frequently must change membership of committees and the resulting lack of continuity makes it more difficult for a committee to do its work. It is almost impossible to reduce the number of committees; the trend is in the opposite direction. Even the most sophisticated scheduling system cannot prevent overlaps in committee meetings. Clearly, in the very near future, the House will be obliged to reduce the size of its committees.

The House will also find it necessary to examine its system of choosing chairmen of committees and of determining their rôle. The present system of determining chairmen—a combination of seniority and politics—does not always produce a chairman with exactly the right skills. Even if it does, chairmen are never certain whether they are mini-Speakers, leaders of investigations, or functionaries of the Government. In Britain, committees do either legislative or investigative work, rather than both, as in Canada. Chairmen on legislative committees are chosen by the Speaker from an all-party panel while investigative committee chairmen are selected in a manner more similar to ours. It may be that we shall have to devise a mixed system of selecting chairmen, just as our committees perform mixed functions.

With an improved system of planning the business of the Commons, a new look must be taken at the time of sittings. Demands from committees and from constituencies are heavy and probably can be met only if it is possible for the House not to sit for brief periods in the middle of a session. These would be made to be seen as short working adjournments, as opposed to the traditional three longer adjournments that are so often called vacations. One also may like to question the contemporary useful-ness of evening sittings. This hangover from the eighteenth and nineteenth centuries could easily be replaced by morning sittings on legislation (Question Period, etc. being kept for the afternoon) although Ministers might object. Finally, there would appear to be a good reason for a short ringing of division bells before a quorum "count out". Quorum bells are used in several legislative bodies, including the United States Congress and the Ontario legislature.

In the final analysis, the essence of reform of the House of Commons is found in preparation and in time. No structural changes can make the House more effective unless Ministers and private members alike prepare themselves well and are able to communicate effectively their views and intelligently respond to the views of others. One can prepare best, how-ever, when a clear time-frame exists. . . .

This revised system will be made to function not so much by good will as by hard work. The advent of broadcasting will force parliamentarians to try to perform well: to be concise, open and responsive. The power of the electronic media will be seen to be far more effective than that of print and if members do not reform their institution they may well expect the public to reform their members.

PRIVATE MEMBERS' BILLS—
CANDIDATES FOR OBLIVION*

Geoffrey Stevens

Do you think prison inmates should have the right to vote? Should the activities of lobbyists be controlled? Would you like the federal minimum wage raised from $1.75 to $3? Do you think the public has a fundamental

* From *The Globe and Mail*, Toronto, October 26, 1974. By permission.

right to information about the way the Government conducts public business? Should the police be compelled to destroy mug shots and fingerprints of suspects who are subsequently acquitted in court? Should it be made illegal to kill polar bears?

If any of these ideas interest you, then you will be interested in the stack of private members' bills—160 of them [there were 268 in 1974] —introduced so far in the current session of Parliament. These bills cover just about every conceivable aspect of federal concern—from statutory holidays to interest rates—and the ones mentioned here are only a random sample.

For example, Jack Horner, the maverick Conservative from Alberta, wants to revoke the right to vote by proxy which is presently enjoyed by a few categories of Canadians—fishermen, mariners, prospectors, full-time students and people who are ill or disabled. Liberal Gaston Isabelle wants to establish in law what is becoming established through practice—that the capital of Canada includes Hull, as well as Ottawa. By coincidence, Dr. Isabelle is the MP for Hull.

Stanley Knowles, the New Democrats' House Leader, seeks to create a constituency of Parliament Hill for the Speaker of the Commons. Of course, Mr. Knowles (who does not give up easily) still wants to abolish the Senate. Conservative Allen McKinnon (Victoria) thinks future Senate appointments should be made on the basis of the number of seats each party holds in the Commons.

Perhaps the private member's bill which, if it became law, would have the most profound impact is one sponsored by Gerald Baldwin, the Conservative house leader. His freedom-of-information bill would give every resident of Canada the right to apply to the Government for copies of records, letters, papers, tapes and so on, compiled in the course of public business. There would be some exceptions: information involving national security, income taxes or legal proceedings, or other information exchanged by public officials which is legitimately confidential.

Mr. Baldwin's bill provides that, if the Government did not produce the information, the applicant could obtain a court order. If the Government failed to comply with the court order, the responsible official would be liable to five years imprisonment. . . .

David Orlikow (NDP, Winnipeg North) is seeking to strengthen civil rights by preventing the police from using any statement obtained from a suspect as a result of threats or promises of special consideration. His bill would also affirm the right to counsel; the poor would be entitled to a legal aid lawyer before being questioned.

MPs of anti-abortion, anti-drinking, anti-smoking persuasions cannot be accused of hiding their convictions. Tory Perrin Beatty's bill would exclude danger to health as a ground for abortion and would specifically enjoin doctors from considering economic and social circumstances. Kenneth Robinson (L, Toronto-Lakeshore) wants liquor bottles to bear a warning that too much of what's inside will do bad things behind the wheel. He would also require planes, ships and buses to have separate seats for non-smokers.

Although some of these bills will eventually be debated (for one hour), they all have one thing in common—none will become law unless the

Government decides to take them over. Unless you subscribe to the quaint notion that the only people in Ottawa who are capable of thinking are those who inhabit the treasury benches, you have to be concerned about the short shrift given private members' bills. It's one more argument for a real reform of parliamentary procedure.

SALARIES AND ALLOWANCES OF MEMBERS OF PARLIAMENT, SENATORS, AND OFFICIALS*

Paul Fox

	Sessional Allowance	Salary	Tax free Allowance	Total[1]
House of Commons				
Members of Parliament	$24,000		$10,600[2]	$34,600
Leader of the Opposition and Speaker	24,000	$20,000	10,600	54,600
Deputy Speaker	24,000	8,000	10,600	42,600
Deputy Chairman, Asst Dep Chmn of Committees, and Ldrs of parties having at least 12 MPs, other than P.M. and Ldr of the Opposition	24,000	5,300	10,600	39,900
Chief Govt Whip, Chief Oppn Whip, Oppn House Ldr	24,000	5,300	10,600	39,900
The Senate				
Senator	24,000		5,300	29,300
Speaker	24,000	12,000	5,300	41,300
Ldr of Govt if not a Minister	24,000	13,300	5,300	42,600
Ldr of the Oppn	24,000	8,000	5,300	37,300
Dep. Ldr Govt	24,000	4,000	5,300	33,300
Dep. Ldr Oppn	24,000	3,200	5,300	32,500

[1] The total equivalent taxable incomes would be considerably larger, e.g. $44,000 for an MP. The Act also provides for an annual increase in salaries and allowances based on increases in the Industrial Composite Index. Beginning in January, 1976 the increase was to be 7 per cent, but on June 15, 1976 royal assent was given to a government bill cancelling the increase for 1976. In 1975 the pensions for MPs were increased by 33.3 per cent. An MP who had contributed and served for 25 years would now receive $18,000 pension per annum; for 10 years' service $12,000.

[2] For MPs from certain remote ridings the tax free allowance is $13,275 per annum; for NWT $14,475 p.a.

[For the prime minister, ministers, and parliamentary secretaries, see Chapter 12, Salaries and Allowances of Federal Ministers and Parliamentary Secretaries, p. 421.]

* From *An Act to Amend the Senate and House of Commons Act, the Salaries Act and the Parliamentary Secretaries Act*, 23-24 Eliz. II, C. 44, 1975, assented to May 8, 1975, but retroactive to July 8, 1974.

INDEMNITIES AND ALLOWANCES OF MEMBERS OF PROVINCIAL LEGISLATURES[1]

Paul Fox

Province	Indemnity	Allowance	Total
Alberta	$10,790	$5,395	$16,185
British Columbia	16,000	8,000	24,000
Manitoba	11,568	6,684	18,252
New Brunswick	8,000	2,500	10,500[2]
Newfoundland	8,000	4,000	12,000
Nova Scotia	9,600	4,800	14,400
Ontario	15,000	7,500	22,500
Prince Edward Island	7,000	3,500	10,500
Quebec	22,700	7,000	29,700
Saskatchewan	6,000	6,500	12,500[3]

[1] As of May 7, 1976. Compiled by the author.
[2] To be increased to $12,000 by a bill introduced into the Legislature on June 11, 1975.
[3] To be increased to $15,520 by a bill introduced into the Legislature on May 4, 1976.

BIBLIOGRAPHY

Parliamentary Procedure
Beauchesne, A., (ed.), *Rules and Forms of the House of Commons*, Toronto, Carswell, 4th ed., 1961.
Bourinot, J. G., *Parliamentary Procedure and Practice in the Dominion of Canada*, Toronto, Canada Law Book Co., 3rd ed. 1903.
Canada, *Standing Orders of the House of Commons, October, 1969*, Ottawa, Queen's Printer, 1969.
Dawson, W. F., *Procedure in the Canadian House of Commons*, Toronto, University of Toronto Press, 1962.

Functioning of Parliament
Aiken, G., *The Backbencher-Trials and Tribulations of a Member of Parliament*, Toronto, McClelland and Stewart, 1974.
Aitchison, J. H., "The Speakership of the Canadian House of Commons," in Clark, R. M., (ed.), *Canadian Issues: Essays in Honour of Henry F. Angus*, Toronto, University of Toronto Press, 1961.
Balls, H. R., "The Public Accounts Committee," *C.P.A.*, Vol. VI, No. 1, March, 1963.
Bishop, P. V., "Restoring Parliament to Power," *Q.Q.*, Vol. LXXVII, No. 2, Summer, 1970.
Black, E. R., "Opposition Research: some theories and practice", *C.P.A.*, Vol. 15, No. 1, Spring, 1972.
Blair, R. S., "What Happens to Parliament?" in Lloyd, T., and McLeod, J. T., (eds.), *Agenda: 1970*, Toronto, University of Toronto Press, 1968.
Brownstone, M., "The Canadian System of Government in the Face of Modern Demands," *C.P.A.*, Vol. XI, No. 4, Winter, 1968.

Burke, E., "Speech to the Electors of Bristol," in *Speeches and Letters on American Affairs*, London, Dent, Everyman's library, 1908.

Byers, R. N., "Perceptions of parliamentary surveillance of the executive: the case of Canadian defense policy", *C.J.P.S.*, Vol. V, No. 2, June, 1972.

Byrne, D., "Some attendance patterns exhibited by members of Parliament during the 28th Parliament", *C.J.P.S.*, Vol. V, No. 1, March, 1972.

Canada, (MacEachen, A. J.), *Members of Parliament and Conflict of Interest*, Ottawa, Information Canada, 1973.

Clarke, H. D.; Price, R. G.; Krause, R., "Constituency Service Among Canadian Provincial Legislators," *C.J.P.S.*, Vol. VIII, No. 4, December, 1975.

Corry, J. A., "Adaptation of Parliamentary Processes to the Modern State," *C.J.E.P.S.*, Vol. XX, No. 1, February, 1954.

Dawson, W. F., "Parliamentary Privilege in the Canadian House of Commons," *C.J.E.P.S.*, Vol. XXV, No. 4, November, 1959.

Forsey, E. A., *Freedom and Order: Collected Essays*, Carleton Library No. 73, Toronto, McClelland and Stewart, 1974.

Franks, C. E. S., "The Dilemma of the Standing Committees of the Canadian House of Commons," *C.J.P.S.*, Vol. IV, No. 4, December, 1971.

Hawkins, G., (cd.), *Order and Good Government*, Proceedings of 33rd Couchiching Conference, Toronto, Canadian Institute on Public Affairs, 1965.

Hockin, T. A., "The Advance of Standing Committees in Canada's House of Commons: 1965 to 1970," *C.P.A.*, Vol. XIII, No. 2, Summer, 1970.

Hoffman, D., and Ward, N., *Bilingualism and Biculturalism in the Canadian House of Commons*, Document 3 of the Royal Commission on Bilingualism and Biculturalism, Ottawa, Queen's Printer, 1970.

Jackson, R. J., and Atkinson, M. M., *The Canadian Legislative System*, Toronto, Macmillan, 1974.

Jewett, P., "The Reform of Parliament," *Journal of Canadian Studies*, Vol. 1, No. 3, November, 1966.

Johnson, J. K., (ed.), *The Canadian Directory of Parliament, 1867-1967*, Ottawa, Public Archives of Canada, 1968.

Kersell, J. E., *Parliamentary Supervision of Delegated Legislation*, London, Stevens and Sons, 1960.

Knowles, Stanley, *The Role of the Opposition in Parliament*, Toronto, Ontario, Woodsworth Memorial Foundation, 1957 (pamphlet).

Kornberg, A., "The Social Bases of Leadership in a Canadian House of Commons," *The Australian Journal of Politics and History*, Vol. XI, No. 3, December, 1965.

Kornberg, A., "Caucus and Cohesion in Canadian Parliamentary Parties," *The American Political Science Review*, Vol. LX, No. 1, March 1966.

Kornberg, A., *Canadian Legislative Behaviour: A Study of the 25th Parliament*, New York, Holt, Rinehart and Winston, 1967.

Kornberg, A., and Mishler, W., *Influence in Parliament: Canada*, Durham, N.C., Duke University, 1976.

Kornberg, A., and Musolf, L., *Legislatures in Developmental Perspectives*, Durham, Duke University Press, 1970.

Kornberg, A., and Thomas, N., "The Purposive Roles of Canadian and American Legislators: Some Comparisons," *Political Science*, Vol. XVIII, No. 2, September, 1965.

Kornberg, A., and Thomas, N., "Representative Democracy and Political Elites in Canada and the United States," *Parliamentary Affairs*, Vol. XIX, No. 1, Winter, 1965-66.

Lamontagne, M., "The Influence of the Politician," *C.P.A.*, Vol. XI, No. 3, Fall, 1968.

Laundy, P., "Procedural Reform in the Canadian House of Commons," in Lankster, R. S., and Dewor, D., (eds.), *The Table: Being the Journal of the Society of Clerks-at-the-Table in Commonwealth Parliaments for 1965*, London, Butterworth, Vol. XXXIV, 1966.

Lloyd, T., "The Reform of Parliamentary Proceedings," in Rotstein, A., (ed.), *The Prospect of Change*, Toronto, McGraw-Hill, 1965.

Lovink, J. A. A., "Parliamentary reform and governmental effectiveness in Canada", *C.P.A.*, Vol. 16, No. 1, Spring, 1973.

Lovink, J. A. A., "Who wants parliamentary reform?", *Q.Q.*, Vol. 79, No. 4, Winter, 1972.

Macdonald, Donald S., "Change in the House of Commons—New Rules," *C.P.A.*, Vol. XIII, No. 1, Spring, 1970.

Mallory, J. R., "The Uses of Legislative Committees," *C.P.A.*, Vol. VI, No. 1, March, 1963.

Mallory, J. R., "Vacation of Seats in the House of Commons: The Problem of Burnaby-Coquitlam," *C.J.E.P.S.*, Vol. XXX, No. 1, February, 1964.

Mallory, J. R., and Smith, B. A., "The Legislative Role of Parliamentary Committees in Canada: The Case of the Joint Committee on the Public Service Bills", *C.P.A.*, Vol. 15, No. 1, Spring, 1972.

March, R., *The Myth of Parliament*, Toronto, Prentice-Hall, 1974.

Normandin, P. G., (ed.), *The Canadian Parliamentary Guide, 1975*, Ottawa, 1975, (annual).

Ontario Commission on the Legislature, *First Report*, May, 1973; *Second Report*, December, 1973; *Third Report*, September, 1974; *Fourth Report*, September, 1975; *Fifth Report*, October, 1975.

Power, C. G., Michener, D. R., *et al.*, "Focus on Parliament," [A collection of articles written on various aspects of Parliament], *Q.Q.*, Vol. XLIII, No. 4, Winter, 1957.

Robertson, R. G., "The Canadian Parliament and Cabinet in the Face of Modern Demands," *C.P.A.*, Vol. XI, No. 3, Fall, 1968.

Schindeler, F. F., *Responsible Government in Ontario*, Toronto, University of Toronto Press, 1969.

Smith, D., *The Speakership of the Canadian House of Commons: Some Proposals*, A paper prepared for the House of Commons' Special Committee on Procedure and Organization, Ottawa, Queen's Printer, 1965.

Turner, J., *Politics of Purpose*, Toronto, McClelland and Stewart, 1968, especially chap. 2, "The Member of Parliament."

Ward, N., "Called to the Bar of the House of Commons," *Canadian Bar Review*, Vol. XXXV, No. 5, May, 1957.

Ward, N., *The Canadian House of Commons: Representation*, Toronto, University of Toronto Press, 2nd ed., 1963.

Ward, N., "The Committee on Estimates," *C.P.A.*, Vol. VI, No. 1, March, 1963.

Ward, N., *The Public Purse: A Study in Canadian Democracy*, Toronto, University of Toronto Press, 1962.

14

THE LEGISLATIVE PROCESS: SENATE

The Senate has been affected by the wave of change and the proposals for reform that have been evident in the Canadian political system in recent years. The second edition of this book noted that between 1962 and 1966 the Senate had been altered in two respects. An amendment to the British North America Act in 1965 (14 Eliz. II, C.4) required senators appointed thereafter to retire at 75 years of age rather than to hold office for life. At the same time generous retirement pensions were offered to encourage former appointees to retire voluntarily if they were 75 years of age or more. The relevant sections of the former statute can be found in the second edition of *Politics: Canada*, pp. 290-293. (It may be noted in passing that this amendment was one of the five enacted by the Canadian Parliament under the authority of the amending power conferred on it by Amendment No. 2 in 1949. See Chapter 2, *supra*, in this present edition.) The second change effected in the period from 1962 to 1966 created a Divorce Commissioner to assist the Senate's Divorce Committee in performing its role. For an article explaining that change, see the second edition, pp. 293-295.

The new retirement provision still holds, of course, but since the second edition appeared the Senate has been deprived entirely of its remaining function in granting divorces by the Divorce Act which went into effect early in 1968. The Senate dealt with its last petition for divorce (most of which had originated from Quebec and Newfoundland) on November 26, 1969, when the courts in these two provinces assumed jurisdiction in this subject, completing the roster of provinces to do so.

The Senate has come under particular criticism recently because it has been accused of being the repository of party workers and business and financial interests. Professor John McMenemy's article, which is published here for the first time, is a strong indictment of these aspects of the upper house.

Meanwhile, proposals for reform continue to be offered, as they have been ever since the creation of the Senate in 1867. (See, for example, a good discussion of reform of the Senate by its own members in one of their debates in 1951, reprinted in part in the first edition of this book, pp. 227-246. See also Senator David Croll's proposals in a debate in the Senate, March 13, 1973.) The subject was revived by the federal government in its white paper, *Federalism for the Future*, Ottawa, Queen's Printer, 1968, p. 26, presented to the first Federal-Provincial Constitutional Conference in February, 1968. Ottawa also offered some specific proposals for reform in its white paper, *The Constitution and the People of Canada*, Ottawa, Queen's Printer, 1969, pp. 28-34 and 76-78, tabled at the Second Meeting of the Constitutional Conference in February, 1969.

The federal proposals are summarized and appraised in detail by Professor E. Donald Briggs in an excellent article which appears in an edited form in this chapter. In 1972 the Special Joint Committee of the Senate and the House of Commons on the Constitution of Canada offered in its *Final Report* a number of proposals for the reform of the second chamber. These recommendations have been reproduced here. Two years later Prime Minister Trudeau proposed some additional changes. Although they were presented rather casually during his contribution to the debate on the Speech from the Throne, the Liberal prime minister subsequently implemented one proposal by appointing a Conservative politician to replace a retiring Conservative senator. Whether this was a unique occurrence or the inauguration of a new convention remains to be seen. The relevant excerpt from the prime minister's speech is published below. A more radical solution has been proffered for many years by Stanley Knowles, a veteran M.P. who advocates abolition. His private member's bill in 1974 proposing such a change is noted in the passage reproduced here. The one actual alteration that has been made in the Senate in this decade is described in the last item; an amendment to the B. N. A. Act in 1975 added one senator each for the Yukon and the Northwest Territories.

The bibliography lists the few recent books and articles that have appeared on the Senate.

INFLUENCE AND PARTY ACTIVITY IN THE SENATE: A MATTER OF CONFLICT OF INTEREST?*

John McMenemy

Some scholarly studies of the Canadian Senate exhibit an unrealistic disregard for the substance of power. R. MacGregor Dawson described the Senate as a "comparatively unimportant and ineffective body" not far removed from "obscurity and obsolescence." In their more recent survey of the Canadian political system, Richard Van Loon and Michael Whit-

* Written in July, 1975, and published here originally with the permission of the author who is Associate Professor of Political Science, Wilfrid Laurier University.

tington reinforced this view that the Senate "is not a very active institution in the policy process."

This attitude towards the Senate ignores the activities of particular senators who have an impact on the informal and formal aspects of the policy process and the electoral fortunes of particular parties. Ironically, their public image of obscurity and obsolescence, reinforced by such academic appraisals, aids the pursuit of their objectives. Prime ministers make some senatorial appointments precisely to facilitate future party service and many senators may be very useful to private corporations which have a direct and continuing interest in federal legislation and administrative regulations and decisions.

In 1975 senators received an annual stipend of almost $30,000, a free office on Parliament Hill, secretarial service, answering service, franking privileges, free long-distance telephone calls, and limited free air travel. Senators appointed before 1965 and still sitting hold life-long tenure while those appointed since then must retire at 75 years of age.

The Corporate Connection

There is no federal law requiring parliamentarians to disclose, let alone restrict, directorates, property and financial holdings, and legal or other activities which might be construed as lobbying. Senators in the cabinet are required to follow existing prime ministerial guidelines for ministers. Most senators, however, are bound only by Senate Rule 49 (1969): "A senator shall not be entitled to vote upon any question to which he has any pecuniary interest whatsoever, not held in common with the rest of the Canadian subjects of the Crown, and the vote of any senator so interested shall be disallowed." Apparently, some senators define "pecuniary interest" in a very narrow sense and recognize that voting in parliament is not the most effective way to influence a legislative issue.

The Trudeau government's concern with conflict of interest began in 1969 during debate in Parliament on tax reform legislation. However, a major storm had blown up five years earlier when the Senate's committee on banking, trade, and commerce considered private legislation to incorporate several new banks and mortgage companies. Senators on this particular committee have been the focus of critical attacks in regard to conflict of interest.

Three bills to incorporate banks and three to create mortgage companies were introduced in 1964. Four directors of established banks were members of the committee, including the chairman, Senator Salter Hayden, then a director and shareholder of the Bank of Nova Scotia. The committee readily passed the three bills to incorporate mortgage companies despite reservations on one bill and serious objections to another by the federal superintendent of insurance. The Bank of Nova Scotia was associated with the companies whose incorporation legislation troubled the superintendent.

On the bill to establish the World Mortgage Corporation, Senator T. A. Crerar announced he was a director of the Eastern and Chartered Trust Company which would be closely connected with the new corpora-

tion and withdrew from the committee. Senator Gordon Isnor acknowledged that he, too, was a director of Eastern and Chartered Trust but
would remain on the committee. Senator Hayden, who was connected
with the application through the Bank of Nova Scotia, stood down as
chairman because his law firm had drafted the legislation and a law
partner had presented it to the committee. However, he remained on the
committee to take issue with the federal superintendent of insurance. The
acting chairman, Senator Paul-Henry Bouffard, then a director of the
Royal Bank of Canada, saw no need to resolve the inconsistency between
Crerar's, Isnor's, and Hayden's positions.

In 1969 the government conceded in the House of Commons that the
conflict of interest provisions were antiquated. At that time, Senator
Hayden and his committee were in the spotlight again during their
consideration of the Investment Companies Bill. Introduced following
the collapse of several financial institutions, the original bill required
many companies borrowing from the public to make special annual
reports, obtain registration certificates and submit to unspecified regulations. Senator Hayden said that none of the 22 companies of which he was
a director was affected by the legislation. However, according to an
account in *The Globe and Mail*, June 7, 1969, the corporate view was
well-represented in his committee:

> Members of Senator Hayden's committee—many of whom are com-
> pany directors—were openly critical of the broad definition of invest-
> ment companies. There was also criticism of the broad discretionary
> powers the bill would give the Government. As a result, a special
> sub-committee headed by Senator Hayden is working with Government
> officials to develop mutually acceptable amendments.

Later that year, the two Houses established a joint committee to examine government proposals for tax reforms occasioned by the Royal
(Carter) Commission on Taxation. The New Democratic Party objected
that the senators on the committee had potential conflicts of interest. *The
Globe and Mail* of July 25, 1969, agreed:

> Which senators will be on the committee? Why, men who, for the most
> part, are directors of some of the largest, most important and powerful
> corporations in the country—banks, financial institutions, distillers,
> insurance companies, co-operatives, industrial concerns and mining
> and petroleum companies. . . . What does the Carter Report recom-
> mend? Why, stiffer tax provisions for most of these corporations. It
> suggests that the general or contingency reserves of banks should not be
> recognized for tax purposes; that financial institutions have been es-
> timating their losses too liberally and should be made to comply with
> more stringent rules: that depletion allowances give mining and pe-
> troleum companies unfair breaks and should be revised. . . . It calls
> for a tax on capital gains.

Prime Minister Trudeau was indifferent. "After all," he told the House,
senators "all have interests as taxpayers in what happens in connection

with tax reform; it might be difficult to eliminate all people with an interest in taxation."

In 1973 the government presented draft legislation to require disclosure of all directorships, regulate the activities of paid lobbyists, and restrict the proportion of a company's stock that a parliamentarian could own. It would also have prohibited parliamentarians from sitting on boards of companies that had more than $1,000 of contracted business annually from the government. An examination of public records by the Canadian Press in 1973 showed that eight of the 22 members of the Senate's committee on banking held 130 company directorships. These 22 senators accounted for 75 per cent of reported directorships of the then 93 senators. The committee members were executives or directors of businesses in banking, investment and insurance, mining, real estate development, and manufacturing and retailing of pulp and paper products, aircraft parts, feed products, clothing, and soft drinks. The draft legislation expired with the Twenty-Ninth Parliament prior to the election in 1974.

In 1975 parliament debated the government's Canadian Business Corporations Act to revise federal private corporation law and amendments to the Combines Investigation Act. Senator Hayden, whose committee acted on both matters, was a director of Jannock Corp. Ltd., which grew out of a merger involving Atlantic Sugar Refineries Ltd. In 1963 Atlantic was fined $25,000 for conspiring to fix the price of sugar. At that time, the judge issued an order prohibiting the directors of Atlantic from repeating the offence. In 1975 Atlantic was again in court charged under the Combines Investigation Act for activities between 1960 and 1973. According to the *Financial Post's Directory of Directors*, Senator Hayden was a director and officer during these years. Another lawyer-director of Jannock Corp. Ltd. was defending Atlantic Sugar. A law partner of the lawyer defending Atlantic Sugar was appointed counsel to Senator Hayden's committee during its examination of changes to the anti-combines law.

After consideration by the House of Commons and acting on the advice of Senator Hayden's committee, the Senate made 27 amendments to the government's Business Corporations Act. The government asked the House to accept the amendments in one motion on short notice. According to the government spokesman, "the Senate committee . . . acted objectively, fairly and reasonably, arguing clearly and forcefully for each proposed amendment. I felt it impossible not to be responsive to their suggestions. . . . "

Stanley Knowles, NDP House leader and long-time foe of the Senate, had been assured that the amendments were administrative. However, reading them for the first time as the debate proceeded, Knowles realized that almost 25 per cent of the packaged amendments effectively removed directors and officers of corporations from legal liability. He said:

> It strikes me that these are amendments we might expect from the other place. . . . The bill which this House sent to the other place included the provision that in certain instances a conviction could be sought against a corporation or against its officers and directors. Considering the

number of officers and directors sitting in the other place, I am not surprised by what has been done.

According to the *Directory of Directors* (1975), the following members of the Senate committee on banking, trade and commerce held these positions:

Louis P. Beaubien: vice-pres. and dir. Beau-bran Corp.; dir. of: Canadair Ltd., Casualty Co. of Canada, Dominion of Canada General Insurance Co., The Empire Life Insurance Co., E-L Financial Corporation Ltd., The Great Lakes Reinsurance Co., Holt, Renfrew and Co. Ltd., Marshall Steel Co. Ltd., Quebecor Inc., Standard Trust Co., Redpath Industries Ltd., Inter City Papers Ltd.

Sidney L. Buckwold: vice-pres. and dir. Buckwold's Ltd.; dir. of: Bank of Montreal, S.E.D. Systems Ltd.; mbr. Saskatoon Advisory Board, Canada Permanent Trust Co.

J. J. Connolly: dir. Scott Misener Steamships Ltd.

Eric Cook: Chm. of T. McMurdo and Co. Ltd., dir. of : Wm. Nosworth Ltd., Heap and Partners (NFLD), Ltd.

Paul Desruisseaux: Chm. of: Melchers Distilleries Ltd., Lucky One Beverages Inc.; pres. of: Desmont Research and Development Ltd., Cablevision (Montreal) Desruisseaux Corp.; dir. of: Royal Bank of Canada, Canadian General Electric Co. Ltd., Westmount Life Insurance Co., PPG Industries Ltd., PPG Foundation, Mondev Corp. Ltd.

Douglas D. Everett: pres. and chief exec. officer The Royal Canadian Securities Co. Ltd.; dir. of: General Foods Ltd., Eaton Group of Funds, Monarch Life Assurance Co.

Jacques Flynn: dir. of: Canada Cement Lafarge Ltd., Savings and Investment Group, Savings and Investment Corporation Mutual Fund of Canada Ltd., Savings and Investment Trust, Savings and Investment American Fund, Le Prêt Hypothécaire, The Trans-Public Advertising Co. Ltd.

Louis-P. Gelinas: vice-pres. and dir. The Mercantile Bank of Canada; dir. of: Canadian International Paper Co., Candiac Development Corp., Delta-Benco Limited, Gerling Global Life Insurance Co., Gerling Global Reinsurance Co., Greyhound Leasing & Financial Ltd., Montreal Refrigerating & Storage Ltd., Manicouagan Power Co., North American Car (Canada) Ltd., Sicard Inc., Hilton of Canada Ltd., Canada Cement Lafarge Ltd., United North American Holdings Ltd., Foster Wheeler Ltd., Crush International Ltd., The Robert Mitchell Co. Ltd., Distillers Corporation-Seagrams Ltd., Hon. dir. John Labatt Ltd.

Salter A. Hayden: vice-pres. International Eveready Co. Ltd.; dir. of Dominion Oxygen Co. Ltd., Domet Ltd., Electric Furnace Products Co. Ltd., National Carbon Ltd., Visking Ltd., Ucar Ltd., Emet Ltd., Jannock Corp. Ltd., Parker Pen Ltd., Provincial Service Agency Ltd., Scott's Restaurants Co. Ltd.; pres. of Nelson Hyland Foundation, Orthopaedic and Arthritic Hospital.

Harry W. Hays: dir. of: Burritt Travel Service Ltd., Canada Permanent Trust Co., Canada Permanent Mortgage Corp., Home Oil Co. Ltd.

D. A. Lang: dir. of: P. L. Robertson Manufacturing Co. Ltd., Procor Ltd.

Alan A. Macnaughton: chm. of: Canadian Offshore Marine Ltd., Pirelli Canada Ltd., pres. of: Milfoy Ltd., Pantene Ltd., Centavia Ltd., Electrofin Construction Investments Ltd.; sec. and director of: Hoffman-LaRoche Ltd., Aviation Electric Ltd.; dir. of: Swiss Corp. for Canadian Investments Ltd., Mirimachi Timber Resources Ltd., The Albion Insurance Co. of Canada, Cunard International Canada Ltd., International Trust Co., The Ontario-Minnesota Pulp and Paper Co. Ltd., SBC Financial Ltd., Sapac Corp., Saelectric Transmission Inc., Federation Insurance Co. of Canada, Brown Boveri (Canada) Ltd., international adviser Swiss Bank Corp. (Basle, Switerzland); chm. The World Wildlife Fund (Canada); trustee World Wildlife Fund.

Hartland de Montarville Molson: chm. The Molson Companies Ltd., vice-pres. and dir. Bank of Montreal; dir. of : Sun Life Assurance Co. of Canada, Canadian Industries Ltd.

David J. Walker: dir. of: The Great Lakes Reinsurance Co., Premier Insurance Co., Anglo Canada Fire and General Insurance Co., Gibraltar Insurance Co.

The matter of lobbying is important because at least 10 members of the committee in 1975 were also lawyers. Disagreeing with the assertion that senators were lobbyists, Senators Walker and Connolly have distinguished between lawyers acting on behalf of clients and lobbyists acting on behalf of clients. The press has noted Senator Connolly's representations on behalf of corporations. Speaking of Connolly, Senator Walker, a colleague in law and on the Senate committee on banking, has said:

> Now in the practice of his [law] profession in Ottawa, as may be expected, he has been consulted by corporate and other clients who have problems to be solved within various departments of the federal Government. These include tax problems, customs matters, contract settlements and other matters requiring the service of lawyers. . . . I am sure that no official in . . . government . . . would ever feel that, because the honourable gentleman happens to be a senator when he appears before them as a lawyer with a client, he is doing any more than his professional duty requires him to do for a client.

Senator Connolly has observed: "When professional people from outside come [to Ottawa] to interview [government lawyers, accountants, engineers], they do not come to seek favours, they come to try to find solutions for the problems of their clients. . . ."

However, this distinction between the activities of lawyers and lobbyists may be less than clear for non-lawyers who are especially concerned when the lawyer in question is a senator and a member of the committee on banking, trade and commerce.

According to journalist Terrence Belford in *The Globe and Mail,*

November 10, 1973, Senator Connolly's clients included Gulf Canada Ltd. and IBM Canada Ltd. Senator Connolly asserted that his relationship with both companies was that of lawyer to client. But Belford quoted Gulf President Jerry McAfee that the senator "occasionally opens doors for us and provides the proper atmosphere" for discussion with government officials: "With his knowledge of the people and scene there . . . he keeps us up to date on who are there, who is who and what is what." Appointed to the upper House in 1953, Senator Connolly, who conceded a thirty-year association with Gulf, was a cabinet minister and government leader of the Senate from 1964 to 1968. Presumably, these laywer-based associations were formally severed or suspended during the senator's tenure in cabinet.

The Active Party Connection

Undeniably, the Senate includes former party activists and leaders. Indeed, Dalton Camp, former president of the national Progressive Conservative party, describes this as "the true value of the senate." According to Camp, "it permits a prime minister to reform his government, to retire ministerial colleagues who are inept or weary, to open seats for newcomers to the cabinet, and to give sanctuary to those who have soldiered in his cause." In 1975, one-third of the sitting senators had been selected by Prime Minister Trudeau. Despite indications of reformist intentions in the early years of his ministry, most of Trudeau's appointments reflect the principle of partisan reward.

The Senate is not well-recognized, however, as a publicly-financed and prestigious repository for party organizers and fund-raisers. Yet in 1975, approximately 25 per cent of the Trudeau-nominated senators, along with at least four colleagues appointed during Lester Pearson's ministry, continued to be active key Liberal party officials. Trudeau's senators included:

Lorne Bonnell: chairman of the national Liberal election campaign committee in Prince Edward Island in 1974.

Jean-Pierre Côté: former minister, president of the Quebec section of the national Liberal party.

John Godfrey: party fund-raiser since 1968.

B. Alasdair Graham: president of the Liberal party in Nova Scotia.

Paul C. Lafond: chief agent for the Liberal party.

Gildas Molgat: former Liberal leader in Manitoba, in 1975 national president of the Liberal Party.

Ray Perrault: former Liberal leader in British Columbia and former MP, chairman of the national election compaign committee in British Columbia in 1974.

Maurice Riel: party fund-raiser in Quebec.

The four active party officials placed in the Senate by Pearson were:

Keith Davey: former national director and co-chairman of several Liberal election campaign committees, including 1974.

Earl Hastings: chairman of the national election campaign committee in Alberta in 1974.

Harry Hays: party fund-raiser.

Richard tanbury: former national president, chairman of the national Liberal party's treasury committee.

Senator J. J. Connolly and former Senator John Nichol were also recent national presidents of the Liberal party during their tenure in the Senate.

The Conservative party has exploited Senate appointments similarly. Former Senator Gunnar Thorvaldson, appointed by Conservative Prime Minister John Diefenbaker, was a fund raiser for the federal and provincial Conservative parties in Manitoba. According to newspaper columnists Douglas Fisher and Harry Crowe, Senator Thorvaldson's role was to seek "contributions from those who got contracts in Manitoba through the Federal [Conservative] Government and from those out-of-province firms which got contracts from the provincial [Conservative] government."

Conclusion

Scholarly surveys of the Senate usually concentrate on the institution and its inactivity and weak impact on policy and legislation, compared with the House of Commons. When senators are discussed, scholars stress their role as superannuated party supporters. Such jejune analyses usually avoid or minimize the intensive and influential activities of nearly a quarter of the senators. These activities relate particularly to the scrutiny of proposed legislation affecting corporate organization, practices, and activities, and political party organization and fund-raising.

In the latter case, the question arises whether the public is well-served by its subsidy of high party officialdom appointed by the government party-of-the-day. In the former case, the public may wonder if it is well served by senators, particularly those on the committee on banking, trade, and commerce, who have extensive corporate interests. We referred to several legislative episodes in which these senators had an important effect on legislation: legislation to incorporate banks and mortgage companies in 1964, legislation affecting investment companies and tax reform in 1969, and federal private corporation law and anti-combines law in 1975. We also noted in passing that the lobby activity of lawyer-senators on behalf of clients may also not be in the public interest. In either case, the Senate is more than a resting place for inactive elder statesmen and party leaders.

REFORM OF THE SENATE: A COMMENTARY ON RECENT GOVERNMENT PROPOSALS*

E. Donald Briggs

. . . Like many of his predecessors, Prime Minister Trudeau promised reform of the upper house when he first took office. Since that time . . . some official suggestions for reform have already been put forward. These are contained in the white paper, *The Constitution and the People of Canada*, published in February 1969. [See *ibid.*, pp. 28-34.]

The suggestions are of two sorts. First, on the organizational side, it is proposed that a review of the distribution of Senate membership be undertaken; that the term of office for Senators be reduced to a set numbers of years, (perhaps six, with a possibility of reappointment); and, probably most important, that Senators be "partly appointed" by the provincial governments. Second, on the functional side, it is suggested that the Senate's powers be curtailed in some respects and extended in others. The curtailment would result from providing that "in the general legislative process" the House of Commons would be enabled to over-rule rejection of a bill by the upper house (p. 32). The extension would come from giving the latter "special responsibility" in dealing with legislative measures concerning human rights and the official languages, as well as the right to approve appointments to the Supreme Court, ambassadorial positions, and the chairmanships of cultural agencies. Over these specific matters it is proposed that the Senate should have an absolute veto.

These proposals are under consideration . . . [But] so far, little public comment of any kind has been made on them.

In putting the proposals forward the Government has been motivated by more than the desire to "improve" the Senate. Senate reform and the revitalization of Canadian federalism are apparently seen as closely linked, and the purpose of the suggested changes is stated to be to enable the Senate "to play a more vital role in reflecting the federal character of our country" (p. 28). In these and other suggestions for constitutional change, however, the Government was also concerned with maintaining the customary responsibility of the cabinet to the House of Commons alone—hence the rejection of such ideas as that for a directly-elected Senate. The proposed Senate changes are consequently described as providing "the best balance between the principles of responsible and representative government and the need in a federal state for the adequate protection of regional and cultural interests" (p. 32).

There are, however, a number of things about these proposals which are both surprising and puzzling. In the first place, it is not entirely obvious that changes in the method of handling many of the matters over which it is proposed to give the Senate special power are either necessary

* From an article by the author in the *Queen's Quarterly*, Vol. LXXVII, No. 1, Spring, 1970. By permission of the author. The author, who is a member of the Department of Political Science at the University of Windsor, wishes to thank his colleagues, Professor K. G. Pryke and C. L. Brown-John, for helpful suggestions during the preparation of this article.

or desirable in and of themselves. To most Canadians the manner in which ambassadors, for instance, have been appointed has been unobjectionable. It is not easy to see, either, how these proposals are related to, or can be expected to solve, the principal problems of federalism, or what value there may be in them if they do not tend in this direction. Finally, the extent to which they would be effective in reforming or upgrading the Senate may also be questioned, particularly since the new duties proposed for the upper house are plainly of no great significance in terms of the general governmental burden of the central administration.

These considerations are not equally relevant to the organizational proposals, of course, but it may be argued that the latter are unlikely to be effective in improving the position or reputation of the Senate either, unless the functional changes succeed in transforming it into an obviously important body. Each of the proposals has its own weaknesses, however, and they are consequently better discussed individually than collectively.

Organizational Reform

The prosposal which by itself seems likely to cause least difficulty is that of a specific term of office for Senators. Sinecures for life or even to age seventy-five have only one thing to recommend them: they ensure that once Senators are appointed they will be relatively immune from pressure by the appointing authority. That this is a principle of paramount importance with respect to judicial and perhaps some other offices is obvious, but its applicability to legislators is considerably more doubtful. It may be argued, in fact, that if the Senate is to become even partly a provincial or regional instrument, then senators should be to some degree responsive to the wishes or policies of their provincial governments. In general, too, a less static membership for the upper house would probably be advantageous. Whether it would prove to be equally desirable to have federally-appointed Senators subject to pressure from the federal cabinet is more problematic, but this problem will be taken up more fully below.

In much the same way, the proposal to review the distribution of Senate seats seems, on the face of it, reasonable enough. As the white paper points out, no such review has been undertaken since confederation, though the original regional balance was upset by assigning Newfoundland an extra six seats when it became a province in 1949. There are admitted inequalities—or at least peculiarities—in the present distribution. Not only does the Atlantic region have thirty seats as compared with twenty-four for each of the other regions, but there are inconsistencies as between individual provinces, particularly between those in the east on the one hand and those in the west on the other. It is difficult, for instance, to reconcile New Brunswick's ten senatorial seats with British Columbia's six when the former has fewer than seven hundred thousand people and the latter close to two million.

It may be argued that since representation in the Senate has always been on a regional basis, comparisons of individual provinces in this way are not relevant. Once the possibility of redistribution is raised, however, such inequalities become a legitimate subject for consideration, particularly as the Government in this case has not revealed the basis on which it thinks redistribution should be undertaken. The fact that some Senators are to be appointed by the provinces also promises to make provincial as against regional representation more important than in the past.

Representation in second legislative chambers, of course, especially in federal systems, is not normally on the basis of population; witness the fact that each state in the United States has two Senators when they vary in population from Alaska's two hundred and fifty thousand to New York's seventeen million. Rather, the idea is that interested blocs or geographical areas should be represented to provide a balance with the population-based representation in the lower house. The simplest and perhaps the most logical way of accomplishing this is to give equal representation to each of the federated units, as has been done in the United States. A Canadian Senate composed of ten representatives from each province would therefore be logical, were it not for the fact that this would mean reducing Quebec's share of the total seats from approximately 23.5 percent to a mere 10 percent at precisely the time that province is demanding recognition of its special linguistic and cultural position within confederation. Granting, then, that Quebec should be accorded special recognition, other difficulties also appear. The west, for example, and perhaps the Maritimes as well, would be less than happy if their strength were to decline in relation to Quebec's. Ontario might also be a problem, but might feel less strongly about it than the west provided a reasonable balance were maintained between French and English Canada as a whole.

Given such difficulties, however, one is tempted to suggest that it might be better to leave things as they are. In view of the Government's declared intention of making the Senate the guardian of regional and cultural interests, however, this would not be without difficulties either. To date, the Senate has not been of any great importance to any of the provinces, and hence the distribution of its seats has not been of much importance in their eyes either. But, obviously, if it is to be rededicated to their use, this will no longer be the case, and redistribution will almost inevitably be demanded by one or more of them. It was undoubtedly recognition of this fact that led to the Government's somewhat tentative inclusion of such a review in its proposals. Needless to say, the same factors which are likely to make review necessary will also intensify the difficulties of achieving it.

With a minimum of good will on all sides, however, a solution should not be beyond the ingenuity of our collective political leadership. Two formulas might be suggested as containing at least some of the elements out of which a solution might be constructed. The first would be to provide for a ninety-seat house in which Quebec would be given one-third, or thirty seats, with the remaining two-thirds being divided equally among the other three regions (twenty seats each). The second, and perhaps from the aesthetic point of view the better, formula would again allow Quebec thirty seats, but out of a total of one hundred and twenty, with each of the other nine provinces having ten. In the first case all three "English" regions would lose strength relative to Quebec, but provided the blocs were equally distributed among the eastern and western provinces (five each) the most glaring inequalities between the provinces of these regions would be eliminated. Under the second formula, Quebec would retain approximately the same proportion of the total seats as she has now (actually a gain of 1.5 percent), while relative to her the east would make a slight gain and the west a considerable one. Ontario would obviously be the big loser relative to all the other regions, but it may be doubted whether there is any good reason for treating her differently from the other largely English provinces. Either of these formulas, or some variation thereon, would be more logical and would reflect existing political realities more precisely than present arrangements.

Theoretically, therefore, redistribution presents no great problem, and it would certainly seem to be desirable from a number of points of view. Of the organizational proposals, however, both the most substantive and the most uncertain in result is that of making appointments partly provincial. Two obvious and interrelated questions arise from this proposal. First, what does, or should, "partly" mean? Second, why, when the declared object of Senate reform is to create a house which will reflect more precisely "the federal character of our country," are the provinces to be allowed to appoint only some of the Senators but not all of them?

The white paper gives no indication whatever of what the Government may have in mind by "partly," but it does indicate the Government's feeling that while it is necessary to give expression to provincial interests, "the interests of the country as a whole should continue to find expression in the Senate to maintain there an influence for the unity of Canada" (p. 30). Presumably it is that portion of the Senate which will continue to be appointed by the federal cabinet which is expected to be such an influence.

One may sympathize with the objective of giving expression to the interests of the country as a whole, but whether the federal appointment of some Senators is necessary to achieve this, or whether Senators so appointed would actually constitute an influence for unity is questionable. The Government appears to anticipate that provincially appointed Senators will be so preoccupied with parochial interests that unless some counter-balance is provided chaos or deadlock or some such catastrophe will result. It should not be forgotten, however, that the senate is and will continue to be only the second legislative chamber, with no independent existence or mandate of its own. Legislation will continue to be initiated largely by the cabinet and discussed by the Commons from a predominantly national viewpoint, and it will be the duty of the Senate to take the traditional "sober, second look" at what is passed to it from the lower house or directly from the cabinet. As long as cabinet and Commons do their work effectively, therefore, there is little chance that "the interests of the country as a whole" will be neglected or that these interests could be ignored by even the most parochially-minded Senate. It is true that provincially-oriented Senators may be inclined to be more critical of federal legislative proposals, and critical from a different point of view, than present ones, but this would seem to be precisely the purpose and value of having them in the Senate in the first place; they would bring a new and different perspective to the work of the central government, and hopefully by so doing would pave the way for better understanding and more co-operation between the different levels of government.

What the Government means by unity, and what the connection is between it, the presence of federal appointees in the Senate, and the expression of "national" interests, is far from clear in any case. Is it unity within the Senate which is sought? Or concurrence of the Senate with the "national" view of the federal cabinet? One might be excused for suspecting that it is the latter which concerns the Government most, since there seems little reason to assume that the provincial or regional orientation of its members would necessarily mean inability to achieve at least sufficient unity to reach decisions in the upper house. Apart from anything else it is reasonable to suppose that voting would ultimately resolve differences in a provincially-oriented Senate as elsewhere in democratic institutions.

The degree to which federal appointees might be able to act as catalysts in reconciling conflicting provincial viewpoints is also doubtful. Federal no less than provincial appointees must be from somewhere, and even if they should in theory be selected at large rather than on a regional or provincial basis; a reasonable distribution over the country would be necessary. When and if federal and provincial views should conflict, minority groups of federal appointees would be likely to find themselves caught between two pressures: to act in accordance with their provinces' interests or views on the one hand, or to conform to central government's view on the other. If they should tend to lean to the latter, they would be less likely to exert influence in the direction of unity than to form simply another faction within the chamber—a "they" group against which opposition might even solidify. If they should tend to "go provincial" on the other hand, any advantage of federal appoinment, except that of patronage, would be lost. In neither case would they contribute to Senate unity in any obvious way.

Assuming the validity of this line of reasoning, and assuming that it could not have been overlooked by the drafters of the reform proposals, it follows that the provision for the continued appointment of some Senators by the federal government is likely to have been intended not only to provide patronage but also a means of preventing or discouraging excessive divergence between the Senate and the cabinet. However, both the need for and the wisdom of attempting to "build in" unity in this fashion must be questioned. Undoubtedly the primary responsibility for governing the country must continue to rest on the federal cabinet and the directly elected representatives in the House of Commons and consequently the forceful expression of their views must be guaranteed. But as it was pointed out above, there is little danger that this would cease to be the case even if the Senate were entirely devoid of "national" spokesmen. Moreover, it must be remembered in this context that except with regard to a very few, not very significant matters, the "new" Senate is not to have a deciding voice in any case: the Commons is to be given power to overrule it in all "general legislative matters." While this is not a power which should be resorted to on any regular basis, it would provide a means whereby the government could, if necessary, ensure that its view of the country's interests would prevail.

Use of this procedure, furthermore, would at least be honest. It would bring differences between federal and provincial authorities into the open and provide an issue upon which voters could ultimately pass judgement. This would be less true if federally appointed Senators either because of their numerical superiority (we are not told that they will not be numerically superior, though we might hope that the Government's intentions are more honourable than that) or for some other reason, were able to circumvent differences within the Senate itself. An "arranged" unity, however, would obviously be no unity at all, and a Senate so constituted as to provide an appearance of unity would, from the point of view of federalism, be no advance over present arrangements. Unfortunately, indications are that the Government is not yet ready to face that fact. But since the Government does not propose giving the Senate sufficiently important functions to cause the provinces to take a very active interest in its deliberations or the performance of its members, all of this becomes somewhat beside the point. The "new" Senate, as it materializes from the present proposals, is simply never likely to be sufficiently concerned with, or important in relation to, the major issues of federalism to make federal-provincial confrontations within it a serious threat to harmony on Parliament Hill. This, of course, makes the Government's concern for unity even more unnecessary.

These factors are of immediate and practical as well as long-term and theoretical importance. Apart from anything else, if the proposed changes in the senate are to be successful at all, it is essential that the provincial governments should be satisfied that they, or their appointees, will have a real and significant role to play in the new institution. If they are not convinced of this from the outset they are unlikely to take seriously such appointive responsibilities as they are finally accorded, and as a result the quality of Senate membership is likely to give far more legitimate cause for concern that it has to date. The white paper obliquely recognized the importance of this when it expressed the hope that federal and provincial governments "would engage in healthy competition" to ensure that the best men available would be appointed to the upper house (p. 34).

Provincial attitudes are likely to be determined largely by two factors: the proportion of Senate membership to be appointed by them, and the importance of the functions to be performed by the house. The first is self-explanatory in that there is a direct relationship between the number of representatives and the importance of their role. On the other hand, numbers alone mean little if the functions of the house are unimportant. We must consquently turn now to an analysis of the proposals for functional reform. These, unfortunately, are perhaps even more open to criticism than the organizational ones.

Functional Reform

The proposal to accord the Senate "special responsibility" with respect to legislation affecting civil rights and the official languages may seem unobjectionable and natural given the special interest which Quebec in particular has in some of these matters. In terms of the extent of the national government's powers and legislative responsibilities, however, it cannot be said to be particularly significant, nor are civil and language rights matters with which the provinces, with the exception of Quebec, are either especially concerned or especially competent to deal.

Moreover, in view of the Government's intention to entrench a comprehensive Charter of Fundamental Rights in the constitution, it may be questioned whether legislative safeguards are necessary even from Quebec's point of view. The proposed Charter is to contain guarantees of linguistic as well as the customary legal and human rights, and once it has been enacted all of these matters will presumably be protected by the courts against legislative encroachments. . . .

Much the same can be said for the confirmation powers which are proposed. On the one hand they seem unlikely to elate the provinces with the opportunities they present for participation in the essentials of the governing process at the national level, and on the other their inherent value also seems open to question.

The proposal to have ambassadorial appointments, for instance, approved by the Senate will almost certainly come as a surprise to most Canadians. Many, it seems safe to say, will find the reasons behind the proposal puzzling, and the benefits to be derived from such a procedure —for the Senate, the provinces, the country, or the diplomatic corps— perhaps even more so. . . . Moreover, . . . there are cabinet prerogatives of far greater potential danger than the right to appoint ambassadors or, for that matter, judges of the Supreme Court, and these proposals would therefore be of comparatively little significance in that connection. . . .

One would not have thought, either, that the provinces would have any great interest in participating in the appointment process. With the possible exception of one, in fact, it seems safe to say that they have not. Quebec, however, has in recent years developed a well-publicized penchant for dabbling in international affairs. . . . While it is by no means clear that Quebec would consider indirect participation in the appointment of ambassadors (and/or, for that matter, the heads of cultural agencies) a satisfactory substitute for the freedom of action which, as a "nation," she claims as her necessary right, it is clearly something of this kind that the Government hopes to achieve. . . . Nevertheless, to institutionalize provincial participation in even such a relatively minor matter as the appointment of ambassadors is surely to concede that the provinces have some legitimate interest in the international field, and such a concession could make additional encroachments more difficult to resist.

The proposal that appointments to the Supreme Court also be subject to confirmation by the Senate has a similar origin and is undoubtedly expected to yield similar advantages. Quebec has also long contested the competence of the Supreme Court to decide constitutional issues between the provinces and the central government. . . . What the Government is now proposing is a compromise, which, as in the case of ambassadors and cultural agencies, concedes the principle but refuses to go the distance. It seems clear, in fact, that the Government's whole design for Senate reform has been motivated primarily by, and is aimed primarily at providing a solution to, the "Quebec problem." . . . .

It may equally be argued that the Government has shown little real interest in Senate reform *per se*. . . . What is more important, however, is that the proposed changes, organizational and functional, collectively constitute only very minor surgery which is at best, calculated to cure some peripheral ills rather than the inherent feebleness of the patient.

By far the most serious and insistent criticism of the present Senate is that it serves no useful function. Unfair as this criticism is in a number of respects, it may be argued that it is the first problem with which reform measures should deal, and that measures which fall short of this goal are not reform in any real sense at all. Since the special tasks visualized for the new Senate are largely ritualistic, and since its power is to be largely confined to these tasks, it seems unlikely that the position or the reputation of the upper house will be substantially improved by the proposed changes.

Both these problems could, at least in principle, be fairly simply solved, and without making the Senate into a rival of Commons in any significant sense. All that would be necessary would be to convert the Senate into what I have elsewhere called a "House of Provinces," [see bibliography for reference] which would be composed of representatives of the provincial governments, and which would be given the power of approving all measures falling within the area of joint federal-provincial responsibility. Such an arrangement would give the Senate the obvious *raison d'être* it has always lacked, and at the same time ensure the continuing interest of more than one province in its operations.

. . . At the constitutional conference of June 1969, the federal government agreed that the provinces should have the power to block federal spending in provincial areas of jurisdiction (i.e., cost-sharing programs). The means, however, by which the provinces would exercise this power was not spelled out. According to press reports, Prime Minister Trudeau had suggested an arrangement under which any two of the four senatorial districts could veto federal spending in areas of provincial jurisdiction, but this, along with alternative formulas proposed by the provinces, was referred for further study. . . .

There seems to be here an obvious opportunity to combine the search for appropriate machinery for federal-provincial co-operation with the movement to make the Senate an instrument of federalism. Why should the upper house not become the continuing federal-provincial conference which could thresh out such matters as well as take responsibility for such specific tasks as are contained in the proposals under discussion here? . . .

. . . The key would be to ensure senatorial responsiveness to provincial policies, and this could be accomplished by seconding members of provincial governments to the Senate on whatever basis individual provinces might think desirable. There would thus be no specific term of office for Senators at all (except perhaps for federal appointees, if these should still be regarded as necessary), and perhaps no specific membership as such. This would provide the maximum of flexibility from the provincial point of view, while the importance of the senatorial responsibilities would at the same time ensure that careful consideration would at all times be given to selecting suitable representatives. From the federal point of view such a

Senate would be powerful, but with a provision that the Commons could overrule except with regard to matters designated as of legitimate provincial concern, its effective strength would be sufficiently channelled so that the authority of the House of Commons and the cabinet's primary responsibility to it would also be preserved.

Nevertheless, there is no doubt that this would be a radical departure from the traditional concept of the Senate and of second chambers generally, and it is not easy to predict all the consequences which might follow if it were adopted. While it would almost certainly bring the Senate publicity and recognition of the kind it has never before enjoyed, it would not be the type of recognition which Senator Martin and some others have been urging and it is perhaps not even certain that a "House of Provinces" of this type could to the same extent carry on the kind of work for which these spokesmen consider it to deserve recognition. As they have rightly pointed out, the Senate at present makes a considerable contribution to the governing process by its extensive committee work, and by giving detailed and in some cases first-instance study to legislative proposals, thus saving much time for the hard-pressed House of Commons. They believe that these functions could and should be extended still further, and it would undoubtedly be useful if they were. Would a House composed largely or entirely of untenured ambassadors of the provinces be able to perform such functions?

The answer is not clear one way or the other, but whether this is the most important consideration may be questioned in any case. The point is that because of a variety of pressures from a variety of sources means have to be found to institute a new kind of federalism. At the same time, for equally varied reasons, Senate reform seems to have been accepted as desirable and necessary. . . .

. . . Is it to be reformed, or is it, in a phrase recently used by Senator Keith Davey on the CBC, merely to be "tinkered with?" Is it to be made a genuine instrument of federalism and protector of provincial and regional interests, or merely a device for spiking the guns of Quebec? The white paper does not give much ground for encouragement on either score. Certainly if the "reforms" are instituted as proposed the result will be that the Senate will be far worse off than before. Its effective power will have been curtailed and confined to a few largely ritualistic tasks, a fact which will not fail to impress the public as confirmation of its inherent uselessness. The quality of its membership is likely to decline since provincial regimes can hardly be expected to devote much energy or care to the selection of people to perform tasks of little direct importance to them, and since political debts at the provincial level are unlikely to be owed to individuals who are very familiar with or interested in federal affairs. Consequently, not even the traditional functions of the Senate referred to above could be expected to be performed as well as at present. Neither, of course, is all this likely to do anything whatever for the state of Canadian federalism in any general sense.

Real Senate reform cannot be accomplished without giving it something of obvious importance to do. Neither can the real needs of Canadian federalism be accommodated by the Senate without giving it authority over matters of substance. Both mean making the Senate powerful in at least some respects. If that is not a prospect which the Government can accept, it would perhaps be better to leave the Senate as it is, concentrate on extending and publicizing its traditional functions, and look elsewhere for solutions to the problems of federalism. It will certainly be unfortunate however, if some more serious attempt is not made to solve both problems with one blow by turning the Senate into something approaching a "House of Provinces."

RECOMMENDATIONS FOR REFORM*

Special Joint Committee

Recommendations

35. The present full veto power of the Senate over legislation should be reduced to a suspensive veto for six months according to the following formula: a bill may become law without the consent of the Senate (1) if the House of Commons, having once passed it, passes it again no less than six months after it was rejected or finally amended by the Senate or, (2) if, within 6 months of third reading of a bill by the House of Commons the Senate has not completed consideration of it, and the House of Commons again passes it at any time after the expiration of the 6 months, but any period when Parliament is prorogued or dissolved shall not be counted in computing the 6 months.

36. The investigative role of the Senate, which has gained more importance in recent years, should be continued and expanded at the initiative of the Senate itself, and the Government should also make more use of the Senate in this way.

37. The Government should be entitled to introduce in the Senate all bills, including money bills but excluding appropriation bills, before their approval by the House of Commons, provided that, in the case of money bills, they should be introduced by the leader of the Government in the Senate on behalf of the Government.

38. The distribution of Senators should be as follows: Newfoundland 6, Prince Edward Island 4, Nova Scotia 10, New Brunswick 10, Quebec 24, Ontario 24, Manitoba 12, Saskatchewan 12, Alberta 12, British Columbia 12, the Yukon Territory 2, and the Northwest Territories 2: a total of 130.

39. All Senators should continue to be appointed by the Federal Government: as vacancies occur in the present Senate, one-half of the Senators from each Province and Territory should be appointed in the same manner as at present; the other half from each Province and

* From the Special Joint Committee of the Senate and of the House of Commons on the Constitution of Canada, *Final Report*, Ottawa, Information Canada, 1972, Chap. 13, p. 33. Reproduced by permission of the Minister of Supply and Services Canada.

Territory should be appointed by the Federal Government from a panel of nominees submitted by the appropriate Provincial or Territorial Government.

40. The personal requirements for appointment to the Senate should be limited to those required for eligibility as an elector in the Canada Elections Act, plus residence in the Province for which a Senator is appointed. The Quebec structure of electoral divisions should be abolished.

41. The compulsory retirement age for all new Senators should be seventy years. Upon retirement, Senators should retain the right to the title and precedence of Senators and the right to participate in the work of the Senate or of its Committees but not the right to vote or to receive the indemnity of Senators.

PROPOSALS FROM THE PRIME MINISTER*

•   •   •

Mr. Trudeau:
Mr. Speaker, I would like to say a word about the Senate. I know that it is not for me to say too much about that subject, but I think that it would not be more than good neighbour policy to suggest that at least a few reforms should be considered, reforms which would in no way interfere with the authority of the provinces, but which could be considered under section 91, subsection (1), of our Constitution. As a matter of fact, I have discussed these reforms with the government leader in the Senate, Mr. Perrault, and I hope that in this area also, this Parliament will accomplish some progress. The two reforms that I have in mind are as follows: First, we should limit the duration of senatorial appointments to a certain number of years, seven, for instance, with the option of reappointing senators when they have well served their country. Secondly, we could follow the example set a long time ago by the British Parliament and give only a suppressive [*sic*, suspensive?] veto to the second House.

Hon. members opposite talk about partisan appointments. This is a serious matter which I have already had the opportunity to discuss several years ago with the authorities of opposition parties, and I had then suggested, and I repeat my suggestion today, that if indeed the senators of the Progressive Conservative party, of the Tory party, who wish to retire from the Higher Chamber, refrain from doing so because they do not want to be replaced by Liberal senators, I repeat what I told several years ago to Senator Flynn who, if I am not mistaken, represents the opposition party in the Senate, that, for my part, I would readily appoint Progressive Conservatives to replace the Progressive Conservatives who voluntarily

* From *House of Commons Debates*, October 2, 1974, p. 44. Reproduced by permission of the Minister of Supply and Services Canada.

retire from the Higher Chamber. I am well aware, Mr. Speaker, that some of them accept my suggestion, but there were many more when I first made this offer several years ago, and if the official opposition party continues to act so speedily, they may be even fewer in four years.

It is a humble start but the House will certainly recall that several years ago the government had proposed a much more thorough reform of the Senate which involved provincial participation. But I will not talk about this today. If, in the context of our constitutional reform, we must come back to this subject, the government always has an open mind to discuss this problem. . . .

[Mr. Trudeau appointed a Conservative former Premier of Nova Scotia, Mr. G. I. Smith, to the Senate in August, 1975 to replace a retiring Conservative Senator.]

ONE SOLUTION—ABOLITION*

Mr. Stanley Knowles (Winnipeg North Centre) moved that Bill C-205, to amend the British North America Act 1867, (abolition of the Senate), be read the second time and referred to the Standing Committee on Justice and Legal Affairs.

He said: . . . A few days ago I had a conversation with a senator who is a friend of mine. . . . I asked . . . whether he would prefer to be reformed by the Prime Minister (Mr. Trudeau) or abolished by me. His answer was immediate. He said he would rather be abolished by me.

As we discussed the matter it became clear that one of the reasons he made that choice is that he feels, as I believe other senators do, that one of the most insulting suggestions that has ever been made to Their Honours in the other place is the proposal of the Prime Minister for Senate reform along the lines of seven-year appointments subject to reappointment. One might ask what would happen to a senator appointed when the Conservatives were in power, if that ever happens again, whose seven-year term should expire when the Liberals were in power. Would the Liberal prime minister say to a Conservative that he has been a good boy and therefore he would be reappointed, or would he pass him by?

For that matter, what would happen to the fortunes of a senator belonging to the party of the prime minister if that same prime minister had some cabinet member he wished to get rid of, or if there should be too many members waiting in the wings? What chance would there be for a firm appraisal of the job done in the other place by those who are there under this seven-year "you are in and then maybe you are out" proposal of the Prime Minister? I suggest that my argument for the outright abolition of the other place is much kinder than what is being proposed by the Prime Minister.

This is not the first time I have moved the second reading of this bill.

* From *House of Commons Debates*, October 17, 1974, pp. 490-491. Reproduced by permission of the Minister of Supply and Services Canada.

It has seldom reached a vote, although on occasion it did. Even though one has not had success in persuading this House to support the abolition of the Senate, I think it is a point which should be considered very seriously. . . .

My basic reason for being against the Senate is that I believe in democracy. To be even more precise, I believe in parliamentary democracy. I believe it is proper for the laws of the country to be made by persons elected by the people of Canada. That is what we are in this House. We are 264 individuals elected by the people of Canada. We can make mistakes, but if we make mistakes we must go back to the people during the next election and answer for our mistakes. We are responsible to the people who sent us here.

The same situation does not exist in respect of the other place. Each one of them is appointed by the prime minister of the day. . . .

[Bill C-205 was "talked out" without a recorded vote.]

TWO SENATORS ADDED FOR YUKON AND NWT*

23-24 Eliz. II, C.53

An Act to amend the British North America Acts, 1867 to 1975

[Assented to 19th June, 1975]

Her Majesty, by and with the advice and consent of the Senate and House of Commons of Canada, enacts as follows:

1. Notwithstanding anything in the *British North America Act, 1867*, or in any Act amending that Act, or in any Act of the Parliament of Canada, or in any order in council or terms of conditions of union made or approved under any such Act,

(a) the number of Senators provided for under section 21 of the *British North America Act, 1867*, as amended, is increased from one hundred and two to one hundred and four;

(b) the maximum number of Senators is increased from one hundred and ten to one hundred and twelve; and

(c) the Yukon Territory and the Northwest Territories shall be entitled to be represented in the Senate by one member each.

2. For the purposes of this Act, the term "Province" in section 23 of the *British North America Act, 1867* has the same meaning as is assigned to the term "province" by section 28 of the *Interpretation Act.*

3. This Act may be cited as the *British North America Act, (No. 2) 1975*, and shall be included among the Acts that may be cited as the *British North America Acts, 1867 to 1975*.

* From *Canada Gazette, Part III*, Vol. 1, No. 9, 19 June, 1975, Ottawa, Queen's Printer, 1975. Reproduced by permission of the Minister of Supply and Services Canada.

BIBLIOGRAPHY

Albinski, H. S., "The Canadian Senate: Politics and the Constitution," *American Political Science Review*, Vol. LVII, No. 2, June, 1963.

Briggs, E. D., "The Senate: Reform or Reconstruction?" *Q. Q.*, Vol. LXXV, No. 1, Spring, 1968.

Canada, *Rules of the Senate of Canada*, Ottawa, Queen's Printer, 1964.

Dawson, W. F., "Parliamentary Privilege in the Senate of Canada," Address to the 38th Annual Meeting of the Canadian Political Science Association, Sherbrooke, P.Q., June 8, 1966.

Hopkins, E. R., "Financial Legislation in the Senate," *Canadian Tax Journal*, Vol. VI, No. 5, September-October, 1958.

Knowles, S., "The only sensible thing to do with the Senate is to abolish it", *Toronto Star*, January 10, 1972.

Kunz, F. A., *The Modern Senate of Canada, 1925-1963, A Re-appraisal*, Toronto, University of Toronto Press, 1965.

Lambert, N., "Reform of the Senate," *Winnipeg Free Press*, Pamphlet No. 30, April, 1950.

Lyon, P. V., "A New Idea for Senate Reform," *Canadian Commentator*, July-August, 1962.

MacKay, R. A., "How to Reform the Senate," *Canadian Commentator*, May, 1963.

MacKay, R. A., *The Unreformed Senate of Canada*, Toronto, McClelland and Stewart, revised edition, 1963.

MacKay, R. A., "To End or Mend the Senate," *Q. Q.*, Vol. LXXI, No. 3, Autumn, 1964.

MacNeill, J. F., "Memorandum for Senator Robertson, re the Senate, Reasons Given by Proponents of Confederation for Constituting a Second Chamber," Ottawa, Senate, February 16, 1950.

Morin, J. Y., "Un nouveau rôle pour un Sénat moribund," *Cité libre*, Vol. XV, juin-juillet, 1964.

Orban, E., *Le Conseil législatif de Québec*, Montréal, Bellarmin, 1967.

Turner, J. N., "The Senate of Canada—Political Conundrum," in Clark, R. M., (ed.), *Canadian Issues: Essays in Honour of Henry F. Angus*, Toronto, University of Toronto Press, 1961.

Watts, R. L., "Second chambers in federal political systems", *Ontario Advisory Committee on Confederation: Background Papers & Reports*, Vol. 2, Toronto, Queen's Printer, 1970.

15

THE ADMINISTRATIVE PROCESS

This chapter has been completely recast in this edition in order to present a synopsis of the essentials of Canadian public administration. Although much of the material refers to the federal government, many of the principles and procedures which are discussed are practised by Canadian provincial governments as well.

The introductory item by Professor Thomas Hockin explains the organizational structure of the federal bureaucracy. It is accompanied by a chart showing in detail the organization of the government of Canada. Within this structure the Treasury Board plays the dominant managerial role. A. W. Johnson's excellent article, "The Treasury Board of Canada and the Machinery of Government of the 1970s", describes how the Treasury Board performs this function in addition to acting as the cabinet's monitor on the budget.

Since the Glassco Commission submitted its report on government organization in 1962-63, Ottawa has adopted a number of new managerial techniques. Professor Hartle's hard-hitting critique assesses the success of these major innovations in procedure, and not surprisingly he finds most of them wanting.

John Kettle's brief article points out how rapidly public employment is growing in Canada. His graphics, which forecast that the increase will continue into the next decade, give some impression of the importance of public employment in Canada. He estimates that by 1986 there will be more than two million Canadians—or about 17 per cent of the total labour force—employed by public authorities. He also notes the significant fact that the greatest increase in public employment is occurring in the provincial and municipal sectors rather than in the federal government.

Since the swelling army of civil servants is involved in more and more aspects of citizens' lives as the administrative and welfare state continues to expand, the problem of the conflict of interest of public servants has become more acute. In 1973 the federal government issued a set of guidelines for its employees. The order-in-council which proclaimed them is reproduced in the chapter.

As state activity has mounted, Canadians have become increasingly concerned about government secrecy. An article from *The Toronto Star* points out some of the problems and some of the reforms that are being proposed.

The growth of state power has also led to popular support for the creation of an ombudsman to protect citizens' rights. Six provinces— Alberta, Quebec, New Brunswick, Nova Scotia, Manitoba, and Ontario— have created such an office in the past decade. An article from *The Financial Post* illustrates the new development by describing how the ombudsman in Alberta performs his job. See also two items on the ombudsman which appeared in the third edition of this book, pp. 391-399.

This chapter omits a number of items which were included in the third edition of this book, pp. 418-434. They dealt with the following subjects: the introduction of collective bargaining in the federal public service, some reflections on this development, the problem of administrative secrecy, the recommendations to control delegated legislation which were contained in the report of the Commons' Special Committee on Statutory Instruments, the granting of political rights to federal public servants, and an article by the Hon. Mitchell Sharp on "The Expert, the Politician, and the Public."

The bibliography is divided into five sections in which relevant works are listed under the following headings: civil service, administration, crown corporations, administrative secrecy, and the ombudsman. The best consistent source of scholarly and professional discussion of administrative issues in Canada is the quarterly journal of the Institute of Public Administration of Canada, *Canadian Public Administration*, referred to in this book as *C.P.A.* For government policy-making, one should refer also to the new journal *Canadian Public Policy*. Several books of readings dealing with public administration and policy-making in Canada are referred to in the bibliography in this chapter.

THE STRUCTURE OF THE FEDERAL BUREAUCRACY*

Thomas A. Hockin

The public service and those government employees outside public service classifications for all three levels of government in Canada account for over 12 percent of the country's work force. By the end of 1974 the total number of Federal government employees reached 450,790. Employment at other levels of government pushed the total over 1 million in 1974. The extent to which government is an employer in Canadian society

* From *Government in Canada*, Toronto, McGraw-Hill Ryerson, 1976, Chapter 5, "The Federal Public Service." By permission.

may not be obvious in Ottawa because of the division of government employment into Federal, provincial and local levels and because of its geographical dispersal. (Considerably less than half of Federal employees work in Ottawa.) Also, a large number of employees are engaged in activity which is not visibly 'governmental,' such as the work of the Crown Corporations (approximately one-third of all Federal employees are engaged in such corporations).

Levels of government employment are an uncertain measure of the significance of the public service in the over-all life of society. More important is the nature and extent of public service activity itself. In Canada at the Federal level the administrative machine is made up of widely disparate units pursuing many different activities. By 1970 the Federal government was made up of twenty-seven departments, twenty-five boards and commissions, and forty-six Crown Corporations.

Let us look first at departments. . . . [See chart "Organization of the Government of Canada".]

All departments except for the Privy Council Office have this much in common: they have been created by statute. This is in contrast to Britain. Yet in Ottawa the cabinet now has liberal discretionary power to alter the duties of departments, thanks to the Transfer of Duties Act of 1918. A department's functions are, of course, defined in large measure by those Acts of Parliament which the minister is expected to administer. The rationale for any group of agencies to be placed into one department or ministry of state varies, from the need to group common functions (such as External Affairs), or common clienteles (Agriculture), or similar processes (Supply and Services), or similar missions (such as the Ministry of State for Science and Technology created in 1971). Other departments are Irish stews, congeries of widely diverse activities (such as the Department of the Secretary of State). Departments also vary widely in size, and in policy influence, from the small but powerful Department of Finance to the enormous yet less powerful Post Office. Some are so enormous and multi-faceted, such as Transport, that they have recently had to be fundamentally reorganized to allow the minister and his top public servants time and opportunity to concentrate on at least a minimum of comprehensive policy assessment. A few new departments comprise a large number of staff and executive personnel who have had little experience in the public service (such as in Consumer and Corporate Affairs). Some departments have been at the centre of the Ottawa scene for decades, such as Finance, Justice and External Affairs, and they have enjoyed a good deal more prestige than either their size or their budgets would suggest. Even more striking is the diversity in the geographical dispersal of departments. Some departments, such as Agriculture, Environment, Veterans Affairs, Transport, Manpower, Immigration and Defence, have over three-quarters of their personnel posted outside Ottawa. Some, such as Finance and Justice, have almost all of their personnel in Ottawa. Some departments are deeply involved in fundamental long-range policy-planning, such as the Department of Finance's research branches (in concert with the Bank of Canada's research branch) and some, such as the Department of External Affairs until the late 1960's have indulged in little long-term policy-planning. These wide differences in departmental characteristics are no doubt typical of most bureaucracies in any country. A striking feature of Canadian departmental history is the prescience of the fathers of confederation. In 105 years the numbers of departments has only grown from fourteen to twenty-seven. Another feature of Federal departments, however, is the tendency to organize departments around what foreign observers would quickly recognize as uniquely Canadian assets: for example the Department of Indian Affairs and Northern Development, the Department of Fisheries and Forestry, and the Department of Energy, Mines and Resources.

That part of the administrative machine most answerable to Parliament is both *de jure* and *de facto* the government department. Within each department are 'branches' or 'divisions' or 'services' which in turn are usually made up of sub-units ranging in name from corporations, to councils, to agencies. At the top of the departmental pyramid is the minister who is responsible to Parliament (and also to the prime minister and the cabinet) for the work of his department. He is chosen by the prime minister, is a member of the prime minister's political party, and is a Member of Parliament or, very infrequently, a senator. Aside from the 'parliamentary secretary' (another MP who assists the minister in ways defined by the individual minister), the minister is the only official 'political' actor in the department . All 'public servants' in a department are constitutionally subordinate to the minister. In public, departmental solidarity and loyalty to the minister is expected. (Unlike the case in Britain, ministers in Canada do not have 'private secretaries' seconded from the public service to help them with personal political and public relations duties. Instead it is the 'executive assistant' who helps the minister most in these functions. These 'EA's' are usually chosen from outside the public service. A large number of these appointments are filled by young men who are party members and look to a career in politics rather than in the public service). [See Tilley's article, Chap. 12.]

Although not appointed under the provisions of the Civil Service Act, the chief public servant in the department, responsible to the minister for running it, is the deputy minister (or in the case of some departments the 'undersecretary'). In the past, the 'DM' was usually a product of many years experience in the public service: more often than not his experience was in the department in which he was the deputy. Now it is no longer unusual for a prime minister who wishes to shake up a department, or who wishes to give it a new sense of mission, to choose someone from outside to be its deputy. A number of deputy ministers were changed after Mr. Trudeau took over from Mr. Pearson as prime minister in 1968. Some were appointed from other departments and some from outside the public service. (For example, a western Canadian businessman was named deputy minister of Energy, Mines and Resources by Mr. Trudeau, and a close personal aide of the prime minister was named a departmental deputy minister in early 1973.) The power of the deputy minister is only what the minister chooses to give him except for some managerial authority delegated to him by the Treasury Board and the Public Service Commission. Underneath the DM there are usually assistant deputy ministers

(ADM's) or assistant undersecretaries. Departments vary in the number of positions at the ADM level (usually around four). Reporting to ADM's are directors of divisions, or similarly senior line managers. These officers, plus those in ranks immediately below, comprise most of the 'executive' class of the public service. (There were 618 members of this class in 1971.)

The most durable image about the bureaucratic part of the government of Canada is that it is a gigantic administrative pie sliced into hermetically sealed, rigorously hierarchical, departments. This way of looking at the Canadian government is useful as an organizing device for budgetary reporting, for coping with parliamentary accountability, and for certain types of administrative convenience; it is only partially useful as an image of how the government's work integrates or fails to integrate. Although this chapter will concentrate on the role of public servants in *departments* in the formation of public policy it would be remiss not to note that the non-departmental branches of the governmental apparatus, the boards, corporations and commissions, account for a large part of the bureaucratic machinery. In fact the administrative part of the government of Canada is a collage of departments, boards, commissions, Crown corporations, supradepartmental control and initiating agencies and Federal-provincial committees and interdepartmental committees. More of this collage is represented not by a list of departments but in the list of the bodies and agencies responsible for the 'Ministry'.

The 'Ministry' of the government of Canada is composed of ministers whose answerability goes beyond the mere obligation to answer for departments in Parliament. Most ministers not only represent departments but are answerable in part for the activities of various boards, corporations and commissions. The [chart on Federal Government Organization] gives the names of the various Ministries of the government of Canada and the departments, boards, commissions and corporations which report through the minister to the House of Commons. It must be noted that although ministers are completely responsible for all work done in departments there are other agencies in his Ministry for which he acts only as a 'spokesman' to Parliament. He is not responsible for their activities.

The Federal government contained seventy-one boards and corporations in 1970, a smaller number than in some provincial governments. For example, by the early 1960s Alberta had 123 such bodies and Ontario had 97.

Canada's Federal Crown corporations are important allocators within the Canadian state. They account for considerable resources and expenditures. For example, in the fiscal year 1969-70, Crown corporations obtained from the Federal government a net amount of $2,162 million, comprised of $1,075 million in loans; $656 million in subsidies and other payments to cover operating and capital expenditures; and $449 million for other purposes such as payments of subsidies to private business. A substantial portion of Federal government resources—equal to about one-fifth of the total Federal budget—went to Crown corporations in that year. There were twenty-seven Crown corporations classified as business enterprises, seventeen of these supporting the infrastructure of the economy in transport, communications and finance. Those not classified as enterprises were on the whole engaged in economic or social support services: these included 'thirteen engaged in economic development and support functions of various kinds, six in health and welfare, four in culture and recreation . . . and three in other functions.' Canadian Federal Crown corporations are not involved in judicial functions or day-to-day political considerations and they 'perform at least one of the functions of managing capital assets, lending, making transfer payments and research'.

The growth in the number of these corporations and commissions is noteworthy, but perhaps not exceptional. All countries try to exempt some functions of government from the restraints and patterns of their public service commissions, such as rules on job classification, promotion, staffing and pay. Exemptions are also sought from Treasury departments with their standardized budgetary and financial procedures. All countries also try to take a number of explicit public functions out of 'politics', so that the minister will not have to be answerable in more detail for the operations of certain public activities than he ordinarily would wish. Canada is no exception. If anything, Canada is becoming unusually prone to those temptations at the Federal and the provincial levels. Still some parliamentary communication is expected from most of these quasi-independent bodies. It has been suggested that the proliferation of such bodies in this century in Canada is in all probability a concession to American influences. Yet apart from a few bodies, such as the Public Service Commission, Canadian agencies bear little resemblance to the 'independent' executive agencies in Washington in that a minister is expected to supply responses from such bodies to Parliament, even if he does not meddle much in their activity. Even the most 'independent' of Canadian agencies is at least expected to provide a minister with information if he asks for it.

Federal boards have considerable independence and power of regulation. The powers of Canadian boards include powers to study, to make policy, to grant licences and to publicize. Some Federal agencies give considerable power to interest groups by giving them representation on the boards; one example is the representation of producers on Federal boards for the marketing of agricultural products. It is also clear that a number of Federal boards wield considerable allocative, structural and regulatory power with little or no cabinet or ministerial influence until the minister decides to change the statutes under which such agencies operate, or unless public or interest-group pressure grows intense enough to force a minister to attempt to persuade such agencies to shift their policy. For example, the powerful Canadian Radio and Television Commission is to be free of political influence, and its mandate includes the power to prescribe classes for broadcast licences, to allocate broadcasting time, to determine time that may be devoted to advertising, and to prescribe the nature of political advertising by political parties. The policy powers of the Canadian Transport Commission are vast. They involve major allocative and regulatory activities. For example under the National Transportation Act (see Bill 231 in 1967) the grant of power to the Commission under Section 3 of the Act is no more detailed than the direction to investigate for the 'public interest'. The guidelines for granting pipeline licences are little more explicit than 'to serve the public convenience and necessity'. Also 'the Commission shall make investigations, including the holding of public hearing, as in its opinion is necessary or desirable in the public interest', or further 'it may disallow acquisitions if in the opinion of the Commission such acquisition will unduly restrict competition or otherwise be prejudicial to the public interest'. In considering an application for a pipeline certificate the Commission 'shall take into account such matters as appear to be relevant'. However, the Commission is expected to be aware of over-all ministry policy in areas concerned.

Most boards, commissions and crown corporations, because of their members' fixed tenure of office and statutory power, are offically expected to operate free of political influence. In practice this expectation is occasionally qualified. First, there is the tendency of the cabinet to appoint to these positions many members who have been party supporters. Second, there is the necessity for many boards or commissions such as the Canadian Transport Commission, to integrate some of their policy emphases within over-all Ministry and government policy. Third, it is politically advisable for good public relations that corporations such as Air Canada or the Canadian Broadcasting Corporation, or regulators such as the St. Lawrence Seaway Authority, agree to explain to parliamentary committees their policies on various matters. Yet these opportunities for parliamentary probing should not lead one to conclude that such agencies are little different from those agencies clearly integrated into departments. Since there are countless issues with which these independent agencies deal and for which the cabinet and the minister would prefer not to be fully 'answerable' in Parliament, ministers are happy, in most instances, to grant them *de facto* power of decision, they simply report their decision to Parliament or let their officers explain the rationale of their decisions in parliamentary committees. . .

[See fold out page at the end of the book: "Organization of the Government of Canada".]

THE TREASURY BOARD OF CANADA AND THE MACHINERY OF GOVERNMENT OF THE 1970s*

A. W. Johnson

The Role and Functions of the Treasury Board

To understand the Treasury Board one must first understand that it is a cabinet committee functioning in two distinct if interrelated areas of government: it is the cabinet's Committee on the Expenditure Budget

* From *Canadian Journal of Political Science*, Vol. IV, No. 3, September, 1971. By permission. (At the time of writing, the author was the Secretary of the Treasury Board.)

and the cabinet's Committee on Management. As the Committee on the Expenditure Budget it is for the Treasury Board to propose to cabinet the allocation of funds as between the myriads of competing programs and projects, taking into account three things: the priorities of the government and its broad policy directions; the effectiveness of the programs in achieving the government's objectives; and the efficiency with which the programs are being administered. The job, in short, is to propose an expenditure plan which at one and the same time represents an expression of the government's policies and priorities, and results in the optimum allocation of the taxpayers' money in terms of value received for each dollar spent.

The job of the Treasury Board as the cabinet Committee on Management, on the other hand, is to establish on behalf of the government the administrative policies or regulations—constraints, in short—which are seen by ministers to be desirable in guiding or governing departments in the use of the public funds which have been allocated to them. In almost all cases the constraints have to do with the "inputs" which are bought to administer the approved programs—personnel, office accommodation, material and equipment, contracts for services, travel and other employee expenses, and the rest. Some of the constraints are designed to ensure the most effective use and development across the Public Service of particularly important inputs—personnel being the prime and the most important example. Others are designed to ensure probity and prudence in the decisions officials make as to the kind and quality of inputs they will acquire. Still other constraints are calculated to assure honesty and economy in the manner in which inputs are acquired—notably the purchasing and contracting methods. Others have to do with public accountability and with the evenness of treatment of public servants across the service.

Popular Perceptions about the Functions of the Treasury Board

The misconceptions which prevail as to the role of the Treasury Board are largely a consequence of this mixing of roles—that is to say of the manner in which the Treasury Board itself has tended to function in years past. The first misconception has to do with the role of the Treasury Board itself: it tends to be looked upon as a central agency devoted to economizing in the use of the particular inputs, whatever the cost to the efficiency of departments, and whatever the consequences in terms of administrative rigidity. Efficiency is judged not in terms of the efficacy of policies in achieving their goals, nor in terms of the efficiency with which individual programs are being administered, but rather in terms of the economies which are or may be effected in the use of manpower, the amount of space employed, the level of travelling expenses incurred, and the rest.

The legitimacy of the Treasury Board's role in evaluating the effectiveness of programs and the efficiency of administration thus tends not to have been established. Under an "input-centred" régime it could not be otherwise. Furthermore the Glassco Commission's concentration on the need for more delegation to departments was widely interpreted as reinforcing the view that the Board had no legitimate role in the evaluation of effectiveness and efficiency. Thus the impression was left that departments alone should determine whether or not their programs were effective and their administration efficient, and Treasury Board intervention—or intervention of any central agency for that matter —came to be regarded as a contravention of the new management slogan, "let the managers manage." It is almost as if the old arbitrariness in budget-making—a 10 per cent cut across the board, or straight percentage cuts or increases in the budgets of the several departments—was to be preferred to hard knowledge on the part of the Treasury Board as to departmental and program operations. Thus has the second popular perception of the Treasury Board come to develop: it is the central agency which arbitrarily determines the allocation of funds between competing programs, without any necessary or clear perception as to the relationship between its actions and the government's goals or policies, and without a proper regard to the effect of its cuts upon the departmental effectiveness.

The third popular perception of the Treasury Board is that far from being a cabinet committee acting for the collectivity of ministers, it is an amorphous mixture of officials and ministers, acting anonymously and beyond the control of departments or ministers, and apparently performing outside of the context of the machinery of cabinet government as a whole. . . .

The Treasury Board as the Cabinet Committee on the Expenditure Budget

The role of the Treasury Board as the cabinet's Committee on the Expenditure Budget is determined partly by the machinery of cabinet government, and partly by the theory of budgeting. The budget is an expression of the government's policies and programs: the best mix of measures which the government has been able to put together at a given point in time for achieving its objectives. It—the budget—is not a disembodied financial document, as some people seem to believe, separated somehow from the central processes of policy formulation: rather it is the meeting point of the decision-making process, the point at which all government's diverse priorities and policies and programs must somehow be brought together into an integrated and hopefully harmonious whole.

This process requires, as has been said, an understanding of the several goals of government and the relative importance attached to each of them by ministers, a knowledge of the myriads of policies and programs of the government—both present and proposed, and an appreciation of how they relate both to the goals they are designed to achieve and to complementary or competing goals. It also calls for reliable information as to the effectiveness with which particular programs—and hopefully alternative ones—are achieving, or can be expected to achieve, the specific goals for which they were designed, as well as information as to the side-effects the programs may have upon the accomplishment of other goals. A clear idea is needed, too, as to the efficiency with which the government's programs are being administered, both of and by themselves and in relation to one another. . . .

It must be remembered, in making this analysis, that virtually every program serves more than one objective, and virtually every objective is served by many programs. Moreover, some objectives are to some extent contradictory, whereas others complement one another. In the evaluation of the social benefits of a particular program, therefore, one must know and understand the extent to which the effectiveness of that program is diminished or enhanced by other programs, and the extent to which it (the program) itself diminishes or enhances the effectiveness of other programs.

The end result of combining all of these facts and all of these judgments is to reach the best allocation of funds which can be achieved at a particular point in time—the annual expenditure plan. This is the purpose and the objective of the Treasury Board as the cabinet Committee on the Expenditure Budget.

The Machinery of Government Involved

It would be wrong to conclude from this that the body which seeks to combine these judgments, the Treasury Board, is the body which makes them all. To begin with, the setting of priorities, and even the development of policies, is very much the business of the political process as a whole—accomplished by the expression by the public of its preferences at the polls, in Parliament, through the press, and by way of various community interest groups. And within government, it is all of the ministers, not any single cabinet committee, who finally must identify the community's (and indeed their own) values and objectives, must consider the principal directions of policy which are called for if the community's problems are to be resolved in a manner consistent with its values, and must evaluate alternative programs and program mixes as instruments for achieving the rather more specific objectives the government has settled upon.

It would also be wrong to conclude from what has been said that the cabinet and a single cabinet committee, the Treasury Board, could today accomplish this immense task alone, as they sought to do in earlier and simpler times. What is required, and what now has been developed, particularly in the last few years, is a complex of cabinet committees which by their several efforts, co-ordinated by the cabinet as a whole, are able together to perform the total job of government.

In this complex cabinet and cabinet committees, the key committee is the Committee on Priorities and Planning. Chaired by the Prime Minister, it is the committee which develops and proposes to cabinet the broad priorities and policy directions of the government. . . .

Next there are what might be called the "functional" committees of the cabinet—those concerned with economic, social, external affairs and defence, and other policy areas. Each of these committees receives from the responsible ministries proposals for program changes in its particular policy area, and evaluates them in terms of their inherent merits, in terms of their relationships to other policies and programs within the field of competence of the committee, and in terms of their bearing upon the overall policy directions of the government. Out of these deliberations emerge both program proposals to the government, and a general set of priorities, or "policy thrusts" as common usage would have it, within the several functional areas of government. . . .

It is for the Treasury Board to take these several priorities and policy directions and program proposals and put them together into annual expenditure plans which will reflect the government's policies and priorities, and at the same time achieve the optimum results for the citizen in the use of his dollar. This is accomplished, as has been said, by allocating funds, in diminishing order, to those programs which are most in accord with the government's priorities and most effective in achieving the goals inherent in those priorities.

There are implicit in this sentence, however, and in what has been said before, two questions which must be answered if the functioning of the Treasury Board as the Committee on the Expenditure Budget is to be understood. The first is this: how, precisely, does the Treasury Board operate in relation to the other cabinet committees? What does it do that the other committees do not do? The second question is this: what mechanisms are employed by the Treasury Board to enable it to make the complex judgments which are involved in seeking to achieve maximum social utility through public expenditures (to use once again the term employed in public finance theory)?

The Functioning of the Treasury Board in Relation to other Cabinet Committees

The first of these questions can be answered by pointing to the organization which is employed to integrate the work of the Treasury Board and the other cabinet committees, and to characteristics of the Treasury Board decisions which distinguish them from the decisions made by other committees.

First, as to the interrelationships, a conscious effort has been made in the Government of Canada to develop mechanisms for ensuring that the Treasury Board and its Secretariat are fully aware of the program decisions and the emerging priorities of other cabinet committees—all of which are approved in principle by the cabinet, usually before they are considered by the Treasury Board. The President of the Treasury Board and his colleagues on the Board obviously are the first link in this relationship, as members of the cabinet, and, each of them, of certain cabinet committees. In addition the Treasury Board Secretariat has an official in attendance at each of the functional committees of cabinet, either as advisers to the President, if he is a member, or to report to him on the financial and other implications of the proposals under discussion. Thus at both the ministerial and the official level the Treasury Board and its Secretariat are aware of the program proposals which have been approved by cabinet committees, and of the factors which entered into these decisions. They are aware, too, of the emerging priorities in each of the policy areas of government, as reflected in the discussions within the functional committees.

Particular care has been taken to integrate the work of the Treasury Board with that of the key cabinet committee—Priorities and Planning. In addition to the organizational arrangements which have just been described, there is a formal exchange of documents between the two committees designed to ensure harmony between the broad policy directions and priorities (commonly called "the guidelines") determined by the Priorities and Planning Committee, and the detailed budget allocations proposed by the Treasury Board. The "guidelines" are transmitted to the Board, when they have been approved by the cabinet, before it begins its deliberations in the expenditure budget, and the Treasury Board in turn reports to the Priorities and Planning Committee, before its expenditure proposals are transmitted to full cabinet, on the relationship between its budget proposals and the broad policy directions it has received from the cabinet. In addition to all this there are the regular exchanges which might be expected between the Privy Council Office Secretariat which serves the Priorities and Planning Committee and the Treasury Board Secretariat.

What distinguishes the decisions of the Treasury Board from those of other committees can best be characterized in a single sentence: the Treasury Board decisions represent those hard choices which finally must be made in arriving at an expenditure plan. At the interfunctional or interdepartmental level, it is not for the Treasury Board to substitute its judgment for that of the cabinet, based on the recommendations of the Committee on Priorities and Planning, respecting the board policy directions which have been decided upon: the role of the Treasury Board is to superimpose upon this general map of social utility, so to speak, the detailed social utility maps which emerge in respect of individual programs and projects. . . .

The same is true *within* the several policy areas of government. The Treasury Board does not attempt to second-guess the functional cabinet committees in respect of the programs they have proposed to cabinet, nor does it seek to substitute its judgment for any ranking of programs, in general policy terms, which may have emerged from individual functional committees. Rather its role is to superimpose upon the program proposals received from these cabinet committees the kinds of choices which must be made in terms (again) of the broad policy directions of the government, in terms of the effectiveness and efficiency of the particular programs proposed, and in terms of their impact on other programs and other government objectives. . . .

The Allocative Mechanisms

. . . The beginning of the process is the establishment of the 'fiscal framework' for a particular fiscal year—the proposed total revenues and total expenditures, both budgetary and non-budgetary. This framework is the product of discussions of the cabinet Committee on Economic

Policy, and then the Committee on Priorities and Planning, based on proposals submitted by the Minister of Finance. It is the Ministry of Finance which prepares at the beginning of the budgetary cycle in respect of each fiscal year proposals as to what the government's overall fiscal policy ought to be for the year. These proposals are based upon the latest evaluation by the ministry of the economic outlook for the fiscal year in question, including prospective revenues and expenditures. Having examined these projections in relation to such criteria as the rate of growth of the economy, employment levels, price stability, stability of the currency, etc., the department then makes specific proposals as to whether the economy should be stimulated or controlled, and the extent to which this should be accomplished by tax or by expenditure changes. Ministers decide, on the basis of these proposals, what the government's fiscal posture should be for the forthcoming fiscal year, and specifically what levels should be set for the budgetary surplus or deficit, and for the total cash requirements of the government. In arriving at these figures the expected levels of revenues are set (both budgetary and non-budgetary) and the target levels of expenditures are established (both budgetary and non-budgetary). These decisions constitute the fiscal framework which, once approved by cabinet, governs the Treasury Board in all of its subsequent work on the expenditure budget for that year. The task of the Board is to allocate the agreed revenues and borrowings among the competing expenditure claims—both budgetary and non-budgetary—of the several departments and agencies of government, within the broad policy directions established by the government. (This is not to suggest that the fiscal framework is "fixed" for the whole of the ensuing fiscal year: in fact it is subject to regular review, as is indicated below.)

These policy directions emerge, as has been said, primarily from the cabinet Committee on Priorities and Planning. Immediately the fiscal framework has been set, the committee meets to consider the policy guidelines which should govern in the preparation of the annual budget. At these meetings the Priorities and Planning Committee brings together its discussions over the year with respect to the community's developing problems, the objectives of the government which emerge from these problems, the major policies of the government serving these objectives, and the manner in which these policies should be shaped in order better to achieve their goals. Out of these meetings there emerge the broad policy directions by which ministers believe the Treasury Board should be guided in the allocation of funds.

Given the myriad of programs involved in government, the range of choices open to the Treasury Board must clearly be identified and even, where possible, narrowed. To this end, the government has adopted a "three budget system" which distinguishes between the programs which have aready been approved and are a part of the present expenditure budget (the "A" budget); those which have yet to be approved or incorporated in the budget (the "B" budget); and the programs which are of the lowest priority and might be dropped to make room for new programs which are expected to contribute more effectively to the government's objectives (the "X" budget). With this distinction it becomes possible in the period during which the expenditure budget is being struck for ministers to concentrate on the "incremental decisions," and to develop a separate and a continuing mechanism for the review of programs which cannot be considered at that time.

This is how the "three budget system" works. The "A" budget, which is arrived at first in the budgetary cycle, reflects the cost of merely continuing present programs at present levels. Increases in expenditure are allowed to finance increases in salaries and in the prices of other inputs, and to finance changes in the volume of services required as a result of increases in the population being served (a rise in the number of children, for example, calls for an increase in family allowance payments). Decreases in expenditures are looked for as a consequence of continuing efforts to increase the productivity of the public service. Because no policy decisions are required respecting the programs in the "A" budget—at least at this juncture in the budget cycle—the "A" budget can be arrived at largely by departmental officials and the Treasury Board Secretariat, with appeals to the Treasury Board being possible in its annual meetings with ministers (see below).

The "B" budget represents the new programs, or improvements in the quality of existing programs, which are being proposed by individual ministers for the next fiscal year (all of which, if they are major in character, will have been or will be discussed by the appropriate functional committee of the cabinet). These are the programs which, along with any potential tax cuts, must compete for any "new" funds estimated to be available in the forthcoming fiscal year—that is to say, the difference between the revenues plus any borrowing (deficit) provided for in the fiscal framework, and the "A" budget level of expenditures. These, in short, are the incremental decisions which must be taken. Table I may serve to illustrate the nature of the operation.

To the extent that the cabinet has found that the expected "fiscal elbow-room" is insufficient (again, the margin between expected revenues plus deficit, if any, and the "A" budget level of expenditures), it may look to the "X" budget for relief. This is the budget which results either from continuing or from periodic examinations of existing programs by departments and the Treasury Board Secretariat, with a view to identifying those which are contributing least to social utility. When some such programs have been identified, the Treasury Board may select certain of them for elimination in favour of new programs which are judged to be of higher priority, or social utility, or in favour of tax cuts.

These, in short, are the incremental decisions which are taken in the course of preparing the annual expenditure budget. An attempt to describe how they are reached was made in earlier paragraphs: in essence it is a matter of ranking the "B" budget proposals in order of their marginal social benefit, taking into account the broad policy directions received from the cabinet and the Priorities and Planning Committee, along with the policy judgments of the functional cabinet committees, and taking into account such evaluation as has been possible as to the relative effectiveness of the proposed program and the efficiency with which it might be expected to be administered.

TABLE I: Fiscal Framework, Year x (millions; estimated)

Budgetary revenues		$ xxx
Budgetary expenditures		
"A" budget	$ xxx	
Available for "B" budget expenditures or tax cut	xx	xxx
Budgetary surplus or deficit		xxx

Non-budgetary transactions have been excluded from this table for purposes of simplification, but the approach followed is not dissimilar from that used in respect of budgetary transactions.

The Evaluation of Program Effectiveness and Administrative Efficiency

It will be evident that so far only "incremental" decision-making has been described: that little has been said about the critical examination of existing programs—those which make up the "A" budget. This is the aspect of government which has received the least attention from Treasury Boards, partly by reason of the difficulties inherent in evaluating the effectiveness of programs in relation to their objectives, and partly by reason of the formidable political obstacles to the elimination of almost any current program.

The development of Planning Programming and Budgeting (PPB) in government heralded in a formal sense the decision to attempt to reverse this tendency, and to examine on a regular and continuing basis the effectiveness of present programs and the efficiency of their administration. This is not to say that such evaluations were unknown in government before. . . .

What is new is the determination to embark upon formal and continuing studies of existing programs, using the sophisticated techniques of analysis which now are available for the purpose, and the decision to use such studies as a basis of decision-making, including the allocation of resources. And what is new for the budgetary process in particular is the recognition that hard information derived from efficiency and effectiveness evaluations, whether done by departments themselves or by departments in association with the Treasury Board Secretariat, is to be preferred to the more informal judgments—on occasion the downright arbitrary judgments—which have tended to characterize Treasury Board operations of the past.

The burden of all this is that PPB is relatively new in the Government of Canada, and that it is too early to describe with precision how its operations will come to affect the examination of the "A" budget. What can be said, however, is that in the field of efficiency evaluation, performance or productivity measures gradually are being introduced across the government, where they are feasible; that information resulting from the management studies commissioned by departments is increasingly becoming an input in the allocative process; and that the Treasury Board Secretariat itself is undertaking a program of organization "audits" designed, again, to provide the Treasury Board with harder information on which to base its judgments. In all of this the prime responsibility for efficiency remains with the operating departments: the role of the Treasury Board Secretariat is to obtain for the Board better information as to the efficiency of several departments, and to ensure that departments have in fact introduced the performance measures and undertaken the management analyses which are seen to be desirable.

As a consequence of these efficiency studies it is possible to reduce or control the "A" budget without the elimination or contraction of whole programs. This, too, has been done in the past, though in a less structured way. It is the effectiveness studies which lead to program changes or indeed the elimination of whole programs. Putting this in terms of the "three budget system," these are the studies which will lead to the identification of the programs which might "qualify" for the "X" budget—the programs which are brought to the attention of ministers for the purpose of examining the possibility of eliminating them, or reducing their scale.

Again, the prime responsibility of these effectiveness studies resides with departments. But the Treasury Board Secretariat has been given the responsibility for working with selected agencies on pilot projects, designed to develop and to adapt techniques for effectiveness evaluation, and then to disseminate them throughout the public service. The Secretariat will also participate in, or audit, departmental effectiveness studies for the purpose of ensuring that the Treasury Board, in its expenditure decisions, is operating with the same information as departments are in respect of the relative effectiveness of the government's several programs. . . .

Formulating the Expenditure Budget

The expenditure for the fiscal year beginning April 1 must be finalized, and the estimates at the press, by the end of the calendar year. The Treasury Board, therefore, receives from its Secretariat, by the summer of each year, the "A" budgets which have tentatively been agreed upon, and the "B" and "X" budgets which have been submitted by departments for consideration by ministers. The Secretariat also submits its views as to which "B" budget programs seem most likely to be in accord with the government's objectives, and most likely to achieve them, as well as some indication as to the programs in the "X" budget which ministers might wish to examine most closely. These views are also made known to the departments concerned.

The Treasury Board then meets with each minister to consider with him the budgets of the agencies for which he is responsible, and to discuss the issues which must be considered in arriving at recommendations. Out of these meetings the Board reaches its conclusions as to which programs should be included in the expenditure plan for the forthcoming year, and at what level, and decides upon the expenditure budget which should be recommended to the Priorities and Planning Committee and the cabinet. When the government has approved the expenditure budget, the printed Estimates are prepared for submission to Parliament.

The same process is followed during the fiscal year. Proposals for program changes are reviewed by the appropriate functional committee of the cabinet, and recommended, or otherwise, to the cabinet. If the programs are approved by the cabinet, in principle, they are referred to the Treasury Board for financial consideration. The Board in turn holds monthly reviews of these new "B" budget items, and proposes to the cabinet which of them ought to be, or can be, included within the approved fiscal framework (as most recently revised). These are the program changes which appear in Parliament in the form of Supplementary Estimates.

This then is how the Treasury Board functions, and the role it is expected to play, as the cabinet's Committee on the Expenditure Budget. . . .

The Treasury Board as the Cabinet Committee on Management

The role of the Treasury Board as the cabinet's Committee on Management is determined by the machinery of cabinet government and by prevalent theories of management, just as its role as a Committee on Expenditures is determined by the machinery of government and the theory of budgeting.

As a Management Committee the Board is concerned with leadership or guidance or regulation respecting the several inputs which enter into program administration, and the manner in which they are combined or organized, rather than with the programs themselves. The question with which this committee is concerned, therefore, given the government's policy decisions, is what quality, or sometimes even quantity, of personnel, equipment, supplies and services it is reasonable to expect departments to acquire in order to implement their programs and what methods they should use in acquiring these inputs.

Theories of management have varied over the years, bringing with them different views as to the extent to which departments should be regulated regarding the acquisition and use of inputs. At one extreme the Treasury Board has been looked upon as "the manager" in government, determining in some detail what quality and quantity of inputs departments would be allowed to acquire, and prescribing how they should be purchased. At the other extreme the departments are looked upon as the "the managers" in government, free to exercise their own good judgment as to which inputs they will acquire and how, and how they will combine them for the purpose of implementing the programs for which they are responsible.

There is no doubt that in this spectrum it is the latter theory which is prevalent in government today. And there is no doubt that given the sheer scale of modern government it is the only viable approach. But it must be said that however much governments may have turned towards this end of the management spectrum, they have been remarkably slow in bringing about the required reforms. And it must be said, too, that however vigorously the theorists have advocated their new approach, they too have been surprisingly slow in adapting it to the needs of cabinet government.

The reason lies partly in the overstatement of the theory. There is no enterprise, public or private, the subdivisions of which enjoy total freedom in their choice and use of inputs. There is scarcely any enterprise which does not impose upon its subdivisions some requirement regarding the acquisition of inputs, designed to achieve economies of scale. Nor are there many enterprises, public or private, which do not provide for their subdivisions, centrally, certain of their administrative requirements (such as pay and collective bargaining systems). The real question is how much freedom the subdivisions should be accorded to the end of achieving optimum results within the context of the total enterprise, given the presence or otherwise of measures by which the performance of the subdivisions can be measured.

The other and more important reason for the apparent slowness with which governments have adapted their operations to the newer theories of management, is the fact that the institutions of the parliamentary system themselves impose constraints upon the freedom which may be accorded the departments and agencies of government. The cabinet as a whole is held responsible by Parliament for the fair and even treatment of the public servants, within the context of what the community regards as being fair and reasonable. The government as a whole is responsible to Parliament for ensuring that the accommodation provided to its civil servants, and the expenses they incur, are within the range of acceptable public standards. The cabinet as a collectivity is responsible to Parliament for ensuring that inputs are acquired in the most economical fashion, and that contracts are let in a way which assures honesty in public administration. The government is and must remain fully accountable to Parliament for the actions of departments, and for the handling of the funds which Parliament has entrusted to them. . . .

The Machinery of Government Involved

The Treasury Board is the cabinet committee which has been chosen to act for the government in discharging these responsibilities. It is the Treasury Board which prescribes the personnel policies, including classification and pay, across the public service. It is the Treasury Board Secretariat which bargains with employee unions on behalf of all departments, and advises the government in respect of such central operations as the Public Service Superannuation Fund. It is the Treasury Board which attempts to give leadership to departments in the development and use of such important and expensive inputs as computing and data processing equipment, and which prescribes guidelines or regulations as to the standards which ought to apply in respect of other inputs such as accommodation, travel, entertainment expenses, and employee benefits such as parking. It is the Board which has determined what contract methods shall be used by departments in acquiring services, equipment, and capital structures, and when materials and supplies should be acquired through central agencies. And it is the Treasury Board, too, along with the Minister of Finance, which prescribes the form of accounts and the manner in which departments are to account to Parliament for the funds which Parliament has appropriated for their use.

In all of this the Treasury Board is acting for the ministers as a collectivity, and is answerable to them for its administrative and personnel policies. In the past is has in fact acted with great independence, as provided for in the Financial Administration Act: only rarely were the policies prescribed by the Board formally reported to the cabinet, and virtually never were they challenged by that body. Only recently has the Board begun reporting to the cabinet its major administrative and personnel policy decisions, and making known to other ministers its willingness to hear their views concerning administrative policies.

As an outgrowth of the promulgation of policies by which departments must be guided in their administrative transactions, the Treasury Board must also approve certain of the transactions themselves before they may be proceeded with. This occurs whenever the Board imposes by regulation the norms or standards which shall apply: by definition departments are not empowered to act beyond the regulations without Treasury Board authority. Moreover there are other transactions, such as contracts valued over a certain amount, which must always be approved by the Board. . . .

It will be evident that to the extent that the Treasury Board promulgates its administrative policies in the form of guidelines instead of regulations, the departments do *not* need to obtain the Board's approval before proceeding with transactions which exceed the norms or standards involved. Instead they are able to exercise their own judgment as to when exceptions to policies are called for subject only to such *ex post* questioning as the Treasury Board may wish to undertake consequent upon its audit of these transactions. Carried to its logical conclusion this approach would remove from the prior approval of the Treasury Board all administrative transactions. It would then be for the government's auditors to draw to ministerial attention the failure of departments to adhere to the spirit of the Treasury Board's guidelines, and for the Auditor General to perform the same function on behalf of Parliament.

The Functioning of the Treasury Board in Relation to Departments

In fact the Treasury Board employs all three of the approaches which have been mentioned in discharging its responsibilities as the cabinet Committee on Management. In some instances it actually provides administrative services to departments, on a centralized basis. In others it establishes regulations by which departments are governed in their administrative transactions, and requires that the transactions which exceed the standards thus established are approved by the Board. In still other cases it establishes guidelines as to the norms of administrative behavior expected of departments, and seeks in its reviews of departmental performance to ensure that there has been reasonable adherence to the norms so prescribed.

To appreciate the role which is seen for the Treasury Board in the 1970s, and to perceive the direction in which the Treasury Board has in fact been moving in the past several years, it is necessary to understand the circumstances under which the Board is tending to employ each of three approaches mentioned above.

First, the Treasury Board itself provides, through its Secretariat, those services which in the view of the government must be performed centrally if the public service is to operate as a single service, and where the alternative of guidelines governing departmental performance has been judged to be largely unadministrable—either by reason of the great difficulty of formulating the guidelines or of seeing to their application. This has applied, specifically, in such areas as the establishment of pay levels across the service, including the classification of positions, the determination of the substitutes for pay which will be provided to employees, including superannuation benefits, and collective bargaining with employee unions. And even within certain of these areas, notably that of classification, once the system has been established and it has been determined that delegation to departments is feasible and capable of being audited, the Treasury Board has delegated to departments the responsibility for administering the system which has been put in place.

Another and rather more obvious criterion for determining when administrative services should be provided centrally is that of pure economy. Traditionally it has been assumed, *prima facie*, that services such as building accommodation, whether provided by construction or by rental, could be acquired more economically by a central agency—notably the Department of Public Works. Similarly it has been assumed that the procurement of supplies and services and capital structures could be done more efficiently and economically by another central agency—the Department of Supply and Services. This proposition, endorsed by the Glassco Commission, has generally been accepted by the Treasury Board.

Increasingly, however, there has been a tendency to look critically at the potential side effects of putting these central agencies in a monopoly position vis-à-vis departments (that is to say, making departments obtain their requirements through them). First, if departments are not obliged to pay the full cost of the services they acquire in this way, there is a tendency to buy more than actually is necessary. With this in mind the Treasury Board has gradually been introducing the requirement that central agencies charge user departments the full cost of the services they purchase. Secondly, the central agencies themselves are undertaking, with the encouragement of the Treasury Board, an evaluation of the efficiency with which they are providing the services, with a view to ensuring that the economies of central procurement (for example) are not being offset by the inefficiencies which tend to creep into enterprises in a monopoly position.

It will be recognized that the central provision of services such as procurement does not determine the input requirements of programs, though it may influence them indirectly. Rather it is the departments themselves who are expected to determine the level of inputs required for the purpose of implementing the programs for which they are responsible. There is one important qualification to this generalization, as has been said: departments may be governed in their decisions by the standards of "probity and prudence" which may be established by the government through the Treasury Board—the standards of honesty, integrity, economy, and discretion which the community expects to see applied in the use of its tax dollars. In these two words—probity and prudence—is to be found the rationale for almost *any* regulation of the inputs departments acquire to implement the programs under their charge. . . .

It is in the imposition of these standards of probity and prudence that the Treasury Board confronts the classical management dilemma: on the one hand the desire to "let the managers (departments) manage" and on the other hand the desire to ensure that community expectations as to standards of behaviour in the public service are realized. The Treasury Board recognizes that the surest way of resolving this dilemma is to impose these standards by way of guidelines instead of regulations. Thus, as has been said, departments would be free to decide when exceptions to the standards were called for, but with the Treasury Board Secretariat setting in place an audit system which would make possible periodic reports to ministers on the actual performance of departments.

This is the direction in which the Treasury Board is moving in the discharge of its responsibilities as the cabinet Committee on Management. The Secretariat has undertaken a review of all of the Board's regulations—a review which will take two years or more to complete —with the objective of determining which of them could properly be converted into guidelines. Two questions are being asked: whether it would be possible to devise an economical system by which departmental performance could be audited, and, if not, what would be the cost, in terms both of efficiency and of government control over the public service, of simply discontinuing the regulations altogether. . . .

Success in this venture will free the Treasury Board, and its Secretariat, to concentrate rather more upon the more constructive elements of its work as the cabinet Committee on Management—namely leadership and co-ordination in the development and use of the really critical resources in government, notably personnel. There have in fact been very substantial changes in this field: an entirely new classification and pay system has been installed, and collective bargaining has been introduced into the Public Service. Now the Treasury Board and its Secretariat are concentrating upon the initiation, in co-operation with the Public Service Commission and operating departments, of a comprehensive manpower development and education program. . . .

Finally, a word should be said about the role of the Treasury Board in respect of the accountability of the government to Parliament for the use of the resources appropriated by that body. Central accounting and auditing has long since given way to a decentralized system, in accordance with the recommendations of the Glassco Commission. But the government remains responsible for ensuring that departments are in a position properly to account to Parliament for their revenues and expenditures and assets and liabilities. To this end the Treasury Board prescribes the form of accounts that shall be used by departments, and assures that the standards of departmental financial administration are adequate to ensure an appropriate accounting to Parliament for the use of public funds.

This in a sense typifies the role of the Treasury Board as the Cabinet's Committee on Management: it is the body responsible for ensuring that the cabinet as a whole is able to answer for the administrative actions of individual ministries, and for ensuring that such actions conform with the standards of probity and prudence which are expected of the government by the community. Different approaches may be used, as has been said, to discharge this responsibility, ranging from leadership and co-ordination to guidelines, to regulations, to the actual provision by the Treasury Board of certain personnel and administrative services. But the goal remains the same: to ensure that the government is in a position to discharge its collective responsibility for the administrative behaviour of all of its ministries. . . .

TECHNIQUES AND PROCESSES OF ADMINISTRATION*

Douglas G. Hartle

I want to say at the outset that, generally speaking, I am not enthusiastic about the new techniques and processes of administration. In my view, those who advocate them are inclined to assume that the problem is much easier than it is. There has been a tendency, which can be traced back to the Hoover Commission in the United States, but which had its counterpart in the Glassco Commission in Canada, which reported in the mid-sixties, to suppose that the public sector was, in some sense, mismanaged relative to the private sector. The basic themes were: 'Let the manager manage' and 'Apply the techniques and processes that have proven successful in the private sector to the public sector.'

Now in my view the idea that public servants are managers is fallacious. In a well-run system, public servants are not managers; they are policy advisers and/or emissaries (negotiators) and/or administrators. To me, the term 'manager' implies a substantial degree of discretion. In a parliamentary system, the bureaucrat should have relatively little decision-making discretion because the minister to whom he reports must take responsibility for the actions of his officials in the House. Any minister who delegates substantial powers to a senior official, who in turn delegates some of these powers to his subordinates, who in turn delegates, ad infinitum, is a fool if he does not specify the ground rules under which they are to proceed. He is, if he does not set forth such rules, inviting political insensitivity at best, and old-fashioned corruption at worst. For the public servant who has a great deal of discretion with little or no accountability is vulnerable both to 'ego trips' on the one hand, where he bestows or withholds favours at his own pleasure, or a candidate for a bribe because the potential beneficiary knows that the power to give or withhold a substantial benefit rests in the hands of a non-elected official. I deplore that substantial body of legislation that confers discretionary powers without any clear methods of holding accountable those who make the decisions.

* From *Canadian Public Administration*, Vol. 19, No. 1, Spring, 1976. By permission of the author and the Institute of Public Administration of Canada. (Professor Hartle was formerly a Deputy Secretary of the Treasury Board.)

It is true, of course, that the legislation usually requires that the minister 'decide.' In fact, as we all know, a minister's time is limited, and he is required, by and large, to accept the recommendations of his officials almost automatically.

The Hoover and Glassco Commissions made a fundamental error in my opinion. They were simple-minded in assuming that the techniques and processes that had proven useful in the private sector could be applied, virtually without modification, to the public sector. They forgot, if they ever understood, that there is a fundamental difference between the two sectors. In the private sector firms that are badly run will ultimately go bankrupt. While no one would claim that the financial statements in the private sector are without their ambiguities, there is a set of accepted accounting conventions that limits the degree of manipulation. For publicly held corporations, if the story told by the profit-and-loss statement is persistently tragic, the shareholders will oust the current corporate managers and replace them with a new set.

In the public sector there is no equivalent to a profit-and-loss statement. The record of assets and liabilities is virtually meaningless. The shareholders—the voters—have only three alternatives if they find the government's policies are unsatisfactory: they can vote the government out of office (when there is a credible alternative); they can revolt; or they can emigrate. But in reaching their decisions the voters cannot simply examine the equivalent of the profit-and-loss statement of the government of the day. No such statement exists or can exist. The 'generally accepted accounting principles' upon which private sector profit-and-loss statements hinge are disputations; I cannot see the day when the same degree of consensus, limited as it is (e.g. inflation adjustments), will exist with respect to the assessment of the policy positions of any government.

The basic conflicts between politicians and bureaucrats, the conflicts among special interest groups; and the conflicts between each of these groups and the political-bureaucratic establishment are inescapable. Those who perceive themselves to be losers are unlikely to acquiesce in their losses: those who perceive themselves to be winners are unlikely to be satisfied with their gains. The losers will fight for redress: the winners will fight to retain what they have, and seek more.

Techniques

In the past decade or so there have been at least six techniques introduced that purported to improve government decision: Program Planning and Budgeting, Operational Performance Measurement Systems, Management by Objectives, Cost/Benefit Analysis, Cost/Effectiveness Studies. I would like to comment on each of them in turn. . . .

Program Planning and Budgeting

While the coroner's report is not yet in, at least in Canada, there seems little doubt the PPB is dead. Some useful things were accomplished, as a comparison of the current *Estimates* with those of a decade ago clearly demonstrates. There is more data presented in a more useful format than there used to be. The new cross-classification of expenditures by agency, by program, by activity, as well as by object of expenditure, is undoubtedly an improvement over the old classification scheme.

Having said this, however, I do not believe that it is an exaggeration to say that the planning and evaluation purposes of PPB have not been realized and are not likely to be. Spending agencies do not take seriously the requests for estimates for their future expenditures. They simply extrapolate the next year's requests at a constant rate. Why should they bother to do otherwise when the numbers are not taken seriously by those responsible for putting together the budget for the coming year? At best, these forecasts are aggregated and presented as one slate to ministers to show that, if restraint is not shown, the system will collapse. This ministers already understand.

Secondly, rarely, if ever, does it make strategic sense for a department to reveal its aspirations during the regular cyclical budgetary review. Better to introduce new initiatives by means of special requests to cabinet outside the regular budgetary cycle where the competition for funds is less and where it can be claimed both that special circumstances warrant emergency action and that funds can be found to finance the new or expanded programs for the balance of the year. To the devil with the financial implications for subsequent years!

Thirdly, the analytical component of PPB, as orginally conceived, has been largely ignored. Typically, no analytical work has been undertaken to assess program efficiency and effectiveness. Where it has been carried out it has had minimal effects on budgetary decisions, for reasons I will elaborate upon later.

Why has PPB not realized its earlier promise? I believe that there are several interrelated answers. 1/ It was naïve to assume that agreement could be reached as to the objective of each program. Most programs have multiple objectives, and some of them cannot be admitted. Different ministers and officials assign quite different weights to these several objectives at any point in time. Then these weights change. Witness the problems involved in closing a defence base located in a depressed area. 2/ What constitutes a program, an activity, a subactivity, or a sub-subactivity is inherently arbitrary. Should our defence spending be considered as one program or as ten programs? What activities should be combined to constitute a program? Why is an activity not a program in its own right, or a subactivity for that matter? 3/ When is it in the interest of the minister and officials responsible to take a hard look at what they are doing? Indeed, is it not dangerous even to collect the basic data upon which such an assessment could be based? 4/ Given the ambiguities about objectives, mentioned above, and the lack of consensus about methods, discussed below, how seriously would an analysis designed to support a PPB submission be taken?

Operational Performance Measurement Systems

When an activity (or should I say subactivity?) results in an output that is sufficiently tangible that it can be measured in both quantitative and qualitative terms, and most of the costs associated with the output are clearly assignable to it, it is feasible to calculate the changes over time in unit costs or, what is essentially the same thing, changes in labour productivity. For the past five or six years the Planning Branch of the Treasury Board has been urging departments with repetitive operations to institute such measurement systems. Using Planning Branch officers as advisers, some progress has been made. While it is certainly a rough estimate, I would suppose that the labour productivity of units accounting for perhaps 30 per cent of government employment is now being estimated. The potential is probably something like 70 percent of federal employment. It must not be forgotten, however, that the wages and salaries paid to this large proportion of federal employers accounts for only a small proportion of federal expenditures. The cost of the Family Allowance would not be materially affected if the application were processed and the cheques issued without labour, materials, space, and equipment. Most of the costs arise because of the dollar amounts stated on the monthly cheques that are distributed to millions of Canadian mothers.

Nevertheless, while not wishing to claim too much for it in terms of potential budgetary-manpower savings, OPMS seems to me a useful advance. Potentially, at least, it can aid the line officer in monitoring the performance of his subordinates; it can also serve as a basis for arguing with the Treasury Board for budgetary increases based on increases in work-load but taking into account some productivity improvements.

There are, however, difficulties. One is the difficulty of measuring the extent to which costs per unit are changing as a result of changes in equipment, space, and materials. Theoretically, this problem is soluble, but to the best of my knowledge there is no department that yet measures its total factor productivity. Another problem is that the method cannot deal with overhead costs. Another is that OPMS only copes with changes over time and does not take into account the legitimacy of the base from which the changes are calculated. Fat operations can appear to have remarkable reductions in unit costs with little effort, while lean ones have to struggle for improvements.

The last problem I wish to mention may, however, be overriding. Unless the dollar and manpower budgets arrived at for those activities to which OPMS has been applied in fact reflect the results, the incentive for agencies to maintain, much less extend, OPMS is, to say the least, minimal. There has been a tendency, I am afraid, to have the Planning Branch of the Treasury Board out flogging OPMS to departments while the Program Branch of the Treasury Board has found it expedient to make its recommendations to ministers as though the information were not available. . . .

Management by Objectives

Except in those operations where it is possible to measure changes in unit costs over time, which means essentially the high volume repetitive operations to which OPMS can be applied, I am highly sceptical about the efficacy of MBO. Too often, in my experience, MBO costs more in time and energy than it produces: endless meetings, haggling over jurisdictional territory, drafts and redrafts of statements of objectives to ensure that they are sufficiently vague, no real monitoring of performance against the stated objectives—sometimes because this is impossible and sometimes because it is uncomfortable for the senior officer.

Who is supposed to monitor the monitors? What is his or her motivation for monitoring? If the subordinate can be neither rewarded nor punished on the basis of the results of the monitoring—at least within extremely wide limits of performance—why bother? We all know of cases where the weak, if not totally incompetent, subordinate is given a glowing letter of recommendation as a way of enticing some unsuspecting agency to take him off the hands of the reviewing officer. Good subordinates are often given weak performance appraisals in order to reduce their mobility. . . .

Cost/Benefit Analysis

As I said before, one could quite easily write a book on the subject of cost/benefit analysis. Indeed many have been written. The last time I checked, the Treasury Board Secretariat was on the sixth or seventh draft of its manual. . . .

I have no quarrel with cost/benefit analysis as a technique for ensuring that none of the factors bearing on a project decision are neglected. I do not think this is a trivial advantage. On the other hand, I deplore the facility with which some analysts are able to conjure up estimates of some of the inputted costs and benefits to obtain the ratio they want. It is not surprising, it seems to me, that this technique is looked upon by decision-makers as a tool in the adversarial process, because they would be foolish in the extreme to take the numbers provided by so-called experts as in some sense sacrosanct. As one of my supervisors once put it: 'if anyone around here is going to be arbitrary, it's me.'

I cannot recall any instance where a cost/benefit study played a decisive role in the decision to proceed with or reject any proposed major federal project. Probably this is as it should be, because the technique does not adequately handle the distributional question: who will bear the costs and who will reap the benefits. And distributional questions are necessarily at the forefront of the minds of politicians.

Having said this, however, I would not want to suggest that cost/benefit analysis is valueless. In addition to ensuring that the logic, as distinct from the numbers, is straight, I believe it should be used much more extensively as a decision rule when decision-making powers are delegated. This implies, of course, that superiors take the time to develop the criteria and accept responsibility for the results on which they want project decisions to be reached by their subordinates.

Cost-Effectiveness Studies

I will not belabour this extremely large and important subject for two reasons: first, it is impossible to do justice to it in short compass. Then, a paper of mine on what I thought were the crucial issues was printed in the Journal some years ago. I have not changed my mind about fundamental theoretical issues. I am, however, more sceptical than ever that we will see, in the near future, the emergence of a large set of social-economic statistical indicators that are perceived by the decision-makers, the opinion-makers, and the voters, to fairly reflect the changes, both favourable and unfavourable, that are taking place in this country. Consensus on the 'right' way to measure the changes in the well-being of Canadians is not going to be easily reached. But until it is reached I am not optimistic that cost-effectiveness studies are going to have much impact. As mentioned at the outset, it is difficult to reach aggreement on the multiple objectives (effects) of programs. It is difficult to obtain the data to estimate their effects quantitatively. It is also difficult to obtain release of the results unless they are favourable in every respect. I strongly believe, however, that as slow and painful as it is likely to be, we must push on in this direction. Only in this way are we likely to get a more informed electorate and hence a more responsible government.

Processes

There are four processes that I wish to comment upon: the personnel selection-promotion process, the budgetary process, the cabinet committee process, the auditing process. My comments must necessarily be too brief relative to the issues. Here too, each one warrants a book rather than a subsection in a paper. I hope, therefore, that you will forgive my impressionistic approach.

Personnel Selection-Promotion Process

. . . First of all, the whole selection procedure, which was designed to minimize political interference, by and large confers instantaneous tenure on public servants. University tenure is seldom granted until after four or five years and then only after an agonizing appraisal process.

Public servants are inclined to sneer at university faculty members, and sometimes rightly so. But there are more research professorships in Ottawa than there are in all the universities in Canada—men and women with effective instant tenure who have the freedom to pose the question they will research, research it, and the file the answer in their own desks with no accountability.

The annual salaries paid in Ottawa to some professional groups (not to mention overtime pay and perquisites) is nothing short of outrageous. While I hesitate to name names, the economist-statistician group immediately comes to mind. Although I obviously cannot prove it, there seems to be a gross distortion brought about by the fact that those groups with weak bargaining power can opt for arbitration while those who have strong bargaining power (e.g. can inconvenience the public by withholding their services) can opt for the strike route. This is a recipe designed to do in the taxpayer. And do not think that the taxpayer is unaware of what is going on. Tails they lose; heads they lose.

The absence in the past of some kind of career-planning system for individuals is notable, particularly at intermediate and senior levels. How many potentially good men and women retire on the job at painfully early ages? How many progress beyond their level of competence because nobody is keeping track of their level of past performance, or lack of performance?

Budgetary Process

The thing that impresses one is the inconsequential nature of the regular budgetary process and the overwhelming importance of decisions made outside of it, through special memoranda to cabinet.

I have no reason to attribute ulterior motives to the Department of Finance. But the fact is that the growth in revenues has been underestimated year after year. Because the revenue estimates of February form the basis of the *Estimates* of the following February, which do not apply until the fiscal year beginning two to three months later, it is not surprising in a period of rapid growth and/or inflation that the realized revenues exceed those estimated fourteen to twenty-four months earlier. The fact is, however, that departments have recognized that they are foolish to compete for additional funds for new or expanded programs at a time when their requests will be arrayed against so many alternatives. Much better to submit a cabinet memorandum during the fiscal year when the windfall revenue gains are being reluctantly revealed by Finance. Then a quickly prepared memorandum to cabinet showing only that funds are available to finance it for the balance of the current year, with no realistic estimates for the implications for ensuing years, will often do the trick. The real trick is, of course, ultimately played on the taxpayer. For, once having been adopted, it is like practising dentistry on a shark to achieve modifications in the program in the future. To change the metaphor: the marshmallows of the current fiscal year become the bricks of the next fiscal year—through the "A" budget. And the bricks of today become the cornerstones of tomorrow as new and expanded programs are erected on this once quivering foundation.

The problem is, of course, that once launched, new initiatives are more like skyrockets than guided missiles—they follow a course dictated more by the shape of the milk bottle from which they were launched (I here reveal my age since even I know that milk bottles have vanished from the scene) than by the intentions of the persons who lit the fuse.

It is pathetic how little impact PPB, DPMS, MBO, and such techniques have had on these crucial decisions. In the vital decisions these techniques are, at the present time, like a well-intentioned funeral director who, through the magic of cosmetics, puts a good face on a man who has just died a slow and agonizing death from cancer. The illusion is nearly complete. But the family knows the horrors that have been disguised, and the visitors to the funeral home have their suspicions.

The indexing of the personal income tax was an important step forward, for it will reduce the income elasticity of the personal income tax and thereby force the government of the day to face more squarely the political costs of increased expenditures. . . .

Cabinet Committee Process

In the past decade or so we have seen the development of a much greater degree of centralization in parliamentary systems. It is true that some departments have been decentralized, notably DREE and the Post Office at the federal level. But in terms of head office, in the federal government and the government of Ontario—the two with which I am familiar—the Prime Minister's Office and the Cabinet Office have much more senior staff, and certainly claim to have much more influence, than they did in the past. Is this an illusion? If not is it good or bad?

I do not think that the centralization of power in a period of majority government is an illusion. A prime minister or a premier with a clear majority has enormous power. He has power that might well be envied by a benevolent dictator—for who is to say him nay? This power attracts, like a magnet, individuals who wish to influence the exercise of this power, for this confers prestige on them.

Whether it be the effect of television or not, although I am inclined to believe that this is far from unimportant, electorates seem to vote a party leader in or out. Ministers in a majority government are therefore elected because of their leader and can be rejected at pleasure. They tend to become, if they were not already, toothless tigers who gum the policy proposals of the senior bureaucracy in general and the cabinet office in particular. Senior ministers may squirm in their chairs, but too often they do not stand up to be counted.

While it is my impression that majority governments confer great powers on the prime minister, and hence on his bureaucratic subordinates, the reverse is also true. Minority governments are highly dependent upon the performance of particular ministers—whether by virtue of the votes they can deliver as individuals from their own riding or the votes they can deliver by virtue of the policies adopted with respect to their particular portfolio.

Canadians, it seems to me, make a fundamental mistake when they assume that minority governments are indecisive and fraught with conflict. Is there not ample evidence that majority governments are both insensitive and dominated by senior bureaucrats who are playing their own games? Are the games of bureaucrats any more attractive than those played by politicians? Frankly, I prefer the latter to the former.

Any prime minister or premier is making a grave error who, by creating a strong Cabinet Office, isolates himself from his own ministers who, if they have been chosen wisely, reflect the views of an important segment of the electorate. Too often the emperor finds he has no clothes only by freezing to death in the harsh Canadian winter. You can imagine which parts freeze first.

In short, I hold the view that too often strong cabinet secretariats, elaborate cabinet briefings prepared by these secretariats, control over cabinet agendas, and so on isolate prime ministers and premiers from the ultimate reality they must face. This is often done in the name of one of the techniques I have briefly discussed above. To lose an election in the name of PPB, or OPMS, or MBO is no better than to lose it in the name of insensitivity, inactivity, and indecisiveness.

Auditor General

Let me end this paper with a plea. Many of the difficulties referred to above arise not because either politicians or bureaucrats are malevolent—indeed the opposite is the case by my observation—but rather because they respond to the implicit incentive systems within which they operate. They are not bad men but good men who cannot face the terribly painful personal costs of doing good.

One way out of this impasse, short of a revolution, is to have much greater public disclosure of information. The public needs the information that will allow it to identify when a good man is doing good—whether it be politician or bureaucrat. In a state of ignorance, fools and knaves are indistinguishable from wise men and saints.

It is rarely in the interest of a particular minister or official to reveal more than his colleagues: 'Better to be silent and thought a fool than to speak up and prove it.' Nevertheless, the conspiracy of silence that prevails in our federal and provincial governments seems to me to put their continued existence in jeopardy. There is, in short, a crisis of confidence. It is not in the interest of any individual to speak up; but it is of vital importance that the system as a whole reveal in the future more than it has in the past if its legitimacy is to be maintained.

For this reason, while sceptical of some of the techniques discussed in the earlier part of this paper, I am strongly in favour of the auditor general reporting to Parliament on the extent to which they have been applied, the actions taken on the basis of the results, and the availability of the information to the public.

It is a most imperfect and complicated world. But undue secrecy will not make it less imperfect or less complicated. We do not know how to assess effectiveness of many programs in realizing the aspirations of a multitude of groups. One thing is clear to me, however, I would prefer to trust the partially informed many to the well informed few. This view is reinforced every time I attend a faculty meeting.

BUREAUCRACY GROWS APACE
IN PROVINCES AND MUNICIPALITIES*

John Kettle

Cries of "empire-building!" always greet the news that more public servants are at work for Ottawa (and us). Hanging over our heads is the awful feeling that the feds are taking over the country, spending all the money, and . . . that more bodies are needed to spend it.

But it ain't so. For years Ottawa has accounted for a declining portion of the labor force as well as a declining portion of total government employment. The empire building (if that's the right word for it) is taking place in the municipal and provincial governments, especially in the provinces. That worried talk in the nation's capital about decentralizing the civil

* From *Executive* magazine, October, 1974. By permission.

service may not be necessary after all if the trends continue, because the bulk of the country's government employees are already as decentralized as they can be, spread evenly through every province and municipality in the country.

(Incidentally, it is still the same few departments of the federal government that dominate the federal public service today as did in the 1960s. . . . The Post Office accounts for 19% of the public service, National Defence's civilian workers for another 15%, National Revenue for 8%, Ministry of Transport for 7%—and that's a total of 49% between the four of them. . . .)

We are getting to be a more governed country, if the number of public servants is acceptable evidence. There are now six or seven government employees for every 100 Canadians, and the figure continues to climb. It is climbing, however, almost exactly in step with the labor force. The reason the labor force is a growing part of the population is the changing mix of age groups—more people of working age compared with those below working age. Government's total share remains remarkably steady, at around one in six of all the people with jobs. So really government as a whole is not empire-building either. But if you worry about the epidemic of bureaucrats, the provinces are the governments to watch.

What we are talking of today is a million and a half government employees in Canada, 7% of a population of 22 million and 17% of the people with jobs.

This is a fairly conservative estimate, by the way. I don't know that anyone has added up the numbers before—certainly they aren't assembled by Statistics Canada. Here's what I included (1973 figures):

Federal level:
Departmental employees	290,000	
Crown corporations	145,000	
Armed forces	80,000	
		515,000
Provincial level:		475,000
Municipal level:		
General employees	225,000	
Teachers	255,000	
		480,000
		1,470,000

The various series from 1961 to 1973 required a little fudging. For instance, the government of B.C. only tells Statistics Canada the number of people it employs in institutes of higher learning, leaving them to guess (but not publicly) the number it employs in its departments, Crown corporations, boards and agencies. I simply assumed the ratio of public servants to population would be the same in that province as in the rest of the country. The figures of municipal employees do not include what I'm sure is a large number of people employed in city transit, city utilities (with the exception of water works employees, who for some reason are counted), and municipal hospitals and school boards. I put in the school teachers on the grounds that they were numerous and easy to isolate. I left the rest because I could see no quick way to uncover national figures or even fake up estimates. One or two of the series had breaks in them when the statisticians decided to collect numbers on a different basis, which required a little juggling.

From these series I found that between 1961 and 1973 federal government employment grew at an average 1.0% a year, provincial government employment at an average 6.9% a year, and municipal government employment at 3.9% a year. Those are big differences, more than enough to skew the old distribution patterns.

I used two different techniques for forecasting. Some of the series are pretty clearly related to the growth of population, the general government or departmental employees most obviously. They grow faster than the population, but then so does the labor force. What I forecast was the ratio of civil servants to citizens; then multiplied by my December 1973 population forecasts. Teachers I related to the number of school-age children, actual and projected. Other series seem to have a life of their own, independent of population growth. The armed forces are winding down, and I simply found an equation that best "explained" or best fit the existing data and extrapolated it. Federal Crown corporation employment has wobbled up and down in the past dozen years, but under the fluctuations there is a faintly growing trend line, and this too I continued.

My extrapolations of employment in 1986:
Federal level:

Departmental employees	450,000	
Crown corporations	145,000	
Armed forces	45,000	
		640,000
Provincial level:		800,000
Municipal level:		
General employees	400,000	
Teachers	300,000	
		700,000
		2,140,000

That's a lot of civil servants, of course, slightly over eight for every 100 Canadians, but still 17% of those forecast to have jobs. What is different about it is the mix between the three levels. In 1986 the provincial governments account for 37% compared with 32% in 1973 and 22% in 1961. Ottawa's share is down to 30% compared with 35% in 1973 and 47% in 1961. Note that the municipal governments' share stays steady throughout the 25 years of records and projections; it is the distribution between the federal and provincial levels that moves steadily in favor of the provinces. That's the main news out of this mess of statistics. . . : different government, rather than just more of the same. Presumably we can expect to see some federal politician try to reverse the trend in the next decade or so. We can expect ambitious career civil servants to look increasingly toward the provinces, where the frog pond is growing so

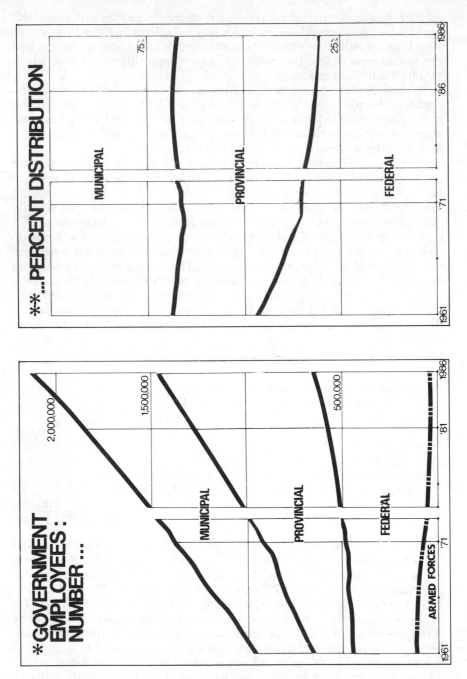

* GOVERNMENT EMPLOYEES : NUMBER ...

2,000,000
1,500,000
500,000

MUNICIPAL
PROVINCIAL
FEDERAL
ARMED FORCES

1961 '71 '81 1986

** ... PERCENT DISTRIBUTION

75%
25%

MUNICIPAL
PROVINCIAL
FEDERAL

1961 '71 '86 1986

* The chart shows dramatically where the growth in the number of government employees has occurred and is forecast to occur — in the provincial governments. Growth in the federal departments is a little more dramatic than at first appears, since the armed forces have declined and the Crown corporations grow very slowly. Municipal growth comes later. Key figures:

	Federal level	of which armed forces	Provincial level	Municipal level	of which teachers
1961	456,953	120,055	213,746	303,362	162,529
1966	471,180	107,467	319,152	379,407	213,067
1971	491,034	89,563	435,686	462,066	256,924
1976	535,671	72,416	548,767	523,054	269,447
1981	582,932	57,835	672,134	591,841	277,488
1986	640,690	45,488	795,513	699,772	300,948

** The different rates of growth at the various levels of government change the distribution pattern, though of course most people have not noticed it yet. We tend to think of the federal civil service as the main body of government employees, and indeed a few years ago they represented the majority; but no longer. Key figures:

	Federal level	Provincial level	Municipal level	Total no. of employees
1961	46.9%	21.9%	31.1%	974,061
1966	40.3	27.3	32.4	1,169,739
1971	35.4	31.4	33.3	1,388,786
1976	33.3	34.1	32.5	1,607,492
1981	31.6	36.4	32.0	1,846,908
1986	30.0	37.2	32.8	2,135,975

*** Here's how the growth in government employees looks on a per-capita basis. The figures are the number of public servants employed at each level for every 100,000 Canadians. At the federal level the ratio actually dropped for a while. Key figures:

	Federal level	Provincial level	Municipal level	Total government
1961	2505	1171	1663	5340
1966	2335	1594	1895	5844
1971	2276	2019	2142	6438
1976	2327	2384	2272	6984
1981	2375	2738	2411	7526
1986	2459	3054	2686	8200

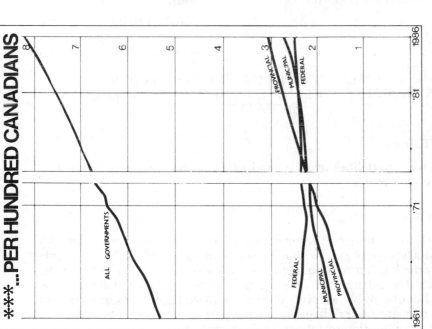

* *Forecasts based on data from Statistics Canada and other public and private sources. In most cases the extrapolations are "naive" (i.e., judgment-free) mathematical extensions of current trends.*

From Executive magazine, October, 1974. By permission.

much faster. We can also surely anticipate more changes in the federal-provincial tax split. And far off on the time horizon is the promise of another change, the growth of the municipal civil service—largely stimulated in my extrapolations by the return of the teachers as a result of the coincidence of a new generation in the classroom and lower pupil-teacher ratios. My figures do, however, also hint at an eventual speed-up in the growth of regular municipal government employment. I would guess at an increasing demand for tax-paid city services, and, along with that, a little municipal empire-building. But that's one or two decades off.

GUIDELINES TO PREVENT CONFLICT OF INTEREST*

Privy Council

P.C. 1973—4065
18 December, 1973

HIS EXCELLENCY THE GOVERNOR GENERAL IN COUNCIL, on the recommendation of the Treasury Board, is pleased hereby to approve the issue of the annexed guidelines to be observed by public servants concerning conflict of interest situations.

Certified to be a true copy
R. G. Robertson
Clerk of the Privy Council

GUIDELINES TO BE OBSERVED BY PUBLIC
SERVANTS CONCERNING CONFLICT OF INTEREST
SITUATIONS

Short Title

1. These guidelines may be cited as the Public Servants Conflict of Interest Guidelines.

Guidelines

2. It is by no means sufficient for a person in a position of responsibility in the public service to act within the law. There is an obligation not simply to obey the law but to act in a manner so scrupulous that it will bear the closest public scrutiny. In order that honesty and impartiality may be beyond doubt, public servants should not place themselves in a position where they are under obligation to any person who might benefit from special consideration or favour on their part or seek in any way to gain special treatment from them. Equally, a public servant should not have a

* From *House of Commons Debates*, December 18, 1973, p. 8883, Appendix "A." Reproduced by permission of the Minister of Supply and Services Canada.

pecuniary interest that could conflict in any manner with the discharge of his official duties.

3. No conflict should exist or appear to exist between the private interests of public servants and their official duties. Upon appointment to office, public servants are expected to arrange their private affairs in a manner that will prevent conflicts of interest from arising.

4. Public servants should exercise care in the management of their private affairs so as not to benefit, or appear to benefit, from the use of information acquired during the course of their official duties, which information is not generally available to the public.

5. Public servants should not place themselves in a position where they could derive any direct or indirect benefit or interest from any government contracts over which they can influence decisions.

6. All public servants are expected to disclose to their superiors, in a manner to be notified, all business, commercial or financial interests where such interests might conceivably be construed as being in actual or potential conflict with their official duties.

7. Public servants should hold no outside office or employment that could place on them demands inconsistent with their official duties or call into question their capacity to perform those duties in an objective manner.

8. Public servants should not accord, in the performance of their official duties, preferential treatment to relatives or friends or to organizations in which they or their relatives or friends have an interest, financial or otherwise.

VEILS OF SECRECY HIDE GOVERNMENT*

John Doig

Politicians of all parties at Queen's Park this week condemned the curtain of secrecy that surrounds government.

But while they were paying lip service to the concept of freedom of information, the Ontario government was working in its usual circumspect way.

John Smith, the minister of correctional services, was still refusing to release a report about the case of an inmate who claimed he'd been sexually assaulted at the Burtch correctional centre.

The minister, who has spoken out in the past about his moral values, said he was keeping the report out of public view because of its "X-rated" language.

Among those angered by the decision was the report's author, Arthur Maloney, Ontario's recently appointed ombudsman.

Maloney said Smith was being unfair to the institution and its guards, who were exonerated by the ombudsman's investigation.

* From *The Toronto Star*, June 19, 1976. By permission.

Confidential Memo

And while MPPs were extolling the merits of open government, members of James Taylor's staff at the ministry of community and social services were referring routine inquiries to the minister's executive assistant.

Their caution stems from a recent confidential memo from Taylor, in which he said departmental "intelligence is not to be public knowledge unless and until considered such by the minister."

Ironically, a copy of the memo was promptly dispatched, in a plain brown envelope, to Opposition Leader Stephen Lewis. . . .

Attempts to open more of government's workings to the scrutiny of the public are being made by opposition legislators in Ottawa and Toronto.

At the federal level, a joint Commons-Senate committee is considering a private member's bill written by veteran Progressive Conservative Gerald Baldwin.

The Ontario Legislature this week debated—for the second time in a year—a private member's bill drafted by former New Democratic Party leader Donald MacDonald.

In both jurisdictions, private bills usually die without action by government.

Baldwin was given some encouragement recently when Mitchell Sharp, president of the Privy Council, said the government is giving "some priority" to planned legislation.

It remains to be seen how far Canadian governments are prepared to go in dismantling centuries of British parliamentary tradition.

But pressure on governments here is being heightened by events in the United States, where freedom of information laws have been on the books since 1974.

In a benchmark ruling a few weeks ago, a U.S. federal judge ordered the administration to release the full, unedited transcript of a 1974 background briefing by Secretary of State Henry Kissinger on the United States-Soviet strategic arms limitation agreement that year.

A citizens' committee, called ACCESS, formed in Ottawa this year, is working in support of Baldwin's bill. It hopes to spawn community groups that would fight for more open government at all levels, from Parliament all the way down to the local town hall.

Advocates of free information laws generally agree that there must be limits on what a government can be expected to reveal. There would be no challenge, obviously, to secrecy regarding information that would endanger national security. At the other end of the scale, Baldwin and MacDonald recognize the need to prevent invasion of individual privacy.

But they see no reasonable grounds for hiding a multitude of facts that would make for a better-informed electorate and, as a result, better government. . . .

For example, it was discovered that milkshakes being served in some restaurants in the Yukon did not measure up to federal health standards. Health Minister Marc Lalonde refused to release details on the ground that disclosure of the information "would interfere with the working rapport" between federal health inspectors and restaurant owners.

Similarly, the federal government conceals results of a wide range of consumer tests dealing with such products as paint, and with important issues such as auto safety—the kind of information now routinely available in the U.S.

'Millions of Dollars'

"As we all know, these are investigations that cost the taxpayers millions of dollars," says Arthur Maloney, "and it is put forward by many that not to make public the findings of these investigations runs contrary to the very purpose for which they are undertaken."

Why have governments in Canada pursued secrecy to the point where even the trivial is stamped "classified?"

It has a lot to do, says Gerald Baldwin, with perpetuation of power.

"We have had a history in Canada of domination by one political party for a great many years," he says.

"Also, civil servants have a natural tendency to avoid embarrassing each other and their ministers," he says.

James Eayrs, University of Toronto professor of international relations, identified public complacency as another important element in Canada's overdeveloped system of secret government. . . .

The government commissioned a senior Privy Council official, Don Wall, to prepare a report on government secrecy—then kept the report itself hidden for more than a year.

In his report, eventually released last year, Wall said that for lack of a comprehensive policy to provide information to the public, "the process of government in Canada is becoming increasingly difficult for those who govern and increasingly incomprehensible to those who are governed."

He said the function of government in providing information is "inseparable" from government itself—"to govern is to inform—to be well-governed is to be well informed . . ."

In Ontario, the committee on government productivity, made up of senior public servants and leading businessmen, concluded that existing secrecy regulations are "an impediment to effective communications."

That view was echoed in a policy paper circulated last month at a weekend conference of the Ontario Progressive Conservative Association by William Neville, who has in the past done public relations work for the Ontario government.

'Feeding Suspicion'

Neville, now chief of staff for federal Conservative leader Joe Clark, said "very little" of the government process in Ontario could be considered "sinister or against the public interest."

But the fact that it is "not open enough," he said, is "feeding ground for suspicion" and "fuel for those who are all too eager to discredit our entire system of government." . . .

Drawing a line on where government secrecy should stop isn't an easy proposition, Baldwin and MacDonald concede.

Their respective bills suggest some limitations in a generally open information policy. The main exemptions would be matters affecting national security, criminal investigations, contract negotiations and individual privacy.

Both MacDonald and Baldwin have reservations about using the courts as a referee in disputes—as in the U.S.—because of the high costs involved.

MacDonald favors strong powers for the provincial ombudsman.

Baldwin is impressed by Sweden's open information system, which uses an independent tribunal to rule on cases in dispute. He thinks Canada might appoint a special panel of judges to the Federal Court for the purpose. . . .

THE OMBUDSMAN—FIGHTING THE SYSTEM THROUGH THE SYSTEM*

John Schreiner

EDMONTON—George B. McLellan, the Western Hemisphere's first legislative ombudsman when he was appointed by Alberta in 1967, retired this spring—5,000 complaints later.

Such is the interest in the idea that five other Canadian provinces and several U.S. states now have legislative ombudsmen. Two American universities are offering courses about ombudsmen, and there were 182 applicants to succeed McLellan.

The man chosen by Alberta was Dr. Randall Ivany, the urbane 41-year-old Anglican Dean of Edmonton. This is the third change of direction in his career. Born in Newfoundland, he was an electrical engineer with Canadian Westinghouse Ltd. before entering the ministry 14 years ago. "In this country, you can do these things. There are no limitations," he says.

When Ivany is asked if he sees the ombudsman's office as an extension of his ministry, the reply has a secular ring. "It is a ministry without religious or denominational barriers. It's got to be that type of service to people which allows them to fight through the bureaucracy."

The ombudsman is the independent person to whom individuals may take complaints involving the *administrative* decisions (as opposed to the policy decisions) of the provincial government.

In 1970 McClellan found his authority being challenged by the provincial attorney general and, as provided for in the Ombudsman Act, sought a ruling from the Alberta Supreme Court. Chief Justice J. V. H. Milvain's judgment has since become a landmark defining why an ombudsman is needed and what he can do.

"I am convinced," Milvain wrote, "that our need for an ombudsman came about as an essential part of what I call impatient efficiency. Or perhaps it should be called efficient impatience. In any event, we have

* From *The Financial Post*, July 20, 1974. By permission.

seen in recent years an increasing body of what we call administrative law . . . Naturally this has brought about an increasing confrontation between individual citizens and the great scheme of things . . ."

The ombudsman in Alberta and in other Canadian provinces is appointed by the legislature, not by the government. This gives him freedom of action comparable to that of the auditor-general.

However, the legislation in some provinces does tend to tie the ombudsman's hands. Ivany refers with scorn to one province where the ombudsman may not touch someone who reports to a cabinet minister. "Who needs access to filing clerks?" he asks.

Yet even under the best of legislation, the ombudsman's power lies in the publicity he can generate where an injustice is done and in the moral suasion and stubborn persistence of the officeholder.

"We have to admit," Ivany says, "that we're not superduck. We sometimes fail . . . But this is a big step in the right direction of getting natural justice."

Milvain wrote that the ombudsman "can bring the lamp of scrutiny to otherwise dark places. If his scrutiny and observations are well founded, corrective measures can be taken in due democratic process."

In the five years to Oct. 31, last year, the Alberta ombudsman received 4,534 complaints. Some 1,551 were investigated and, of these, McLellan judged 390 were justified.

That set of figures tells two things. First, the ombudsman has no authority to deal with complaints—and there are many—involving municipal or federal governments or private businesses or the courts of law. Second, the ombudsman is not immune from frivolous complaints.

The inmates of provincial jails and other institutions are the largest single source of complaints. By law, their letters to the ombudsman must be forwarded without being opened. A recent unjustified complaint on Ivany's desk came from an inmate of a jail who had not been allowed to watch a late-night movie on television. "Watching television is a privilege, not a right," Ivany observes.

The largest number of complaints used to involve decisions of the Workmen's Compensation Board. That source is less prolific since the province gave the board a major overhaul—quite possibly stimulated by McLellan's investigation.

That frequently is the sort of impact the ombudsman can have. A case is recounted in McLellan's last annual report involving a destitute inmate of a mental home whose husband neglected to provide her with pocket money.

This investigation led ultimately to the province deciding to provide $10 a month pocket money for all such destitute inmates.

"We help many people in the future," Ivany says. "For the guy who has to have some sort of justification at the end of each day, this is not the job."

Indeed, the investigations may run for years. McLellan reported another case in which the first letter was written to him in mid-1970 and the complaint (a claim for crop damages) arose from a drainage ditch dug by the government in 1962.

When the case was concluded in February, 1973, the file was two inches thick. And the complainant (who had suffered a heart attack in 1972) received a $1,500 settlement.

This case aside, a major cause for delays in individuals settling complaints with bureaucrats is the failure of the latter to answer their correspondence.

"I have exactly the same trouble myself with some government departments," the exasperated McLellan wrote in his last annual report.

The first important innovation Ivany is bringing to the office is to take it closer to rural Alberta, with periodic visits to temporary storefront offices in the smaller centres. Now, 12 members of the ombudsman's staff are in Edmonton, in a downtown office tower, and the other four are in Calgary.

"We've got to do something, something really serious, to get the office better known in rural areas," Ivany says.

BIBLIOGRAPHY

Civil Service

Armstrong, R., "Some Aspects of Policy Determination in the Development of the Collective Bargaining Legislation in the Public Service of Canada," *C.P.A.*, Vol. XI, No. 4, Winter, 1968.

Blackburn, G. A. "A Bilingual and Bicultural Public Service," *C.P.A.*, Vol. XII, No. 1, Spring, 1969.

Callard, K. B., *Advanced Training in the Public Service*, Governmental Studies Number 1, Toronto, The Institute of Public Administration of Canada, 1958.

Carson, J. J., "The Changing Scope of the Public Servant," *C.P.A.*, Vol. XI, No. 4, Winter, 1968.

Civil Service Commission, *Personnel Administration in the Public Service*, Report of the Civil Service Commission of Canada [Heeney Report], 1958.

Cloutier, S., "Le Statut de la Fonction publique du Canada: Son histoire," *C.P.A.*, Vol. X, No. 4, December, 1967.

Cloutier, S., "Senior Public Service Officials in a Bicultural Society," *C.P.A.*, Vol. XI, No. 4, Winter, 1968.

Cole, Taylor, *The Canadian Bureaucracy, 1939-1947*, Durham, N.C., Duke University Press, 1949.

Cole, Taylor, *The Canadian Bureaucracy and Federalism, 1947-1965*, Denver, University of Denver, 1966.

Côté, E. A., "The Public Services in a Bicultural Community," *C.P.A.*, Vol. XI, No. 3, Fall, 1968.

Crispo, J., "Collective bargaining in the public service," *C.P.A.*, Vol. 16, No. 1, Spring, 1973.

Deutsch, J. J., "Some Thoughts on the Public Service," *C.J.E.P.S.*, Vol. XXIII, No. 1, February, 1957.

Deutsch, J. J., "The Public Services in a Changing Society," *C.P.A.*, Vol. XI, No. 1, Spring, 1968.

Frankel, S. J., *A Model for Negotiation and Arbitration between the Canadian Government and Its Civil Servants*, Montreal, McGill University Press, 1962.

Frankel, S. J., *Staff Relations in the Civil Service: The Canadian Experience*, Montreal, McGill University Press, 1962.

Gosselin, E., Lalande, G., Dozois, G., Boyd, R., "L'administration publique dans un pays bilingue et biculturel: actualités et propos," *C.P.A.*, Vol. VI, No. 4, December, 1963.

Government of Canada, *Organization of the Government of Canada*, Ottawa, Information Canada, 1975, tenth edition.

Heeney, A. D. P., "Civil Service Reform, 1958," *C.J.E.P.S.*, Vol. XXV, No. 1, February, 1959.

Hodgetts, J. E., *Pioneer Public Service: An Administrative History of the United Canadas, 1841-1867*, Toronto, University of Toronto Press, 1955.

Hodgetts, J. E., "The Civil Service and Policy Formation," *C.J.E.P.S.*, Vol. XXIII, No. 4, November, 1957.

Hodgetts, J. E., "Challenge and Response: A Retrospective View of the Public Service of Canada," *C.P.A.*, Vol. VII, No. 4, December, 1964.

Hodgetts, J. E. and Dwivedi, O. P., "The Growth of Government Employment in Canada," *C.P.A.*, Vol. VII, No. 4, December, 1964.

Hodgetts, J. E., McCloskey, W., Whitaker, R., and Wilson, V.S., *The Biography of an Institution: The Civil Service Commission of Canada, 1908-1967*, Montreal, McGill-Queen's University Press, 1972.

Hodgetts, J. E., *The Canadian Public Service: A Physiology of Government, 1867-1970*, Toronto, University of Toronto Press, 1973.

Hodgetts, J. E., "The Public Service: Its past and the challenge of its future", *C.P.A.*, Vol. 17, No. 1, Spring, 1974.

Hodgetts, J. E., and Dwivedi, O. P., *Provincial Governments as Employers*, Montreal and London, McGill-Queens University Press, 1974.

House of Commons, *Minutes of Proceedings and Evidence, Special Committee on the Civil Service Act*, March 20-June 23, 1961, Ottawa, Queen's Printer, 1961.

Institute of Public Administration of Canada, *Collective Bargaining in the Public Service*, Toronto, I.P.A.C., 1973.

Kwavnick, D., "French Canadians and the Civil Service of Canada," *C.P.A.*, Vol. XI, No. 1, Spring, 1968.

Robertson, G., "Official Responsibilities, Privileges, Conscience and Public Information", *Proceedings and Transactions of the Royal Society of Canada*, Vol. X, 1972, Toronto, University of Toronto Press, 1973.

Tunnoch, G. V., "The Bureau of Government Organization," *C.P.A.*, Vol. VIII, No. 4, December, 1965.

Vaison, R. A., "Collective Bargaining in the Federal Public Service: The Achievement of a Milestone in Personnel Relations," *C.P.A.*, Vol. XII, No. 1, 1969.

Administration

Aucoin, P., and French, R., "The Ministry of State for Science and Technology", *C.P.A.*, Vol. 17, No. 2, Fall, 1974.

Baker, W. A., "Management by Objectives: A Philosophy and Style of Management for the Public Sector," *C.P.A.*, Vol. XII, No. 3, Fall, 1969.

Baker, W. A., "Administrative reform in the federal public service: the first faltering steps", *C.P.A.*, Vol. 16, No. 3, Fall, 1973.

Balls, H. R., "Improving Performance of Public Enterprise through Financial Management and Control," *C.P.A.*, Vol. XIII, No. 1, Spring, 1970.

Barr, J. J., "A Despotism of Boards Choking Alberta," *The Edmonton Journal*, Feb. 21-22-23, 1966 (in three parts).

Bieler, J. H., Burns, R. M., Johnson, A. W., "The Role of the Deputy Minister," *C.P.A.*, Vol. IV, No. 4, December, 1961.

Bridges, The Rt. Hon. Lord, "The Relationship Between Ministers and the Permanent Departmental Head," *C.P.A.*, Vol. VII, No. 3, September, 1964.

Bryden, M., and Gurney, M., "Royal Commission Costs," *Canadian Tax Journal*, Vol. XIV, No. 2, March-April, 1966.

Canada, *Report of the Royal Commission on Government Organization* [Glassco Report], Ottawa, Queen's Printer, 1962-3, 5 vols.

Courtney, J. C., "In Defence of Royal Commissions," *C.P.A.*, Vol. XII, No. 2, Summer, 1969.

Denham, R. A., "The Canadian Auditors General—What is their role?", *C.P.A.*, Vol. 17, No. 2, Summer, 1974.

Des Roches, J. M., "The Evolution of the Organization of Federal Government in Canada," *C.P.A.*, Vol. V, No. 4, December, 1962.

Doern, G. B., and Aucoin, P., *The Structures of Policy-Making in Canada*, Toronto, Macmillan, 1971.

Doern, G. B., and Wilson, V. S., *Issues in Canadian Public Policy*, Toronto, Macmillan, 1974.

Doern, G. B., "Recent Changes in the Philosophy of Policy-making in Canada," *C.J.P.S.*, Vol. IV, No. 2, June, 1971.

Doern, G. B., "The Role of Royal Commissions in the General Policy Process and the Federal-Provincial Relations," *C.P.A.*, Vol. X, No. 4, December, 1967.

Donnelly, M. S., *et al.*, "Aspects of Municipal Administration: A Symposium," *C.P.A.*, Vol. XI, No. 1, Spring, 1968.

Dussault, R., and Bernatchez, R., "La fonction publique canadienne et québécoise", *C.P.A.*, Vol. 15, No. 1, Spring, 1972, and Vol. 15, No. 2, Summer, 1972.

Fera, N., "Review of administrative decisions under the Federal Court Act (1970)," *C.P.A.*, Vol. 14, No. 4, Winter, 1971.

Forrest, D. G., "Performance Appraisal in Government Services," *C.P.A.*, Vol. XII, No. 3, Fall, 1969.

Grasham, W. E., *Canadian Public Administration Bibliography*, Toronto, The Institute of Public Administration of Canada, 1972.

Hanson, H. R., "Inside Royal Commissions," *C.P.A.*, Vol. XII, No. 3, Fall, 1969.

Heeney, A., *The Things that are Caesar's: The Memoirs of a Canadian Public Servant*, Toronto, University of Toronto Press, 1972.

Henderson, G. F., *Federal Royal Commissions in Canada 1867-1966: A Checklist*, Toronto, University of Toronto Press, 1967.

Hicks, M., "The Treasury Board of Canada and its clients: five years of change and administrative reform 1966-1971," *C.P.A.*, Vol. 16, No. 2, Summer, 1973.

Hodgetts, J. E., "The Role of Royal Commissions in Canadian Government," *Proceedings of the Third Annual Conference*, The Institute of Public Administration of Canada, Toronto, 1951.

Hodgetts, J. E., "Should Canada Be De-Commissioned? A Commoner's View on Royal Commissions," *Q.Q.*, Vol. LXX, No. 4, Winter, 1964.

Hodgson, J. S., "Management by Objectives: The Experience of a Federal Government Department," *C.P.A.*, Vol. XVI, No. 3, Fall, 1973.

Hodgson, J. S., *Public Administration*, New York, McGraw-Hill, 1969.

Jolliffe, E. B., "Adjudication in the Canadian Public Service," *McGill Law Journal*, Vol. 20, No. 3, 1974.

Kernaghan, W. D. K., "An Overview of Public Administration in Canada Today," *C.P.A.*, Vol. XI, No. 3, Fall, 1968.

Kernaghan, W. D. K., and Willms, A., (eds.), *Public Administration in Canada*, 2nd ed., Toronto, Methuen, 1971.

Kernaghan, W. D. K., (ed.), *Bureaucracy in Canadian Government*, Toronto, Methuen, 1973, second edition.

Kernaghan, K., "Responsible public bureaucracy: a rationale and a framework for analysis", *C.P.A.*, Vol. 16, No. 4, Winter, 1973.

Kernaghan, K., "Codes of ethnics and administrative responsibility", *C.P.A.*, Vol. 17, No. 4, Winter, 1974.

Kuruvilla, P. K., "Administrative Culture in Canada: some perspectives", *C.P.A.*, Vol. 16, No. 2, Summer, 1973.

Laframboise, H. L., "Administrative reform in the federal public service: signs of a saturation psychosis", *C.P.A.*, Vol. 14, No. 3, Fall, 1971.

Lamontagne, M., "The Influence of the Politician," *C.P.A.*, Vol. XI, No. 3, Fall, 1968.

Lyngseth, D. M., "The Use of Organization and Methods in Canadian Government," *C.P.A.*, Vol. V, No. 4, December, 1962.

Mallory, J. R., "The Minister's Office Staff: An Unreformed Part of the Public Service," *C.P.A.*, Vol. X, No. 1, March, 1967.

McKeough, W. Darcy, "The Relations of Ministers and Civil Servants," *C.P.A.*, Vol. XII, No. 1, Spring, 1969.

McLeod, T. H., "Glassco Commission Report," *C.P.A.*, Vol. VI, No. 4, December, 1963.

Mitchell, H., *et al.*, "To Commission or Not to Commission," *C.P.A.*, Vol. V, No. 3, September, 1962.

Ontario, *Committee on Government Productivity*, Report Number Ten, a Summary, Ontario, Queen's Printer, 1973.

Pitfield, M., "The Shape of Government in the 1980's: Techniques and Instruments for Policy Formulation at the Federal Level," *C.P.A.*, Vol. 19, No. 1, Spring, 1976.

Rea, K. J., and McLeod, J. T., (eds.), *Business and Government in Canada: Selected Readings*, Toronto, Methuen, 1976, second edition.

Ritchie, R. S., Heeney, A. D. P., MacKenzie, M. W., Taylor, M. G., "The Glassco Commission Report," *C.P.A.*, Vol. V, No. 4, December, 1962.

Rowan, M., "A Conceptual Framework for Government Policy-Making," *C.P.A.*, Vol. XIII, No. 3, Autumn, 1970.

Santos, C. R., "Public Administration as Politics," *C.P.A.*, Vol. XII, No. 2, 1969.

Self, P., *Administrative Theories and Politics*, Toronto, University of Toronto Press, 1973.

Shoyama, T. K., "Advisory Committees in Administration," *Proceedings of the Ninth Annual Conference*, The Institute of Public Administration of Canada, Toronto, 1957.

Sharp, M., "Decision-making in the Federal Cabinet," *C.P.A.* Vol. 19, No. 1, Spring, 1976.

Steele, G. G. E., "The Treasury Board as a Control Agency," *C.P.A.*, Vol. IV, No. 2, June, 1961.

Steele, G. G. E., "The Role of the Treasury Board," *Canadian Chartered Accountant*, November, 1961.

Tellier, P. M., "Pour une réforme des cabinets de ministres fédéraux," *C.P.A.*, Vol. XI, No. 4, Winter, 1968.

Tunnoch, G. V., "The Glassco Commission: Did It Cost More Than It Was Worth?" *C.P.A.*, Vol. VII, No. 3, September, 1964.

Walls, C. E. S., "Royal Commissions—Their Influence on Public Policy," *C.P.A.*, Vol. XII, No. 3, Fall, 1969.

White, W. L. and Strick, J. C., "The Treasury Board and Parliament," *C.P.A.*, Vol. X, No. 2, June, 1967.

White, W. L., and Strick, J. C., *Policy, Politics and the Treasury Board in Canadian Government*, Don Mills, Ontario, Science Research Associates, 1970.

Willis, J., "Canadian Administrative Law in Retrospect," *University of Toronto Law Journal*, Vol. 24, 1974.

Willis, J., Eades, J. E., Angus, H. F., *et al.*, "The Administrator as Judge," *Proceedings of the Eighth Annual Conference*, The Institute of Public Administration of Canada, Toronto, 1956.

Willms, A. M., "The Administration of Research on Administration in the Government of Canada," *C.P.A.*, Vol. X, No. 4, December, 1967.

Wilson, H. T., "Rationality and Decision in Administrative Science", *C.J.P.S.*, Vol. VI, No. 2, June, 1973.

Crown Corporations

Ashley, C. A., *The First Twenty-five Years: A Study of Trans-Canada Air Lines*, Toronto, Macmillan, 1963.

Ashley, C. A., and Smails, R. G. H., *Canadian Crown Corporations*, Toronto, Macmillan, 1965.

Barbe, R. P., "Le contrôle parlementaire des enterprises au Canada," *C.P.A.*, Vol. XII, No. 4, Winter, 1969.

Black, E. R., "Canadian Public Policy and the Mass Media," *Canadian Journal of Economics*, Vol. I, No. 2, May, 1968.

Beke, J. A., "Government Regulation of Broadcasting in Canada," *Saskatchewan Law Review*, Vol. 36, No. 1, Fall, 1971, and No. 2, Spring, 1972.

Bridges, The Rt. Hon. Lord, "The Relationship Between Government and Government-Controlled Corporations," *C.P.A.*, Vol. VII, No. 3, September, 1964.

Canada, *Report of the Committee on Broadcasting*, [The Fowler Report], Ottawa, Queen's Printer, 1965.

Corbett, D., *Politics and the Airlines*, Toronto, University of Toronto Press, 1965.

Friedman, W., (ed.), *The Public Corporation: A Comparative Symposium*, Toronto, Carswell, 1954.

Hull, W. H. N., "The Public Control of Broadcasting: The Canadian Australian Experiences," *C.J.E.P.S.*, Vol. XXVIII, No. 1, February, 1962.

Hull, W. H. N., "The Fowler Reports Revisited: A Broadcasting Policy for Canada," Address to the 38th Annual Meeting of the Canadian Political Science Association, Sherbrooke, P.Q., June 9, 1966.

Irvine, A. G., "The delegation of authority to crown corporations," *C.P.A.*, Vol. 14, No. 4, Winter, 1971.

Kristjanson, K., "Crown Corporations: Administrative Responsibility and Public Accountability," *C.P.A.*, Vol. XI, No. 4, Winter, 1968.

Peers, F. W., *The Politics of Canadian Broacasting 1920-51*, Toronto, University of Toronto Press, 1965.

Shea, A. A., *Broadcasting, The Canadian Way*, Montreal, Harvest House, 1963.

Spry, G., "The Decline and Fall of Canadian Broadcasting," *Q.Q.*, Vol. LXVIII, No. 2, Summer, 1961.

Weir, E. A., *The Struggle for National Broadcasting in Canada*, Toronto, McClelland and Stewart, 1965.

Administrative Secrecy

Abel, A. S., "Administrative Secrecy," *C.P.A.*, Vol. XI, No. 4, Winter, 1968.

Canada, Privy Council Office, *The Provision of Government Information*, [The Wall Report], Ottawa, April, 1974, printed as an appendix to the Minutes of Proceedings and Evidence of the Standing Joint Committee on Regulations and Other Statutory Instruments, June 25, 1975.

Premont, J., "Publicité de documents officiels," *C.P.A.*, Vol. XI, No. 4, Winter, 1968.

Rowat, "How Much Administrative Secrecy?", *C.J.E.P.S.*, Vol. XXXI, No. 4, November, 1965. (See also "Comments", *ibid.*, Vol. XXXII, No. 1, February, 1966.)

Thomas, P. G., "Secrecy and Publicity in Canadian Government," *C.P.A.*, Vol. 19, No. 1, Spring, 1976.

Ombudsman

Anderson, S. V., *Canadian Ombudsman Proposals*, Berkeley, University of California, 1966.

Friedmann, K. A., *Complaining: Comparative Aspects of Complaint Behaviour and Attitudes Towards Complaining in Canada and Britain*, Beverley Hills, Sage, 1974.

Friedmann, K. A., "Controlling Bureaucracy: Attitudes in the Alberta Public Service Towards the Ombudsman," *C.P.A.*, Vol. 19, No. 1, Spring, 1976.

Rowat, D. C., "An Ombudsman Scheme for Canada," *C.J.E.P.S.*, Vol. XXVII, No. 4, November, 1963.

Rowat, D. C., "Recent Developments in Ombudsmanship," *C.P.A.*, Vol. X, No. 1, March, 1967.

Rowat, D. C., *The Ombudsman: Citizen's Defender*, Toronto, University of Toronto Press, 1965.

Rowat, D. C., *The Ombudsman Plan: Essays on the World-wide Spread of an Idea*, Carleton Library No. 67, McClelland and Stewart, 1973.

16

THE JUDICIAL PROCESS

The judiciary and the judicial process do not usually attract as much attention from political scientists and the public as do certain other aspects of Canadian politics. However, in recent years there has been considerable interest displayed in legal matters, no doubt in part because of the increased popular concern since the nineteen sixties with civil rights and the judicial process and partly because Prime Minister Trudeau, himself a former legal scholar, has attempted to initiate a number of constitutional and juridical changes.

One positive result of this new interest has been the improvement of the administration of justice by the federal government and a number of provinces. Sufficient progress has been made in this regard that it did not seem fair or accurate to repeat in this edition the scathing criticisms of the judicial process that were levelled against it by Sidney Katz in an article which appeared in the second edition (pp. 247-255), although it is too much to believe that some of his strictures do not still apply to some jurisdictions.

This chapter begins with Professor Peter Russell's original article on the Supreme Court's interpretation of the written Canadian constitution, the British North America Act, since the Court became the final appellate tribunal in 1949. Students who wish to read the actual decisions by the Judicial Committee of the Privy Council or by the Supreme Court of Canada in major constitutional cases should consult the references to sources in the bibliography in this chapter. They will find two paperbacks readily available and very helpful. Both appear in the Carleton Library Series. They are Professor Russell's *Leading Constitutional Decisions*, and Professor W. R. Lederman's *The Courts and the Canadian Constitution*.

The second item in this chapter is new. Professor Russell has written it for this edition of *Politics: Canada*. The article continues Professor Russell's analysis of the Supreme Court for the period from 1960 to the present. It should be noted that it contains a section on recent significant cases dealing with civil rights, which is the subject of Chapter 17.

The four items which follow explain some of the major changes that have been effected or proposed in our judicial system recently. The first article summarizes briefly the essentials of the new Federal Court of Canada, which was created in 1970 to replace the Exchequer Court. The next item notes the principal suggestions that have been offered in the past few years for reforming the Supreme Court of Canada. At the time of writing the subject is still under discussion. The appointment procedure, however, has been improved, as Geoffrey Stevens' article explains. Salaries for federal judges have been augmented also.The new salary scale is summarized in a table. The chapter concludes with an amusing account of one of the few instances in which a federal judge has been removed from the bench.

The bibliography in this chapter includes references to the judiciary in general, as well as to judicial interpretation. The bibliography on civil liberties will be found at the end of Chapter 17.

THE SUPREME COURT'S INTERPRETATION OF THE CONSTITUTION FROM 1949 to 1960*

Peter H. Russell

In December, 1949 the Supreme Court of Canada became the final court of appeal for Canada. This was accomplished by the simple expedient of an Act of the Dominion Parliament, the constitutional validity of which had been previously established by a 1947 decision of the Privy Council. With the exception of cases in which the litigation had begun prior to December, 1949, no longer could aggrieved litigants carry their case across the Atlantic and plead before the Judicial Committee of the Privy Council that the decision of a Canadian court be reversed. Now a Canadian court, appointed by the Canadian Government, staffed by Canadian jurists, was Canada's highest judicial organ. Canada had passed another —almost the final—milestone on her road to nationhood.

At the time this change was affected it was only logical that interest in it was focussed primarily on the area of constitutional law. In a federal state with a written constitution defining the boundaries of the national and regional legislatures, the court of last resort, through the process of judicial review, can have an enormous influence on the legislative policies pursued by both levels of government. As Professor Kelsen has said, "A court which has the power to annul laws is consequently an organ of legislative power." Indeed, it was as the arbiter of our Constitution— the British North America Act—that the Judicial Committee had become a centre of controversy in Canada. Now, with that tribunal giving way to the Supreme Court of Canada, there was a great deal of speculation as to

* Published originally in this book with permission of the author, who is a member of the Department of Political Economy, University of Toronto.

how this transition would affect the interpretation of the B.N.A. Act.

Looking forward to the new era of judicial autonomy, two rival patterns of hopes and fears were evident. By far the most vociferous viewpoint was expressed by the Privy Council's critics. They had attacked the Judicial Committee for what they regarded as its unjustified and unwise reduction of Dominion power and they now hoped that an indigenous highest court would emancipate Canada from the stultifying effects of their Lordships' constitutional conceptions. On the other hand, there were those, mainly in French-speaking Canada, who cherished the Privy Council's constitutional handiwork as a vital bulwark of provincial autonomy against the onslaught of centralizing forces. To these, the abolition of appeals looked ominous. The inclusion of a provision in the Supreme Court Amendment Act of 1949, which guaranteed that three of the nine Supreme Court judges would always come from Quebec, did little to offset their fears. They were more impressed by the fact that the Dominion executive appointed all the judges. Hence, those who subscribed to this school of thought were inclined to heed the warnings of those theoreticians of federalism who insisted that to permit one level of government the exclusive power of appointing the umpire of the federal system constituted a serious deviation from "pure federalism."

It is against this background of speculations that we shall examine the Supreme Court's record of constitutional adjudication from the abolition of appeals in 1949 until the end of 1960. The cases discussed deal only with questions concerning the division of legislative powers. With each of the major issues some attempt has been made to indicate the major contrasts, if any, between the Supreme Court's approach and that of the Privy Council.

The most serious charge in the traditional indictment of the Privy Council's interpretation of the B.N.A. Act was that it had reduced Parliament's power to legislate for "the peace, order and good government of Canada" from the position of a residual clause in the division of powers to the status of an emergency power. For those centralists who pressed for a reinstatement of the Dominion's General power, Lord Simon's judgment in the *Canadian Temperance Federation case* of 1946 had provided a new ray of hope. There, Lord Simon, in maintaining the validity of what was virtually the same statute as was involved in Russell v. The Queen, had gone a long way towards undermining the authority of the emergency doctrine. The true test, he stated, of whether the Dominion's General power could be invoked to uphold legislation was not the existence of an emergency but "the real subject matter of the legislation: if it is such that it goes beyond local or provincial concern or interests and must from its inherent nature be the concern of the Dominion as a whole. . . ." The impact of this dictum was partially offset by two later decisions of the Privy Council which returned to the emergency doctrine as the justification for bringing legislation under the General power. Nevertheless, Lord Simon's words were now part of the record, so that, even if the newly emancipated Supreme Court were to assume the yoke of *stare decisis* and consider itself bound by its predecessor's decisions, this opinion could provide the necessary support for extending the scope of the Peace, Order, and Good Government clause beyond emergency situations.

Despite the apparent centrality of "Peace, Order, and Good Government," it has been a key issue in only two of the constitutional cases that have been before the Supreme Court in the past decade. In the first of these cases, *Reference re. Validity of Wartime Leasehold Regulation* (1950), the court was asked to pass on the constitutionality of the Federal Government's rent-control regulations. These orders-in-council had been made under the authority of the National Emergency Transitional Powers Act, which continued those provisions of the War Measures Act that Parliament had deemed necessary for dealing with the economic dislocations arising out of the war. Although the court referred to the Peace, Order, and Good Government clause as the constitutional support for the regulations, in doing so it did not have to go beyond the emergency doctrine. Even this was significant in as much as a number of judges stated that unless there was "clear and immutable" evidence to the contrary, they would not question Parliament's declaration (in the preamble to the Act) that an emergency exists. This policy in the context of an enduring "cold war" situation might well make even the emergency conception of the General power a more fertile source of legislative capacity. It is worth noting that during the 1950s two of the statutes which entailed the widest extension of Dominion power were the Defence Production Act and the Emergency Powers Act.

It was the case of *Johannesson v. West St. Paul* (1952) that provided a more revealing test of the Supreme Court's treatment of "Peace, Order, and Good Government." Here, the constitutional issue revolved around the competing claims of the Dominion Parliament and the Manitoba Legislature to make laws regulating the location of aerodromes. The court was unanimous in sustaining the Dominion's Aeronautics Act and in finding the Manitoba legislation and regulations *ultra vires*. Certainly the most significant aspect of this decision was the test that the court used to determine whether the regulation of civil aviation was a subject-matter of legislation embraced by the "Peace, Order, and Good Government" clause. On this point, four of the five judges who wrote opinions explicitly accepted Lord Simon's test of national importance. Mr. Justice Kellock used these words: "Once the decision is made that a matter is of national importance, so as to fall within the peace, order and good government clause, the provinces cease to have any legitimate jurisdiction with regard thereto and the Dominion jurisdiction is exclusive." Of course the court could dress up this approach in the cautious language of *stare decisis* by referring to Lord Simon's formulation of the national aspect test and Lord Sanky's allusion to the national importance of Aeronautics in the Aeronautics Reference of 1932. But this cannot disguise the fact that in selecting these cases a choice was exercised between contrasting judicial traditions. *Stare decisis* might just as easily have permitted resort to the 1937 Reference cases in which national importance, aside from emergency situations, was rejected as a proper test for invoking the General power.

But it would be a mistake to accept the Johannesson case as a decisive breakthrough. It must be pointed out that the court's validation of the Dominion's Aeronautics Act did not, in itself, constitute an expansion of the central legislature's powers. The Aeronautics Act had been validated previously by the Privy Council in 1932 (although on that occasion Section 132—the treaty implementing power—rather than the General power had been singled out as the basis of the Act's constitutionality). The effect of the national importance test in the Johannesson case was essentially negative; it prevented a province from encroaching upon a field of legislation already occupied by the Dominion. It may well be that the Supreme Court would be less prepared to adopt Lord Simon's conception of "Peace, Order, and Good Government" if it was required to support the entry of Parliament into an activity already subject to provincial law.

Supreme Court cases since Johannesson v. West St. Paul throw no light on this conjecture. Thus, for the centralist cause, the Johannesson case represents encouragement but hardly victory. The enumerated powers of Section 91, far more than "the residuary power," have served as the vehicle for judicial initiatives. These initiatives, as we shall now see, have generally leaned towards the expansion of the Dominion's powers.

The Judicial Committee's attenuation of the Dominion's Trade and Commerce power had come in for almost as much criticism as its treatment of the General power. There had never been much quarrel with the assumption that some limits would have to be set to Section 91 (2) if a reasonable measure of provincial autonomy were to be preserved. But the restrictive nature of those limits and the inflexible way in which they had been delineated by the judiciary had been the source of much discontent. Although the Trade and Commerce power was occasionally employed by the Privy Council to circumscribe the provinces' powers of trade regulation and as one of a number of supports for Dominion legislation, its emasculation has proceeded so far that as an independent source of constitutional power for significant legislation in the field of economic regulation it had been rendered very nearly useless. Further, for the purpose of drawing a clear line between those forms of trade which could be regulated by the Dominion and those which could be regulated by the provinces, the Privy Council had adopted the categories of inter-provincial and intra-provincial trade. These categories when applied uncritically to the activities of an interdependent economy resulted in a division of jurisdiction which precluded efficacious legislation by either the Dominion or the Provinces. The debilitating effects of this approach were felt most severely in connection with marketing legislation. Where produce at the point at which regulation was desirable could not be segregated into that destined for the provincial market and that destined for the extra-provincial market, and where delegation of legislative powers between Parliament and provincial legislatures was precluded, it appeared that judicial construction of the B.N.A. Act had produced a constitutional hiatus.

Since 1949 the Supreme Court has delivered two judgments that cast some light upon its treatment of the Trade and Commerce power. While neither case marks a revolutionary approach, taken together they suggest, to use Professor Laskin's words, "a decided thaw in the hitherto frozen federal commerce power." In the first of these cases, *Reference re. (Ontario) Farm Products Marketing Act* (1957), the court was asked to answer eight questions concerning certain provisions of and regulations under an Ontario marketing Act. Since it was provincial legislation whose validity was being examined, the Dominion's Trade and Commerce power was referred to only negatively as limiting the application of Ontario's marketing schemes to intra-provincial trade. Even so, the way in which a majority of judges elucidated the distinction between intra-provincial trade (subject to provincial jurisdiction) and inter-provincial or export trade (subject to Dominion jurisdiction) suggested a large area in which Head No. 2 of Section 91 could serve as a constitutional foundation for national economic policies. The court's relatively liberal appraisal of Section 91 (2) did not have any direct bearing upon the outcome of the case: all the judges accepted at face value the wording of the opening question of the Reference Order, to the effect that the "Act applies only in the case of intra-provincial transactions." The significance of this case, then, is to be measured not in terms of its substantive results but in terms of the pragmatic approach to constitutional adjudication which it implies. This approach was most evident in Mr. Justice Rand's opinion from which the following passage is quoted:

> Trade arrangements reaching the dimensions of world agreements are now a commonplace; interprovincial trade, in which the Dominion is a single market, is of similar importance, and equally vital to the economic functioning of the country as a whole. The Dominion power implies responsibility for promoting and maintaining the vigour and growth of trade beyond provincial confines, and the discharge of this function must remain unembarrassed by local trade impediments.

What stands out here by way of contrast with earlier judicial efforts to divide jurisdiction over trading activities is that the point of departure is not fixed categories of Dominion and Provincial economic responsibility but rather judicial notice of the evolving requirements of a national economy.

In the second case, *Murphy v. C.P.R. and A. G. Canada* (1958), the Trade and Commerce power was invoked as the basis for the constitutionality of the Canadian Wheat Board Act. Here, the court showed that it was prepared to regard the federal commerce power as an independent source of legislative authority broad enough to sustain a Dominion marketing Act, which is of crucial importance to the national economy. However, the facts of this case were such as to qualify the significance of the court's use of Section 91 (2). The impugned provisions of the Act came clearly under the heading "Regulation of international and inter-provincial trade in wheat" and the plaintiff, Murphy, who was challenging the C.P.R.'s refusal to handle his wheat because he had failed to comply with the provisions of the Act, was clearly shipping wheat across provincial boundaries.

The implications of this decision appeared of much greater consequence when the Manitoba Court of Appeal referred to it in the case of *Regina v. Klassen* (1959). Here, in contrast to the Murphy case, the facts posed a more severe challenge to the traditional bifurcation of legislative authority over trade into intra-provincial and extra-provincial compartments. The issue in the Klassen case was whether regulations made under the Canadian Wheat Board Act could be applied to a feed-mill whose business was carred on entirely within a province. Drawing upon the Supreme Court's decision in the Murphy case, the Manitoba court upheld this application of the Dominion statute to *intra-provincial* transactions on the pragmatic grounds that, if the intra-provincial market was severed from the scope of the Act, the whole attempt to create an orderly scheme for marketing the annual wheat crop would be rendered impossible. Considerations of economic policy took precedence over legalistic categories.

From the above cases it seems fair to conclude that if since 1949 there has not been a positive expansion of the scope of the federal commerce power, the Supreme Court has at least demonstrated a more pragmatic and less legalistic approach to the general problem of adjusting national and local interests in marketing matters. Even so, much of the court's work in this area may now be rendered largely academic by its treatment of the delegation question.

During the 1930s and 1940s many of those who viewed the Privy Council's "watertight compartments" treatment of the division of powers as a frustrating obstacle to the effective handling of some of Canada's major social and economic problems looked to the delegation device as the most likely way of hurdling the constitutional barrier. If the Judicial Committee in the course of interpreting the B.N.A. Act had effected a division of authority inappropriate to the needs and resources of the provinces and the Dominion, then, it was argued, at least the legislatures and Parliament should be free to delegate their powers to one another. As for the constitutionality of the delegation device, this question, prior to 1949, had not be canvassed by either the Privy Council or the Supreme Court. The Privy Council's only pronouncement on the subject was made by Lord Watson in 1899, and this was to the effect that delegation by a provincial legislature to Parliament or vice versa was invalid. However, this was simply a remark thrown out in the course of argument and was not central to the case. In his Appendix to the Sirois Commission Report, J. A. Corry, after a thorough examination of the issue, had concluded that it was still an open question.

Thus, when the Supreme Court in 1951 and 1952 was directly faced with the delegation issue, it was breaking rather new and significant ground. The net result of these two cases was paradoxical: first, direct delegation was banned, and, then, indirect delegation was approved. In the first case, the *Nova Scotia Inter-delegation* case (1951), the court declared Nova Scotia's Bill 136 *ultra vires*. This Bill constituted an attempt by the Nova Scotia legislature to delegate a part of its law-making authority (in this case in the field of labour law) directly to the Parliament of Canada. In addition, the Bill looked forward to Parliament delegating part of its legislative authority to the Nova Scotia legislature. The judges based their decision on the "watertight compartments" view of federalism. In Mr. Justice Rand's words, this type of delegation was "utterly foreign to the conception of a federal organization."

If the advocates of flexible federalism were at all dismayed by this decision, their anguish was short-lived. The following year, in the case of *P.E.I. Potato Marketing Board v. H. B. Willis Inc.,* the Supreme Court designed an escape from its doctrine of the Nova Scotia Inter-delegation case. Here the issue concerned an attempt by the Dominion in the Agricultural Products Marketing Act (1949) to delegate to provincial marketing boards the power of regulating inter-provincial and export trade in agricultural products. The court ruled that this manner of delegation was constitutionally valid. In order to reach this decision the court distinguished the Nova Scotia case on the grounds that, there, legislative power was being delegated to other legislatures, whereas, in this case, the recipient of the delegated power was the subordinate agency of another legislature. The latter was justified because it involved merely an attempt by Parliament "to employ as its own a Board, or agency, for the purpose of carrying out its own legislation."

Whether or not one agrees with the logic of this distinction, it must be acknowledged that the decision in the Willis case opened a significant chink in the dike which separates Section 91 of the B.N.A. Act from Section 92. Indeed, on at least two occasions since then the Provinces and the Dominion have resorted to this device of "indirect delegation" to circumvent the effects of other judicial decisions. The most striking example of this occurred after the Privy Council brought down its decision in the case of *A.-G. Ont. v. Winner* (1954). Since the original litigation in the Winner case had begun prior to the abolition of appeals, it was possible to appeal the Supreme Court's decision to the Privy Council. The outcome of this appeal was a victory for the Dominion: the Judicial Committee amended the Supreme Court's judgment and found that the Dominion alone had the power to regulate the operations of inter-provincial bus lines. Within two months representatives of the Federal Government and nine Provinces met to consider the implications of the Winner case. As a result of this meeting the Dominion Parliament passed the Motor Vehicle Transport Act, which was designed to delegate back to provincial licensing boards any of the powers over extra-provincial motor carriers that the Dominion might have won in the Winner case.

Parliament used the same technique again in 1957 to overcome the consequences of another judicial decision. This time, the ruling to be circumvented was part of the decision in Reference re. Ontario Farm Products Marketing Act (see above). In answer to one of the questions in this Reference, the court found that Ontario's incorporation of licensing fees, in its marketing regulations, which were designed to equalize the returns of producers, constituted indirect taxation and was therefore *ultra vires*. Following this, the Dominion Parliament, working on the assumption that a legislative power denied to the Provinces is within the Dominion's orbit, amended its Agricultural Products Marketing Act and delegated the power of imposing equalization levies to provincial marketing agencies. The ironic finale to this episode occured four years later,

when the Supreme Court in the case of *Crawford & Hillside Farm Dairy Ltd.,
et al. v. A.-G. B.C.* (1960) apparently reversed its position on provincial
marketing levies. In this case the court ruled that where a provincial
marketing scheme attempts to equalize the returns of producers this is
still legislation in relation to trade and not indirect taxation. Consequently, provincial marketing levies such as had been declared *ultra vires*
were now valid so long as they applied only to intra-provincial trade. This
decision thus rendered superfluous Parliament's earlier amendment to
the Agricultural Products Marketing Act.

The Supreme Court's validation of the "indirect delegation" device has
undoubtedly opened up another channel of legislative co-operation in the
Canadian federal system. This device, when both levels of government
are willing to use it, makes it much easier for the national and local
legislatures to overcome the difficulties of divided jurisdiction or, as the
aftermath to the Winner case suggests, enables them to accommodate
political pressures which are not recognized by the courts. In a word,
where it is applicable, this device removes the sense of finality from the
process of constitutional adjudication.

One of the major laments of the centralist critics of the Privy Council
was that tribunal's invalidation of the Dominion's Industrial Disputes
Investigation Act (the Lemieux Act) in the Snider case of 1925. The basic
purpose of the Lemieux Act was to establish collective bargaining
machinery that would be applicable to all mines, transportation and
communication agencies, and public service utilities. By finding this statute *ultra vires*, the Privy Council had apparently disqualified the
Dominion's efforts to provide a procedure for handling industrial disputes that were national in scope.

In 1955 the Supreme Court in yet another Reference case was confronted with the task of delineating legislative authority in relation to
collective bargaining arrangements. In this *Reference re. Validity of Industrial Relations and Disputes Investigation Act* the court unanimously found
the federal statute *intra vires*. The decisive difference between this Act and
the Lemieux Act which it had replaced was that it applied only to those
activities that were within the legislative authority of Parliament. Consequently, this judgment confirmed the bifurcation of power in the field of
labour relations. Whether labour relations in a particular industry are
subject to federal or provincial law depends on whether that industry is
one that can generally be brought under one of the heads of Section 91 or
of Section 92. For instance, in the 1955 Reference, the court was also
asked to decide whether employees of a Toronto stevedoring company
were subject to the Dominion's Industrial Relations and Disputes Investigations Act. A majority of the court answered this question in the
affirmative on the grounds that, since the Company serviced only boats
engaged in foreign trade, its activities were subject to Head 10 (Navigation and Shipping) of Section 91.

Mr. V. C. MacDonald has described the Supreme Court's treatment of
the labour relations question as "a truly gigantic step from the conclusion
of the Privy Council in Snider's case. . . ." This perhaps overstates the
case. Certainly the 1955 Reference contrasts with the Snider case to the

extent that it denies provincial jurisdiction over collective bargaining in *some* industries. But it must also be noticed that the Supreme Court judgment does not uphold the argument that had prevailed in the lower courts in Canada prior to the appeal of the Snider case to the Privy Council; namely, that the settlement of major industrial disputes was a distinct and independent area of legislative activity and as such was subject to the Dominion's power to legislate for the Peace, Order, and Good Government of Canada. The principal way in which the 1955 decision might lead to an expansion of Federal jurisdiction over labour relations is through the judiciary adopting a generous construction of those industrial activities that are subject to Dominion authority. This has already happened on more than one occasion. In the *Pronto Uranium case*, for example, Judge McLennan of the Ontario Supreme Court ruled that labour relations in uranium mines were subject to the Dominion's legislation because activities related to the production of atomic energy came under the Peace, Order, and Good Government clause.

In the B.N.A. Act there is, of course, nothing comparable to the American Bill of Rights, which explicitly prohibits local and federal legislatures from violating certain basic rights. However, judicial review can affect civil liberties by determining whether the Dominion or the Provinces have the power to restrict fundamental freedom. Prior to 1949 this issue had not been explored in a definitive way by the Privy Council. Consequently, the three constitutional cases in the 1950s which raised civil liberty questions provided rather fertile soil for indigenous judicial seeds.

The three leading cases in this area are also of special interest to the political scientist because they tended to push the Supreme Court into a definite posture in regard to one of the most significant areas of conflicting values in Canadian life. On the surface the three cases would appear admirably suited to play such a role. They all concerned provincial legislation that curtailed some aspect of religious or political freedom; in all three cases it was the Province of Quebec whose legislation was under attack; in all three cases that province's Court of Appeal had upheld the legislation; in all three cases the Supreme Court reversed the decision of the lower court.

Saumur v. Quebec (1953) was the most perplexing of the three. In this case, Saumur, a Jehovah's Witness, challenged a Quebec City by-law forbidding the distribution in the streets of any book, pamphlet, or tract without the permission of the Chief of Police. In a narrow sense Saumur won his case. The Supreme Court on a five to four vote found that the by-law did not prohibit the Jehovah's Witnesses from distributing their literature in the streets. In a broader and more significant sense Saumur and those who view with alarm provincial laws authorizing the police to control the dissemination of opinions lost their case. In the opinions of five of the judges, including the three from Quebec, it was within provincial competence to limit freedom of religious expression. The other four, rejecting the view that the phrase "civil rights" in Section 92 (13) refers to liberties such as freedom of religion, ruled against provincial competence in this matter. Saumur's victory, then, did not turn upon constitutional grounds but upon the much narrower opinion of Mr. Justice Kerwin. The latter conceded the constitutional validity of the by-law but reasoned that it did not apply to the Jehovah's Witnesses because it had to give way to the Quebec Freedom of Worship Act. Given the narrow basis of Kerwin's judgment, the Quebec legislature made quick work of the Saumur decision by amending the Freedom of Worship Act so that Jehovah's Witness publications would be clearly classified under the exceptions to the Act.

In contrast to the Saumur case, the case of *Birks & Sons v. Montreal* (1955) was more productive of solid constitutional fruit. The Quebec statute attacked in this case by Henry Birks & Co. required that store-keepers should close their shops on six Catholic Holy days. In a surprising display of unanimity all nine members of the court found the legislation *ultra vires*. Two elements of this decision stand out. In the first place, the court's basic point of departure from the Quebec Court of Queen's Bench lay in classifying the Act as one whose main concern was religious observance and not the regulation of working hours. Second, and this is the important constitutional doctrine, the court ruled that such legislation, which makes the failure to observe a certain religious practice a crime, falls under Parliament's power to enact criminal law (Section (91)).

Certainly the court's most prominent treatment of political freedoms arose in the case of *Switzman v. Elbling and A.-G. Quebec* (1957), which invalidated Quebec's Communist Propaganda Act. This Act, popularly known as the "Padlock Law," prohibited the use of houses for Communist meetings and banned the printing and publication of literature propagating the Communist ideology. The Supreme Court's decision here was in line with its earlier decision in the Birks case. With only Mr. Justice Taschereau dissenting, the court determined that the "pith and substance" of the Act was the suppression of Communism and, as such, it was beyond provincial jurisdiction. Once again it was the Dominion's power to legislate in relation to Criminal Law to which the majority referred as the constitutional basis for legislation restricting civil liberty. But, more spectacular and potentially of greater importance to the question of civil liberties in the Canadian Constitution was the doctrine formulated by Mr. Justice Rand and supported by two of his fellow judges, Kellock and Abbott.

Mr. Justice Rand, who has been described by Professor Laskin as the "greatest expositor of democratic public law which Canada has known," throughout these cases attempted to discover within the B.N.A. Act an implicit Bill of Rights that would at least protect fundamental liberties from abridgement by provincial legislatures. In the Winner case of 1951, Rand first brought up the notion of the "Rights of a Canadian Citizen." According to this doctrine, the institution of a common Canadian citizenship was an essential by-product of the nation created by the constitutional Act of 1867. This "citizenship" bears in its wake certain fundamental rights which all Canadians must enjoy and which are constitutionally beyond the range of provincial power. In this case, the particular "Right of a Canadian Citizen," which Rand elucidated as grounds for limiting the scope of New Brunswick's Motor Carrier Act, was the right to the use of highways. In the Saumur case, Rand referred to the phrase "a constitution similar in principle to that of the United Kingdom," which appears in the preamble to the B.N.A. Act, as the constitutional support of fundamental freedoms. This phrase, he reasoned, implies government by parliamentary institutions, a necessary condition of which is freedom of the press and freedom of public discussion. Rand developed this thesis further in the Padlock Law case. Again, he saw in the preamble to the B.N.A. Act a political theory that demands free speech and a free press as essential conditions of a Parliamentary Democracy. Mr. Justice Abbott went one step further than Rand and suggested that this implicit guarantee of free speech meant that "Parliament itself could not abrogate this right of discussion and debate."

Impressive as Rand's ideas may be as exercises in political philosophy, it must be noted that they are still some way from becoming a settled part of our Constitutional Law. In none of the cases in which Rand enunciated his thesis was it either endorsed by a majority or the turning point in the decision. Indeed, the late Chief Justice Mr. Kerwin in the Saumur case explicitly disavowed Rand's use of the preamble to the B.N.A. Act. Nevertheless, while the court as a whole may have declined to be as adventurous as Mr. Justice Rand, it has still partially clarified the constitutional position of civil liberties. After the Birks case and the Padlock Law case, the Dominion's Criminal Law power looms as an effective constitutional restraint on provincial laws that aim at circumscribing political and religious liberties.

Thus far we have examined Supreme Court decisions in those areas of constitutional interpretation which have traditionally attracted the attention of students of Canadian federalism. But these cases by no means give a full picture of the Supreme Court's performance as the umpire of the federal system. In addition to the 12 cases mentioned above, there were 26 other constitutional cases before the Supreme Court in the period under review. While these cases may not have raised what have come to be regarded as the classic issues of judicial review, in many instances they did result in decisions that had a significant impact on the legislative capacities of the Provinces and the Dominion. In the past, political scientists have often been so dazzled by the court's treatment of the General power and Property and Civil Rights that they have been somewhat blind to the importance of some of the other enumerated powers as sources of legislative authority and issues of judicial review.

Two of these rather neglected issues which were prominent in the 1950s were the Dominion's Criminal Law power (Section 91 (27)) and the question of taxation. We have already seen in the Civil Liberties cases how Parliament's Criminal Law power was invoked against provincial attempts to legislate with respect to religious practice and political freedoms. In nine other cases the Criminal Law power was at the centre of the constitutional dispute. In two of these cases the court invoked Section 91 (27) to uphold Dominion statutes. The most important of these was *Goodyear Tire & Rubber Co. v. the Queen* (1956) in which the court used Head 27 of Section 91 to sustain provisions of the Combines Investigation Act. This judgment served as a reminder of the extent to which 91 (27) can support legislation pursuing economic policy goals. Mr. Justice Rand declared that "it is accepted that head (27) of Section 91 . . . is to be interpreted in its widest sense. . . ." Against this broad interpretation of the Criminal Law power must be balanced the court's tendency to uphold provincial legislation that was being attacked as an infringement of Head 27 of Section 91. This was the basic question in the seven other "criminal law" cases, and in all but one the court found the impugned provincial legislation *intra vires*.

The constitutional prohibition of indirect provincial taxation was the central issue in five cases. It is beyond the scope of this article to examine these cases in any detail, but two cases are significant enough to merit some comment. In *Cairns Construction Ltd. v. Government of Saskatchewan* (1960) the court ruled that Saskatchewan's Education & Hospitalization Tax was *intra vires*. This was a retail sales tax, so that the court's decision provided a further constitutional underpinning for what has become an increasingly important source of provincial revenue. On the other hand, in *Texeda Mines Ltd. v. A.-G. B.C.*, by invalidating British Columbia's Mineral Property Tax, the Court, through Mr. Justice Locke, indicated a severe limitation to the province's powers of taxation. In this instance, although the B.C. tax in form resembled a Saskatchewan tax that had been found valid by the court in 1952, in substance it was ten times higher than the Saskatchewan tax and, consequently, it was distinguished and invalidated.

When the Privy Council was Canada's final court of appeal, the method it employed in constitutional adjudication came in for almost as much discussion as the substance of its decisions. Most of the Privy Council's English-speaking critics were advocates of judicial activism. According to this conception of judicial review, the court's function in a country with a written constitution was to adjust the terms of the constitutional text to the rapidly changing requirements of a dynamic environment. These judicial activists singled out the Privy Council's apparently strict adherence to the principle of *stare decisis* and its literalistic interpretation of the B.N.A. Act as the aspects of its method which precluded the kind of judicial statesmanship they advocated. While the Privy Council's critics looked forward with some optimism to the Supreme Court's emancipation, there were others, not surprisingly associated with the provincial rights view of federalism, who were alarmed at the prospect of any major deviation by the Supreme Court from the Privy Council's traditions. Parliamentary spokesmen of this school of thought went so far as to move, unsuccessfully, an amendment to the Act abolishing appeals which would have made previous Privy Council decisions binding on the Supreme Court.

It is extremely difficult to summarize with any degree of precision the Supreme Court's record with regard to these matters of method. As far as *stare decisis* is concerned, it is clear that the court is under no statutory compulsion to adopt the earlier rulings of the Privy Council as the bases for its own judgments. At the same time it is also clear that *in practice* the Supreme Court since 1949 has never explicitly overruled a Privy Council decision or, indeed, any of its own previous judgments. Thus, the court appears to be somewhere between the position of the United States Supreme Court and its own position prior to the abolition of appeals: unlike its American counterpart it has not officially declared its readiness to discard old judicial precedents when they no longer seem suitable but, in contrast to its own pre-1949 position, it is relatively free to work out its own policy of interpreting and applying Privy Council precedents. This rather ambiguous position becomes, perhaps, more comprehensible if we acknowledge that even when a court formally follows a practice of *stare decisis* this does not necessarily result in as inflexible and predictable a course of decisions as is sometimes suggested. Given rival precedents on the same general question and the art of distinguishing previous cases as different from the one at hand, it is entirely possible for a court, while looking exclusively to past cases for the premises of its reasoning, in fact so to select, ignore and distinguish cases that it is able to evolve its own doctrines of constitutional law.

Stare decisis is naturally linked to that other controversial aspect of judicial review—the unimaginative, literalistic interpretation of the B.N.A. Act as opposed to the statesmanlike adaptation of the constitutional text. Which of these alternative approaches has the Supreme Court tended to follow? Again it is impossible to give a simple answer. It would be misleading to brand the Supreme Court's approach as either distinctively literal or distinctively liberal. If any contrast can be drawn here between the Supreme Court's record and that of its predecessor, it would be in terms of an increasing degree of pragmatism in the court's interpretation of the division of powers, especially in areas affecting economic welfare. In a number of cases, individual judges have based their reasoning not so much on the words of the B.N.A. Act as on the adverse practical consequences they felt would flow from an alternative decision to the one they were giving. For instance, Mr. Justice Locke, in the Johannesson case, based his opinion against provincial regulation of aerodromes partly on his estimation of the "intolerable" state of affairs that would result if the national development of airlines was obstructed by local regulations. Similarly, the court's examination of the concepts of intra-provincial and extra-provincial trade in the Ontario Farm Products Marketing Reference was much more concerned with elaborating a workable scheme for the division of legislative authority than with a close textual scrutiny of the B.N.A. Act. Of course, these are only isolated examples, but still it is in these occasional outbursts of functionalism that we are apt to find some vindication of Edward Blake's opinion that the great merit of a Canadian Course of last resort would be in its possession of "the daily learning and experience which Canadians, living under the Canadian Constitution, acquire . . . and which can be given only by residence on the spot."

There is one other aspect of the Supreme Court's method that calls for some comment; that is its practice of having a number of judges write opinions in each case—even in cases where all the judges reach the same result. This is in marked contrast to the Judicial Committee's custom of publishing only one opinion for every case. No matter how divided their Lordships may have been in private, their public face was always one of unanimity. In contrast to this, the Supreme Court, in the 37 constitutional cases it handled in the period under review, on the average included four opinions in each case.

This rather different practice has been a mixed blessing. The inclusion of the minority's opinion, when the court is split, has the undoubted advantage of displaying the alternative principles of interpretation upon which the case hinged. Also, we know from American experience that the minority opinion of today can be become the majority opinion of tomorrow. But, unfortunately, the Canadian Supreme Court has failed to combine this practice of multi-opinion writing with any procedure for co-ordinating the separate opinions. Unlike the United States Supreme Court, the Canadian court does not present a majority opinion which at least indicates the common ingredients of those judgments that determined the outcome of the case. This means that when several judges, constituting the majority in a given case, all write separate opinions, it is extremely difficult to ascertain the common grounds of their disparate arguments and, hence, the basic principles established by the case. For example, in the Saumur case, the five judges who made up the majority all wrote separate opinions and, while they all agreed to allow the appeal, their opinions represented at least three different viewpoints on the central constitutional issue. This disjointed system of opinion writing not only might make it perplexing for the professional lawyer who must somehow determine the net effect of the different opinions, but also, in many cases, it prevents the court from performing what should surely be a necessary adjunct of the process of constitutional adjudication; namely, the clarification of constitutional principles for the public at large.

THE SUPREME COURT SINCE 1960*

Peter H. Russell

Since 1960 the Supreme Court has played an increasingly prominent role in Canadian public life, although it is still far from assuming as important a position as that occupied by the Supreme Court of the United States. In contrast to its American counterpart, the Canadian Supreme Court's decisions in the area of constitutional law constitute only a minor portion of its work. Still, Canadian expectations about the importance of the Supreme Court's constitutional work have been stimulated rather than tempered by the Court's performance since 1960. These rising expectations have stemmed mostly from the enactment of the Bill of Rights in 1960. But even on the more traditional federal issues, the Court, especially in its more nationalist decisions, has been a focus of political controversy and has continued to have an important influence on the balance of power in Canadian federalism.

Federalism

So far as the classic issues of Canadian constitutional law are concerned—the scope of federal power to legislate for peace, order and good

* Prepared for this edition in March, 1974 and published originally here with the permission of the author, who is a member of the Department of Political Economy, University of Toronto.

government and the regulation of trade and commerce, as against provincial jurisdiction over property and civil rights or matters of a merely local or private nature—the Supreme Court's decisions have continued to bear a distinct centralist accent. By the mid-1960s there had been more than a 50 per cent turnover in the personnel of the Court since 1952 when the Court in the *Johannesson* case adopted Lord Simon's "inherent national importance" test for invoking the peace, order and good government power. In the *Munroe* case in 1965 and the *Offshore Minerals Reference* of 1967, a very differently constituted Court indicated that the "inherent national importance" test had replaced Haldane's much more restrictive emergency doctrine as the key to the Supreme Court's understanding of peace, order and good government. Regardless of the attraction of these decisions to those of a centralist persuasion, the style if not the substance of these decisions is disappointing. The "national importance" test cries out for judicial opinions like Justice Locke's in the *Johannesson* case, which go beyond purely conceptual and legalistic considerations to the reasons for holding that a particular subject must necessarily be the concern of the national government. But in neither case did the Court accept the challenge of providing a reasoned basis for what were inescapably policy decisions.

In the *Munroe* case, this failure was less objectionable. Here the federal legislation at stake was the National Capital Commission Act, and it was not so unreasonable for Justice Cartwright simply to assert that it is "difficult to suggest a subject matter of legislation which more clearly goes beyond local or provincial interests and is the common concern of Canada as a whole than the development, conservation and improvement of the National Capital Region. . . ."

But the Court's use of the national importance argument to uphold federal rights in the *Offshore Minerals Reference* was far more provocative. It is interesting that the Court's opinion in this highly political case was *per curiam*, that is, unanimous and anonymous—so far as I know the first time in the Court's history that a constitutional decision had been so rendered. Most of the judgment, in fact 23 of its 29 pages, focussed on the question of whether the territory of British Columbia extended past the provincial shore line. After reviewing a body of conflicting statutory and common law authorities, the Court concluded that the provincial territory did not include the sea or the sea-bed adjacent to its coast. The Court might have rested its case there, since not even B.C.'s Premier W. C. Bennett was inclined to press for extra-territorial provincial rights. But the Court went on to offer a positive basis for federal power. With a short nationalist flourish, it asserted towards the end of its judgment that "the mineral resources of our lands underlying the territorial sea are of concern to Canada as a whole and go beyond local or provincial concerns or interests."

The *Offshore Mineral Rights* case was already political enough without this display of dogmatic centralism. Prime Minister Pearson had shown questionable judgment in referring this matter to the Supreme Court at a time when it was the centre of a hot political controversy between Ottawa and a number of provinces. There is no question of the Supreme Court's right to adjudicate a legal controversy between two parties which turns on the question of the ownership of offshore minerals. The rule of law in our constitutional system requires such adjudication. And this adjudication must be authoritative. But there was no case or controversy in the courts on offshore mineral rights. Mr. Pearson chose to take advantage of the reference case procedure and ask the Court for an advisory opinion, presumably with the hope of obtaining a Supreme Court decision favourable to federal interests. This use of the Court was strenuously objected to by both Premier Bennett of British Columbia and Premier Lesage of Quebec. The latter declared that "Quebec is not prepared to allow this question to be decided by the courts, it must be settled by political negotiation." Following the Supreme Court decision in March 1967, Mr. Lesage said that "if French-speaking Canadians' constitutional rights are to be protected, the Supreme Court of Canada, which rules on constitutional questions, must be either changed or altered." Daniel Johnson, who succeeded Lesage as Premier of Quebec, reiterated this position in November 1967.

In the intensely political atmosphere that surrounded this case it is unfortunate that the Supreme Court employed, so glibly, the national dimensions test of peace, order and good government. If the Supreme Court is to retain its effectiveness as the arbiter of our federal constitution, politicians must be careful in exploiting the easy access to the Court which the reference case gives them and the Court itself must take pains to be convincing in justifying decisions which are bound to be highly unpopular in certain quarters. One measure of the ineffectiveness of the Court's decision in the *Offshore Mineral Rights* case is the simple fact that the Court's holding has not been followed.

Turning now to the trade and commerce power, the major breakthrough of the 1950s should be recalled—that is, the Supreme Court's discovery that commerce flows (at least that "commerce" which only the federal parliament can regulate). In the words of Chief Justice Kerwin in the 1957 *Ontario Farm Products Marketing Act* case, "Once an article enters into the flow of interprovincial or external trade, the subject-matter and all its attendant circumstances cease to be a mere matter of local concern." Two cases upholding the federal scheme for marketing the prairie wheat crop followed on the heels of this decision—*Murphy* v. *C.P.R.* (1958) and, in Manitoba's Court of Appeal, *Regina* v. *Klassen* (1959). These cases, involving the hard facts of real-life litigation, indicated that with the "flow of commerce" incorporated into our constitutional law, the judiciary might no longer approach the division of powers in the field of economic regulation in terms of the mutually exclusive water-tight compartments of intra-provincial and extra-provincial transactions.

There was no further action on this front until the late 1960s and early 1970s when four cases, three of which concerned Quebec, came before the Supreme Court. The Court's decision in the first of these, *Carnation Co. Ltd.* v. *Quebec Agricultural Marketing Board* (1968), was favourable to the province. Justice Martland, writing for a unanimous Court, dismissed an attack on Quebec price supports for milk sold to the Carnation Company, most of whose products were exported from the province. Justice Martland acknowledged that the provincial regulations might well have an effect on the company's export trade but that this was not the aim of the legislation. Its prime purpose was to strengthen the bargaining position of milk producers within the province and this was within provincial jurisdiction.

But in the two cases which followed in 1971, the Supreme Court upheld national economic interests which were in conflict with Quebec policies. In both cases, the Court was unanimous. In *Caloil Inc.* v. *Attorney General of Canada*, the Court upheld the national energy policy which at that time was designed to protect western Canadian producers from competition with cheaper imported oil. The regulations drew a line in Ontario through the Ottawa Valley and banned the sale west of that line of products from Eastern Canadian refineries served by foreign suppliers of crude oil. Justice Pigeon, at the time the newest appointee to the Court, wrote the opinion. He was content simply to classify the federal regulations as being "in pith and substance" concerned with the control of imports and therefore under the federal trade and commerce power. He did not examine the economic aims and consequences of the regulations—in fact, for instance, that the regulations were primarily concerned with the preservation of an appropriate market in central Canada for oil produced in western Canada. Nor did he weigh the need, from a national point of view, of giving this policy priority over provincial interests in local markets and manufacturing. Immediately after the decision, Jacques Parizeau, a well-known separatist economist, at a press conference in Montreal, announced that many of the 1200 workers might be laid off at Caloil's Montreal refinery. This refinery had recently been built largely on the expectation of developing an extensive network of gasoline stations in a market embracing the "golden horseshoe" of south-west Ontario.

The third of the cases, *Attorney General for Manitoba* v. *Manitoba Egg and Poultry Association*, was a reference case. If all reference cases can be said to be hypothetical, this one must be considered super-hypothetical. Manitoba initiated this reference by asking its own Court of Appeal to assess the constitutional validity of a provincial egg-marketing scheme under which quotas could be applied to any or all of the eggs sold in the province, including those imported from other provinces. Manitoba, in fact, was not an importer of eggs, nor was there any intention of putting this scheme into force in Manitoba. But Quebec was an egg-importer and had imposed quotas on eggs coming on to the Quebec market from Ontario and Manitoba. But no one had challenged the validity of the Quebec scheme in the courts. Hence, Manitoba simply drafted marketing legislation similar to Quebec's and referred it to the courts, hoping, of course, that its own draft scheme (and therefore Quebec's as well) would be held unconstitutional. The Manitoba Court and, on appeal, the Supreme Court of Canada obliged and ruled against the provincial scheme.

The Supreme Court's decision in this case provided the occasion for Justice Bora Laskin's first full-length opinion on a central issue in Canadian constitutional law. Justice Laskin before coming to the bench had for many years been a professor of law at the University of Toronto and in that capacity had established himself as one of the country's leading scholars in the field of constitutional law. He was noted for his trenchant criticism of both the form and substance of the Privy Council's interpretation of the Canadian constitution. He was appointed to the Supreme Court of Canada in 1970 (after five years on the Ontario Court of Appeal) and within three years was to become its Chief Justice.

In many respects his opinion in this case came up to the expectations of those who had applauded his elevation to the Court. The opinion contains a masterful review of the previous cases dealing with trade and commerce. It traces the early reduction of trade and commerce as an all-embracing source of federal power to its virtual attenuation and finally the recent endeavour of the Supreme Court to restore a "necessary balance." The Court's opinion in this case crystallizes this restoration of the federal trade and commerce power as a constitutional basis for national economic policy. The provincial scheme was held to be *ultra vires* because in attempting to impede the flow of commerce across provincial boundaries, it infringed on Parliament's exclusive jurisdiction over trade and commerce. In the words of Justice Laskin, provincial trade wars of the kind which inspired the Manitoba egg marketing scheme "deny one of the objects of Confederation . . . namely, to form an economic unit of the whole of Canada."

Justice Laskin's opinion produced some important dicta on the scope of the federal trade and commerce power, but the case as a whole was seriously flawed by the total absence of any factual evidence to support the Court's view of the legislation's purpose and effect. Justice Laskin himself pointed out at the beginning of his opinion how factual data concerning the importance of imported eggs in the Manitoba egg-market would be relevant to determining the pith and substance of the Manitoba scheme. But even though there were no such data, he was able to satisify his judicial conscience and reach the conclusion that "the proposed scheme has as a direct object the regulation of the importation of eggs."

Two years later in *Burns Foods Ltd., et al.* v. *A. G. Manitoba*, the federal trade and commerce power was employed again to cut down a provincial marketing regulation. But on this occasion the Supreme Court's opinion (written by Justice Pigeon) seemed something of a throwback to the earlier, more rigid approach to the division of powers in economic matters. The regulation in question required Manitoba processors to purchase all their hogs from a provincial board. The aim of the regulation was to strengthen the bargaining position of hog producers in the province against the large meat-packing firms. About four per cent of the hogs involved were imported from Saskatchewan. But because the regulation applied directly to this interprovincial trade, it was ruled null and void by the Court. It is interesting that Mr. Justice Laskin did not take part in this decision.

Besides trade and commerce, and peace, order and good government, there has been the usual trickle of cases on other heads of power. Throughout the 60s and in the 70s, constitutional cases have continued to reach the Supreme Court at the rate of three to four a year. On a purely box-score basis, the outcomes have been considerably more favourable to federal than to provincial interests, as the table below indicates.

Outcome of Supreme Court's Constitutional Decisions, 1950-72

	1950-60	1960-72
Federal law valid	7	13
Federal law invalid	0	0
Provincial law valid	16	18
Provincial law invalid	14	6

Federal authorities have yet to lose a constitutional decision before an independent Supreme Court of Canada, whereas provincial claims have been defeated on numerous occasions. These statistics, coupled with the Court's liberal construction of the key sources of federal power, may be grist for the mill of provincial rights critics of the Supreme Court. Provincial distrust of the Supreme Court was manifest at the Victoria Conference in June 1971. The lengthiest section of the Charter for constitutional reform which emerged from that Conference concerned provincial participation in appointments to the Supreme Court of Canada.

But it would be a mistake to infer from these statistics that in fact the Supreme Court's interpretation of the constitution has consistently embodied a nationalist bias. In a number of the Court's decisions on particular heads of power, a mood of permissiveness and flexibility has been more evident than a pro-federal orientation. On five occasions in the 1960s, the Supreme Court upheld provincial administrative arrangements which were attacked on the ground that they usurped the powers of courts to which the federal government appoints the judges. In five other cases, provincial laws with punitive sections were attacked as infringing exclusive federal jurisdiction over criminal law. All but one of these laws survived judicial review. The device of delegation from the legislature at one level to a board or commission at the other level, a device sanctioned by the Supreme Court in the 1950s, was upheld in two further cases—the *Coughlin* case in 1968 and *The Queen* v. *Smith* in 1972. In the area of business regulation, Saskatchewan legislation concerning promissory notes (*Duplain* v. *Cameron*, 1961), an Ontario Act aimed at preventing "unconscionable" interest charges (*A. G. Ont.* v. *Barfreid Enterprises Ltd.*, 1963), a provincial tax on mining profits (*Nickel Rim Mines Ltd.* v. *A. G. Ont.*, 1967), and an Alberta Act affecting banks (*Breckenridge Speedway Ltd.* v. *The Queen*, 1970) were all upheld by the Supreme Court, although each ran up against exclusive federal powers.

An optimistic reading of this relatively charitable treatment of provincial legislation would see it as contributing to "co-operative federalism". It might be more realistic to acknowledge that this judicial restraint has the effect of adding to the areas of law in which the provinces and Ottawa have concurrent jurisdiction. While this trend undoubtedly increased the legislative capacities of federal and provincial legislators, and may in that way contribute to the flexibility of our federal system, it may also make life somewhat more confusing to the Canadian citizen by subjecting him to a welter of legislation on a single subject.

Civil Liberties

[For an extended discussion of Civil Liberties, see also Chapter 17, where in particular the decision in *Lavell and Bedard* is given *verbatim*, abridged.]

The Supreme Court's decisions on civil liberties have attracted far more attention in recent years than have its decisions on the classical issues of federalism. Certainly its decisions in this area have been more divisive of the Court itself. In contrast to the Court's unanimity on most federal issues, it has been closely divided on nearly all cases dealing with civil liberties. Its civil liberties decisions should be divided into two categories: those having to do with the B.N.A. Act and those which concern the Bill of Rights.

Beginning with the 1938 Alberta Press case, the Supreme Court had been evolving two doctrines upon which constitutional protection for certain civil liberties might be derived from the B.N.A. Act. First was Chief Justice Duff's notion of the rights required for the operation of parliamentary government which, among other things, would include freedom of speech and of the press to debate government policy. A second approach simply relied on exclusive federal jurisdiction over criminal law to preclude provincial legislation attaching penalties to non-conformance with religious customs (*Birks* case, 1955) or outlawing the expression of certain political beliefs (*Switzman* case, 1957). Only the second of these approaches ever gained the support of a majority on the Supreme Court.

Since 1960, there has been little further development of these constitutional "guarantees". The Duff doctrine of implied parliamentary rights has not become established as part of our constitutional law. In the *Oil, Chemical and Atomic Workers International Union* case of 1963, the Court split four to three on the constitutionality of Premier Bennett's legislation preventing trade unions from using union funds collected through a check-off to support a political party. The majority decided that the law in pith and substance concerned labour relations in the province and therefore was constitutional. But the minority acknowledged that the law could in effect cripple labour-supported political parties and so emphasized its effect on federal elections. Even so, only one of the dissenters, Justice Abbott, saw the issue in terms of fundamental political rights beyond curtailment by both levels of government. The other two dissenting judges, Justices Cartwright and Judson, merely held that provincial legislation relating to federal elections was beyond provincial jurisdiction. Justice Cartwright's minority position was adopted by the majority two years later in *McKay* v. *The Queen*. The issue here was whether a by-law restricting the posting of signs in a Toronto suburb could validly prohibit the posting of signs by candidates in a federal election. The Court split five to four, the majority holding that this application of a municipal by-law would be an unconstitutional infringement of exclusive federal jurisdiction over Dominion elections. But, again, there was no reliance by the Court on the notion of an implied bill of parliamentary rights in the B.N.A. Act.

In 1969, in *Walter* v. *A. G. Alberta*, the justices of the contemporary Supreme Court gave further evidence that they are not prepared to find a great deal of constitutional protection for civil liberties in the B.N.A. Act. In this case, Alberta's Communal Property Act, which regulates land purchases by Hutterites and other communitarian sects, was attacked as an unconstitutional provincial restriction of religious freedom. The Hutterites based their argument on the Supreme Court's decision in the 1950s in the *Birks, Switzman,* and *Saumur* cases. But the Supreme Court, in a unanimous decision, held that the Alberta legislation was valid as being primarily in relation to property management.

By 1960 many Canadians were looking beyond the B.N.A. Act to the Canadian Bill of Rights as an instrument through which the judiciary might better protect fundamental rights and freedoms. Granted, the Bill of Rights did not apply to the provinces, and as an ordinary act of Parliament could be set aside at any time by Parliament, still, its enactment in 1960 aroused great expectations.

For many observers, the Supreme Court's treatment of the Bill of Rights adds up to a strange tale of prevarication and confusion. The most consistent element in the Supreme Court's interpretation of the Bill of Rights, until 1973, is that the same judge, Justice Ritchie, has written the majority opinion in the three landmark decisions—*Robertson and Rosetanni* in 1963, *Drybones* in 1969, and the *Lavell and Bedard* case in 1973. Unlike some members of the Court, Justice Ritchie does not admit to changing his mind about the meaning of the Bill of Rights during this period. But it is a challenging exercise in analytical jurisprudence to work out the consistent principles of his decisions.

In *Robertson and Rosetanni*, Justice Ritchie took a conservationist approach to the Bill of Rights. In his view, the Bill's aim was to conserve the basic rights and freedoms Canadians had enjoyed prior to 1960. The Canadian Bill of Rights, he insisted, "is not concerned with 'human rights and fundamental freedoms' in any abstract sence, but rather with such 'right and freedoms' as they existed in Canada immediately before the statute was enacted." In the case at hand, Robertson and Rosetanni were claiming that their conviction under the federal Lord's Day Act for operating a bowling alley on Sunday violated the freedom of religion clause in the Bill of Rights. Justice Ritchie, following his conservationist approach, found that before 1960 the courts of Canada had on a number of occasions declared that Canada enjoyed "freedom of religion" and that when such declarations were made, Canadians also lived under compulsory Lord's Day observance legislation. Therefore, he concluded, freedom of religion as traditionally understood in Canada was not violated by the Lord's Day Act.

Six years later when the *Drybones* case reached the Supreme Court, many observers expected that Justice Ritchie's historical perspective would defeat Drybones' claim for equality under the law as provided for in the Bill of Rights. Drybones, an Indian in the Northwest Territories, had been convicted under a section of the Indian Act which makes it a crime for Indians to have intoxicants or be intoxicated off a reserve. This legislation had been on the statute book for many years prior to 1960. But even so, the mere fact that the law was passed before 1960 did not in Justice Ritchie's view make it immune to the Bill of Rights. Presumably, what was lacking here, in contrast to *Robertson and Rosetanni*, were authoritative statements making it clear that the traditional Canadian conception of equality before the law was compatible with this kind of discrimination against Indians. Justice Ritchie went on to hold that "an individual is denied equality before the law if it is made an offence punishable at law, on account of his race, for him to do something which his fellow Canadians are free to do. . . ." For the first time the Court ruled that federal legislation was rendered inoperative because it violated the Canadian Bill of Rights.

The dissenting opinions in the Supreme Court's *Drybones* decision were as interesting as the majority opinion. Chief Justice Cartwright, who had taken the more radical position in *Robertson and Rosetanni* and written the only dissenting opinion, dissented again. He had given the Bill of Rights question "a most anxious reconsideration" since 1963 and had now concluded that his earlier position had been an "error". To put real teeth in the Bill of Rights would impose a tremendous responsibility on every court in the country, a revolution in our system of government which it could not be assumed Parliament intended to bring about by enacting the Bill of Rights. Justice Pigeon, the newest Quebec justice on the Court, wrote an even more ardent dissent defending the retention of the British system of parliamentary supremacy.

The *Lavell and Bedard* case, the third land-mark decision, seemed to many to constitute another dramatic turn-about by the Supreme Court. Mrs. Lavell, and another Indian woman, Mrs. Bedard, after leaving an Indian reserve and marrying non-Indians, wished to return and live as members of Indian bands. But under section 12 (1) of the Indian Act, an Indian woman who had married a non-Indian was not entitled to be registered as a member of an Indian band, although an Indian man could marry a non-Indian without relinquishing his Indian status. Thus, counsel for the two women hoped to benefit from Justice Ritchie's decision in *Drybones* and claim that the Indian Act by discriminating against women violated the "equality before the law" provision of the Bill of Rights. But Justice Ritchie disappointed them. Writing the majority opinion for a closely divided Court (five to four), he was able to distinguish this case from *Drybones* and dismiss the claim.

For Justice Ritchie, the crucial difference in this case was that the discrimination here applied only within Indian reserves whereas in *Drybones* it pertained to all Indians as members of the Canadian community. Under the B.N.A. Act, there was explicit authorization for federal laws regulating the status of Indians and for over a century the Indian Act had contained this patriarchal provision. Parliament, he argued, could not have intended to change such an established and traditional policy when it passed the Bill of Rights. Later in his judgment he appeared to back away from the definition of "equality before the law" he had given in Drybones. There, equality before the law seemed to require a degree of equality *of* the law itself. But now he looked to A.V. Dicey's English definition which emphasizes equality in the way the law is applied rather than of the law itself. "Equality before the law," he wrote, "is to be treated as meaning equality in the administration and enforement of the law by the law enforcement authorities and the ordinary courts of the land." In his opinion, no such inequality in treatment between Indian men and women resulted from section 12(1) of the Indian Act.

Justice Laskin, soon to become Chief Justice of Canada, wrote a vigorous dissent in the *Lavell* case. The majority's reasoning, he contended, by permitting sex discrimination among Indians "compounds racial inequality even beyond the point that the *Drybones* case found unacceptable." In his view, the Canadian Bill of Rights goes even further than the American Constitution's due process and equal protection guarantees, in that it explicitly prohibits discrimination on the basis of race, national origin, colour, religion or sex. Justice Pigeon's and Justice Abbott's decisions were ironic: Justice Pigeon now concurred with Justice Ritchie for the very reasons he had disagreed with him in *Drybones*, while Justice Abbott disagreed with Justice Ritchie because reluctantly he felt obliged to follow Ritchie's earlier *Drybones* decision. No wonder the public felt confused!

The Supreme Court of Canada certainly cannot be given high marks for clarifying the meaning of the Canadian Bill of Rights. But to be fair, it must be acknowledged that the Bill of Rights imposes on the Canadian Supreme Court a most difficult task—to apply a long list of very abstract ideals to a statute book which is more than a century old. Even in a country where the public and the Court are accustomed to the judiciary's playing a large role in the revision of legislation this would be a remarkable challenge. It is not surprising that in Canada, where traditionally the courts have not been perceived as playing such a role, the Justices of the Supreme Court have been rather wavering and cautious in responding to this challenge.

Their basic caution is further evidenced by the five other Bill of Rights cases the Court decided between *Drybones* in 1969 and *Lavell* in 1973. All concerned various aspects of fair legal procedure. In only one did the Court uphold a claim under the Bill of Rights. This was a case involving the breathalizer amendments to the Criminal Code (*Brownridge* v. *The Queen*, 1972) where the majority agreed that a person should not be convicted of refusing without reasonable excuse to take a breathalizer test when the refusal is based on the police's denial of the accused's right to counsel. In all of these cases involving the rights of accused persons as against the rights of the police and the prosecution, the Court showed a real reluctance to move boldly in the directions which the Warren Court had taken in the United States, a direction which had done so much to spike the guns of the "law and order" opponents of the U.S. Supreme Court. In Canada, most political criticism of the Supreme Court has come from the other direction, from those who expect the Supreme Court through the application of the Bill of Rights to intervene much more decisively as a reforming influence on legislation and the conduct of government. Even under Chief Justice Laskin's leadership these critics are unlikely to receive much satisfaction in the future.

Organization and Procedure

A few changes in the organization and procedures of the Supreme Court have been made in recent years, all of which reflect the Court's greater self-consciousness of its responsibilities as the nation's final court of appeal. The extremely individualistic pattern of opinion-writing has moderated somewhat. Instead of every justice writing his own opinion, there has been (at least in public law cases) a greater tendency for the majority group of judges to support a single majority opinion. The Court has also been somewhat more inclined to sit as a full court in constitutional cases. In approximately 60 per cent of the constitutional cases it has heard since 1960, all nine judges participated in the decisions, whereas the full court sat for less than 50 per cent of the constitutional cases it heard in the previous decade.

Two other "reforms" should be reported. The Court's bilingual capacities have been enlarged. Since 1970, all of the Court's reported cases have been printed in both French and English in the official reports. Before this, many of the Court's decisions were available in one language only (usually English). For oral presentations, instantaneous interpretation facilities have been installed in the court room. But these are seldom used. The English-speaking judges still seem overly shy about admitting the need for interpretation of French-speaking lawyers' presentations. The other reform is the provision of legal secretaries as research assistants for each of the justices. Law clerks are essentially an American institution. They are usually young law graduates personally selected by each justice. Their introduction to the Supreme Court emphasizes the "research" dimension of the Supreme Court's role. As the second and final court of appeal, its function is not to hear every contested trial decision but to settle those difficult legal questions which often require extensive research and deliberation.

Late in 1974 a much more significant change in the Court's operations was finally implemented. Following many years of agitation by students of the Court and a recent inquiry by a Committee of The Canadian Bar Association, Parliament enacted legislation which will eliminate the automatic right to appeal from the highest provincial courts to the Supreme Court in civil cases involving at least $10,000. In the past this right of appeal accounted for more than half of the cases heard by the Supreme Court. As a result, much of the Court's time was taken up with settling suits which did not raise significant legal issues. This change will free the Supreme Court to devote most of its energies to deciding cases which a panel of three judges has determined raise legal questions of major importance. The establishment of the Federal Court in 1970-71, with an appeal division, also freed the Court from the burden of hearing routine tax appeals. These reforms should enable the Supreme Court of Canada to attain a higher level of performance in a more collegiate manner on an agenda of increasing significance to the nation.

THE NEW FEDERAL COURT OF CANADA

The Federal Court of Canada was created in 1970, replacing the former Exchequer Court. It is one of the two senior courts established by the federal government under enabling Section 101 of the British North America Act, the other being the Supreme Court of Canada.

The Federal Court has two divisions, a Trial and an Appeal Division. Its judicial members are appointed and can be removed in the same manner as Supreme Court judges, except that after June 1, 1971, the former hold office only until they reach 70 years of age. There are nine judges and an associate chief justice in the Trial Division, and five judges and a chief justice in the Appeal Division.

The new body has all of the jurisdiction of its predecessor, the Exchequer Court, and some additional responsibilities. Thus the Trial Division has original jurisdiction in all claims by and against the crown in Canada, claims against crown officials, litigation seeking relief from decisions of federal boards, commissions, and other tribunals, in certain interprovincial and federal-provincial disputes, in cases involving industrial property (e.g. copyright, trade marks), admiralty, income tax and estate tax appeals, citizenship appeals, and aeronautics. The Appeal Division hears appeals from the Trial Division and appeals arising from such legislation as the Broadcasting Act, the National Energy Board Act, the Immigration Appeal Board Act, and the Canada Shipping Act. It also has some appellate function in reviewing decisions of federal boards, commissions and other tribunals.

RECENT PROPOSALS FOR REFORM OF THE SUPREME COURT

Proposals in the Constitution and the People of Canada, 1969

[See *Politics: Canada*, third edition, pp. 452-455.]

Proposals in the Canadian Constitutional Charter, Parts IV and V, 1971

[See Chapter 2, *supra*, pp. 24-27.]

Proposals in the Special Joint Committee of the Senate and of the House of Commons on the Constitution of Canada, Final Report, 1972*

Recommendations

44. The existence, independence and structure of the Supreme Court of Canada should be provided for in the Constitution.

45. Consultation with the Provinces on appointments to the Supreme

---

* From the Special Joint Committee of the Senate and of the House of Commons on the Constitution of Canada, *Final Report*, Ottawa, Information Canada, 1972, Chap. 15, p. 39. Reproduced by permission of the Minister of Supply and Services Canada.

Court of Canada must take place. We generally support the methods of consultation proposed in the Victoria Charter, but the Provinces should also be allowed to make nominations to the nominating councils which would be set up under the Victoria proposals if the Attorney-General of Canada and the Attorney General of a province fail to agree on an appointee.

46. The Provinces should be given the right to withdraw appeals in matters of strictly provincial law from the Supreme Court of Canada and to vest final decision on such matters in their own highest courts, thus leaving to the Supreme Court of Canada jurisdiction over matters of Federal law and of constitutional law, including the Bill of Rights. The issue of whether a matter was one of strictly provincial law would be subject to determination by the Supreme Court of Canada.

APPOINTMENT SYSTEM IMPROVED*

Geoffrey Stevens

Less Patronage

. . . It is a pleasure and a relief to note that quality has replaced patronage as the guiding principle in the most vital area of federal appointments —the naming of judges. Almost exactly 500 judicial positions are filled by the federal Minister of Justice; besides the judges of the Federal and Supreme Courts of Canada, these include 201 country and district judges from one end of the country to the other and 277 provincial Supreme Court judges.

The effort to upgrade the calibre of the bench can be traced to 1967 when the then Minister of Justice, Pierre Trudeau, adopted the practice of submitting the names of prospective judges to the judicial committee of the Canadian Bar Association. This procedure was continued by the next Justice Minister, John Turner, who also did a great deal of personal bird-dogging to seek out able, experienced lawyers for judicial appointments.

Under Mr. Turner's successor, Otto Lang, the selection of judges has been made more systematic. Last year, Mr. Lang appointed a young University of Windsor law professor, Ed Ratushny, as special adviser with responsibility for receiving and seeking out recommendations for appointments and for gathering information about the individuals recommended.

From this bank of names, Mr. Lang selects those he wants to submit to the judicial committee. The committee then reports back to Mr. Lang whether, in its opinion, each candidate is well qualified, qualified, or not qualified.

Although its opinions are not binding on the Government, the judicial

---

* From a two-part article in *The Globe and Mail*, Toronto, March 7-8, 1974. By permission.

committee, in effect, has the power to blackball potential judges. Its reports are secret, but as far as can be determined only once since 1967 has an individual been appointed who was deemed to be not qualified; that was to a county court in Ontario.

Some of the appointments have been outstanding—so much so that Mr. Lang and his predecessors win praise not only from the legal profession but from opposition politicians as well. . . .

That's not to say partisan political considerations play no role at all in appointments to the bench; it's doubtful whether any Minister of Justice could ever insulate himself completely from the pressures of his party and his Cabinet colleagues. Appointments are discussed in Cabinet, often heatedly, before they are made. "In the process we may have hair all over the place," says Mr. Lang. "It could be anybody's hair."

Two recent appointments in which politics may have been more than a passing consideration were those last year of former Liberal MP Russell Honey to the county court in Belleville and former Liberal Cabinet minister Patrick Mahoney to the Federal Court. Both had lost their seats in the 1972 election. But other appointments have crossed party lines. Mr. Turner, for example, appointed the former provincial New Democratic Party Leader, Tom Berger, to the Supreme Court of British Columbia and another CCF-NDP stalwart, John Osler, to the Supreme Court of Ontario. Mr. Lang named Charles Dubin, a Conservative, and Allan Goodman, a New Democrat, to the Supreme Court in Ontario and former Conservative Justice Minister Davie Fulton to the same court in British Columbia. . . .

Better Qualifications

. . . Mr. Lang says he looks first at the prospective appointee's human qualities, including sympathy, generosity and charity. He also looks for an even temperament, integrity, ability to listen and an impeccable personal life.

Next, in Mr. Lang's order of priorities, come legal ability and experience (under the Judges Act federally-appointed judges must have been members of the bar for at least 10 years). "I rate ability above experience," says Mr. Lang, "and I try to match both to a willingness to work and a desire to do a job well."

Other considerations include religion and ethnic origin (although these are less crucial than they once were), specialized ability (a particular court may need strengthening in, say, bankruptcy or criminal law), public service (political activity is not an automatic entree, but it doesn't hurt), age and sex.

The Government is making a conscious effort to lower the average age of the nation's judges, by recruiting them younger and retiring them earlier. Mr. Lang feels 37 to 50 years is the ideal age range for a new judge, depending on the level of the court. The retirement age on county and district courts has already been lowered from 75 to 70, and the Justice Department encourages judges to move to a supernumerary or part-time status when they reach 65.

It is not easy, however, to interest younger lawyers in the bench. For many, a judgeship means a drastic reduction in income at a time when their family requirements are greatest and their earning power is at its peak. . . .

Sex is an even more difficult problem for the Justice Minister—politically and ministerially speaking. Women's Lib has had virtually no impact. In the four years prior to Mr. Lang's appointment in January, 1972, Ottawa named 116 male judges and only two females. Since then, Mr. Lang has appointed 99 males and five females—a slight but unimpressive improvement. Today, there are no women on the Supreme Court of Canada or the Federal Court of Canada and only four (out of 277 positions) on provincial Supreme Courts. Until last year, there were only two.

There are special problems, Mr. Lang says, in recruiting women judges. Women account for only 3 per cent of the practicing lawyers in Canada. Many of them are in fairly narrow specialties, such as institutional work (with trust companies and the like) and family law; relatively few do litigation work. Although women are entering law schools in ever-increasing numbers, the 10-year rule means that it will be some time before there is a large pool to draw from. "At the present time," says Mr. Lang, "if I'm looking at an equal man and woman for an appointment, I'll appoint the women."

Without question, Mr. Lang's most dramatic appointment was the elevation late last year of Bora Laskin to Chief Justice of Canada, over the heads of other, more senior, Supreme Court justices. But in terms of improving the calibre of the bench, three appointments in January and February, 1973, may have a more far-reaching effect. That was when Mr. Lang persuaded three of the most prominent lawyers in Ontario—Charles Dubin, Willard Z. Estey and G. Arthur Martin—to join the Ontario Court of Appeal.

"That was a real coup for the courts in Canada," says the Justice Minister. "It made it a little easier for other good men to give up their practices to become judges."

INCREASED JUDICIAL SALARIES, 1975

Salaries for federally appointed judges were increased greatly by 23-24 Elizabeth II, An Act to amend the Judges Act and certain other Acts. . . , Chapter 48, which was given royal assent on June 19, 1975.

The new annual salary scales are as follows:

Supreme Court of Canada	
Chief Justice	$65,000
Puisne judges	60,000
Federal Court of Canada	
Chief Justice and Associate C.J.	55,000
Other judges, Appeal and Trial Divisions	50,000
Provincial Supreme Courts	
Chief Justice, Appeal and Trial Divisions	55,000

Other judges, Appeal and Trial Divisions	50,000

County and District Courts

Chief Judge	48,000
Other judges	43,000

In addition, judges may be paid allowances for certain purposes such as travelling and professional conferences. Some federal judges may also receive additional remuneration for duties performed under provincial legislation, up to a maximum of $3,000 per year.

The salary increases, which are retroactive to April 1, 1974, are the first federal increases since 1971. They are to be staged in over a period of two years for the supreme courts and over three years for county courts.

LEWIS ST. G. STUBBS, JUDICIAL REBEL*

Lewis St. George Stubbs, 79, removed from the bench in 1933 in the course of a legal and political career that made his name known across Canada, died last night.

His dramatic removal from the bench was due mainly to charges concerning his actions in 1929 and 1930 as Manitoba Surrogate Court judge. He had refused to grant letters of administration in the estate of Alexander Macdonald, millionaire Winnipeg merchant, to Mr. Macdonald's daughter, Mrs. Grace Anne Forlong, and her husband.

The Manitoba Court of Appeal granted the letters over his head and, he charged, clandestinely. He held a public meeting in a Winnipeg theatre and a resolution was passed asking the Legislature to invalidate the Appeal Court action.

Superior Court judges asked the federal justice minister to remove Judge Stubbs from the bench and Mr. Justice Frank Ford was appointed Royal Commissioner to investigate.

The 24-day hearing created intense interest across the country. Judge Stubbs suggested that the inquiry be held in the Winnipeg auditorium and that admission be charged.

After hearing 600,000 words of evidence, Mr. Justice Ford found him guilty of judicial misconduct.

Testimony included the fact that Judge Stubbs often had said that "there is one law for the rich and another for the poor." One commission attorney described him as a judicial rebel.

In his own defense, Judge Stubbs said: "I would much rather have done what I did and go off the bench, than not to have done what I did and stay on the bench."

He topped the poll in Winnipeg in 1936 when 21 candidates were seeking 10 seats in the Manitoba Legislature. He sat as Independent member of the provincial House until 1949.

* From *The Canadian Press*, May 13, 1958. By permisson.

BIBLIOGRAPHY

The Courts and Judicial Review

Angus, W. H., "The Individual and the Bureaucracy: Judicial Review—Do We Need It?", *McGill Law Journal*, Vol. 20, No. 2, 1974.

Barnes, J., "The Law Reform Commission of Canada," *Dalhousie Law Journal*, Vol. 2, No. 1, February, 1975.

Bossard, J., *La Cour Suprême et la Constitution*, Montréal, les Presses de L'Université de Montréal, 1968.

Browne, G. P., *The Judicial Committee and the British North America Act*, Toronto, University of Toronto Press, 1967.

Cairns, A. C., "The Judicial Committee and Its Critics", *C.J.P.S.*, Vol. IV, No. 3, September, 1971.

Canada, Law Reform Commission, *Working Papers*, No. 1-14, 1974-75.

Cheffins, R. I., "The Supreme Court of Canada: The Quiet Court in an Unquiet Country," *Osgoode Hall Law Journal*, Vol. IV, No. 2, September, 1966.

Cheffins, R. I., and Tucker, R. N., *The Constitutional Process in Canada*, Toronto, McGraw-Hill Ryerson, second ed., 1976.

Gibson D., "—and One Step Backward: The Supreme Court and Constitutional Law in the Sixties," *Canadian Bar Review*, Vol. LIII, No. 3, September, 1975.

Gower, L. C. B., "Reflections on Law Reform," *University of Toronto Law Journal*, Vol. 23, 1973.

Grant, J. A. C., "Judicial Review in Canada: Procedural Aspects," *Canadian Bar Review*, Vol. XLIII, No. 2, May, 1964.

Hall, E. M., "Law Reform and the Judiciary's Role," *Osgoode Hall Law Journal*, Vol.10, No. 2, 1972.

Hogarth, J., *Sentencing as a Human Process*, Toronto, University of Toronto Press, 1971.

Hunter, I. A., "Judicial Review of Human Rights Legislation: McKay v. Bell", *University of British Columbia Law Review*, Vol. 7, No. 1, 1972.

Joanes, A., "Stare Decisis in the Supreme Court of Canada," *Canadian Bar Review*, Vol. XXXVI, No. 2, May, 1958.

Laskin, B., *Canadian Constitutional Law: Cases, Text and Notes on Distribution of Legislative Power*, Toronto, Carswell, 3rd ed., 1966.

Laskin, B., "The Supreme Court of Canada: A final Court of and for Canadians," *Canadian Bar Review*, Vol. XXIX, No. 10, December, 1951.

Laskin B., "The Role and Functions of Final Appellate Courts: The Supreme Court of Canada," *Canadian Bar Review*, Vol. LIII, No. 3, September, 1975.

Laskin B., "The Supreme Court: The First Hundred Years," *Canadian Bar Review*, Vol., LIII, No. 3, September, 1975.

Lederman, W. R., *The Courts and the Canadian Constitution*, Toronto, McClelland and Stewart, 1964.

Logan G. R., "Historical Sketch of the Supreme Court of Canada," *Osgoode Hall Law Journal*, Vol. III, 1964.

MacDonald, V. C., "The Privy Council and the Canadian Constitution," *Canadian Bar Review*, Vol. XXIX, No. 10, December, 1951.

MacDonald, V. C., *Legislative Power and the Supreme Court in the Fifties*, Toronto, Butterworth, 1961.

MacGuigan, M., "Precedent and Policy in the Supreme Court," *Canadian Bar Review*, Vol. XLV, 1967.

MacKinnon, F., "The Establishment of the Supreme Court of Canada," *Canadian Historical Review*, Vol. XXVII, 1946.

McNaught, K., "Political Trials and the Canadian Political Tradition," *University of Toronto Law Journal*, Vol. 24, 1974.

McWhinney, E., "A Supreme Court in a Bicultural Society: The Future Role of the Canadian Supreme Court," in Ontario Advisory Committee on Confederation, *Background Papers and Reports*, Toronto, Queen's Printer, Vol. I, 1967.

McWhinney, E., "The new, Pluralistic Federalism in Canada," *La Revue Juridique Thémis*, Vol. II, 1967.

McWhinney, E., *Judicial Review in the English-Speaking World*, Toronto, University of Toronto Press, 4th ed., 1969.

Mitchell, C. M., "The Role of the Courts in Public Policy Making: A Personal View," *University of Toronto Faculty of Law Review*, Vol. 33, No. 1, Spring, 1975.

Morin, J.-Y., "A Constitutional Court for Canada," *Canadian Bar Review*, Vol. XLIII, 1965.

Mullan, D. J., "The Federal Court Act: A Misguided Attempt at Administrative Law Reform," *University of Toronto Law Journal*, Vol. 23, 1973.

Olmsted, R. A., *Decisions relating to the BNA Act, 1867, and the Canadian Constitution, 1867-1954*, Ottawa, Queen's Printer, 1954, 3 vols.

Peck, S. R., "A Behavioural Approach to the Judicial Process: Scalogram Analysis," *Osgoode Hall Law Journal*, Vol. V, No. 1, April, 1967.

Peck, S. R., "The Supreme Court of Canada, 1958-1966: A search for Policy through Scalogram Analysis," *The Canadian Bar Review*, Vol. XLV, December, 1967.

Read, H., "The Judicial Process in Common Law Canada," *Canadian Bar Review*, Vol. XXXVII, 1959.

Russell, P. H., "The Jurisdiction of the Supreme Court of Canada: Present Policies and a Programme for Reform," *Osgoode Hall Law Journal*, Vol. VI, No. 1, October, 1968.

Russell, P. H., *Bilingualism and Biculturalism in the Supreme Court of Canada*, Document of the Royal Commission on Bilingualism and Biculturalism, Ottawa, Queen's Printer, 1970.

Russell, P. H., "The Political Role of the Supreme Court in its First Century," *Canadian Bar Review*, Vol. LIII, No. 3, September, 1975.

Russell, P. H., (ed.), *Leading Constitutional Decisions*, Rev. ed., Carleton Library No. 23, Toronto, McClelland and Stewart, 1973.

Slayton, P., "Quantitative Methods and Supreme Court Cases," *Osgoode Hall Law Journal*, Vol. 10, No. 2, 1972.

Strayer, B. L., *Judicial Review of Legislation in Canada*, Toronto, University of Toronto Press, 1969.

Scott, F. R., "Centralization and Decentralization in Canadian Federalism," *Canadian Bar Review*, Vol. XXIX, No. 10, December, 1951.

Senate of Canada, *Report to the Honourable the Speaker Relating to the Enactment of the British North America Act, 1867*, (O'Connor Report), Ottawa, Queen's Printer, 1939.

Tarnopolsky, W. S., "The Supreme Court and the Canadian Bill of Rights," *Canadian Bar Review*, Vol. LIII, No. 4, December, 1975.

Weiler, P., *In the Last Resort*, Toronto, Carswell-Methuen, 1974.

Weiler, P., "The Supreme Court and the Law of Canadian Federalism," *University of Toronto Law Journal*, Vol. 23, 1973.

Judiciary

Angus, W. H., "Judicial Selection in Canada,—The Historical Perspective," Address to the Annual Meeting of the Association of Canadian Law Teachers, Sherbrooke, P.Q., June 10, 1966.

Clark, J. A., "Appointments to the Bench," *Canadian Bar Review*, Vol. XXX, No. 1, January, 1952.

Jaffary, S. K., *Sentencing of Adults in Canada*, Toronto, University of Toronto Press, 1963.

Kinnear, H., "The County Judge in Ontario," *Canadian Bar Review*, Vol. XXXII, No. 1, January, 1954, and No. 2, February, 1954.

Lederman, W. R., "The Independence of the Judiciary," *Canadian Bar Review*, Vol. XXXIV, No. 7, August-September, 1956 and No. 10, December, 1956.

Russell, P. H., "Constitutional Reform of the Canadian Judiciary," *Alberta Law Review*, Vol. VII, No. 1, January, 1969.

Turner, J., *The Federal Court of Canada, A Manual of Practice*, Ottawa, Information Canada, 1971.

17

PROTECTING CIVIL RIGHTS

The question of whether Canada should have a formal Bill or Charter of Human Rights has been under much discussion in recent years. The British North America Act of 1867 contained no declaration of rights, similar, for instance, to that found in the Bill of Rights attached as the first ten amendments to the American constitution. This omission from the B.N.A. Act reflected, of course, the British tradition that an individual's rights were protected more satisfactorily by judicial interpretation of common law and by specific legislative enactments than by being enshrined in a formal, "written" constitution.

In Canada the argument has centred on two major questions: first, whether the conventional British approach should continue to hold sway over the example set by American practice, and second, if it were thought advisable to move in the latter direction, whether a bill of rights should be entrenched within a written constitution—for instance, within a revised B.N.A. Act—or whether it should be enacted merely as ordinary statutory law. The second question raises another consideration in a federal country such as Canada, namely, the thorny issue of divided jurisdiction. Since some of the subjects which would be included within either an entrenched, constitutional bill of rights or an ordinary statute would fall within the competence of the federal Parliament and others would fall within the jurisdiction of provincial legislatures, there would be a need for agreement on subject matter between the federal government and presumably all the provincial governments if one wished to achieve a uniform, pan-Canadian charter of rights. Such a bill of rights would entail also the additional difficulty of arriving at a method of amendment of the charter which was acceptable to all jurisdictions.

Because of problems of this sort, Mr. Diefenbaker, when he was prime minister, fulfilled his long-standing ambition to attain a bill of rights for Canada by settling for the enactment by Parliament of an ordinary statute. Thus, the "Diefenbaker" Canadian Bill of Rights came into being as a federal law in 1960. It is reprinted in its statutory form *infra*. For an excellent, extensive study of its history, contents, and the issues involved, see in particular the book by Professor Walter Tarnopolsky noted in the bibliography in this chapter.

The entire subject was raised again for active discussion in 1968 when Mr. Trudeau, who was then the minister of justice, presented vigorously to the first of a series of federal-provincial constitutional conferences his arguments for a constitutionally entrenched charter of rights, which he had long regarded as a superior form to a mere statute. His views were expressed in writing to the conference in a federal government position paper which appeared under his name and was entitled *A Canadian Charter of Human Rights.* An extract from this document, giving the gist of his arguments and an outline of the rights which he suggested ought to be included in any bill of rights, follows in this chapter.

Most of the provincial governments have been cool to Mr. Trudeau's proposals but the most incisive critique yet available of both the general arguments for such a charter and the specific contents of the federal paper have come from Professor Donald Smiley. He presented his views in a major article which is reprinted here in a slightly reduced version.

Discussions about the advisability of entrenching rights in a constitution tended to be the focus of attention during the late nineteen-sixties. The "Diefenbaker" Bill of Rights was regarded as a dead letter by virtually all commmentators because although it had been on the statute books since 1960, it had seldom been cited by counsel in pleading cases or been weighed heavily by courts in rendering decisions. Then, suddenly, in late 1969 it took a new lease on life when the Supreme Court of Canada made much of it in handing down what appears to be a leading civil libertarian decision in "the Drybones case." An account of this interesting case and its possible implications appeared in a lively newspaper article contained in this chapter.

In 1973 the Supreme Court rendered another important decision regarding the Bill of Rights. In the Lavell and Bedard cases a majority of five justices appeared to reverse the essence of the Drybones decision by finding that the Bill of Rights did not override the Indian Act. However, a minority of four justices held otherwise. The details of the cases and the substance of the majority's and minority's reasoning are given in the concluding item in this chapter.

Thus, there is a large question mark over the course that is likely to be pursued now in protecting civil liberties in Canada. Will there be a continuation of the effort to entrench rights constitutionally, or will there be a tendency to return to reinforced interpretation of the existing Canadian Bill of Rights?

A reader should consult also Chapter 16 for a discussion of the Supreme Court's role in civil libertarian cases. Students should see also the comments and proposals about fundamental rights made by the Special Joint Committee of the Senate and of the House of Commons on the Constitution of Canada in its *Final Report*, Ottawa, Information Canada, 1972, Chapter 9.

The bibliography in this chapter deals not only with civil rights but the following social issues also: environment, native peoples, poverty, resources, urban problems, women's rights, and other.

DIEFENBAKER'S CANADIAN BILL OF RIGHTS*

8-9 ELIZ. II, C. 44

[*Assented to 10th August, 1960*]

An act for the Recognition and Protection of Human Rights and Fundamental Freedoms

The Parliament of Canada, affirming that the Canadian Nation is founded upon principles that acknowledge the supremacy of God, the dignity and worth of the human person and the position of the family in a society of free men and free institutions;

Affirming also that men and institutions remain free only when freedom is founded upon respect for moral and spiritual values and the rule of law;

And being desirous of enshrining these principles and the human rights and fundamental freedoms derived from them, in a Bill of Rights which shall reflect the protection of these rights and freedoms in Canada.

Therefore Her Majesty, by and with the advice and consent of the Senate and House of Commons of Canada, enacts as follows:

Part I

Bill of Rights

1. It is hereby recognized and declared that in Canada there have existed and shall continue to exist without discrimination by reason of race, national origin, color, religion or sex, the following human rights and fundamental freedoms, namely,

(a) The right of the individual to life, liberty, security of the person and enjoyment of property, and the right not to be deprived thereof except by due process of law;

(b) The right of the individual to equality before the law and the protection of the law;

(c) Freedom of religion;

(d) Freedom of speech;

(e) Freedom of assembly and association; and

(f) Freedom of the press.

2. Every law of Canada shall, unless it is expressly declared by an Act of the Parliament of Canada that it shall operate notwithstanding the Canadian Bill of Rights, be so construed and applied as not to abrogate, abridge or infringe or to authorize the abrogation, abridgement or infringement of any of the rights or freedoms herein recognized and declared, and in particular, no law of Canada shall be construed or applied so as to

---

* From *Statutes of Canada*, 1960, Vol. I, pp. 519-522. By permission of the Queen's Printer.

(a) Authorize or effect the arbitrary detention, imprisonment or exile of any person;

(b) Impose or authorize the imposition of cruel and unusual treatment or punishment;

(c) Deprive a person who has been arrested or detained

  (i) of the right to be informed promptly of the reason for his arrest or detention,

  (ii) of the right to retain and instruct counsel without delay, or

  (iii) of the remedy by way of habeas corpus for the determination of the validity of his detention and for his release if the detention is not lawful;

(d) Authorize a court, tribunal, commission, board or other authority to compel a person to give evidence if he is denied counsel, protection against self crimination or other constitutional safeguards;

(e) Deprive a person of the right to a fair hearing in accordance with the principles of fundamental justice for the determination of his rights and obligations;

(f) Deprive a person charged with a criminal offense of the right to be presumed innocent until proved guilty according to law in a fair and public hearing by an independent and impartial tribunal, or of the right to reasonable bail without just cause; or

(g) Deprive a person of the right to the assistance of an interpreter in any proceedings in which he is involved or in which he is a party or a witness, before a court, commission, board or other tribunal, if he does not understand or speak the language in which such proceedings are conducted.

3. The Minister of Justice shall, in accordance with such regulations as may be prescribed by the Governor in Council, examine every proposed regulation submitted in draft form to the Clerk of the Privy Council pursuant to the Regulations Act and every Bill introduced in or presented to the House of Commons, in order to ascertain whether any of the provisions thereof are inconsistent with the purposes and provisions of this part and he shall report any such inconsistency to the House of Commons at the first convenient opportunity.

4. The provisions of this part shall be known as the Canadian Bill of Rights.

Part II

5. (1) Nothing in Part I shall be construed to abrogate or abridge any human right or fundamental freedom not enumerated herein that may have existed in Canada at the commencement of this Act.

(2) The expression "law of Canada" in Part I means an Act of the Parliament of Canada enacted before or after the coming into force of this Act, any order, rule or regulation thereunder, and any law in force in Canada or in any part of Canada at the commencement of this Act that is subject to be repealed, abolished or altered by the Parliament of Canada.

(3) The provisions of Part I shall be construed as extending only

to matters coming within the legislative authority of the Parliament of Canada.

6. Section 6 of the War Measures Act is repealed and the following substituted therefor:

"6. (1) Sections 3, 4 and 5 shall come into force only upon the issue of a proclamation of the Governor in Council declaring that war, invasion or insurrection, real or apprehended, exists.

(2) A proclamation declaring that war, invasion or insurrection, real or apprehended, exists shall be laid before Parliament forthwith after its issue, or, if Parliament is then not sitting, within the first fifteen days next thereafter that Parliament is sitting.

(3) Where a proclamation has been laid before Parliament pursuant to subsection (2), a notice of motion in either House signed by ten members thereof and made in accordance with the rules of that House within ten days of the day the proclamation was laid before Parliament, praying that the proclamation be revoked, shall be debated in that House at the first convenient opportunity within the four sitting days next after the day the motion in that House was made.

(4) If both Houses of Parliament resolve that the proclamation be revoked, it shall cease to have effect, and Sections 3, 4 and 5 shall cease to be in force until those sections are again brought into force by a further proclamation but without prejudice to the previous operation of those sections or anything duly done or suffered thereunder or any offense committed or any penality or forfeiture or punishment incurred.

(5) Any act or thing done or authorized or any order or regulation made under the authority of this Act, shall be deemed not to be an abrogation, abridgement or infringement of any right or freedom recognized by the Canadian Bill of Rights."

PROPOSAL FOR A CONSTITUTIONAL CHARTER OF HUMAN RIGHTS*

Pierre-Elliott Trudeau

The Need

Canada's main constitutional documents—the British North America Act, 1867 and its amendments—contain few guarantees of specific liberties. The courts have from time to time been invited to find in the B.N.A. Act some implied guarantee that fundamental rights are constitutionally protected from either federal or provincial encroachment, but such an interpretation has never since been the basis of a majority judgment in the higher courts. At this time in their history, Canadians are not afforded any guarantees of fundamental rights which (a) limit governmental

* From *A Canadian Charter of Human Rights*, Ottawa, Queen's Printer, 1968. Reproduced by permission of the Minister of Supply and Services Canada.

power *and* (b) possess a large measure of permanence because of the requirement that it be amended not by ordinary legislative process but only by more rigorous means of constitutional amendment.

The 1960 Canadian Bill of Rights has served to inhibit Parliament from amending the terms of that Bill and from violating its principles, but this is not a constitutional limitation on Parliament, only an influence. Additionally, that Bill has in practice had a limited application because the Courts have held that it does not expressly over-ride any provisions inconsistent with it which may be contained in earlier federal statutes. . . . [However, see *infra*, Rae Corelli, "How An Indian Changed Canada's Civil Rights Laws."]

Nor can any other human rights legislation (federal or provincial) be considered truly "constitutional": all of it is subject to amendment or repeal by the enacting legislature; none of it attempts to affect the validity or effect of other conflicting laws. Such legislation, in addition, is generally directed against the invasion of human rights by individuals, not by governments or legislatures (though in some cases it does bind the Crown).

To overcome these shortcomings while preserving the essential purpose of the present Bill, a constitutionally entrenched Bill of Rights is required which will declare invalid any existing or future statute in conflict with it. Language in this form would possess a degree of permanence and would over-ride even unambiguous legislation purporting to violate the protected rights.

In addition to these considerations of permanency, there is an even more pressing reason why a bill of rights, in order to be effective, must assume a constitutional—rather than a merely legislative—form. This arises out of the Canadian constitutional division of legislative competence as between Parliament and the provincial legislatures. In Canada, authority to legislate with respect to some of the rights regarded as fundamental lies with the provinces, authority to legislate with respect to others of these rights lies with Parliament, and authority with respect to the balance is shared by the two. Only by a single constitutional enactment will the fundamental rights of all Canadians be guaranteed equal protection. A bill of rights so enacted would identify clearly the various rights to be protected, and remove them henceforth from governmental interference. Such an amendment, unlike most proposed constitutional amendments, would not involve a transfer of legislative power from one government to another. Instead, it would involve a common agreement to restrict the power of governments. The basic human values of all Canadians—political, legal, egalitarian, linguistic—would in this way be guaranteed throughout Canada in a way that the 1960 Canadian Bill of Rights, or any number of provincial bills of rights, is incapable of providing.

The Contents

. . . Existing human rights measures in Canada are limited in scope. The Canadian Bill of Rights emphasizes political freedoms (speech, assembly, religion) and legal rights (freedom from arbitrary deprivation of life, liberty or property, and equality before the law). Other federal legislation and most provincial legislation is confined to prohibitions against discrimination in employment, admission to trade union membership, or the provision of accommodation. Some do go further. The Saskatchewan Bill of Rights, for example, embraces political and legal rights as well as a wider range of egalitarian rights, and the old Freedom of Worship Act (enacted during the pre-Confederation Union and still in effect in Ontario and Quebec) gives some guarantee of freedom of religion.

It is now suggested that there be included in a constitutional bill those rights which have been legislatively protected in Canada, and to add to them those linguistic rights which are recommended by the Royal Commission on Bilingualism and Biculturalism in the first volume of the Commission's report.

Rights which may be included in a bill of the sort under consideration here fall into five broad categories: political, legal, egalitarian, linguistic, and economic. . . .

1. Political Rights

This term is used in a broad sense to cover matters of belief, their expression and advocacy. The several political rights (here called "freedoms") are enumerated; following each there is a short discussion of the major legal considerations which attach thereto.

(a) *Freedom of expression*

These freedoms are presently protected legislatively in Section 1 of the Canadian Bill of Rights and in section 4 of the Saskatchewan Bill of Rights. The cases which have been decided to date indicate that these freedoms are largely subject to control by Parliament in the exercise of its criminal law power. There are, however, aspects of freedom of expression which may be subject to provincial limitation, as for example through the law of defamation, or through laws regulating advertising in provincial and municipal elections. For this reason adequate protection can only be offered in the form of a constitutional bill.

The means of definition of this freedom are of equal importance to its declaration. The question arises whether freedom of expression is best guaranteed in simple terms without qualification, or whether the limitations of this freedom ought to be specified. Opponents of an unconditional declaration fear that such wording might restrict the application of Criminal Code prohibitions against obscene or seditious publications, or provincial laws pertaining to defamation or film censorship. This is unlikely, however, for free speech as it developed in England was never equated with complete license. . . .

In Canada, existing federal laws against sedition and obscenity have been construed so narrowly that it is unlikely they would be held to conflict with a guarantee of free speech. The obscenity provisions of the Criminal Code have been applied since the enactment of the Canadian Bill of Rights without any conflict being recognized.

It is also unlikely that existing provincial laws against defamation would be upset by a free speech guarantee. As long as such legislation is confined to protecting long-recognized private rights of reputation there would be no conflict with the concept of "free speech.". . . .

The alternative to a broad, unqualified description of "freedom of speech" is an enumeration of specific exceptions. An example of this more detailed type of language is found in Article 10 of the European Convention on Human Rights. . . . By specifying the grounds for permissible limitations upon the right, possible uncertainties have been removed. The disadvantage of this technique, however, is its lack of flexibility and the difficulty of adapting the language to changed circumstances. For this reason the simple form of description is recommended.

(b) Freedom of conscience and religion

There is some legislative protection now. The Canadian Bill of Rights, section 1, recites "freedom of religion". The Saskatchewan Bill of Rights, section 3, declares the right to "freedom of conscience, opinion, and belief, and freedom of religious association, teaching, practice and worship". The Freedom of Worship Act (applicable in Ontario and Quebec) declares the right to "the free exercise and enjoyment of religious profession and worship". It is arguable, however, that a guarantee of "freedom of religion" does not protect the freedom of the person who chooses to have no religion. To protect such persons, consideration could be given to widening the guarantee to protect, for example, "freedom of conscience".

Freedom with respect to the individual's internal belief or conscience might well be considered absolute and not qualified in any way. It is the external manifestation of the exercise or furtherance of beliefs which may give rise to problems and the need for limitations in the interest of public safety and order.

In these areas, for example, no one would dispute that federal laws should be able to prevent acts in the exercise of religious beliefs which would constitute obscenity, sedition, bigamy, or homicide. It is more debatable, however, what further powers Parliament should possess to permit it to restrict other religiously-motivated acts. An example is the imposition of Sunday closing of businesses on Christians and non-Christians alike. . . .

(c) Freedom of assembly and association

These freedoms are now legislatively protected by section 1 of the Canadian Bill of Rights and by section 5 of the Saskatchewan Bill of Rights. They are closely related to freedom of expression and many of the comments made with respect to legislative jurisdiction over freedom of expression are equally applicable here. As with freedom of expression, they are not usually considered to be absolute but rather are subject to limitations in the interest of public order. Present federal limitations of this nature are mainly found in the Criminal Code relating to unlawful assembly, riot, conspiracy, watching and besetting, and disturbing the peace. Provincial limitations exist in laws dealing with the incorporation or regulation of commercial, educational, charitable and other organizations otherwise within provincial control, in the use of roads and parks for public assemblies, and the like. All these limitations appear to be consistent with freedom of assembly and association as long as they are clearly related to the preservation of public safety and order.

2. Legal Rights

These rights go to the very root of the concept of the liberty of the individual, so highly prized in Canada. They are dealt with now, to a certain extent, in sections 1 and 2 of the Canadian Bill of Rights and in section 6 of The Saskatchewan Bill of Rights. They are recognized as well by other statutory provisions and by rules of statutory interpretation developed by the courts. There is not, however, any constitutional protection of the rights.

These rights and their protection fall within both federal and provincial jurisdiction, depending on the context. . . .

The Canadian Bill of Rights lists most of the legal rights which need protection; with modification its provisions could form the basis for similar guarantees in a constitutional bill. Using it as a frame of reference, it is suggested that the rights enumerated below should be guaranteed:

(a) General security of life, liberty and property

The Canadian Bill of Rights declares

> The right of the individual to life, liberty, security of the person and enjoyment of property, and the right not to be deprived thereof except by due process of law.

. . . The words "due process of law" have been given a double interpretation in the United States. The first of these is as a guarantee of procedural fairness. In this respect, similar words used in the Canadian Bill of Rights are intended to guarantee the specific requirements of fair procedure. The words "due process" have, in addition, been given a substantive interpretation in the United States' courts with the result that the words have been employed as a standard by which the propriety of all legislation is judged. At one time the words used in this latter sense resulted in the judicial invalidation of minimum wage legislation, laws against child labour, and hours-of-work statutes. . . .

In examining American experience with "due process", it appears that the guarantee as applied to protection of "life" and personal "liberty" has been generally satisfactory, whereas substantive due process as applied to "liberty" of contract and to "property" has created the most controversy. It might therefore be possible to apply the due process guarantee only to "life", personal "liberty" and "security of the person". The specific guarantees of procedural fairness set out elsewhere in the bill would continue to apply to any interference with contracts or property. In this fashion the possibility of any substantive "due process" problems would be avoided.

In the alternative, if "due process" is to remain applicable to "liberty" of contract and to "property", there should be spelled out in some detail what is involved. . . .

(b) Equal protection of the law

The Canadian Bill of Rights, section 1(b) declares "the right of the individual to equality before the law and the protection of the law".

It might be argued that this wording serves to overlap other provisions. . . . [But] because the basic concept is sound, it is desirable to retain some such guarantee. . . .

(c) Cruel punishment, etc.

Section 2(b) of the Canadian Bill of Rights now provides that no law of Canada is to be deemed to "impose or authorize the imposition of cruel and unusual treatment or punishment". . . . While a court would likely be extremely reluctant to substitute its opinion of a proper punishment for that of the legislature, the power to do so could prove useful in extreme cases.

(d) Rights of an arrested person

Section 2(c) of the Canadian Bill of Rights states that no law of Canada shall be deemed to

deprive a person who has been arrested or detained

(i) of the right to be informed promptly of the reason for his arrest or detention,
(ii) of the right to retain and instruct counsel without delay, or
(iii) of the remedy by way of *habeas corpus* for the determination of the validity of his detention and for his release if the detention is not lawful. . . .

It is recommended that the same rights be protected in a constitutional bill. . . .

(e) Right of a witness to counsel

Section 2(d) of the Canadian Bill of Rights provides that no law of Canada is to be deemed to

authorize a court, tribunal, commission, board or other authority to compel a person to give evidence if he is denied counsel, protection against self-crimination or other constitutional safeguards. . .

and this right should appear in a constitutional bill.

(f) Fair hearing

Section 2(e) of the Canadian Bill of Rights provides that no law of Canada shall be deemed to

deprive a person of the right to a fair hearing in accordance with the principles of fundamental justice for the determination of his rights and obligations. . .

This is a fundamental requirement which is already generally recognized in the public law of Canada. In a new constitutional bill of rights it might well be placed in association with the fundamental rights of life, liberty and property.

(g) Presumption of innocence

Section 2(f) of the Canadian Bill of Rights states that no law of Canada is to be deemed to

> deprive a person charged with a criminal offence of the right to be presumed innocent until proved guilty according to law in a fair and public hearing by an independent and impartial tribunal, or of the right to reasonable bail without just cause . . .

The presumption of innocence is a fundamental ingredient of Canadian criminal justice, and must be guaranteed. . . .

(h) The right to an interpreter

Section 2(g) of the Canadian Bill of Rights states that no law of Canada is deemed to "deprive a person of the right to the assistance of an interpreter. . . ."
This is an important right, and should be retained.

(i) Other legal rights for possible inclusion

There are other legal rights which might be included in a constitutional bill of rights which were not included in the 1960 Canadian Bill. Following are some examples.

(i) Guarantee against *ex post facto* laws creating crimes retroactively. . .

(ii) Guarantee against unreasonable searches and seizures. . . .

(iii) Guarantee of the right of a citizen not to be exiled. . . . It is suggested that any exile, whether arbitrary or not, should be prohibited. . . .

3. Egalitarian Rights

. . . Existing legislation shows a widespread concern about racial and similar discrimination. The Canadian Bill of Rights declares that the rights listed in Section 1 . . . exist without discrimination by "race, national origin, colour, religion or sex". Federal legislation and legislation in eight provinces and both territories prohibit discrimination in employment. Seven provinces and the two territories also prohibit discrimination in public accommodation. The greater number of these statutory provisions, however, are designed to affect only private conduct. A constitutional bill of rights would serve to limit discriminatory activities on the part of governments as well.

The prohibited criteria of discrimination, as well as the areas of activity where discrimination is forbidden, should be considered in any antidiscrimination clauses:

(a) Prohibited criteria of discrimination

It is suggested that the bill should provide that the criteria listed in section 1 of the Canadian Bill of Rights—race, national origin, colour, religion, sex—should be retained as prohibited criteria for discrimination. Additional prohibited criteria might be considered, as for example, ethnic origin.

(b) Areas of activity where discrimination might be forbidden
  (i) voting or the holding of public office;
  (ii) employment—here it is suggested that there be added a qualification to the effect that distinctions based on a *bona fide* occupational qualification are not prohibited. In this way, possible difficulties concerning, for example, provincial legislation authorizing the hiring of teachers for denominational schools on the basis of their religious belief will be avoided;
  (iii) admission to professions where admission is controlled by professional bodies acting under legislative authority;
  (iv) education—special provisions will be required here to avoid inconsistencies with guarantees of separate or denominational schools contained in section 93 of the B.N.A. Act and corresponding sections in other constitutional statutes relating to other provinces. . . . ;
  (v) use of public accommodation, facilities and services;
  (vi) contracting with public agencies;
(vii) acquiring of property and interests in property. . . .

4. Linguistic Rights

Section 133 of the British North American Act, 1867 provides . . . a constitutional guarantee of the use of both languages in governmental processes, but this extends only to the legislature and courts of Quebec and to the Parliament and courts of Canada. In matters of education, it has been held that the guarantees of separate or denominational schools do not include any guarantee of the right to use either language as a medium of instruction.

It is submitted that these language guarantees be extended to other institutions of government and to education as has been recommended by the Royal Commission on Bilingualism and Biculturalism. These guarantees would prove effective, it is suggested, if incorporated into a constitutional bill of rights. . . .

5. Economic Rights

The kind of rights referred to here are those which seek to ensure some advantage to the individual and which require positive action by the state. The Universal Declaration of Human Rights, for example, included such rights as the right to work, the right to protection against unemployment, the right to form and join trade unions, the right to social security, the right to rest and leisure, the right to an adequate standard of living, the right to education, and the right to participate in the cultural life of the community. The United Nations Covenant on Economic, Social and Cultural Rights adopted by the General Assembly in 1966 included and elaborated upon these rights.

The guarantee of such economic rights is desirable and should be an ultimate objective for Canada. There are, however, good reasons for putting aside this issue at this stage and proceeding with the protection of political, legal, egalitarian and linguistic rights. It might take considerable time to reach agreement on the rights to be guaranteed and on the feasibility of implementation. The United Nations recognized these problems when it prepared two separate Covenants on Human Rights—one on Civil and Political Rights and one on Economic, Social and Cultural Rights, thus giving nations an opportunity to accede to them one at a time.

It is therefore suggested that it is advisable not to attempt to include economic rights in the constitutional bill of rights at this time.

THE CASE AGAINST THE CANADIAN CHARTER OF HUMAN RIGHTS*

Donald V. Smiley

. . . Proposals that there be the entrenchment in the Canadian constitution of what are variously regarded as fundamental human rights have come from several quarters since the Second World War. The scheme laid before the federal-provincial constitutional conference by the government of Canada in February 1968 recommended an entrenched charter of what was classified as political, legal, egalitarian, and linguistic rights. . . .

It might plausibly be argued that the opposition of most of the provinces to the constitutional entrenchment of human rights as recommended by the federal authorities makes the adoption of such a measure very improbable in the foreseeable future. . . .

In clearing the ground for my skirmish with supporters of the Charter, I may say that I agree that the protection of human rights is the final end of government and that the degree to which human rights are safeguarded is the final test by which any polity should be judged. . . .

My disagreement with the supporters of the Charter is thus not on the basis of final values but rather of evidence and the prudential political judgments based on such evidence. If and when the chips are down, I am a liberal rather than a democrat, but unlike Mr. Trudeau I find little in the contemporary situation in Canada which makes it necessary for me to choose between these two commitments.

Although human rights are primary, it is elemental to realize that at different times and under different circumstances humane societies recognize different rights and order those so recognized according to quite different priorities, and that the rights won in one generation often become in quite unintended ways the bastions of reaction and privilege in the next. . . .

Part of the processes of change to which we are being subjected is the assertion of new human rights and demands that we rank the existing ones differently. For purely illustrative purposes here are some of the areas where the reordering of human rights is occurring or may reasonably be expected in the near future:

* From the Presidential Address to the Canadian Political Science Association, 1969 published in the *Canadian Journal of Political Science/Revue Canadienne de Science politique*, Vol. II, No. 3, September, 1969. By permission of the author and the publisher.

First, we must redefine the permissible kinds of political participation and protest and the physical means that those charged with the security of the organized community may use against those persons who exceed such limits to protest and participation as are set by law. We have passed rapidly from the politics of pressure and influence to the politics of confrontation; confrontation in some cases going no further than to dramatize what protesters believe to be intolerable situations and in others going to subject all or part of the community to inconvenience, financial penalty, or danger. In defining these new limits there are some hard questions to be answered about whether these are to be the same for all or, alternatively, whether some can demonstrate that the normal workings of the political system are so unresponsive to their demands—or that these demands are so inherently righteous—that these people are allowed to press their interests in ways not permitted to others. The escalation in the intensity of domestic political conflict has led to new means of surveillance and coercion by those charged with maintaining internal order and security, and it seems inevitable that the increasing incidence of radical protest will lead to new and more restrictive definitions of loyalty and new ways of enforcing these limits. Increasingly sophisticated methods of crowd-control are now upon us, methods which both make such control more effective and allegedly do not subject those against whom they are used to more than temporary physical or psychological impotence. And if liberally minded people are successful in having fluorides put in the common water-supply perhaps the rest of us in the future will be able to think up convincing reasons for preventing the authorities from being granted permission to pour mild depressants into the same reservoirs to becalm communities inflamed by racial or other tensions!

Second, in the reordering of human rights we are experiencing changes in the way in which equality is defined. It has become accepted as universal morality that persons should not be discriminated against because of their race, ethnic origin, sex, or religion. From time to time the law adds new categories deemed to be irrelevant to how people are to be treated such as the age or marital circumstances of those seeking employment. But if people may not legitimately be disadvantaged because they fall in one of these categories, may public policies be designed to confer advantage on them? And if this is done cannot those not within such classifications validly complain of discrimination? In the United States, for example, judicial decision has brought about a "colour-blind Constitution" just at the time when there are new demands that race be regarded as one of the most important categories for determining how people are to be treated. An increasing number of negroes define their blackness as their most important identification and assert that for the foreseeable future compensatory measures are needed to mitigate the effects of centuries of exploitation. . . .

In Canada we are locked in debate among contradictory definitions of linguistic and cultural equality. Various kinds of "two nations" formulations assert that the crucial equality is that between the historic French-and English-speaking communities. The major thrust of the recommendations of the Royal Commission on Bilingualism and Biculturalism is towards defining equality as the right of individuals to affiliate themselves with the linguistic community of their choice in such provinces or areas as have official language concentrations of significant size. In some areas of English-speaking Canada equality is understood to mean the right of French Canadians and members of other minority groups to assimilate into the Anglo-Saxon community without penalties because of their previous cultural and linguistic backgrounds. Problems both of theory and practice arise in the relation between the indigenous people and other Canadians. The Hawthorn-Tremblay Report of 1966 recommends that the Indian be treated as a "citizen plus," that he have the option to enter the wider society without discrimination or, alternatively, to retain his membership in a traditional community whose welfare and integrity are protected by public policy. As in the case of other historically disadvantaged groups, to begin to treat Canadian Indians today as if their background and affiliations were irrelevant is perhaps not equality.

Third, new measures are needed to redress the alarming imbalances in mutual information between citizens and bureaucracies. We are just now beginning to realize the frightening possibilities for surveillance in closed-circuit television and various electronic listening devices. We are becoming aware of the potentialities for social control in the increasingly more refined data-collection and data-retrieval procedures of public and private agencies. Radical protest leads almost inevitably to more widespread infiltration of organizations by those charged with internal security and the attendant invasions of privacy and corrosions of human relations. But as the dimensions of individual privacy are progressively restricted, governments continue to assert the privilege of carrying on many of their own most crucial processes in secret and to determine unilaterally, and in accord with their own convenience, the information about these processes to be made available to the public. In the period ahead, some of the most critical struggles for human freedom may revolve around the citizen's right to privacy on the one hand and his right to public information on the other. . . .

In the field of material needs, we are just beginning to recognize the urgency of consumer rights. Former societies did not have to worry about privacy and up to the present neither democratic theory nor democratic practice emphasized what has now become this compelling necessity of human dignity. Perhaps we are even being faced with the more basic question, "When is a human being?" The current controversey over abortion raises the old question of whether human life comes into existence at conception, at birth, or sometime between these two events. At the other end of the line, so to speak, perhaps a fundamental human right in the future will be an assurance to the individual that his carcass will not be used as a handy source of spare parts unless and until he has been pronounced dead by procedures less casual then those commonly now used. And when the geneticists and/or the computer scientists put together forms of existence having some, but likely not all, the distinctive characteristics of humans, in what ways will these creatures be granted the rights previously enjoyed only by those having their origins in the traditional process of human procreation?

In a period where there is a rapid reordering of human rights, the ways by which rights are finally and authoritatively defined are the most crucial activities of government. If the proposed Charter were enacted some or all of the following might happen:

First, certain provisions might be stated so unequivocally as not to permit any subsequent dispute or interpretations as to their meaning.

Second, the constitution might subsequently be amended so as to change the scope of entrenched human rights. On the whole, it is less likely that previously entrenched rights would be removed or restricted than that new rights would be given such protection. It is also likely that any acceptable amending procedure will make such amendments subject to unanimous provincial consent. Thus the entrenchment of human rights at any particular time imposes the formulations of that time on the future in the sense that a small minority can obstruct future changes.

Third, the Charter might be overridden by Parliament's emergency powers. . . . Thus, unlike the American Bill of Rights and despite the absolutist claims made for the Charter, constitutionally entrenched rights in Canada are under emergency conditions to be subject to the will of the federal legislature.

Fourth, the generalized provisions of the Charter are given their meaning by judicial interpretation. This is the crucial feature of the proposal. Supporters of the Charter have been peculiarly reticent in explaining that its effect is to confer on the judiciary new and extended powers; in misleading language drawn from the French and American political traditions rather than our own this measure is alleged to transfer power not from legislatures to courts but rather to "the people" from governments. . . .

In defining and ordering human rights the judicial method as it has developed in Canada suffers from major disabilities:

First, judicial review is sporadic. Unlike legislatures and executives, the courts have a narrow range of discretion in timing the decisions they make, either in the course of litigation or in giving advisory opinions when directed by the federal or provincial cabinets. Thus enactments which are later declared unconstitutional can and often do remain in effect for long periods before cases involving their validity come before the courts. Further, in interpreting the constitution the courts ordinarily decide only the issues in the particular case before them and leave for later decision the consequences for cases which are somewhat similar and, in denying the validity of laws, whether and in what ways the offending legislature could attain broadly the same objectives by enactments framed somewhat differently.

Second, under present circumstances most Canadians do not have the financial resources to undertake legal action to protect their rights. We have no national organizations corresponding to the American Civil Liberties Union or the National Association for the Advancement of Colored People which have at their disposal large resources of specialized legal talent to defend those whose constitutional rights are challenged. Provisions for legal aid to those without the funds to pay for such services are to a greater or lesser degree inadequate everywhere in Canada. . . .

Third, in our judicial tradition the courts in coming to decisions take into explicit account a restricted range both of facts and values. For the most part, the courts apply to the constitution the same rules of interpretation that are used in determining the meaning and effect of other statutes. Although I am here over-simplifying, the raw materials of the decision are the facts of the case, the usual and accepted meaning of the words of the enactment and what courts at the same or at higher levels in the judicial hierarchy have decided in previous cases deemed to be similar. In some cases the courts proceed further and examine the intent of the legislature which enacted the statute and the surrounding circumstances, although whether this is appropriate is a matter of dispute both among members of the Canadian judiciary and legal scholars. There are of course Canadian constitutional decisions where broader considerations than those mentioned above have been taken into account, and many scholars argue that the usual rules of statutory interpretation are by themselves inadequate guides when questions involving the constitution are under review.

However, the broad thrust of Canadian constitutional interpretation is positivist. This is not good enough in our present circumstances. For example, if individual privacy is to be protected effectively decisions will have to be made largely on the basis of an up-to-date appreciation of the technology of surveillance devices. In ordering the relations between the Canadian Indian and the rest of the community the public authorities need the most sophisticated analyses that social scientists can provide. The Canadian judiciary is badly equipped both by its traditional procedures and by training and inclination to use scientific knowledge creatively in the making of public policy. The legal realists assert that the courts in coming to decisions do in fact take into account a broader range of factors than the canons of statutory interpretation imply. Particularly in a review of the constitution, where the range of judicial discretion is often wider than when other statutes are involved, it is inevitable that judges will be influenced by their formulations of the essential nature of the polity and their evaluations of the public consequences of their decisions. However, within the Canadian tradition these considerations are seldom made explicit and are concealed in decisions within a morass of legal verbiage unintelligible to the average interested citizen. Again this will not do. If our courts are given the task of making the final and authoritative definitions of human rights it is essential that they, along with other organs of government, enter into a continuing dialogue with the Canadian public about the premises of these decisions. It is my assumption that the ethos of democracy has so permeated the public consciousness that no public body which proceeds otherwise will have its powers regarded as legitimate.

Fourth, the courts have few resources to enforce their decisions. The proposed Charter implies that on occasion the judiciary will challenge elected bodies representing deeply felt sentiments in the national or provincial communities. Under contemporary circumstances the effective exercise of human rights often requires positive action from legislatures and executives. The American experience indicates that when the courts clash with other organs of government the implementation of judicial decisions is by no means automatic or certain.

The general disabilities of the judicial method in defining human rights are reinforced by the more specific characteristics of the Canadian legal culture. It is my impression that Canadian legal education and scholarship have been for the most part technical in nature and have not on the whole concerned themselves deeply with broader matters of public policy and political philosophy. Despite the very great advances that are reportedly being made in enhancing the quality of judicial appointments, I remain unconvinced that the Canadian courts are a sufficient repository of superior wisdom and statesmanship to entrust with the new functions. There is in the federal proposals a thinly disguised enthusiasm for the Supreme Court of the United States in the past generation. But the differences between the two experiences are vast. The United States constitution has developed a central and symbolic role in fostering allegiance to the polity as ours has not. The American political formula is a creedal one based on natural law foundations leading to the authoritative definition of constitutional orthodoxy by an authority removed from overt partisan influences. Much of the activity of the Supreme Court of the United States in defining human rights has been in the direction of a national system of criminal law, something Canadians have had from the first under the existing constitution. Perhaps most crucially, the Supreme Court of the United States works within the environment of an enormously rich and sophisticated tradition of legal-philosophical debate about the most fundamental matters, an environment largely absent in Canada.

Another of the many questions which the supporters of the Charter have not raised is the compatibility or otherwise between the new tasks being assigned to the courts and the effective performance of other judicial functions. The American experience—and I would argue that it is here relevant—is that a final court of review which makes important and controversial public policy decisions inevitably becomes the object of partisan political debate. . . . The Canadian judiciary has maintained a high reputation for impartiality, a reputation that persists even when judges leave their courtrooms and involve themselves in contentious matters where legal standards in the strict sense do not apply, as when they sit on labour conciliation boards, participate in redefining electoral districts, and become members of royal commissions and other inquiries dealing with controversial public issues. . . . These kinds of activities are already putting the reputation of judicial impartiality under strain, and the new and controversial tasks suggested for the courts by the Charter would almost inevitably contribute to these influences.

Supporters of the Charter might agree with much of the argument I have made but still maintain that, on balance, the constitutional entrenchment of rights was justified on the double grounds that it would introduce a measure of certainty into what rights are recognized in Canada and that, again on balance, courts can be expected to be more zealous than elected politicians in safeguarding human rights.

It is undeniable that there are many uncertainties with respect to human rights in Canada. Part of these relate to the division of legislative powers—for example, how far might Parliament go in defining racial or religious discrimination as criminal offences? The question has never been resolved as to whether the preamble of the British North America

Act constitutes the elements of an implied bill of rights limiting the powers of the provinces and perhaps of Parliament as well. In matters within federal jurisdiction the status of the 1960 Bill of Rights is unclear. Nearly a decade of experience indicates to me that the major difficulty with the bill is not, as its critics claim, that it can be amended or repealed by the ordinary legislative processes but rather that the courts have not found in it an unambiguous directive for interpreting and perhaps invalidating federal legislation. This is so even though the language of the bill appears clear to the effect that "Every law of Canada shall, unless it is expressly declared by an Act of Parliament of Canada that is shall operate notwith-standing the Canadian Bill of Rights, be so construed and applied as not to abrogate, abridge or infringe or to authorize the abrogation, abridgement or infringement of any of the rights and freedoms herein recognized and declared . . ." So far as legislative intent is concerned, the evidence indicates that the government of the day—and in particular the Prime Minister and his Minister of Justice—regarded the Bill of Rights as a constitutional statute by whose terms other federal enactments were to be judged and, if found wanting, invalidated by the courts. But if the proposed Charter resolved some or all of the existing uncertainties it would almost inevitably create even more serious ones in the several decades it would take for the new traditions of judicial interpretation to evolve. What could we expect in the meantime? Would the courts exercise a high degree of self-restraint in striking down legislation alleged to be contrary to the Charter? Or would judges come rampaging out to do battle for human rights? Or, alternatively, would they develop towards a presumption of constitutionality with respect to some provision of the Charter and put other provisions in a "preferred position"? Would judges in interpreting the Charter take into account the cultural duality of Canada? And in particular what recognition, if any, would they give to the circumstances that in some important respects the civil and common law systems define rights in quite different ways? As the Canadian constitution moved toward a definition of individual rights what doctines of judicial standing would evolve, that is, what persons would be regarded as having a sufficiently direct interest in particular legislation or executive acts to challenge their validity in the courts? It is the goal of a democratic polity that individuals, at least with the assistance of normally competent lawyers, can at any time determine with some precision what their rights are under the law. However, the answer to existing uncertainties lies not with the Charter but in the clearer definition from time to time of human rights by Parliament and the provincial legislatures, preferably aided by some form of ongoing federal-provincial collaboration in such matters. The courts have, and will continue to have, a crucial role in the protection of human rights. But it seems to me that this role can best be fulfilled when the juciciary proceeds from the traditional protections of the two legal systems supplemented and extended from time to time by precise and detailed legislative enactments.

Is it reasonable to expect that Canadian courts will be more zealous than legislatures in the protection of human rights? The incumbent judiciary does not impress me in this respect. In the few cases when federal actions have been challenged as infringing upon the provisions of the 1960 Bill of Rights the higher courts have shown an extraordinary degree of self-restraint. But the pervasive major premise of those who support the charter is a distrust of legislatures, executives, voters, and the whole democratic political process. The federal proposal of 1968 nowhere recommends entrenching the right to vote—although almost parenthetically it suggests that where this right exists persons should not be discriminated against in its exercise because of race, religion, national origin, colour, or sex. (Significantly, those latter safeguards do not appear in the revised Charter as proposed by Mr. Trudeau in February 1969). It is revealing that the federal government did not see as desirable the extension in the Charter to the provinces of the existing provisions of the BNA Act which require an annual session of Parliament and, except under defined conditions of national emergency, a general election every five years. The proposed Charter recommends several important restrictions on the existing powers of the provinces. However, such restrictions do not include those governing the provincial franchise, annual legislative sessions, and periodic elections and these can be altered or amended by the usual legislative processes. Thus in the federal proposal the whole process of democratic political debate and political conflict are seen exclusively in the perspective of the hazards they contain for human rights rather than in their potentialities for protecting and extending these rights.

Whatever general dispositions toward human rights that elected bodies in Canada may be assumed to have, it is undeniable that in this decade there has been a legislative recognition of such rights unprecedented in Canadian history. Parliament and most of the provinces have enacted bills of rights and in some jurisdictions specialized administrative agencies have been established to implement these purposes. Both Ontario and Quebec have royal commissions at work inquiring in a detailed way into human rights and important legislative action is expected on the basis of their recommendations; in the latter province many of the "obstacles to democracy" which Mr. Trudeau so well analysed a decade ago have been removed and there is reportedly to be a bill of rights incorporated into the revised civil code. Alberta, New Brunswick, and now Quebec have appointed ombudsmen and it is likely that other Canadian jurisdictions will soon experiment with this institution. Parliament has liberalized Canadian law in respect to capital punishment, divorce, abortion, birth control, and homosexuality. In Ottawa and most of the provinces there has been a legislative and executive recognition of the French language that not even the most sanguine would have predicted as recently as, say, five years ago. There has been a belated and as yet insufficient effort toward bettering the circumstances of the Indian and Eskimo peoples. Perhaps the most dramatic victory for human rights in Canada during this decade occurred during March 1964 in Ontario when the Attorney General introduced into the legislature a bill to extend vastly the *in camera* investigatory powers of the Ontario Police Commission; the reaction of the public to this repressive measure was almost instantaneous and resulted in the quick withdrawal of the bill and the resignation of the cabinet minister responsible for it. In general, there can never be any reasonable complacency about human rights but *in toto* legislative and administrative action in Canada during this decade constitute significant achievements for freedom and dignity.

It is likely that a stronger case can be made for the Charter than its supporters have formulated. Such a reasoned argument might proceed along two lines: First, new and illiberal influences are upon us and it is probable that Canadian legislators will be less solicitous of human rights than in the recent past. Second, Canadian judges will respond, and quickly, to the challenge of the Charter and transform themselves into zealous and sophisticated libertarians. But such a case has not been made and the rationale of the Charter published under the name of Mr. Trudeau has been made in terms which are pretentious, misleading, and intellectually shoddy. . . .

First, in the document *A Canadian Charter of Human Rights* there is a pretentious three-and-a-half-page summary of the whole of the western tradition in politics. . . . Nowhere is the elementary analytical distinction made between natural and positive law. There is no substance in this pseudo-erudition except the assertion that in the western tradition there has been a continuing disposition toward the protection of human rights by law. So far as I know, there is no challenge to the principle in Canada, and the principle in itself gives no guidance in determining the appropriate "mix" of common or civil law safeguards, legislative enactments, and constitutional entrenchment in protecting human rights.

Second, in the document referred to above this sentence occurs: "An entrenched bill of rights would offer this constitutional protection [to human rights], although at the price of some restriction on the theory of legislative supremacy." But who cares about the *theory* of legislative supremacy? The proposal is no more and no less than to transfer certain kinds of crucial policy decisions from legislatures to courts. What are the inhibitions against saying so clearly and without equivocation?

Third, here is a sentence from *The Constitution and the People of Canada*, published under Mr. Trudeau's name in February 1969. "A constitutional guarantee of human rights would thus represent a commitment by all governments to the people—a commitment that, whatever their legislative powers, they will not deny the fundamental values which make life meaningful for Canadians" (p. 16). On a personal basis, I find repugnant some of the values "which make life meaningful" for some Canadians. If there is one value in Canadian life which I cherish it is that no one has yet prescribed any set of values to which I am required to assent. I hope that all citizens of perverse and independent spirit will unite to put down the arrogance of politicians who would inflict this kind of creedal Canadianism—or un-Canadian creedalism—upon us. . . .

Fourth, in the 1969 document we find this sentence: "To enshrine a right in a constitutional charter is to make an important judgment, to give to the right of the individual a higher order of value than the right of government to infringe upon it." Nowhere is the superficiality of the case made for the Charter so clearly shown. No reasonable person believes that in all cases individual rights even though constitutionally entrenched, are to take precedence over other claims which have no such protection. Mr. Trudeau's argument proceeds on the assumption that encroachments on human rights are always unequivocal and that disinterested and liberal persons will be able to agree when such encroachments have been made. This is, of course, not so. In a society generally committed to liberal values—and this is the only kind of society where procedural safeguards of human rights are of more than marginal consequences—men sharing these values can and will weigh conflicting claims differently. When does a particular kind of expression become a "clear and present danger" to society? How far do constitutional prohibitions extend to private organizations operating under public regulation or with public financial assistance? How is the fine line to be drawn between *predicting* that certain conditions can be righted only by violence and *advocating* violence? What kinds of restrictions can a liberal community impose on aliens wanting to enter that community as visitors, residents, or citizens? How does freedom of expression relate to means of expression which are inherently quasi-monopolistic? What are the kinds of overt conduct that can be justified in the name of freedom of religion, and when privileges are granted in these directions, should they be extended only to members of organized religious groups? How does one strike a balance between the claims of procedural regularity and the need for speedy, expert, and inexpensive adjudication of disputes? There are manifold complexities in the delicate balancing of social priorities which is the essence of protecting human rights. Unfortunately, none of these yield to superficial sloganeering about the rights of individuals preceding those of governments.

In a time of turbulence when the things which we most value are under attack it is understandable that some will come forward to promise us certainty. Only such impulses can explain the misleading and absolutist language in which the Charter is presented. The rights which it is to recognize are "basic" and "fundamental"—although no serious attempt is made to demonstrate that these claims are more essential than others which are not to be so protected. So far as fundamental rights are concerned, we are to "guarantee" them, to "entrench" them, and finally to "enshrine" them. Perhaps the more accurate term is "entomb." For in the nature of things there is no sure and certain way to protect human rights—no certainty that courts will be more zealous than legislatures in meeting the future requirements of human freedom and dignity and no certainty, but rather the reverse, that a judiciary intent on defending such rights will long be able to restrain a community bent on their destruction. We can only say with Judge Learned Hand, "this much I think I do know—that a society so riven that a spirit of moderation is gone, no court *can* save, that a society where that spirit flourishes, no court *need* save, that in a society which evades its responsibility by thrusting upon courts the nature of that spirit, that spirit will in the end perish."

To end, one of the most intractable dilemmas confronting the responsible man is how to act prudently today without foreclosing the possibilities of tomorrow. Those who would enact a charter of human rights are confident enough of their own judgments to wish to press on future generations of Canadians—if there be such—a particular formulation of the requirements of human dignity. . . . But there is another way than that of the Charter. The master tradition of the British parliamentary system affirms that with one exception a legislature can enact as it chooses, either as sovereign or within the restrictions imposed by a federal division of legislative powers. That single exception is that it cannot bind future Parliaments. There is here elemental wisdom we would do well to ponder.

Postscript (1975)

The breakdown of the process of constitutional reform at the Victoria Conference in June 1971 makes it very unlikely that there will be any further constitutional entrenchment of human rights in Canada in the forseeable future. Yet the role of the courts in the protection of human rights remains a matter of doubt and debate, particularly the measures that the judiciary will and should take in invalidating federal legislation deemed contrary to the Bill of Rights of 1960.

Judicial interpretation of the Diefenbaker Bill of Rights has been relatively ineffective in the protection of human rights, in part because of the few important cases brought before the courts under this Bill and in part because of the disposition of the judges themselves to defer to the will of Parliament as expressed in more explicit statutes. However, in this 15-year period Parliament and provincial legislatures have enacted a very large number of statutes giving further protection to human rights. In these crucial matters, I would hope that Canadians will continue to look primarily to their elected legislatures rather than the courts of law to decide what human claims are to be regarded as rights.

The Lavell-Bedard case posed in a clear-cut way two conflicting sets of rights: those of Indian communities for autonomy and those of sexual equality. As I explained in my article, I believe that courts of law work under severe institutional disabilities in deciding such matters of public policy.

HOW AN INDIAN CHANGED CANADA'S CIVIL RIGHTS LAWS—THE DRYBONES CASE*

Rae Corelli

It was a fateful moment for Canada when, early in the morning of April 10, 1967, Joe Drybones was convicted of having been drunk in a public place (viz., the lobby floor in the Old Stope Hotel in Yellowknife) and fined $10.

Because that was the first act in a 2½ year courtroom drama which was to propel Canada onto the threshold of a revolution in the field of law and civil rights.

The last act was performed six weeks ago by the Supreme Court of

* From *The Toronto Star*, January 2, 1970. By permission of the publisher.

Canada which ordered the conviction quashed and the fine refunded on the grounds that the 42-year-old bespectacled and illiterate Indian had been denied equality before the law.

The court's authority for that historic decision?

None other than the much-maligned and ridiculed Canadian Bill of Rights. From the day it was enacted by John Diefenbaker's Progressive Conservative government nearly 10 years ago, the bill had been so thoroughly shunned by the courts that it had virtually no force or effect in Canadian law.

Lawyers had despaired of ever winning a case on the strength of it even though its guarantees of human rights and fundamental freedoms were supposed to take precedence, or so it seemed, over all other federal laws.

The trouble was that no court had ever placed that interpretation on it—until six weeks ago, that is, when the Supreme Court of Canada said that's exactly what the words in the bill meant.

Legal scholars and constitutional law experts across the nation have been excitedly studying the 6-to-3 decision for weeks and now they say it may have an impact on the administration of justice in Canada far beyond their first impressions.

For instance, these experts say, by giving to the Bill of Rights the meaning it did, the Supreme Court of Canada has also given itself—and all other courts in the country—the unprecedented power to over-rule Parliament and throw out unjust federal laws. (The Bill of Rights doesn't apply to provincial law.)

The significance of that is that the day may come when you will be freed by a court—not because you are necessarily innocent but because the law under which you were charged has been found to be discriminatory or manifestly unjust or unduly restrictive.

Says Justice Minister John Turner: "This extremely important decision by the Supreme Court of Canada establishes the paramountcy in law of the Bill of Rights as it relates to federal legislation . . . "

To understand why the decision excites legal experts and where it may conceivably lead, let's examine the bizarre saga of Joe Drybones.

After the RCMP lugged the unconscious Indian away from the Old Stope Hotel (where owner Fred Rasche used to quell mutineers by raining blows on the splintered bar with a five-pound sledge-hammer), they charged him with violating a section of the Indian Act which makes it unlawful for Indians to be drunk off a reservation.

(Since there are no reservations in the Northwest Territories, it's impossible for an Indian to be legally drunk anywhere, including his own home.)

Joe Drybones was convicted, fined the statutory minimum of $10 and let go the following Monday morning (he got boiled on Saturday night). Later that day, lawyer Brian Purdy, a 27-year-old native of Toronto and a graduate of Halifax's Dalhousie University law school, noticed the record of Drybones' conviction in the Yellowknife court office.

It suddenly struck him, Purdy said afterward, that the Indian Act was discriminatory because it contained harsher penalties for drunkenness than those contained in the territorial liquor ordinance under which white men were prosecuted. (For one thing, the white man's law contains no minimum fines.)

Purdy went to see Drybones and explained through an interpreter the law as he saw it. Joe, who didn't have a lawyer at his trial, decided to appeal the conviction.

The appeal was heard June 5 at Yellowknife by Mr. Justice William G. Morrow of the Territorial Court. Purdy based his case largely on section 1 of the Bill of Rights which guarantees "the right of the individual to equality before the law."

Drybones, Purdy said, had enjoyed no such equality. Moreover, he argued, the Bill of Rights is supposed to take precedence over every other law of Canada unless Parliament explicitly decrees otherwise.

Since the Indian Act contained no such decree, Purdy said, the section had to give way to the Bill of Rights and the conviction against Drybones should therefore be set aside.

Morrow agreed. "This portion of the Indian Act is to me a case of discrimination of sufficient seriousness that I must hold that the intoxication sections of the Indian Act (violate) the Canadian Bill of Rights," he said in his judgment.

The crown appealed Morrow's decision to the Territorial Court of Appeal which comprised Chief Justice Sidney Bruce Smith of the Alberta Court of Appeal and two of his colleagues.

Drybones won again. The appeal court said that while it was Canadian government policy to treat Indians differently (often for their own protection) "one would have hoped that that could have been done without subjecting Indians to penalties and punishments different to those imposed on other races."

That judgment finally got the attention of the federal justice department in Ottawa and it launched last-ditch appeal proceedings before the Supreme Court of Canada.

On Oct. 28, 1968, G. Brian Purdy, three years at the bar, found himself in the panelled chambers of the highest court in the nation. Opposing him was a justice department team headed by Assistant Deputy Attorney-General Donald H. Christie.

Chief Justice John R. Cartwright, believing the issue had far-reaching implications for both the courts and the law of the country, had taken the unusual step of assembling all nine judges to hear the argument. Grave and attentive, they gazed down from the 35-foot-wide elevated bench ranged across the end of the chamber.

"It was enough to scare you right out of your socks," said Purdy.

Purdy's entire case was a single sentence 13 typewritten lines long. In it, he repeated his contention that because the Indian Act imposed a more severe penalty than the territorial liquor ordinance, it therefore violated the Bill of Rights and its offending sections should be declared "inoperative."

Then Christie presented the government's case, the court rose and everyone went home to await the decision.

On New Year's Day, 1969, the Old Stope Hotel caught fire and burned to the ground.

All over the Northwest Territories, drunk prosecutions under the Indian Act piled up but were not proceeded with because the crown was awaiting word on the fate of the law.

Joe Drybones, meanwhile, had long since got his $10 back and had lost interest in the whole affair. Purdy says he doubts whether Joe really comprehended what was going on or, for that matter, if he really knew or cared that there was such a thing as the Supreme Court of Canada.

(In January, 1968, Purdy and a bush pilot spent most of one day scouting the snow desert around Yellowknife by plane, looking for Joe so they could serve him with the notice of the crown's appeal to the Ottawa court. They finally found him by following his dog-team tracks. "Since he already had his 10 bucks back, I think he thought we were all nuts," said Purdy).

Then last Nov. 20, more than a year after the case was argued, the Supreme Court delivered its ruling. The 29 foolscap pages shot holes in the Indian Act and transformed the Bill of Rights from a dusty and half-forgotten relic into one of the most important laws in the country.

Mr. Justice Roland A. Ritchie, who wrote the majority opinion dismissing the crown's appeal, said "an individual is denied equality before the law if it is made an offence punishable at law, on account of his race, for him to do something which his fellow Canadians are free to do without having committed an offence. . . ."

The drunkenness section of the Indian Act, he said, created just that kind of offence and therefore it had to go. . . .

Mr. Justice Emmett M. Hall, agreeing with Ritchie, went so far as to liken the "philosophic concept" of the majority decision to the historic school desegregation order of the United States Supreme Court in 1954. Said Hall:

> The Canadian Bill of Rights is not fulfilled if it merely equates Indians with Indians in terms of equality before the law, but can have validity and meaning only when . . . it is seen to repudiate discrimination in every law of Canada by reason of race, national origin, color, religion or sex . . . in whatever way that discrimination may manifest itself, not only as between Indian and Indian but as between all Canadians. . . .

A judge of the provincial Supreme Court, who asked that his name be withheld, says the Drybones decision is the first time in history that the Supreme Court of Canada has gone beyond its traditional constitutional role of settling arguments over legislative jurisdiction between the provinces and the federal government.

"The court has added a new dimension," he said. "That dimension is that even though the federal government may pass legislation that is completely within its jurisdiction, that legislation shall not stand if its language is such as to create discrimination or the lack of equality before the law.

"The Supreme Court of Canada now employs its own test of a law. It superimposes the Bill of Rights on the statute at issue and if that statute offends, out it goes. It's the biggest decision we've had in years, perhaps ever. Any legislation that affects human rights will be fair game.". . .

THE LAVELL AND BEDARD DECISIONS*

[See also Chapter 16, pp. 542-546, for a discussion of the Supreme Court's recent role in these and other civil libertarian cases.]

Introduction

The Indian Act is a statute of the Parliament of Canada which is chiefly concerned with the internal regulation of the lives of Indians on reserves. Such persons enjoy the use and benefit of Crown lands and have other privileges.

For the purposes of the Indian Act, the definition of "Indian" is laid down in section 2(1) of the Act as follows: "'Indian' means a person who pursuant to this Act is registered as an Indian or is entitled to be registered as an Indian."

Section 12(1) of the Indian Act refines the above definition further: "The following persons are not entitled to be registered, namely . . . (b) a woman who married a person who is not an Indian."

In contrast, the Canadian Bill of Rights, also a statute of the Parliament of Canada, makes the following provision in Section 1 [italics added]:

> It is hereby recognized and declared that in Canada there have existed and shall continue to exist without discrimination by reason of race, national origin, colour, religion *or sex*, the following human rights and fundamental freedoms, namely . . .
> (b) the right of the individual to equality before the law and the protection of the law; . . . .

The Lavell and Bedard cases raise the question of whether Section 1(b) of the Canadian Bill of Rights renders inoperative Section 12(1b) of the Indian Act.

Background

Jeannette Lavell, originally a member of the Wikwemikong Band of Indians, married a non-Indian. Accordingly, her name was duly deleted from the Indian Register pursuant to Section 12(1b) of the Indian Act. Mrs. Lavell brought legal action against her exclusion from the Register, first before a judge acting as *persona designata* under the Indian Act, and then before the Federal Court of Appeal. The latter court found in favor of Mrs. Lavell, holding that Section 12(1b) of the Indian Act offended against the Canadian Bill of Rights and was therefore rendered inoperative. The Attorney General of Canada thereupon appealed this decision to the Supreme Court of Canada.

Yvonne Bedard was born and raised on the Six Nations Indian Reserve in the County of Brant until she married a non-Indian in May of 1964. She then resided off Reserve and had two children, but separated from

* From "Attorney General of Canada v. Lavell," *Canada Supreme Court Reports*, Part 10, 1974, Ottawa, Queen's Printer, 1975, pp. 1349-1392. Reproduced by permission of the Minister of Supply and Services Canada.

her husband in June of 1970. At this time, she returned to the Reserve to live on a property bequeathed to her by her mother. Thereupon the Council of the Six Nations, whose members were Richard Isaac and eighteen other individuals, served notice that she must dispose of the property, and she duly conveyed her interest in the property to her brother, a registered Indian who then allowed her to continue to occupy the property rent free. Soon, however, the Council of the Six Nations passed a further resolution that Mrs. Bedard must be given notice to quit the Reserve. Mrs. Bedard took action before the Supreme Court of Ontario, which found in favor of Mrs. Bedard, basing its decision on the judgment of the Federal Court of Appeal in the Lavell case. The Council of Six Nations appealed this decision to the Supreme Court of Canada.

The Decision of the Supreme Court of Canada

Having dealt with the two cases together, the Supreme Court found in favor of the respective appellants, namely the Attorney General of Canada and the Council of Six Nations, and against Mrs. Lavell and Mrs. Bedard. Accordingly, this decision reversed the judgments that had been rendered in these two cases by the Federal Court of Appeal and the Supreme Court of Ontario. The final decision was reached by a vote of five justices (CJ. Fauteux and JJ. Judson, Martland, Pigeon and Ritchie) to four (JJ. Abbott, Hall, Laskin and Spence). Reasons for the majority decision were expressed by the written opinion of Mr. Justice Ritchie and supplemented by an additional opinion written by Mr. Justice Pigeon. Reasons for the minority view were given by Mr. Justice Laskin, and supplemented by Mr. Justice Abbott.

The Opinions of the Justices

RITCHIE J.   These appeals, which were heard together, are from two judgments holding that the provisions of s.12(1)(b) of the *Indian Act,* R.S.C. 1970, c. I-6, are rendered inoperative by s.1(b) of the *Canadian Bill of Rights,* 1960 (Can.), c.44, as denying equality before the law to the two respondents. . . .

The contention which formed the basis of the argument submitted by both respondents was that they had been denied equality before the law *by reason of sex*, and I propose to deal with the matter on this basis. . . .

In my opinion the exclusive legislative authority vested in Parliament under [the *B.N.A. Act*] s.91(24) could not have been effectively exercised without enacting laws establishing the qualifications required to entitle persons to status as Indians and to the use and benefit of Crown "lands reserved for Indians". The legislation enacted to this end was, in my view, necessary for the implementation of the authority so vested in Parliament under the constitution.

To suggest that the provisions of the *Bill of Rights* have the effect of making the whole *Indian Act* inoperative as discriminatory is to assert that the Bill has rendered Parliament powerless to exercise the authority entrusted to it under the constitution of enacting legislation which treats

Indians living on Reserves differently from other Canadians in relation to their property and civil rights. The proposition that such a wide effect is to be given to the *Bill of Rights* was expressly reserved by the majority of this Court in the case of *The Queen v. Drybones*, [1970] S.C.R. 282 at 298, to which reference will hereafter be made, and I do not think that it can be sustained.

What is at issue here is whether the *Bill of Rights* is to be construed as rendering inoperative one of the conditions imposed by Parliament for the use and occupation of Crown lands reserved for Indians. These conditions were imposed as a necessary part of the structure created by Parliament for the internal administration of the life of Indians on Reserves and their entitlement to the use and benefit of Crown lands situate thereon. They were thus imposed in discharge of Parliament's constitutional function under s.91(24) and in my view can only be changed by plain statutory language expressly enacted for the purpose. It does not appear to me that Parliament can be taken to have made or intended to make such a change by the use of broad general language directed at the statutory proclamation of the fundamental rights and freedoms enjoyed by all Canadians, and I am therefore of opinion that the *Bill of Rights* had no such effect. . . .

The contention that the *Bill of Rights* is to be construed as overriding all of the special legislation imposed by Parliament under the *Indian Act* is, in my view, fully answered by Pigeon J. in his dissenting opinion in the *Drybones* case where he said, at page 304:

> If one of the effects of the *Canadian Bill of Rights* is to render inoperative all legal provisions whereby Indians as such are not dealt with in the same way as the general public, the conclusion is inescapable that Parliament, by the enactment of the *Bill*, has not only fundamentally altered the status of the Indians in that indirect fashion but has also made any future use of federal legislative authority over them subject to the requirement of expressly declaring every time "that the law shall operate notwithstanding the *Canadian Bill of Rights*". I find it very difficult to believe that Parliament so intended when enacting the *Bill*. If a virtual suppression of federal legislation over Indians as such was meant, one would have expected this important change to be made explicitly not surreptitiously so to speak.

•   •   •

In considering the meaning to be given to section 1(b) of the *Bill of Rights*, regard must of course be had to what was said by Mr. Justice Laskin, speaking in this regard for the whole of the Court in *Curr v. The Queen*, [1972] S.C.R. 889 at pages 896 and 897, where he interpreted sections 1(a) and 1(b) of the *Bill* in the following passage:

> In considering the reach of s.1(a) and s.1(b), and, indeed, of s.1 as a whole, I would observe, first, that the section is given its controlling

force over federal law by its referential incorporation into s.2; and, second, that I do not read it as making the existence of any of the forms of prohibited discrimination a *sine qua non* of its operation. Rather, the prohibited discrimination is an additional lever to which federal legislation must respond. Putting the matter another way, federal legislation which does not offend s.1 in respect of any of the prohibited kinds of discrimination may nonetheless be offensive to s.1 if it is violative of what is specified in any of the clauses (a) to (f) of s.1. It is, *a fortiori*, offensive if there is discrimination by reason of race so as to deny equality before the law. That is what this Court decided in *Regina v. Drybones* and I need say no more on this point.

It is, therefore, not an answer by the appellant of s.1(a) and s.1(b) of the *Canadian Bill of Rights* that s.223 does not discriminate against any person by reason of race, national origin, colour, religion or sex. The absence of such discrimination still leaves open the question whether s.223 can be construed and applied without abrogating, abridging or infringing the rights of the individual listed in s.1(a) and s.1(b).

My understanding of this passage is that the effect of section 1 of the *Bill of Rights* is to guarantee to all Canadians the rights specified in paragraphs (a) to (f) of that section, irrespective of race, national origin, colour or sex. . . .

It was stressed on behalf of the respondents that the provisions of section 12(1)(b) of the *Indian Act* constituted "discrimination by reason of sex" and that the section could be declared inoperative on this ground alone even if such discrimination did not result in the infringement of any of the rights and freedoms specifically guaranteed by section 1 of the Bill.

I can find no support for such a contention in the *Curr* case in which, in any event, no question of any kind of discrimination was either directly or indirectly involved. My own understanding of the passage which I have quoted from that case was that it recognized the fact that the primary concern evidenced by the first two sections of the *Bill of Rights* is to ensure that the rights and freedoms thereby recognized and declared shall continue to exist for all Canadians, and it follows, in my view, that those sections cannot be invoked unless one of the enumerated rights and freedoms has been denied to an individual Canadian or group of Canadians. Section 2 of the *Bill of Rights* provides for the manner in which the rights and freedoms which are recognized and declared by section 1 are to be enforced and the effect of this section is that every law of Canada shall "be so construed and applied as not to abrogate, abridge or infringe or authorize the abrogation, abridgment or infringement of any of the rights and freedoms herein recognized and declared. . . ." (i.e. by section 1). There is no language anywhere in the *Bill of Rights* stipulating that the laws of Canada are to be construed without discrimination unless that discrimination involves the denial of one of the guaranteed rights and freedoms, but when, as in the case of *Regina v. Drybones*, denial of one of the enumerated rights is occasioned by reason of discrimination, then, as Mr. Justice Laskin has said, the discrimination affords an "additional lever to which federal legislation must respond."

The opening words of section 2 of the *Bill of Rights* are, in my view, determinative of the test to be applied in deciding whether the section here impugned is to be declared inoperative. The words to which I refer are:

> 2. Every law of Canada shall, unless it is expressly declared by an act of the Parliament of Canada that it shall operate notwithstanding the *Canadian Bill of Rights*, be so construed and applied as not to abrogate, abridge or infringe or authorize the abrogation, abridgment or infringement of the freedoms herein recognized and declared. . . .

In the course of the reasons for judgment rendered on behalf of the majority of this Court in *The Queen v. Drybones supra*, this language was interpreted in the following passage at page 294:

> It seems to me that a more realistic meaning must be given to the words in question and they afford, in my view, the clearest indication that s.2 is intended to mean and does mean that if a law of Canada cannot be "sensibly construed and applied" so that it does not abrogate, abridge or infringe one of the rights and freedoms, recognized and declared by the Bill, then such a law is inoperative "unless it is expressly declared by an Act of the Parliament of Canada that it shall operate notwithstanding the *Canadian Bill of Rights*".

Accordingly, in my opinion, the question to be determined in these appeals is confined to deciding whether the Parliament of Canada in defining the prerequisites of Indian status so as not to include women of Indian birth who have chosen to marry non-Indians, enacted a law which cannot be sensibly construed and applied without abrogating, abridging or infringing the rights of such women to equality before the law.

In my view the meaning to be given to the language employed in the *Bill of Rights* is the meaning which it bore in Canada at the time when the Bill was enacted, and it follows that the phrase "equality before the law" is to be construed in light of the law existing in Canada at that time. . . . [Mr. Justice Ritchie proceeds to quote various authorities.]

The relevance of these quotations to the present circumstances is that "equality before the law" as recognized by Dicey as a segment of the rule of law, carries the meaning of equal subjection of all classes to the ordinary law of the land *as administered by the ordinary courts*, and in my opinion the phrase "equality before the law" as employed in section 1(b) of the *Bill of Rights* is to be treated as meaning equality in the administration or application of the law by the law enforcement authorities and the ordinary courts of the land. This construction is, in my view, supported by the provisions of subsections (a) to (g) of section 2 of the Bill which clearly indicate to me that it was equality in the administration and enforcement of the law with which Parliament was concerned when it guaranteed the continued existence of "equality before the law".

Turning to the *Indian Act* itself, it should first be observed that by far the greater part of that Act is concerned with the internal regulation of the lives of Indians on Reserves and that the exceptional provisions dealing with the conduct of Indians off Reserves and their contacts with other Canadian citizens fall into an entirely different category. . . .

Provision for the loss of status by women who marry non-Indians was first introduced in 1869 by section 6 of chapter 6 of the Statutes of Canada of that year. . . . It is thus apparent that the marital status of Indian women who marry non-Indians has been the same for at least one hundred years and that their loss of Band status on marriage to a member of another Band and acquisition of status in that Band, for which provision is made under s.14 of the *Indian Act*, has been in effect for the same period.

•   •   •

A careful reading of the Act discloses that section 95 (formerly 94) is the only provision therein made which creates an offence for any behaviour of an Indian *off* a Reserve and it will be plain that there is a wide difference between legislation such as s.12 (1)(b) governing the civil rights of designated persons living on Indian Reserves to the use and benefit of Crown lands, and criminal legislation such as s.95 which creates an offence punishable at law for Indians to act in a certain fashion when *off* a Reserve. The former legislation is enacted as a part of the plan devised by Parliament, under s.91(24) for the regulation of the internal domestic life of Indians on Reserves. The latter is criminal legislation exclusively concerned with behaviour of Indians *off* a Reserve.

Section 95 (formerly s.94) reads, in part, as follows:

> 95. An Indian who . . .
>   (b) is intoxicated . . .
> Off a reserve, is guilty of an offence and is liable on summary conviction to a fine of not less than ten dollars and not more than fifty dollars or to imprisonment for a term not exceeding three months or to both fine and imprisonment.

These were the provisions that were at issue in the case of *The Queen v. Drybones, supra*, where this Court held that they could not be construed and applied without exposing Indians as a racial group to a penalty in respect of conduct as to which the Parliament of Canada had imposed no sanctions on other Canadians who were subject to Canadian laws regulating their conduct, which were of general application in the Northwest Territories where the offence was allegedly committed and in which there are no Indian Reserves.

In that case the decision of the majority of this Court was that the provisions of s.94(b), as it then was, could not be enforced without bringing about inequality between one group of citizens and another and that this inequality was occasioned by reason of the race of the accused. It was there said, at page 297:

> . . . I am . . . of opinion that an individual is denied equality before the law if it is made an offence punishable at law, on account of his race, for him to do something which his fellow Canadians are free to do without having committed any offence or having been made subject to any penalty.

It is only necessary for the purpose of deciding this case for me to say that in my opinion s.94(b) of the *Indian Act* is a law of Canada which creates such an offence and that it can only be construed in such manner that its application would operate so as to abrogate, abridge or infringe one of the rights declared and recognized by the *Bill of Rights*. For the reasons which I have indicated, I am therefore of opinion that s.94(b) is inoperative.

For the purpose of determining the issue raised by this appeal it is unnecessary to express any opinion respecting the operation of any other section of the *Indian Act*.

And it was later said:

The present case discloses laws of Canada which abrogate, abridge and infringe the right of an individual Indian to equality before the law and in my opinion if those laws are to be applied in accordance with the express language used by Parliament in s.2 of the *Bill of Rights*, then s.94(b) of the Indian Act must be declared to be inoperative.

It appears to me to be desirable to make it plain that these reasons for judgment are limited to a situation in which, under the laws of Canada, it is made an offence punishable at law on account of race, for a person to do something which all Canadians who are not members of the race may do with impunity; in my opinion the same considerations do not by any means apply to all the provisions of the *Indian Act*.

Having regard to the express reservations contained in these passages, I have difficulty in understanding how that case can be construed as having decided that any sections of the *Indian Act*, except s.94(b), are rendered inoperative by the *Bill of Rights*.

The *Drybones* case can, in my opinion, have no application to the present appeals as it was in no way concerned with the internal regulation of the lives of Indians *on* Reserves or their right to the use and benefit of Crown lands thereon, but rather deals exclusively with the effect of the *Bill of Rights* on a section of the *Indian Act* creating a crime with attendant penalties for the conduct by Indians *off* a Reserve in an area where non-Indians, who were also governed by federal law, were not subject to any such restriction.

The fundamental distinction between the present case and that of *Drybones*, however, appears to me to be that the impugned section in the latter case could not be enforced without denying equality of treatment in the administration and enforcement of the law before the ordinary courts of the land to a racial group, whereas no such inequality of treatment between Indian men and women flows as a necessary result of the application of s.12(1)(b) of the *Indian Act*.

To summarize the above, I am of opinion:

1. that the *Bill of Rights* is not effective to render inoperative legislation, such as 12(1)(b) of the *Indian Act*, passed by the Parliament of Canada in discharge of its constitutional function under s.91(24) of the *B.N.A. Act*, to specify how and by whom Crown lands reserved for Indians are to be used;

2. that the *Bill of Rights* does not require federal legislation to be declared inoperative unless it offends against one of the rights specifically

guaranteed by section 1, but where legislation is found to be discriminatory, this affords an added reason for rendering it ineffective;

3. that equality before the law under the *Bill of Rights* means equality of treatment in the enforcement and application of the laws of Canada before the law enforcement authorities and the ordinary courts of the land, and no such inequality is necessarily entailed in the construction and application of s.12(1)(b). . . .

LASKIN J.   In my opinion, unless we are to depart from what was said in *Drybones*, both appeals now before us must be dismissed. I have no disposition to reject what was decided in *Drybones*; and on the central issue of prohibited discrimination as catologued in s.1 of the *Canadian Bill of Rights*, it is, in my opinion, impossible to distinguish *Drybones* from the two cases in appeal. If, as in *Drybones*, discrimination by reason of race makes certain statutory provisions inoperative, the same result must follow as to statutory provisions which exhibit discrimination by reason of sex. . . .

•   •   •

The contentions of the appellants in both cases in appeal, stripped of their detail, amount to a submission that the *Canadian Bill of Rights* does not apply to Indians on a Reserve, nor to Indians in their relations to one another whether or not on a Reserve. This submission does not deny that the effect of s.12(1)(b) of the *Indian Act* is to prescribe substantive discrimination by reason of sex, a differentiation in the treatment of Indian men and Indian women when they marry non-Indians, this differentiation being exhibited in the loss by the women of their status as Indians under the Act. It does, however, involve the assertion that the particular discrimination upon which the two appeals are focussed is not offensive to the relevant provisions of the *Canadian Bill of Rights*; and it also involves the assertion that the *Drybones* case is distinguishable or, if not, that it has been overcome by the re-enactment of the *Indian Act* in the Revised Statutes of Canada, 1970, including the then s.94 (now s.95) which was in issue in that case. I regard this last-mentioned assertion, which is posited on the fact that the *Canadian Bill of Rights* was not so re-enacted, as simply an oblique appeal for the overruling of the *Drybones* case.

The *Drybones* case decided two things. It decided first—and this decision was a necessary basis for the second point in it—that the *Canadian Bill of Rights* was more than a mere interpretation statute whose terms would yield to a contrary intention; it had paramount force when a federal enactment conflicted with its terms, and it was the incompatible federal enactment which had to give way. This was the issue upon which the then Chief Justice of this Court, Chief Justice Cartwright, and Justices Abbott and Pigeon, dissented. Pigeon J. fortified his view on this main point by additional observations, bringing into consideration, *inter alia*, s.91(24) of the *British North America Act*. The second thing decided by *Drybones* was that the accused in that case, an Indian under the *Indian Act*, was denied equality before the law, under s.1(b) of the *Canadian Bill of Rights*, when it was made a punishable offence for him, on account of his race, to do something which his fellow Canadians were free to do without being liable to punishment for an offence. . . .

It would be unsupportable in principle to view the *Drybones* case as turning on the fact that the challenged s.94 of the *Indian Act* created an offence visited by punishment. The gist of the judgment lay in the legal disability imposed upon a person by reason of his race when other persons were under no similar restraint. If for the words "on account of race" there are substituted the words "on account of sex" the result must surely be the same where a federal enactment imposes disabilities or prescribes disqualifications for members of the female sex which are not imposed upon members of the male sex in the same circumstances.

It is said, however, that although this may be so as between males and females in general, it does not follow where the distinction on the basis of sex is limited as here to members of the Indian race. This, it is said further, does not offend the guarantee of "equality before the law" upon which the *Drybones* case proceeded. I wish to deal with these two points in turn and to review, in connection with the first point, the legal consequences for an Indian woman under the *Indian Act* when she marries a non-Indian.

It appears to me that the contention that a differentiation on the basis of sex is not offensive to the *Canadian Bill of Rights* where that differentiation operates only among Indians under the *Indian Act* is one that compounds racial inequality even beyond the point that the *Drybones* case found unacceptable. In any event, taking the *Indian Act* as it stands, as a law of Canada whose various provisions fall to be assessed under the *Canadian Bill of Rights*, I am unable to appreciate upon what basis the command of the *Canadian Bill of Rights*, that laws of Canada shall operate without discrimination by reason of sex, can be ignored in the operation of the *Indian Act*.

The *Indian Act* defines an Indian as a person who is registered as an Indian pursuant to the Act or is entitled to be so registered. It is registration or registrability upon a Band list or upon a general list that is the key to the scheme and application of the Act. The Registrar, charged with keeping the membership records, is the person to whom protests may be made by a Band Council or by an affected person respecting the inclusion or deletion of a name from the Indian Register. By s.9(2) his decision on a protest is final subject to a reference to a judge under s.9(3). The *Lavell* case arose in this way. Section 11 of the Act enumerates the persons entitled to be registered, and it is common ground that both Mrs. Lavell and Mrs. Bedard were so entitled prior to their respective marriages. Section 12 lists the classes of persons not entitled to be registered and the only clause thereof relevant here is subsection 1(b) which I have already quoted. Section 14 has a peripheral relevance to the present case in its provision that a woman member of a Band who marries a person outside that Band ceases to be a member thereof but becomes a member of the Band of which her husband is a member. There is no absolute disqualification of an Indian woman from registrability on the Indian Register (that is, as a member on the general list) by marrying outside a Band unless the marriage is to a non-Indian.

Registration or registrability entitles an Indian as a member of a Band

(and that was the status of both Mrs. Lavell and Mrs. Bedard prior to their respective marriages) to the use and benefit of the Reserve set aside for the Band. This may take the form of possession or occupation of particular land in the Reserve under an allotment by the Council of the Band with the approval of the responsible Minister, and it may be evidenced by a certificate of possession or a certificate of occupation, the latter representing possession for a limited period only. Indians may make wills disposing of their property, and it may also pass on intestacy, in either case subject to approval or control of the Minister or of a competent court; and in the case of a devise or descent of land in a Reserve the claimant's possession must be approved by the Minister under s.49. Section 50 has only a remote bearing on the *Bedard* case in providing that a person who is not entitled to reside on a Reserve does not by devise or descent acquire a right to possession or occupation of land in that Reserve. It begs the question in that the issue here is whether or not Mrs. Bedard became disentitled to reside on the land in the Reserve which was left to her by her mother upon the latter's death in 1969. The fact that the respondent's brother now holds a certificate of possession of all the land formerly possessed by the mother, that certificate having been issued after the respondent transferred her interest to her brother in February, 1971, does not affect the overriding question of the respondent's right to reside on the land, having her brother's consent to residence thereon.

Indians entitled to be registered and to live on a Reserve are members of a society in which, through Band Councils, they share in the administration of the Reserve subject to overriding governmental authority. There is provision for election of councillors by Band members residing on a Reserve, and I note that there is no statutory discrimination between Indian men and women either as qualified electors or as qualified candidates for election as councillors. Other advantages that come from membership in the social unit relate to farm operations and to eligibility for governmental loans for various enumerated purposes.

Section 12(1)(b) effects a statutory excommunication of Indian women from this society but not of Indian men. Indeed, as was pointed out by counsel for the Native Council of Canada, the effect of ss.11 and 12(1)(b) is to excommunicate the children of a union of an Indian woman with a non-Indian. There is also the invidious distinction, invidious at least in the light of the *Canadian Bill of Rights*, that the *Indian Act* creates between brothers and sisters who are Indians and who respectively marry non-Indians. The statutory banishment directed by s.12(1)(b) is not qualified by the provision in s.109(2) for a governmental order declaring an Indian woman who has married a non-Indian to be enfranchised. Such an order is not automatic and no such order was made in relation to Mrs. Bedard; but when made the woman affected is, by s.110, deemed not to be an Indian within the *Indian Act* or any other statute or law. It is, if anything, an additional legal instrument of separation of an Indian woman from her native society and from her kin, a separation to which no Indian man who marries a non-Indian is exposed.

It was urged, in reliance in part on history, that the discrimination embodied in the *Indian Act* under s.12(1)(b) is based upon a reasonable classification of Indians as a race, that the *Indian Act* reflects this classification and that the paramount purpose of the Act to preserve and protect the members of the race is promoted by the statutory preference for Indian men. Reference was made in this connection to various judgments of the Supreme Court of the United States to illustrate the adoption by that Court of reasonable classifications to square with the due process clause of the Fifth Amendment and with due process and equal protection under the Fourteenth Amendment. Those cases have at best a marginal relevance because the *Canadian Bill of Rights* itself enumerates prohibited classifications which the judiciary is bound to respect; and, moreover, I doubt whether discrimination on account of sex, where as here it has no biological or physiological rationale, could be sustained as a reasonable classification even if the direction against it was not as explicit as it is in the *Canadian Bill of Rights*.

I do not think it is possible to leap over the telling words of s.1, "without discrimination by reason of race, national origin, colour, religion or sex", in order to explain away any such discrimination by invoking the words "equality before the law" in clause (b) and attempting to make them alone the touchstone of reasonable classification. That was not done in the *Drybones* case; and this Court made it clear in *Curr v. The Queen*, [1972] S.C.R. 889 that federal legislation, which might be compatible with the command of "equality before the law" taken alone, may nonetheless be inoperative if it manifests any of the prohibited forms of discrimination. In short, the proscribed discriminations in s.1 have a force either independent of the subsequently enumerated clauses (a) to (f) or, if they are found in any federal legislation, they offend those clauses because each must be read as if the prohibited forms of discrimination were recited therein as a part thereof.

This seems to me an obvious construction of s.1 of the *Canadian Bill of Rights*. When that provision states that the enumerated human rights and fundamental freedoms shall continue to exist "without discrimination by reason of race, national origin, colour, religion or sex" it is expressly adding these words to clauses (a) to (f). Section 1(b) must read therefore as "the right of the individual to equality before the law and the protection of the law without discrimination by reason of race, national origin, colour, religion or sex". It is worth repeating that this is what emerges from the *Drybones* case and what is found in the *Curr* case.

There is no clear historical basis for the position taken by the appellants, certainly not in relation to Indians in Canada as a whole, and this was in effect conceded during the hearing in this Court. In any event, history cannot avail against the clear words of ss.1 and 2 of the *Canadian Bill of Rights*. It is s.2 that gives this enactment its effective voice, because without it s.1 would remain a purely declaratory provision. Section 2 brings the terms of s.1 into its orbit, and its reference to "every law of Canada" is a reference, as set out in s.5(2), to any Act of the Parliament of Canada enacted before or after the effective date of the *Canadian Bill of Rights*. Pre-existing Canadian legislation as well as subsequent Canadian legislation is expressly made subject to the commands of the *Canadian Bill of Rights*, and those commands, where they are as clear as the one which is relevant here, cannot be diluted by appeals to history. Ritchie J. in his reasons in the *Drybones* case touched on this very point when he rejected the contention that the terms of s.1 of the *Canadian Bill of Rights* must be circumscribed by the provisions of Canadian statutes in force at the date of the enactment of the *Canadian Bill of Rights:* see [1970] S.C.R. 282, at pp. 295-296. I subscribed fully to the rejection of that contention. Clarity here is emphasized by looking at the French version of the *Canadian Bill of Rights* which speaks in s.1 of the enumerated human rights and fundamental freedoms "pour tout individu au Canada quels que soient sa race, son origine nationale, sa couleur, sa religion ou son sexe".

In my opinion, the appellants' contentions gain no additional force because the *Indian Act*, including the challenged s.12(1)(b) thereof, is a fruit of the exercise of Parliament's exclusive legislative power in relation to "Indians, and Lands reserved for the Indians" under s.91(24) of the *British North America Act.* Discriminatory treatment on the basis of race or colour or sex does not inhere in that grant of legislative power. The fact that its exercise may be attended by forms of discrimination prohibited by the *Canadian Bill of Rights* is no more a justification for a breach of the *Canadian Bill of Rights* than there would be in the case of the exercise of any other head of federal legislative power involving provisions offensive to the *Canadian Bill of Rights.* The majority opinion in the *Drybones* case dispels any attempt to rely on the grant of legislative power as a ground for escaping from the force of the *Canadian Bill of Rights*. The latter does not differentiate among the various heads of legislative power; it embraces all exercises under whatever head or heads they arise. Section 3 which directs the Minister of Justice to scrutinize every Bill to ascertain whether any of its provisions are inconsistent with ss.1 and 2 is simply an affirmation of this fact which is evident enough from ss.1 and 2.

There was an intimation during the argument of these appeals that the *Canadian Bill of Rights* is properly invoked only to resolve a clash under its terms between two federal statutes, and the *Drybones* case was relied on in that connection. It is a spurious contention, if seriously advanced, because the *Canadian Bill of Rights* is itself the indicator to which any Canadian statute or any provision thereof must yield unless Parliament has declared that the statute or the particular provision is to operate notwithstanding the *Canadian Bill of Rights*. A statute may in itself be offensive to the *Canadian Bill of Rights*, or it may be by relation to another statute that it is so offensive. . . .

PIGEON J. (supporting Ritchie J.):   I agree in the result with Ritchie J. I certainly cannot disagree with the view I did express in *The Queen v. Drybones* ([1970] S.C.R. 282, at p. 304) that the enactment of the *Canadian Bill of Rights* was not intended to effect a virtual suppression of federal legislation over Indians. My difficulty is Laskin J.'s strongly reasoned opinion that, unless we are to depart from what was said by the majority in *Drybones*, these appeals should be dismissed because, if discrimination by reason of race makes certain statutory provisions inoperative, the same result must follow as to statutory provisions which exhibit discrimination by reason of sex. In the end, it appears to me that, in the circumstances, I need not reach a firm conclusion on that point. Assuming the situation is such as Laskin J. says, it cannot be improper for me to adhere to what was my dissenting view, when a majority of those who did not agree with it in respect of a particular section of the *Indian Act*, now adopt it for the main body of this important statute.

I would observe that this result does not conflict with any of our decisions subsequent to *Drybones*. In no case was the *Canadian Bill of Rights* given an invalidating effect over prior legislation.

In *Lowry and Lepper v. The Queen* ((1972), 26 D.L.R. (3d) 224) and in *Brownridge v. The Queen* ([1972] S.C.R. 926), the application of criminal legislation, past and subsequent, was held to be subject to provisions respecting a "fair hearing" and "the right to retain and instruct counsel". These decisions are important illustrations of the effectiveness of the Bill without any invalidating effect.

In *Smythe v. The Queen* ([1971] S.C.R. 680) it was held that provisions for stiffer penalties depending on the method of prosecution were not rendered inoperative by the *Canadian Bill of Rights* as infringing equality before the law, although the choice of the method of prosecution always depends on executive discretion.

In *Curr v. The Queen* ([1972] S.C.R. 889) recent *Criminal Code* provisions for compulsory breath analysis were held not to infringe the right to the "protection of the law" any more than the right to the "protection against self-crimination".

Finally, in *Duke v. The Queen* ([1972] S.C.R. 917) these same provisions were said not to deprive the accused of a "fair trial" although proclaimed without some paragraphs contemplating a specimen being offered and given on request to the suspect.

ABBOTT J. (supporting Laskin J.): I am in agreement with the reasons of Laskin J. and wish to add only a few observations.

I share his view that the decision of this Court in *R. v. Drybones* cannot be distinguished from the two cases under appeal although in these two appeals the consequences of the discrimination by reason of sex under s.12(1)(b) of the *Indian Act* are more serious than the relatively minor penalty for the drinking offence under s.94 of the *Act* which was in issue in *Drybones*.

In that case, this Court rejected the contention that s.1 of the *Canadian Bill of Rights* provided merely a canon of construction for the interpretation of legislation existing when the Bill was passed. With respect I cannot interpret "equality before the law" as used in s.1(b) of the Bill as meaning simply "the equal subjection of all classes to the ordinary law of the land as administered by the ordinary courts" to use the language of Dicey which is quoted in the reasons of Ritchie J.

Unless the words "without discrimination by reason of race, national origin, colour, religion or sex" used in s.1 are to be treated as mere rhetorical window dressing, effect must be given to them in interpreting the section. I agree with Laskin J. that s.1(b) must be read as if those words were recited therein.

In my view the *Canadian Bill of Rights* has substantially affected the doctrine of the supremacy of Parliament. Like any other statute it can of course be repealed or amended, or a particular law declared to be applicable notwithstanding the provisions of the Bill. In form the supremacy of Parliament is maintained but in practice I think that it has been substantially curtailed. In my opinion that result is undesirable, but that is a matter for consideration by Parliament not the courts.

Ritchie J. said in his reasons for judgment in *Drybones* that the implementation of the *Bill of Rights* by the courts can give rise to great difficulties and that statement has been borne out in subsequent litigation. Of one thing I am certain the Bill will continue to supply ample grist to the judicial mills for some time to come. . . .

BIBLIOGRAPHY

Protecting Civil Rights

Borovoy, A., "Civil Liberties in the Imminent Hereafter", *The Canadian Bar Review*, Vol. LI, No. 1, March, 1973.

Canada, (Trudeau, P. E.), *A Canadian Charter of Human Rights*, Ottawa, Queen's Printer, 1968.

Cosman, R. W., "A Man's House is his Castle—'Beep': a Civil Law Remedy for the Invasion of Privacy", *University of Toronto Faculty of Law Review*, Vol. 29, August, 1971.

Devall, W. B., "Support for Civil Liberties among English-speaking Canadian University Students", *C.J.P.S.*, Vol. III, No. 3, September, 1970.

Haggart, R., and Golden, A. E., *Rumours of War*, Toronto, New Press, 1971.

Hogg, P. W., "The Canadian Bill of Rights—Equality Before the Law"—A.-G. Can. V. Lavell, *The Canadian Bar Review*, Vol. LII, No. 2, May, 1974.

Hunter, I. A., "Judicial Review of Human Rights Legislation: McKay v. Bell", *University of British Columbia Law Review*, Vol. 7, No. 1, 1972.

MacGuigan, M., "The Development of Civil Liberties in Canada," *QQ*. Vol. LXXII, No. 2, Summer, 1965.

Marx, H., "Emergency Power and Civil Liberties in Canada," *McGill Law Journal*, Vol. 16, No. 1, 1970.

Russell, P. H., "A Democratic Approach to Civil Liberties," *University of Toronto Law Journal*, Vol. XIX, 1969.

Schmeiser, D. A., *Civil Liberties in Canada*, London, Oxford University Press, 1964.

Schmeiser, D. A., "The Case Against Entrenchment of a Canadian Bill of Rights," *Dalhousie Law Journal*, Vol. 1, No. 1, September, 1973.

Scott, F. R.; et al., "A collection of articles on the Canadian Bill of Rights," *Canadian Bar Review*, Vol. XXXVII, No. 1, March, 1959.

Scott, F. R., *Civil Liberties and Canadian Federalism*, Toronto, University of Toronto Press, 1959.

Sharp, J. M., "The public servant and the right to privacy", *C.P.A.*, Vol. 14, No. 1, Spring, 1971.

Smith, D., *Bleeding Hearts . . . Bleeding Country: Canada and the Quebec Crisis*, Edmonton, Hurtig, 1971.

Tarnopolsky, W. S., "Emergency powers and civil liberties", *C.P.A.*, Vol. 15, No. 2, Summer, 1972.

Tarnopolsky, W. S., *The Canadian Bill of Rights*, 2nd rev. ed., Carleton Library, No. 83, Toronto, McClelland and Stewart, 1975.

Tarnopolsky, W. S., "The Supreme Court and the Canadian Bill of Rights," *Canadian Bar Review*, Vol. LIII, No. 14, December, 1975.

University of British Columbia Law Review, Vol. 7, No. 1, 1972. (See articles pp. 17-137.)

Whyte, J. D., "The Lavell Case and Equality in Canada", *Q.Q.*, Vol. 81, No. 1, Spring, 1974.

Social Issues

Environment

Chant, D. A., (ed.), *Pollution Probe*, Toronto, New Press, 1972.

Dales, J. H., *Pollution, property & prices*, Toronto, University of Toronto Press, 1968.

Freeman, M. M. R., *People Pollution*, Montreal & London, McGill-Queen's University Press, 1974.

Larkin, P. A., *Freshwater Pollution, Canadian Style*, Montreal & London, McGill-Queen's University Press, 1974.

Lundquist, L. J., "Do political structures matter in environmental politics? The Case of air pollution control in Canada, Sweden, and the United States", *C.P.A.*, Vol. 17, No. 1, Spring, 1974.

McNairn, C. H., "Airport Noise Pollution: The Problem and the Regulatory Response", *The Canadian Bar Review*, Vol. L, No. 2, May, 1972.

Marsden, L. R., *Population Probe: Canada*, Toronto, Copp Clark, 1972.

Raynauld, A., "Protection of the environment: economic perspectives", *C.P.A.*, Vol. 15, No. 4, Winter, 1972.

Richardson, A. H., *Conservation by the People*, Toronto, University of Toronto Press, 1974.

Stein, S. B., "Environmental control and different levels of government", *C.P.A.*, Vol. 14, No. 1, Spring, 1971.

Native Peoples

Canada, *A Survey of the Contemporary Indians of Canada*, (Hawthorn-Tremblay Report), Ottawa, Queen's Printer, 1966.

Cardinal, H., *The Unjust Society: The Tragedy of Canada's Indians*, Edmonton, Hurtig, 1969.

Chrétien, J., *Statement of the Government of Canada on Indian Policy*, 1969, Ottawa, Queen's Printer, 1969.

Cox, B., (ed.), *Cultural Ecology: Readings on the Canadian Indians and Eskimos*, Toronto, McClelland and Stewart, 1973.

Cumming, P. A., and Mickenberg, N. H., (eds.), *Native Rights in Canada*, 2nd ed., Toronto, Indian-Eskimo Association, 1972.

Davis, R., and Zannis, M., *The Genocide Machine in Canada—The Pacification of the North*, Montreal, Black Rose, 1973.

Denton, T., "Migration from a Canadian Indian reserve", *Journal of Canadian Studies*, Vol. VII, No. 2, May, 1972.

Dosman, E. J., *Indians, The Urban Dilemma*, Toronto, McClelland and Stewart, 1972.

Eisenberg, J., and Troper, H., *Native Survival*, Toronto, Ontario Institute for Studies in Education, 1973.

Frideres, J. S., *Canada's Indians: Contemporary Conflicts*, Scarborough, Ontario, Prentice-Hall, 1974.

La Violette, P., *The Struggle for Survival, Indian Cultures and the Protestant Ethic in B.C.*, Toronto, University of Toronto Press, 1973.

Manuel, G., *The Fourth World: An Indian Reality*, Toronto, Collier-Macmillan, 1974.

Robertson, H., *Reservations are for Indians*, Toronto, James, Lewis & Samuel, 1970.

Smith, D. G., (ed.), *Canadian Indians and the Law: Selected Documents, 1663-1972*, Carleton Library No. 87, Toronto, McClelland and Stewart, 1975.

Poverty

Adams, I., *The Poverty Wall*, Toronto, McClelland and Stewart, 1970.

Adams, I., *et al.*, *The Real Roverty Report*, Edmonton, Hurtig, 1972.

Canada, Senate, Special Committee on Proverty, *Poverty in Canada*, Ottawa, Queen's Printer, 1972.

Dennis, M., and Fish, S., *Programs in Search of a Policy; Law Income Housing in Canada*, Toronto, Hakkert, 1972.

Harp. J., and Hofley, J. R., (eds.), *Poverty in Canada*, Scarborough, Ontario, Prentice-Hall, 1971.

Johnson, L. A., *Incomes, Disparity and Improvement in Canada Since World War II*, Toronto, New Hogtown Press, 1973.

Lithwick, N. H., "Proverty in Canada: recent empirical findings", *Journal of Canadian Studies*, Vol. VI, No. 2, May, 1971.

Lithwick, N. H., *Urban Poverty*, Research Monograph No. 1 in the *Urban Canada, problems and prospects series*, Ottawa, Central Mortgage & Housing Corporation, 1971.

New Brunswick, *Participation and Development: The New Brunwick Task Force Report on Social Development and Social Welfare*, Fredericton, Queen's Printer, 1971.

Ryan, T. J., *Poverty and the Child—a Canadian Study*, Toronto and Montreal, McGraw-Hill Ryerson, 1972.

Swidinsky, R., and Wales, T. J., "Poverty and the Welfare State I & II", *BC Studies*, No. 13, Spring, 1973.

Resources

Bocking, R. C., *Canada's Water: For Sale?*, Toronto, James, Lewis & Samuel, 1972.

Bourassa, R., *James Bay*, Montreal, Harvest House, 1973.

Crabbé, P., and Spry, I. M., (eds.), *Natural Resource Development in Canada: A Multi-Disciplinary Seminar*, Ottawa, University of Ottawa Press, 1973.

Cross, M. S., *et al.*, *"Energy Sell-out: A Counter-Report"*, *The Canadian Forum*, Vol. LIII, No. 629-30, June-July, 1973.

Editorial Board, *et al.*, "Energy Policy," *Canadian Public Policy*, Vol. 1, No. 1, Winter, 1975.

Kilbourn, W., *Pipeline*, Toronto, Clarke, Irwin, 1970.

Laxer, J., *Canada's Energy Crisis*, Toronto, James, Lewis & Samuel, 1974.

Pearse, P., (ed.), *The Mackenzie Pipeline: Arctic Gas and Canadian Energy Policy*, Toronto, McClelland and Stewart, 1974.

Rohmer, R., *The Arctic Imperative: an overview of the energy crisis*, Toronto, McClelland and Stewart, 1973.

Rowland, W., *Fuelling Canada's Future*, Toronto, Macmillan, 1974.

Salisbury, R. F., *et al.*, *Development and James Bay: socio-economic implications of the Hydro-Electric Project*, Montreal, McGill University, 1972.

Scott, A., *Natural Resources; the Economics of Conservation*, Carleton Library No. 67, Toronto, McClelland and Stewart, 1973.

Sykes, P., *Sellout: The Giveaway of Canada's Energy Resources*, Edmonton, Hurtig, 1973.

Urban Problems

Axworthy, L., and Gillies, J. M., (eds.), *The City: Canada's Prospects and Canada's Problems*, Toronto, Butterworth, 1973.

Burns, R. M., "Government in an urban society", *C.P.A.*, Vol. 14, No. 3, Fall, 1971.

Chevalier, M., and Choukroun, J.-M., "Urban change and the urban future", *C.P.A.*, Vol. 14, No. 3, Fall, 1971.

Goldrick, M. D., "Present issues in the growth of cities", *C.P.A.*, Vol. 14, No. 3, Fall, 1971.

Gordon, D. R., *City Limits: Barriers to Change in Urban Government*, Don Mills, Ontario, Musson, 1973.

Harvey, E. R., *Sydney, Nova Scotia*: an urban study, Toronto, Clarke, Irwin, 1971.

Jackson, *The Canadian City*, Toronto, McGraw-Hill Ryerson, 1973.

Lithwick, N. H., (ed.), *Urban Canada—problems and prospects*, Ottawa, Central Mortgage and Housing Corporation, 1970.

Lithwick, N. H., "A economic interpretation of the urban crisis", *Journal of Canadian Studies*, Vol. VII, No. 3, August, 1972.

Lithwick, N. H., "Urban policy-making: shortcomings in political technology", *C.P.A.*, Vol. 15, No. 4, Winter, 1972.

Powell, A., (ed.), *The City: Attacking Modern Myths*, Toronto, McClelland and Stewart, 1972.

Richardson, B., *The Future of Canadian Cities*, Toronto, New Press, 1972.

Stewart, W., "Why Cities Don't Work", *Macleans*, January, 1974.

Wolforth, J. R., *Urban Prospects*, Toronto, McClelland and Stewart, 1971.

Women's Rights

Bohnen, L. S., "Women Workers in Ontario: A Socio-Legal History", *University of Toronto Faculty of Law Review*, Vol. 31, August, 1973.

Canada, "Cultural Tradition and Political History of Women in Canada", *Studies of the Royal Commission on the Status of Women in Canada*, No. 8, Ottawa, Information Canada, 1971.

Cleverdon, C. L., *The Woman Suffrage Movement in Canada*, Toronto, University of Toronto Press, 1974, First Published 1950.

Stephenson, M., (ed.), *Women in Canada*, Toronto, New Press, 1973.

Other

Canada, Senate, *A Science Policy for Canada: Report of the Senate Special Committee on Science Policy: Volume 2, Targets and Strategies for the Seventies*, Ottawa, Information Canada, 1972.

Canada, Senate, Special Committee on Aging, *Final report and proceedings*, Ottawa, Queen's Printer, 1966.

Clairmont, D. H., and Magill, D. W., *Africville; The Life and Death of a Canadian Black Community*, Toronto, McClelland and Stewart, 1974.

Doern, G. B., *Science and Politics in Canada*, London & Montreal, McGill-Queen's University Press, 1972.

Finnigan, B., and Gonick, C., (eds.), *Making It: The Canadian Dream*, Toronto, McClelland and Stewart, 1972.

La Pierre, L., McLeod, J., Taylor, C., Young, W., *Essays on the Left*, Toronto, McClelland and Stewart, 1971.

Lewis, D., *Louder Voices: The Corporate Welfare Bums*, Toronto, James, Lewis & Samuel, 1972.

Lithwick, N. H., *Canada's Science Policy and the Economy*, Toronto, Methuen, 1969.

Lloyd, T., and McLeod, J. T., (eds.), *Agenda 1970*, Toronto, University of Toronto Press, 1969.

Manzer, R., *Canada: A Socio-Political Report*, Toronto, McGraw-Hill Ryerson, 1974.

Marchak, M. P., *Ideological Perspectives on Canada*, Toronto, McGraw-Hill Ryerson, 1975.

Martell, G., (ed.), *The Politics of the Canadian Public School*, Toronto, James Lorimer, 1974.

Massey, H. J., (ed.), *The Canadian Military*, Toronto, Copp Clark, 1972.

Ossenberg, R., (ed.), *Canadian Society: Pluralism, Change & Conflict*, Toronto, Prentice-Hall, 1971.

Rea, K. J., and McLeod, J. T., (eds.), *Business and Government in Canada: Selected Readings*, Toronto, Methuen, 1969.

Rotstein, A., (ed.), *The Prospect of Change*, Toronto, McGraw-Hill, 1965.

Roussopoulos, D., (ed.), *Canada and Radical Social Change*, Montreal, Black Rose, 1973.

Stewart, W., *Hard to Swallow: Why food prices keep rising and what can be done about it*, Toronto, Macmillan, 1974.

Teeple, G., (ed.), *Capitalism and the National Question in Canada*, Toronto, University of Toronto Press, 1972.

Winks, R. W., *The Blacks in Canada; A History*, New Haven, Conn., Yale University Press, McGill-Queens University Press, 1971.

Ziegel, J. S., "The Future of Canadian Consumerism", *The Canadian Bar Review*, Vol. LI, No. 2, May, 1973.

18

PROVINCIAL ELECTION RESULTS

A SURVEY OF CANADIAN PROVINCIAL ELECTION RESULTS, 1905-1976*

Loren M. Simerl

The election survey presented here provides a guide to provincial voting statistics, as well as to the nature of the franchise and electoral systems in Canada's provinces over the past seventy years. With a few noted exceptions, all voting information in this survey came directly from provincial records and publications. Where accurate party identifications were unavailable from government sources, they were taken from *The Canadian Parliamentary Guide*, newspapers, and the *Canadian Annual Review*.

The choice of 1905 as the starting point for this survey is intended to give the reader a view of provincial elections before the era of third parties began in 1919 in Canada. Moreover, much early provincial election data is unavailable. Only Ontario and Quebec kept voter turnout statistics before 1905. Finally, the provinces of Saskatchewan and Alberta were created in 1905.

Where earlier tabulations of provincial voting data are available, they have been used as a check on the data given here. Inconsistencies have been double-checked.

Efforts have been made to make the percentage of votes for each party reflect its true voting strength. In the provinces of Newfoundland, Nova

* The author, who is a former post-graduate student in the Department of Political Economy, University of Toronto, is indebted to Canada's provincial electoral officers and archivists who provided much of the data in this survey, and the Canada Council, which helped make this research possible.

Scotia, New Brunswick, Ontario, Saskatchewan, Alberta, and British Columbia, where the electoral system tended to distort the relative popularity of the various parties, described adjustments in the party percentages removed this distortion. However, the unadjusted, valid votes by party are given for all provincial elections.

Where available, the details of voter turnout are given for each province. They have been adjusted to exclude possible distortions caused by acclamations or missing data. Rejected ballots are included in voter turnout figures for all provinces.

While the election data are set out in comparative format, caution should be exercised in making certain comparisons regarding voter turnout, since voter franchises vary by province and period, as does the thoroughness and method of enumeration.

Explanation of the Voter Code: The Criteria for Voter Eligibility in Canadian Provincial Elections

Voter Code	Age	Sex	Citizen- ship	Reservation Indian Voting	Nature of Other Criteria
a	21	Male	Br. Sub.	no	Wealth
b	21	Male	Br. Sub.	yes	—
c	21	Male	Br. Sub.	no	Anti-Asiatic
d	21	Male	Br. Sub.	no	—
e	21	Male	Br. Sub.	yes	Wealth
f	21	*	Br. Sub.	yes	Wealth
g	21	Both	Br. Sub.	no	—
h	21	Both	Br. Sub.	yes	—
i	21	Both	Br. Sub.	yes	Wealth
j	19	Both	Br. Sub.	no	—
k	21	Both	Br. Sub.	no	Anti-Asiatic
l	21	Both	Canadian	no	—
m	21	Both	Br. Sub.	no	Wealth
n	21	Both	Canadian	no	Wealth
o	18	Both	Br. Sub.	yes	—
p	19	Both	Br. Sub.	yes	—
q	**	Both	Br. Sub.	yes	—
r	18	Both	Canadian	no	—
s	21	Both	Canadian	yes	—
t	18	Both	Canadian	yes	—
u	18	Both	Br. Sub.	no	—

Source: The statutes of the ten provinces.
* Both sexes voted, but not married women.
** The voting age was 21 for men and 25 for women.
Notes: *Sex:* The word "Male" indicates that only men voted.
Citizenship: In 1947 the legal category of "Canadian Citizen" was established. Most provinces, however, continue to allow "British Subjects" to vote, a term which includes members of all Commonwealth countries including Canada.
Reservation Indians: This term excludes specially "enfranchised" Indians and those living off reservations, who could qualify to vote.
Asiatic Law: While in Saskatchewan this law forbade voting by Chinese persons, in British Columbia it applied to Chinese and Japanese persons (1907-1945) and to "Hindu" persons 1909-1945).

Wealth Laws: This is a general category of restrictions which had the effect of denying the vote to the poor and those who received public support, including Indians. Nova Scotia, New Brunswick, and Quebec passed laws to prevent most Indians from voting after they had ended or greatly reduced wealth qualifications. The legal criteria to establish "wealth" usually involved one or more of the following: personal property, real estate, or income, each of which might vary with occupation or locality. Ontario's 1905 "wealth" law applied to only 9 northern ridings.

Language: Although not part of the voter code, British Columbia requires its voters to have an "adequate knowledge" of either English or French (1949-1972).

Abbreviations Used Throughout:

Accl.	Acclamations	Nat.	Nationalist
CCF	Cooperative Commonwealth Federation	NDP	New Democratic Party
		O.	Others
Comm.	Communist	P./Prog.	Progressive
C./Con.	Conservative	PC	Progressive Conservative
Farm.	Farmer	Proh.	Prohibitionist
El.	Elected	SC	Social Credit
F-L	Farmer-Labour	Soc.	Socialist
I./Ind.	Independent	Temp.	Temperance
Lab.	Labour	UF	United Farmer
L./Lib.	Liberal	3rd	Third Party
L-P	Liberal Progressive	4th	Fourth Party
LPP	Labour Progressive Party		

Prince Edward Island Provincial Elections

Election Date	Seats	Candidates				Elected			Popular Vote							ACCL	Voter Code
		L	C	O	Tot	L	C	O	L	%	C	%	O	%	Total		
Nov. 18, 1908	30	30	28	—	58	16	14	—	15,488	51.6	14,541	48.4	—	—	30,029	2	e
Jan. 3, 1912	30	24	30	—	54	2	28	—	10,686	39.8	16,189	60.2	—	—	26,875	6	e
Sept. 16, 1915	30	30	30	—	60	13	17	—	17,097	49.9	17,179	50.1	—	—	34,276	—	e
July 24, 1919	30	28	30	2	60	25	4	1	19,241	51.7	17,028	45.7	956	2.6	37,225	—	e
July 24, 1923	30	30	30	7	67	5	25	—	23,087	43.8	27,144	51.5	2,442	4.7	52,673	—	m
June 25, 1927	30	30	30	—	60	24	6	—	34,004	53.1	30,072	46.9	—	—	64,076	—	m
Aug. 6, 1931	30	30	30	—	60	12	18	—	33,833	48.3	36,229	51.7	—	—	70,062	—	m
July 23, 1935	30	30	30	—	60	30	0	—	43,824	58.0	31,780	42.0	—	—	75,604	—	m
May 18, 1939	30	30	30	—	60	27	3	—	40,205	53.0	35,600	47.0	—	—	75,805	—	m
Sept. 15, 1943	30	30	30	12	72	20	10	—	35,396	51.3	31,849	46.1	1,815	2.6	69,060	—	m
Dec. 11, 1947	30	30	30	17	77	24	6	—	40,758	49.8	37,461	45.8	3,598	4.4	81,817	—	m
Aug. 26, 1951	30	30	30	5	66	24	6	—	40,847	51.6	36,971	46.7	1,336	1.7	79,154	—	m
May 25, 1955	30	30	30	—	60	27	3	—	44,918	55.0	36,705	45.0	—	—	81,623	—	n
Sept. 1, 1959	30	30	30	—	60	8	22	—	42,214	49.1	43,845	50.9	—	—	86,059	—	n
Dec. 10, 1962	30	30	30	—	60	11	19	—	43,603	49.4	44,707	50.6	—	—	88,310	—	n
May 30, 1966	32	32	32	—	64	17	15	—	47,056	50.5	46,118	49.5	—	—	93,174	—	s
May 11, 1970	32	32	32	—	64	27	5	—	64,484	58.3	46,075	41.7	—	—	110,559	—	t
Apr. 29, 1974	32	32	32	20	84	26	6	—	61,967	53.9	46,315	40.3	6,786	5.9	115,068	—	t

Sources: *Canadian Parliamentary Guide* (1908-1919); Official unpublished results first published by H. A. Scarrow (1923-1955); *Results*, Provincial Secretary Department (1959-1966); *Report of the Chief Electoral Officer* (1970-1974). No adequate check upon the party vote is possible for the elections from 1923 to 1955 since the official unpublished results are not available from P.E.I. sources.

Note: The figures given here are based on the combined results for both houses in P.E.I., the Assembly and the Council with half of the total seats in each. Until 1963, voting for candidates of either house was limited by property restrictions, but the restrictions for voting for Councillors were somewhat greater. From 1908 to 1962, an average of 31% of the voters who voted for Assemblymen did not cast a vote for a Councillor.

Note: Before 1970 no records were kept regarding voter turnout.

Acclamations: 1908: 2 Liberals, 1912: 6 Conservatives.

Electoral System: A Single-member, plurality system for each house.

Explanation of Party Totals:
1919: Others: I. (2) 965 (1 El.).
1923: Others: Prog. (5) 1,765; I. (2) 677.
1943: Others: CCF (9) 1,436; I.L. (3) 379.
1947: Others: CCF (16) 3,509; I. (1) 89.
1951: Others: CCF (5) 1,336.
1974: Others: NDP (20) 6,786.

Year	Voter Turnout		
	Registered Electorate	Voters who Voted	%
1970	65,201	56,937	87.3
1974	71,429	58,750	82.2

Newfoundland Provincial Elections

Election Date	Seats	Candidates					Elected				Popular Vote			
		L.	C.	NDP	O.	Tot.	L.	C.	O.	A C C L	L.	%*	C.	%*
May 27, 1949	28	28	28	—	2	58	22	5	1	—	109,802	70.0	55,111	28.0
Nov. 26, 1951	28	28	23	—	3	54	24	4	—	5	83,628	69.0	46,782	29.9
Oct. 2, 1956	36	35	31	—	11	76	32	4	—	4	75,883	66.7	36,591	31.6
Aug. 20, 1959	36	32	32	18	12	94	31	3	2	1	75,560	58.2	33,002	24.8
Nov. 19, 1962	42	42	35	6	3	86	34	7	1	3	72,319	58.7	45,055	36.4
Sept. 8, 1966	42	42	38	3	7	90	39	3	—	3	91,613	59.9	50,316	32.7
Oct. 28, 1971	42	42	42	19	5	108	18	22	1	—	102,775	44.4	118,899	51.3
Mar. 24, 1972	42	41	41	3	10	95	9	33	—	1	77,849	38.0	126,508	59.9
Sept. 16, 1975	51	51	51	17	32	151	16	30	5	—	82,270	37.1	101,016	45.5

Source: Chief Electoral Officer, *Report on the Provincial General Election* (1949-1975)

Notes: * The percentages given for party vote are adjusted to exclude the distortions caused by the electoral system. In multi-member ridings, the party per cent is changed by dividing the party vote by the number of members to be elected in each riding.

The vote by party for one riding in which the 1971 election was declared void are not available, although the total vote is known and the results are included in the voter turnout figures.

In two-member ridings the number of "Voters who Voted" is determined by adding the highest candidate vote for each full slate of candidates. Where a party did not run a full slate, the vote is divided by two.

Acclamations: All acclamations were won by Liberals with the exception of one Progressive Conservative in each of the elections of 1956 and 1972.

Electoral System: All ridings used the single-member, plurality system of voting except as described for those elections listed below. In all two-member ridings, voters could mark their ballot twice.

　　1949-51: Three ridings elected two members each.

　　1956-72: One riding elected two members.

Newfoundland

NDP	%*	O.	%*	Total	Total Registered Electorate	Voter Turnout			Voter Code
						Registered Electorate in Contested Seats	Voters who Voted	%	
—	—	2,642	2.0	167,555	176,281	176,281	133,189	75.6	q
—	—	1,156	1.2	131,566	176,281	153,318	102,102	66.6	q
—	—	1,964	1.8	114,438	189,240	169,940	111,996	65.9	h
9,352	7.3	12,411	9.7	130,325	189,240	183,434	128,028	69.8	h
4,479	3.8	1,378	1.2	123,231	211,921	200,912	120,394	59.9	h
2,725	1.8	3,548	2.2	148,202	239,616	227,711	145,832	64.0	p
4,075	1.8	5,804	2.6	231,553	265,653	265,653	229,486	86.4	p
410	.2	4,307	1.8	209,074	265,653	255,165	204,033	80.0	p
9,653	4.4	28,879	1.3	221,818	306,247	306,247	222,786	72.7	t

Explanation of Party Vote:

1949:   Others: I. (2) 2,642 (1 El.).

1951:   Others: I. (3) 1,156.

1956:   Others: I. (3) 696; CCF (7) 661; I.L. (1) 607.

1959:   The votes polled in the NDP column were by pro-labour candidates who ran as the "Newfoundland Democratic Party". Others: United Newfoundland Party (9) 10,639 (2 El.); I. (3) 1,772. (The two elected U.N.P. members had both been previously elected as Progressive Conservatives in 1956.)

1962:   Others: I. (2) 740 (1 El.); United Newfoundland Party (1) 638.

1966:   Others: I. (7) 3,548.

1971:   Others: New Labrador Party (3) 5,645 (1 El.); I. (2) 159.

1972:   Others: New Labrador Party (3) 2,548; I.L. (2) 1,259; I. (5) 500.

1975:   Others: Lib. Reform Party (28) 26,378 (4 Elec); I.L. (1) 2,185 (El.); I (3) 316.

Nova Scotia Provincial Elections

Date	Seats	Candidates					Elected					Popular Vote	
		L.	C.	3rd.	O.	Tot.	L.	C.	3rd.	O.	A C L	L.	%*
June 20, 1906	38	38	31	—	5	74	32	5	—	2	2	84,359	53.2
June 14, 1911	38	38	37	2	3	80	27	11	—	—	—	99,192	51.1
June 20, 1916	43	43	43	2	1	89	30	13	—	—	—	136,315	50.6
July 27, 1920	43	40	34	12	14	100	29	3	4	7	—	154,627	46.0
June 25, 1925	43	43	41	10	2	96	3	38	—	2	—	161,158	36.9
Oct. 1, 1928	43	43	43	2	—	88	20	23	—	—	—	209,380	48.2
Aug. 22, 1933	30	30	30	3	3	66	22	8	—	—	—	166,170	52.5
June 29, 1937	30	30	30	—	1	61	25	5	—	—	—	165,397	53.6
Oct. 28, 1941	30	30	29	6	—	65	23	4	3	—	—	138,915	53.6
Oct. 23, 1945	30	30	30	20	3	83	28	—	2	—	—	153,513	53.0
June 9, 1949	37	37	37	21	1	96	27	7	2	—	—	174,604	50.8
May 26, 1953	37	37	37	16	1	91	22	13	2	—	—	169,118	49.2
Oct. 30, 1956	43	43	43	11	1	98	18	24	1	(1)	—	159,656	48.0
June 7, 1960	43	43	43	34	1	121	15	27	1	—	—	147,951	42.3
Oct. 8, 1963	43	43	43	20	—	106	4	39	—	—	—	134,873	39.4
May 30, 1967	46	46	46	24	2	118	6	40	—	—	—	142,945	41.8
Oct. 13, 1970	46	46	46	23	2	117	23	21	2	—	—	174,943	46.3
Apr. 2, 1974	46	46	46	46	6	144	31	12	3	—	—	206,648	47.3

Sources: *Journal of the House of Assembly* (1906-45) and *Return of the General Election* 1933-1974.

Notes: * The percentages given for party vote are adjusted to exclude the distortions caused by the electoral system. In multi-member ridings, the party per cent is changed by dividing the party vote by the number of members to be elected in each riding.

Notes: * In 1949 the election of one Liberal was declared void and is listed in the Other (O.) Column. No vote figures were given.

Acclamations: 1906: Two Liberals.

Electoral System: In all multi-member ridings voters could place an "X" on the ballot for each of the total number of candidates to be elected.

The number of single and multi-member ridings by the number of members for each riding. (M = Members)

Elections	1M	2M	3M	4M	5M
1906-11	0	16	2	0	0
1916-20	0	14	2	1	1
1925-28	0	16	2	0	1
1933-45	22	4	0	0	0
1949-53	27	5	0	0	0
1956-63	37	3	0	0	0
1967-74	40	3	0	0	0

Nova Scotia Provincial Elections

C.	%*	3rd	%*	O.	%*	Total	Voter Turnout			Voter Code
							Registered Electorate	Voters who Voted	%	
66,638	41.6	—	—	7,423	5.2	158,420	—	—	—	f
88,114	45.6	3,410	1.3 Lab.	3,441	2.0	194,157	—	—	—	f
131,844	48.7	1,488	.4 Lab.	727	.3	270,374	—	—	—	f
86,054	26.6	58,727	12.7 Lab.	48,546	14.7	347,954	—	—	—	i
253,697	56.6	12,260	3.1 Lab.	16,847	3.3	443,962	261,570	180,612	69.0	h
218,974	50.3	4,862	1.4 Lab.	—	—	433,216	253,199	179,393	70.9	h
145,107	45.5	2,336	.9 CCF	2,469	1.0	316,082	295,957	254,233	85.9	h
143,670	45.0	—	—	3,396	1.4	312,463	312,817	249,215	79.7	h
106,133	37.5	18,583	8.8 CCF	—	—	263,631	341,788	215,491	63.0	h
97,774	31.7	39,637	15.1 CCF	634	.2	291,558	370,945	238,966	64.4	h
134,312	37.6	32,869	11.3 CCF	749	.3	342,534	369,117	286,694	77.7	h
150,480	41.9	23,700	8.2 CCF	2,065	.7	345,363	370,293	280,661	75.8	h
161,016	48.5	9,932	3.2 CCF	812	.3	331,416	376,894	302,421	80.5	h
168,023	48.0	31,036	9.6 CCF	650	.1	347,660	388,805	318,900	82.0	h
191,128	56.2	14,076	4.4 NDP	—	—	340,077	400,078	311,562	77.9	h
180,498	52.5	17,873	5.6 NDP	498	.1	341,814	405,704	312,647	77.1	h
177,986	46.2	25,259	7.3 NDP	1,464	.2	379,652	453,727	350,852	77.3	p
166,388	38.5	55,902	13.6 NDP	2,220	.5	431,158	507,190	395,089	77.9	p

Others (votes polled):

1906:	I. (5) 7,423. (2 El.).
1911:	I. (3) 3,441.
1916:	I. (1) 727.
1920:	Farmers candidates (14) 48,546. (With one exception Farmer and Labour groups supported each others' candidates.) Elected: Farmer (7).
1925:	I. Lab. (1) 8,267, Farm. Con. (1) 8,580. (Both elected with Conservative support.)
1933:	United Front (3) 2,469.
1937:	Lab. (1) 3,396.
1945:	Lab. Prog. (2) 505, I. (1) 129.
1949:	I. (1) 749.
1953:	I. (1) 2,065.
1956:	I. (1) 812.
1960:	I. (1) 650.
1967:	I. (2) 498.
1970:	I. (2) 1,464.
1974:	I. (6) 2,220.

New Brunswick Provincial Elections

Election Date	Seats	Candidates					Elected					Popular Vote			
		L.	C.	3rd	O.	Tot.	L.	C.	3rd	O.	ACCL	L.	%*	C.	%*
Mar. 3, 1908	46	43	43	—	10	96	12	28	—	6	—	87,611	43.5	95,319	46.7
June 20, 1912	48	47	46	—	2	95	2	46	—	—	—	80,532	39.9	123,176	58.6
Feb. 24, 1917	48	48	48	—	—	96	27	21	—	—	—	106,948	52.3	98,469	47.7
Oct. 9, 1920	48	47	27	25	7	106	24	13	9	2	2	147,393	46.5	82,427	27.1
Aug. 10, 1925	48	45	48	3	2	98	11	37	—	—	—	184,700	44.6	217,904	53.2
June 19, 1930	48	48	48	—	1	97	17	31	—	—	2	221,396	47.5	242,922	52.4
June 27, 1935	48	48	48	—	2	98	43	5	—	—	—	340,621	59.0	229,690	40.6
Nov. 20, 1939	48	48	48	1	1	98	29	19	—	—	—	296,838	54.4	243,607	45.3
Aug. 28, 1944	48	52	48	41	—	137	37	11	—	—	—	282,397	47.4	233,371	39.6
June 28, 1948	52	52	40	20	13	125	47	5	—	—	5	332,321	57.2	179,690	32.3
Sept. 22, 1952	52	52	52	12	7	123	16	36	—	—	—	372,140	48.1	369,919	50.1
June 18, 1956	52	52	52	18	2	124	15	37	—	—	—	346,021	45.0	391,775	53.2
June 27, 1960	52	52	52	—	2	106	31	21	—	—	—	418,043	52.4	362,171	46.9
Apr. 22, 1963	52	52	52	—	1	105	32	20	—	—	—	395,543	50.9	367,673	49.1
Oct. 23, 1967	58	58	58	3	—	119	32	26	—	—	—	396,354	50.9	354,070	49.0
Oct. 26, 1970	58	58	58	32	5	153	26	32	—	—	—	354,944	46.2	354,441	51.0
Nov. 18, 1974	58	58	58	35	24	175	25	33	—	—	—	147,272	47.5	145,304	46.9

Source: *Journal of the Legislative Assembly* 1908-1963, *Report of the Chief Electoral Officer* 1967-1974.

Notes: *The percentages given for party vote are adjusted to exclude the distortions caused by the electoral system. In multi-member ridings, the party per cent is changed by dividing the party vote by the number of members to be elected in each riding. The total provincial vote which is used in the calculation of percentages is given separately in the column labeled "Adjusted Total Vote", which represents the minimum number of voters who cast valid ballots.

—The 1967 voter turnout figures exclude rejected ballots. Voters who voted in advance polls in 1967 are estimated by adding together the highest vote polled by one candidate in each party. 1967 estimate is 2,372. In addition 414 ballots are excluded from the 1967 "Voters who Voted" column because there were no accurate comparative figures for registered electorate.

Note: Before 1967 no records were kept regarding voter turnout.

Acclamations: The acclamations in 1920 and 1948 were by Liberals.

Electoral System: In all multi-member ridings voters could place an "X" on the ballot for each of the total number of candidates to be elected.

The number of single and multi-member ridings by the number of members for each riding. (M = Members)

Elections	1M	2M	3M	4M	5M
1908	—	7	4	5	—
1912-20	1	7	3	6	—
1925	3	7	5	4	—
1930-44	1	7	3	6	1
1948-63	—	6	5	5	2
1967-70	4	7	6	3	—
1974	58	—	—	—	—

New Brunswick (con't)

3rd.	%*	Party	O.	%*	Total	Adjusted Total Vote*	Voter Turnout Registered Electorate	Voter Turnout Voters who Voted	Voter Turnout %	Voter Code
—	—	—	20,723	9.8	203,653	62,374	—	—	—	e
—	—	—	1,907	1.5	205,615	64,175	—	—	—	e
—	—	—	—	—	205,417	64,416	—	—	—	d
64,451	19.6	UF	19,272	6.8	313,543	98,119	—	—	—	g
7,927	1.9	UF	1,330	.4	411,861	141,450	—	—	—	g
—	—	—	183	.1	464,501	147,756	—	—	—	g
712	.1	CCF	1,482	.4	571,793	181,458	—	—	—	g
68,248	13.0	CCF	562	.2	541,719	171,833	—	—	—	g
34,415	5.7	CCF	—	—	584,016	186,187	—	—	—	g
9,490	1.2	CCF	28,634	4.8	575,060	178,196	—	—	—	g
11,828	1.7	SC	4,858	.6	756,407	221,940	—	—	—	g
—	—	—	726	.1	750,350	222,283	—	—	—	g
—	—	—	3,185	.7	783,399	233,865	—	—	—	g
—	—	—	7	.0	763,223	228,880	—	—	—	h
1,247	.1	NDP	—	—	751,671	245,181	313,253	261,135	83.4	h
20,383	2.6	NDP	1,762	.2	731,530	242,559	331,643	269,306	81.2	h
9,092	2.9	NDP	8,322	2.7	309,990	309,990	408,182	312,475	76.6	o

Explanation of Party Vote:

1908: In 1908 and in 1912 the Conservative column refers to both Conservatives and Liberal-Conservatives who supported the Government of Premier Hazen, himself a Liberal-Conservative.

Others: 3 Conservatives ran as pro-Liberal (Government) candidates with Liberal backing, 4004; 3 Ind. (El.) were pro-Conservative, 9,674; I.L. (3) 6,665 (El.) pro-Conservative; Other (1) 380.

1912: Others: I.L. (2) 1,907.

1920: There were no official returns for 12 candidates and their vote was taken from newspaper reports. In 31 of the 48 seats the Liberals faced a unified opposition slate composed of Conservatives, Farmers, or Conservatives and Farmers.

Others: Lab. (4) 16,135 (2 El.); I. (2) 2,682; Soldier(1) 455.

1925: Others: I. (2) 1,330.

1930: Others: I. (1) 183.

1935: Others: I. (2) 1,482.

1939: Others: I.L. (1) 562.

1948: Others: I. (8) 25,500; SC (5) 3,134.

1952: Others: I. (7) 4,858.

1956: Others: I. (2) 1,196.

1960: Others: I. (2) 3,185.

1963: Others: I. (1) 7.

1970: Others: I. (5) 1,762.

1974: Others: Parti Acadien (13) 3,607; I. (7) 3,905; Canada Party (4) 810.

Quebec Provincial Elections

Election Date	Seats	Candidates					Elected					Popular Vote	
		L.	C/UN	3rd.	O.	Tot.	L.	C/UN	3rd.	O.	ACCL	L.	%
June 8, 1908	74	74	64	—	13	151	57	13	—	4	6	131,065	53.5
May 15, 1912	81	83	76	—	11	170	63	15	—	3	1	155,799	53.5
May 22, 1916	81	85	54	—	2	141	75	6	—	—	26	133,473	64.0
June 23, 1919	81	97	21	7	7	132	74	5	2	—	45	87,478	67.5
Feb. 5, 1923	85	88	67	—	24	179	64	19	—	2	8	154,568	53.2
May 16, 1927	85	85	67	—	15	167	73	9	—	3	12	187,799	59.1
Aug. 24, 1931	90	88	90	—	18	196	77	11	—	2	—	260,938	53.3
Nov. 25, 1935	90	90	33	52	28	203	47	17	25	1	3	249,586	46.5
Aug. 17, 1936	90	88	90	—	27	205	14	76	—	—	1	224,344	39.4
Oct. 25, 1939	86	86	84	57	21	248	69	14	4	3	—	301,631	53.5
Aug. 8, 1944	91	90	90	80	72	332	37	48	—	2	—	523,316	39.3
July 28, 1948	92	92	91	92	36	311	8	82	—	2	—	547,478	36.2
June 16, 1952	92	92	92	23	29	236	23	68	—	1	—	768,539	45.8
June 20, 1956	93	91	93	26	62	272	20	72	—	1	—	827,268	44.8
June 22, 1960	95	95	95	—	63	253	52	42	—	1	—	1,077,135	51.4
Nov. 14, 1962	95	95	95	—	34	224	63	31	—	1	—	1,205,253	56.4
June 5, 1966	108	108	108	73	129	418	50	56	—	2	—	1,099,435	47.3
Apr. 29, 1970	108	108	108	108	141	465	72	17	7	12	—	1,304,341	45.4
Oct. 29, 1973	110	110	110	110	148	478	102	—	6	2	—	1,623,734	54.7
Nov. 15, 1976	110	110	108	110	228	556	26	11	71	2	—	1,134,997	33.8

Source: Reports of the Chief Returning Officer of Quebec.

Notes: The C/UN column refers to the Conservative Party from 1908 to 1935 when Maurice Duplessis, the then Conservative leader, merged his party with the ALN (National Liberal Action) to form the UN (Union Nationale), which, in effect, displaced the Conservative Party from 1936 to 1973.

Abbreviations (Quebec): *Nat.* (Nationalist); *BPC* (Bloc Populaire Canadien); *RIN* (Rassemblement pour L'Indépendance Nationale); *PQ* (Parti Québécois).

Electoral System: Single-member, plurality system.

Acclamations: All acclamations were by Liberals except 3 Conservatives in each of the elections of 1916 and 1919.

Explanation of Party Vote:

1908: Others: I. (9) 7,786 (1 El.); I.L. (2) 3,871 (1 El.); I. Nat. (1) 1,362 (El.); C. Nat. (1) 966 (El.).

1912: Contested the same seat: 3 Liberals in one riding; 2 Liberals in each of two ridings; 2 Labour in one riding. Others: Lab. (4) 3,751 (1 El.); I. L. (3) 3,385 (1 El.); Nat. (2) 2,703 (1 El.); I. (2) 757.

1916: Contested the same seat: 3 Liberals in one riding; 2 Liberals in each of five ridings. Others: Lab. (2) 1,832.

1919: Contested the same seat: 3 Liberals in each of four ridings; 2 Liberals in each of eleven ridings. Others: Democratic Liberals (5) 4,399; Lab. L. (1) 1,457; I.L. (1) 1,716.

1923: Contested the same seat: 2 Liberals in each of five ridings; 2 Conservatives in one riding. From 1923 to 1939 candidates declared whether they * were Pro-Government (G), Opposition (OP), or Other (O).* Others: (G): Lab. (2) 4,204; I.L. (6) 2,100. (OP): I. (7) 5,386; Lib (3) 4,167 (2 El.); Farm. (3) 3,180; Lab. (2) 1,777. (O): Lab. (1) 925.

1927: Others: (G): I.L. (5) 8,232 (2 El.); I. (3) 1,365. (OP): I. (5) 4,686; Lab. (1) 4,432 (El.). (O) Lab. (1) 2,342.
*

1931: Others: (G): I.L. (3) 8,037 (2 El.); I. (2) 2,787; I.C. (1) 711 (OP): I.C. (6) 1,459; Lab. (1) 1,630; I. (1) 106. (O): Lab. (1) 416; I. (1) 323; I. Lab. (1) 65.
*

1935: Others: (G): I.L. (1) 1,541 (El.); L.Lab. (1) 998; I. (3) 615. (OP); ALN; I.L. (1) 1,532. (O): I.L. (4) 3,331; Lab. (2) 2,238; I. (1) 94; I.C. (1) 37.
*

1936: Others: (G): I.L. (11) 9,746; I. (2) 3,765. (OP): I.UN (3) 1,928; C. (2) 1,703; I.C. (1) 167. (O): CCF (1) 1,469; Comm. (3) 1,045; I. (2) 767; People's * (1) 470; Lab. (1) 79.

Quebec

C./UN	%	3rd	%	Party	O.	%	Total	Total Registered Electorate	R.E. in Contested Seats	Voters who Voted	%	Voter Code
99,789	40.8	—	—	—	13,985	5.7	244,839	415,801	391,581	247,091	63.1	e
124,693	42.8	—	—	—	10,596	3.6	291,088	479,521	474,446	294,424	62.1	e
73,147	35.1	—	—	—	1,832	.9	208,452	486,136	336,696	211,229	62.7	a
21,990	17.0	12,596	9.7	Lab.	7,572	5.8	129,636	480,120	238,050	131,084	55.1	a
114,344	39.3	—	—	—	21,737	7.5	290,649	513,224	474,794	294,417	62.0	a
109,105	34.3	—	—	—	21,057	6.6	317,961	567,907	514,857	320,855	62.3	a
213,223	43.5	—	—	—	15,534	3.2	489,695	639,005	639,005	493,885	77.3	a
103,596	19.3	156,078	29.1	ALN	27,101	5.1	536,361	726,551	711,618	551,589	77.5	a
323,812	56.9	—	—	ALN	21,139	3.7	569,295	734,025	734,025	574,255	78.2	a
217,413	38.6	25,523	4.5	ALN	18,730	3.3	563,297	753,310	741,131	570,631	77.0	d
505,651	38.0	191,564	14.4	BPC	109,418	8.2	1,329,949	1,864,692	1,864,518	1,361,109	73.0	g
775,747	51.2	140,036	9.3	UE	50,716	3.3	1,513,977	2,036,576	2,036,576	1,531,753	75.2	l
855,327	50.9	16,039	1.0	CCF	39,358	2.3	1,679,263	2,246,889	2,246,889	1,704,924	75.9	l
956,082	51.8	11,232	.6	SD	51,147	2.8	1,845,729	2,393,350	2,393,350	1,874,508	78.3	l
977,318	46.6	—	—	—	42,144	2.0	2,096,597	2,608,439	2,608,439	2,130,109	81.7	l
900,817	42.2	—	—	—	30,896	1.4	2,136,966	2,721,933	2,721,933	2,166,475	79.6	l
948,928	40.8	129,045	5.6	RIN	147,481	6.3	2,324,889	3,222,302	3,222,302	2,370,510	73.6	r
564,544	19.7	662,404	23.1	PQ	341,681	11.9	2,872,970	3,478,891	3,478,891	2,929,999	84.2	t
146,209	4.9	897,809	30.2	PQ	303,226	10.2	2,970,978	3,758,111	3,758,111	3,025,736	80.5	t
611,678	18.2	1,390,363	41.4	PQ	223,189	6.6	3,360,227	4,023,490	4,023,490	3,430,257	85.3	t

Explanation of Party Vote (Con't):

1939: Others: (G): C. (1) 2,989 (El.); I.UN (3) 469. (OP): Nat. (1) 3,074 (El.); I.L. (2) 539. (O): I. (5) 6,281; CCF (1) 2,513; C. (3) 1,679; I.ALN (1) 617; Lab. (2) 281; Comm. (1) 159; I.Lab. (1) 129.

1944: Others: CCF (24) 33,986 (1 El.); SC (12) 16,542; I. (16) 12,766; I.L. (7) 8,656; I.Workers (2) 8,355; LPP (3) 7,873; I.UN (3) 6,775; Nat. (1) 6,587 (El.); I.CCF (1) 3,015; People's (1) 2,583; Nat. I.(1) 2,124; I.BPC (1) 156.

1948: Others: I. (10) 23,401 (2 El.); CCF (7) 9,016; I.UN (8) 8,649; LPP (1) 4,899; I.L. (7) 2,968; Lab. (1) 1,098; People's (1) 575; I.CCF (1) 110.

1952: Others: I. (6) 14,138 (1 El.); Nat. (1) 9,734; I.UN (7) 5,220; I.L. (7) 4,799; LPP (4) 3,932; I.LAB. (3) 1,027; I.Nat. (1) 508.

1956: The CCF ran under th label "Social Democrat"(SD). Others: I. (7) 33,205 (1 El.); LPP (32) 6,517; I.L. (8) 5,434; I.UN (11) 4,624; Lab. (3) 1,274. L.Lab. (1) 93.

1960: Others: I. (14) 21,563 (1 El.); I.UN (22) 11,155; I.L. (2) 8,205; Comm. (2) 536; Republican L. (1) 188; Soc. (1) 166; Capital Familial (1) 144; UN Lab. (1) 134; I.Lab. (1) 50.

1962: Others: I. (10) 17,835 (1 El.); I.L. (10) 11,209; L'Action Provinciale (11) 1,445; I.UN (2) 336; Comm. (1) 71.

1966: Others: Le Ralliement National (90) 74,670; I. (23) 62,466 (2 El.); C. (5) 6,737; I.L. (2) 2,056; Soc. (4) 905; Comm. (4) 502; Le Partie de la Democratisation Economique (1) 125.

1970: Others: Ralliement des Créditistes (98) 321,370 (12 El.); NDP (13) 4,374; I. (30) 15,937.

1973: Others: Parti Créditiste (108) 294,706 (2 El.); I. (26) 7,195; Parti Communiste du Quebec (Marxiste-Leniniste) (14) 1,325.

1976: Others: Ralliement Créditiste (109) 155,508 (1 El.); Parti Nationale Populaire (36) 31,045 (1 El.); Alliance Democratique (13) 17,444; I. (15) 10,740; Coalition; nouveau Parti Democratique du Quebec: Regroupement des Miliants Syndicaux (21) 3,101; Parti Communiste du Quebec (14) 1,770; Parti des Travailleurs du Quebec (12) 1,248; No Party Label (8) 2,333.

Ontario Provincial Elections

Election Date	Seats	Candidates					Elected				ACCL	Popular Vote			
		L.	C.	3rd	O.	Tot.	L.	C.	3rd	O.		L.	%*	C.	%*
Jan. 25, 1905	98	95	98	—	17	210	28	69	—	1	—	198,595	44.4	237,603	53.5
June 1, 1908	106	90	106	7	29	232	19	86	1	—	6	177,719	41.0	248,194	54.1
Dec. 11, 1911	106	78	106	7	16	207	22	82	1	1	17	142,245	40.1	205,338	54.6
June 29, 1914	111	90	111	4	35	240	24	84	1	2	4	186,284	37.7	270,881	53.8
Oct. 20, 1919	111	67	103	66	52	288	28	25	44	14	4	311,395	24.5	392,389	32.7
June 25, 1923	111	77	103	71	41	292	14	75	17	5	2	202,697	22.1	474,819	48.3
Dec. 1, 1926	112	50	112	20	59	241	14	72	13	13	3	203,966	17.8	638,567	55.7
Oct. 30, 1929	112	84	112	10	30	236	13	90	4	5	8	326,960	32.2	574,730	56.7
June 19, 1934	90	83	90	37	51	261	65	17	1	7	—	735,489	47.1	621,218	39.8
Oct. 6, 1937	90	86	89	39	52	266	63	23	—	4	—	773,608	49.2	619,610	39.4
Aug. 4, 1943	90	89	90	86	17	282	15	38	34	3	—	397,014	30.2	469,672	35.7
June 4, 1945	90	79	90	89	59	317	11	66	8	5	—	475,029	26.9	781,345	44.2
June 7, 1948	90	88	90	81	30	289	13	53	21	3	—	515,795	29.3	725,799	41.3
No. 22, 1951	90	88	90	77	16	271	7	79	2	2	—	551,794	31.1	860,898	48.5
June 9, 1955	98	94	98	81	41	314	10	84	3	1	—	577,774	32.8	853,625	48.5
June 11, 1959	98	97	98	80	21	296	21	71	5	1	—	682,590	36.3	868,815	46.2
Sept. 25, 1963	108	107	108	97	25	337	23	77	7	1	—	757,950	35.0	1,052,740	48.6
Oct. 17, 1967	117	115	117	117	17	366	27	69	20	1	—	760,096	31.4	1,022,967	42.3
Oct. 21, 1971	117	117	117	117	33	384	20	78	19	—	—	913,742	27.8	1,465,313	44.5
Sept. 18, 1975	125	125	125	125	60	435	36	51	38	—	—	1,135,103	34.3	1,193,075	35.8

Source: Chief Electoral Officer, *Ontario Election Returns* (1905-1975).

Notes: * The percentages given for party vote from 1905 to 1923 are adjusted to exclude the distortions caused by the electoral system. In multi-member ridings, the party per cent is changed by dividing the party vote by the number of members to be elected in each riding.

During the period 1905-1923 no figures for registered electorate were kept in ridings won by acclamation and in certain other ridings. For such ridings which were contested, the number of ballots cast has been deleted from the "Voters who Voted" column. The number of contested ridings for which there is no figure for registered electorate is as follows (by year): 1905: (2); 1914 (1); 1919: (9); 1923: (4); 1926: (1). Registered electorate in ridings won by acclamation was 47,809 in 1926 and 102,688 in 1929.

Acclamations: 1908: 6 Con.; 1911: 17 Con.; 1914: 3 Con., 1 Lib.; 1919: 4 Con.; 1923: 1 Con., 1 Lab.; 1926: 3 Con.; 1929: 8 Con.

Electoral System: All ridings used the single-member, plurality system with the following two exceptions.

1905: There was one two-member riding in which voters could mark their ballots twice.

1908-1923: There were four two-member ridings in which each voter could cast one ballot for each of the two members to be elected.

Explanation of Party Vote:

1905: Others: I.L. (3) 5,362 (1 El.); Proh. (2) 1,906; Soc. (7) 1,273; I. Temp. (1) 160; I. (1) 100; I.C. (1) 95; Temp. (1) 90.

1908: Others: I.C. (5) 6,107; I. (5) 3,042; Soc. (14) 2,891; Prog. (1) 2,187; I.L. (2) 1,470; L. Temp. (1) 1,017; I. Lab. (1) 544.

1911: Others: I.C. (2) 3,593; I. (5) 3,327; Soc. (7) 3,206; C. Temp. (1) 1,604; Lib. Con. (1) 1,130 (El).

1914: Others: I. Temp. (5) 6,545; Temp. (4) 6,519; Soc. (10) 3,919; I. (5) 4,807; I.C. (3) 2,896; L. Temp. (1) 2,733 (El); I.L. (2) 2,236 (1 El); I. Proh. (1) 1,302; Temp. Con. (1) 1,213; Anti-Temp. Lib. (1) 691; I. Soc. (2) 577.

1919: Others: Labour (20) 107,775 (10 El); Lab. UFO (5) 25,324 (1 El); Lab. UFO (2) 7,448 (1 El) (The votes of the three preceding groups plus the regular (UFO) United Farmers of Ontario vote totals 395,470 or 36.1% of the adjusted vote.) The remaining votes in "Others" were cast for: I. (14) 38,377; I.C. (3) 14,213; Soldier-Lab. (2) 9,088; Soldier-Ind. (1) 7,472 (El); I.L. (1) 5,354 (El); Soldier (1) 2,146; Soc. (3) 637.

Ontario

3rd	%*	Party	O.	%*	Total	Registered Electorate in Contested Seats	Voters Who Voted	%	Voter Code
—	—	—	8,986	2.1	445,184	604,666	428,083	70.8	d&a
7,298	1.5	Lab.	17,258	3.4	450,469	622,751	427,131	68.6	d
8,965	1.8	Lab.	12,860	3.5	369,408	583,909	352,455	60.4	d
6,535	1.4	Lab.	33,438	7.1	497,138	697,935	462,649	66.3	d
254,923	23.6	UFO	217,834	19.3	1,176,541	1,378,721	1,028,161	74.6	g
199,393	21.8	UFO	76,183	7.8	953,092	1,655,312	875,032	52.9	g
87,862	7.7	Prog.	216,107	18.8	1,146,502	1,792,757	1,144,617	63.8	g
34,507	3.4	Prog.	78,113	7.7	1,014,310	1,804,932	1,021,229	56.6	g
108,951	7.0	CCF	96,158	6.2	1,561,826	2,130,420	1,577,547	74.0	g
87,490	5.7	CCF	90,425	5.8	1,571,133	2,228,030	1,587,027	71.2	g
415,441	31.6	CCF	31,812	2.4	1,313,939	2,269,895	1,323,712	58.3	g
395,708	22.4	CCF	113,711	6.4	1,765,793	2,469,960	1,781,930	72.1	g
466,274	26.5	CCF	50,169	2.9	1,758,037	2,623,281	1,773,446	67.6	g
339,376	19.1	CCF	24,548	1.4	1,776,616	2,750,709	1,794,922	65.3	g
291,410	16.5	CCF	38,716	2.2	1,761,525	2,905,760	1,784,147	61.4	h
313,834	16.7	CCF	17,334	.9	1,882,573	3,196,801	1,903,845	59.6	h
336,290	15.5	NDP	18,793	.9	2,165,773	3,437,834	2,184,078	63.5	h
626,429	25.9	NDP	10,218	.4	2,419,710	3,685,755	2,439,710	66.2	h
893,879	27.1	NDP	19,783	.6	3,292,717	4,503,142	3,310,776	73.5	o
953,238	28.8	NDP	23,359	.7	3,304,775	4,853,998	3,324,334	68.1	o

Explanation of Party Vote (con't)

1923: Two Conservatives contested the same seat. Two Liberals contested the same seat. Others: Lab. (22) 44,904 (4 El.); Prog. (3) 10,122; I. (14) 16,116 (1 El.); I.L. (2) 5,041.

1926: Two Conservatives contested the same seat in each of two ridings. Others: Proh. (26) 87,814; L.Prog. (9) 45,733 (4 El.); I.C. (7) 22,110 (2 El.); I.L. (7) 20,984 (4 El.); Lab. (3) 14,794 (1 El.); I.Prog. (1) 5,861 (El.); L.Proh. (1) 4,407 (El.); Prog.L. (1) 3,941; I. (1) 3,532; L.Lab. (1) 2,392; L.Lab. Proh. (1) 2,298; Lab. Lib. (1) 2,241.

1929: Two Conservatives contested the same seat. Others: Proh. (8) 25,807; I.C. (7) 21,947 (2 El.); UFO (3) 12,752 (1 El.); Lab. (4) 10,029 (1 El.); L.Prog. (1) 5,449 (El.); Comm. (5) 1,542.

1934: Others: L.Prog. (4) 38,161 (4 El.); I. (15) 17,462 (1 El.); I.L. (5) 12,984; Comm. (14) 9,775; UFO (2) 8,648 (1 El.); Lab. (1) 5,877 (El.); Lab. Soc. (4) 1,526; Farm. Lab. (1) 608; I. Lab. (1) 534; I.C. (2) 344; I. Worker (1) 158; Scc. (1) 81.

1937: Others: I.L. (8) 20,776 (1 El.); L.Prog. (3) 16,920 (2 El.); Farm. Lab. (6) 14,675; I.C. (5) 8,270; UFO (1) 7,296 (El.); I. Lab. (2) 6,377; Lab. (5) 5,455; I. (8) 4,108; LPP (1) 3,343; Social Lab. (11) 2,199; SC (1) 538; Comm. (1) 408.

1943: Two Liberals contested the same seat. Others: LPP (3) 12,037 (2 El.); I.L. (3) 8,252 (1 El.); L.Prog. (1) 4,042; I. (3) 2,593; I. Lab. (2) 2,215; I.CCF (1) 1,513; Soc. Lab. (2) 591; I. Soldier (2) 569.

1945: Others: LPP (29) 43,170 (2 El.); L.Lab. (7) 41,163 (3 El.); I. (14) 11,895; L.Prog. (2) 10,241; Lab. (4) 6,285; Soc. Lab. (2) 710; SC (1) 247.

1948: Others: LPP (2) 17,654 (2 El.); Union of Electors (12) 8,844; I.CCF (1) 8,613; L.Lab. (2) 7,682 (1 El.); I.PC (3) 3,340; I. (1) 1,766; SC (3)1,104; Soc. Lab. (5) 913; I.Lab. (1) 258.

1951: Others: LPP (6) 11,914 (1 El.); L.Lab. (2) 7,989 (1 El.); I. (4) 1,869; I.Lab. (1) 1,375; I.PC (2) 1,080; Soc.Lab. (1) 371.

1955: One unendorsed PC is counted as a Progressive Conservative. Others: LPP (31) 20,875; I. (5) 9,169; L.Lab. (2) 7,305 (1 El.); I. Lab. (1) 641; I.SC (1) 602; Soc. Lab. (1) 124.

1959: Others: L. Lab. (1) 6,559 (El.); LPP (9) 4,304; I.PC (2) 2,119; SC (5) 1,740; Lab.CCF (1) 1,512; I. (2) 832; White Canada Party (1) 268.

1963: Others: L. Lab (1) 6,774 (El.); I.PC (1) 5,190; I. (6) 2,656; SC (9) 2,313; Comm. (6) 1,654; I.L. (1) 103; Soc. Lab. (1) 103.

1967: Others: L. Lab. (2) 5,051 (1 El.); I. (5) 2,382; SC (7) 1,906; Comm. (2) 592; Soc.Lab. (1) 287.

1971: Others: I. (23) 16,959; Comm. (5) 1,620; SC (5) 1,204.

1975: Others: I (15) 10,427; Comm. (33) 9,451; SC (12) 3,481.

Manitoba Provincial Elections

Election Date	Seats	Candidates						Elected					ACCL	Popular Vote			
		L.	C.	3rd	4th	O.	Tot.	L.	C.	3rd	4th	O.	L.	L.	%	C.	%
Mar. 7, 1907	41	40	41			1	82	13	28				1	29,426	47.9	31,067	50.6
June 11, 1910	41	39	41			6	86	13	28				1	33,092	44.3	38,056	50.9
July 10, 1914	49	49	45			9	103	20	28			1	3	62,798	42.8	68,434	46.6
Aug. 9, 1915	47	44	46			10	100	38	5			4	1	63,251	54.1	38,623	33.0
June 29, 1920	55	52	30	18	25	23	148	21	7	11	12	4	3	51,659	35.9	24,210	16.9
July 18, 1922	55	40	27	20	50	18	155	9	7	6	28	5	—	37,071	24.4	25,043	16.5
June 28, 1927	55	41	40	9	47	17	154	7	15	3	29	1	3	34,472	21.1	44,291	27.1
June 16, 1932	55	12	48	20	52	15	147	—	10	5	38	2	2	5,544	2.2	90,152	35.5
July 27, 1936	55	49	39	20	20	7	135	23	16	7	5	4	—	91,357	36.0	71,927	28.4
Apr. 22, 1941 (*) C:	55	40	18	15	3	14	90	27	13	3	3	5	16	57,245	35.0	27,524	16.8
AC:		1	4	—	9	6	20	—	2	—	—	2	—	701	.4	7,430	4.5
Oct. 15, 1945 C:	55	35	19	—	2	9	65	25	13	—	2	3	7	72,087	32.9	35,704	16.3
AC:		—	—	40	2	18	60	—	—	10	—	2	—	—	—	—	—
Nov. 10, 1949 C:	57	45	17	—	—	6	68	30	10	—	—	3	16	79,833	40.5	24,985	12.7
AC:		—	6	25	—	13	44	—	4	7	1	3	—	—	—	—	—
June 8, 1953	57	50	38	25	43	18	174	33	12	5	1	6	—	105,958	39.6	56,278	21.0
June 16, 1958	57	56	56	43	12	12	179	19	26	11	—	1	—	101,763	35.0	117,822	40.5
May 14, 1959	57	57	57	45	—	6	165	11	36	10	—	—	—	95,452	30.3	147,140	46.7
Dec. 14, 1962	57	57	57	39	12	5	170	13	36	7	1	—	—	108,261	36.4	134,147	45.2
June 23, 1966	57	56	57	53	17	2	185	14	31	11	1	—	—	107,841	33.1	130,102	40.0
June 25, 1969	57	57	57	57	5	7	183	5	22	28	1	1	—	80,288	24.0	119,457	35.7
June 28, 1973	57	50	52	57	3	24	186	5	21	31	—	—	—	88,907	19.0	171,553	36.7

Sources: Canadian Parliamentary Guide (1907, 1910, 1915), Manitoba Sessional Papers (1914), Summary of Election Results (1920-1973).

Notes: The third party (3rd) column refers to Labour (1920-1932), the Ind. Labour Party (1936), and finally to the CCF/NDP (1941-73). The fourth party (4th) column refers to the Farmer candidates (1920), the United Farmers of Manitoba (UFM) (1922), The Progressives (1927), the Liberal-Progressives (LP) (1932). These farmer-oriented parties (after 1922 led by John Bracken) formally merged with the Liberal Party in the 1936 election and retained their new label of "Liberal-Progressive" until 1961, when the word "Progressive" was dropped. The 4P column refers to (SC) Social Credit (1936-73).

* Note: Voter turnout figures exclude rejected ballots from 1914 to 1931.

(*) In 1940 Premier Bracken formed a coalition government and during the next three elections candidates declared whether they were for Coalition (C:) or against Coalition (AC:).

Electoral System: All ridings in Manitoba used a single-member, plurality system of voting with the following exceptions.
1914-15: 3 Two-member districts in which voters could mark two "X's" on their ballot.
1920-45: A 10-member district in Winnipeg used the Hare system of Proportional Representation.
1927-36: All 45 single-member ridings used the alternate system of voting.
1949-53: 1 Two-member district and 3 Four-member districts used the Hare system.

Acclamations:		
1907: 1 Con.	1920: 1 Farm., 1 I., 1 Lib.	1936: 1 L-P
1910: 1 Con.	1922: 2 UFM.	1941: 10 L-P, 5 Con. 1 S.C.
1914: 3 Con.	1927: 2 Prog.	1945: 3 L-P, 3 Con., 1 I.
1915: 1 I.		1949: 12 L-P, 4 Con.
		1953: 1 L-P

Manitoba Provincial Elections

3rd	%	Party	4th	%	Party	O.	%	Total	Voter Turnout: Registered Electorate in Contested Seats	Registered Voters who Voted	%	Voter Code
						939	1.5	61,432		61,432		d
						3,564	4.8	74,712		74,712		d
29,869	20.8	Lab.	22,739	15.8	Farm.	15,654	10.7	146,886	131,179	112,892	86.1	d
24,290	16.0	Lab.	49,767	32.8	UFM	15,073	12.9	116,947		93,685		d
15,540	9.5	Lab.	53,939	33.1	Prog.	15,163	10.6	143,640	206,317	143,640	69.6	g
43,365	17.0	Lab.	100,801	39.6	L-P	15,603	10.3	151,774	218,720	151,774	69.4	g
30,983	12.2	ILP	23,413	9.2	SC	14,927	9.1	163,169	235,689	163,169	69.2	g
28,280	17.3	CCF	2,723	1.7	SC	14,800	5.8	254,662	350,481	255,812	73.0	g
			9,156	5.6	SC	35,756	14.1	253,436	391,902	258,960	66.1	g
77,235	35.3	CCF	2,953	1.3	SC	18,948	11.6	134,720	329,734	164,672	49.9	g
			1,548	.7	SC	11,601	7.1	28,888				
50,120	25.4	CCF				7,144	3.3	117,888	396,332	221,039	55.8	g
44,332	16.6	CCF	35,750	13.4	SC	22,374	10.2	101,157				
58,671	20.2	CCF	5,174	1.8	SC	7,924	4.0	112,742	396,644	199,481	54.0	g
69,594	22.1	NDP				34,201	17.4	84,321				
45,430	15.3	NDP	7,495	2.5	SC	25,318	9.5	267,636	451,905	273,069	60.4	h
75,333	23.1	NDP	11,635	3.6	SC	7,471	2.6	290,901	480,083	292,932	61.0	h
128,080	38.3	NDP	4,304	1.3		2,902	.9	315,088	484,467	317,581	65.6	h
197,585	42.3	NDP	1,709	.4		1,776	.6	297,109	491,632	299,867	61.0	h
						638	.2	325,549	509,469	327,574	64.3	h
						2,764	.8	334,893	523,179	336,386	64.3	h
						7,290	1.6	467,044	599,712	469,798	78.3	o

Explanation of Party Totals and Others:

1907: Others: Lab. (1) 939.

1910: Others: Lab. (1) 1,939; Soc. (3) 1,237; I. (2) 388.

1914: Others: (Pro-Lib.) I. Lab. (1) 8,205 (El.); Soc. (4) 5,870; I. (2) 570.

1915: Others: I. Lib. (2) 7,615 (El.); I. (4) 3,400 (2 El.); Soc. (3) 3,254; Lab. (1) 840.

1920: Two Liberals contested the same seat in each of four ridings. Two Farmers contested the same seat. Others: I. (23) 15,163 (4 El.).

1922: Others: Fusion (1) 3,281 (El.); I. (17) 12,322 (4 El.).

1927: Others: I. (15) 12,346 (1 El.); I. Prog. (1) 566; Comm. (1) 2,015.

1932: Two L-P contested the same seat in two ridings. Others: I. (14) 14,627 (2 El.); I. Con. (1) 173.

1936: Others: I. (5) 29,206 (2 El.); I. Lib. (1) 686 (El.); Comm. (1) 5,864 (El.).

1941: Others: Coalition: I. (13) 17,998 (5 El.); Lib. (1) 814; Unallocated (0) 136. Anti-C.: I. (2) 5,848 (1 El.); Workers (1) 4,889 (El.); Sound Money (3) 864.

1945: Others: Coalition: I. (4) 2,810 (2 El.); I. Lib. (4) 2,944; I. Con (1) 1,390 (El.). Anti-C.: LPP (13) 10,566 (1 El.); I. (3) 9,936 (1 El.); I.CCF (1) 1,650; Soc (1) 222.

1949: Others: Coalition: I. (4) 5,391 (3 El.); I.L-P (1) 1,673; I. Lib. (1) 860. Anti-C.: I.PC (5) 14,735 (4 El.); I. (4) 6,892 (1 El.); I. Lib. (4) 5,109 (1 El.); LPP (2) 5,243 (1 El.); I.L-P (1) 952; I.CCF (1) 1,171; I.Lab. (1) 99.

1953: Others: I.L-P (6) 11,929 (3 El.); LPP (1) 3,812 (1 El.); I. (11) 9,577 (2 El.).

1958: Others: I. (3) 1,207 (1 El.); LPP (1) 1,207; I.PC (3) 1,223.

1959: Others: I. (3) 1,171; LPP (3) 1,731.

1962: Others: I. (2) 849; Comm. (2) 816; Lib.Lab. (1) 111.

1966: Others: Comm. (2) 638.

1969: Others: I. (5) 2,020 (1 El.); Comm. (2) 744.

1973: Others: I. (18) 6,969; Comm. (3) 252; Comm. Marxist-Leninist (3) 69.

Saskatchewan Provincial Elections

Election Date	Seats	Candidates						Elected						Popular Vote			
		L.	C.	3rd	SC	O.	Tot.	L.	C.	3rd	SC	O.	ACC L	L.	%*	C.	%*
Dec. 4, 1905	25	25	24	—	—	1	50	17	8	—	—	—	1	17,783	52.2	16,180	47.5
Aug. 14, 1908	41	41	40	—	—	3	84	27	14	—	—	—	—	29,798	50.8	28,102	47.9
July 11, 1912	53	53	53	—	—	5	111	45	8	—	—	—	—	50,004	57.1	36,648	41.8
June 26, 1917	59	58	54	—	—	17	129	51	7	—	—	1	3	106,087	56.8	68,899	36.9
June 9, 1921	63	60	4	7	—	48	119	45	2	6	—	10	17	92,775	51.1	7,133	3.5
June 2, 1925	63	62	18	40	—	9	129	50	3	6	—	4	—	127,542	52.7	45,508	14.4
June 6, 1929	63	62	40	16	—	22	140	28	24	5	—	6	8	164,510	46.9	131,701	33.2
June 19, 1934	55	56	52	53	—	8	169	50	—	5	—	—	—	206,188	48.3	114,936	25.9
June 8, 1938	52	53	24	31	41	11	160	38	—	10	2	2	—	200,370	45.8	52,366	9.9
June 15, 1944	52	52	39	52	1	9	153	5	—	47	—	—	—	140,901	36.0	42,511	9.9
June 24, 1948	52	41	9	52	36	11	149	19	—	31	—	2	—	152,394	33.0	37,985	5.5
June 11, 1952	53	53	8	53	24	7	145	11	—	42	—	—	—	211,463	40.7	10,648	1.9
June 29, 1956	53	52	9	53	53	4	171	14	—	36	3	—	—	167,419	32.4	10,955	1.8
June 8, 1960	55	55	55	55	55	5	225	17	—	38	—	—	—	222,066	34.2	94,713	13.5
Apr. 4, 1964	59	58	43	59	2	1	163	32	1	26	—	—	—	269,402	42.5	127,410	16.6
Oct. 11, 1967	59	59	41	59	6	—	165	35	—	24	—	—	—	193,871	45.6	41,583	9.8
June 23, 1971	60	60	16	60	—	2	138	15	—	45	—	—	—	193,864	42.8	9,659	2.1
June 11, 1975	61	61	61	61	—	5	188	15	7	39	—	—	—	142,853	31.7	124,573	27.6

Sources: Chief Electoral Officer: *Returns from the Records of Saskatchewan General Elections, 1905-1948; Election Summaries (1952-1971);* Saskatchewan Archives Board, *Saskatchewan Executive and Legislative Directory 1905-1970; Election Summaries 1952-1975.*

* The percentages given for party vote are adjusted to exclude the distortions caused by the electoral system. In the determination of party percentages, the party vote in multi-member ridings is divided by the number of members to be elected.

Notes: All Voter Turnout data have been calculated from the "Returns from the Records" from 1908-1948. The "Voters who Voted" column excludes votes from polls or ridings where the figures for "Registered Voters" are missing or unreliable. After the Voter Turnout % column a column is included (entitled "Used Seats") which gives the number of seats contested which were used to calculate Voter Turnout.

In multi-member ridings from 1921-29, the number of "Voters who Voted" are determined by adding the highest candidate vote for each full slate of candidates. Where a party did not run a full slate, the vote is divided by the number of members to be elected. After 1930 voters were required to place an "X" on their ballot for as many candidates as there were members to be elected. All turnout figures include rejected ballots.

Acclamations: 1905: 1 Liberal; 1917: 2 Liberals, 1 Ind.; 1921: 16 Liberals, 1 Ind. Prog.; 1925: 8 Liberals.

Electoral System:

All ridings used the single-member, plurality system of voting except as described for those elections listed below. In all multi-member ridings voters placed an "X" by the names of as many candidates as there were members to be elected.

1921-1948: Three ridings elected two members each.

1952-1956: Two ridings elected two members each. One riding elected three members.

1960:   One riding elected two members. One riding elected three members.
           One riding elected four members.

1964:   Three ridings elected two members each. One riding elected five members.

Saskatchewan

3rd	%*	Party	SC	%*	O.	%*	Total	Voter Turnout			S UE SA ET DS	Voter C O D E
								Registered Electorate in Contested Seats	Voters who Voted	%		
—	—	—	—	—	94	.3	34,057	—	—	—	—	d
—	—	—	—	—	781	1.3	58,681	64,903	45,578	70.2	34	c
—	—	—	—	—	934	1.1	87,586	138,632	80,142	57.8	48	c
—	—	—	—	—	11,664	6.2	186,650	187,718	134,652	71.7	46	k
13,613	8.8	Prog.	—	—	67,262	36.6	180,783	159,256	101,948	65.2	33	k
57,104	25.7	Prog.	—	—	17,605	7.1	247,759	324,909	212,549	65.4	53	k
24,988	7.9	Prog.	—	—	40,061	12.0	361,260	382,509	309,560	80.9	60	k
103,050	24.6	F-L	—	—	5,554	1.2	429,728	443,831	377,363	85.0	54	k
82,568	21.5	CCF	69,720	16.3	35,249	6.5	440,273	448,246	374,589	83.6	49	k
211,365	53.4	CCF	249	.0	2,777	.7	397,803	403,799	322,007	79.7	51	g
236,920	46.4	CCF	40,299	9.1	30,513	6.1	498,111	503,793	419,870	83.3	50	u
290,557	52.4	CCF	21,002	4.3	4,292	.7	537,962	505,679	419,373	82.9	53	u
249,576	43.5	CCF	118,498	21.7	5,250	.6	551,698	510,064	427,918	83.9	53	u
276,897	39.5	CCF	83,761	12.6	1,806	.2	679,243	527,144	443,434	84.1	55	o
268,752	40.2	CCF	2,621	.6	68	.0	668,253	536,392	450,301	83.9	55	o
188,653	44.3	NDP	1,296	.3	—	—	425,403	549,256	427,341	77.8	60	o
248,978	55.0	NDP	—	—	235	.1	452,736	550,850	458,415	83.2	60	o
180,700	40.1	NDP	—	—	2,897	.6	451,023	564,390	453,075	80.3	61	o

Explanation of Party Vote:

1905: In 1905 and 1908 Conservatives ran as "Provincial Rights" candidates. Others: I. (1) 94.

1908: Others: I.L. (1) 394; I. (2) 387.

1912: The election was declared void in one riding and is not referred to in the tables above. All "Provincial Rights" candidates in 1908 who ran again in 1912 did so as Conservatives. Others: I. (5) 934.

1917: The tables exclude the election of three armed service representatives (votes polled: 12,655). Others: Non-Partisan (6) 5,750; I. (9) 4,440 (1 El.); Lab. (2) 1,474.

1921: Others: I. (35) 46,593 (7 El.); I.C. (3) 6,298 (1 El.); Lab. (3) 6,034 (1 El.) Non-Partisan (4) 5,137; I.Lab. (1) 1,690; Government (1) 1,510; I. Pro-Government (1) (El. by acclamation).

1925: Others: I. (6) 8,703 (2 El.); Lab.L. (1) 4,704 (El.). I.L. (1) 2,653 (El.); I.C. (1) 1,545.

1929: Conservatives, Progressives, and Independents formed a coalition government after the election. Two Progressives contested the same seat. Others: I. (17) 32,778 (6 El.); L.Lab. (1) 4,181; Economic Group (3) 1,942; I.L. (1) 1,160.

1934: Two Liberals contested the same seat. Others: I. (3) 2,949; Lab. (1) 1,420; United Front (3) 1,052; I.L. (1) 133.

1938: Two Liberals contested the same seat. Two Social Credit candidates contested the same seat. Others: I. Lab (3) 12,047; Unity (4) 11,421 (2 El.); LPP (2) 8,502; I. (1) 2,451; I.C. (1) 828.

1944: The tables exclude the election of 3 armed service representatives (votes polled: 11,610). Others: LPP (3) 2,067; I. (5) 705; I.L. (1) 5.

1948: Others: I. (5) 11,088 (1 El.); Lib.Con. (3) 9,574 (1 El.); I.L. (1) 3,299; LPP (1) 1,301.

1952: Others: I.PC (1) 1,529; I. (3) 1,517; LPP (2) 1,143; I.L. (1) 103.

1956: Others: I. (2) 4,714; Comm. (2) 536.

1960: Others: I. (3) 1,427; Comm. (2) 379.

1964: Others: LPP (1) 68.

1971: Others: I. (1) 189; Comm. (1) 46.

1975: Others I. Socialist (1) 1,492; I. (2) 1,232; Comm. (2) 173.

Alberta Provincial Elections

Election Date	Seats	Candidates						Elected						Popular Vote			
		L.	C.	3rd	4th	O.	Tot.	L.	C.	3rd	4th	O.	ACCL.	L.	%	C.	%
Nov. 9, 1905	25	27	21	—	—	6	54	22	3	—	—	0	1	14,057	60.7	7,589	32.8
Mar. 22, 1909	41	42	29	—	3	8	82	36	2	—	1	2	9	29,634	59.3	15,848	31.7
Apr. 17, 1913	56	56	56	—	5	15	132	38	18	—	0	0	—	47,544	49.0	43,922	45.3
June 7, 1917	56	49	48	—	1	16	114	34	19	—	1	2	11	54,212	48.1	47,055	41.8
July 18, 1921	61	57	13	43	10	34	157	15	1	38	4	3	2	99,518	34.2	34,548	5.5
June 28, 1926	60	54	56	46	13	14	183	7	4	43	6	0	—	44,722	25.5	40,091	22.9
June 19, 1930	63	36	18	47	11	29	141	11	6	39	4	3	4	46,275	24.6	25,449	13.5
Aug. 22, 1935	63	61	39	45	63	31	239	5	2	0	56	0	—	69,845	23.1	19,358	6.4
Mar. 21, 1940	57	2	0	36	56	71	165	1	—	0	36	20	—	2,755	.9	—	—
Aug. 8, 1944	57	0	0	57	57	70	184	—	—	2	51	4	—	—	—	—	—
Aug. 17, 1948	57	49	0	51	57	16	173	2	—	2	51	2	—	52,655	17.9	—	—
Aug. 5, 1952	61	55	12	41	61	14	183	4	2	2	52	1	1	66,738	22.4	10,971	3.7
June 29, 1955	61	53	26	38	62	23	202	15	3	2	37	4	—	117,741	31.1	34,757	9.2
June 18, 1959	65	51	60	32	64	9	216	1	1	0	62	1	—	57,408	13.9	98,730	23.9
June 17, 1963	63	55	33	56	63	18	225	2	0	0	60	1	—	79,709	19.8	51,278	12.7
May 23, 1967	65	45	47	65	65	14	236	3	6	0	55	1	—	53,845	10.8	129,552	26.0
Aug. 30, 1971	75	20	75	70	75	3	243	0	49	1	25	0	—	6,475	1.0	296,934	46.4
Mar. 26, 1975	75	46	75	75	70	27	293	0	69	1	4	1	—	30,036	5.0	375,670	62.9

Sources: *Returns* (1905-1971), *Statement of Votes* (1930-1948), Edmonton Journal(1975).

Notes: — Excluded from the tables above are the results of at-large elections in 1917 and 1944 to elect, respectively, two and three non-partisan armed services representatives.

— The party percentages in 1921 only are adjusted to exclude the distortions caused by the electoral system. For that election in multi-member ridings, the party percent is changed by dividing party vote by the number of members to be elected in each riding.

— The number of "Voters who Voted" from 1905 to 1926 exclude rejected ballots, and for the elections of 1909 and 1913 the vote in multi-member ridings has been estimated using the procedure of adding the highest vote by one candidate for each party.

Acclamations: 1905: 1 Liberal; 1909: 9 Liberals; 1917: 6 Liberals and 5 Conservatives; 1921: 2 Liberals; 1930: 4 UFA;

Electoral System:

All ridings used the single-member, plurality system of voting except as described for those elections listed below.

1909: Two ridings had two members where voters could mark their ballot twice.

1913: One riding had two members where voters could mark their ballot twice.

1921: Two ridings had five members each and one riding had two members where voters could mark their ballot once for each member to be elected.

1926: Two ridings elected five members each using the Hare system of proportional representation (P.R.). The single-member ridings used the alternate system.

1930-35: Two ridings had six members each (Hare P.R.). Others: single-member, alternative.

1940-48: Two ridings had five members each (Hare P.R.). Others: single-member, alternative.

1952-55: One six-member riding and one seven-member riding (Hare P.R.). Others: single member, alternative.

Explanation of Party Vote

Contested the same seat: Two Liberals in each of two ridings. Others: I. (6) 1,508.

1909: Contested the same seat: Two Liberals in each of two ridings. Others: I. (6) 1,695 (1 El.); I L. (2) 1,311 (1 El.); Lab. (1) 214.

1913: Others: I. (14) 3,639; I.L. (1) 47.

Alberta

3rd	%	Party	4th	%	Party	O.	%	Total	Registered Electorate in Contested Seats	Voters who Voted	%	Voter Code
—	—	—	—	—	—	1,508	6.5	23,154	—	23,154	—	d
—	—	—	1,302	2.6	Soc.	3,220	6.4	50,004	—	43,187	—	d
—	—	—	1,814	1.9	Soc.	3,686	3.8	96,966	—	87,554	—	d
—	—	—	1,328	1.2	Lab.	10,017	8.9	112,612	—	112,612	—	g
83,773	45.4	Farm	33,987	6.3	Lab.	46,351	8.5	298,177	—	175,980	—	g
70,968	40.5	UFA	14,123	8.1	Lab.	5,233	3.0	175,137	—	175,137	—	g
74,187	39.4	UFA	14,354	7.6	Lab.	27,954	14.9	188,219	293,758	197,141	67.1	g
33,063	11.0	UFA	163,700	54.2	SC	15,786	5.2	301,752	378,249	312,331	82.6	g
34,316	11.1	CCF	132,507	42.9	SC	139,286	45.1	308,864	427,245	320,403	75.0	j
70,307	24.9	CCF	146,367	51.9	SC	65,432	23.2	282,106	421,051	291,908	69.3	j
56,387	19.1	CCF	164,003	55.6	SC	21,748	7.4	294,793	489,311	313,481	64.1	j
41,929	14.1	CCF	167,789	56.2	SC	10,908	3.7	298,335	537,170	318,948	59.4	j
31,180	8.2	CCF	175,553	46.4	SC	18,948	5.0	378,179	589,409	401,018	68.0	j
17,899	4.3	CCF	230,283	55.7	SC	9,195	2.2	413,515	649,678	415,113	63.9	j
38,133	9.5	NDP	221,107	54.8	SC	13,217	3.3	403,444	720,910	404,808	56.2	p
79,593	16.0	NDP	222,271	44.6	SC	13,080	2.6	498,341	779,822	501,108	64.3	p
73,038	11.4	NDP	262,953	41.1	SC	462	.1	639,862	895,442	644,504	72.0	p
78,017	13.1	NDP	106,245	17.8	SC	7,299	1.2	597,367	—	—	—	

1917: Totals exclude 25,601 votes cast by 13,286 Soldiers and Nurses in an "at-large" district for two special representatives. A special act of the Assembly re-elected by acclamation 11 sitting members who enlisted in the armed services. Others: I. (8) 3,625; Soc. (4) 1,570; I.L. (1) 1,296; Non-Partisan (1) 839 (El.); I.Farmer (1) 439 (El.); Unknown (1) 2,248.

1921: Others: I. (14) 29,691 (3 El.); I.L. (6) 3,666; I.Lab. (5) 5,483; Soc. (2) 2,628; I.Farmer (5) 2,376; I. Prog. (1) 1,744; Non-Partisan (1) 763.

1926: Farmers ran as the (UFA) United Farmers of Alberta. Others: I.L. (5) 2,728; I. (3) 1,254; I. UFA (4) 626; L.Prog. (1) 252; I.Farmer (1) 373.

1930: Others: I. (29) 27,954 (2 El.).

1935: Others: Comm. (9) 5,771; Lab. (10) 5,086; I. (7) 2,740; I.L. (1) 955; United Front (1) 560; I. Lab. (1) 224; I.C. (1) 258; Economic Reconstruction (1) 192.

1940: Others: Ind. Movement (59) 131,172 (19 El.) A grouping of Conservatives, Liberals, and some U.F.A. candidates; Lab. (3) 3,509 (1 El.); I. Prog. (4) 1,726; Comm. (1) 1,067; I.L. (1) 1,136; I.SC (1) 362; I. Farmer (2) 314.

1944: Others: Ind. Movement (36) 47,239 (3 El.); LPP (3) 12,003; Veteran (1) 3,532 (El.); Lab. Union (1) 1,788; Single Tax (1) 480; Farmer-Lab. (1) 390.

1949: Others: I. (7) 9,014 (1 El.); Ind. Citizen's Association (2) 3,969; Lab. (1) 3,579; I.SC (3) 2,958 (1 El.); LPP (2) 1,372; United Lab. (1) 856.

1952: The Conservative column includes : Con. (5) 6,271 (2 El.) and PC (7) 4,700. Others: I.SC (6) 4,203 (1 El.); LPP (2) 1,132; Farmer (1) 655; Lab. (1) 527; Non-Partisan Farmer (1) 463; I. Lab. (1) 2,927; People's (1) 296.

1955: Others: Coalition (2) 4,581 (1 El.); I. (7) 4,225 (1 El.); Lib.-Con. (2) 4,001 (1 El.); LPP (9) 3,420; I.SC (3) 2,721 (1 El.).

1959: Others: I. (2) 3,640; I.SC (2) 2,392 (1 El.); Coalition (1) 2,279; LPP (4) 884.

1963: Others: I. (3) 3,966; I.SC (6) 3,178; Alberta Unity Movement (3) 2,233; Coalition (1) 2,179 (El.); Comm. (4) 527; PC-Lib. (1) 1,134.

1967: Others: I. (7) 6,916 (1 El.); Coalition (2) 3,654; I.PC (2) 1,118; Other (1) 699.

1971: Others: I. (3) 462.

1975: The results given are unofficial. The turnout percent excluding rejected ballots was 61.3. Others: I.SC (1) 4,428 (El.); I.PC (3) 1,057; Comm. (14) 766; I. (4) 558; I.L. (2) 412; Constitutional Socialist Party (3) 113.

British Columbia Provincial Elections

Election Date	Seats	Candidates						Elected					ACCL	Popular Vote			
		L.	C.	3rd	4th	O.	Tot.	L.	C.	3rd	4th	O.		L.	%*	C.	%*
Feb. 2, 1907	42	40	42	22	—	8	112	12	27	3	—	—	—	23,560	38.0	31,068	47.0
Nov. 25, 1909	42	39	42	20	—	3	104	3	36	3	—	—	—	36,472	33.8	52,462	53.3
Mar. 28, 1912	42	18	46	18	—	6	88	—	40	2	—	—	9	21,261	19.4	51,181	64.6
Sept. 14, 1916	47	46	46	—	—	24	116	37	8	1	—	1	—	90,380	50.9	72,834	41.3
Dec. 1, 1920	47	46	43	14	—	52	155	26	14	2	—	5	1	134,591	36.9	111,380	32.8
June 20, 1924	48	46	48	17	45	12	168	25	16	3	2	2	—	108,322	32.5	102,433	31.6
July 18, 1928	48	46	48	8	—	15	117	12	35	1	—	—	—	146,552	40.9	192,867	52.4
Nov. 2, 1933	47	47	6	46	29	82	210	34	—	7	2	4	—	159,131	42.0	7,114	1.5
June 1, 1937	48	48	43	46	18	31	186	31	8	7	—	2	—	156,074	38.3	119,521	25.7
Oct. 21, 1941	48	48	43	45	—	20	156	21	12	14	—	1	—	149,525	33.6	140,282	28.8
Oct. 25, 1945	48	47*	—	48	16	36	147	37*	—	10	—	1	—	261,147	53.8	(Coalition)*	
June 15, 1949	48	48*	—	48	16	26	138	39*	—	7	—	2	—	428,773	58.9	(Coalition)*	
June 12, 1952	48	48	48	48	47	22	213	6	4	18	19	1	—	180,289	23.3	129,439	15.8
June 9, 1953	48	48	39	47	48	47	229	4	1	14	28	1	—	171,671	23.0	40,780	5.0
Sept. 19, 1956	52	52	22	51	52	22	199	2	—	10	39	1	—	177,922	20.8	25,373	2.8
Sept. 12, 1960	52	50	52	52	52	24	230	4	—	16	32	—	—	208,249	19.5	66,943	6.7
Sept. 30, 1963	52	51	52	52	52	6	205	5	—	14	33	—	—	193,363	17.8	109,090	11.1
Sept. 12, 1966	55	53	3	55	55	15	181	6	—	16	33	—	—	152,155	17.5	1,409	.2
Aug. 27, 1969	55	55	1	55	55	12	178	5	—	12	38	—	—	186,235	18.4	1,087	.1
Aug. 30, 1972	55	50	45	55	55	5	210	5	2	38	10	—	—	185,640	15.5	143,450	13.1
Dec. 11, 1975	55	49	29	55	55	33	221	1	1	18	35	—	—	93,379	6.9	49,796	4.1

Source: Chief Electoral Officer.

* The percentages given for party vote are adjusted to exclude the distortions caused by the electoral system. When determining party percentages, the party vote in multi-member ridings is divided by the number of members to be elected.

Notes: The number of "Voters who Voted" in 1920 and 1924 exclude rejected ballots and have been estimated in multi-member ridings by adding the top candidate vote for each party which ran a full slate. The vote for candidates which were not part of a full slate were divided by 4 in Victoria and 6 in Vancouver.

The given "Registered Electorate" in 1920 excludes 1,965 persons in one riding won by acclamation.

Acclamations: 1912: 9 Conservatives; 1920: 1 Liberal.

Electoral System: In multi-member ridings voters could place an "X" on the ballot for each of the total number of candidates to be elected, except for the elections of 1952 and 1953 when all ridings used the "alternate" (or preferential) system of voting.

The number of single and multi-member ridings by the number of members for each riding. (M = Members)

Elections	1M	2M	3M	4M	5M	6M
1907-12	31	1	—	1	1	—
1916-20	37	—	—	1	—	1
1924-28	38	3	—	1	—	1
1933	34	3	1	1	—	—
1937	35	3	1	1	—	—
1941-49	36	3	2	—	—	—
1952-53	36	3	2	—	—	—
1956-66	34	6	2	—	—	—
1969-72	41	7	—	—	—	—
1969-75	41	7	—	—	—	—

Explanation of Party Vote:

1907: The vote for 21 candidates came from newspaper report. Others: Lab. (6) 1,972; I.L. (1) 197; I. (1) 147.

1909: The vote for 3 candidates came from newspaper report. Others: Lab. (2) 222; I.C. (1) 154.
* Contested the same seat: 2 Conservatives in each of 2 ridings, 3 Conservatives in one riding.

1912: Others: I. (3) 1,695; I.C. (3) 405.

1916: Others: I. (12) 9,035; Lab. (1) 2,487; I.C. (1) 539 (E.).

1920: The Lab. column includes 10 Federated Lab. 29,582 (1 El.) and 4 Lab. 2,461 (1 El.). Others: I. (18) 35,980 (3 El.); Soc. (7) 12,414 (1 El.); Soldier-Lab. (7) 7,225; Government Aid (2) 5,441; Farmer (4) 3,565; I. Soldier (2) 2,265; (con't)

British Columbia

3rd	%*	Party	4th	%*	Party	O.	%*	Total	Voter Turnout			Voter Code
									Registered Electorate	Voters who Voted	%	
6,300	11.1	Soc.	—	—	—	2,316	3.9	63,244	—	—	—	c
11,493	12.1	Soc.	—	—	—	376	.8	100,803	—	—	—	c
9,987	13.9	Soc.	—	—	—	2,100	2.0	84,529	—	—	—	c
4,487	3.5	Soc.	—	—	—	12,061	4.3	179,762	—	—	—	c
31,993	8.7	Lab.	83,517	22.6	PP	76,124	21.6	354,088	199,407	154,818	77.6	k
39,577	8.7	Lab.	—	—	PP	11,759	4.6	345,608	225,675	153,289	67.9	k
16,627	4.7	Lab.	—	—	NP	5,768	2.1	361,814	245,240	174,934	71.3	k
120,248	31.1	CCF	38,524	11.9	NP	56,206	13.5	381,223	323,540	236,415	73.1	k
119,400	29.5	CCF	4,812	.9	SC	18,122	5.5	417,929	372,781	265,446	71.2	k
151,440	34.4	CCF	—	—	SC	12,646	3.2	453,893	417,839	303,901	72.7	k
175,960	39.1	CCF	6,627	1.4	SC	24,013	5.6	467,747	476,222	298,387	62.7	k
245,248	36.9	CCF	11,536	1.9	SC	13,230	2.3	698,823	649,019	477,999	73.6	h
236,562	31.5	CCF	209,049	27.9	SC	13,222	1.6	768,561	793,074	543,456	68.5	h
224,513	32.2	CCF	274,771	37.6	SC	16,104	2.1	727,839	740,006	522,052	70.5	p
231,511	29.4	CCF	374,711	46.0	SC	7,880	1.0	817,397	778,587	509,409	65.4	p
326,094	33.7	CCF	386,886	39.4	SC	8,232	.8	996,404	874,267	628,031	71.8	p
269,004	29.0	NDP	395,079	41.9	SC	1,139	.1	967,675	873,140	608,672	69.7	p
252,753	34.5	NDP	342,751	47.3	SC	2,808	.4	751,876	873,927	596,716	68.3	p
331,813	34.2	NDP	457,777	47.2	SC	1,444	.1	978,356	1,152,598	794,696	68.9	p
448,260	40.1	NDP	352,776	31.2	SC	2,046	.2	1,132,060	1,343,357	929,632	69.2	p
505,396	38.7	NDP	635,482	49.8	SC	6,398	.4	1,290,451	1,559,633	1,088,001	69.8	p

1920: (Con't) I.L. (2) 2,702; Soldier Farm. (3) 1,944; Soldier (2) 1,740; People's (1) 1,354 (El.); I.C. (1) 697; Farm. Lab. (2) 378; Lab. Soc. (1) 419.

1924: Others: Soc. (2) 4,364; I.L. (4) 3,324 (2 El.); I. (4) 3,570; I.C. (1) 276; I. Lab. (1) 225.

1928: The 3rd party Lab. column includes: Lab. (5) 6,062 (1 El.) and I. Lab. (3) 10,565. Others: I. (13) 4,704; I.C. (2) 1,064.

1933: The Non-Partisans were led by the former leader of the Conservatives, however only 11 of the 35 Conservatives elected in 1928 ran in 1933 and only 6 of those 11 were clearly Non-Partisan candidates. Others: Unionist (11) 14,394 (1 El); United Front of Workers and Farmers (20) 4,584; I. (33) 31,435 (2 El.); I. CCF (7) 1,990; Lab. (3) 2,261 (1 El.); Soc. (5) 370; I.L. (2) 1,076; I. Lab. (1) 96.

1937: Others: I. (11) 7,341 (1 El.); Lab. (2) 1,787 (1 El.); Comm. (1) 567; Soc. (2) 287; Financial Justice (1) 54; B.C. Constructive (14) 8,086. Social Credit (SC) was known as the Social Credit League.

1941: Others: I. Lab. (2) 3,899; Lab. (4) 2,975 (1 El.); Official Con. (1) 2,161; I. (4) 1,638; Soc. Lab. (4) 950; I. Farm. (1) 388; Emancipation (1) 265; Victory without Debt (1) 209; Religious Political Brotherhood (1) 105; I. Soc. (1) 56.

1945: The Liberals and Conservatives formed a coalition for the 1945 and 1949 elections. Others: LPP (21) 16,479; People's CCF (2) 2,786; I. (2) 1,532; Lab. (1) 1,289 (El.); I.PC (1) 473; Democratic (1) 423; Soc. Lab. (3) 285; PC (1) 275; I.L. (1) 199; I. Lab. (1) 106; Soc. (1) 105; Prog. L. (1) 61.

1949: Others: I. (7) 5,163 (1 El.); Union of Electors (12) 2,790; LPP (2) 1,660; Lab. (1) 1,483 (El.); Con. (1) 1,241; People's (2) 607; Soc. Lab. (1) 286.

1952: Others: LPP (5) 2,514; Christian Democratic (8) 7,176; I. (6) 1,312; Lab. (1) 1,290 (El.); Lab. Rep. (1) 654; Soc. (1) 276.

1953: Others: LPP (25) 7,496; Christian Democratic (14) 5,036; I. (6) 1,951; Lab. (1) 1,601 (El.); People's (1) 20.

1956: Others: LPP (14) 3,381; Lab. (1) 1,321 (El.); I. (6) 3,005; People's (1) 173.

1960: Others: Comm. (19) 5,675; I. (5) 2,557.

1963: Others: Comm. (4) 849; I. (1) 215; Soc. (1) 75.

1966: Others: I. (6) 1,711; Comm. (6) 1,097.

1969: Others: I. (6) 831; Comm. (4) 482; Social Con. (1) 131.

1972: Others: I. (9) 1,184; Comm. (5) 862.

1975: Others: I (16) 4,816; Comm. (13) 1,441; N.Am Labour Party (4) 141.

19

GOVERNMENT PUBLICATIONS

Professor Land's article is self-explanatory. It is a very useful guide for those who wish to find material in the voluminous and confusing world of federal and provincial governmental publications. The author explains the origins of most major publications and the nature of their contents. He also lists a number of bibliographical works that give additional information about governmental publications.

A DESCRIPTION AND GUIDE TO THE USE OF CANADIAN GOVERNMENT PUBLICATIONS*

Brian Land

A government publication has been defined as "any printed or processed paper, book, periodical, pamphlet or map, originating in, or printed with the imprint of, or at the expense and by the authority of, any office of a legally organized government".[1] Government publications range in scope from the formal papers, debates and journals of our legislatures, and from the annual reports of the various departments and agencies to the

---

* Revised February, 1977, for this book by the author who is Professor of Library Science, University of Toronto.

[1] American Library Association, Committee on Library Terminology, *A.L.A. Glossary of Library Terms, with a Selection of Terms in Related Fields*, Chicago: American Library Association, 1943, p. 65.

more popular periodicals and pamphlets for tourists, and to "how to do it" booklets for the handyman or housewife.

The following paragraphs describe some of the more important serial publications of the federal government such as the debates, journals, departmental reports, statutes, and gazettes, and review some of the guides, catalogues, indexes and checklists of government publications.

The Major Serial Publications

Debates of the House of Commons

The most familiar of the legislative publications are the debates which give a verbatim account of what is said in Parliament. The several volumes each session record the daily debates of the House, messages of the Governor-General and varying information such as lists of members of the House and of the Ministry. Like those of the British Parliament, the Canadian *Debates* are referred to as *Hansard* in honour of the printer, T. C. Hansard, who reported the British *Debates* in the early nineteenth century.

The only example of printed debates as we know them today which were published before Confederation are the *Parliamentary Debates on the Subject of the Confederation of the British North American Provinces*, published in 1865 and republished in 1951. This volume was indexed by the Public Archives Canada under the title *Index to Parliamentary Debates on the Subject of the Confederation of the British North American Provinces*, compiled by M. A. Lapin and edited and revised by J. S. Patrick.

The debates of the early Canadian Parliaments, as in most countries, were not officially reported and the only records are, with a few exceptions, the so-called *Scrapbook Debates* which are in the library of Parliament. These debates consist of clippings from contemporary newspapers, which have been mounted in scrapbooks and for which handwritten indexes have been made. The *Scrapbook Debates* cover the period from Confederation to 1874, and are available on microfilm, published by the Canadian Library Association, Ottawa, 1954. From 1870 to 1872, three volumes of debates of both Houses were published but were unofficial in origin. These are referred to as the *Cotton Debates* after the name of the Ottawa *Times* reporter, John Cotton, who covered the sessions. Not until 1875 did the House of Commons itself begin reporting its debates. From 1875 to 1879, the contract for reporting these debates was awarded to private reporters, but from 1880 on, an official staff of reporters was appointed to secure continuity and uniformity.

As a Centennial project of the Parliament of Canada under the auspices of the Library of Parliament, the *Debates* of the House of Commons for 1867-1868 were edited by Professor Peter B. Waite of Dalhousie University and published in one volume by the Queen's Printer in 1967. This volume covers the first session of the first Parliament, November 6, 1867 to May 22, 1868, and is principally a collation by Professor Waite of the debates published during these years in the Ottawa *Times* and Toronto

Globe. The *Debates* for 1869 were published in 1975. The debates for the years 1870-1874 are also being reconstituted from the same sources for publication.

The daily edition of the *Debates: Official Report* is issued in pamphlet form during each session of Parliament on the morning following each day's sitting and contains the speeches in English as delivered and the English translation of speeches delivered in French. Similarly, a daily edition of the *Debates* containing the speeches in French as delivered and the French translation of speeches delivered in English is also issued on the day following delivery. Following publication of the daily edition, proofs of their speeches or remarks are sent to members for suggested changes which must be confined to the correction of errors and essential minor alterations. At the end of each session, revised bound volumes are published. At the present time, each Wednesday's edition of the daily *Debates* includes an alphabetical list of members with their constituencies, party affiliations and addresses; a complete list of standing, special and joint committees with the membership of each; members of the Ministry according to precedence; and a list of parliamentary secretaries.

In recent years, an index to the daily House of Commons *Debates* has been issued in pamphlet form at intervals during the session. The complete index is either included in the final bound volume of the *Debates* for the session or published separately.

Debates of the Senate

This series is also referred to as *Hansard* from its prototype, the Parliamentary debates of Great Britain. For the years 1870-1872 inclusive, unofficial non-verbatim versions of the Senate debates appear in the *Cotton Debates* referred to above. In 1871 the Senate began publishing its own *Debates*. From 1871 to 1899 they were published in English only, and from 1871 to 1916 the contract for reporting was awarded to various persons, but in 1917 an official reporter was appointed. The *Debates* of the Senate covering the first session of the first Parliament, November 6, 1867 to May 22, 1868, have been edited by Professor Waite and were published in 1968 as part of the Centennial project of the Parliament of Canada referred to above. The *Debates* for 1869 were published in 1975. Debates for the years 1870-1874 are being reconstituted for publication.

The *Debates: Official Report (Hansard)* of the Senate are, like those of the House of Commons, recorded and printed day by day and the same opportunity is afforded its members to amend or correct errors and omissions in the daily *Debates*, so that the bound volume at the end of the session can be complete and correct. The amount and extent of corrections in *Hansard* are subject to discussion and agreement in each House respectively. When a change in membership of the Senate occurs, a revised roster is usually published in the next Tuesday issue of the daily *Debates* listing the Senators according to seniority, alphabetically, and by province. Officers and committees of the Senate are also listed.

In recent years, an index to the daily *Debates* of the Senate has sometimes been issued in pamphlet form at intervals during the session. The complete index is included in the final bound volume of the *Debates* for each session.

Votes and Proceedings and Journals of the House of Commons

The *Votes and Proceedings* of the House of Commons are published daily when the House is in session and constitute the official records of the House. The *Votes and Proceedings* include the daily transactions of the House, accounts of the introduction of bills, referral of questions to committees, resolutions amended or carried, votes taken, debates adjourned, proclamations and rosters of committee members. Everything printed above the Speaker's signature in the daily *Votes and Proceedings* appears at the end of each session in the bound *Journals* of the House of Commons, which then become the official records of the House. Everything printed below the Speaker's signature in the *Votes and Proceedings*, such as notices of committee meetings, are omitted from the *Journals*. The *Journals* are so named because they provide a complete and concise record of the proceedings of the House in chronological order, day by day.

The bound *Journals* contain a numerical "List of Appendices" consisting mainly of a list of reports of standing committees. Occasionally, the report of a special joint committee of the House of Commons and the Senate is published in the bound *Journals*. An example is the *Final Report* of the Special Joint Committee on the Constitution of Canada presented to the House on March 16, 1972, which was also published as a separate monograph. An index to the *Journals* is included in the final volume for each session. To locate a Commons committee report in its *Journals*, it is necessary to look in the index under the name of the committee concerned.

Minutes of the Proceedings and Journals of the Senate

The *Minutes of the Proceedings* of the Senate, the official record of proceedings, are issued daily when the Senate is in session and correspond to the *Votes and Proceedings* of the House of Commons. At the end of each session, the *Minutes of the Proceedings* and such appendices as it is decided to include are published with an index in the *Journals* of the Senate. In the 1964-65 session, the *Journals* of the Senate began to be issued in two parts: Part I deals with all matters coming before the Senate with the exception of "Resolutions for Dissolution and Annulment of Marriages", which are contained in Part II.

As in the case of the House of Commons, reports of standing committees of the Senate are included in the *Journals*. An example is the report of the Committee on National Finance presented to the Senate on March 23, 1972. To locate a Senate committee report in its *Journals*, it is necessary to look in the index under "Committees" where the references to various committees are gathered together.

Daily Agenda

The *Order Paper and Notices* (which superseded *Routine Proceedings and Orders of the Day*) is issued daily in bilingual form by the House of Commons when it is in session. On Monday or on the first sitting day of the week, it is comprehensive and includes the present and past status of all business of the House plus unresolved notices of motions for the production of papers or unanswered questions. For the other sitting days of the week, it is abbreviated, giving only routine proceedings, government orders, private members' business for that day, and notices. The *Order Paper and Notices* is not cumulated or republished.

In the case of the Senate, a section dealing with "Orders of Business" appears each day in the *Minutes of the Proceedings*. This section constitutes the agenda for each day's business of the Senate and is not subsequently republished in its *Journals*.

Sessional Papers, 1867/68-1925

This series included most of the reports that came before Parliament and were ordered printed, with the exception of the reports of committees which were printed as appendices to the *Journals* of each House. There were several volumes of sessional papers for each session, and each volume includes both an alphabetical and numerical list of the papers for that session. They are not paged continuously and indexes refer to the number of each document rather than to pages. Much of the material published in the *Sessional Papers* was also published elsewhere, e.g., a branch report might appear in the *Sessional Papers*, be published separately, and published as part of a departmental report as well as being issued in both English and French. The government ceased publication of the *Sessional Papers* series in 1925 after having published some 923 volumes since Confederation, but the departmental reports formerly included were continued in the series of *Annual Departmental Reports*. Although there is no longer an official printed set of sessional papers, individual items are still tabled daily in the House of Commons and are subsequently deposited in the Sessional Papers Office of the House of Commons.

General Indexes to the Journals of the House and to Sessional Papers

In order to facilitate their use, a consolidated *General Index to the Journals of the House of Commons of Canada, and of the Sessional Papers of Parliament* was published on five occasions covering the following periods: 1867-1876; 1877-1890; 1891-1903; 1904-1915; and 1916-1930. General indexes to the *Journals* of the House of Commons are being prepared to cover the periods 1930-1945, 1946-1962, and subsequent years.

Annual Departmental Reports, 1924/25-1929/30.

This series included reports of some commissions as well as continuing the departmental reports issued in *Sessional Papers* up in 1924. Since this series also duplicated material issued in other forms, it was dropped in 1930 as an economy measure.

Acts of Parliament

All *Bills* originating in the House of Commons or Senate are printed after first reading. *Bills* originating in the House are distinguished by the letter C and numbered chronologically; those of the Senate, by the letter S and numbered chronologically. Beginning with the thirtieth Parliament in 1974, the numbers from C-2 to C-200 have been reserved for government bills in the Commons; numbers from C-201 have upward have been allocated to private members' bills. If successful, *Bills* are printed after the third reading as passed. When Royal Assent has been given, these *Bills* become *Acts* and are assigned individual chapter numbers along with the name of the reigning sovereign and the year of reign, e.g., 21 Eliz. II, c. 11. *Acts* may be issued separately as well as being published in bound form in the *Acts of the Parliament of the Dominion of Canada*, or, as they are more commonly known, the *Statutes of Canada*. Since the first session of the twenty-eighth Parliament in September, 1968, all *Bills* and *Statutes* have been printed in both the official languages of Canada, the English text in the left-hand column of each page and the French in the right-hand column.

Since 1875, the volumes of the *Statutes of Canada* have been divided into two parts, one devoted to Public General Acts, and the other to Local Private Acts. A preliminary section includes proclamations, despatches, appointments, etc. From 1874 to 1939, Orders-in-Council were also included. The government issues no bound volume of bills which have failed to pass, and most libraries do not keep them beyond the session in which they were proposed. For special compilations and indexes to legislation of the federal government prior to 1932, one should consult Marion V. Higgins, *Canadian Government Publications*, described below.

Since December 1974, the Public Acts of each session of Parliament have been published as soon as practicable after receiving Royal Assent in a new Part III of *The Canada Gazette*. Formerly, statutes passed in a given session of Parliament had not normally been published in general form until the end of the session. The new system of publication will largely eliminate this delay. The normal publication of bound volumes of statutes at the end of each session of Parliament is to continue as in the past.

Revised Statutes of Canada

The *Revised Statutes of Canada*, which bring legislation amended since its original passage up to date, have been issued five times since Confederation: 1886, 1906, 1927, 1952, and 1970. When the 1970 *Revised Statutes* were proclaimed in force, the proclamation had the effect of repealing those public general statutes included in the revision and replacing them by the statutes in the revision. For the first time in the history of the Canadian Parliament, the 1970 *Revised Statutes* were tabled in the House of Commons both in the form of magnetic tape containing the machine-readable data base used in their production, as well as in the traditional form of bound volumes. The 1970 revision is in a two-language, English-French page format for the first time and each volume contains a table of contents and index. There is also a separate index volume which forms part of the eleven-volume set of the 1970 *Revised Statutes*.

Special Compilations of Statutes and Regulations

After third reading and Royal Assent, an Act may be published in pamphlet form as a "separate chapter" for public distribution. From time to time, the government also issues "office consolidations" of certain statutes and regulations for the convenience of court officials, lawyers, and the public generally. Examples of office consolidations are the *Canadian Corporations Act and Regulations*, published in 1972, and the *Criminal Code* published in 1973.

The Canada Gazette

The Canada Gazette, published in three parts in a bilingual format, is the official gazette of Canada. All proclamations issued by the Governor-General under the authority of the Governor-in-Council, and all official notices, Orders-in-Council, regulations, advertisements, and documents relating to the government of Canada, or matters under the control of Parliament thereof, and requiring publication, are published in *The Canada Gazette* unless some other mode of publication thereof is required by law.

The Canada Gazette, Part I, is published every Saturday and contains notices of a general character, proclamations, certain Orders-in-Council and various other classes of statutory notices. Orders-in-Council are designated by the letters PC (for Privy Council), followed by the year and a chronological number. Each issue of *Part I* is indexed and there are also non-cumulative quarterly indexes but currently there is no annual index.

The Canada Gazette, Part II, is published under the authority of the Statutory Instruments Act, (which came into force January 1972), on the second and fourth Wednesday of each month with special editions as required. It contains all regulations, as defined by the Statutory Instruments Act, and certain other classes of statutory instruments and documents required to be published therein. Certain regulations and classes of regulations are exempted from publication by Section 14 of the Statutory Instruments Regulations. Each item in *Part II* is listed by its registration number assigned in the Privy Council Office as either SOR (regulations) or SI (other than regulations) and the numbers are consecutive within each series and year. All statutory instruments and regulations made under statutory authority and published in *The Canada Gazette, Part II*, and in force at any time since January 1 and of the current calendar year, are indexed in the *Consolidated Index of Statutory Instruments*, a quarterly publication.

Since December 1974, a new *Part III* of *The Canada Gazette* has been published. Starting with the first session of the thirtieth Parliament (1974), the Acts of Parliament are to be printed individually or in groups as *Part III* of *The Canada Gazette*. From time to time, *Part III* is to contain an updated Table of Public Statutes and, when necessary, a Table of Proclaimed Acts as in the annual volumes so that relevant information concerning the statutes will be more rapidly available to recipients as *Part III* of *The Canada Gazette*. In addition, it is expected that a table will be published from time to time in *Part III* identifying the Minister responsible for administering each Public Statute.

Orders-in-Council and Statutory Instruments and Regulations

Orders-in-Council were first published in the *Statutes of Canada* for 1872. From 1874 to 1939, statutory orders and regulations having the force of law were published in the preliminary section of the *Statutes of Canada*. On two occasions during this period, consolidations were published by the federal government: *Orders-in-Council, Proclamations, Departmental Regulations, etc., having the Force of Law in the Dominion of Canada* (1875), and *Consolidated Orders-in-Council of Canada* (1889).

Since 1939, there has been a steady increase in the number of statutes which confer power on the Minister to make orders and regulations. The systematic publication of statutory orders "of general or widespread interest or concern" is a fairly recent development. It began in 1940 with the publication of *Proclamations and Orders-in-Council [relating to the War]*. Eight volumes of this series were published covering the period from August 26, 1939 to September 30, 1942. During the period from 1940 to 1942, the federal government also published three volumes of the consolidated *Defence of Canada Regulations*. In October 1942, a new publication, *Canadian War Orders and Regulations* began. Its title changed to *Statutory Orders and Regulations* in October 1945 and it ceased publication in January 1947.

Since January 1, 1947, provision has been made for publication of statutory orders and regulations in *Part II* of the *Canada Gazette*. In 1950, a *Statutory Orders and Regulations Consolidation* was published bringing together all statutes which conferred the power to make orders or regulations, and all orders and regulations having a general effect. A later consolidation was published in 1955. For information about statutory instruments and orders in force since 1955, reference should be made to the latest December issue of the *Consolidated Index of Statutory Instruments* previously mentioned.

For the period 1867-1965, the Privy Council Office has prepared an *Annual Index of Orders in Council* which is available on microfilm from the Public Archives of Canada.

A monthly *Summary of Orders-in-Council Passed during the Month* is tabled in the House of Commons and is listed in the *Votes and Proceedings*.

Report of Committees, Commissions and Task Forces

Reports of Parliamentary Committees

Unlike the royal commission or commission of inquiry, which are creatures of the executive, the parliamentary committee is a vital part of the legislative arm of government—the House of Commons and Senate. Parliamentary committees are of three kinds: the Committee of the Whole House, standing committees, and special committees.

The main function of the Committee of the Whole House is deliberation, rather than inquiry, and clause-by-clause discussion of the bills under consideration, which is facilitated by relaxation of the formal rules of debate and party discipline. The proceedings of the Committee of the Whole House are reported without a break in the *Debates* and in the *Journals* and there is no special problem in locating them.

The first session of the twenty-eighth Parliament, 1968-69, adopted major changes in the Standing Orders of the House concerning the business of supply and the business of ways and means formerly dealt with in the Committee of Supply and in the Committee of Ways and Means respectively. As a result of these changes, detailed scrutiny of government estimates and consideration of bills arising out of budget tax proposals are now given by the appropriate committees of the House of Commons. Under the Standing Orders of the House of Commons adopted January 1976, all public bills except those based on a supply or ways and means motion are referred at the end of second reading to a standing committee of the House or to a special or joint committee. In addition, all governmental estimates for expenditures are also referred to a standing committee.

The effect of recent changes in House procedure has been to extend significantly the functions of its standing committees and, as a consequence, their influence and importance. The standing committees are permanently provided for in the Standing Orders, and are set up at the commencement of each session of Parliament to consider all subjects of a particular type arising or likely to arise in the course of the session, e.g., agriculture; broadcasting, films and assistance to the arts; external affairs and national defence; finance, trade and economic affairs; fisheries and forestry; health, welfare and social affairs; Indian affairs and northern development; justice and legal affairs; labour, manpower and immigration; management and members' services; miscellaneous estimates; miscellaneous private bills and standing orders; national resources and public works; privileges and elections; procedure and organization; public accounts; regional development; transport and communications; and veterans' affairs. The deliberations of standing committees are published as *Minutes of Proceedings and Evidence* as their meetings occur.

Special committees are frequently set up to consider and report on particular bills or upon special subjects. A recent example is the Special Committee on Trends in Food Prices. The chief function of the special committee is to investigate, and it is the legislative prototype of the executive's commission of inquiry except that its members must be Members of Parliament. Deliberations of special committees are also published as they occur as *Minutes of Proceedings and Evidence*.

In the past, special committees occasionally have been converted into quasi-standing committees called "sessional committees" by enlarging their original orders of reference which provide them with a greater degree of permanence than ordinary special committees, e.g., the Sessional Committee on Railways, Air Lines and Shipping Owned and Controlled by the Government.

A "joint committee" is one appointed from the membership of both the Senate and House of Commons, e.g., the Joint Committee on Regulations and Other Statutory Instruments, and may be either a standing or special committee.

Reports of standing committees are published in the daily *Votes and Proceedings*; reports of most special committees, however, are published separately. A list of committee reports appears in the "List of Appendices" in the *Journals* of the House of Commons for each session. These are indexed under the name of the committee.

Standing committees of the Senate are: agriculture; banking, trade and commerce; internal economy, budgets and administration; foreign affairs; health, welfare and science; legal and constitutional affairs; national finance; standing rules and orders; and transport and communication. Reports of standing committees of the Senate are usually published in its *Minutes of the Proceedings*, frequently as an appendix, and are republished in the *Journals* of the Senate. Reports of special committees of the Senate may be published separately as monographs.

Committee reports of the House of Commons and of the Senate that are published separately are listed in the catalogues described below.

Reports of Royal Commissions or Commissions of Inquiry

Royal commissions, or commissions of inquiry as they are now generally called, are appointed under the terms of the *Inquiries Act* by the executive arm of government, i.e., the Cabinet, to carry out full and impartial investigations of specific problems and to report their findings so that decisions might be reached and appropriate action taken. When the Cabinet has approved of the setting up of a royal commission or commission of inquiry it issues an Order-in-Council which is published in *The Canada Gazette, Part I*, giving the terms of reference, powers and names of the commissioners. The commission is usually empowered to call witnesses and to hold public hearings. When the commission has completed its investigation and made its report to the Prime Minister, the report is subsequently published. There has been a recent trend towards the commissioning of special studies which are prepared as supplements to the main report; for example, 26 special studies were published as supplements to the *Report* of the Royal Commission on Health Services. Usually commissions are popularly referred to by the names of their chairmen; hence the so-called "LeDain report" is the *Final Report* of the Commission of Inquiry into the Non-Medical Use of Drugs, whose chairman was Gerald LeDain.

A useful reference work for locating royal commission reports is *Federal Royal Commissions in Canada, 1867-1966; a Checklist*, by George F. Henderson, published by the University of Toronto Press. From 1940 to 1970-71, each edition of the *Canada Year Book* contained a list of newly appointed royal commissions, both federal and provincial, indicating their terms of reference and their date of appointment. This feature was resumed with the 1974 edition.

Reports of Task Forces

The term "task force" became a common expression during World War II when it was used to describe a military force, frequently involving different services, assembled to undertake a specific task. In the jargon of government, the term is used to describe a group of experts gathered together to tackle a particular problem of public concern. In Canada, the use of task forces to help formulate government policy on such topics as labour relations, the government's role in sport, and housing, became fashionable in the late 1960s. In its composition and operation, the task force stands somewhere between a royal commission and a Parliamentary committee. Usually, the task force is made up of academics and other experts from outside government who work closely with senior civil servants. The task force may commission special studies, invite briefs and hold public hearings.

Examples of task force reports are: *To Know and Be Known; the Report of the Task Force on Government Information*, published in 1969 and containing valuable material on government publishing; and *Branching Out; Report of the Canadian Computer/Communications Task Force*, published in 1972.

Publications of the Federal Courts

The principal publications of the judicial arm of the federal government consist of the reports of cases tried before the two federal courts, the Federal Court of Canada (formerly known as the Exchequer Court of Canada), and the Supreme Court of Canada. From 1876 to 1922, there was a series of *Reports of the Exchequer Court of Canada*; from 1923 to 1969, the series was known as *Canada Law Reports: Exchequer Court of Canada*; in 1970, the title was changed to *Canada Exchequer Court Reports*; and when the Federal Court replaced the Exchequer Court in 1971, its judgements were contained in a new series called *Canada Federal Court Reports*. From 1876 to 1922, there was also a series known as the *Reports of the Supreme Court of Canada*; from 1923 to 1969, the series was called *Canada Law Reports: Supreme Court of Canada*; and, since 1970, the series has been known as *Canada Supreme Court Reports*.

Bibliographies and Catalogues of Government Publications

Bibliographies

A useful guide is *Canadian Federal Government Publications; a Bibliography of Bibliographies*, by Mohan Bhatia, which was published in 1971 by the University of Saskatchewan and is divided into three parts: general bibliographies, bibliographies of parliamentary publications, and bibliographies of departmental publications.

Although out-of-date, the manual on *Canadian Government Publications*, compiled by Marion V. Higgins and published in 1935 by the American Library Association, remains the outstanding descriptive bibliography in its field. It includes federal publications beginning with the united province of Canada, 1841-1867. Publications are arranged according to the issuing office, and brief histories of the various governmental agencies are supplied along with a list of their publications. These publications are divided into two large groups: serial publications and special publications. For serials, inclusive dates of publication are shown with a note as to whether or not the reports appeared in the *Sessional Papers* and *Annual Departmental Reports*. The section on special publications includes all those publications issued by each governmental agency which were not published in the *Journals* or *Sessional Papers*. There is a general subject index.

Government Catalogues Issued Before 1953

For federal government publications issued prior to 1953, the indexes and catalogues available were incomplete, spasmodic, and originated from many different sources. From 1892 to 1938, the *Annual Report* of the Department of Public Printing and Stationery contained a list of government pamphlets and miscellaneous monographs issued during the fiscal year arranged according to the issuing agency. No bibliographical details were given except paging. From 1894 to 1927, this department also issued a *Price List of Government Publications* which was superseded in 1928 by the *Catalogue of Official Publications of the Parliament and Government of Canada*. This latter publication was issued from 1928 to 1948 in different forms, later being known as the *Government Publications Annual Catalogue*. It was simply a list of titles and prices of all official publications procurable from the King's Printer and no bibliographical details were supplied. It had supplements at intervals up to 1952, when it was replaced by the current series of daily, monthly and annual catalogues.

Government Catalogues Issued Since 1953

In 1953, the Queen's Printer published the *Canadian Government Publications Consolidated Annual Catalogue*, a basic work which superseded the old *Annual Catalogue* of 1948 and its supplements to 1952. The *Consolidated Annual Catalogue* attempted to include all federal government publications in print as of September, 1953. The *Canadian Government Publications Annual Catalogue*, 1954, supplemented the *Consolidated Annual Catalogue*, 1953, and listed federal government publications issued between October 1953 and December 1954. Both the 1953 and 1954 editions were also published separately in French.

Since 1955, a bilingual *Annual Catalogue* has been published. The *Annual Catalogue* supersedes issues of the bilingual *Canadian Government*

Publications Monthly Catalogue which, in turn, cumulates issues of the bilingual *Daily Checklist of Government Publications*. The purpose of these catalogues is to provide a comprehensive listing of all official publications, public documents and papers, not of a confidential nature, printed or processed at government expense by authority of Parliament or of a government agency, or bought at public expense for distribution to members of Parliament, public servants, or the public. These publications make it possible to check the bibliographic details, price and distribution policy of any current federal government publication. The *Monthly Catalogue* and the *Annual Catalogue* are indexed by personal author, title and subject. Since 1963, the *Monthly Catalogue* has also indexed articles in about two dozen Canadian government periodicals by personal author, title and subject. This index is cumulated in the *Annual Catalogue*.

The federal government has published a series of *Sectional Catalogues* which provide a more detailed subject approach to the many thousands of government publications. To date, the following *Sectional Catalogues* have been published: Labour, Northern Affairs and National Resources, Mines Branch, Forestry, Dominion Bureau of Statistics (since superseded), Canada Treaty Series, and National Museums of Canada.

In 1976, the Publishing Centre of the Department of Supply and Services began to issue a new series of bilingual *Subject Lists* of priced Canadian government publications. Each *Subject List* is devoted to a topic of current interest such as Energy, Environment, and Business. Periodically, the Publishing Centre also issues a *Special List of Government Publications*, a bilingual pamphlet highlighting selected publications available free from the issuing department, as well as a selection of publications for sale by the Publishing Centre.

Certain federal government departments and agencies such as the Department of Agriculture, the Geological Survey, and the National Research Council of Canada have issued excellent guides or indexes to their publications giving greater detail than is possible in the general catalogues mentioned above. The Dominion Bureau of Statistics (now know as Statistics Canada) issued an *Historical Catalogue of Publications, 1918-1960*, designed as a guide to its publications since its inception. Since 1972, Statistics Canada has periodically published a two-part *Catalogue*: Part I—"Publications", lists approximately 1,375 publications grouped by subject areas; Part II—"Unpublished Information", includes information which may be useful to a limited number of individuals or organizations, but which is not published because interest in it is not sufficiently broad.

Canadiana

In 1951, the National Library of Canada (then known as the Canadian Bibliographic Centre) began issuing *Canadiana*, a national monthly bibliography listing books about Canada, published in Canada, or written by Canadians. Since 1952, one part of *Canadiana* has been devoted to federal government publications and all listings are in full bibliographic form giving author, title, edition, publisher, date and place of publication, paging, series notes, and other pertinent information. Coverage of federal government publications in *Canadiana* is not quite as comprehensive nor listings as quick to appear as is the case with the *Monthly Catalogue*. Nevertheless, the bibliographical description for each item listed is considerably more complete, often supplying details about previous publications in the same series. Since 1953, another part of *Canadiana* has listed current publications of the ten provincial governments. The monthly issues of *Canadiana* are cumulated annually and the monthly indexes are cumulated quarterly, semi-annually, and annually.

The Publicat Index

Micro Media Ltd. of Toronto began publication in January 1977 of *Publicat Index*, a new Canadian federal documents service designed to supplement the *Daily Checklist of Government Publications* issued by the Publications Centre of the Department of Supply and Services. Scheduled to be published monthly and cumulated annually, *Publicat Index* lists selected current federal government documents published after November 1, 1976, such as: annual reports, research reports and special studies, policy announcements and important press releases, position papers, proceedings of selected government-sponsored conferences, working papers and planning studies, public documents prepared for commissions of inquiry, significant statements and speeches, bibliographies and catalogues, manuals and directories, and serials of reference value for which indexing is unavailable from other sources. Full cataloguing information is supplied along with indexes by title, subject, personal name, non-government corporate name, and geographic area.

Provincial Government Publications

In general, publications of the provincial governments parallel the types issued by the federal government. Most provinces publish debates, votes and proceedings, journals, sessional papers, annual departmental reports, and gazettes. Because of a dearth of published indexes or catalogues, provincial government publications have in the past been much more difficult to locate than those of the federal government. The situation has improved considerably in recent years but some provinces still do not publish catalogues of their publications. A useful reference work is *Canadian Provincial Government Publications; Bibliography of Bibliographies*, compiled by Mohan Bhatia and published by the Library of the University of Saskatchewan, 1971. Another valuable reference work is *ProFile Index*, issued monthly since January 1973 and cumulated annually by Micro Media Ltd. of Toronto, which indexes Canadian provincial publications and makes them available in microfiche.

Retrospective bibliographies have been compiled for most of the provinces:

Publications of the Government of British Columbia, 1871-1947, was compiled by Marjorie C. Holmes and published in 1950 by the Provincial Library in Victoria.

Government Publications Relating to Alberta; A Bibliography of Publications of the Government of Alberta from 1905 to 1968, and of Publications of the Government of Canada Relating to the Province of Alberta from 1867 to 1968, compiled by Joseph Forsyth, is a multi-volume work completed in 1971 and available in microform or photocopy through the Library Association of Great Britain.

Publications of the Governments of the North-West Territories, 1876-1905, and of the Province of Saskatchewan, 1905-1952, compiled by Christine MacDonald, was published in 1952 by the Legislative Library, Regina.

Publications of the Government of the Province of Canada, 1841-1867, compiled by Olga B. Bishop and published by the National Library in 1963, covers the geographic area of what is now Ontario and Quebec.

Publications of the Government of Ontario, 1867-1900, compiled by Olga B. Bishop, was published by the Ontario Ministry of Government Services in 1976. *Publications of the Government of Ontario, 1901-1955,* a checklist compiled for the Ontario Library Association by Hazel I. MacTaggart, was published by the University of Toronto Press in 1964. A supplement compiled by Hazel MacTaggart with the assistance of Kenneth E. Sundquist covering the years 1956-1971 was published in 1975 by the Ontario Ministry of Government Services.

Répertoire des Publications Gouvernementales du Québec de 1867 à 1964, compiled by André Beaulieu, Jean-Charles Bonefant and Jean Hamelin, was published by Imprimeur de la Reine du Québec in 1968. A *Supplément 1965-1968* compiled by Beaulieu, Hamelin and Gaston Bernier was published by Editeur officiel du Québec in 1970.

Publications of the Governments of Nova Scotia, Prince Edward Island, New Brunswick, 1758-1952, complied by Olga B. Bishop, was published in 1957 by the National Library of Canada, Ottawa.

Guide to Official Publications of New Brunswick 1952-1970, was compiled by Claude Guilbeault in 1974 as a M.L.S. thesis for the University of Ottawa Library School.

Most provinces now issue periodic lists of their current publications:

British Columbia Government Publications Monthly Checklist began January 1970 but limits its distribution to B.C. libraries, the legislative libraries of other provinces, and to certain other libraries. It is compiled by the Provincial Library.

In 1974, the Alberta Public Affairs Bureau issued a *Publications Catalogue* for 1973 and began publishing a quarterly *Publications Catalogue* dating from January 1974.

At present, Saskatchewan issues no current list of government publications.

Manitoba Government Publications Received in the Legislative Library began publication in 1971 and was issued three times a year. It was superseded by *Manitoba Government Publications* which has been issued monthly since 1975 by the Department of Tourism, Recreation and Cultural Affairs.

Ontario Government Publications Checklist has been issued monthly by the Ministry of Government Services since May 1971. It is cumulated into an annual, *Ontario Government Publications,* the first one of which was issued for the year 1972.

Bibliographie du Québec; Liste Mensuelle des Publications Québecoises ou Relatives au Québec, published since 1968 by the Bibliothèque Nationale du Québec, Montréal, contains a section on current publications of the province of Québec. *Catalogue de l'Editeur Officiel* has been issued since 1966 and lists legislative and departmental publications for sale by that office. It was formerly titled *Publications*. Québec also issues a list of free publications, *Répertoire des publications gouvernementales gratuites*, which is published by Communication-Québec, as well as a selective list of publications which provides abstracts and author, title and subject indexes, *Répertoire analytique des publications gouvernementales*, published by Editeur officiel du Québec.

New Brunswick Government Documents is a checklist of provincial publications received at the Legislative Library in Fredericton and has been issued annually since 1955.

Publications of the Province of Nova Soctia is an annual checklist of provincial publications compiled by the Legislative Library. The first issue covered the year 1967. A semi-annual supplement is distributed to a limited number of research libraries. In 1976, the Communications and Information Centre issued a *Publications Catalogue* of material available from the Nova Scotia Government Bookstore.

Significant Publications of the Government of Prince Edward Island covering the years 1967-1968 and 1969-1970 was issued by the Legislative Library. *Publications and Reports Tabled in the Legislative Assembly* appeared annually from 1971-1974. In 1976, the Island Information Service began issuing a monthly *PEI Provincial Government Publications Checklist*.

In June 1974, the Newfoundland Information Services began issuing a *List of Publications of the Government of Newfoundland and Labrador* on a monthly basis. Suspended in October 1974, the *List* resumed publication on an irregular basis in July 1975.

BIBLIOGRAPHY

Banks, M. A., "Statutes", *Using a Law Library: A Guide for Students and Lawyers in the Common Law Provinces of Canada*, 2d ed., Toronto, Carswell Co. Ltd; 1974, pp. 15-32, 59-75.

Boucher, Alain, *Le Service des Publications Gouvernementales*, 2d ed., La Pocatière, Collège de Sainte-Anne-de-la-Pocatière, 1970.

Childs, J. B., "Canadian Government Publications; Developments in Control, Use and Bibliography", *Australian Library Journal*, 18 (August, 1969), pp. 256-61.

Hardisty, A. P., "Some Aspects of Canadian Official Publishing", *Government Publications Review*, 1 (Fall, 1973), pp. 7-17.

Jarvi, Edith, *Access to Canadian Government Publications in Canadian Academic and Public Libraries*, Ottawa, Canadian Library Association, 1976.

Murray, F. B., "Reference Use of Canadian Documents", *Library Resources and Technical Services*, 5 (Winter, 1961), pp. 48-52.

Presser, Carolynne, "Canadian Provincial and Municipal Documents; The Mystery Explained?", *Government Publications Review*, 2 (Winter, 1975), pp. 17-25.

Pross, A. P., and Pross, C. A., *Government Publishing in the Canadian Provinces; a Prescriptive Study*, Toronto: University of Toronto Press, 1972.

Scollie, F. B., "Every Scrap of Paper: Access to Ontario's Municipal Records", *Canadian Library Journal*, 31 (January-February, 1974), pp. 8-16.

Tripp, Pat, "On the Tracks of Municipal Government Publications in Canada", *Canadian Library Journal*, 28 (November-December, 1971), pp. 464-67.